Health

PSYCHOLOGY

EDITED BY *Ad Kaptein and John Weinman*

BPS Blackwell

BLACKWELL PUBLISHING
350 Main Street, Malden, MA 02148-5020, USA
108 Cowley Road, Oxford OX4 1JF, UK
550 Swanston Street, Carlton, Victoria 3053, Australia

First published 2004 by The British Psychological Society and Blackwell Publishing Ltd

Library of Congress Cataloging-in-Publication Data

Health psychology / edited by Ad Kaptein and John Weinman.—1st ed.
p. cm.
Includes bibliographical references and index.
ISBN 0-631-21441-0 (hbk : alk. paper) — ISBN 0-631-21442-9 (pbk : alk. paper)
1. Clinical health psychology. I. Kaptein, A. A. (Adrian A.) II. Weinman, John.

R726.7.H433 2004
616'.001'9–dc22
2004003062

A catalogue record for this title is available from the British Library.

Set in Rotis Serif 10/12^{1}/$_{2}$pt
by Graphicraft Limited, Hong Kong
Printed and bound in the United Kingdom
by TJ International, Padstow, Cornwall

For further information on
Blackwell Publishing, visit our website:
http://www.blackwellpublishing.com

Contents

Notes on Contributors

Paul Bennett, Bristol Doctoral Training Programme in Clinical Psychology, University of Bristol, UK.

J. M. Bensing, NIVEL (Netherlands Institute of Primary Health Care), Utrecht, the Netherlands.

Nicola W. Burton, Australian Centre for Physical Activity and Health, School of Movement Studies, University of Queensland, St Lucia, Australia.

Linda D. Cameron, Department of Psychology, University of Auckland, New Zealand.

Kazuyo Enomoto, Unit of Health Psychology, Centre for Behaviour and Social Sciences in Medicine, Royal Free and University College Medical School, University College London, UK.

Ad Kaptein, Psychology Unit, Leiden University Medical Centre, and Department of Clinical and Health Psychology, Leiden University, Leiden, the Netherlands.

Nina Knoll, Department of Health Psychology, Freie Universität Berlin, Germany.

Stan Maes, Department of Health Psychology, Leiden University, the Netherlands.

Hannah McGee, Health Services Research Centre, Department of Psychology, Royal College of Surgeons in Ireland, Dublin, Ireland.

Susan Michie, Centre for Outcomes Research and Effectiveness, Department of Psychology, University College London, UK.

Rona Moss-Morris, Division of Health Psychology, University of Auckland, New Zealand.

Lynn B. Myers, Unit of Health Psychology, Centre for Behaviour and Social Sciences in Medicine, Royal Free and University College Medical School, University College London, UK.

Stanton P. Newman, Unit of Health Psychology, Centre for Behaviour and Social Sciences in Medicine, Royal Free and University College Medical School, University College London, UK.

Brian Oldenburg, School of Public Health, Queensland University of Technology, Kelvin Grove, Australia.

Denise de Ridder, Department of Health Psychology, Utrecht University, the Netherlands.

Nina Rieckmann, Department of Psychiatry, Mount Sinai School of Medicine, New York, USA.

Ralf Schwarzer, Department of Health Psychology, Freie Universität Berlin, Germany.

Suzanne M. Skevington, Department of Psychology, University of Bath, UK.

Andrew Steptoe, Psychobiology Group, Department of Epidemiology and Public Health, University College London, UK.

Wolfgang Stroebe, Research School of Psychology and Health, and Department of Social and Organizational Psychology, University of Utrecht, the Netherlands.

Margot van der Doef, Department of Health Psychology, Leiden University, the Netherlands.

P. F. M. Verhaak, NIVEL (Netherlands Institute of Primary Health Care), Utrecht, the Netherlands.

Ad Vingerhoets, Department of Psychology and Health, University of Tilburg, the Netherlands.

Claus Vögele, School of Psychology and Therapeutic Studies, University of Surrey, Roehampton, London, UK.

Jane Wardle, Health Behaviour Unit, Department of Epidemiology and Public Health, University College London, UK.

John Weinman, Health Psychology Section, Department of Psychology, Institute of Psychiatry, Guy's Hospital, London, UK.

John de Wit, Research School of Psychology and Health, and Department of Social and Organizational Psychology, University of Utrecht, the Netherlands.

Preface

It seems remarkable that it is only 25 years since the first 'official' health psychology text appeared. Within a relatively short period of time health psychology has become established as one of the most active and rapidly developing areas within the whole of psychology. This is very much reflected in the numbers of new specialist journals and books, as well as professional developments across a very wide range of countries.

In planning the contents of this edited overview we have been very mindful not only of the broad range topics within health psychology but also of the considerable health psychology expertise which now exists around the world. Thus we have included expert overviews of the many core topics across the whole discipline. The structure of the book and the choice of topics have been strongly guided by the definition of health psychology as the study of psychological processes in health, illness and health care, a tripartite view which originated in the UK and is now generally held in Europe and many other countries. Therefore, the book is divided into three sections (1) health and illness behaviour, (2) process and outcome in illness, and (3) health-care contexts and the practice of health psychology.

In our selection of authors, we have very deliberately drawn upon experts from within Europe and other major health psychology centres outside the USA. This is because we are very keen to provide the book with a broad perspective, as an acknowledgement of the considerable health psychology expertise which now exists in these countries. In doing this, we are not overlooking the fact that the largest aggregate of health psychology research lies within the USA, which is clearly reflected in the balance of studies and research evidence cited by our authors. Nevertheless, we hope that our choice of authors has ensured that readers will be presented with an excellent blend of research findings and ideas, originating from a much broader range of countries than is often found in existing texts from a single geographic source.

The book is aimed at different audiences, including undergraduate and graduate psychology students, young and experienced health psychology researchers, and both researchers and practitioners from a number of related disciplines, such as those with a public health or medical background who are keen to get a picture of developments within health psychology. By providing 'Discussion Points', references to 'Key Studies', and suggestions of important studies for further reading, we have attempted to make the chapters attractive for the reader, and for teachers who use the book. We decided not to include internet addresses in the various chapters, as they tend to become obsolete fairly rapidly, but chapter 1 has three web addresses that will be helpful in guiding the reader through major areas covered in the book.

The editors are very grateful to the authors for their very valuable contributions and for their cheerful cooperation with 'two grumpy old men' who kept asking them to revise their chapters. We also thank the staff at Blackwell for their help and support. The editors and authors of this book enjoy teaching health psychology and doing health psychology research. We very much hope that this book will enable you, the reader, to share our enjoyment and enthusiasm.

Ad Kaptein   *John Weinman*
Leiden   *London*
Spring 2004

Part I

INTRODUCTORY OVERVIEW

Chapter One

HEALTH PSYCHOLOGY: SOME INTRODUCTORY REMARKS

Ad Kaptein and John Weinman

'Everyone who is born holds dual citizenship, in the kingdom of the well and in the kingdom of the sick.'

(Sontag, 1979: 3)

Health psychology is concerned with the study of psychological processes in health, illness and health care. Health psychologists study behavioural factors associated with staying healthy, and they examine how patients with health problems can be helped to improve their quality of life. They may also examine individuals in an experimental setting, work with groups in real-life settings, or observe social inter-actions taking place between health-care professionals and patients in a variety of health-care contexts.

Health psychology is one of the fastest-growing subdisciplines in psychology, if not the fastest. In the next paragraphs we will provide a brief and concise intro-duction to the area of health psychology, with some illustrations of its main foci of interest, both theoretically and empirically.

HEALTH PSYCHOLOGY IN CONTEXT

Health and illness have long been the object of scientific and clinical interest for psychologists. The separation between 'psychological' on the one hand, and 'phys-ical, medical or somatic' on the other, is quite superficial and unhelpful – modern developments in the area of psycho-neuro-immunology, for example, or in the area of interrelationships between genetic and behavioural factors in staying healthy or becoming ill, are just some illustrations of this statement.

The relatively successful application of learning-theory principles to patients or clients with psychological problems (e.g. phobias, neurotic symptoms) inspired psychologists to apply these principles to patients with various physical disorders, and examine the effects of those interventions (see the special issue of *Journal of Consulting and Clinical*

Psychology (1982) on 'Behavioral Medicine' (Blanchard, guest editor) and the special issue on 'Behavioral Medicine and Clinical Health Psychology' published 20 years later (Smith, Kendall, & Keefe, guest editors, 2002) to gauge the progress made). The development of health psychology was also greatly stimulated by publications that demonstrated the impact of behaviour on health status. Physicians and governments were quick in involving psychologists in programmes aimed at encouraging populations and individuals to adopt lifestyles that are conducive to health (Conner & Norman, 2001).

Most authors of the chapters in this book are too old to have had the relative luxury of being able to buy books on health psychology or read journals focusing specifically on health psychology when they were students or postgraduates, as they simply did not exist prior to the 1980s. Relevant knowledge had to be discovered, and was hidden in books and papers on clinical or social psychology, or, for instance, endocrinology, neurology or sociology. Health psychology was first used in a book title in 1979 (Stone, Cohen & Adler). Some 25 years on, one would need a large bookcase to hold all the books that have 'health psychology' in their titles or that belong to the category of health psychology. The year 1979 was an important year for the formal establishment of the subdiscipline. The book by Stone et al. (1979) was published, and in September 1979, Matarazzo presented his presidential address to the Division of Health Psychology at an APA meeting. The title of his address was 'Behavioral Health and Behavioral Medicine – Frontiers for a New Health Psychology' (Matarazzo, 1980). He defined health psychology as 'the aggregate of the specific educational, scientific, and professional contributions of the discipline of psychology to the promotion and maintenance of health, the prevention and treatment of illness, and the identification of etiologic and diagnostic correlates of health, illness, and related dysfunction' (p. 815). In the 1982 definition, the following text was added: '. . . and to the analysis and improvement of the health care system and health policy formation' (Matarazzo, 1982: 4).

Health psychology is sometimes confused with a number of related disciplines (Weinman & Petrie, 2000). Figure 1.1 summarizes the position of health psychology and those disciplines in a grid with 'psychology–medicine' on the *x*-axis, and 'mental disorders–physical disorders' on the *y*-axis. Of course, separating 'mental problems' from 'physical disorders' is artificial, and the allocation of the different disciplines into their positions in the four quadrants may be somewhat forced.

The quadrant with 'psychology' and 'physical disorders' constitutes *health psychology*. As we will discuss in detail in the next section, in health psychology, psychological theories and methods are applied in order to examine how to ensure that people stay healthy or achieve better adaptation to or recovery from illness.

Clinical psychology focuses on patients, or clients, with mental health problems (e.g. phobias, anxiety disorders, depression, substance abuse problems). The theoretical models and interventions that clinical psychologists apply to clients with these problems have been shown to be quite effective (White, 2001). This has encouraged clinicians and researchers to apply these models to individuals with physical health problems as well. In this sense, health psychology and behavioural medicine were influenced

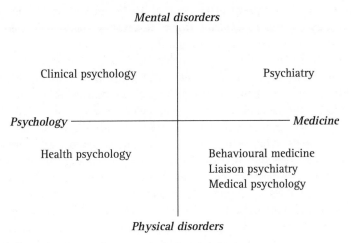

Figure 1.1 Health psychology and related disciplines

and shaped by clinical psychology, and there are now many clinical psychologists who work in the area of clinical health psychology (e.g. Bennett Johnson, Perry & Rozensky, 2002; Llewelyn & Kennedy, 2003).

Psychiatry also focuses on patients with mental health problems. Psychiatrists mainly adopt a biomedical approach to patients with such disorders, applying medication and medical treatment. Currently, psychiatry appears to be dominated by biomedical, genetic and molecular views on disturbed behaviour: the journal *Molecular Psychiatry*, for instance, has one of the highest impact factors in the psychiatry field. However, within psychiatry there are practitioners who make use of psychological treatments, either on their own or more commonly in conjunction with medical approaches.

Behavioural medicine, liaison psychiatry and medical psychology are in the quadrant 'physical disorders' and 'medicine'. These three disciplines all focus on physical disorders and diseases, although there are differences in their emphasis and theoretical background. *Behavioural medicine* is defined as 'the interdisciplinary field concerned with the development and integration of behavioural, psychosocial, and biomedical science, knowledge and techniques, relevant to the understanding of health and illness, and the application of this knowledge and these techniques to prevention, diagnosis, treatment and rehabilitation' (Outlook SBM, 1995: 1). In an earlier definition of Behavioural Medicine, a sentence was added to the definition: 'Psychosis, neurosis and substance abuse are included only insofar as they contribute to physical disorders as an endpoint' (Schwartz & Weiss, 1978: 249), clearly delineating clinical psychology and behavioural medicine. Central to behavioural medicine is its interdisciplinary nature, and the emphasis on integration of behavioural and biomedical knowledge. In addition, although behavioural medicine also incorporates (primary) prevention, just like health psychology, behavioural medicine's emphasis is more on treatment and rehabilitation. A comparison of the content of the major journals in behavioural medicine (*Annals of Behavioral Medicine, Behavioral Medicine, International Journal of Behavioral Medicine, Journal of Behavioral Medicine*) with the major journals in health psychology (*Health Psychology, British Journal of Health Psychology, Psychology & Health*) easily demonstrates this point.

Liaison psychiatry is a subspecialty within psychiatry, focusing on patients in a medical setting whose responses to illness – for medical or psychological reasons – lead to problems for the patient themselves and/or the medical staff. Although liaison psychiatry and health psychology have developed over a similar period of time with a number of overlapping interests and concerns, there are some important differences between the two fields. Whereas liaison psychiatry has its major focus on patients with physical health problems and who are experiencing psychological difficulties, health psychology has a much broader remit since it is concerned with all behaviours which influence health and illness in all individuals. Thus, while health psychology has focused on the development of theoretically based explanations and interventions for health-related and illness-related behaviours, liaison psychiatry has been concerned primarily with the diagnosis and treatment of people with either unexplained symptoms or with psychiatric disorders occurring in the context of a physical health problem.

Medical psychology used to be the term for describing the disciplinary area for psychologists who worked in medical settings (medical schools and hospitals), and who diagnosed and managed patients with physical health problems and were often involved with teaching and training of medical students and staff about psychology as applied to health and illness. However, this term is used much less frequently now, as most psychologists working in these contexts tend to be called health or clinical health psychologists.

HEALTH PSYCHOLOGY AND ITS FOUR FIELDS

We now move on from defining and demarcating scientific disciplines to illustrations of the four core elements of health psychology.

The *first* element of health psychology, given Matarazzo's definition, is the promotion and maintenance of health. Studies in this area are aimed at healthy individuals, and where health psychology is instrumental in achieving this aim. Wardle (2000) has labelled this 'public health psychology', and has outlined various areas where health psychology can play a role. These include understanding and modifying health behaviours (cf. Chapter 2 in this book), mass communication about health, or elucidating the pathways through which population-level factors affect health (Hardey, 1998).

Kaplan pointed out how 'promotion and maintenance of health' have very different connotations in medicine and (health) psychology (Kaplan, 2000). Prevention in the medical context pertains to 'identifying an existing disease at an early stage and eliminating the problem before it gets out of control', while prevention in behavioural models pertains to 'maneuvers that reduce the chances that a health problem will ever develop' (Kaplan, 2000: 382). Physicians and others working with a medical model of health and illness define activities that scientists and clinicians who work in a behavioural model would call 'secondary prevention' as 'primary prevention'.

This is a matter that is not only limited to a semantic issue, or to confusion in medical students and behavioural-science teachers when they teach about prevention. As Kaplan emphasizes, 'Secondary prevention is typically based on a traditional biomedical model that requires the diagnosis and treatment of an existing condition and that usually involves one or more of the following: medical diagnosis, surgery, or use of medications. Primary prevention is usually based on a behavioral rather than a disease model. Diagnosis plays a lesser role because there is no disease to diagnose. Intervention is typically behavioral and might include exercise, dietary change, or the avoidance or reduction of alcohol use. Interventions might also include public policy changes' (2000: 383). However, in the context of secondary prevention, reduction of disease risk or progression may be achieved by behaviour changes, such as smoking cessation or dietary changes (see also below). Chapter 2 on health behaviour, Chapter 13 on primary prevention and Chapter 15 on worksite health promotion in this book contain empirical illustrations of this first field of health psychology: promotion and maintenance of health.

The *second* element, prevention and treatment of illness, has some overlap with the first area, but more obviously focuses on people who have been identified to be at risk for disease (e.g. those who have been screened to be at risk for coronary heart disease or stroke from blood pressure screening, or for colorectal, cervical or breast cancer as the result of screening programmes involving testing for faecal occult blood, the cervical smear test and mammography, respectively). Here the aim is to detect risk or early signs of disease at an early enough stage in order to eliminate or slow down its development. Prevention may then be achieved through behavioural changes and/or medical options, such as anti-hypertensive or lipid lowering medication, which also involve a major behavioural component (i.e. adherence to the treatment).

Health psychologists have an excellent track record when it comes to psychological interventions in people who are ill. Meta-analyses, Cochrane reviews, and handbooks on this subject are available. The *Handbook of Clinical Health Psychology*, edited by Millon, Green and Meagher (1982), is the first of a long and impressive list of books in the area of (clinical) health psychology (e.g. Baum, Revenson & Singer, 2001; Bennett-Johnson et al., 2003; Llewelyn & Kennedy, 2003; Sutton, Baum & Johnston, 2004). Many chapters in these books deal extensively with theoretical, methodological and empirical issues in the area of 'chronic somatic disorders – coping, assessment, and interventions'.

If we consider three of the major physical illnesses and some of the best intervention studies from a (clinical) health psychology point of view, a number of important papers illustrate what the field has to offer. Linden, Stossel and Maurice (1996), in a meta-analysis of behavioural interventions in cardiovascular disease, conclude, 'The *addition* of psychosocial treatments to standard cardiac rehabilitation regimens reduces mortality and morbidity, psychological distress, and some biological risk factors' (p. 745). In the area of cancer, Rehse and Pukrop (2003) and Meyer and Mark (1995) present two meta-analyses on the effects of psychosocial interventions on 'quality of life' and other major outcome measures. The conclusions by Meyer and Mark are of the utmost importance: 'it would be an inefficient use of research resources to conduct more studies . . . to ask the simple question: Is there an effect of behavioral, educational, social support, and non-behavioural counselling and therapy interventions on the emotional adjustment, functional adjustment, and treatment- and disease-related symptoms of cancer patients? These interventions have a consistent beneficial effect on all three areas' (p. 106). In the area of the third leading cause of death in developed societies, chronic obstructive pulmonary disease (COPD), Lacasse et al. (2003) in a Cochrane review conclude that psychosocial interventions 'relieve dyspnea and fatigue, and enhance patients' sense of control over their condition. These improvements are moderately large and clinically significant' (p. 1; see also Kaptein & Creer, 2002).

Two issues deserve discussion. The first has to do with the kind of outcome measures which health psychologists choose as dependent variables in the intervention studies examining effects of psychological or psychosocial treatment on various conditions. As outlined by Kaplan (1990) in his important paper 'Behavior as the Central Outcome in Health Care', choosing observable outcome measures which make sense in the real world is his preferred type of dependent variable. It is important to consider Kaplan's views when planning a study, or when studying the research literature in health psychology. All too often, health psychologists fall victim to the 'self-report predicts self-report trap', and so it is no surprise to find high correlations between self-reports of, for example, self-efficacy, and self-reported quality of life. Self-reports are highly susceptible to self-presentation bias and it is equally important to try and predict more 'objective' indicators, such as survival, resumption of work and social activities (Petrie et al., 2002). Secondly, various authors, health psychologists themselves, increasingly publish critical papers on various major issues in health psychology. For example, Ogden (2003) has critically reviewed the social cognition theories developed in the health psychology domain, and concluded that 'If social cognition models are to be given the status of theories, then it is recommended that the critical eye that psychologists place on other areas of research also be cast on this one' (p. 427). Similarly, Salmon and Hall (2003) have critically reviewed one of the pet concepts of health psychologists ('patient empowerment and control') – these papers illustrate the coming of age of health psychology: the area is being criticized by scientists who contribute to the further development of health psychology.

The *third* element of health psychology in Matarazzo's definition is 'etiologic and diagnostic correlates of health and illness'. Illustrations of these two topics can be found in almost any recent issue of a health psychology journal. Appels' work on 'vital exhaustion' as a contributor to the incidence of myocardial infarction is a very good example of the role of a psychological factor in the aetiology of a major illness (van Diest et al., 2002). A study on patient-controlled analgesia is an example of 'diagnostic correlates of health and illness' (Lang et al., 2000). Patients who had to undergo invasive diagnostic procedures were randomized into three groups: (*a*) standard care, (*b*) structured attention, and (*c*) self-hypnotic relaxation. Pain, anxiety, analgesia use and 'theatre time' were all significantly lower in the structured attention condition.

The *fourth* and final element is 'health care system and health policy'. Health psychology research aiming at examining or changing the health-care system and/or health policy is rather scarce. The *Journal of Health Psychology* is an important source of debate on this issue. The topic of 'critical health psychology' (Radley & Chamberlain,

2001) is dealt with in that journal quite frequently. The journal *Sociology of Health and Illness* publishes important papers on this fourth element of health psychology, albeit – of course – with a sociological emphasis.

TYPES OF HEALTH PSYCHOLOGY RESEARCH

As in every other area of psychology, there are very different types of research conducted within health psychology. A broad distinction can be made between four broad categories of study, namely those which are descriptive, explanatory, predictive or intervention-based.

At the most basic level are the *descriptive studies*, which represent a very useful first step in research since they provide accounts of the nature and range of key behaviours or other psychological processes. For example, descriptions of the levels of engagement in different health behaviours such as daily exercise or dietary intake (see Chapter 2, by Steptoe & Wardle, in this volume), or of the ways in which people cope with stressors, including major health problems (e.g. Scharloo et al., 1998) provide an important database for the discipline. Thus descriptive research in health psychology may involve accounts of types of different health or illness behaviours (see for example Chapters 2 and 4 in this volume), or descriptions of processes, such as doctor–patient communication (see Chapter 11, this volume).

However, more valuable for the long-term progress of the discipline are the insights and the potential provided by explanatory, predictive and intervention studies. Typically, *explanatory and predictive studies* will involve either the development or application of psychological theories (see the next section below). A large number of theories have been developed for explaining variations in health- and illness-related behaviour, and these continue to be refined in order to improve their explanatory and predictive power. Theories have been borrowed from other areas of psychology, particularly from social psychology, and applied to the explanation of different health behaviours. For example, the theory of planned behaviour (TPB) (Ajzen, 1991), a general theory developed for showing how individual and social contextual attitudes explain variations in behaviour, has been successfully adopted for explaining a wide range of health behaviours (Godin & Kok, 1996). Similarly, self-regulation models, which have been developed to explain goal-directed, adaptive responses to general threats (e.g. Carver & Scheier, 1998), have also been derived in very specific formats to explain patterns of response to health-related threats (e.g. Leventhal, Nerenz & Steele, 1984). In a discussion of general and health-specific models of self regulation, Cameron and Leventhal (2003) draw attention to the importance of having models which capture the unique aspects of the illness experience, such as the primary role of symptoms, the major threats of illness and the complexities of decision-making associated with treatment adherence. Nevertheless, they also point to the important interchange between general and health-specific models, and the potential which this can offer for enhancing the flow of information between the fields of social cognition and personality and health psychologies. In this way health psychology research can effectively inform the development of theory in these other fields; and so the fields can develop in synchrony.

Despite the importance of descriptive and explanatory studies for establishing the empirical and theoretical basis of health psychology, a more definitive test of theory or of a proposed explanatory model needs to involve experimental or quasi-experimental methodologies. Increasing levels of confidence in explaining health and illness behaviour can be gained from studies in which independent variables (e.g. arousal, emotion, knowledge, beliefs, etc.) are experimentally manipulated in order to see whether this results in predicted/hypothesized changes in behaviour or other outcomes, including health. This can be achieved using laboratory-type experimental methods where tight control can be exercised over the manipulation of independent variables and where dependent variables can be observed and/or measured with precision. For example, psycho-physiological studies have been conducted to establish relations between such factors as stressors and both physiological (e.g. blood pressure; salivary control; immune function) and psychological outcomes (e.g. mood; information processing). Similarly there is increasing use of analogue or vignette studies, which not only allow the researcher to investigate how individuals respond to imagined scenarios (e.g. being provided with a genetic test result – Senior et al., 1999) but also to see how responses are affected by the manipulation of specific variables, such as the type of information presented or the way in which it is framed. Inevitably these types of study can be criticized as not being real or as lacking in ecological validity (Parkinson & Manstead, 1993), but there is now increasing evidence about their utility (e.g. Lanza et al., 1997).

In the longer term, the most valuable types of experimental or quasi-experimental study in health psychology will be those involving *interventions* based on the findings from earlier explanatory studies. For example, building on the growing evidence that beliefs play an important role in explaining difference in health- or illness-related behaviour, there are now a small but growing number of intervention studies designed to modify beliefs as a basis for changing behaviour and related outcomes (see Petrie et al., 2002; Rutter & Quine, 2002). These not only provide a test of the intervention but can also allow the researcher to assess the role of the underlying theory.

Another important distinction in health psychology research is between the use of qualitative and quantitative research methods, which can differ considerably in their approach and function. Quantitative approaches typically involve the use of structured methods for measuring and/or manipulating variables, and for defining relationships between them in order to describe processes, test hypotheses or examine the impact of an intervention. In contrast, qualitative research is more concerned with understanding the meaning of experience or situations as they are interpreted by the individuals participating in a study.

Traditionally, psychology research, and health psychology research in particular, have relied more on theory-based quantitative methods, but there is increasing use of qualitative methods for guiding research and developing theory (e.g. Murray & Chamberlain, 1999). There is not space here to discuss the assumptions underlying qualitative research or to map out the range of approaches, which can be used for data collection or analysis. Nevertheless it is important to note that many methods exist, including interview, focus groups and observational methods, and these typically but not exclusively involve the use of audio- or video-recording for the collection of data. For example, many of the studies of doctor–patient interaction referred to in Chapter 11, by Bensing and Verhaak, in this book, are based on audio or videotaped analyses of medical consultations. These can be analysed either quantitatively by counting the frequency of different types of utterance, or qualitatively by examining the ways in which doctor and patient interact or interpret their roles. Most commonly, qualitative research involves the use of in-depth interviews or focus group discussions to generate data, which then can be analysed in a range of ways, which vary in their level of imposed structure and their underlying assumptions.

The qualitative/quantitative distinction is sometimes presented or perceived as a competitive, either–or issue, and this is both absurd and pointless. The two approaches differ in their intent and underlying assumptions, and researchers need to be clear about the overall aims of their research in order to select the appropriate method. While there are some research questions in health psychology where one particular approach is clearly most appropriate, there are many others which can be answered by either method or both. Thus one is not superior to the other but it is important to recognize the value of both and to make choices according to the nature and scope of the research question.

THEORY IN HEALTH PSYCHOLOGY

A core part of the evolution of any discipline involves the development, application and evaluation of theory in order to be able to explain why and in what circumstances specific phenomena occur. Theories are crucial not only for providing agreed structural descriptions of key processes, but also for providing guidelines for designing research studies at all the levels outlined in the previous section. Hence theories can and should shape the design of research, as well as providing frameworks for the interpretation of research findings which, in turn, provide evidence for assessing the adequacy of theory.

Early work in health psychology often made reference to the importance of the bio-psychosocial model (Schwartz, 1982) as the basis for developing research or intervention studies. At that time, this broad concept might have been helpful to make a contrast between the aims and approaches which needed to be adopted in health psychology and those used in medicine, but this model does little more than highlight the broad domains which need to be considered.

A wide range of theories of differing levels of specificity and complexity have now been developed within health psychology. This range is very much reflected within the chapters in this book, where many different types of theory are alluded to, or presented in some detail. Some of these have been developed specifically for use in health behaviour research, whereas others have been developed and used more broadly in psychological research.

Some areas of health psychology, such as the investigation of health-related behaviour (Conner & Norman, 1996), have been dominated by theoretical approaches, and this has allowed health psychologists to evaluate and compare the explanatory or predictive value of different theories. This, in turn, has led to very active theory testing and development in order to improve the explanatory power of the theories. The proliferation of social cognition theories for explaining health-related behaviour has recently resulted in attempts to categorize or group the theories according to the stage or component of the behavioural process which the theory is attempting to explain. For example, Armitage and Conner (2000) have presented a three-way classification of the social cognition models which have been used in health behaviour research. They distinguish between motivational, behavioural-action and multi-stage models, and then attempt not only to evaluate the contribution of each type but also to determine the extent to which core constructs can be identified and integrated across the models.

In contrast, other research areas in health psychology, such as the investigation of health-care practitioner–patient communication, or the study of effects of stress on immunity, have been less dominated by theoretical development and may involve studies with little or no theoretical basis. The absence of theory in research is generally to be regretted since this creates inherent difficulties for developing and evaluating research, as well as for assessing the progress made within any research field. In this latter sense, the evaluation of theories is one way of providing a record of the progress made in developing adequate explanation and prediction.

Theories in health psychology incorporate a wide range of explanatory variables within models with very different levels of complexity. Some, such as social cognitive theory (Bandura, 1986), place a major explanatory emphasis on a small number of key variables, for which well-developed measures are available. Others, such as Leventhal's self-regulation model (Leventhal et al., 1984), incorporate more variables within a looser framework. Although many theories acknowledge the importance of cultural and social contextual variables, very few have made serious attempts to incorporate these in meaningful ways. Nevertheless, a very wide range of explanatory constructs can be found in the theories currently used in health psychology. These include very specific constructs such as reinforcement from behavioural theory, social cognitive variables with a focus on beliefs and attitudes, as well as other major processes such as emotions, self-goals and broad dispositional variables such as personality and intelligence. In this way, the explanations of health and illness behaviours are informed by explanations and general theories of behaviour in order to capture the diversity of factors which determine how people respond in health and illness contexts.

As better ways of explaining processes, behaviours and outcomes in health psychology are developed, this should inform the development of more effective interventions. Theory-based interventions should result in more structured and informed approaches for modifying health or illness behaviours, provided that the theory on which they are based has been shown to have sufficient explanatory power. As we discussed earlier, many interventions in clinical health psychology have been based on the cognitive-behavioural theories and methods originally developed in clinical psychology. However, with the development of more elaborate social cognition and self-regulatory models in health psychology, there is now a greater possibility for using constructs from these models for refining interventions and for explaining how interventions do or do not achieve their effects.

Using theory for creating new interventions to change health or illness behaviours should be a careful process involving a number of steps and stages (e.g. see Campbell et al., 2000) in order to ensure that the intervention is developed and will work in a true theory-based way. Although attempts have been made to develop theory-based interventions (see Hardeman et al., 2002; Rutter & Quine, 2002), work in this area is still at a very early stage. An additional problem arises from the fact that many interventions which have been used in health psychology involve multiple components to achieve a range of outcomes. For example, interventions which have been developed to improve coping or self-management in patients with a chronic illness, such as rheumatoid arthritis, typically involve a package with components such as goal-setting, teaching cognitive coping skills and stress management amongst others (see Astin et al., 2002). With these it is often very difficult to tease out why and how the intervention has or has not been effective, and to identify the key ingredients of a successful intervention on either theoretical or empirical grounds.

There is still much to be learned about the best ways of structuring interventions to incorporate theoretical constructs, which are presumed to be explaining a particular health or illness behaviour. As yet, we know relatively little about the most effective ways of modifying social-cognitive or self-regulatory processes in ways which will result in long-term changes in behavioural, emotional, symptomatic or other health outcomes. This is particularly true in areas of health psychology such as psycho-neuro-endocrinology, where theory is much less developed and where attempts to use psychological intervention to enhance immune function have so far proven rather inconclusive (Miller & Cohen, 2001).

JOURNALS AND BOOKS IN HEALTH PSYCHOLOGY

A growing number of journals focusing on health psychology have been established in the past 10 to 20 years, helping the field to develop. *Health Psychology* is the subdiscipline-linked journal with the highest number of subscriptions of all APA (American Psychological Association) journals, and it has the highest impact factor score of journals in the specific health psychology area (American Psychologist, 2003; http://isi4.newisiknowledge.com). The other key journals include *Psychology & Health, British Journal of Health Psychology, Journal of Health Psychology*, and *Psychology, Health & Medicine*. In addition, health psychologists publish papers in journals with a more or less explicit multi-disciplinary focus such as *Journal of Psychosomatic Research, Psychosomatic Medicine, Social Science & Medicine, Behavioral Medicine, Patient Education & Counseling, Quality of Life Research*, or in general psychology or medical journals (e.g. *Psychological Bulletin, Lancet, Archives of Internal Medicine*). Some non-English-language national journals publish important health psychology papers as well. These include *Zeitschrift für Gesundheitspsychologie* (Journal of Health Psychology) in Germany, and *Gedrag & Gezondheid* (Behaviour & Health) in the Netherlands.

Books on health psychology are published at an impressive rate (e.g. Bennett Johnson, Perry & Rozensky, 2002, *Handbook of Clinical Health Psychology*; Johnston & Johnston, 2001, *Health Psychology*; Llewelyn & Kennedy, 2003, *Handbook of Clinical Health Psychology*; Nezu, Nezu & Geller, 2003, *Health Psychology*; Sutton, Baum & Johnston, 2004, *Handbook of Health Psychology*). The present volume is another illustration of the virtual explosion of information in the area of psychology as applied to health and illness. Universities all over the world have initiated health psychology tracks, including Masters of Science Health Psychology courses. Societies for Health Psychology have been established in the USA (Division 38, APA; www.health-psych.org), Europe (European Health Psychology Society; www.ehps.net), and in the UK (the Division of Health Psychology within the British Psychological Society; www.health-psychology.org.uk).

HEALTH PSYCHOLOGY – DISCIPLINE OR PROFESSION?

In recent years, health psychology has developed strongly as a discipline, but there is still uncertainty about the nature of the professional roles and training needs of health psychology practitioners. One important step in this process was the publication of *Health Psychology: A Discipline and a Profession* (Stone et al., 1987), a collection of papers from a conference which brought together leading US health psychologists in a discussion of training-related issues. The contributors attempted to define the knowledge and skills base of health psychology, as well as identify the contexts where these could be applied. This early volume is therefore something of a landmark in the attempt to map out the disciplinary and professional basis of health psychology.

Earlier in this chapter we outlined the emergent knowledge base of health psychology, and we also referred to the many textbooks and journals devoted to the discipline which provide strong evidence of its scope and quality. The professional development of health psychology has inevitably taken longer, but this is now clearly beginning to happen in many countries. Textbooks in clinical health psychology (e.g. Bennett Johnson et al., 2002) and on health-psychology-based interventions (e.g. Rutter & Quine, 2002) provide clear indications of the ways in which health psychology approaches can be applied in preventive or clinical settings. Despite this, there is still a lack of consensus as to the best way to train psychology graduates for the professional roles which are now recognized within health psychology.

One example of a training model is the tripartite approach to professional training in health psychology which originated in the UK, with its view of professional practice in terms of research, teaching and training, and consultancy, and this has been mapped out and developed in a companion volume by Michie and Abraham (2004). In addition to these three core areas of professional practice, there are a range of other roles involving interventions at all sorts of levels from delivering primary prevention to providing support and behaviour change initiatives in people with major health problems, as we have outlined earlier in this chapter.

Within Europe there have been attempts to define the core areas of training for professional health psychology, and some common themes are emerging (Marks et al., 1998; McIntyre et al., 2000). As the key aims and methods of professional training in health psychology are mapped out, and as professional roles emerge, there will be a greater understanding of what health psychologists can and should be doing to improve health and health care.

In this book, we have been very fortunate in obtaining very high-level contributions on the main areas of health psychology from major experts in the field. In addition to providing current, critical overviews of these key areas, many have also provided excellent examples of the wide range of professional roles which are possible for health psychologists. Over the next few years, there will need to be further development and agreement about the content and best methods for implementing professional health psychology training. As health psychologists branch out and apply their knowledge and skills more widely to the improvement of health and health care, this will provide an excellent real-world test of the adequacy and applicability of their knowledge and theoretical base. Inevitably the result is that we will become more aware of the gaps in the knowledge base as well as the limitations in the explanatory value and relevance of current theories. This, in turn, will provide the impetus for further work incorporating refinements in research methods and theoretical models, in the continuing attempts to improve our understanding of the role of psychological factors in health, illness and health care. Although health psychology is still in its relative infancy, so much has already been achieved and there is the promise of so much more to follow. We very much hope that the present volume provides both a representative account of the progress in the discipline and serves as a foundation for the development of professional roles and training.

DISCUSSION POINTS

1. Summarize the reasons underlying the emergence of health psychology, and relate these to the limitations of a narrowly biomedical view of health and health care.
2. Write down in a few sentences how the disciplines in figure 1.1 would conceptualize myocardial infarction, how each of the disciplines would go about reducing distress in patients with a myocardial infarction, and which theoretical approach each discipline would be using.
3. Find out what the most important journals are respectively for the six disciplines (figure 1.1), based on SSCI and SCI impact factors.
4. Find, study and critically review an empirical paper on what health psychologists would designate 'primary prevention'. Find, study and

> critically review an empirical paper on what physicians would desig-
> nate 'primary prevention'. Analyse similarities and differences.
> 5. Design the outline, by giving chapter titles, of a book that introduces
>   health psychology to undergraduate psychology students; design the
>   outline, by giving chapter titles, of a book that introduces health psycho-
>   logy to graduate psychology students; and a book that introduces health
>   psychology to medical students.

REFERENCES

Ajzen, I. (1991). The theory of planned behavior. *Organizational Behavior and Human Decision Processes* 50, 179–211.

American Psychologist (2003). Summary report of journal operations, 2002. *American Psychologist* 58, 663.

Armitage, C. J. and Conner, M. (2000). Social cognition models and health behaviour: a structured review. *Psychology & Health* 15, 173–89.

Astin, J. A., Becker, W., Soeken, K., Hochberg, M. C. and Berman, B. (2002). Psychological interventions for rheumatoid arthritis: a meta-analysis of randomised controlled trials. *Arthritis Care & Research* 47, 291–302.

Bandura, A. (1986). *Social Foundations of Thought and Action.* Englewood Cliffs, NJ: Prentice Hall.

Baum, A., Revenson, T. A. and Singer, J. E., eds. (2001). *Handbook of Health Psychology.* Mahwah, NJ: Lawrence Erlbaum.

Bennett Johnson, S., Perry, N. W. and Rozensky, R. H., eds. (2002). *Handbook of Clinical Health Psychology.* Washington, DC: American Psychological Association.

Blanchard, E. B., ed. (1982). Special issue: behavioral medicine. *Journal of Consulting and Clinical Psychology* 50, 795–1053.

Cameron, L. D. and Leventhal, H. (2003). Self-regulation, health, and illness: an overview. In L. D. Cameron and H. Leventhal, eds., *The Self-regulation of Health and Illness Behaviour.* London: Routledge, 1–13.

Campbell, M., Fitzpatrick, R., Haines, A., Kinmonth, A. L., Sandercock, P., Spiegelhalter, D. and Tyrer, P. (2000). A framework for the design and evaluation of complex interventions to improve health care. *British Medical Journal* 321, 694–6.

Carver, C. S. and Scheier, M. F. (1998). *On the Self-regulation of Behavior.* New York: Cambridge University Press.

Conner, M. and Norman, P., eds. (1996). *Predicting Health Behaviour.* Buckingham, UK: Open University Press.

Conner, M. and Norman, P. (2001). Health behavior. In D. W. Johnston and M. Johnston, eds., *Health Psychology.* Amsterdam: Elsevier, 1–37.

Godin, G. and Kok, G. (1996). The theory of planned behavior: a review of its applications to health-related behaviors. *American Journal of Health Promotion* 11, 87–98.

Hardeman, W., Johnston, M., Johnston, D. W., Bonetti, D., Wareham, N. J. and Kinmonth, A. L. (2002). Application of the theory of planned behaviour in behaviour change interventions: a systematic review. *Psychology & Health* 17, 123–58.

Hardey, M. (1998). *The Social Context of Health*. Buckingham: Open University Press.

Johnston, D. W. and Johnston, M., eds. (2001). *Health Psychology*. Amsterdam: Elsevier.

Kaplan, R. M. (2000). Two pathways to prevention. *American Psychologist* 55, 382–96.

Kaplan, R. M. (1990). Behavior as the central outcome in health care. *American Psychologist* 45, 1211–20.

Kaptein, A. A. and Creer, T. L., eds. (2002). *Respiratory Disorders and Behavioral Medicine*. London: Martin Dunitz.

Lacasse, Y., Brosseau, L., Milne, S., Martin, S., Wong, E., Guyatt, G. H., Goldstein, R. S. and White, J. (2003). Pulmonary rehabilitation for chronic obstructive pulmonary disease (Cochrane Review). In *The Cochrane Library*, issue 3. Oxford: Update.

Lang, E. V., Benotsch, E. G., Fick, L. J., Lutgendorf, S., Berbaum, M. L., Berbaum, K. S., Logan, H. and Spiegel, D. (2000). Adjunctive non-pharmacological analgesia for invasive medical procedures: a randomised trial. *The Lancet* 355, 1486–90.

Lanza, M. L., Carifio, J., Pattison, I. and Hicks, C. (1997). Validation of a vignette simulation of assault on nurses by patients. *Journal of Nursing Scholarship* 29, 151–4.

Leventhal, H., Nerenz, D. R. and Steele, D. J. (1984). Illness representations and coping with health threats. In A. Baum, S. E. Taylor and J. E. Singer, eds., *Handbook of Psychology and Health: Vol. IV*. Hillsdale, NJ: Lawrence Erlbaum, 219–52.

Linden, W., Stossel, C. and Maurice, J. (1996). Psychosocial interventions for patients with coronary artery disease: a meta-analysis. *Archives of Internal Medicine* 156, 745–52.

Llewelyn, S. and Kennedy, P., eds. (2003). *Handbook of Clinical Health Psychology*. Chichester, UK: Wiley.

Marks, D., Brucher-Albers, C., Donker, F., Jepsen, Z., Rodriguez-Marin, J., Sidot, S. and Backman, B. (1998). Health psychology 2000: the development of professional health psychology. *Journal of Health Psychology* 3, 149–60.

Matarazzo, J. D. (1980). Behavioral health and behavioral medicine: frontiers for a new health psychology. *American Psychologist* 35, 807–17.

Matarazzo, J. D. (1982). Behavioral health's challenge to academic, scientific, and professional psychology. *American Psychologist* 37, 1–14.

McIntyre, T., Maes, S., Weinman, J., Wrzesniewski, K. and Marks, D. (2000). *Post-graduate Programmes in Health Psychology in Europe: A Reference Guide*. Leiden: European Health Psychology Society.

Meyer, T. J. and Mark, M. M. (1995). Effects of psychosocial interventions with adult cancer patients: a meta-analysis of randomized experiments. *Health Psychology* 14, 101–8.

Michie, S. and Abraham, C., eds. (2004). *Health Psychology in Practice*. Oxford: Blackwell.

Michie, S., Miles, J. and Weinman, J. (2003). Patient-centredness in chronic illness: what is it and does it matter? *Patient Education and Counseling* 51, 197–206.

Miller, G. E. and Cohen, S. (2001). Psychological interventions and the immune system: a meta-analytic review and critique. *Health Psychology* 20, 47–63.

Millon, T., Green, C. and Meagher, R., eds. (1982). *Handbook of Clinical Health Psychology*. New York: Plenum Press.

Murray, M. and Chamberlain, K., eds. (1999). *Qualitative Health Psychology: Theories and Methods*. Sage: London.

Nezu, A. M., Nezu, C. M. and Geller, P. A., eds. (2003). *Health Psychology*, vol. 9. Chichester, UK: Wiley.

Ogden, J. (2003). Some problems with social cognition models: a pragmatic and conceptual analysis. *Health Psychology* 22, 424–8.

Outlook Society of Behavioral Medicine (1995). President's message (1). Knoxville, TN: SBM.

Parkinson, B. and Manstead, A. S. R. (1993). Making sense of emotion in stories and social life. *Cognition and Emotion* 7, 295–323.

Petrie, K. P., Cameron, L. D., Ellis, C. J., Buick, D. and Weinman, J. (2002). Changing illness perceptions after myocardial infarction: an early intervention randomized controlled trial. *Psychosomatic Medicine* 64, 580–6.

Radley, A. and Chamberlain, K. (2001). Health psychology and the study of the case: from method to analytic concern. *Social Science & Medicine* 53, 321–32.

Rehse, B. and Pukrop, R. (2003). Effects of psychosocial interventions on quality of life in adult cancer patients: meta-analysis of 37 published controlled outcome studies. *Patient Education and Counseling* 50, 179–86.

Rutter, D. and Quine, L., eds. (2002). *Changing Health Behaviour – Intervention and Research with Social Cognition Models.* Buckingham, UK: Open University Press.

Salmon, P. and Hall, G. M. (2003). Patient empowerment and control: a psychological discourse in the service of medicine. *Social Science & Medicine* 57, 1969–80.

Scharloo, M., Kaptein, A. A., Weinman, J., Hazes, J. M., Willems, L. N. A., Bergman, W. and Rooijmans, H. G. M. (1998). Illness perceptions, coping and functioning in patients with rheumatoid arthritis, chronic obstructive pulmonary disease and psoriasis. *Journal of Psychosomatic Research* 44, 573–85.

Schwartz, G. (1982). Testing the biopsychosocial model: the ultimate challenge facing behavioural medicine? *Journal of Consulting and Clinical Psychology* 50, 1040–53.

Schwartz, G. E. and Weiss, S. M. (1978). Behavioral medicine revisited: an amended definition. *Journal of Behavioral Medicine* 1, 249–51.

Senior, V., Marteau, T. M. and Weinman, J. (1999). Impact of genetic testing on causal models of heart disease and arthritis: an analogue study. *Psychology & Health* 14, 1077–88.

Smith, T. W., Kendall, P. C. and Keefe, F. J. (2002). Special issue: behavioral medicine and clinical health psychology. *Journal of Consulting and Clinical Psychology* 70, 459–856.

Sontag, S. (1979). *Illness as Metaphor.* New York: Vintage Books.

Stone, G. C., Cohen, F. and Adler, N. E., eds. (1979). *Health Psychology – A Handbook.* San Francisco: Jossey-Bass.

Stone, G. C., Weiss, S. M., Matarazzo, J. D., Miller, N. E., Rodin, J., Belar, C. D., Follick, M. J. and Singer, J. E. (1987). *Health Psychology: A Discipline and a Profession.* Chicago: University of Chicago Press.

Sutton, S., Baum, A. and Johnston, M., eds. (2004). *Handbook of Health Psychology.* London: Sage.

Van Diest, R., Hamulyak, K., Kop, W. J., van Zandvoort, C. and Appels, A. (2002). Diurnal variations in coagulation and fibrinolysis in vital exhaustion. *Psychosomatic Medicine* 64, 787–92.

Wardle, J. (2000). Editorial: public health psychology: expanding the horizons of health psychology. *British Journal of Health Psychology* 5, 329–36.

Weinman, J. and Petrie, K. J. (2000). Health psychology. In M. G. Gelder, J. J. Lopez-Ibor Jr. and N. C. Andreasen, eds., *New Oxford Textbook of Psychiatry.* Oxford: Oxford University Press, 1225–36.

White, C. A. (2001). *Cognitive Behaviour Therapy for Chronic Medical Problems.* Chichester, UK: Wiley.

Chapter Two

HEALTH-RELATED BEHAVIOUR: PREVALENCE AND LINKS WITH DISEASE

Andrew Steptoe and Jane Wardle

CHAPTER OUTLINE

Two of the central issues in health psychology are understanding the determinants of health behaviour, and improving methods of promoting behaviour change and healthier lifestyles. This chapter focuses on what we mean by health behaviours, how they are related to disease and disability, and how they are patterned in the population. The chapter begins with an outline of why health behaviours are important for public health. A historical summary of the development of the health behaviour concept is provided, and definitions of health behaviour are offered. The chapter then discusses several major health behaviours, including tobacco use, food choice, physical activity, alcohol consumption, cancer screening, sexual behaviour, and hazardous driving behaviour. In each case, we describe the associations with disease, the prevalence of the behaviours in various countries of the developed world, and how the behaviours are patterned in relation to gender and socio-economic status. The chapter concludes with a description of the large number of factors that contribute to health behaviour, ranging from sociocultural and economic influences, right through to aspects of the individual's health and biology.

KEY CONCEPTS

AIDS/HIV

Alameda County study

alcohol consumption

cancer screening

carcinogenesis

chronic disease

drinking and driving

driving speed

family determinants

food choice

health service provision

leading causes of death

legislation

measurement of behaviour

obesity

physical activity

preventive health behaviours

sexually transmitted disease

socio-economic status

standardized death rate

tobacco epidemic

INTRODUCTION

Health behaviours are increasingly recognized as pivotal factors in health promotion and the prevention of disease, with behavioural factors estimated to account for half of the premature death from the 10 leading causes in the developed world (Gruman & Follick, 1998). What causes most death and disability? Table 2.1 summarizes the main causes of death in the countries of the European Union averaged together, and in two illustrative individual countries, the United Kingdom and Germany (World Health Organization, 2002). It can be seen that cardiovascular diseases and cancer are by far the most common causes of death, together accounting for 66 per cent of male and 67 per cent of female deaths. The most frequent individual diagnosis is coronary heart disease in men and women, but stroke, lung cancer and breast cancer are also very common, while a significant proportion of people die from respiratory diseases such as chronic obstructive pulmonary disease. The other leading causes are accidents and unintentional injury, from incidents such as road traffic accidents, injury in the home and accidental poisoning. The pattern is very similar in the US, where recent figures indicate that 37 per cent of men and 38 per cent of women died from cardiovascular disease, and 24 and 23 per cent respectively from cancers (National Center for Health Statistics, 2001).

What this means is that efforts to improve health in the population must tackle this set of health problems. The terrible scourges of past eras that still pervade the developing world, such as infectious illnesses, account for no more than 1 per cent of deaths in Europe and the US. For the diseases that beset modern society, behaviours such as smoking, dietary choice, alcohol consumption and regular physical activity make a significant contribution. Although many factors are involved in the development of cardiovascular disease, cancers and chronic respiratory diseases, it is recognized that

Table 2.1 Percentage of deaths from major causes in European countries – 1998

	European Union average		United Kingdom		Germany	
	Men	Women	Men	Women	Men	Women
Standardized death rate per 100,000	896.4	531.6	905.3	597.3	926.9	556.2
All cardiovascular diseases	38%	40%	40%	37%	43%	46%
Coronary heart disease	17	14	25	18	21	18
Stroke	8	11	8	11	8	11
All cancers	28	27	27	28	27	27
Lung cancer	8	3	7	5	7	3
Breast cancer		5		5		5
Respiratory diseases	9	8	15	15	7	5
Accidents and injuries	7	4	4	3	6	4
Road traffic accidents	2	<	1	<	1	<

Notes: < = less than 1%
Source: World Health Organization, 2002.

healthier lifestyles are the key to reducing the incidence of these conditions, while early detection through screening and other medical assessments can improve outcome.

Of course, everybody must die of something, so the fact that these medical conditions cause most deaths may be because they are diseases of old age. Table 2.2 makes some additional points about the importance of health behaviour, by summarizing the leading causes of death in middle-aged men and women aged 45–54 years, and teenagers and young adults (15–24 years). There are important differences between the causes of total deaths in table 2.1, and the pattern of premature mortality in the middle-aged shown in table 2.2. Cardiovascular diseases are much less prominent, causing 26 per cent instead of 38 per cent of deaths in men and 16 per cent instead of 40 per cent of deaths in women. Interestingly, mortality from coronary heart disease is preserved in men, reflecting the importance of this illness for premature mortality as well. Conversely, the proportion of deaths attributable to cancers is higher in the middle-aged compared with the entire population, particularly among women. The difference in factors accounting for deaths is even more striking for teenagers and young adults. In this age group, death rates from chronic diseases such as coronary heart disease, stroke and lung cancer are very low. Instead, deaths from accidents and injuries figure prominently, with about a third of all deaths resulting from road traffic accidents.

Again, this pattern is not unique to Europe. In the US, the leading causes of death among 45- to 64-year-olds are cancers (35 per cent), stroke and diseases of the heart (29 per cent), followed by unintentional injuries (5 per cent) and respiratory diseases

Table 2.2 Causes of death in young and middle-aged adults: European Union, 1998

	Middle-aged adults (45–54 years)		Teenagers and young adults (15–24 years)	
	Men	Women	Men	Women
Standardized death rate per 100,000	473.1	243.1	82.0	30.4
All cardiovascular diseases	26%	16%	4%	7%
Coronary heart disease	15	5	<	<
Stroke	4	5	<	<
All cancers	35	53	7	13
Lung cancer	10	6	<	<
Breast cancer		17		<
Accidents and injuries	13	8	69	52
Road traffic accidents	3	2	39	30

Notes: < = less than 1%
Source: World Health Organization, 2002.

(4 per cent). In young people aged 15–24 years, unintentional injuries are most common (44 per cent) followed by murder (16 per cent) and suicide (13 per cent), with cancers and cardiovascular disease accounting for less than 10 per cent (National Center for Health Statistics, 2001).

The figures in table 2.2 describe the relative importance of different causes of death, and not absolute rates. The 'standardized death rate', shown at the top of the table, indicates how many people died in each category. It can be seen that far fewer young people died overall, so although accidents and injuries dominate in younger groups, the absolute number of deaths is not so large in comparison with older cohorts. In addition, we must recognize that the postponement of death is only one aspect of health, and that chronic but non-lethal medical conditions are also important. Nevertheless, the point of these comparisons is to show up the relevance of health-related behaviours to the major causes of death throughout the lifespan.

The development of the health behaviour concept

The modern concept of health behaviour can be dated back to the pioneering research of the epidemiologist Sir Richard Doll on the health impact of smoking. His study of many thousands of British doctors started in the 1950s, and identified smoking as a major precursor of premature mortality (Doll & Hill, 1964). Since then, numerous epidemiological and laboratory studies have investigated dietary choices, alcohol consumption, patterns of physical exercise, sexual behaviour and safety practices in relation to specific health outcomes. The notion that health behaviours might cluster together into a healthy lifestyle owes its scientific foundation to the Alameda County study. This investigation of just under 7,000 adults living in Alameda County, California, began in 1965 with a postal questionnaire, followed by regular surveys of death and illness. When the factors measured at baseline were analysed against later mortality, seven aspects of lifestyle predicted death: not being physically active, smoking, sleeping for either short (less than 7 hours) or long (more than 8 hours) periods nightly, skipping breakfast, eating snacks between meals, regularly drinking more than 5 units of alcohol at one session, and being either overweight or underweight (Belloc, 1973). Importantly, it was also found that the more positive health habits that people reported, the lower their risk of death. These same behaviours were also related to future disability (Breslow & Enstrom, 1980). Work of this kind has stimulated researchers to look beyond individual risk factors for particular illnesses, and think of health behaviour as a broader construct. Habits such as cigarette smoking and excessive alcohol consumption have a range of health effects that are not limited to a single disease endpoint, and different behaviours may have common determinants.

THE DEFINITION OF HEALTH BEHAVIOUR

There are two broad types of health behaviour: those that increase risk and those that promote health. Health risk behaviour can be defined as *any activity undertaken by people with a frequency or intensity that increases risk of disease or injury*. Common health risk behaviours include cigarette smoking, taking narcotic drugs, excessive alcohol consumption, some sexual behaviours, and drink-driving. Our definition indicates that the amount or 'dose' of the behaviour may be important. This is not the case for most behaviours, but there are instances in which moderate levels may be beneficial; as will be seen later in the chapter, there is evidence that moderate alcohol consumption is associated with more favourable health outcomes than either heavy drinking or complete abstinence.

The definition of positive health behaviour is more controversial. The first to attempt a formal definition were Kasl and Cobb (1966), who stated that health behaviour was 'any activity undertaken by a person believing himself to be healthy for the purpose of preventing disease or detecting it at an asymptomatic stage.' This definition is orientated towards the detection and prevention of disease by healthy individuals, and does not include actions by people who are already ill. However, much health behaviour is carried out by people with a diagnosed condition, and is aimed at delaying the further progression of the disorder. Kasl and Cobb's definition also regards a health behaviour as one that is consciously carried out for health-enhancing purposes. But both positive and risk health behaviours are important irrespective of whether the individual carries out the activity for health reasons. Exercising on most days would be regarded as a positive health behaviour, whether the person does this for health reasons, or because they are sports fans, play in teams, enjoy the social aspects or are trying to look good. We would therefore define health behaviours as *activities that may help to prevent disease, detect disease and disability at an early stage, promote and enhance health, or protect from risk of injury.* Common positive health behaviours include regular physical exercise, various dietary choices, using sunscreen, using a seatbelt, driving sensibly, and taking advantage of medical and dental screening opportunities.

Several general points emerge from these definitions of health behaviour:

1) The concept of health behaviour is fluid, and the activities that are included can change as medical knowledge develops. In the 1950s in Britain, children were encouraged to eat the fat on meat, and refusal to do so was considered a sign of fussy eating. The use of a condom when having sex with a person whose sexual history is unknown only emerged as a preventive health behaviour within the past 25 years. There is much current interest in the role of folic acid in coronary heart disease because of its effects on plasma homocysteine, so it is possible that dietary supplementation with folate will soon be seen as a positive health behaviour (Schnyder et al., 2001). It is also likely that there are other activities that many people do now without a moment's thought that may turn out to have adverse health effects.

2) The strength of evidence relating behaviours with health outcome is extremely variable. Some findings have emerged from case-control studies, comparing people who do and do not have an illness, while others are backed by prospective epidemiological research, studies of trends over time, and experimental work on the biological mechanisms through which the behaviour affects the disease process. A basic principle of research is that association is not the same as cause. An association between a behaviour and a health outcome may be a chance occurrence, or due to some third underlying factor that is related both to the behaviour and the illness. It is essential that results are replicated with different samples, and that there is some understanding of the biological mechanisms responsible, before we can be confident about health behaviours. An epidemiological article in 1988 listed 56 associations that had been observed in case-controlled studies, but had not been confirmed in subsequent investigations (Mayes, Horwitz & Feinstein, 1988). These included associations between coffee-drinking and congenital birth defects, owning a dog and developing multiple sclerosis, and the use of saccharine and the development of bladder cancer. We need to be certain that any health education advice we provide is based on sound scientific data, otherwise there is a danger that we reinforce the sceptical public's view that scientists can't make up their minds, and say something is dangerous one day and safe the next.

3) As noted earlier, our definitions of health behaviour recognize that these activities may be done for non-health reasons. Some healthy habits such as toothbrushing and limiting fat in the diet may be driven by non-health motives like concern about appearance. This means that health motives may be relatively unimportant in many cases, reducing the probable impact of any programme of behaviour change that is founded on attempts to provide health knowledge or change health-related attitudes. Health psychologists need to view behaviour in a broad context, and recognize that health motivations and cognitions are part of a wider set of influences on health behaviour. A summary of these wider influences is provided later in the chapter.

IMPORTANT HEALTH BEHAVIOURS IN THE MODERN WORLD

The next sections of this chapter provide information about the main health risk and positive health behaviours that are relevant to the population at large. In each case, we provide information about the prevalence or frequency of the behaviour, with particular reference wherever possible to the European populations. We also specify the medical conditions affected by the behaviour, and outline some of the pathways through which the behaviour exerts its effects. Finally, we summarize how the behaviours are distributed in the population, focusing on sex differences, variations in the behaviour with age, and the impact of socio-economic status or social class. There are a number of other important health behaviours, including sunscreen use, sleep patterns, drug use, dental health behaviour, and breast self-examination. We have not discussed these in the interests of space, and because we have focused on the behaviours that are of greatest importance to the health of the public, and for which the most evidence is available.

TOBACCO USE

Tobacco smoking must take pride of place among health risk behaviours. The burden of disease attributable to smoking in developed countries is greater than for all other health behaviours. Cigarette smoking leads to increased risk of coronary heart disease, lung cancer, and cancers of the larynx, oesophagus, mouth, bladder and cervix. It also causes a number of pregnancy complications, including detached placenta, bleeding during pregnancy, premature delivery, and low birth weight. It has been estimated that smoking 1–6 cigarettes per day during pregnancy increases the risk of having a low birth weight infant by 60 per cent (Institute of Medicine, 2001). Other problems related to tobacco use include stroke, vascular disease in the legs, and chronic obstructive pulmonary diseases such as bronchitis and emphysema. An effect on bone mineral density and risk of hip fractures in older age groups is now acknowledged as well (Law & Hackshaw, 1997). Smokers tend to have poorer psychological well-being than non-smokers, and score more highly on measures of depressive symptoms and psychiatric problems. Researchers at the World Health Organization have estimated that tobacco accounts for 14.9 per cent of deaths in the developed world, and for 17 per cent of disability (Murray & Lopez, 1996).

Several different biological mechanisms are responsible for the impact of smoking on health. Tobacco smoke contains about 4,000 chemicals, at least 40 of which are carcinogenic. These lead to mutations in the cells of different tissues, some of which proliferate clonally in an uncontrolled fashion. The effects of smoking on cardiovascular disease are due in part to damage done to the vascular endothelium, the single layer of cells lining blood vessels. The impact of smoking on pregnancy outcomes results from changes in blood flow and supply of nutrients from the mother to the foetus, leading to growth retardation. Some mechanisms are not yet understood;

for instance, the effects of tobacco on calcium absorption and the formation of new bone are probably not large enough to account for effects of smoking on hip fractures.

Does smoking have any health benefits? It has been suggested that dementia and Alzheimer's disease are less common in smokers than non-smokers. However, this supposed benefit is probably illusory, since larger prospective studies have shown no reduced rate of dementia among smokers (Doll et al., 2000).

The good news about smoking is that many of the adverse health effects are reversible. Although timing varies, for many conditions the increased risk associated with smoking disappears a short time after giving up.

The prevalence of smoking

The proportion of people who smoke in a range of developed countries is summarized in table 2.3. These figures are derived from self-report surveys, but it is also possible to measure carbon monoxide in expired air or metabolites of tobacco such as cotinine in blood or saliva. The different methods typically come up with similar results in general surveys. The smoking rate is just under 30 per cent in men, and slightly lower in women, but there are wide variations between countries. Smoking rates have levelled off or declined over the past 20 years in many countries, but rates in children have not decreased, and may even have risen. As table 2.3 shows, the proportion of 15-year-olds who smoke is rather high, indicating that a new generation of heavier smokers may be emerging (Currie et al., 2000). It can also be seen from table 2.3 that in many countries there is a slightly higher proportion of female than male adolescent smokers, while the gender difference is in the opposite direction in adults.

Table 2.3 Smoking in the adult population and in 15-year-old school students (per cent)

	Adult population[1]		School students[2]	
	Men	Women	Boys	Girls
Australia	27	23		
Belgium	31	26	20	21
England	28	26	24	21
Germany	43	30	25	22
Greece	46	28	14	13
The Netherlands	37	30		
Sweden	17	22	16	10
US	28	22	12	13

Notes: All percentages refer to the proportion of people smoking at least one cigarette a day.
[1] Latest available year; from Corrao et al., 2000.
[2] Data from 1997–8 WHO Cross-national Study of Health Behaviour in School-aged Children (Currie et al., 2000).

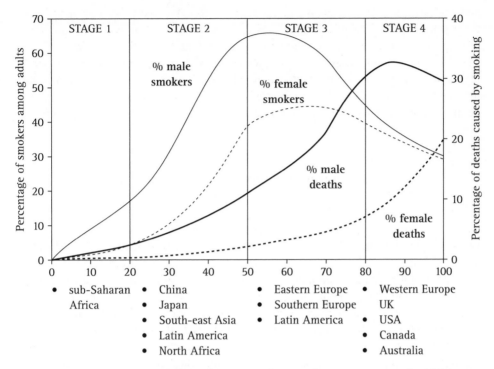

Figure 2.1 The stages of the tobacco epidemic; from Lopez et al., 1994

The general pattern of smoking depends on the stage of economic development of the country. Figure 2.1 summarizes the model developed by the World Health Organization to describe the tobacco epidemic of the twentieth and twenty-first centuries (Lopez, Collishaw & Piha, 1994). This model proposes there are four major stages of tobacco use in the world, each of which may continue for 20–30 years, and that countries will progress through stages unless fundamental steps are taken to alter the pattern. Stage 1 is characterized by a smoking prevalence of less than 20 per cent in men and little smoking in women. The prevalence of lung cancer and other smoking-related diseases is low. This pattern is typical of developing countries that have yet to be drawn into the global tobacco economy. Countries in Stage 2 show increases in smoking up to more than 50 per cent in men, and a growing proportion of female smokers, together with rising death rates from lung cancer among men as the consequences of smoking habits emerge. Tobacco control activities are not well developed in these countries, and many individuals do not understand the health risks. This pattern is thought to be present in many countries in Asia, Latin America and north Africa. Stage 3 sees the peak in male smoking and the beginning of a downturn in prevalence, while levels in women typically peak a few years later. There is a continuing rise in mortality from smoking and a narrowing gap in the proportion of male and female smokers. Many countries of eastern and southern Europe appear to be at this stage. Stage 4 is marked by decreases in smoking in both men and women, and the beginning of a decrease in smoking-attributable deaths among men. However, deaths among women continue to rise. Countries in Stage 4, which include much of western Europe, Canada, Australia, New Zealand, and the US, have vigorous anti-smoking educational programmes, and often legislation against smoking in public places. It remains to be seen whether this pattern is borne out in practice, but it does highlight the importance that international health promotion policies play in preventing developing countries from going through the same miserable experience as the Western World.

Socio-economic position and smoking

One of the strongest influences on smoking in the developed world is socio-economic position. Socio-economic position has affected death and illness for more than 2,000 years. People who come from more deprived social backgrounds, have less education and lower-prestige jobs, tend to die sooner and suffer from more chronic medical conditions and psychiatric problems. The causes of this gradient have varied through history – at one time, it could be attributed to the sheer amount people had to eat, and then in later eras to hygienic problems that followed from crowded urban living. But over the past half century, it has been realized that health behaviours play an important role (Adler et al., 1999). The measurement of socio-economic status is complicated, but common markers include occupational class, income, educational attainment, and scales of deprivation. Figure 2.2 shows the pattern of cigarette smoking in the UK in adults classified on two socio-economic indices: occupational class and educational attainment (Jarvis & Wardle, 1999). Odds ratios are presented rather than

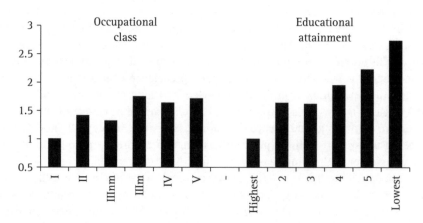

Figure 2.2 The relationship between cigarette smoking and socio-economic status as defined by occupational social class (left panel) and educational attainment (right panel) in the UK. Values represent odds ratios, with Class 1 and the highest educational group as the reference categories. Nm = non-manual, m = manual. From Jarvis and Wardle, 1999

absolute rates, so the figure shows the likelihood that someone will smoke in each socio-economic position, compared with the reference rate of 1 in the highest occupational group, or most educated group. It can be seen that for both criteria, there is a rather orderly increase in smoking with decreasing socio-economic status, so that less privileged people are much more likely to smoke. This pattern is due partly to higher rates of starting smoking in lower status groups, and to higher rates of stopping smoking in the better off sectors of the population. Both factors seem to be involved. The implication for health psychology is that prevention and intervention are equally important.

DIET

If tobacco smoking takes first place among health risk behaviours, a healthy diet is the front-runner in positive health behaviours. Food has always been of fundamental importance for health, mostly obviously getting enough food to provide for energy needs, but also getting the right balance of foods to supply nutrient requirements. In the wealthier parts of the world in the twentieth century, a new dietary problem arose as a consequence of the advances in food manufacturing and preservation. These made many energy-dense foods more accessible, cheap, and designed to appeal to the eye and the palate, than ever before. The modern food supply, combined with an increasingly sedentary lifestyle, has led to an epidemic of over-consumption, not only of energy, but also of fat, sugar and salt. In parallel, high fibre, nutrient-rich, plant-based foods such as vegetables and fruits, are under-consumed. The changes in both diet and physical activity have led to epidemic increases in obesity in both adults and children (Kumanyika et al., 2002; Strauss & Pollack, 2001).

Diet is generally measured in surveys using food frequency questionnaires, in which people indicate how often they eat a range of foodstuffs. This method is quick and easy, but is prone to error, since respondents may not accurately recall how often they eat different foods, and the measure may not include all the foods in their diets. Another common method is to carry out a 24-hour dietary recall, in which people indicate exactly what and how much they ate over the past day. This method is more specific, but involves complicated dietary analysis, and the previous day may not have been typical for the individual. More elaborate methods, such as food diaries or weighed records, are necessary if very precise information is needed (Calfas, Zabinski & Rupp, 2000).

Fat intake

The weight of evidence that saturated fat intake is directly associated with serum cholesterol levels, which in turn are strongly and linearly related to risk of atherosclerosis and heart disease, has generated a huge drive for research into the determinants of fat intake. While we know that heart disease is a multi-factorial condition,

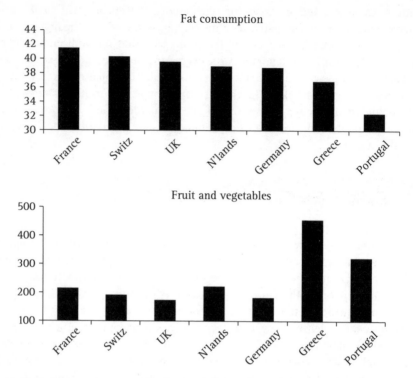

Figure 2.3 Percentage energy derived from fat (upper panel), and availability of fruit and vegetables (kg per person) in selected countries. Figures from the World Health Organization, 2002

a high fat diet appears to be the necessary condition for its development. In areas like rural China where fat intake is very low and population cholesterol levels are well below the typical values found in the West, heart disease is extremely rare (Campbell, Parpia & Chen, 1998). The process whereby saturated fat increases coronary heart disease involves the oxidization of one type of cholesterol (low density lipoprotein), and its deposition in the walls of blood vessels, increasing the amount of atherosclerosis.

Fat intake is also strongly linked to the energy content of the diet, since fat is the most energy-dense of the macronutrients, and thereby to weight gain. Higher-fat diets promote weight gain in rats. Human studies show that low-fat diets are almost always associated with some weight loss – since without significant amounts of fat in the diet, it is much more difficult to keep energy intake levels high (Astrup, 2001).

Figure 2.3 summarizes fat consumption in a number of countries, presented in terms of percentage of energy (calories) derived from fat. The target for *Healthy People 2010* in the US is that adults and children derive no more than 30 per cent of calories from fat, and there are similar guidelines elsewhere in the world (US Department of Health and Human Services, 2000; World Health Organization, 1999a). It is clear from figure 2.3 that fat consumption is well above recommended levels in most European countries, especially those in northern and central Europe. However, the use of lower-fat versions of foods is increasingly popular, and consumption of semi-skimmed milk, for example, is now more common than full-fat milk. Similarly, as awareness that saturated fats are the principal cause of higher blood cholesterol has become more widespread, consumption of animal fats in the form of butter or lard has been reduced in favour of spreads derived from plant oils such as sunflower or olive. Choosing lower-fat foods has become one of the most commonly reported health behaviours, with more than 50 per cent of adults in the UK saying that they try to limit fatty foods in their diet (Wardle & Griffith, 2001).

Women tend to consume more lower-fat foods than men, which appears to be primarily due to their greater use of deliberate weight control strategies, but also their greater concern about diet and health. However, overall there are not striking differences in energy intake from fat. Likewise there are some socio-economic differences in food choices, but this does not result in a consistent socio-economic gradient for fat intake (Gregory et al., 1990).

Fruit and vegetable intake

The other area of dietary behaviour which is attracting increasing interest from researchers is under-consumption of fruit and vegetables. Fruits and vegetables are nutrient-rich foods that are also low in energy density. The idea that they are healthy elements of the diet is not new, having its scientific origin in the eighteenth-century observation that sailors who had little or no fresh food while at sea for long periods developed scurvy. Providing limes – and thereby vitamin C in the diet – prevented this. Oddly this snippet of dietary history seems to have become surprisingly embedded in the national consciousness, at least in the UK, with many adults still linking scurvy with eating too little fruit and vegetables.

Fruit and vegetable consumption has been linked with low rates of development of heart disease and many cancers in a number of large-scale studies (Ness & Powles, 1997; Peto, 2001). The primary nutritional mechanism is believed to involve their anti-oxidant content. Anti-oxidant vitamins such as vitamin C, beta carotene and vitamin E scavenge the oxidated products of metabolic processes, which would otherwise damage cells. Anti-oxidants are thought to protect the endothelial lining of blood vessels from oxidative damage, and also to protect other cells (especially epithelial cells) from DNA damage which can lead to a higher risk of lung, skin and cervical cancer. Plasma vitamin C levels have been shown to be linked prospectively with mortality (Khaw et al., 2001). Interestingly, no studies have yet been able to achieve the same benefits with administration of vitamin supplements, which suggests that the form in which the anti-oxidants come, or some other co-factor in fruits and vegetables, is required for the positive effects. On the basis of existing epidemiological research, the World Health Organization recommended an intake of at least 400 grams of fruit and vegetables a day. This has been translated in many countries into five servings a day (at least three of vegetables and two of fruit).

The average intake in most countries is well below the recommended level. The National Food Survey in the United Kingdom reported a mean intake of 3.85 portions per day across all households in 1999, with fewer than 25 per cent eating five or more servings, while surveys in the US indicate that only 32 to 35 per cent of adults eat five or more a day (US Department of Health and Human Services, 2000). Southern European countries, where fruits and vegetables are plentiful, cheap and an established element of the normal meal, tend to have higher consumption than northern European countries – although there is a fear that the spread of the fast-food culture, processed meals and fat-based desserts, will erode this advantage. This pattern is illustrated in the lower panel of figure 2.3, which shows that fruit intake is far higher in southern countries like Greece and Portugal in comparison with northern and central European countries.

It is not clear why consumption of fruit and vegetables is so low. It could be related to the relative tastiness of processed foods, which may make fruits and vegetables appear bland by contrast. In addition, fruit and vegetables have a relatively low energy density, and this could put them at a disadvantage in the complex psycho-biological processes governing food choices. For example, it has been shown that 2- to 5-year-old children develop preferences for novel flavours when they are paired with more energy-dense yoghurts or drinks, indicating that energy density contributes to how much foods are liked (Birch et al., 1990).

Women tend to eat more fruit and vegetables than men (Li et al., 2000). This is partly due to women's greater investment in healthy dietary choices. Households with children eat less fruit and vegetables than adult households, suggesting that children's reluctance to eat these foods could influence the family meal patterns (Ministry of Agriculture, 2000). Low socio-economic status groups tend to eat strikingly less fruit and vegetables than high status groups. This is also reflected in serum vitamin levels, which are strikingly lower in men and women of lower socio-economic status (Gregory et al., 1990).

In summary, the food choices of most people in the developed world put them at risk for serious chronic medical conditions. Fat intake is too high, while the consumption of fruit and vegetables is lower than recommended. The limited intake of fruit and vegetables in lower socio-economic status groups may be one reason why they are at greater disease risk.

PHYSICAL ACTIVITY

Regular physical activity has a wide range of positive effects on health. Since obesity arises from an imbalance between energy intake (food) and energy expenditure (activity), lack of regular exercise is a major determinant of weight gain and obesity. Physical inactivity is related to premature mortality, particularly death from coronary heart disease. It has been estimated that sedentary adults are twice as likely to develop premature heart disease than active people, after controlling statistically for other factors. The mechanism underlying this effect is probably a combination of influences on the major risk factors for heart disease, including body weight, high blood pressure, blood cholesterol levels and diabetes. Effects on cancer are less certain, but there is evidence for a lower risk of cancer of the colon in physically active people. Physical activity also contributes to the maintenance of bone mass and bone mineral density. The added strength and flexibility associated with regular exercise is thought to reduce the risk in older people of falling and suffering from fractures. In addition, the evidence is reasonably strong that exercise has positive effects on mood and psychological well-being (Biddle & Mutrie, 2001). Certainly, physically active people report more positive mood profiles than the sedentary, feeling less tense, anxious and depressed, and have a greater capacity to cope with stress.

How much is enough exercise? This is a difficult issue that has been studied for many years. Until the 1990s it was thought that exercise did not confer health benefits unless the person improved their physical fitness – this normally requires vigorous activity (running, swimming, dancing) continuously for 20 minutes or more on at least three days of each week. However, other studies indicate there is a dose-response relationship between the amount of exercise performed and premature mortality, with health effects progressively increasing with exercise levels (Blair et al., 1995). Over the last decade, it has been agreed that lower levels of activity are also beneficial, provided that they are carried out frequently. For example, a study of 72,000 middle-aged nurses in the US suggested that brisk walking for at least three hours each week reduced risk of coronary heart disease by 30–40 per cent (Manson et al., 1999). The current advice in many countries is that people accumulate 30 minutes of moderately intense exercise like brisk walking on at least five days of each week.

Exercise can have negative effects on health as well. Sudden death while exercising is documented, although it is very rare. More common are musculoskeletal injuries. Many of these instances are due to activity that is too intense for the person, or to unfortunate cases in which an individual has a physiological abnormality of which they were not aware. In the population at large, the health gains from exercise outweigh these adverse effects. Unfortunately, the health benefits of exercise are not lasting. Someone who changes from being very active to becoming sedentary soon loses the advantages of their earlier lifestyle. For health psychologists, this means that encouraging people to maintain activity is just as important as helping them to start in the first place.

Physical activity is another difficult health behaviour to quantify. Most studies rely on self-report, and people may overestimate their activity so as to present themselves in a positive light. In addition, the same activity (e.g. soccer, dancing) can be carried out at quite different levels of intensity. A lot of activity occurs in everyday life, perhaps when walking to and from work or climbing stairs at home, and this is difficult to record accurately. In some countries, there are large variations in physical activity over the year, since people exercise more in the summer. Objective measurements of activity are possible, involving motion sensors or even global positioning systems. Heart rate is sometimes monitored as an index of physical activity, on the grounds that vigorous activity stimulates large increases in heart rate. These objective methods are very helpful, but difficult to apply in large-scale studies (Sallis & Owen, 1999).

Andrew Steptoe and Jane Wardle

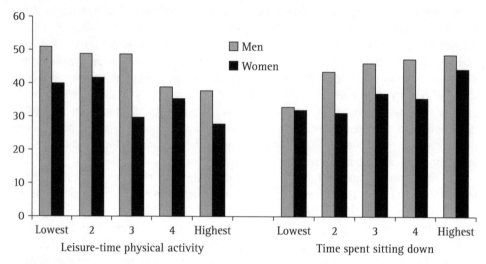

Figure 2.4 The proportion of adults in the European Union who are overweight or obese (body mass index > 25) in relation to physical activity. The left panel shows the population divided into quintiles of leisure-time physical activity, and it can be seen that excessive body weight is more common in those who carry out least physical activity. The right panel shows the division on the basis of leisure time spent sitting down (watching television, reading, listening to music), and excessive body weight is more common in more sedentary individuals. From Martinez-González et al., 1999

It has been estimated that in the US only 27 per cent of adults exercise to recommended levels, and at the other extreme, 29 per cent report no leisure-time activity at all (Pratt, Macera & Blanton, 1999). In the UK, 48 per cent of men and 31 per cent of women aged 25–34 years are active at recommended levels, declining to 32 per cent men and 21 per cent of women aged 55–64 years (Erens & Primatesta, 1999). A recent survey of a representative sample of adults from the 15 European Union member states showed that the proportion of adults carrying out any leisure-time physical activity ranged from 90 per cent in Sweden and 84 per cent in the Netherlands, to 77 per cent in the United Kingdom, 66 per cent in France, and 41 per cent in Portugal (Martinez-González et al., 2001). Among 15-year-old students there are also big variations, ranging from 70 per cent of girls and 85 per cent of boys in Germany exercising two or more hours a week, compared with 51 per cent of girls and 67 per cent of boys in the US, and 40 per cent of girls and 61 per cent of boys in England (Currie et al., 2000).

Associations between physical activity and body weight can be seen in cross-sectional studies. Figure 2.4 summarizes data from adults in the European Union. It is apparent that either overweight or obesity is more common in individuals who do little leisure-time physical activity, and in those who spend much of their time in sedentary pursuits (Martinez-González et al., 1999).

Men tend to be more physically active than women. This is one of the few health behaviours in which men have an advantage, but the difference appears not to be related to health concerns. Rather, men participate in sporting activities more than women, and are also more likely to have active manual jobs. As far as leisure-time physical activities are concerned, there is a social gradient in both men and women, with people of higher socio-economic status being more physically active (Martinez-González et al., 2001).

ALCOHOL

Alcoholic beverages are made from a wide range of grains and fruits, and are consumed throughout the world. The health risks of alcohol can be divided into problems that result directly from excessive intake such as alcohol dependence, foetal alcohol syndrome and alcoholic liver cirrhosis, and illnesses in which alcohol is one of a number of important causal factors. The latter include risk of high blood pressure, cardiac arrhythmias, and cancers of the mouth, throat, colon and rectum. The mechanisms responsible for some of these effects are beginning to be understood. For example, ethanol is broken down by cells and bacteria in the mouth and digestive system to create a potent carcinogen called acetaldehyde. Alcohol also contributes in a crucial way to road traffic accidents and domestic violence, and is associated with problems like sexually transmitted disease.

Assessing the health impact of alcohol is complicated for two reasons. Firstly, many adverse effects depend not only on how much is drunk overall, but also on the pattern of consumption. Binge drinking has particular health risks; drinking heavily on just two nights a week may lead to worse health outcomes than drinking the same total amount evenly over all seven days of the week. Secondly, there appears to be a U-shaped relationship between alcohol use and mortality in the United States and western Europe (Marmot, 2001). The explanation of this pattern is almost certainly due to a protective effect of moderate intake on coronary heart disease.

Estimating the amount of alcohol drunk in different countries is not easy, because there are variations in the preferred type of beverage – beer, wine or spirits – and in some cultures the amount of home brewing and illicit production is high. Table 2.4 summarizes data from the US and some European countries (World Health Organization, 1999b). There are wide variations even between these few countries, with the highest per capita consumption in Denmark and the lowest in the United Kingdom. We can also see that the proportion of people who drink several times a week is higher in countries like Portugal, Greece and France than in the US and Denmark. It is likely that countries with a higher overall consumption level will have more problem drinkers, but there may also be cultural differences in the amount of binge drinking. In the US, it has been estimated that 5.4 per cent of adults are heavy drinkers, consuming five or more drinks on at least five days every month, and 17 per cent of drinkers meet the diagnostic criteria for alcohol dependence or alcohol abuse (Institute of Medicine, 2001).

Table 2.4 Alcohol consumption in the adult population and in 15-year-old school pupils

	Total population		School pupils (%)[3]	
	Per capita consumption (litres)[1]	Frequent drinkers (%)[2]	Boys	Girls
Belgium	11	19	38	22
Denmark	15.2	16	46	38
France	14.6	30	31	15
Greece	12.5	36	52	31
Portugal	13.5	39	29	9
United Kingdom	9.5	19	17	11
US	11	15.5	23	15

[1] Per capita consumption per year in litres in adults aged 15 or older.
[2] Typically defined as drinking at least 3 times a week; from World Health Organization, 1999b.
[3] Students who report drinking beer, wine or spirits at least weekly; from Currie et al., 2000.

Alcohol consumption is more common in men than women, though the gap is smaller in developed countries than in the developing world. This pattern begins early in life, with more male than female adolescents being regular drinkers. The age at which people start drinking predicts the likelihood of later problems. As can be seen in table 2.4, more than a third of 15-year-old boys in Belgium, France and Greece drink at least once a week.

There is good evidence that heavy alcohol consumption is more common in lower social status groups, particularly among men. Deaths from diseases caused by alcohol show a clear social gradient, with higher rates in less privileged groups. This is illustrated in figure 2.5 with the death rate by social class from two causes: alcohol dependent syndrome, and chronic liver disease and cirrhosis. Rates increase with lower occupational position, but the slope is comparatively small until the lowest stratum (that of unskilled manual workers) is reached. There is rather less of a social gradient in moderate than in heavy alcohol consumption.

Drinking alcohol is deeply embedded within Western culture, and a significant proportion of the economy is devoted to alcohol production and distribution. Nevertheless, the amount of alcohol consumed has been declining throughout the developed world since around 1980, suggesting that publicity about the risk of excessive drinking has had an impact on consumption. By contrast, there is serious concern that in Russia and eastern Europe, heavy drinking has become more common in unskilled male workers, possibly in response to the disintegration of familiar social structures that occurred with the collapse of communism. This may be responsible in part for the high premature mortality rates in these countries over the past 15 years (McKee & Shkolnikov, 2001).

In conclusion, alcohol is a difficult health behaviour to manage since it is both socially acceptable and possibly even medically beneficial at moderate levels, and

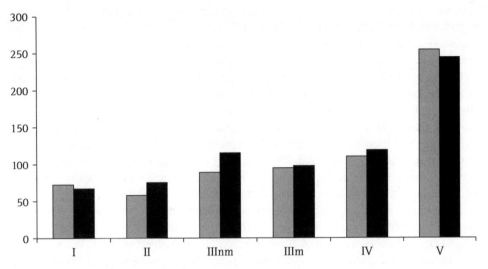

Figure 2.5 Standardized mortality ratio (SMR) by social class for alcohol dependence syndrome (grey bars) and chronic liver disease and cirrhosis (solid bars) for men aged 20–64 in England and Wales (1991–3). Social class ranges from professional (I) to unskilled manual (V). The SMR is the death rate standardized to an average of 100 for the population, so values less than 100 indicate better than average, while values over 100 are worse than average. From Drever and Whitehead, 1997

sustains a significant sector of the economy. This means that simple messages such as 'do not drink' are not feasible, and health promotion efforts need to be more sophisticated.

CANCER SCREENING

Cancer is a multi-stage process, involving a sequence of probably 4–6 mutations in the cells before they develop their full damaging and invasive potential. The purpose of screening is to detect abnormalities before the disease process is manifest in symptoms. Its value in cancer comes from detecting the malignant or, better still, pre-malignant transformations at a stage before there is significant damage to surrounding tissues or metastases (migration of cancer cells to other regions of the body through the lymphatic or blood system to set up secondary cancers at the new sites). Each cancer has a different developmental process and medical technology has developed strategies for identifying the earliest stages better for some cancers than others. In colorectal cancer, the early abnormalities (adenomatous polyps) can be visualized directly during sigmoidoscopic examination and removed quickly and easily, thereby entirely eliminating the risk of further malignant transformation at that site (UK Flexible Sigmoidoscopy Screening Trial Investigators, 2002). Cervical cancer also has an established pre-malignant stage, and the use of Papanicolaou (Pap) smears has clearly been linked with reduced mortality (Sasieni & Adams, 1999). Testing for the viral causal agent, human papillomavirus or HPV, should also contribute to a reduction in the incidence of cervical cancer (Cuzick et al., 2000).

For some other cancers (e.g. breast and prostate cancer), techniques are not yet available to detect a pre-malignant stage, so the aim of screening is to identify the area of cell proliferation before the cells have mutated to their metastasizing form. In these cases, the screening identifies malignancy rather than pre-malignancy, and so treatment in the form of surgery and chemotherapy is likely to be required whenever any abnormality is detected. The benefit of screening in these cases depends on the availability of treatments which are either more effective at that early stage, or offer equivalent benefit with less associated toxicity.

Some cancers are also known to develop more readily in individuals who have inherited specific mutations from one of their parents (e.g. BRCA1 for breast cancer; HNPCC for colorectal cancer). Advances in genetic technologies are making it feasible to screen for these mutations, either by mutation testing (testing for the risky polymorphisms in the individual's DNA) or, where the gene is not yet cloned, comparing the DNA of the individual to be tested with that of affected and unaffected relatives. If the individual has the susceptible genotype, they can be offered frequent surveillance to give the maximum chance of detecting cancer at the earliest possible stage. Higher risk individuals could also take steps to avoid exposure to aspects of the environment that increase cancer risk (e.g. tobacco) and might consider chemoprevention (e.g. tamoxifen for women at higher risk of breast cancer). In cases where the risk is even higher, some individuals have prophylactic surgery such as prophylactic mastectomy or oophorectomy, to reduce the likelihood of the malignant transformations starting in the at-risk organs (Kauff et al., 2002).

The benefits of screening to public health depend on reducing mortality and treatment costs. There is consensus that regular cervical screening reduces cervical cancer mortality, and reductions in cervical cancer incidence have been seen in many countries as they implement an effective screening programme. Both randomized controlled trial evidence and case-control studies support the value of faecal occult blood screening to detect colorectal cancer (Scholefield et al., 2002), while the use of flexible sigmoidoscopy screening should result in significant reductions in incidence (UK Flexible Sigmoidoscopy Screening Trial Investigators, 2002). Randomized trial evidence supports the efficacy of mammography screening (Nystrom et al., 2002), although benefits are probably not as great as had been hoped. There is controversy about the costs and benefits of other forms of cancer screening, especially prostate screening (Parkinson et al., 2002).

Uptake of screening

The value of screening in a community depends crucially on high rates of utilization among the at-risk population. Most developed countries have public education campaigns which advise on screening regimens. Some countries such as the UK record participation and send invitations to individuals when their screening is due, which tends to result in good attendance rates across the board. Others countries (e.g. the US) publicise screening recommendations, but individuals must make their own arrangements.

There is evidence that groups with lower income and lower levels of education are less likely to participate in screening (*Bostick* et al., 1994; McCaffery et al., 2002). The fact that there are socio-economic differences in participation even where screening is free to all citizens suggests that the barriers are not only financial. In general, public attitudes towards screening are positive; most people accept the view that earlier detection is likely to lead to a better outcome. In fact there are often strong public pressures to introduce new screening programmes, even where there is still doubt among clinicians and epidemiologists about whether earlier detection is useful. This is usually because some of the cancers detected would probably never have become problematic and meanwhile the treatment is likely to have adverse effects, resulting in no net benefit. Screening for prostate cancer may fall into this category (Parkinson et al., 2002).

Individually, however, there are variations in the perception of the value of, or need for, screening. Attitudinal factors associated with non-attendance include feeling healthy and not in need of medical checks (demonstrating the failure of the message that screening is to pick up problems *before* symptoms develop), being frightened of cancer, and being embarrassed about the test procedure (Wardle et al., 2000). Factors such as fear of cancer and concerns about the test procedure may lie behind the socio-economic differences in attendance. There is also an important issue of gender differences. By reputation, men are less willing than women to involve themselves with medical care. However, research into participation in colorectal cancer (one of the few cancers that are screened for in both men and women) documents very little differences in men's and women's participation rates (UK Flexible Sigmoidoscopy Screening Trial Investigators, 2002).

SEXUAL BEHAVIOUR

The HIV/AIDS epidemic of the past quarter century has transformed the impact of sexual behaviour on health. Before infection with human immunodeficiency virus (HIV) was identified in 1981, the most serious sexually transmitted disease had been syphilis, and this had largely been eliminated with antibiotics. But the spread of HIV has been such that in 1995, 43,000 people died from AIDS in the US. It was the eighth most common cause of death in the US, and the leading cause among 25- to 44-year-olds (Institute of Medicine, 2001). The situation in many other parts of the world is far more bleak. Overall, more than 33 million adults and 1.3 million children live with HIV/AIDS. An estimated 24.5 million of these individuals live in sub-Saharan Africa, compared with 520,000 in western Europe and 900,000 in North America.

Other unpleasant but not life-threatening conditions such as gonorrhoea and genital herpes are highly prevalent sexually transmitted diseases. In the US, it has been estimated that some 20 per cent of the population have genital herpes (Tanne, 1998). Sexually transmitted infections are more common in teenagers and young adults than in older groups. HIV/AIDS contribute fewer than 1 per cent of the total new cases of sexually transmitted infection every year.

An aspect of sexual behaviour that is becoming increasingly recognized is its contribution to spreading viruses that are linked with cancer risk. As noted earlier in the section on cancer screening, types of human papilloma virus (HPV) are responsible for cervical cancer. Hepatitis B is linked with liver cancer, and is also sexually transmitted.

All these sexually transmitted infections are driven by behaviour. Factors such as early age of first intercourse, multiple sexual partners, the failure to use condoms, and sexual practices such as anal intercourse affect the likelihood of transmission. The occurrence of sexually transmitted infections is directly related to the number of sexual partners. A national survey in the US estimated that the lifetime occurrence of sexually transmitted infection rises from 4 per cent for those with only one partner after the age of 18 years, to 40.4 per cent for those who have had more than 20 partners (Laumann, 1994).

Information about sexual behaviours is available in national surveys from many countries. In the UK, for example, 13.8 per cent of men and 6.8 per cent of women in the age range 16–49 years report having had at least one sexual partner other than their regular partner in the past 12 months (Johnson et al., 1994). The comparable figures for the Netherlands are 18 and 17 per cent for men and women respectively (Leridon, Van Zessen & Hubert, 1998). In high-risk groups, unsafe sexual practices are common. Thus, it has been found that about one-third of both HIV positive and negative gay and bisexual men have had recent unprotected anal intercourse (Lemp et al., 1994). A study of HIV positive women reported that more than 40 per cent had engaged in unprotected vaginal intercourse, and 10 per cent in unprotected anal intercourse, in the previous six months (Kalichman, 1999). The occurrence of risky sexual behaviour is particularly high among intravenous drug users, homeless people and others at the margins of society.

HAZARDOUS DRIVING BEHAVIOUR

Road traffic crashes are the leading cause of death for children and young adults in the US and Europe. In the 15 European Union countries, some 45,000 people are killed and 1.6 million injured in road crashes every year. In the year 2000, more than 41,000 people were killed in traffic crashes in the US. Three behaviours are particularly important in increasing the risk of the vehicle crashes and injury: drink-driving, not using a seatbelt, and driving too fast. In the year 2000, it is thought that alcohol was involved in 40 per cent of fatal crashes in the US (National Highway Traffic Safety Administration, 2000). The problem is particularly marked among the

Table 2.5 Hazardous driving behaviour in European populations (per cent)

	Driving over the speed limit		Drink-driving[1]	Seatbelt use[2]
	Motorways	Urban areas		
Germany	18	7	3.4	82
Greece	38	7	13.1	15
Hungary	15	8	0.6	61
Italy	23	11	5.6	15
The Netherlands	27	8	1.1	64
Spain	30	7	5.0	51
United Kingdom	29	6	1.9	89

[1] Driving after drinking over the legal limit at least once in the past week.
[2] Always wearing a seatbelt in urban areas.
Source: Data from the Project on Social Attitudes to Road Traffic in Europe, 1998.

young, since drivers aged 21 to 24 had the highest intoxication rates. The risk of involvement in fatal crashes rises with blood alcohol concentration in all age groups, but the slope is steepest in the young (Zador, Krawchuk & Voas, 2000).

Seatbelts are one of the most important means of reducing injury. It has been estimated that seatbelts are 45–60 per cent effective in reducing deaths, 50–65 per cent effective in reducing serious injury in accidents (National Highway Traffic Safety Administration, 2000). In contrast, speeding is one of the most important factors contributing to crashes. Again in the US, speeding contributed to 29 per cent of all fatal crashes, and more than half a million people received injuries in speeding-related crashes. Of all drivers involved in fatal crashes, young men are the most likely to be speeding. The speed a vehicle is travelling on impact determines the severity of injury in pedestrians. It has been estimated that 5 per cent of pedestrians hit at 20 miles per hour are killed, increasing to 85 per cent of those hit at 40 miles per hour (World Health Organization, 2001).

Table 2.5 summarizes data collected in the mid-1990s from seven European countries (Social Attitudes to Road Traffic Risk in Europe, 1998). The figures were collected by self-report, so probably underestimate the extent of hazardous behaviour. However, it is evident that a significant proportion of drivers in these countries disobey speed limits, have driven after drinking too much even over the past week, and do not regularly use seatbelts when sitting in the front of a vehicle. Large differences between countries are also evident. In the UK and Germany, the vast majority of respondents reported using seatbelts, compared with the minority in Italy and Greece. High rates of disobeying speed limits were found in Italy, Spain and Greece, and in these countries the prevalence of drink-driving was also greatest. Comparison with figures in other parts of the world is difficult because of varying methods of data collection. However, surveys in the US show a prevalence among university students of drink-driving at least once over the past year of more than 30 per cent (Institute of Medicine, 2000). A survey in the US in 2000 involving measures by observers in several hundred sites showed that overall, 75 per cent of drivers and 70 per cent of passengers were using seatbelts when sitting in the front of cars (Waller, 2002).

Hazardous driver behaviours are a great deal more common in men than women. They are also typically associated with age and socio-economic status, such that older drivers and those of higher social status tend to be more safe in their behaviour.

DETERMINANTS OF HEALTH BEHAVIOUR

Health behaviours take place within a cultural and social context. The psychological factors that influence health behaviour are detailed in Chapter 3. However, it is important to appreciate the broader context, not only for a fuller understanding of why people act in the way they do, but because non-psychological factors may limit the impact that interventions can have on changing behaviour. The broader determinants also remind us that most people do not carry out positive health practices or indulge in risk behaviours primarily for health reasons, or often even for conscious reasons at all. In this section, we therefore summarize the wider determinants of health behaviour, beginning with the broadest national and even international factors, narrowing down to issues that are influential within the individual.

Sociocultural and national factors

One reason that there are wide variations in the frequency of different positive and risk behaviours is national, cultural and religious tradition. Most countries have a distinctive cuisine, with preferences for particular foods and methods of preparation. Some religions and cultures disapprove of alcohol and smoking, while others proscribe the eating of meat from particular animals. Cultural factors also affect the behaviour of young adults prior to marriage, and place limits on sexual expression.

Legislative factors

Several health-compromising behaviours are affected by laws. In many countries, for example, it is illegal to sell tobacco to children. While this does not prevent children from smoking, the difficulty of obtaining cigarettes may affect rates of uptake. Laws also govern the purchasing of alcohol, while various drugs and sexual practices may be outlawed. There is good evidence that laws concerning drink-driving and seatbelt use have an impact on these behaviours (DeJong & Hingson, 1998). The method of law enforcement is also relevant. Laws concerning selling alcohol to minors have little deterrent effect if they are not constantly monitored. In the case of driving, primary enforcement, when police officers are allowed to stop a vehicle solely for something like a seatbelt violation, has substantially greater effects than secondary enforcement, when a violation can only be cited after the vehicle has been stopped for another suspected misdemeanour (Dinh-Zarr et al., 2001). Laws concerning the fitting of seatbelts to cars, or the presence of physical education within the school curriculum, again influence the occurrence of the behaviour.

Macro-economics

Many health behaviours cost money. Cigarettes, alcohol, food, exercise facilities and access to health care (in some countries) have to be purchased. Economic factors such as the buoyancy of the economy and availability of disposable income, together with taxes on tobacco and alcohol, have perceptible effects on behaviour.

Systems of provision and services

Some health behaviours are dependent on the availability of goods and services. If manufacturers do not make palatable low-fat foods, and these are not stocked in retail outlets, then people are not likely to eat them. If people live in dense, urban environments without sport and leisure facilities, their physical activity levels will suffer. There has been a striking increase in the availability of high protection sunscreen in many countries over recent years which has a direct association with protection from damaging sun exposure. The provision of smoke-free environments reduces smoking levels, and may help deter a proportion of smokers altogether.

Health service provision

Many of the methods that people use to prevent disease depend on the availability of appropriate health services. Even if they want to, people cannot get screened for cancer if there are no facilities, cannot have their teeth checked if they have no access to dental services, and similar factors apply to immunization programmes and health checks for markers like blood pressure and cholesterol.

Socio-demographic factors

As we have illustrated at several points in this chapter, health behaviours are strongly associated with age, sex and socio-economic status.

Health status

The ability to carry out many health behaviours is affected by personal health, while illness may provide additional motivation for behaviour change. For example, many people with disabilities or chronic lung disease are limited in the physical exercise they can carry out. People with diabetes and other metabolic disorders may have particular dietary requirements. The effectiveness of medications taken by people with HIV can be affected by alcohol and diet. Diagnosis with a condition like coronary heart disease or non-insulin-dependent diabetes may provide the stimulus for weight reduction through dietary change and physical exercise.

Social and family factors

Health behaviours are strongly affected by peer group influences, family habits and social networks (Baranowksi, 1997). Family habits have a strong impact on food choice, cigarette smoking, alcohol consumption and physical exercise habits. For example, children of adults who smoke are more likely to become smokers (Biglan et al., 1995). Health behaviours have been successfully modified through social support interventions, as in the studies involving supportive lay health advisers to encourage breast cancer screening among rural African American women (Earp et al., 2002).

Psychological factors

These are detailed in Chapter 3.

Biological factors

Finally, it should be emphasized that some health behaviours are determined in part by biological factors. Factors such as nicotine and opiate dependence are strong determinants of smoking and drug use respectively. Dietary choice may be influenced in part by the metabolic or psychological effects of particular nutrients, while alcohol has an important reciprocal relationship with biological stress responses (Sayette, 1993). There is also increasing interest in investigating the impact of genetic factors on health-related behaviours, with evidence from twin studies that there is a heritable component to smoking initiation and nicotine addiction, as well as to body weight and obesity, which probably reflect genetic effects on food intake and physical activity (Plomin et al., 2000).

SUMMARY AND CONCLUSIONS

Health behaviours are a central topic in health psychology. A wide range of everyday activities are relevant to health risk and health promotion. The occurrence of health behaviours varies systematically in relation to culture, gender, age and socioeconomic status. Health behaviours are determined by a range of personal and sociocultural factors, and need to be understood within the broad context of people's lives.

DISCUSSION POINTS

1. How do we know whether an activity is a 'health behaviour'?
2. What is the best way to inform the public about health behaviours?
3. Why is low socio-economic status associated with less healthy behaviours?
4. Is there such a thing as a 'healthy lifestyle'?
5. Should the way people drive really be described as health behaviour?
6. Are health risk behaviours such as smoking a matter of free choice?
7. Should we legislate against health risk behaviours?

FURTHER READING

Baranowksi, T. (1997). Families and health actions. In D. S. Gochman, ed., *Handbook of Health Behavior Research, Vol 1: Personal and Social Determinants*. New York: Plenum, 179–206.

DeJong, W. and Hingson, R. (1998). Strategies to reduce driving under the influence of alcohol. *Annual Review of Public Health* 19, 359–78.

Institute of Medicine (2001). *Health and Behavior: The Interplay of Biological, Behavioral, and Societal Influences*. Washington, DC: National Academy of Sciences.

McKee, M. and Shkolnikov, V. (2001). Understanding the toll of premature death among men in eastern Europe. *British Medical Journal* 323, 1051–5.

Social Attitudes to Road Traffic Risk in Europe (1998). European drivers and traffic safety. Available at http://sartre.inrets.fr. Accessed Oct. 8, 2001.

Strauss, R. S. and Pollack, H. A. (2001). Epidemic increase in childhood overweight, 1986–1998. *Journal of the American Medical Association* 286, 2845–8.

KEY STUDIES

Belloc, N. B. (1973). Relationship of health practices and mortality. *Preventive Medicine* 2, 67–81.

Lopez, A. D., Collishaw, N. E. and Piha, T. (1994). A descriptive model of the cigarette epidemic in developed countries. *Tobacco Control* 3, 242–7.

REFERENCES

Adler, N. E., Marmot, M., McEwen, B. S. and Stewart, J., eds. (1999). *Socio-economic Status and Health in Industrial Nations: Social, Psychological and Biological Pathways* (vol. 896). New York: New York Academy of Sciences.

Astrup, A. (2001). The role of dietary fat in the prevention and treatment of obesity: efficacy and safety of low-fat diets. *International Journal of Obesity* 25 Suppl 1, S46–50.

Baranowksi, T. (1997). Families and health actions. In D. S. Gochman, ed., *Handbook of Health Behavior Research, Vol 1: Personal and Social Determinants*. New York: Plenum, 179–206.

Belloc, N. B. (1973). Relationship of health practices and mortality. *Preventive Medicine* 2, 67–81.

Biddle, S. J. H. and Mutrie, N. (2001). *Psychology of Physical Activity*. London: Routledge.

Biglan, A., Duncan, T. E., Ary, D. V. and Smolkowski, K. (1995). Peer and parental influences on adolescent tobacco use. *Journal of Behavioral Medicine* 18, 315–30.

Birch, L. L., McPhee, L., Steinberg, L. and Sullivan, S. (1990). Conditioned flavor preferences in young children. *Physiology and Behavior* 47, 501–5.

Blair, S. N., Kohl, H. W., Barlow, C. E., Paffenbarger, R. S., Gibbons, L. W. and Macera, C. A. (1995). Changes in physical fitness and all-cause mortality: a prospective study of healthy and unhealthy men. *Journal of the American Medical Association* 273, 1093–8.

Bostick, R. M., Sprafka, J. M., Virnig, B. A. and Potter, J. A. (1994). Predictors of cancer prevention attitudes and participation in cancer screening examinations. *Preventive Medicine* 23, 816–26.

Breslow, L. and Enstrom, J. E. (1980). Persistence of health habits and their relationship to mortality. *Preventive Medicine* 9, 469–83.

Calfas, K. J., Zabinski, M. F. and Rupp, J. (2000). Practical nutrition assessment in primary care settings: a review. *American Journal of Preventive Medicine* 18, 289–99.

Campbell, T. C., Parpia, B. and Chen, J. (1998). Diet, lifestyle, and the etiology of coronary artery disease: the Cornell China study. *American Journal of Cardiology* 82, 18T–21T.

Core Institute (2000). 2000 Statistics on Alcohol and Other Drug Use on American Campuses. Available at http://www.siu.edu/departments/coreinst/public_html/recent.html. Accessed Dec. 17, 2001.

Corrao, M. A., Guindon, G. E., Sharma, N. and Shokoohi, D. F., eds. (2000). *Tobacco Control Country Profiles*. Atlanta, GA: American Cancer Society.

Currie, C., Hurrelmann, K., Settertobulte, W., Smith, R. and Todd, J., eds. (2000). *Health and Health Behaviour among Young People*. Copenhagen: World Health Organization.

Cuzick, J., Sasieni, P., Davies, P., Adams, J., Normand, C., Frater, A., van Ballegooijen, M. and van den Akker-van Marle, E. (2000). A systematic review of the role of human papilloma virus (HPV) testing within a cervical screening programme: summary and conclusions. *British Journal of Cancer* 83, 561–5.

DeJong, W. and Hingson, R. (1998). Strategies to reduce driving under the influence of alcohol. *Annual Review of Public Health* 19, 359–78.

Dinh-Zarr, T. B., Sleet, D. A., Shults, R. A., Zaza, S., Elder, R. W., Nichols, J. L., Thompson, R. S. and Sosin, D. M. (2001). Reviews of evidence regarding interventions to increase the use of safety belts. *American Journal of Preventive Medicine* 21, 48–65.

Doll, R. and Hill, A. B. (1964). Mortality in relation to smoking: ten years' observations of British doctors. *British Medical Journal* 1, 1399–1410, 1460–7.

Doll, R., Peto, R., Boreham, J. and Sutherland, I. (2000). Smoking and dementia in male British doctors: prospective study. *British Medical Journal* 320, 1097–102.

Drever, F. and Whitehead, M., eds. (1997). *Health Inequalities*. London: The Stationery Office.

Earp, J. A., Eng, E., O'Malley, M. S., Altpeter, M., Rauscher, G., Mayne, L., Mathews, H. F., Lynch, K. S. and Qaqish, B. (2002). Increasing use of mammography among older, rural African American women: results from a community trial. *American Journal of Public Health* 92, 646–54.

Erens, B. and Primatesta, P., eds. (1999). *Health Survey for England: Cardiovascular Disease '98*. London: The Stationery Office.

Gregory, J., Foster, K., Tyler, H. and Wiseman, M. (1990). *The Dietary and Nutritional Survey of British Adults. A Survey of the Dietary Behaviour, Nutritional Status and Blood Pressure of Adults Aged 16–64 Living in Great Britain*. London: The Stationery Office.

Gruman, J. and Follick, M., eds. (1998). *Putting Evidence into Practice: The OBSSR Report of the Working Group on the Integration of Effective Behavioral Treatments into Clinical Care*. Bethesda, MD: Office of Behavioral and Social Sciences Research, NIH.

Institute of Medicine (2001). *Health and Behavior: The Interplay of Biological, Behavioral, and Societal Influences*. Washington, DC: National Academy of Sciences.

Jarvis, M. J. and Wardle, J. (1999). Social patterning of individual health behaviours: the case of cigarette smoking. In M. G. Marmot and R. G. Wilkinson, eds., *Social Determinants of Health*. Oxford: Oxford University Press, 240–55.

Johnson, A. M., Wadsworth, J., Wellings, K. and Field, J. (1994). *National Survey of Sexual Attitudes and Lifestyles*. London: Penguin Books.

Kalichman, S. C. (1999). Psychological and social correlates of high-risk sexual behaviour among men and women living with HIV/AIDS. *AIDS Care* 11, 415–27.

Kasl, S. V. and Cobb, S. (1966). Health behavior, illness behavior, and sick role behavior, I: Health and illness behavior. *Archives of Environmental Health* 12, 246–66.

Kauff, N. D., Satagopan, J. M., Robson, M. E., Scheuer, L., Hensley, M., Hudis, C. A., Ellis, N. A., Boyd, J., Borgen, P. I., Barakat, R. R., Norton, L., Castiel, M., Nafa, K., and Offit, K. (2002). Risk-reducing Salpingo-oophorectomy in Women with a BRCA1 or BRCA2 mutation. *New England Journal of Medicine* 346, 1609–15.

Khaw, K. T., Bingham, S., Welch, A., Luben, R., Wareham, N., Oakes, S. and Day, N. (2001). Relation between plasma ascorbic acid and mortality in men and women in EPIC-Norfolk prospective study: a prospective population study. European Prospective Investigation into Cancer and Nutrition. *Lancet* 357, 657–63.

Kumanyika, S., Jeffery, R. W., Morabia, A., Ritenbaugh, C. and Antipatis, V. J. (2002). Obesity prevention: the case for action. *International Journal of Obesity* 26, 425–36.

Laumann, E. (1994). *The Social Organization of Sexuality*. Chicago: University of Chicago Press.

Law, M. R. and Hackshaw, A. K. (1997). A meta-analysis of cigarette smoking, bone mineral density and risk of hip fracture: recognition of a major effect. *British Medical Journal* 315, 841–6.

Lemp, G. F., Hirozawa, A. M., Givertz, D., Nieri, G. N., Anderson, L., Lindegren, M. L., Janssen, R. S. and Katz, M. (1994). Seroprevalence of HIV and risk behaviors among young homosexual and bisexual men. The San Francisco/Berkeley Young Men's Survey. *Journal of the American Medical Association* 272, 449–54.

Leridon, H., Van Zessen, G. and Hubert, M. (1998). The Europeans and their sexual partners. In M. Hubert, N. Bajos and T. Sandfort, eds., *Sexual Behaviour and HIV/AIDS in Europe: Comparisons of National Surveys*. London: UCL Press.

Li, R., Serdula, M., Bland, S., Mokdad, A., Bowman, B. and Nelson, D. (2000). Trends in fruit and vegetable consumption among adults in 16 US states: Behavioral Risk Factor Surveillance System, 1990–1996. *American Journal of Public Health* 90, 777–81.

Lopez, A. D., Collishaw, N. E. and Piha, T. (1994). A descriptive model of the cigarette epidemic in developed countries. *Tobacco Control* 3, 242–7.

Manson, J. E., Hu, F. B., Rich-Edwards, J. W., Colditz, G. A., Stampfer, M. J., Willett, W. C., Speizer, F. E. and Hennekens, C. H. (1999). A prospective study of walking as compared with vigorous exercise in the prevention of coronary heart disease in women. *New England Journal of Medicine* 341, 650–8.

Marmot, M. G. (2001). Alcohol and coronary heart disease. *International Journal of Epidemiology* 30, 724–9.

Martinez-González, M. A., Martinez, J. A., Hu, F. B., Gibney, M. J. and Kearney, J. (1999). Physical inactivity, sedentary lifestyle and obesity in the European Union. *International Journal of Obesity* 23, 1192–1201.

Martinez-González, M. A., Varo, J. J., Santos, J. L., De Irala, J., Gibney, M., Kearney, J. and Martinez, J. A. (2001). Prevalence of physical activity during leisure time in the European Union. *Medicine and Science in Sports and Exercise* 33, 1142–6.

Mayes, L. C., Horwitz, R. I. and Feinstein, A. R. (1988). A collection of 56 topics with contradictory results in case-control research. *International Journal of Epidemiology* 17, 680–5.

McCaffery, K., Wardle, J., Nadel, M. and Atkin, W. (2002). Sociodemographic variation in participation in flexible sigmoidoscopy screening for colorectal cancer. *Journal of Medical Screening*
9, 104–8.

McKee, M. and Shkolnikov, V. (2001). Understanding the toll of premature death among men
in eastern Europe. *British Medical Journal* 323, 1051–5.

Ministry of Agriculture, Food and Fisheries. (2000). *National Food Survey 1999*. London: The
Stationery Office.

Murray, C. J. L. and Lopez, A. (1996). *Quantifying Global Health Risks: The Burden of Disease
Attributable to Selected Risk Factors*. World Health Organization/Harvard University Press.

National Center for Health Statistics. (2001). *Health, United States, 2001*. Hyattsville, MD: National
Center for Health Statistics.

National Highway Traffic Safety Administration (2000). Traffic Safety Facts 2000. Available at
http://www-nrd.nhtsa.dot.gov/pdf/nrd-30/ncsa/tsf2000/2000occfacts.pdf. Accessed Oct. 8,
2001.

Ness, A. R. and Powles, J. W. (1997). Fruit and vegetables, and cardiovascular disease: a review.
International Journal of Epidemiology 26, 1–13.

Nyström, L., Andersson, I., Bjurstam, N., Frisell, J., Nordenskjöld, B. and Rutqvist, L. E. (2002).
Long-term effects of mammography screening: updated overview of the Swedish randomised
trials. *Lancet* 359, 909–19.

Parkinson, M. C., Bott, S. R., Montironi, R. and Melia, J. (2002). Screening for prostatic cancer and its evolution within Britain. *Journal of Pathology* 197, 139–42.

Peto, J. (2001). Cancer epidemiology in the last century and the next decade. *Nature* 411, 390–5.

Plomin, R., DeFries, J. C., McClearn, G. E. and McGuffin, P. (2000). *Behavioral Genetics*, 4th
edn. New York: W. H. Freeman.

Pratt, M., Macera, C. A. and Blanton, C. (1999). Levels of physical activity and inactivity in
children and adults in the United States: current evidence and research issues. *Medicine and
Science in Sports and Exercise* 31, S526–33.

Sallis, J. F. and Owen, N. (1999). *Physical Activity and Behavioral Medicine*. Thousand Oaks,
CA: Sage.

Sasieni, P. and Adams, J. (1999). Effect of screening on cervical cancer mortality in England
and Wales: analysis of trends with an age period cohort model. *British Medical Journal* 318,
1244–5.

Sayette, M. A. (1993). An appraisal-disruption model of alcohol's effects on stress responses
in social drinkers. *Psychological Bulletin* 114, 459–76.

Schnyder, G., Roffi, M., Pin, R., Flammer, Y., Lange, H., Eberli, F. R., Meier, B., Turi, Z. G. and
Hess, O. M. (2001). Decreased rate of coronary restenosis after lowering of plasma homocysteine levels. *New England Journal of Medicine* 345, 1593–1600.

Scholefield, J. H., Moss, S., Sufi, F., Mangham, C. M. and Hardcastle, J. D. (2002). Effect of
faecal occult blood screening on mortality from colorectal cancer: results from a randomised
controlled trial. *Gut* 50, 840–4.

Social Attitudes to Road Traffic Risk in Europe. (1998). European drivers and traffic safety.
Available at http://sartre.inrets.fr. Accessed Oct. 8, 2001.

Strauss, R. S. and Pollack, H. A. (2001). Epidemic increase in childhood overweight, 1986–
1998. *Journal of the American Medical Association* 286, 2845–8.

Tanne, J. (1998). US has epidemic of sexually transmitted disease. *British Medical Journal* 317,
1616.

UK Flexible Sigmoidoscopy Screening Trial Investigators. (2002). Single flexible sigmoi-doscopy screening to prevent colorectal cancer: baseline findings of a UK multicentre ran-domised trial. *Lancet* 359, 1291–1300.

US Department of Health and Human Services (2000). *Healthy People 2010.* Washington, DC: US Department of Health and Human Services.

Waller, P. F. (2002). Challenges in motor vehicle safety. *Annual Review of Public Health* 23, 93–113.

Wardle, J. and Griffith, J. (2001). Socio-economic status and weight control practices in British adults. *Journal of Epidemiology and Community Health* 55, 185–90.

Wardle, J., Sutton, S., Williamson, S., Taylor, T., McCaffery, K., Cuzick, J., Hart, A. and Atkin, W. (2000). Psychosocial influences on older adults' interest in participating in bowel can-cer screening. *Preventive Medicine* 31, 323–34.

World Health Organization. (1999a). *Health 21 – Health For All in the 21st Century.* Copenhagen: WHO Regional Office for Europe.

World Health Organization. (1999b). *Global Status Report on Alcohol.* Geneva: World Health Organization.

World Health Organization. (2001). *A 5-year WHO Strategy for Road Traffic Injury Prevention.* Geneva: World Health Organization.

World Health Organization. (2002). *Health for All Mortality Data Base.* Copenhagen: World Health Organization.

Zador, P. L., Krawchuk, S. A. and Voas, R. B. (2000). Alcohol-related relative risk of driver fatalities and driver involvement in fatal crashes in relation to driver age and gender: an update using 1996 data. *Journal of Studies in Alcohol* 61, 387–95.

Chapter Three

SOCIAL COGNITION MODELS OF HEALTH BEHAVIOUR

John de Wit and Wolfgang Stroebe

CHAPTER OUTLINE

Social cognition models consider the beliefs that individuals hold about the outcomes of their actions as key determinants of health-impairing and health-protective behaviours. In the first part of this chapter we will provide readers with an overview and discussion of a range of theories of (health) behaviour that have been developed from this social cognition perspective. In our discussion of prevailing models we distinguish between models that were specifically developed to explain health behaviours and those that were not. Key issues concern the types of beliefs that are included in the models, the way these beliefs are thought to combine to explain behaviour, and the empirical evidence that supports or refutes the theories' assumptions. In the remainder of the chapter we will explain and illustrate how social cognition models can be used in approaches to change health behaviours. Social cognition models of health behaviour generally focus on increasing individuals' motivation to change by targeting relevant beliefs, mostly through persuasive communication. This approach is limited in scope and effect, and in our application of social cognition models to behaviour change interventions we will also consider the translation of motivation into action, as well as the potentially staged nature of behaviour change.

KEY CONCEPTS

attitude
beliefs
coping appraisal
evaluation of the recommended action
expectancy–value principle
Health Belief Model
implementation intention
intention
models of health behaviour
models of social behaviour
perceived behavioural control
perceived health threat
principle of compatibility

Protection-Motivation Theory
salient beliefs
social cognitions
stage models
stage of change
subjective norm
tailoring
Theory of Planned Behaviour
Theory of Reasoned Action
threat appraisal
trans-theoretical model
volitional control

INTRODUCTION

In the first half of the twentieth century, infectious diseases lost their dominant position as causes of morbidity and mortality in industrialized countries (Armstrong, Conn & Pinner, 1999). Together with other relevant social changes, such as improved nutrition, this resulted in a substantial increase in life expectancy in these countries (Fielding, 1999; Matarazzo, 1984). Today, the leading causes of death are cardiovascular diseases and cancers, conditions that are increasingly being linked to health-impairing behaviours, such as smoking, drinking too much alcohol, poor nutrition, and lack of physical exercise (McGinnis & Foege, 1993).

In response to the increasing importance placed on lifestyle factors as determinants of health and illness, psychologists set out to develop an empirical and theoretical understanding of psychological determinants of health behaviour. *Health behaviour* has traditionally been defined as behaviour undertaken by individuals to enhance or maintain their health (e.g. Kasl & Cobb, 1966). However, since much behaviour with implications for one's health is often undertaken for reasons unrelated to health (e.g. dieting to look good; drinking alcohol to feel good), Stroebe (2000) argued that health behaviours should be defined in terms of their objective impact on health rather than in terms of the intentions of the individuals engaging in these behaviours. Researchers further distinguish between *health-impairing behaviours* (e.g. smoking, unprotected sex), which have a negative effect on health, and *health-protective behaviours* (e.g. exercising, eating a healthy diet), which have a positive effect (Matarazzo, 1984). Understanding the factors underlying health behaviours should help health researchers to develop successful strategies that contribute to *health promotion* and *disease prevention*.

As any other meaningful social behaviour, health behaviour is thought to be determined by a multitude of factors. The social-psychological approach to health behaviour emphasizes social-cognitive factors, in particular the class of social cognitions that concern beliefs about the consequences of a given behaviour or set of behaviours. *Beliefs* are socially acquired and shared expectancies that reflect, among others, thoughts about the attributes of some situation or condition (e.g. the perceived likelihood and severity of health consequences resulting from a lack of exercise), as well as considerations of the outcomes of specific courses of action (e.g. the advantages and disadvantages of exercising more regularly). For several reasons these and other *social cognitions* to be introduced later are considered important determinants of behaviour (Conner & Norman, 1996). First, social cognitions are thought of as relatively enduring characteristics of individuals that have the potential to shape behaviour. Secondly, social cognitions differentiate between individuals with a similar background, suggesting that social cognitions are proximal behavioural determinants that may mediate the impact of more structural intrinsic aspects of a person, such as sociodemographic characteristics and personality, as well as of factors extrinsic to the individual. Thirdly, social cognitions are generally shared within social groups, and thought to be socially acquired and open to change.

In this chapter we will review four social cognition models of health behaviour (for a more extensive review see Armitage & Conner, 2000), of which two deal specifically and exclusively with health behaviour (the Health Belief Model; Protection Motivation Theory), and two are more general models of social behaviour (Theory of Reasoned Action; Theory of Planned Behaviour). All these behaviour models are based on an *expectancy–value principle.* This principle starts from the assumption that decisions between different courses of action are based on two types of cognition: (1) subjective probabilities that a given action will lead to a set of expected outcomes (beliefs or expectancies), and (2) the evaluation of the action outcomes (values). Individuals are assumed to choose from various alternative courses of action that action which will be most likely to lead to positive consequences or avoid negative consequences.

The theories to be described in this chapter elaborate this basic expectancy–value model by specifying the types of *beliefs* that should be used in predicting a particular class of behaviour. They differ both in the types of beliefs included as determinants of intention and behaviour, and in the assumptions made about the way in which the different types of beliefs combine to influence behaviour. All theories can be used both to predict and explain behaviour, and as a basis for the development of interventions for health behaviour change. Both these aspects will be discussed in this chapter.

SOCIAL COGNITION MODELS OF HEALTH BEHAVIOUR

The Health Belief Model

In an attempt to understand why many individuals did not practise preventive health behaviours, in particular why they did not use available health services, such as screening tests to detect diseases at an early stage, a group of social psychologist in the

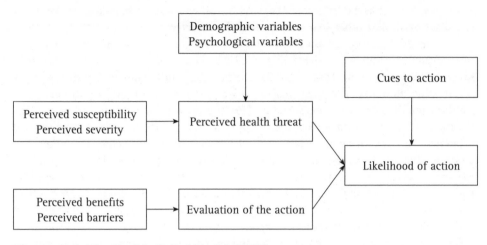

Figure 3.1 The Health Belief Model (HBM)

US Public Health Service developed the Health Belief Model (Rosenstock, 1974; Strecher, Champion & Rosenstock, 1997). Originating in the 1950s, the Health Belief Model (HBM) is 'the grandparent of all health behaviour change models' (Fisher & Fisher, 2000: 5). Moreover, the model has been used in a substantial body of research, and set the stage for subsequent theorizing (Sheeran & Abraham, 1996).

The HBM assumes that whether or not an individual engages in any particular health behaviour depends on a number of health beliefs (figure 3.1). In particular, the model suggests that the likelihood that an individual will engage in any given health behaviour to avert potential health problems is determined jointly by his or her *perception of the health threat* posed by the current situation he or she is in, and the individual's *evaluation of a recommended course of action* (Becker et al., 1977).

The extent of threat an individual experiences results from his or her *perceived susceptibility* to a particular illness or disability, in combination with the *perceived severity* of this illness or disability. The combined level of susceptibility and severity is assumed to provide the *motivation to act*. Whether a person will subsequently adopt a health-protective action is posited to depend on the subjective likelihood that the *benefits* resulting from that action, in particular its efficacy in avoiding the negative health consequences, outweigh the *barriers* that may have to be overcome, and the costs that may be incurred. For example, a sexually active student who enjoys having unprotected sex with a variety of partners may fear that he or she runs the risk of contracting a sexually transmitted disease (perceived vulnerability). Obviously, getting such a disease would have severe medical and social consequences (perceived severity). However, whether this student will decide to use condoms will depend on whether the perceived benefits of condom use (i.e. protection) outweigh the disadvantages, such as the reduction in sexual enjoyment and the embarrassment of having to negotiate condom use with a partner.

The HBM proposes further that *cues to action* may be needed to trigger behaviour (Rosenstock, 1974). Such behavioural triggers include internal cues, such as perceived symptoms, as well as external cues, such as health education campaigns or the death of a liked or similar other (e.g. a close friend or relative).

Since the original formulation of the model, a number of suggestions have been made for inclusion of additional variables into the HBM (e.g. Becker et al., 1977; Rosenstock, Strecher & Becker, 1988). To account for the fact that individuals may differ in terms of the value they attach to their health, as well as in their willingness to engage in health-promoting activities, Becker et al. (1977) proposed the inclusion of a category of variables termed *health motivation*. Health motivation was defined as representing differences in concern about health matters, and proposed to encompass rather disparate motivational factors, such as concerns about health and getting sick, willingness to seek diagnosis, positive health activities, and intention to comply. More recently, it was suggested that *self-efficacy*, a construct introduced by Bandura (1977) to reflect individuals' confidence in their ability to perform a given behaviour, should be added to the HBM in order to increase its explanatory power (Rosenstock et al., 1988).

The HBM is an abstract theoretical framework that is not specified with respect to a given behavioural domain. Therefore, there is no standard HBM questionnaire that can readily be obtained and used. Rather, the general constructs proposed by the HBM need to be operationalized in the context of a particular research question and study sample. Detailed information regarding the construction of a questionnaire to measure the constructs specified in the HBM is provided by Sheeran and Abraham (1996), who include a sample questionnaire taken from a study by Champion (1984), which they consider an example of good practice.

In her study on breast self-examination, Champion (1984) first generated an item pool in collaboration with experts in the behavioural field. Alternatively, items can be derived from interviews with members of the target population. After pilot testing, Champion (1984) retained 5–12 items to measure each of the distinct constructs. All items could be answered on 5-point Likert scales, ranging from 'strongly disagree' to 'strongly agree'. Susceptibility was measured with six items, one of which was 'my chances of getting breast cancer are great'. The severity measure encompassed 12 items, for instance 'the thought of breast cancer scares me'. Benefits were assessed with 5 items, such as 'doing self-breast exams prevents future problems for me'. Barriers were tapped with 8 items, such as 'it is embarrassing for me to do monthly breast exams'.

An extensive narrative review (Sheeran & Abraham, 1996), as well as two quantitative reviews of studies using the HBM, generally obtained results favourable to the model (Harrison, Mullen & Green, 1992; Janz & Becker, 1984). The one meta-analysis conducted on studies testing the HBM (Harrison et al., 1992) included only 16 (out of 234 studies) in their review that presented measurements of all four major, original, health belief components. Harrison et al. (1992) found average effect sizes, based on the weighted average correlation statistic ($r+$), of 0.15 (susceptibility), 0.08 (severity), 0.13 (benefits) and 0.21 (barriers), which are considered small. This suggests that although the components specified by the HBM are often significant predictors of behaviour, their individual effects are rather small.

An issue not addressed by the Harrison et al. (1992) meta-analysis, however, is the size of the combined effect of specified health beliefs. It is this combination of beliefs that according to the HBM shapes behaviour, and the joint effect may be larger than the sum of individual effects (Sheeran & Abraham, 1996). A problem in establishing the joint effect of health belief components, however, is that the relation between the distinct variables has never been formalized, and an additive combination has been generally used, even though multiplicative combinations seem more plausible (Stroebe, 2000). Furthermore, cues to action and general health motivation were not included in the meta-analysis presented by Harrison et al. (1992), probably because they have not been studied as frequently as other HBM components (Sheeran & Abraham, 1996).

Protection-Motivation Theory

The original version of Protection-Motivation Theory (PMT) constituted an attempt to specify the mathematical relationships between the core components of the HBM, as well as to provide a comprehensive account of the persuasive effects of fear-arousing health communications. Fear appeals include three crucial informational components: the noxiousness of the health-threatening event, the probability of occurrence of the event, and the efficacy of the protective response proposed to avert negative consequences. Rogers (1975) assumed that each of these three communication variables initiated corresponding appraisal processes in the individual. Protection motivation, a concept generally measured as an individual's intention to adopt a given behaviour (Rippetoe & Rogers, 1987), was conceived of as a multiplicative function of *perceived vulnerability*, *perceived severity* and *response efficacy* (i.e. benefits of the action). This assumption followed from the plausible consideration that protection motivation should not be aroused if any of the three factors was zero. However, empirical support for this multiplicative combination has been weak and inconsistent (Boer & Seydel, 1996).

In a reformulation, Rogers (1983) developed PMT into a more general theory of cognitive change. According to Rogers (1983; Rippetoe & Rogers, 1987), environmental or intrapersonal information sources signalling a threat initiate two appraisal processes, namely *threat appraisal* and *coping appraisal* (figure 3.2). Each of these appraisal processes involves multiple cognitive processes.

Threat appraisal is concerned with the factors that determine the occurrence of the response that elicited the danger; that is, the *maladaptive response* (Rippetoe & Rogers, 1987). The likelihood of a maladaptive response is thought to be positively related to the *perceived rewards* of that response, either intrinsic or extrinsic, and expected to be reduced as a result of the perceived severity of the threat and the vulnerability to the threat resulting from the behaviour. Rogers (1983) further assumed that when the perceived threat resulting from a maladaptive response outweighs the advantages of this behaviour, threat appraisal should promote protection motivation. For example, a newspaper report about a substantial increase in the incidence of sexually transmitted diseases may make a sexually active student, who is not using condoms, anxious about the risk of contracting such a disease. In the course of his appraisal of the threat of sexually transmitted diseases, the young person will evaluate her or his vulnerability to the disease and the severity of the condition, and weigh this against

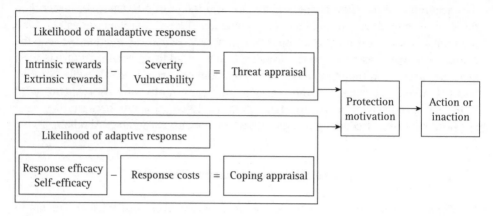

Figure 3.2 Protection-Motivation Theory (PMT)

the rewards (i.e. sexual enjoyment) that would accrue from continuing to have sex without condoms (maladaptive response). To the extent that the perceived threat resulting from the maladaptive response outweighs the advantages of this behaviour, threat appraisal should promote protection motivation.

In addition, protection motivation is posited to depend also on an individual's coping appraisal, referring to a person's ability to avert the danger, which is to enact the adaptive response (Rippetoe & Rogers, 1987). The likelihood of an adaptive response is assumed to increase to the extent that an individual holds the beliefs that the response is effective in avoiding danger, and he or she is capable of performing the recommended behaviour. Adaptive responses are inhibited by any *costs* related to their enactment. Our sexually active student is, thus, expected to initiate consistent condom use to the extent that (s)he is convinced of their efficacy in reducing the risk of contracting sexually transmitted diseases, and finds her or himself capable of procuring them in advance, negotiating their use when needed, and using them as required. Any costs potentially incurred, such as reduced sensation, negative reactions from the partner, and the product price, reduce the odds of condom use.

The *combinatorial rules* to be used to relate the specified multiple cognitive processes to protection motivation and subsequent behaviour are less clear for revised PMT than they were for the original formulation. As we have seen, variables resulting from the same appraisal process combine additively, according to the revised model (Rogers, 1983; Rippetoe & Rogers, 1987). Factors resulting from different appraisal processes are assumed to combine multiplicatively. Thus, increasing threat appraisal is assumed to increase protection motivation only if the individual believes that he or she is able to perform a coping response, this response is effective in eliminating the danger (i.e. if self-efficacy and response efficacy are both high), and the costs incurred are low or acceptable. An increase in perceived threat should not increase protection motivation if individuals believe that they are unable to perform the protective action, if the action would be ineffective in reducing or eliminating the danger, or unacceptably high costs are involved.

As was true for the HBM, no standard questionnaire is available to measure the social-cognitive factors specified in PMT, and these mediational processes have been assessed in a variety of ways (Boer & Seydel, 1996). Nevertheless, a general outline of this measurement and sample items are provided by Boer and Seydel (1996). In general, multiple item assessment of the different constructs should be preferred over measurement based on single items because such measures are likely to be more reliable. The constructs' severity and vulnerability overlap with the factors' severity and susceptibility in the HBM, and assessments are conceptually similar. Severity of the threat reflects an individual's sense of seriousness of a threat (e.g. 'I think breast cancer is a serious disease'), and vulnerability indicates the subjective likelihood of contracting the condition (e.g. 'It is rather probable that I will ever get breast cancer'). Response efficacy refers to the expected positive consequences of an adaptive response and can be measured by a set of beliefs pertaining to behavioural outcomes (e.g. 'Regular breast self-examination leads to early detection of small abnormalities'). Self-efficacy measures attempt to assess the extent to which a person feels capable of performing a given act and could include items such as 'It is difficult for me to engage in breast cancer screening because I feel awkward about it.' Finally, protection motivation can be measured as a person's intention to perform a behaviour in the future (e.g. 'I plan to engage regularly in breast self-examination in the future'). Sheeran and Abraham (1996) suggest using 5-point Likert response alternatives ranging from 'strongly disagree' to 'strongly agree'.

Two recent meta-analytic studies have reviewed the overall success of PMT as a model of health-related intentions and behaviour (Floyd, Prentice-Dunn & Rogers, 2000; Milne, Sheeran & Orbell, 2000). Milne et al. (2000) found that all studied variables (i.e. perceived vulnerability, severity, fear, self-efficacy, response efficacy and response costs) were significantly correlated with behavioural intention, as indexed by the computed weighted average correlations ($r+$). The associations between threat appraisal variables and *intention* were small to medium (vulnerability: 0.16; severity: 0.10; fear: 0.20), while the relation between coping appraisal variables and intention was medium (response efficacy: 0.29; self-efficacy: 0.33; response costs: 0.34).

With respect to the prediction of *behaviour*, Milne et al. (2000) conducted separate analyses for cross-sectional studies that measured behaviour at the same time as the predictors (concurrent behaviour), and longitudinal studies that measured behaviour prospectively. Milne et al. (2000) found that, apart from intention that was most consistently and most robustly associated with concurrent behaviour (0.82), self-efficacy (0.36) and response costs (–0.32) were the PMT variables most strongly and most often related to behaviour measured concurrently. Regarding subsequent behaviour, intention was, as hypothesized by protection-motivation theory, again found to be the strongest, most consistent and most robust predictor (0.40). Perceived vulnerability (0.12), self-efficacy (0.22) and response costs (–0.25) were the only threat and coping appraisal variables prospectively associated with behaviour.

Floyd et al. (2000) did not calculate separate effect sizes for intentions, concurrent behaviour and subsequent behaviour. Based on the *d*-statistic, which reflects the standardized mean difference between groups, these authors computed a composite mean effect-size (*d+*) for each predictor variable tested, irrespective of the nature of the outcome variable. Combining all predictor variables for all outcomes, Floyd et al. (2000) obtained a mean effect size in the moderate range (*d+* = 0.52), suggesting that components of threat and coping appraisal are substantially related to protection motivation. The variables that had the strongest impact on protection motivation were self-efficacy (*d+* = 0.88), response efficacy (*d+* = 0.54), combined threat vulnerability and severity (*d+* = 0.54) and response costs (*d+* = 0.52), with generally smaller effect sizes found for threat appraisal variables than for coping appraisal variables. Thus, the findings of both meta-analyses indicate that protection motivation is more strongly associated with coping appraisal than with threat appraisal, and that self-efficacy appears to be the strongest determinant of protection motivation.

Summary and conclusions

The HBM suggests a limited number of modifiable psychological factors that can easily be used to understand individual differences in health-related actions, and that translate readily in health promotion interventions. In addition, the common-sense constructs are well understood by non-experts, adding to the ease of use of the model in health promotion (Sheeran & Abraham, 1996). Despite its inherent plausibility and frequent use, however, the HBM suffers from serious empirical and theoretical limitations that raise doubts as to its adequacy as a conceptual framework to understand health behaviour.

Two problems with the theoretical account given by the HBM are (1) the narrow focus of the beliefs included in the model, and (2) the failure to specify the relationship between the different components of the model. First, the exclusive focus on health consequences of behaviour disregards the fact that many health behaviours are performed for reasons unrelated to health (e.g. exercising to look good). Second, although the model indicates for each of the different constructs whether they have a positive or negative impact on health behaviour, it fails to specify how the different constructs should be combined. Specifically, it is unclear whether perceived vulnerability and severity should be treated as one or rather separate constructs, and if treated separately, whether they combine additively or multiplicatively. In addition, there is lack of clarity as to whether benefits and barriers should be combined by subtraction or treated as different constructs. Moreover, both benefits and barriers may encompass qualitatively distinct types of beliefs that may not readily be combined in these global constructs (e.g. benefits can include beliefs about the efficacy of any recommended behaviour as well as additional benefits, such as social approval) (Sheeran & Abraham, 1996).

Some of these deficits have been addressed in the development of PMT. In fact, the original version of PMT constituted an attempt to specify the mathematical relationship between the core components of the HBM. However, since empirical tests of the multiplicative combination assumed between perceived susceptibility, perceived severity of the threat, and response efficacy resulted in inconsistent patterns, the revised version of the model abandoned these assumptions. Although the revision substantially broadened the types of health beliefs included in the model, it lacks the conceptual clarity and parsimony that was characteristic of Rogers' (1975) original formulation. Moreover, the simplified combinatorial rule proposed by revised PMT (e.g. Rippetoe & Rogers, 1987) seems intuitively implausible, and is at odds with theoretical assumptions specified by the underlying expectancy–value approach. Furthermore, there is little empirical evidence to support these assumptions. Although the meta-analyses pertaining to the HBM (Harrison et al., 1992), and to PMT (Floyd et al., 2000; Milne et al., 2000) found support for the assumption that the variables included in these models are significantly related to health-protective intentions or behaviour, none of these meta-analyses assessed the validity of the combinatorial rules of either the original or the revised version of PMT.

In conclusion, the social cognition models developed in the context of health psychology identify a set of social-cognitive variables that appear to be important determinants of health behaviour. However, neither of the two theories discussed here succeeded in clarifying the relationships that exist between the distinct variables in shaping intentions and behaviour. Whereas the HBM did not make any such assumptions in the first place, the assumptions made by PMT lack empirical support.

SOCIAL COGNITION MODELS OF SOCIAL BEHAVIOUR

The basic model

Central to the more general social-psychological analysis of social behaviour is the now classic assumption that attitudes are the major determinant of behaviour. An *attitude* is defined as a person's tendency to evaluate a particular entity, such as another person, or group, an abstract issue or a specific behaviour, with some degree of favour or disfavour (Eagly & Chaiken, 1993). The assumption that attitudes are a major determinant of behaviour was challenged in the late sixties by reviews of the literature that appeared to indicate that attitudes were frequently unrelated to behaviour (e.g. Wicker, 1969). However, in their influential analysis, Ajzen and Fishbein (1977) pointed out that attitudes and behaviour are related, provided that the measures employed to assess both concepts are not only reliable but also compatible. Every instance of behaviour involves four specific elements: (*a*) a specific action, (*b*) performed with respect to a given target, (*c*) in a given context, and (*d*) at a given point in time. The *principle of compatibility* specifies that measures of attitude and behaviour are compatible to the extent that their target, action, context, and time elements are assessed at identical levels of generality or specificity.

Since attitudes were often measured at a very global level, such measures were incompatible with observations of specific behaviour. For example, a person's attitude towards a healthy lifestyle only specifies the target, but leaves action, context and time elements unspecified. A healthy lifestyle comprises numerous health practices that can be performed in many different contexts at many different times. A behavioural measure that would be compatible with this global attitude would have to aggregate a wide range of health behaviours across different contexts and times. Consistent with this assumption, Ajzen and Timko (1986) reported that a measure of (global) attitude towards health maintenance did not correlate significantly with the self-reported frequency with which respondents performed *specific* health-protective behaviours. However, as predicted, this global attitude measure did show a substantial correlation with a behavioural index that aggregated the performance of a wide variety of different health-protective behaviours. These behaviours related to different aspects of health and had been performed in a wide variety of contexts and times.

If we were interested in predicting specific behaviours, an attitude measure would be compatible if it assessed the attitude towards performing the specific behaviour. Thus, if we want to predict a specific health-related action, we should not base our prediction on the global attitude towards health or healthful behaviour, but should assess the specific attitude towards performing the behaviour we would like to predict. In line with this assumption, Ajzen and Timko (1986) were able to predict specific health behaviours from equally specific attitudes towards these behaviours. For example, the reported frequency with which respondents had regular dental check-ups correlated 0.46 with respondents' attitudes towards having regular dental check-ups. In a recent meta-analysis of studies that manipulated compatibility between measures of attitude and behaviour, Kraus (1995) reported a mean correlation of 0.13 at the lowest level of compatibility as compared to 0.54 when compatibility was high.

The Theory of Reasoned Action

The Theory of Reasoned Action (TRA) was developed to improve our understanding of the underlying psychological processes by which attitudes might serve as causes of behaviour (Eagly & Chaiken, 1993). Basic to the TRA is the assumption that much behaviour in everyday life can be thought of as largely under *volitional control* (Ajzen, 1988; Fishbein & Ajzen, 1975). That is, individuals can choose to perform or not perform many behaviours of interest to social psychologists, at will. The TRA posits that individuals' deliberations result in an intention to engage or not engage in a given behaviour, and that this behavioural intention is the most *proximal determinant* of action. Intentions presumably reflect individuals' motivation with respect to the behaviour and are thought to have an impact on how hard one is willing to try and how much effort one is likely to exert to perform the behaviour. Given the appropriate time and opportunity, behavioural intentions will translate into behaviour (Ajzen, 1988).

Fishbein and Ajzen (1975; Ajzen & Fishbein, 1980) propose that a person's intention to engage in a specific behaviour depends on his or her attitude with respect to the behaviour, as well as his or her perceived social norm regarding the behaviour (figure 3.3). Thus, algebraically, the TRA could be presented as follows:

$$B \sim BI = w_1 A_B + w_2 SN$$

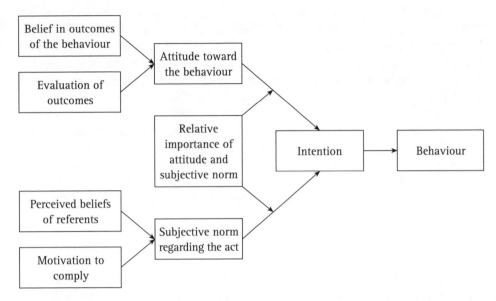

Figure 3.3 The Theory of Reasoned Action (TRA) (cf. Ajzen & Fishbein, 1980)

where B is behaviour, BI is behavioural intention, A_B is attitude towards the behaviour, *SN* reflects the individual's *subjective norm* with regard to that behaviour, and w_1 and w_2 are empirical weights indicating the relative importance of the determinants of intentions.

A person's attitude towards a behaviour is assumed to be a reflection of his or her subjective evaluation of the outcomes of any action to be undertaken (e.g. Fishbein, 1967). More specifically, the TRA holds that a person's attitude towards a given behaviour follows from his or her *salient beliefs* about that behaviour (i.e. behavioural beliefs). A *behavioural belief* links the behaviour to a specific outcome, and includes a *belief-strength* dimension representing the subjective likelihood of occurrence of any given outcome, and a dimension representing the *evaluation* of the relevant outcomes. For any specific behaviour, a person may hold a variety of behavioural beliefs of which some may pertain to likely outcomes and others to less likely consequences, that, in addition, can vary in *valence* (i.e. their degree of (un)favourability). A person's attitude towards the behaviour is therefore conceptualized as the sum of the products of the probability and evaluation judgements. Thus,

$$A_B = \sum_{i=1}^{i=x} b_i * e_i$$

where A_B is the attitude towards the behaviour, b_i is a behavioural belief reflecting the subjective probability that the behaviour B has the consequence i, e_i is the evaluation of the consequence i, and x is the total number of salient consequences.

The TRA acknowledges that individual behaviour occurs in the context of social influence and pressure to perform or not perform a particular behaviour. This social influence is represented in the theory by the concept of subjective norm, the proposed second determinant of behavioural intentions. According to the TRA, a person's subjective norm with respect to a given behaviour reflects the person's (normative) belief that people who are important to him or her think that he or she should or should not perform the behaviour. Each *normative belief* is weighted by the person's *motivation to comply* with the referents' opinions. Thus, whether normative beliefs will influence a person's behaviour depends on the person's motivation to comply. In essence then, Fishbein and Ajzen (1975) propose an expectancy–value formulation of their subjective norm construct in that it is conceived of as the sum of salient normative expectancies, weighted for the value attached to these expectancies. Thus,

$$SN = \sum_{j=1}^{j=y} nb_j * mc_j$$

where SN is the subjective norm, nb_j is a normative belief indicating the subjective probability that some referent person j thinks one should perform the behaviour, mc_j is the motivation to comply with referent j, and y is the total number of salient referents.

Fishbein and Ajzen (1975) originally argued that most behaviours of interest to social psychology were those that allowed complete volitional control. Moreover, they assumed that individuals are unlikely to intend to perform behaviours that are beyond their ability, thus suggesting that their model offers adequate behavioural prediction in most but extreme cases. As meta-analyses of the great number of studies based on the TRA demonstrated, their theory made good predictions for a wide range of actions (Randall & Wolff, 1994; Sheppard, Hartwick & Warshaw, 1988). It has, nevertheless, become accepted that most socially relevant behaviour, even that as mundane as buying groceries, may involve incomplete volitional control of an individual (Sheppard et al., 1988). Ajzen (e.g. 1988) therefore proposed an extension of the TRA that can account for the more general class of behaviours that involve the attainment of a specified goal.

The Theory of Planned Behaviour

Ajzen (1988) suggested that any behaviour could be placed on a continuum of the amount of control that a person has over the respective actions. He distinguished between two general classes of factors that promote or inhibit *behavioural control*: *Internal factors* include level of information, skills and ability, as well as emotions and compulsions. *External factors* refer to the extent of opportunity an individual has for engaging in the behaviour, as well as the extent to which performance of the behaviour depends on the cooperation of others. Collectively, these factors represent the amount of actual control an individual has over a given behaviour in a specific context. To the extent that actual control is high, performance of behaviour depends only on the person's intention to engage in it. With lower levels of control, however, the predictive utility of intention is thought to diminish.

Conceptually, Ajzen (e.g. 1988; Ajzen & Madden, 1986; Schifter & Ajzen, 1985) addressed the issue of incomplete volitional control in the Theory of Planned Behaviour (TPB) by adding *perceived behavioural control* as a third determinant of intention to the two determinants assumed by the TRA. The concept of perceived behavioural control refers to the perceived ease or difficulty of performing a behaviour, and is thought to reflect past experience as well as anticipated impediments and obstacles. As such (cf. Ajzen, 1991), perceived behavioural control is very similar to Bandura's (e.g. 1986, 1997) concept of self-efficacy that is concerned with people's beliefs in their capabilities to perform a specific action to attain a desired outcome (also see Schwarzer & Fuchs, 1996). Thus, according to the TPB, behavioural intentions are determined by the additive combination of three factors:

$$BI = w_1 A_b + w_2 SN + w_3 PBC$$

where BI is a persons' behavioural intention, A_b is his or her attitude towards, the behaviour, *SN* is subjective norm, *PBC* is perceived behavioural control and w_1, w_2 and w_3 represent the empirical weights indicating the relative importance of the three predictors of behavioural intention.

Perceived control is thought to take into account some of the reality constraints that may be at work when contemplating enactment of a given behaviour, and is assumed to have motivational properties. That is, to the extent individuals believe that they have neither the resources nor the opportunities to perform a behaviour, they are unlikely to form strong intentions to engage in the behaviour or strive for a goal. Like attitude and subjective norm, a person's perceived behavioural control is posited to reflect his or her *belief structure*. A person is assumed to hold a set of beliefs regarding factors that may promote or inhibit the performance of a given behaviour. These beliefs may vary in terms of the estimated likelihood of occurrence of the respective inhibiting or facilitating factors, a dimension labelled *control belief,* as well as the potential of the distinct factors to inhibit or promote behaviour, a dimension referred to as *power* (Ajzen, 1991; Conner & Sparks, 1996). The model quantifies these beliefs by suggesting multiplying the frequency or likelihood of occurrence of a given factor by the evaluation of the power of that factor to facilitate or inhibit the performance of the behaviour (Conner & Sparks, 1996). Thus,

$$PBC = \sum_{k=1}^{k=z} c_k * p_k$$

where PBC is perceived behavioural control, c_k is the perceived frequency or likelihood of some factor k, p_k is the perceived power of the factor k to facilitate or inhibit a behaviour k, and z is the total number of control factors.

John de Wit and Wolfgang Stroebe

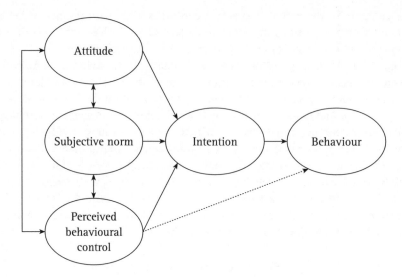

Figure 3.4 The Theory of Planned Behaviour (TPB) (cf. Ajzen, 1991)

The TPB posits that perceived behavioural control may also have a *direct* link with behaviour because it is considered to, at least partially, represent an individual's actual control over the behaviour (figure 3.4). It is important to note that this proposed direct link of perceived behavioural control to behaviour has a somewhat different theoretical status from the link that is mediated by intention. Whereas perceived behavioural control is thought to have a *causal* influence on intentions (e.g. after many unsuccessful attempts, an addicted smoker may be unwilling to form the intention to stop smoking), it is not the perceived but the *actual* lack of control that causally influences behaviour (via the direct route). For example, if after a recent move, the only way a person can attend an early morning class in winter is to come by train, and if the trains are unreliable, then (s)he might often be prevented from attending this class. However, it is not the person's perception of the unreliability of the train service that prevents him or her from attending class, but the actual unreliability of the trains.

Taking individuals' control over their environment into account in assessing the success of their actions (e.g. class attendance) will improve predictions of behaviour only to the extent that individuals' perception of control is accurate. This has been nicely demonstrated by Ajzen and Madden (1986) in a study of students' intention to get an A (best grade) in a course, as well as their actual grades. In line with the assumption that perceived behavioural control only adds to the prediction of behaviour when it adequately reflects actual control, they found that the direct link between perceived behavioural control and behaviour only emerged when perceived behavioural control was assessed towards the end of the semester; that is, after students had had considerable experience of how they could perform in this course, and their perceived behavioural control more accurately reflected their actual control. Perceived control as assessed at the start of the term did not improve the prediction of behaviour, presumably because it was not an adequate reflection of reality.

Operationalizations of the TRA and the TPB are discussed extensively by Ajzen and Fishbein (1980) and Ajzen (1988), who stress the importance of the principle of compatibility in measuring attitudes, subjective norms, intentions and behaviours. That is, these constructs need to be measured at the same level of specificity regarding action, target, context and time aspects. A clear specification of the target behaviour thus is a prerequisite for a valid operationalization of social-cognitive determinants. Conner and Sparks (1996) give an overview of the operationalization of the model, which includes a set of sample items. They present a hypothetical study designed to predict the eating (action) of fruit (target) as a part of a mid-day meal (context) tomorrow (time). This target behaviour could be assessed by obtaining self-reports the following day of whether participants had fruit for their midday meal. The intention measure might be formulated as 'I intend to eat fruit as part of my midday meal tomorrow', with answers measured on a 5- or 7-point scale ranging from 'unlikely' to 'likely'. Attitudes are measured as a set of semantic differential items assessing respondents' global evaluations on 5- or 7-point scales in terms of, for instance, 'good–bad', 'harmful–beneficial' and 'pleasant–unpleasant'. Subjective norms are often measured by a single item such as 'Most people who are important to me think I should–should not eat fruit as a part of my mid-day meal tomorrow'. Scoring can again be done on 5- or 7-point scales. Perceived behavioural control items should reflect the extent to which a person feels able to perform the behaviour as desired (e.g. 'Whether I do or do not eat fruit as part of my mid-day meal tomorrow is entirely up to me', 1 = strongly disagree, 7 = strongly agree). In addition to these global evaluations, the theories of reasoned action and planned behaviour also specify the measurement of beliefs and evaluations. Details of this assessment and examples of multi-item measures of all TPB constructs can be found in Conner and Sparks, 1996.

The TPB has been applied to a variety of behaviours ranging from academic grades to shoplifting. The first published test was a study of weight loss (Schifter & Ajzen, 1985). Female college students were asked at the beginning of the study to express their attitudes, subjective norms, perceived behavioural control and intentions with respect to losing weight during a 6-week period. Consistent with the theory, these factors predicted the intention to lose weight quite accurately. However, intentions and perceived behavioural control were only moderately successful in predicting the amount of weight that participants actually lost during the six weeks, with perceived behavioural control being the better predictor. There was also an interaction between perceived behavioural control and intention on weight reduction: A strong intention to lose weight increased weight reduction only for those participants who believed that they would be able to control their calorie intake if they wanted to. However, although this interaction is theoretically plausible, most research has found only main effects of perceived control on behaviour.

Recent meta-analyses of applications of the TPB have been conducted by Armitage and Conner (2001) and Godin and Kok (1996). Armitage and Conner (2001) analysed 185 independent studies published up to the end of 1997 and conclude that TPB accounts for 39 per cent of the variance in intention and 27 per cent of the variance in behaviour. TPB accounted for more variance in behaviour when this was self-reported (31 per cent) than when objective or observational measures were used (21 per cent). Godin and Kok (1996), who focused exclusively on health behaviour, equally found that the model performed well for the explanation of intention; a proportion of explained variance of 0.41 was observed. The model performed less well with respect to the prospective prediction of behaviour, but nonetheless a proportion of explained variance of 0.34 was obtained. For a subset of studies Godin and Kok (1996) were able to calculate the additional contribution of perceived behavioural control, and they found that it added substantially to the prediction of intention (13.1 per cent increment in explained variance), as well as behaviour (11.5 per cent increment), over and above the determinants specified in the TRA. Godin and Kok (1996) concluded that the theory is successful in explaining intentions across a wide range of health action categories. However, with respect to the prediction of behaviour they observed considerable differences in the efficiency of the model, depending on the specific behavioural domain. The model performed well in the prediction of behaviours in the domain of HIV/AIDS, addictions and exercise (R^2's 0.42, 0.41 and 0.36, respectively). The model succeeded less well in predicting behaviour in domains including clinical screening, eating, and oral hygiene (R^2's 0.16 to 0.26).

Godin and Kok (1996) suggested that the difference in fit of the TPB for distinct behavioural domains may be related to the inability to enact one's intentions in some areas but not in others. They reasoned that clinical and screening behaviours involved a succession of the steps before the target behaviour is realized. For instance, obtaining a mammogram involves making an appointment with a physician, going to this appointment, obtaining a prescription for the mammogram, making an appointment for this screening, going to this screening and obtaining results. This reasoning explains why the intention–behaviour link may be weaker for some domains, but it fails to explain why the inclusion of perceived control into the prediction of behaviour does not compensate for this difference. According to the TPB, actual control becomes an important predictor of behaviour whenever control over enactment of a behaviour is incomplete, as in the mammogram example provided by Godin and Kok (1996). Thus, even though the predictive utility of intention may be lower under such conditions, the addition of perceived behavioural control should compensate for this deficit. However, as Ajzen and Madden (1986) have shown, one condition for perceived behavioural control to improve the prediction of behaviour, is that it be an adequate reflection of actual control. We would therefore argue that the variation in the strength of the intention–behaviour link across different domains may be due to variations in the accuracy with which individuals' perception of control reflects their actual control. Individuals may have substantial experience with relatively common behaviours in the field of addiction (e.g. smoking) or HIV/AIDS (e.g. negotiating condom use), while they have less experience with more infrequently enacted clinical or screening behaviours, such as obtaining an X-ray.

Several recent reviews specifically focus on the predictive utility of TPB as a theoretical framework for understanding condom use. In one of the first of such meta-analyses, Sheeran and Orbell (1998) found a medium to strong effect of intentions on condom use ($r+ = 0.44$). This intention–behaviour relationship, however, was moderated by several variables, including type of partner (i.e. casual versus steady), age of the sample, and time interval between assessments of intention and behaviour. In a more encompassing meta-analysis of predictors of condom use, Sheeran, Abraham and Orbell (1999) found that intention was one of the most important predictors of behaviour, together with attitude and communication about condoms, a factor not included in TRA and TPB, nor in any of the other social cognition models of behaviour. Finally, Albarracin et al. (2001) compared TRA and TPB as models of condom use. Consistent with TRA, these authors found a strong relation between intention and condom use ($r+ = 0.45$), similar to the effect size reported by Sheeran and Orbell (1998). Intentions were based on attitudes ($r+ = 58$), and, to a lesser extent, subjective norm ($r+ = 0.39$) (see Armitage & Conner, 2001, for a similar weaker effect of subjective norms). As predicted by TPB, Albarracin et al. (2001) found that intention was also significantly related to perceived behavioural control ($r+ = 45$). Actual condom use was also related to perceived behavioural control ($r+ = 0.25$), but contrary to what would be expected, perceived behavioural control did not improve the multivariate prediction of condom use.

Summary and conclusions

In our discussion of the four models of behaviour, we focused mainly on three issues, namely the range of beliefs that were included in the various models, the internal structure of these models, and their empirical validation. On all of these comparisons, the model of planned behaviour has been found superior to the other models.

The HBM and PMT identified five common determinants of health behaviour. According to these theories, individuals are likely to engage in health-protective behaviour if they perceive a health threat which appears to be serious, and if they feel able to perform some action that is likely to alleviate the health threat and that is not too effortful or costly. But whereas the HBM assumes a direct impact of these beliefs on behaviour, the PMT conceives of them as determinants of intentions. The conception of intention as the proximal determinant of behaviour is even more central in the TRA and the TPB.

The TRA assumes that the performance or non-performance of a given behaviour only depends on one's intention to perform that behaviour. Behavioural intentions are in turn assumed to be determined by one's attitude towards performing the behaviour and by one's subjective norms. Although attitudes towards a health behaviour are likely to be influenced by both the person's perception of a health threat and his or her evaluation of the efficacy of a health-protective behaviour in alleviating the threat, we have argued that these may not be the only, and often even not the most important, beliefs associated with the attitude. With subjective norms, the TRA also takes account of the fact that people often engage in behaviour to meet the expectations of others that are important to them. Finally, Ajzen (1988) added the concept of perceived behavioural control to the TRA, to account for the fact that the execution of much behaviour depended on resources, skills and/or opportunity. Thus, the TPB does not only incorporate all the variables specified in the HBM and the PMT, but it also includes a number of non-health beliefs that are not part of these other theories.

Conceptually the TPB also compares favourably to both these health behaviour models. The relationship between the various components of the TPB is clearly specified, and the model assumes an explicit and testable mechanism through which social-cognitive predictors relate to behaviour. Finally, the TPB stands out well with regard to empirical validation.

Using Social Cognition Models to Improve Health Behaviour

The most obvious strategy to improve health behaviour is the persuasion of those who have no intention to engage in a given health behaviour to change their intention. However, the fact that approximately half of the individuals with good intentions fail to act on them (Orbell & Sheeran, 1998; Sheeran, 2001) suggests that strategies aimed at increasing the intention–behaviour link should also be highly effective in improving health behaviour. We will first consider strategies aimed at helping individuals to act on their good intentions, before we discuss the use of social cognition models to develop interventions aimed at changing health intentions. Health behaviour interventions may be more successful in promoting change when they are *tailored* to the needs of the targeted individuals. This notion is central to so-called *stage models of behaviour change* (e.g. Prochaska, DiClemente & Norcross,1992; Weinstein & Sandman, 1992), and we will consider the implications of this approach for health behaviour interventions.

Translating intentions into action

The research reviewed in this chapter has indicated that intentions are by far the best predictor of behaviour. However, this research has also demonstrated that the correlation between intention and behaviour is less than perfect. In a meta-analysis of meta-analyses, Sheeran (2001) concluded that in prospective studies, intentions account for 28 per cent of the variance in behaviour. Even though this value probably underestimates the 'true' association between intention and behaviour, due to a variety of measurement artefacts which reduced the observed relationship (e.g. the artificial dichotomization of measures of behaviour and intention; unreliability of measures of intention and behaviour), it suggests a fair amount of inconsistency between intention and behaviour (Sheeran, 2001), even though social cognition models might do better than this apparent inconsistency suggest (see Sutton, 1998).

Logically, there are two groups of individuals responsible for the intention–behaviour gap, namely those who act, despite intending to abstain, and those who abstain, despite intending to act. It is hardly surprising that the intention–behaviour gap is largely due to people who fail to act on their good intentions (Sheeran, 2001). In a re-analysis of studies of the intention–behaviour relationship as assessed in research on condom use and cancer screening, Sheeran (2001) found that nearly 50 per cent of individuals with good intentions fail to act on them, as compared to 11 per cent of individuals who act despite the intention not to act.

These findings suggest that any strategy that increased the percentage of individuals who enact their intentions would substantially reduce the intention–behaviour gap. One set of strategies involves training programmes to provide individuals with the skills necessary to act on their intentions. For example, with regard to condom use, training in negotiation skills and other social skills has proven highly effective in increasing condom use among homosexual men and also among heterosexual women (for a review, see Stroebe 2000).

However, lack of relevant skills is not the only reason why individuals fail to act on their intentions. Other reasons are forgetting to act when the occasion arises, or a weakening of the action motivation at the relevant point in time. One strategy likely to overcome these problems is the induction of an *implementation intention* (Gollwitzer, 1999). In contrast to goal intentions, which specify a certain end state (i.e. a desired performance or an outcome), implementation intentions specify when, where and how the intended behaviour should be performed. Implementation intentions are of an 'if–then' form, and can be induced by asking individuals, after they have reported their intention to perform a specific behaviour, also to specify the time and place for performing that action. This would, for instance, result in resolutions such as 'if I have breakfast in the morning, I will also take my vitamin pills'. Expressed in the terminology of Ajzen and Fishbein (1977), the induction of implementation intentions serves to reduce the compatibility gap that exists between behaviour, which is always performed at a given time and a given place, and intentions that are usually formulated at a more general level.

The first study in which implementation intentions have been manipulated predates the formulation of the concept (Gollwitzer, 1993) by several decades. In a study of the effectiveness of fear-arousing communications, students were given high or low fear communications to persuade them to take tetanus shots at their university health service (Leventhal, Singer & Jones, 1965). Implementation intentions were induced by asking students to review their daily schedule and to locate within it a time that was convenient for action. Even though these specific action instructions had no effect on intentions, they led to an increase in behaviour: 29 per cent of the students who had received specific instructions took tetanus shots, as compared to 3 per cent of respondents without specific instructions.

Since then, studies have demonstrated that, despite equivalent intentions, individuals who form implementation intentions are more likely to act on their intentions (for a review see Sheeran, 2001). These recent studies also focused on more complex health behaviours, and found that implementation intentions promote the performance of breast self-examination over a period of a month (Orbell, Hodgkins & Sheeran, 1997), regular intake of vitamin pills (Sheeran & Orbell, 1999), attendance at cervical cancer screening (Sheeran & Orbell, 2000) and eating healthily (Verplanken & Faes, 1999). Based on a meta-analysis of studies manipulating implementation intentions, Sheeran (2001) computed a weighted correlation between implementation intentions and behaviour of $r+ = 0.34$. This suggests that inducing implementation intention results in a considerable increase in the variance in behaviour accounted for by intentions. In a controlled test of this expectation Milne, Orbell and Sheeran (2002) compared the effect of a motivational intervention on exercise participation with that of the same motivational intervention supplemented with implementation intentions. The motivational intervention was based on PMT and significantly increased threat and coping appraisals, as well as intentions to engage in exercise. It did not, however, increase exercise behaviour. The combined intervention, on the other hand, had a dramatic effect on behaviour, but not on behavioural intention or any other motivational variable. This latter finding indicates that the formation of implementation intentions indeed complements the effect of goal or behavioural intentions.

Gollwitzer (1999) reasoned the formulation of simple plans in the form of implementation intentions could support people in overcoming problems in translating their goals into action, because they delegate the control over behavioural responses to situational cues, which helps people in getting started. Gollwitzer (1999) assumes that the formation of implementation intentions entails the selection of a suitable future opportunity. This selection process makes the mental representation of the situation highly activated, and thus more easily accessible in memory. Subsequent encountering of a relevant situational cue will automatically result in the specified behavioural response (Gollwitzer, 1999).

We contend that there are two alternative pathways by which implementation intentions may affect behaviour, namely memory and motivation. Implementation intentions are likely to cause the mental representation of the anticipated situation to become highly activated, and thus easily accessible (Gollwitzer, 1999). For example, if rather than forming the general intention to phone my doctor for an appointment, I make the specific plan to phone tomorrow morning at 10 a.m., immediately after a meeting with a Ph.D. student, I am much more likely to remember this plan. Furthermore, it is very likely that I will remember the phone call to my doctor as soon as the student has left my office. In fact, Sheeran (2001) reported findings that indicate that two-thirds of the respondents in a study on cervical cancer smears who had been induced to form implementation intentions, acted on their intentions precisely on the time that they had specified in their implementation intentions. However, as our example suggests, this could be the result of either an automatic or a deliberate process resulting from a more conscious decision to enact one's goal intention.

Although there is less evidence, so far, we further suspect that the effects of implementation intentions go beyond the (mnemonic) increase in the accessibility of relevant memory traces. Forming the implementation intention to perform the behaviour Y, once the situation X arises, not only helps to remind one of this commitment. Once the situation X has arisen, it also reminds us that not performing the behaviour Y would constitute a failure to act. Thus, one of the important side-effects of making specific plans about *when* and *where* to act on an intention is that one also specifies criteria that allow the identification of a 'goal violation'. Since these motivational effects are assumed to arise only at the time when intentions need to be translated into action, this interpretation is consistent with the finding that the induction of implementation intentions has no impact on intentions or any of the other components of the model of planned behaviour (Sheeran, 2001).

As Sheeran (2001) pointed out, one of the neglected problems in applying the concept of implementation intention to the area of health behaviour concerns the specific behaviour, which should be specified in inducing the implementation intention. When a single action is to be performed, as in the case of taking a pill, then the intention to take the pill can easily be supplemented by the implementation intention to take the pill each morning, before brushing one's teeth. However, if a person intends to achieve goals or outcomes which can be reached by a number of different strategies, such as eating more healthily or losing weight, the specific behaviour which should be specified is less clear.

Verplanken and Faes (1999) solved this problem in their study of healthy eating by asking research participants to choose one of the next 5 days as their healthy eating day and to formulate in detail what they planned to eat and drink during that day. Although individuals who had formed this type of healthy-eating intention exhibited a higher degree of healthy eating during a 5-day period, one wonders to what extent this effect might not have been due to a self-induced attitude change with regard to healthy eating rather than the specific effect of the intention to, for example, eat carrots for lunch next Tuesday. However, the important point is that the induction of implementation intentions was effective in changing eating behaviour, even if the precise process underlying the impact of an induction of implementation intentions under such circumstances requires further research.

In summary then, when people encounter problems in translating their goals into action, they can strategically call on implementation intentions to secure goal attainment. This can be achieved by formulating specific plans which link anticipated critical situations to goal-directed responses. Similarly, the impact of the behaviour change interventions discussed in the next section can be substantially increased if the message does not only aim at changing in behavioural intentions but also at inducing implementation intentions by persuading respondents to form specific plans about where and when to act on their intentions.

Designing interventions to change intentions and behaviour

Social cognition models of health and social behaviour, as discussed in the previous part of this chapter, can also be used for the development of behaviour change interventions (see Hardeman et al., 2002, for a review of approaches based on TPB). Once these models have helped us to identify the major cognitive determinants underlying a given behaviour, this information can be used to develop interventions aimed at changing these determinants. Interventions generally either consist of persuasive messages directed at beliefs to change intentions or of training programmes that help individuals to recognize and change factors that determine their (actual) control over their behaviour. The first part of our discussion of these strategies will be based on the model of planned behaviour and will be guided by analyses published by Sutton (2002) and by Fishbein, Middlestadt and Hitchcock (1994). In a second section we will focus on stage theories of behaviour change (e.g. Prochaska, DiClemente & Norcross, 1992) to extend this analysis.

Interventions based on the Theory of Planned Behaviour

Suppose some governmental agency has asked us to develop an intervention aimed at persuading people to eat a healthier diet. How would we proceed? Since eating a healthier diet is a global behavioural goal that can be reached by various behaviours, our first step would have to be to define the *target behaviour* – that is, the specific behaviour we would like to change. In choosing this behaviour, we would have to rely on epidemiological evidence for what constitutes healthy or unhealthy eating, and for the prevalence of such healthy or unhealthy eating habits among our target population. Let us suppose that, on the basis of this evidence, we decided on 'eating five portions of fruits and vegetables per day' as our target behaviour.

The second step would be to conduct an *elicitation study* aimed at identifying modal salient beliefs with respect to the target behaviour. These beliefs are elicited with open-ended questions. For example, to elicit behavioural outcome beliefs, we would ask the respondents to list all the advantages and disadvantages of eating five portions of fruit and vegetables per day. For normative referents, individuals would be asked to list the people who are important to them and would approve or disapprove of them engaging in the target behaviour. Finally, control beliefs would be elicited by asking respondents to list the factors or circumstances that might make it easier (or more difficult) for them to eat five portions of fruit and vegetables per day. *Individual* salient beliefs would be the first 5 to 7 beliefs listed by each individual. *Modal* salient beliefs would be the beliefs that are most frequently mentioned by our sample of respondents.

The third step would be to conduct a study applying the TPB to the target behaviour in a second sample of people drawn from the target population. In this study all the variables of the TPB (including the modal salient beliefs and the target behaviour) are assessed using closed-ended questions. The data from this study are used to identify the determinants of the target behaviour in our target population. We would first check whether the target behaviour is under volitional control (i.e. determined by intentions). For this purpose, we regress a measure of behaviour on intention and perceived behavioural control. We would use the two regression weights as indicators of the relative strength of the association of intention and perceived behavioural control with behaviour. Let us for now assume that behaviour is strongly determined by intention, and that perceived behavioural control has a minimal association with behaviour. (We will later discuss the situation where behaviour is only weakly or not at all related to intention.)

Lack of motivation as impediment to action

Once we have ascertained that the target behaviour is under volitional control, we move to our next step, to find out which of the components of the TPB is the main determinant of the *intention* to eat five portions of fruit and vegetables per day. For this purpose, we regress intention on attitude, subjective norms and perceived behavioural control, and again use the regression weights as an indicator for the strength of these associations. This analysis will enable us to decide whether the proposed intervention should target only one specific component (i.e. attitudinal, normative or control beliefs) or more than one component.

Once one (or more than one) component has been identified as the major determinant of intention, we now identify those modal salient beliefs underlying this component, which are likely to be the major determinants of our target behaviour. We use the data from the same study to identify those modal salient beliefs which best discriminate between respondents who intend to engage in the target behaviour and those who do not intend to do so (or between those who subsequently perform the behaviour and those who do not). This is usually done by dividing the respondents into two groups, and comparing them on each of the relevant measures. We select those salient beliefs as targets for our intervention that differentiate the two groups, because beliefs which the two groups share cannot be determinants of their fruit and vegetable eating intention or behaviour. For example, if people do not eat sufficient fruit and vegetables even though they believe that eating fruit and vegetables is healthy, it would be of little use to develop messages aimed at persuading them of the health benefits of eating fruit and vegetables. A second criterion for the selection of a target belief should be that the chosen beliefs can be modified through persuasive communication.

As the next step, we have to develop persuasive messages aimed at changing the target beliefs. For this task we will have to rely on our own creativity, because the model of planned behaviour does not provide any 'formal guidelines for choosing arguments to include in messages designed to influence a specific belief' (Eagly & Chaiken, 1993: 240). However, a group of health education scientists recently developed an *intervention mapping* methodology to assist practitioners in the systematic development of interventions (Bartholomew, Parcel & Kok, 1998). Once we have developed a persuasive message, it is important to pre-test it with another sample from our target population to make sure that the message is really persuasive (i.e. succeeds in changing the targeted belief). Since this pre-testing can be done with a relatively small sample, it is an economical way to eliminate ineffective messages. If a message is ineffective in changing targeted beliefs of captive audiences under laboratory conditions, it is unlikely to have an impact under field conditions. Unfortunately, however, the opposite is not necessarily true.

Lack of control as impediment to action

Sometimes behaviour is only weakly or not at all related to intentions, but strongly predicted by perceived behavioural control. This is unlikely to be the case for behaviours such as eating fruit and vegetables which most people who can take care of their own shopping and preparation of meals would perceive as largely under their own control. Control over this type of behaviour should only be limited to the extent that one depends on other persons, such as parents or spouses, for buying and preparing food. In a more general sense, behavioural control is incomplete when enacting the behaviour requires the cooperation of others (see Liska, 1984, for a more extensive discussion of limited control). This cooperation of others is needed when a person wants to engage in safe sex. In a study of consistent condom use among homosexual men, De Wit et al. (2000) even found that whether these men engaged in safe sex with casual partners was largely predicted by perceived behavioural control and not significantly related to their intentions. The likely reason for this pattern was that most men intended to have safe sex, but that some were unable to negotiate these safety rules with a casual partner. Obviously, these men knew themselves well enough to anticipate these problems.

If behaviour is not determined by intentions but *predicted* by perceived control, changing control beliefs should have little impact on behaviour, because this association does not reflect a causal relationship. As argued before, behaviour is not determined by the individual's control beliefs, but by personal and environmental factors which are not under the volitional control of these individuals. However, since it is assumed that the direct association between perceived behavioural control and behaviour does only occur when the individual's perceived control is a realistic reflection of their actual control over the behaviour, their control beliefs should give us some indications of the aspects of actual control which are interfering with their performance of a given behaviour. In the case of homosexual men, one strategy which has often proved to be effective, is to increase their actual control by giving training to improve their sexual negotiation skills (for reviews, see Kelly, 2000; Stroebe, 2000).

Interventions based on stages theories of behaviour change

Implicit in the model of planned behaviour is the assumption that it is the characteristics of a behaviour that determine whether or not it is mainly under motivational control. Thus, behaviours which are difficult to enact because they involve negotiations with a partner (as in the case of condom use) or because they involve breaking with an addiction (as in the case of stopping smoking or reducing alcohol consumption) are likely to be under external control, whereas 'easy' behaviours such as brushing one's teeth or eating more fruit and vegetables are mainly under volitional control. An alternative perspective that has been taken by stage theorists (e.g. Prochaska et al., 1992; Weinstein & Sandman, 1992) assumes that individuals move through stages of attitude and behaviour change from a situation where they are not even aware of the existence of a risk, to a situation where they are changing their behaviour and fighting relapse.

According to one of the best-known stage theories of change, the *trans-theoretical model* (e.g. Prochaska et al., 1992), behaviour change involves five stages. Individuals begin at a stage of *pre-contemplation*, in which they are not aware of a risk and have no intention to change. The next stage is *contemplation*, where people are aware that there may be a health risk and are thinking of changing their behaviour, without reaching a definite decision. From there individuals move to a stage of *preparation*, at which they have not only formed the firm intention to change but have also begun to make small behavioural adjustments in preparation for a change. This leads to an *action* stage, where they are changing their behaviour, and finally to a *maintenance* stage, at which they are fighting relapse.

The major implication for interventions to be derived from stage models of change is that the nature of the intervention has to be matched to the stage of change of the target individuals (see Weinstein, Rothman & Sutton, 1998, for an extensive discussion of essential characteristics of stage models). For example, information about the health consequences associated with a given health-impairing behaviour is most likely to be effective for individuals who are in a pre-contemplation or contemplation stage. Once a decision to act has been taken, action- or maintenance-oriented information, for example information that enhances the self-efficacy of the individual with regard to changing the behaviour, is likely to be more effective.

Thus, whereas interventions derived from the TPB would be aimed at the most typical members of the target population and based on aggregate information of behavioural determinants, stage models suggest tailoring messages to particular individuals on the basis of their *stage of change*. However, beyond the difference in focus on either health outcome or self-efficacy information, stage models give little guidance with regard to the types of beliefs one should focus on. Since this information on types of beliefs to be targeted can be derived from applying the model of planned behaviour, it would appear useful to combine both approaches in designing an intervention. For example, if the analysis in terms of the TPB indicates that for this particular target population, the health behaviour assessed is partly determined by intention and partly by (actual) control, one could design two interventions, a persuasive message aimed at changing the attitudinal, normative and/or control beliefs of individuals who are in the pre-contemplation and contemplation stages, and a training targeted for those who are already in the action and maintenance stages.

FINAL COMMENTS

This chapter described four social cognition models and discussed their use for the prediction of health behaviour as well as for the development of interventions aimed at improving health behaviour. However, we would like to conclude this section with some words of caution. Even if we succeed in changing salient beliefs that have been identified as determinants of our target behaviour, this belief change is unlikely to result in dramatic behaviour change. According to the meta-analysis of meta-analyses reported earlier (Sheeran, 2001), behavioural intentions account only for 28 per cent of the variance in behaviour, and the determinants of the model of planned behaviour account only for about 40 to 50 per cent of the variance in intentions. Thus, the percentage of variance in behaviour explained by more distal variables such as an individual's beliefs is likely to be relatively small. Sutton (2002) estimated the effective variance explained to be around 5 per cent for behavioural and 3 per cent for normative beliefs.

Since the impact of an intervention should not be judged solely on the basis of the impact it has on individuals (i.e. its efficacy), but also by the number of individuals that can be targeted (i.e. its reach), even such small effects would be useful from a public health perspective. Nevertheless, considerations regarding the limited impact of health education interventions should motivate us to search for strategies that would increase the impact of public health campaigns. On the basis of the research discussed in the last section, one such strategy could be the inclusion of implementation intentions in a message. As we have seen, inducing respondents to form specific plans on *where*, *when* and *how* to execute the target behaviour is likely to increase the correspondence between intention and behaviour.

A second strategy suggested by Stroebe (2000) is to combine health education campaigns whenever possible with changes in the incentive structure so as to increase the costs to the individual of the behaviour one wants to change. Thus, governments can use fiscal and legal measures to alter the contingencies affecting individuals as they drink, smoke or engage in other health-damaging behaviours. Sometimes persuasion and incentive-modification strategies can be combined. Thus, a health promotion campaign aimed at preventing alcoholism might involve health education campaigns focusing on beliefs about alcoholism and alcohol intake, as well as changes in incentives, such as increases in the tax on alcohol or legal restrictions on the sale of alcoholic beverages. It is worthwhile noting that the finding that changes in the incentive structure, and thus in the consequences of engaging in a given behaviour, affect individual behaviour is consistent with the model of planned behaviour, at least if we assume that individuals are likely to be aware of these changes which would then represent negative value outcomes.

DISCUSSION POINTS

1. The theoretical approach outlined in this chapter emphasizes one category of factors that determine health behaviours. Which category is this and why are these factors considered important determinants of behaviour?
2. Explain the general principle that underlies the theoretical models that are presented.

3. Which main types of theoretical models to explain health behaviours are distinguished? How do these types of models differ?

4. The Health Belief Model and Protection-Motivation Theory belong to the same class of theories. What do the original theories have in common and how are they different?

5. Explain what is meant by threat appraisal and coping appraisal in the reformulation of Protection-Motivation Theory.

6. What is an attitude and when do attitudes predict behaviour?

7. The Theory of Reasoned Action distinguishes a proximal determinant of behaviour. What is this proximal determinant and by which other factors is it influenced?

8. Explain what the concept of volitional control entails. How does this distinguish between the Theory of Reasoned Action and the Theory of Planned Behaviour?

9. What are salient beliefs? How can these be assessed? Explain the difference between modal salient beliefs and individual salient beliefs.

10. Which theoretical approaches give the best account of health behaviours? Why?

11. Explain what implementations are and how they can be used to change behaviour.

12. What is the main assumption of stage models of behaviour? What consequence does this have for strategies to change behaviour?

FURTHER READING

Armitage, C. J. and Conner, M. (2000). Social cognition models and health behaviour: a structured review. *Psychology and Health* 15, 173–189.

Bartholomew, L. K., Parcel, G. S. and Kok, G. (1998). Intervention mapping: a process for developing theory- and evidence-based health education programs. *Health Education and Behavior* 25, 545–63.

Conner, M. and Norman, P., eds. (1996). *Predicting Health Behaviour*. Buckingham, UK: Open University Press.

Gollwitzer, P. M. (1999). Implementation intentions: strong effects of simple plans. *American Psychologist* 54, 493–503.

Sheeran, P. (2001). Intention–behaviour relations: a conceptual and empirical review. In W. Stroebe and M. Hewstone, eds., *European Review of Social Psychology*, vol. 12. Chichester: Wiley.

Stroebe, W. (2000). *Social Psychology and Health*, 2nd edn. Buckingham, UK: Open University Press.

Sutton, S. (1998). Predicting and explaining intentions and behavior: how well are we doing? *Journal of Applied Social Psychology* 28, 1317–38.

Weinstein, N. D., Rothman, A. J. and Sutton, S. R. (1998). Stage theories of health behavior: conceptual and methodological issues. *Health Psychology* 17, 290–9.

KEY STUDIES

De Wit, J. B. F., Stroebe, W., De Vroome, E. M. M., Sandfort, T. G. M. and Van Griensven, G. J. P. (2000). Understanding AIDS preventive behavior with casual and primary partners in homosexual men: the Theory of Planned Behaviour and the Information–Motivation–Behavioral-Skills Model. *Psychology and Health* 15, 325–40.

Milne, S., Orbell, S. and Sheeran, P. (2002). Combining motivational and volitional interventions to promote exercise participation: protection motivation theory and implementation intentions. *British Journal of Health Psychology* 7, 163–84.

Orbell, S. and Sheeran, P. (1998). 'Inclined abstainers': a problem for predicting health-related behaviour. *British Journal of Social Psychology* 37, 151–65.

Schifter, D. E. and Ajzen, I. (1985). Intention, perceived control, and weight loss: an application of the theory of planned behavior. *Journal of Personality and Social Psychology* 49, 843–51.

Verplanken, B. and Faes, S. (1999). Good intentions, bad habits, and effects of forming implementation intentions on healthy eating. *European Journal of Social Psychology* 29, 591–604.

REFERENCES

Ajzen, I. (1988). *Attitudes, Personality, and Behavior.* Buckingham, UK: Open University Press.

Ajzen, I. (1991). The theory of planned behavior. *Organizational Behavior and Human Decision Processes* 50, 179–211.

Ajzen, I. and Fishbein, M. (1977). Attitude–behavior relations: a theoretical analysis and review of empirical research. *Psychological Bulletin* 84, 888–918.

Ajzen, I. and Fishbein, M. (1980). *Understanding Attitudes and Predicting Social Behavior.* Englewood Cliffs, NJ: Prentice Hall.

Ajzen, I. and Madden, T. J. (1986). Prediction of goal-directed behavior: attitudes, intentions, and perceived behavioral control. *Journal of Experimental Social Psychology* 22, 453–74.

Ajzen, I. and Timko, C. (1986). Correspondence between health attitudes and behavior. *Basic and Applied Social Psychology* 7, 259–76.

Albarracin, D., Johnson, B. T., Fishbein, M. and Muellerleile, P. A. (2001). Theories of reasoned action and planned behavior as models of condom use: a meta-analysis. *Psychological Bulletin* 127, 142–61.

Armitage, C. J. and Conner, M. (2000). Social cognition models and health behaviour: a structured review. *Psychology and Health* 15, 173–89.

Armitage, C. J. and Conner, M. (2001). Efficacy of the Theory of Planned Behaviour: a meta-analytic review. *British Journal of Social Psychology* 40, 471–99.

Armstrong, G. L., Conn, L. A. and Pinner, R. W. (1999). Trends in infectious disease mortality in the United States during the 20th century. *Journal of the American Medical Association* 281, 61–6.

Bandura, A. (1977). Self-efficacy: toward a unifying theory of behavioral change. *Psychological Review* 84, 191–215.

Bandura, A. (1986). *Social Foundations of Thought and Action.* Englewood Cliffs, NJ: Prentice Hall.

Bandura, A. (1997). *Self-efficacy: The Exercise of Control.* New York: Freeman.

Bartholomew, L. K., Parcel, G. S. and Kok, G. (1998). Intervention Mapping: a process for developing theory- and evidence-based health education programs. *Health Education and Behavior* 25, 545–63.

Becker, M. H., Maiman, L. A., Kirscht, J. P., Haefner, D. P. and Drachman, R. H. (1977). The health belief model in the prediction of dietary compliance: a field experiment. *Journal of Health and Social Behavior* 18, 348–66.

Boer, H. and Seydel, E. R. (1996). Protection motivation theory. In M. Conner and P. Norman, eds., *Predicting Health Behaviour*. Buckingham: Open University Press, 95–120.

Champion, V. L. (1984). Instrument development for health belief model constructs. *Advances in Nursing Science* 6, 73–85.

Conner, M. and Norman, P. (1996). The role of social cognition in health behaviours. In M. Conner and P. Norman, eds., *Predicting Health Behaviour*. Buckingham, UK: Open University Press, 1–22.

Conner, M. and Sparks, P. (1996). The theory of planned behaviour and health related behaviours. In M. Conner and P. Norman, eds., *Predicting Health Behaviour*. Buckingham, UK: Open University Press, 1–22.

De Wit, J. B. F., Stroebe, W., De Vroome, E. M. M., Sandfort, T. G. M. and Van Griensven, G. J. P. (2000). Understanding AIDS preventive behavior with casual and primary partners in homosexual men: the Theory of Planned Behaviour and the Information-Motivation-Behavioral-Skills Model. *Psychology and Health* 15, 325–40.

Eagly, A. H. and Chaiken, S. (1993). *The Psychology of Attitudes*. Fort Worth, TX: Harcourt Brace Jovanovich.

Fielding, J. E. (1999). Public health in the twentieth century: advances and challenges. *Annual Review of Public Health* 20, xii–xx.

Fishbein, M. (1967). Attitude and the prediction of behavior. In M. Fishbein, ed., *Readings in Attitude Theory and Measurement*. New York: John Wiley and Sons, 477–92.

Fishbein, M. and Ajzen, I. (1975). *Belief, Attitude, Intention and Behavior: An Introduction to Theory and Research*. Reading, MA: Addison-Wesley.

Fishbein, M., Middlestadt, S. E. and Hitchcock, P. J. (1994). Using information to change sexually transmitted disease-related behaviors: an analysis based on the theory of reasoned action. In R. J. DiClemente and J. L. Peterson, eds., *Preventing AIDS: Theories and Methods of Behavioral Interventions*. New York: Plenum Press, 61–78.

Fisher, J. D. and Fisher, W. A. (2000). Theoretical approaches to individual-level change in HIV risk behavior. In J. L. Peterson and R. J. DiClemente, eds., *Handbook of HIV Prevention*. New York: Kluwer Academic/Plenum, 3–55.

Floyd, D. L., Prentice-Dunn, S. and Rogers, R. W. (2000). A meta-analysis on protection-motivation theory. *Journal of Applied Social Psychology* 30, 407–29.

Godin, G. and Kok, G. (1996). The theory of planned behavior: a review of its applications to health related behavior. *American Journal of Health Promotion* 11, 87–97.

Gollwitzer, P. M. (1993). Goal achievement: the role of intentions. In W. Stroebe and M. Hewstone, eds., *European Review of Social Psychology*, vol. 4. New York: Wiley, 141–85.

Gollwitzer, P. M. (1999). Implementation intentions: strong effects of simple plans. *American Psychologist* 54, 493–503.

Hardeman, W., Johnston, M., Johnston, D. W., Bonetti, D., Wareham, N. J. and Kinmoth A. L. (2002). Application of the Theory of Planned Behaviour in behaviour change interventions: a systematic review. *Psychology and Health* 17, 123–58.

Harrison, J. A., Mullen, P. D. and Green, L. W. (1992). A meta-analysis of studies of the health belief model with adults. *Health Education Research* 7, 107–16.

Janz, N. K. and Becker, M. H. (1984). The health belief model: a decade later. *Health Education Quarterly* 11, 1–47.

Kasl, S. V. and Cobb, S. (1966). Health behavior, illness behavior, and sick role behavior. *Archives of Environmental Health* 12, 246–66.

Kelly, J. A. (2000). HIV prevention interventions with gay or bisexual men and youth. *AIDS* 14 (suppl. 2), 34–9.

Kraus, S. J. (1995). Attitudes and the prediction of behavior: a meta-analysis of the empirical literature. *Personality and Social Psychology Bulletin* 21, 58–75.

Leventhal, H., Singer, R. P. and Jones, S. (1965). The effects of fear and specificity of recommendation upon attitudes and behavior. *Journal of Personality and Social Psychology* 2, 20–9.

Matarazzo, J. D. (1984). Behavioral health: a 1990 challenge for the health sciences profession. In J. D. Matarazzo, S. M. Weiss, J. A. Herd, N. E. Miller and St. M. Weiss, eds., *Behavioral Health: A Handbook of Health Enhancement and Disease Prevention*. New York: Wiley, 3–40.

McGinnis, J. M. and Foege, W. H. (1993). Actual causes of death in the United States. *Journal of the American Medical Association* 270, 2207–12.

Milne, S., Orbell, S. and Sheeran, P. (2002). Combining motivational and volitional interventions to promote exercise participation: protection motivation theory and implementation intentions. *British Journal of Health Psychology* 7, 163–84.

Milne, S., Sheeran, P. and Orbell, S. (2000). Prediction and intervention in health-related behavior: a meta-analytic review of protection-motivation theory. *Journal of Applied Social Psychology* 30, 106–43.

Orbell, S., Hodgkins, S. and Sheeran, P. (1997). Implementation intentions and the Theory of Planned Behavior. *Personality and Social Psychology Bulletin* 23, 945–54.

Orbell, S. and Sheeran, P. (1998). 'Inclined abstainers': a problem for predicting health-related behaviour. *British Journal of Social Psychology* 37, 151–65.

Prochaska, J. O., DiClemente, C. C. and Norcross, J. C. (1992). In search of how people change: applications to addictive behavior. *American Psychologist* 47, 1102–14.

Randall, D. M. and Wolff, J. A. (1994). The time interval in the intention–behaviour relationship: meta-analysis. *British Journal of Social Psychology* 33, 405–18.

Rippetoe, P. A. and Rogers, R. W. (1987). Effects of components of protection motivation theory on adaptive and maladaptive coping with a health threat. *Journal of Personality and Social Psychology* 52, 596–604.

Rogers, R. W. (1975). A protection motivation theory of fear appeals and attitude change. *Journal of Psychology* 91, 93–114.

Rogers, R. W. (1983). Cognitive and physiological processes in fear appeals and attitude change: a revised theory of protection-motivation. In J. T. Cacioppo and R. E. Petty, eds., *Social Psychophysiology: A Source Book*. New York: Guilford Press, 153–76.

Rosenstock, I. M. (1974). Historical origins of the health belief model. *Health Education Monographs* 2, 1–8.

Rosenstock, I. M., Strecher, V. J. and Becker, M. H. (1988). Social learning theory and the health belief model. *Health Education Quarterly* 15, 175–83.

Schifter, D. E. and Ajzen, I. (1985). Intention, perceived control, and weight loss: an application of the theory of planned behavior. *Journal of Personality and Social Psychology* 49, 843–51.

Schwarzer, R. and Fuchs, R. (1996). Self-efficacy and health behaviours. In M. Conner and P. Norman, eds., *Predicting Health Behaviour*. Buckingham, UK: Open University Press, 163–96.

Sheeran, P. (2001). Intention–behaviour relations: a conceptual and empirical review. In W. Stroebe and M. Hewstone, eds., *European Review of Social Psychology*, vol. 12. Chichester: Wiley.

Sheeran, P. and Abraham, C. (1996). The health belief model. In M. Conner and P. Norman, eds., *Predicting Health Behaviour*. Buckingham, UK: Open University Press, 23–61.

Sheeran, P., Abraham, C. and Orbell, S. (1999). Psychosocial correlates of heterosexual condom use: a meta-analysis. *Psychological Bulletin* 125, 90–132.

Sheeran, P. and Orbell, S. (1998). Do intentions predict condom use? Meta-analysis and examination of six moderator variables. *British Journal of Social Psychology* 37, 231–50.

Sheeran, P. and Orbell, S. (1999). Implementation intentions and repeated behaviour: augmenting the predictive validity of the theory of planned behaviour. *European Journal of Social Psychology* 29, 349–69.

Sheeran, P. and Orbell, S. (2000). Using implementation intentions to increase attendance for cervical cancer screening. *Health Psychology* 19, 283–9.

Sheppard, B. H., Hartwick, J. and Warshaw, P. R. (1988). The theory of reasoned action: a meta-analysis of past research with recommendations for modifications and future research. *Journal of Consumer Research* 15, 325–43.

Strecher, V. J., Champion, V. L and Rosenstock, I. M. (1997). The health belief model and health behavior. In D. S. Gochman, ed., *Handbook of Health Behavior Research I: Personal and Social Determinants*. New York: Plenum Press, 71–91.

Stroebe, W. (2000). *Social Psychology and Health*, 2nd ed. Buckingham, UK: Open University Press.

Sutton, S. (1998). Predicting and explaining intentions and behavior: how well are we doing? *Journal of Applied Social Psychology* 28, 1317–38.

Sutton, S. (2002). Using theories of reasoned action and planned behaviour to develop health behaviour interventions: problems and assumptions. In D. R. Rutter and L. Quine, eds., *Changing Health Behaviour: Research and Practice with Social Cognition Models*. Buckingham, UK: Open University Press, 193–208.

Verplanken, B. and Faes, S. (1999). Good intentions, bad habits, and effects of forming implementation intentions on healthy eating. *European Journal of Social Psychology* 29, 591–604.

Weinstein, N. D., Rothman, A. J. and Sutton, S. R. (1998). Stage theories of health behavior: conceptual and methodological issues. *Health Psychology* 17, 290–9.

Weinstein, N. D. and Sandman, P. M. (1992). A model of the precaution adoption process: evidence from home radon testing. *Health Psychology* 11, 170–80.

Wicker, A. W. (1969). Attitude versus action: the relationship of verbal and overt behavioural responses to attitude objects. *Journal of Social Issues* 25, 41–78.

Chapter Four

ILLNESS-RELATED COGNITION AND BEHAVIOUR

Linda D. Cameron and Rona Moss-Morris

CHAPTER OUTLINE

This chapter focuses on the self-regulation model of illness cognition and behaviour. This model specifies that patients' hold cognitive representations of their illness which include beliefs about the identity, cause, time-line, consequences, cure/controllability and cause of their conditions. The purpose of the chapter is to show how these beliefs influence the ways in which patients respond to their illness-related experiences. The responses include whether or not patients seek help for symptoms, adhere to treatment recommendations, avoid dealing with the problem altogether or remain engaged in various daily activities. Patients' illness representations are also shown to be important determinants of psychological adjustment to illness. The chapter also discusses how people's perceptions of illness risk act as catalysts for health-protective behaviours such as cancer screening and regular medical check-ups. The final sections of the chapter look at the inter-relationships between emotional and cognitive representations of illness and the influence of culture on the development of illness representations.

KEY CONCEPTS

adherence

appraisals

attributions

causal beliefs

common-sense models of illness

control beliefs

coping behaviour

chronic illness

cultural influences

egocentric cultures

emotional adjustment

emotional regulation

emotional representations

emotional responses

health behaviours

illness beliefs

illness cognitions

illness consequences

illness identity

illness perceptions

illness prototypes

illness representations

illness schemata

mood states

psychological adjustment

risk perceptions

self-efficacy

self-regulation theory

socio-centric cultures

symptom perception

timeline beliefs

unrealistic optimism

Imagine waking up one morning with a splitting headache. The sharp, pounding pain flares as you try to lift your head off the pillow. You then notice that your eyes hurt when you move them, and that your throat feels a little scratchy. You immediately try to figure out what is wrong: Could it be a migraine headache, or the beginning of the flu? Or is it fatigue and over-exertion from too much work? What you do next will depend on your beliefs about the nature of this episode. These beliefs will determine whether you spend the day in bed with the lights out and the curtains pulled, drink lots of fluids and take vitamin C tablets, or press on with your busy schedule after taking some aspirin and promising yourself an early bedtime that night.

As this scenario illustrates, illness-related beliefs critically shape our illness experiences and behaviours. Illness beliefs are assumed to be organized in memory into schemas or *representations* – that is, mental models for how a condition, event or object usually functions. An *illness representation*, therefore, is an organized set of beliefs regarding how the illness affects the body, its likely impact on life activities and experiences, whether it can be cured, and so on. A number of other terms are often used in the research literature: illness cognitions, illness perceptions, illness beliefs and illness schemata are some of the more common ones. These terms are considered to be synonyms of illness representations (Scharloo & Kaptein, 1997). In this chapter, we will use the term 'illness representations' in discussing this large area of research.

People vary markedly in their representations of an illness. For example, one person may erroneously believe that HIV can be spread through mosquito bites or sharing eating utensils with an infected person, and that new treatments can cure AIDS. In contrast, another person may have more accurate beliefs that HIV is spread through the exchange of bodily fluids by sexual intercourse and the use of contaminated intravenous needles, and that new treatments may prolong survival but not eliminate AIDS.

Individuals differ not only in the medical accuracy of their illness representations, but also in the level of development of their representations. Some may have an elaborate and detailed understanding about an illness whereas others may know very little about it. Illness representations can also vary in terms of their coherence, or the extent to which they make sense to a person (Moss-Morris et al., 2002). For example, one person may have beliefs about her diabetes that seem logical to her, whereas another person with diabetes may be perplexed as to how her obesity could have contributed to its development, how insulin relates to her body functioning, and why nothing can be done to cure it. This second person can have many beliefs about her diabetes which nevertheless seem confusing and mysterious.

Illness representations are critically important because they guide our reactions to symptoms, diagnoses and other types of illness-related information. For example, a person's decision regarding whether or not to seek medical care for an unusual set of symptoms will depend primarily on her beliefs about the likely illnesses creating those symptoms. Inaccurate illness representations can lead to problems such as excessive delay in seeking medical care, non-adherence to medical prescriptions and undue emotional distress.

A SELF-REGULATION MODEL OF ILLNESS COGNITION AND BEHAVIOUR: AN OVERVIEW

The self-regulation model of illness cognition and behaviour (proposed by Leventhal and associates) specifies how illness representations guide responses to illness-related experiences (see figure 4.1; Leventhal, Nerenz & Steele, 1984). It is a self-regulation

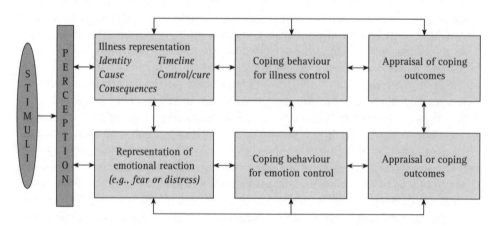

Figure 4.1 Leventhal's self-regulation model of illness cognition and behaviour; from Leventhal et al., 1984

model in that it focuses on how individuals select and monitor their behaviour over time in order to make progress towards their goals (e.g. being healthy, avoiding pain and suffering; Cameron & Leventhal, 2003). It is often called the *common sense model* because of its emphasis on personal, common-sense beliefs about illnesses.

This model identifies five key components or dimensions of illness representations. These components are:

Identity: These beliefs concern the illness label or diagnosis (e.g. 'migraine headache') and associated symptoms (e.g. throbbing headache, nausea and visual disturbances).

Cause: These beliefs concern the factors or conditions believed to have caused the illness (e.g. hereditary factors or stress).

Timeline: These beliefs concern the expected duration of the illness. Beliefs about illness timelines can vary from acute, or of limited duration (e.g. the flu); to cyclic, with episodes that come and go over time (e.g. migraines); and chronic, or of long-term duration (e.g. diabetes).

Consequences: These beliefs concern the expected effects of an illness on physical, social and psychological well-being (e.g. migraines interfere with performance at work or school, and they limit one's ability to attend social gatherings).

Control/Cure: These beliefs concern the extent to which the illness can be controlled or cured through treatment measures and behaviours (e.g. medication will control the migraines effectively; controlling stress levels will reduce the frequency of migraines).

Illness representations develop from exposure to a variety of social and cultural sources of information – news stories, education in schools, personal experiences of illness, witnessing illness experiences of family members and friends, portrayals of illness in books and movies, and other experiences. Representations include both abstract, conceptual information (represented by the linguistic phrases in memory, such as 'medication will control my migraines') and concrete, emotionally evocative images (such as vivid memories of experiencing a migraine, taking the pills, and feeling the pain eventually subside).

Figure 4.1 illustrates the role of illness representations in the self-regulation of health threats – that is, the process of selecting and monitoring behaviour aimed at controlling or reducing health threat conditions. Perceptions of stimuli (such as symptoms or disease-related information) activate illness representations stored in memory, and a representation of the individual's present condition is formed through matching and integrating current symptoms and contextual information with these pre-existing beliefs. This representation guides the selection of coping behaviours, and the outcomes of these actions are appraised in terms of their success in controlling or eliminating the illness and its consequences. These outcome appraisals lead to refinements of the representation (e.g. its controllability, its likely consequences, etc.) and the selection of new coping behaviours (e.g. maintaining the same action or switching to an alternative course of action).

At the same time that symptoms or other cues trigger the activation and development of cognitive representations, they can also induce emotional responses (see the lower level of the model in figure 4.1). For example, the discovery of a large, unusual lump may automatically induce a response of fear and the activation of an illness representation (e.g. cancer) can further fuel distress and worry. Awareness of these emotional responses (the emotional representation) prompts the selection and use of strategies for controlling these emotions. These responses are then appraised for their success, and these appraisals guide further efforts in emotional regulation. Illness representations therefore play an important role in generating emotional experiences and influencing behaviours aimed at controlling them.

Although illness representations are activated by symptoms, diagnoses and other cues that one is sick, they can also be evoked when a person is asymptomatic and free of the illness. Beliefs regarding one's risk of illness can develop through matching beliefs about one's health status, health habits and family history with beliefs about the causes of the illness. Risk perceptions and their activation of illness representations can play an important role in influencing health-related behaviours such as exercise, diet, safe-sex practices and the use of immunizations. Moreover, they critically influence the use of screening practices such as mammography, blood pressure checks, cholesterol level checks and HIV testing.

In the following sections, we focus more closely on the each of the illness representation components. As will become clear, each component plays an important role in influencing behaviours, emotions and health outcomes.

IDENTITY BELIEFS: LABEL AND SYMPTOMS

An illness label is closely linked with beliefs about associated symptoms; indeed, when asked to define an illness such as a cold, we almost invariably describe the physical experiences we associate with it. Moreover, when we experience atypical symptoms, we automatically try to determine whether they represent a specific illness by searching for possible matches with one of our illness representations. Research indicates that illness identity beliefs have a prototype structure (Bishop & Converse, 1986). A prototype is a mental model of the most representative case of a particular condition or entity, and it is used as the standard with which to determine whether a presented case is a member of that category. If you experience six symptoms that closely match the prototypical symptoms of your representation of strep throat, then you may readily label your condition as strep throat. If, however, only two out of your six symptoms match your prototype for strep throat, then you may suspect that your condition is something other than strep throat.

The process of matching symptoms with disease labels is often not an easy one. There may be considerable overlap among disease prototypes, making it difficult to discern which illness is more likely to be responsible for a particular symptom experience. In addition, the same disease can cause markedly different types of symptoms in different people. For example, symptoms associated with blood glucose levels vary across diabetes patients to such an extent that no one symptom is linked with blood glucose levels for all patients (Gonder-Frederick et al., 1986). Moreover, symptoms can be caused by other factors besides illness – fatigue may produce headaches and lethargy, exercise may cause vague muscle or nerve pains, and insect bites can produce large lumps.

Individuals recognize that stress can cause a variety of symptoms, and they often attribute symptoms occurring during a stressful time to stress rather than to illnesses. Stress attributions are more likely to occur if the symptoms are unfamiliar or ambiguous rather than highly prototypical of a specific disease, and if the stressor is highly salient (Baumann et al., 1989) and of recent onset. In a study illustrating this stress attribution process (Cameron, Leventhal & Leventhal, 1995), community residents were asked about their naturally occurring symptoms and how they treated them. At the same time, they were asked about any current stressful events. Residents who were experiencing stressful events were more likely to believe that their symptoms were due to stress rather than to illness if the symptoms were ambiguous in nature, but not if they were highly distinctive of particular illnesses. Moreover, residents were less likely to seek care for ambiguous symptoms when facing stressful events that had started recently.

Just as individuals experiencing atypical symptoms rely on identity beliefs to determine a 'diagnosis', individuals who receive an illness diagnosis (such as from a doctor) use identity beliefs to detect associated symptom experiences. When a woman is told that she has heart disease, for example, she will automatically go over her current and recent symptom experiences in her mind to identify symptoms that are likely to be caused by this condition. This process can lead to erroneous attributions of symptoms to a diagnosed illness. Consider, for example, the case of hypertension. Hypertension is an asymptomatic condition – there are no clearly identifiable symptoms of high blood pressure, and people are not able to tell when their blood pressure is high or low (Baumann & Leventhal, 1985). Nevertheless, people diagnosed with hypertension can and do find symptoms to associate (erroneously) with this illness label. This tendency is highlighted by the findings of a study in which university students had their blood pressure taken and were then informed that their blood pressure was either high or normal. In fact, this information was fictitious and not at all based on their actual blood pressure levels. Students who received a high reading reported experiencing a higher number of symptoms commonly believed to be associated with hypertension (such as dizziness, heart palpitations and headache) than did students receiving a normal reading (Baumann et al., 1989). This tendency to identify symptoms is clearly evident among patients with hypertension. One study found that 80 per cent of hypertension patients agreed that people with hypertension cannot tell when their blood pressure is elevated. Yet 88 per cent of these same patients reported that *they* could tell when their blood pressure was elevated, and they identified symptoms that they believed corresponded with their high blood pressure (Meyer, Leventhal & Gutmann, 1985).

Illness identity beliefs critically influence decisions to seek medical care for symptoms. It is important to note that symptoms in and of themselves do not stimulate care-seeking – indeed, most of us experience a number of symptoms at any given time and yet we only infrequently seek care. Rather, it is the label we ascribe to these symptoms that generally determines whether or not we seek care. One study (Cameron, Leventhal & Leventhal, 1993) found that individuals seeking care for atypical symptoms reported just as many symptoms as did individuals with atypical symptoms who were not seeking medical care. However, the care-seekers were significantly more likely than those not seeking care to have an illness label for their symptoms. Having a personal diagnosis for symptoms stimulates care-seeking, whereas not identifying a specific illness label inhibits seeking care for new symptoms.

Labelling symptoms as illness related can also influence patients' treatment decisions. A study of patients with moderate to severe asthma showed that up to 60 per cent of patients ascribed non-asthma-specific symptoms such as fatigue and headache to their asthma (Main et al., 2003). The tendency to label non-specific symptoms as asthma-related was strongly associated with the number of times per day that patients used their reliever medication. Interestingly, this relationship was independent of objective measures of lung functioning, suggesting that patients' symptom reports do not clearly reflect underlying patho-physiological processes. This has important treatment implications, as overuse of relievers has been shown to have a number of negative consequences. Patients are often taught to rely on their symptom reports to assess their lung functioning, which may in itself lead to an overuse of medication.

Inaccurate labelling of symptoms can also lead to dangerous delays in seeking care for serious symptoms, such symptoms of a heart attack. People tend to have clear beliefs about heart attack symptoms as including breathlessness, crushing chest pain and sudden collapse. In fact, heart attack symptoms can vary markedly from this prototype. Common symptoms include nausea, coughing and flu-like symptoms; moreover, chest pain caused by a heart attack can develop gradually or be relatively mild in nature. Individuals often fail to recognize these as heart attack symptoms and end up delaying seeking care for many hours (Dracup et al., 1995). Among heart attack patients, discrepancies between their beliefs about symptoms associated with a heart attack and their actual symptom experiences are associated with longer delays in getting to the hospital (Perry et al., 2001). These delays may critically affect survival, as the risk of mortality is reduced by 40 per cent if treatment is started within the first hour after the onset of symptoms (Newby et al., 1996).

CAUSAL BELIEFS

Illnesses by their very nature are threatening and unwanted conditions, and a natural response to a diagnosis is to ask, 'Why me? Why did I get this illness?' Attempts to identify the causes of an illness can be motivated by efforts to make sense of the experience. Being able to identify the causes also may provide a sense of predictability and control over the illness (Turnquist, Harvey & Anderson, 1988), such as by enabling one to determine whether aspects of one's life can be changed to alter the course of the disease or to prevent recurrences. For certain illnesses, almost all patients develop some beliefs about likely causes. For example, Taylor and her colleagues (Taylor, Lichtman & Wood, 1984) found that over 95 per cent of breast cancer patients had developed strong beliefs about the likely causes of their illness, many of which were discrepant with medical science. For other illness experiences, there may be less motivation to formulate causal attributions. Sissons Joshi (1995) found that over one-third of patients with diabetes were disinclined to identify causes of their diabetes, apparently because they did not believe that it was important or helpful to do so.

What kinds of causes are identified by patients? People commonly attribute their illnesses to heredity, the actions of other people, the environment, fate or chance, and their own character and actions (Michela & Wood, 1986). Beliefs that God's will and sin play a causal role in the development of illnesses such as AIDS are also common, even among US university students (Klonoff & Landrine, 1994). Stress is implicated as a causal factor for a wide variety of illnesses. In fact, stress is one of the most commonly reported perceived causes among individuals with breast cancer (Taylor et al., 1984), heart disease (French et al., 2001), diabetes (Hampson, 1997), rheumatoid arthritis and multiple sclerosis (Moss-Morris et al., 2002).

How do causal beliefs affect coping behaviours and emotional responses? Weiner's theory of causal attribution (Weiner, 1986) identifies three aspects of causal beliefs that are associated with coping behaviours and emotional adjustment: the *locus* of causality (whether the cause is an internal feature of the person or an external aspect of the environment), the *stability* (whether the cause changes over time), and the *controllability* (whether the cause is under volitional control). Beliefs that causes are stable and uncontrollable (such as intelligence or environmental pollution) are associated with the use of avoidance coping and, in turn, poor psychological adjustment (Roesch & Weiner, 2001). Blaming others for an illness (external, uncontrollable causes) is also associated with poor adjustment (Taylor et al., 1984; Tennen, Affleck & Gershman, 1986). In contrast, attributions to internal, unstable and controllable causes are associated with the use of problem-focused coping and emotion-focused coping, and with positive psychological adjustment (Roesch & Weiner, 2001). This general relationship between causal attributions and adjustment may not hold under all conditions; in particular, the influence of causal attributions on adjustment may depend on whether or not the illness is perceived as controllable or curable. For example, an individual may believe that her heart disease was caused by internal, unstable and controllable factors (high-fat diet) and that the illness is uncontrollable and incurable. Individuals with this combination of causal and control beliefs may be particularly susceptible to feelings of guilt, lowered self-esteem and poorer psychological adjustment.

Finally, there is some evidence that causal beliefs may predict subsequent health outcomes. Affleck and colleagues have found that patients who attributed their heart attack to stress had greater disease progression 8 years later compared to patients who did not make stress attributions. Moreover, those who blamed the initial heart attack on other people were more likely than those who did not to suffer another heart attack (Affleck et al., 1987).

TIME-LINE

The time-line component constitutes the perceived time frame for the development and duration of the illness. As mentioned earlier in the chapter, patients tend to define illnesses in terms of three major time-line models: acute, cyclical and chronic (Leventhal et al., 1984). However, we often start out with an acute model of illness because our childhood experiences with infectious diseases lead us to develop implicit acute models for most illnesses (Leventhal, Brissette & Leventhal, 2002). For instance, the experience of illnesses such as colds, influenza, chicken pox, measles or mumps is almost ubiquitous during childhood. These illness episodes tend to be of relatively short duration, and in most cases people recover from these conditions with no residual effects. These experiences may lead people to develop a heuristic or implicit 'rule of thumb' that illnesses are acute and can be cured. When faced with a diagnosis of a more chronic condition, such as heart disease or diabetes, the adjustment to a chronic model can pose difficulties for many people. In some instances, it may take repeated symptom flare-ups and remissions or ongoing complications before patients realize the chronicity of their condition. A chronic illness often means accepting that the illness may not be amenable to cure and that the illness and the symptoms have to be managed over the long term.

It is therefore not surprising that the time-line component influences adherence to treatment. For example, patients who perceive their asthma to be a cyclical rather than chronic condition often fail to use their preventive medication as prescribed, apparently because they do not believe that the medication is necessary (Horne & Weinman, 2002). Research on patients with hypertension revealed that up to 70 per cent of those holding an acute illness model dropped out of treatment prematurely (Meyer et al., 1985). For these patients, the need for ongoing treatment may have conflicted with their belief that the illness would be of short duration. Hypertension poses particular problems with regards to chronicity beliefs because of its asymptomatic nature. It is often the ongoing experience of symptoms which facilitates the development of a chronic model.

In other instances, an acute model can be advantageous for patients. A study of illness perceptions in first-time myocardial infarction patients demonstrated that patients who believed that their illness would last a short time were more likely to return to work within six weeks of their heart attack (Petrie et al., 1996). Other studies on patients with Addison's disease (Heijmans, 1999) and psoriasis (Scharloo et al., 1998) have shown that patients who have a strong belief that their illness is chronic report higher levels of disability and poorer psychological adaptation to their condition.

Time-line also shows logical relationships with the other illness representation components (Moss-Morris et al., 2002). For example, a strong belief that the illness can be cured or controlled is typically associated with perceptions of short duration and relatively minor consequences. In contrast, beliefs that an illness will last a long time and has a number of symptoms tend to be associated with more severe consequences and lower beliefs about cure or control of the disease.

CONSEQUENCES

Beliefs about the consequences of one's illness include physical, social and economic consequences, and in some cases, the prospect of imminent death (Ditto, Jemmott & Darley, 1988). In a series of studies, Jemmott and his colleagues demonstrated that individuals use their perceived prevalence of a disorder as a heuristic device to determine the seriousness of its consequences (Ditto et al., 1988; Jemmott, Croyle & Ditto, 1988; Jemmott, Ditto & Croyle, 1986). The perception that a disease is rare tends to be associated with higher estimates of its seriousness and greater emotional distress than if the illness is perceived as common.

The type and nature of symptoms experienced is also related to people's beliefs about the consequences of their illness. Many chronic illnesses, such as heart disease and cancer, have few symptoms in the early stages of the illness, yet we are conditioned from childhood to view symptoms as reflecting severity and progress of disease. Studies on cancer and chemotherapy have shown that the consequences of treatment can be perceived as more harmful and serious than the disease itself (Nerenz, Leventhal & Love, 1982). The concrete side-effects of nausea and vomiting can override the more abstract consequences of having a life-threatening illness. In general, medical perceptions of severity may not always be reflected in patients' beliefs about the severity of their illness. A classic example of this discrepancy occurs in diabetes, an illness that is often regarded as a 'silent killer' by the medical profession. Poorly controlled diabetes can have severe consequences such as blindness, gangrenous limbs, renal failure and even death. However, patients with poorly controlled diabetes may not experience many symptoms (Gonder-Frederick and Cox, 1991). For these patients, the long-term consequences may be too abstract to motivate adherence behaviours which require patients to carefully monitor their blood glucose levels, regulate their medication use, and adhere to a strict dietary regimen.

On the other end of the spectrum are medically unexplained illnesses such as chronic fatigue syndrome and fibromyalgia, which are not life-threatening illnesses and are generally not regarded as serious illnesses by the medical profession. Yet patients with these illnesses experience a wide range of symptoms which they believe signify a serious disease (Fink, 1992; Moss-Morris & Petrie, 2001; Robbins & Kirmayer, 1990). The number of symptoms ascribed to the illness is highly correlated with the belief that the illness is a serious condition (Moss-Morris, Petrie & Weinman, 1996). In addition, studies comparing these patient groups to patients with chronic illnesses such as rheumatoid arthritis and diabetes have found that the chronic fatigue and fibromyalgia patients believe that their illnesses have had a more profound impact on their lives (Robbins & Kirmayer, 1990; Weinman et al., 1996).

Patients' perceptions of the consequences of their illness are important predictors of both behavioural responses to the illness and adjustment to the condition. In fact, beliefs about consequences are often more important than timeline beliefs as predictors of outcome. A prospective study showed that early return to work following a heart attack was related to the belief that the illness would have fewer grave consequences for the patient (Petrie et al., 1996). A longitudinal study of patients with rheumatoid arthritis showed that even when controlling for medical indices of illness severity, belief in the adverse consequences of the illness was associated with more visits to the outpatient clinic, more tiredness and higher anxiety (Scharloo et al., 1999). A study of psoriasis patients showed that beliefs about the serious consequences of the illness were associated with pathological worry (Fortune et al., 2000). However, worry was unrelated to the actual clinical severity of the condition, and beliefs about the severity of the condition were also unrelated to clinical indices. Finally, a study on patients with multiple sclerosis showed that severity beliefs were associated with poorer adjustment to MS even when controlling for more objective measures of disability and the length and type of multiple sclerosis (Jopson & Moss-Morris, 2003). Of particular interest is the consistent finding from these latter studies that patients' beliefs about the severity of the illness have a greater association with outcome than do clinical measures of illness severity. This pattern reinforces the idea that the patients' beliefs may be just as important as the predictions of the medical profession in ultimately determining the prognosis for the patient.

CURE (CONTROLLABILITY)

The fifth illness representation component refers to beliefs about the controllability and/or curability of the illness and is closely related to inferences about the severity of the illness. A more severe illness is seen as less controllable and less curable than an illness that is perceived to be less severe (Lau & Hartman, 1983). Perceptions of control are also important indicators of coping behaviour. People with a strong sense of control over their illness may be more prepared to engage in an active treatment programme to recover or to prevent further relapses from the illness. This is certainly true for patients who have experienced a heart attack. Prospective studies have shown that these patients' attendance at cardiac rehabilitation programmes is related to a stronger belief at admission that their heart condition can be cured or controlled (Cooper et al.,1999; Petrie et al., 1996).

On the other hand, patients who believe that the course of their illness is largely uncontrollable are more likely to engage in the use of passive coping strategies to deal with their illness such as cognitive or behavioural avoidance (Heijmans, 1999; Moss-Morris et al., 1996). Perceptions of low controllability are also related to higher hospital admissions in rheumatoid arthritis and psoriasis patients (Scharloo et al., 1999, Scharloo et al., 2000), which may reflect in part a greater reliance on hospital care than on self-care to manage the illness. Patients who lack confidence that self-care measures will be effective may fail to make behavioural changes to manage their illness. They may end up going to hospital more frequently as a consequence because they are sicker and because they feel a greater need to be taken care of by hospital staff.

There is strong evidence that high control beliefs are associated with better psychological adjustment and greater functional abilities in patients with chronic illness, particularly in those with more severe disease conditions (Helgeson, 1992; Orbell et al., 1998; Tennen et al., 1992). Perceptions of high controllability may promote adaptive coping efforts and reduce distress, which results in better adjustment and functional well-being.

Recent research suggests that it may be useful to separate control beliefs into two dimensions: personal control and treatment control (Moss-Morris et al., 2002). Personal control includes beliefs that one's own actions will help to control the illness, whereas treatment control includes beliefs that one's prescribed treatments will be effective in controlling or curing the condition. More work needs to be done to ascertain whether these beliefs predict different coping responses. We might hypothesize, for instance, that perceptions of high treatment control will result in increased adherence to treatment regimens, whereas perceptions of high personal control might lead to lifestyle changes.

A recent study on multiple sclerosis suggests that these control dimensions have different effects on the fatigue experienced by these patients (Jopson & Moss-Morris, 2003). Mental fatigue was associated with higher beliefs of personal control over the illness, but lower beliefs of treatment control. It may be that maintaining a strong sense of personal control over an illness that can be unpredictable requires substantial mental effort, leading to mental fatigue. Having faith that treatment may control the illness may offer a more external source of control, which has positive benefits for mental fatigue. Although personal control appeared to tax mental stamina in these patients, it did have positive benefits for their psychological adaptation. Patients with a strong sense of personal control had higher self-esteem, were less distressed by their illness, and were less depressed in general.

It is useful to consider how personal control and treatment control beliefs relate to two other types of beliefs: *self-efficacy* and *outcome efficacy*. Self-efficacy refers to beliefs that one has the ability to engage in a particular action (Bandura, 1977), and it is likely to be an important determinant of both personal control beliefs ('Can I do these actions?') and treatment control beliefs ('Do I have the ability to successfully complete this treatment regimen?'). Self-efficacy beliefs have been found to be strong predictors of a variety of behaviours, including adherence to treatment regimens for patients with diabetes (Kavanagh, Gooley & Wilson, 1993) and patients with arthritis (Marks, 2001). Outcome efficacy refers to beliefs that a particular course of action will successfully lead to a particular goal state or outcome (Bandura, 1977). Within the context of illness experiences, outcome efficacy refers to beliefs that a behaviour or treatment will successfully control or cure the illness. As with self-efficacy, outcome efficacy is expected to be an important determinant of both personal control beliefs and treatment control beliefs. For example, patients with cancer who believe that exercise can reduce the risk of recurrence may be highly motivated to engage in regular physical activity. Similarly, patients with asthma who have high outcome efficacy beliefs about a medication are very likely to view that medication as necessary for controlling their asthma (Horne & Weinman, 2002).

ILLNESS REPRESENTATIONS AND CLINICAL INTERVENTIONS

Taken together, there is now substantial evidence to suggest that the identity, cause, time-line, consequences and cure/control beliefs all have a unique contribution to behavioural and psychological outcomes in chronic illnesses. Of even greater clinical significance are recent findings that interventions specifically designed to address patients' illness representations may be able to alter their adaptation to the illness. For example, a randomized controlled trial of a brief illness perceptions intervention for patients who had recently experienced a myocardial infarction showed that the intervention enhanced control/cure beliefs and reduced time-line and serious consequences beliefs (Petrie et al., 2002). A three-month follow-up showed that patients in the intervention group returned to work sooner and experienced less angina compared to those in the control condition.

In another trial, myocardial infarction patients received a cardiac rehabilitation programme either alone or in combination with an educational manual that provided detailed information about consequences, control and other facets of heart disease. Those who received the manual reported greater increases in their control beliefs and lower depression levels relative to patients who received only the cardiac rehabilitation programme (O'Rourke & Hampson, 1999).

MEASURING ILLNESS REPRESENTATIONS

One of the key issues facing researchers in this area is the selection of a good measure of illness representations. Although a number of assessment strategies have been used (Kaptein, Scharloo & Weinman, 2001), one of the more popular tools has been the 'Illness Perceptions Questionnaire' (IPQ; Weinman et al., 1996). The IPQ consists of subscales that tap into each of the five components of illness representations: identity, cause, consequences, time-line and control/cure. This measure can be adapted to assess representations of a wide variety of chronic and acute illnesses.

More recently, the designers have introduced a revised version of the IPQ: the IPQ-R (Moss-Morris et al., 2002). The IPQ-R has improved versions of the original IPQ subscales, a number of which have higher levels of internal consistency relative to the original subscales. An important change is the way in which the identity component is measured. The IPQ identity subscale asked patients to rate the extent to which they experienced a number of symptoms as part of their illness. This meant that the identity subscale was potentially confounded with measures of somatization or distress, as distress is positively associated with symptom severity ratings (Watson & Pennebaker, 1989). In order to address this problem, the IPQ-R identity subscale asks patients whether they associate each of the symptoms with their illness on a yes/no scale. In other words, it measures the symptoms patients label as illness-related and not the extent to which they experience the symptoms.

The IPQ-R also includes new subscales. The control/cure subscale has been replaced with two subscales assessing personal control and treatment control. The IPQ-R also includes new subscales assessing cyclical timeline beliefs, illness coherence (the extent to which the representation 'makes sense' to the individual), and emotional representations (anxiety, depression, and other affective responses associated with the illness). The addition of this last subscale allows the IPQ-R to measure both cognitive and emotional representations.

RISK PERCEPTIONS

Perceptions of illness risk are regarded as essential catalysts of health-protective action by many theoretical models of health behaviour, including the health belief model and protection motivation theory (see Chapter 3, this volume). Risk perceptions are positively associated with a wide variety of health behaviours, including regular medical check-ups, use of immunizations, and use of cancer screening techniques such as mammograms and Pap tests (Floyd, Prentice-Dunn & Rogers, 2000). Risk perceptions are often discrepant with actual risk estimates (Wilcox & Stefanick, 1999), however, and these inaccuracies may lead to inappropriate use of health-care procedures and protective behaviours.

What factors influence the development of risk perceptions?

Beliefs about illness risk are, to an extent, reasoned estimates based on perceptions of personal risk factors (Glik et al., 1999). For example, people who smoke generally believe that they are at greater risk of lung cancer than do non-smokers (Weinstein, 1998), and adolescents report increases in their perceived risk of lung cancer after they begin smoking (Gerrard et al., 1996). Risk perceptions do not reflect purely rational deductions, however. A number of social and psychological factors influence risk perceptions in ways that often lead to biased beliefs. For example, the mere act of engaging in a risky behaviour may actually lower perceptions of its riskiness. Individuals who have driven while drunk report lower perceptions of risk for car accidents when driving drunk than do those who have never driven while drunk (Halpern-Felsher et al., 2001). On the other hand, mere exposure to cases of illnesses – even through watching television – is associated with inflated risk perceptions (Wober, 1987).

Perceptions of risk for contracting HIV and other sexually transmitted diseases (STDs) through unprotected sex are susceptible to a variety of biases. These risk perceptions tend to be lower when under the influence of alcohol, when the partner is attractive, and when the partner 'looks like' he or she is the type of person who is unlikely to have had sex with infected people or used intravenous drugs (Blanton & Gerrard, 1997; Gordon, Carey & Carey, 1997). In a study illustrating how sexual attractiveness can influence these risk perceptions (Blanton & Gerrard, 1997), male undergraduates received profiles of various women describing key aspects of their sexual history and background. The men then estimated their risk of contracting HIV and other STDs if they were to have unprotected sex with these women. Later, the men were asked to repeat the exercise – but this time, they also were given pictures of the women that were either high or low in sex appeal. Men viewing the pictures of sexually attractive women significantly lowered their risk perceptions, although they only did so if they were also given additional information about the women's personalities – which was irrelevant to HIV and STD risk – so that they could justify their change in beliefs. Men who were given pictures with low sex appeal did not change their risk perceptions.

People generally exhibit unrealistic optimism in their risk perceptions. That is, they have a biased tendency to perceive their own risk for illnesses as lower than the risk levels of others (Eiser, Eiser & Pauwels, 1993). For example, university students believe that they have a lower risk for diseases – especially serious, life-threatening ones – compared to others like them (Lek & Bishop, 1995). This phenomenon has long been suspected to reflect a developmental tendency for young people to harbour an 'illusion of invulnerability' to disease. However, a study comparing risk perceptions of adolescents with those of their parents found that it was the parents who had the higher levels of unrealistic optimism (Cohn et al., 1995). Although the observed differences in risk perception reflect unrealistic optimism among those who engage in risky behaviours, there is also evidence of unrealistic pessimism among those who do not engage in risky behaviour. Individuals with little experience of risky behaviour (such as unprotected sex or driving while drunk) tend to overestimate the risk of associated disorders (Halpern-Felsher et al., 2001).

Unrealistic optimism appears to reflect a defensive bias aimed at protecting one's self-concept and minimizing perceptions of potential threats to well-being (Taylor & Brown, 1988). This bias appears to affect risk perceptions by influencing the accessibility of risk factor information about oneself and others. When making risk assessments of themselves and others, people tend to pay more attention to the risk-increasing factors in others (such as hereditary risk and risky behaviours) than to their own risk-increasing factors. Conversely, they give more emphasis to their own risk-reducing factors (such as exercise and healthy weight status) than to those of others (Weinstein & Klein, 1995).

How do risk beliefs influence illness representations and experiences?

Heightened perceptions of disease risk induce a variety of defensive biases in illness cognition. Upon learning that they are at significant risk for an illness, individuals tend to alter other illness beliefs in ways that minimize the potential threat or severity of the illness.

Evidence regarding how risk information induces defensive biases has been provided through the use of an experimental paradigm in which individuals are given false information about their risk for a fictitious digestive disorder. Participants are told about 'Thioamine Acetylase (TAA) enzyme deficiency', which is described as a genetic enzyme deficiency that is a risk factor for a pancreatic disorder. Participants are then 'tested' for TAA enzyme deficiency, and they receive information that they either do or do not have the disorder. Researchers have found that participants who are told that they have the TAA deficiency (relative to those who are told that their results are 'normal') appraise the pancreatic disorder as being less serious (Jemmott et al., 1986). Moreover, they tend to derogate the validity and the accuracy of the test, expressing less confidence that the results are correct (Ditto & Lopez, 1992). These defensive biases have been observed in responses to accurate risk factor information as well. For example, community residents who received (accurate) high cholesterol readings rated high cholesterol as a less serious condition than did residents who had normal cholesterol levels. This *minimization effect* was not simply a short-term effect, as this group difference endured for up to three months following the cholesterol test (Croyle, Sun & Louie, 1993). These defensive biases may not necessarily inhibit or curtail protective action; rather, they may help to control emotional distress and thus enable the individual to engage in protective action without the emotional disruption.

Risk perceptions can influence other aspects of health-related experiences as well. Individuals with high risk perceptions are susceptible to excessive worry and rumination about their disease risk, even to the point where it significantly intrudes on their general well-being and daily activities (Lerman et al., 1993). Risk perceptions can also influence reactions to health campaigns or messages aimed at motivating individuals to engage in protective action. High-threat messages that stress the serious consequences of an illness tend to motivate health behaviours for individuals with perceptions of low disease risk, but not for individuals with high risk perceptions. For people with high risk perceptions, reassuring messages that stress how the protective action will help to maintain wellness and stay healthy are most effective in motivating protective behaviour (Cameron & Leventhal, 1995; Gintner et al., 1987).

CONCRETE-EMOTIONAL ASPECTS OF ILLNESS COGNITIONS

Illness representations include not only conceptual, abstract information; they also incorporate vivid images and memories of experiences. These concrete-emotional cognitions can have particularly powerful effects on reactions. Someone who has vivid memories of a friend struggling with AIDS may have the same conceptual beliefs about AIDS identity, consequences, cause, duration and control/cure as another person, but these vivid memories may trigger more powerful emotional reactions and stronger motivations to take protective action.

Emotions themselves play an important role in illness cognition. As we have seen, illness perceptions and beliefs can evoke powerful emotional experiences, and these experiences can significantly influence coping responses and adjustment to illness. But cognitions and emotions are highly interactive: just as illness cognitions can activate emotions such as worry and distress, emotions can influence illness cognitions.

For example, negative mood states can influence the perception and interpretation of physical symptoms. In studies in which people's moods have been experimentally manipulated through the use of mood induction techniques, people who are made to feel sad report more physical symptoms and greater discomfort from them than do those who are made to feel happy (Salovey & Birnbaum, 1989). Mood can also influence risk perceptions. Happy moods have been found to lower levels of perceived risk for health problems, whereas sad moods increase these risk perceptions (Johnson & Tversky, 1983; Salovey & Birnbaum, 1989).

Why do mood states influence these illness cognitions? There may be a number of reasons. First, people rely on their moods as indicators of how well they are doing. If they feel happy, they may perceive this mood as a sign that things are going well and there is little danger or need for worry. Positive mood states may also enhance confidence that one is able to protect oneself from potential dangers. Moreover, negative mood enhances self-focus, turning attention inward and away from the external environment (Salovey, 1992). This inward self-focus may increase awareness of bodily symptoms and stimulate worries about their implications for health and illness (Pennebaker, 1982). Finally, mood-congruent memory effects may be at work, such that negative moods may increase the accessibility of worrying, health-related thoughts, and memories (Forgas, 2000).

Worry about a disease is an emotional factor that significantly influences illness cognition and behaviour (Cameron, 1997). Worry can promote rumination about the illness and motivate one to search for relevant information, and so it can foster the development of more extensive and elaborate illness representations. Moreover, worry can heighten the accessibility of these cognitive representations in memory; one consequence of this heightened accessibility is that one may be more likely to remember to engage in protective behaviours, such as taking medications or scheduling medical appointments.

Worry has been found to be associated with a greater propensity to seek medical care and to use screening procedures such as mammograms and Pap tests (Cameron, 1997). It appears, however, that very high levels of worry can sometimes be a barrier to undergoing screening procedures (Lerman et al., 1993). For individuals with very high worry, the potential for finding evidence of disease may be too anxiety-arousing and so they may delay and avoid the use of these screening tests.

CULTURAL INFLUENCES

So far we have focused primarily on research concerning mental representations of illness held by individuals in Western societies in Europe, the United States, Canada, New Zealand and Australia. These societies make up a small minority of the world's peoples, however, and research exploring illness beliefs in cultures around the globe reveals a diverse array of beliefs about health and illness. This is not surprising when you consider that illnesses are, to a large extent, culturally defined experiences. Although most diseases involve biological processes that are universal and thus give rise to similar biological disruptions, cultural differences in the perception of symptoms and the illness beliefs that develop about them can lead to dramatic differences in illness experiences.

Illness beliefs are highly linked in with the culture's philosophical and spiritual views regarding one's role in the world and universe. If a culture believes that supernatural forces govern the fates of individuals on the basis of their moral behaviour, then illness representations will tend to implicate moral transgressions as the cause of illness and atonement or good deeds as the appropriate means to cure it. Cultures adopting the Western biomedical model of illness, which emphasizes the causal role of viruses, bacteria and mechanistic malfunctions of the body in illness development, tend to rely on medicines and surgical procedures to treat illnesses. Consequently, they may give less emphasis to changing lifestyle habits as a means of controlling disease (Leventhal, Leventhal & Cameron, 2001).

Cultural researchers have noted fundamental differences in the patterns of illness beliefs held by sociocentric cultures and egocentric cultures (Landrine & Klonoff, 2001). Sociocentric cultures (which include many Asian, Native American, Latino and Central American cultures) hold holistic worldviews in which there is little or no distinction between self and others, mind and body, humans and the environment, and science and spirituality. The person is seen as existing in relation to others, the environment, and spiritual forces. In contrast, egocentric cultures (such as European and American cultures) construe a separateness, or dualism, between these concepts, and they place an emphasis on the individual. These distinctive worldviews directly shape the nature of beliefs about health and illness. Sociocentric cultures share the view that health is determined by maintaining balance or harmony among the physical, psychological, social and spiritual factors and that disease results from imbalances among these factors. Conversely, egocentric cultures place a primary emphasis on the physiological processes of illness, and see these processes as easily distinguishable from emotional, social and environmental events (Fabrega, 1974; Landrine & Klonoff, 2001).

The indigenous Maori in New Zealand are an example of a sociocentric culture in which illness beliefs connect with broader, holistic worldviews. The traditional Maori approach identifies four interrelated dimensions of health: Te Taha Wairua, or spiritual being; Te Taha Hinengaro, or mental being; Te Taha Tinana, or physical being; and Te Taha Whanau, or family well-being. Illness is believed to be caused by an imbalance of these four components, and treatment therefore requires taking measures to achieve balance (Durie, 1994). Moreover, *tapu* (supernatural influence or sacred restriction) is a pervasive aspect of Maori life, and violating the lore of *tapu* can lead to harm from evil spirits, angry Gods, and *makutu* (witchcraft). A breach of *tapu* laws (either by oneself or family members) is seen as a predominant cause of disease. Treatment methods may be regarded as unacceptable if they break *tapu* rules; for example, if they involve mixing *tapu* materials, such as body parts, with *noa* materials (things not under supernatural influence), such as bowls or other items used for cooking. Beliefs regarding Te Taha Whanau and the interconnectedness among family members are reflected in the common practice of numerous family members accompanying the sick individual to medical consultations and being involved in treatment decisions.

Cultural worldviews provide the framework within which representations of illness identity, cause, time-line, consequences and control/cure develop. The causal component is particularly variable across cultures. Causal beliefs can be grouped into three general categories: natural causes (such as infection, accidents or deterioration), supernatural causes (such as sorcery, bewitchment or mystical retribution for transgressions or violations of taboos), and emotional causes (such as stress, fear or worry). Studies of traditional world cultures reveal that, overall, supernatural causes have far outweighed natural causes of illness (Murdock, 1980).

Stress and emotions are believed to be primary causes of illness in most sociocentric cultures. In traditional Mexican culture, for example, carrying an excessive load of emotions causes illness, and the emotions of anger and worry are particularly unhealthy because they tend to persist for long periods of time. It is believed that emotions – even positive ones such as joy – should be discharged quickly, through prompt expression and taking quick action to resolve them. Similar beliefs that strong emotions cause illness are held by Chinese and other Asian cultures, where emotional equanimity is the desired (healthy) state – in fact, it is unhealthy to display strong emotions, as these displays can disrupt social harmony and thus cause illness (Spector, 1996).

'Mal de ojo' or 'evil eye', an illness common in many Latino, Asian and African cultures, highlights the perceived riskiness of strong emotions. This illness occurs when a person stares enviously or admiringly at another, causing a sudden onset of headache, anxiety, crying, rashes and other symptoms; advanced stages involve uncontrollable coughing, vomiting and death. 'Susto' ('fright' or 'soul loss') is another emotion-induced illness that is common in Mexican, Central American and South American cultures (Landrine & Klonoff, 2001). A frightening or traumatic experience is believed to cause the soul to become dislodged from the body, resulting in a state of anxiety, lethargy, loss of appetite, and even wasting away to death.

Today, there are many traditional cultures in which Western medicine has been integrated into society, and this integration has led to the development of *medical pluralism* in illness beliefs in which traditional illness beliefs are combined with, rather than replaced by, the Western biomedical beliefs. The New Zealand Maori, for example, distinguish between Maori illnesses, which are well-defined in their traditional culture, and 'Pakeha' illnesses, which have been introduced along with Western medicine by those of European descent. Identifying an illness as a Maori or Pakeha illness provides a cultural validity for the illness experience, and it connects strongly with beliefs about treatment control and cure (White, Mavoa & Bassett, 1999). If the illness is identified as a Pakeha disease, then the individual can seek Western treatment – which often is seen as a relatively simple 'quick fix' for alleviating symptoms. Medical pluralism in treatment beliefs is also evident in the health-care systems of other cultures. For example, Chinese hospitals can have Western medical pharmacies and traditional Chinese herb dispensers side by side, with patients making use of both (Moyers, 1993). Pluralistic beliefs about illness causes often integrate biomedical and traditional views by regarding the biomedical causes (e.g. a virus) as *how* the body became ill, and the traditional causes (e.g. spirit possession or a hex) as *why* the illness occurred (Spector, 1996).

SUMMARY AND CONCLUSIONS

The self-regulation model of illness cognition and behaviour developed by Leventhal identifies five key components of illness representations: identity (illness label and symptoms), cause, time-line, consequences and control/cure. These illness beliefs guide the selection and use of procedures for coping with the illness-related experience, and they critically determine emotional reactions to the experiences. Illness identity beliefs include a diagnostic label for the disorder and prototypical symptoms. The process of determining the appropriate label for the condition causing a set of symptoms is influenced by many factors, including the ambiguousness of the symptoms and the presence of stressors that make plausible an attribution of the symptoms to stress. Individuals who receive illness diagnoses search for associated symptom experiences, and they may inaccurately identify bodily sensations as illness symptoms. Identity beliefs influence decisions to seek medical care for symptoms, and inaccurate labelling of symptoms can lead to inappropriate use of medical services, such as delaying to seek care for symptoms associated with life-threatening conditions. Causal beliefs vary in terms of their locus (internal or external), stability and controllability. Attributions of illness to internal, stable and controllable causes often are associated with more active, problem-focused coping and better psychological adjustment. Time-line beliefs tend to reflect an acute model, a cyclical model, or a chronic model of the illness. For most individuals, the majority of illness experiences are with acute illnesses such as colds, measles or the flu. These experiences may make it difficult for individuals newly diagnosed with a chronic condition to adjust to a chronic model of illness. Chronic patients who have an acute model of their illness may exhibit difficulties in adhering to on-going treatment regimens. Beliefs about consequences of an illness are influenced by factors such as perceptions of disease prevalence and number of symptoms. These consequence beliefs can be important predictors of behavioural responses, such as functional activities and use of medical services, and psychological adjustment, such as worry and anxiety. Associations between perceptions of serious consequences and poor illness-related outcomes remain even after accounting for clinical indicators of illness severity. Beliefs about the controllability and curability of an illness are also related to coping behaviour and psychological adjustment, with high controllability beliefs associated with more active coping, lower distress, and better health outcomes.

Perceptions of illness risk are another important type of illness cognition, and they are positively associated with use of health-protective behaviours. Risk perceptions can be biased by a number of social and psychological factors, including defensive biases that motivate the development of unrealistic optimism in one's perceptions of illness risk. Perceptions of heightened disease risk can lead, in turn, to defensive biases in perceptions of illness consequences and other representational components. Concrete-emotional aspects of illness representations, such as vivid mental images and strong reactions of anxiety, can enhance motivations to take protective action. Emotional experiences may influence illness cognitions by serving as information about how well one is doing, altering attention to bodily symptoms, and influencing the accessibility of relevant thoughts and memories.

Illness beliefs are profoundly shaped by the surrounding culture. There are fundamental differences in the general illness beliefs held by members of sociocentric cultures and egocentric cultures. Sociocentric cultures, which make little distinction between the person, surrounding social group, environment and spiritual forces, view illness as an imbalance among these elements. Egocentric cultures, which place an emphasis on the individual, generally view illness in terms of physiological processes. These cultural frameworks lead to distinctive beliefs about illness identity, cause, consequences, time-lines and control/cure. The introduction of Western medicine into traditional cultures has led to the development of medical pluralism in illness beliefs, in which biomedical and traditional beliefs become integrated.

DISCUSSION POINTS

1. According to the self-regulation model, how do illness representations influence health and illness behaviours?
2. How may the process of receiving a diagnostic label influence a patient's symptom reports?
3. What role do patients' beliefs about the causes of their illness play in their psychological adjustment to their condition?
4. How might childhood experiences with illness influence people's time-line and consequences beliefs of chronic illnesses such as heart disease and diabetes?
5. How do beliefs about controllability of illness as defined by Leventhal's self-regulation model overlap with Bandura's concepts of self-efficacy and outcome efficiency?
6. What role does unrealistic optimism play in people's perceptions of heath risks?
7. How might people's emotional reactions to their illness influence their cognitive illness representations?
8. According to cultural researchers, how do the patterns of illness beliefs differ in sociocentric and egocentric cultures?

FURTHER READING

Cameron, L. D. and Leventhal, H., eds. (2003). *The Self-Regulation of Health and Illness Behaviour.* London and New York: Routledge.

Landrine, H. and Klonoff, E. A. (2001). Cultural diversity and health psychology. In A. Baum, T. Revenson and J. Singer, eds., *Handbook of Health Psychology*. Mahwah, NJ: Lawrence Erlbaum, 851–92.

Leventhal, H., Leventhal, E. A. and Cameron, L. (2001). Representations, procedures, and affect in illness self-regulation: a perceptual-cognitive model. In A. Baum, T. Revenson and J. Singer, eds., *Handbook of Health Psychology*. Mahwah, NJ: Lawrence Erlbaum, 19–47.

Moss-Morris, R., Weinman, J., Petrie, K. J., Horne, R., Cameron, L. D. and Buick, D. (2002). The Revised Illness Perception Questionnaire (IPQ-R). *Psychology and Health* 17, 1–16.

Petrie, K. J. and Weinman, J. A., eds. (1997). *Perceptions of Health and Illness*. Reading, UK: Harwood Academic.

Roesch, S. C. and Weiner, B. (2001). A meta-analytic review of coping with illness: do causal attributions matter? *Journal of Psychosomatic Research* 50, 205–19.

Scharloo, M., Kaptein, A. A., Weinman, J., Hazes, J. M., Willems, L. N. A., Bergman, W. and Rooijmans, H. G. M. (1998). Illness perceptions, coping and functioning in patients with rheumatoid arthritis, chronic obstructive pulmonary disease and psoriasis. *Journal of Psychosomatic Research* 44, 573–85.

Weinstein, N. E. and Klein, W. M. (1996). Unrealistic optimism: present and future. *Journal of Social & Clinical Psychology* 15, 1–8.

KEY STUDIES

Blanton, H. and Gerrard, M. (1997). Effect of sexual motivation on men's risk perception for sexually transmitted disease: there must be 50 ways to justify a lover. *Health Psychology* 16, 374–9.

Petrie, K. J., Cameron, L. D., Ellis, C., Buick, D. and Weinman, J. (2002). Changing illness perceptions following myocardial infarction: an early intervention randomized controlled trial. *Psychosomatic Medicine* 64, 580–6.

REFERENCES

Affleck, G., Tennen, H., Croog, S. and Levine, S. (1987). Causal attribution, benefits, and morbidity after a heart attack: an 8-year study. *Journal of Consulting & Clinical Psychology* 5, 339–55.

Bandura, A. (1977). Self-efficacy: towards a unifying theory of behavior change. *Psychological Review* 84, 191–215.

Baumann, L. J., Cameron, L. D., Zimmerman, R. S. and Leventhal, H. (1989). Illness representations and matching labels with symptoms. *Health Psychology* 8, 449–69.

Baumann, L. J. and Leventhal, H. (1985). I can tell when my blood pressure is up, can't I? *Health Psychology* 4, 203–18.

Bishop, G. D. and Converse, S. A. (1986). Illness representations: a prototype approach. *Health Psychology* 5, 95–114.

Blanton, H. and Gerrard, M. (1997). Effect of sexual motivation on men's risk perception for sexually transmitted disease: there must be 50 ways to justify a lover. *Health Psychology* 16, 374–9.

Cameron, L. D. (1997). Screening for cancer: illness worry and illness perceptions. In K. J. Petrie and J. Weinman, eds., *Perceptions of Health and Illness*. Reading, UK: Harwood Academic, 291–322.

Cameron, L. and Leventhal, H. (1995). Vulnerability beliefs, symptom experiences, and the processing of health threat information. *Journal of Applied Social Psychology* 25, 1859–83.

Cameron, L. D. and Leventhal, H., eds. (2003). *The Self-Regulation of Health and Illness Behaviour.* London and New York: Routledge.

Cameron, L. D., Leventhal, E. A. and Leventhal, H. (1993). Symptom representations and affect as determinants of care seeking in a community-dwelling, adult sample population. *Health Psychology* 12, 171–9.

Cameron, L. D., Leventhal, H. and Leventhal, E. A. (1995). Symptom ambiguity, life stress, and decisions to seek medical care. *Psychosomatic Medicine* 57, 37–47.

Cohn, L. D., Macfarlane, S., Yanez, C. and Imai, W. K. (1995). Risk-perception: differences between adolescents and adults. *Health Psychology* 14, 217–22.

Cooper, A., Lloyd, G., Weinman, J. and Jackson, G. (1999). Why patients do not attend cardiac rehabilitation: role of intentions and illness beliefs. *Heart* 82, 234–6.

Croyle, R. T., Sun, Y. C. and Louie, D. H. (1993). Psychological minimization of cholesterol test results: moderators of appraisal in college students and community residents. *Health Psychology* 12, 503–7.

Ditto, P. H., Jemmott, J. B. and Darley, J. M. (1988). Appraising the threat of illness: a mental representational approach. *Health Psychology* 7, 183–201.

Ditto, P. H. and Lopez, D. F. (1992). Motivated skepticism: the use of differential decision criteria for preferred and nonpreferred conclusions. *Journal of Personality & Social Psychology* 63, 568–84.

Dracup, K., Moser, D. K., Eisenberg, M., Meischke, H., Alonzo, A. A. and Braslow, A. (1995). Causes of delay in seeking treatment for heart attack symptoms. *Social Science & Medicine* 40, 379–92.

Durie, M. H. (1994). Maori perspectives of health and illness. In J. Spicer, A. Trlin and J. A. Walton, eds., *Social Dimensions of Health and Disease: New Zealand Perspectives.* Palmerston North, NZ: Dunmore Press, 194–203.

Eiser, J., Eiser, C. and Pauwels, P. (1993). Skin cancer: assessing perceived risk and behavioural attitudes. *Psychology & Health* 8, 393–404.

Fabrega, H. (1974). *Disease and Social Behavior.* Cambridge, MA: MIT Press.

Fink, P. (1992). Physical complaints and symptoms of somatizing patients. *Journal of Psychosomatic Research* 36, 125–36.

Floyd, D. L., Prentice-Dunn, S. and Rogers, R. W. (2000). A meta-analysis of research on protection motivation theory. *Journal of Applied Social Psychology* 30, 407–29.

Forgas, J. P. (2000). Affect and information processing strategies: an interactive relationship. In J. P. Forgas, ed., *Feeling and Thinking: The Role of Affect in Social Cognition.* Cambridge, U.K.: Cambridge University Press, 253–80.

Fortune, D. G., Richards, H. L., Main, C. J. and Griffiths, C. E. M. (2000). Pathological worrying, illness perceptions and disease severity in patients with psoriasis. *British Journal of Health Psychology* 5, 71–82.

French, D. P., Senior, V., Weinman, J. and Marteau, T. (2001). Causal attributions for heart disease: a systematic review. *Psychology & Health* 16, 77–98.

Gerrard, M., Gibbons, F. X., Benthin, A. C. and Hessling, R. M. (1996). A longitudinal study of the reciprocal nature of risk behaviors and cognitions in adolescents: what you do shapes what you think, and vice-versa. *Health Psychology* 15, 344–54.

Gintner, G., Rectanus, E., Achord, K. and Parker, B. (1987). Parental history of hypertension and screening attendance: effects of wellness appeal versus threat appeal. *Health Psychology* 6, 432–44.

Glik, D. C., Kronenfeld, J. J., Jackson, K. and Zhang, W. (1999). Comparison of traffic accident and chronic disease risk perceptions. *American Journal of Health Behavior* 23, 198–209.

Gonder-Frederick, L. A. and Cox, D. J. (1991). Symptom perception, symptom beliefs, and blood glucose discrimination in the self-treatment of insulin-dependent diabetes. In J. A. Skelton and R. T. Croyle, eds., *Mental Representations in Health and Illness.* New York: Springer-Verlag, 220–46.

Gonder-Frederick, L. A., Cox, D. J., Bobbitt, S. A. and Pennebaker, J. (1986). Blood glucose symptom beliefs in type I diabetic adults. *Health Psychology* 3, 327–41.

Gordon, C. M., Carey, M. P. and Carey, K. B. (1997). Effects of a drinking event on behavioral skills and condom attitudes in men: implications for HIV risk from a controlled experiment. *Health Psychology* 16, 490–5.

Halpern-Felsher, B. L., Millstein, S. G., Ellen, J. M., Adler, N. E., Tschann, J. M. and Biehl, M. (2001). The role of behavioral experience in judging risks. *Health Psychology* 20, 120–6.

Hampson, S. E. (1997). Illness representations and the self-management of diabetes. In K. J. Petrie and J. A. Weinman, eds., *Perceptions of Health and Illness.* Reading, UK: Harwood Academic, 323–47.

Heijmans, M. J. W. M. (1999). The role of patients' illness representations in coping and functioning with Addison's disease. *British Journal of Health Psychology* 4, 137–49.

Helgeson, V. S. (1992). Moderators of the relation between perceived control and adjustment to chronic illness. *Journal of Personality & Social Psychology* 63, 656–66.

Horne, R. and Weinman, J. (2002). Self-regulation and self-management in asthma: exploring the role of illness perceptions and treatment beliefs in explaining non-adherence to preventer medication. *Psychology & Health* 17, 17–32.

Jemmott, J. B., Croyle, R. T. and Ditto, P. H. (1988). Common sense epidemiology: self-based judgements from laypersons and physicians. *Health Psychology* 4, 54–73.

Jemmott, J. B. III, Ditto, P. H. and Croyle, R. T. (1986). Judging health status: effects of perceived prevalence and personal relevance. *Journal of Personality & Social Psychology* 50, 899–905.

Johnson, E. J. and Tversky, A. (1983). Affect, generalization, and the perception of risk. *Journal of Personality & Social Psychology* 45, 20–33.

Jopson, N. and Moss-Morris, R. (2003). The role of illness severity and illness representations in adjusting to multiple sclerosis. *Journal of Psychosomatic Research* 54(6), 503–11.

Kaptein, A. A., Scharloo, M. and Weinman, J. A. (2001). Assessment of illness perceptions. In A. Vingerhoets, ed., *Assessment in Behavioral Medicine.* Hove, UK: Brunner Routledge, 179–94.

Kavanagh, D. J., Gooley, S. and Wilson, P. H. (1993). Prediction of adherence and control in diabetes. *Journal of Behavioral Medicine* 16, 509–22.

Klonoff, E. A. and Landrine, H. (1994). Culture and gender diversity in commonsense beliefs about the causes of six illnesses. *Journal of Behavioral Medicine* 17, 407–18.

Landrine, H. and Klonoff, E. A. (2001). Cultural diversity and health psychology. In A. Baum, T. A. Revenson and J. E. Singer, eds., *Handbook of Health Psychology.* Mahwah, NJ: Lawrence Erlbaum, 851–92.

Lau, R. R. and Hartman, K. A. (1983). Common sense representations of common illnesses. *Health Psychology* 2, 167–85.

Lek, Y. and Bishop, G. (1995). Perceived vulnerability to illness threats: the role of disease type, risk factor perception and attribution. *Psychology & Health* 10, 205–19.

Lerman, C., Daly, M., Sands, C., Balshem, A., Lustbader, E., Heggan, T., Goldstein, L., James, J. and Engstrom, P. (1993). Mammography adherence and psychological distress among women at risk for breast cancer. *Journal of the National Cancer Institute* 85, 1074–80.

Leventhal, H., Brissette, I. and Leventhal, E. A. (2003). The common-sense model of self-regulation of health and illness. In L. D. Cameron and H. Leventhal, eds., *The Self-Regulation of Health and Illness Behaviour.* London and New York: Routledge, 42–65.

Leventhal, H., Leventhal, E. A. and Cameron, L. (2001). Representations, procedures, and affect in illness self-regulation: a perceptual-cognitive model. In A. Baum, T. A. Revenson and J. E. Singer, eds., *Handbook of Health Psychology.* Mahwah, NJ: Erlbaum, 19–47.

Leventhal, H., Nerenz, D. R. and Steele, D. J. (1984). Illness representations and coping with health threats. In A. Baum, S. E. Taylor and J. E. Singer, eds., *Handbook of Psychology and Health*, vol. 4. Hillsdale, NJ: Lawrence Erlbaum Associates, 219–52.

Main, J, Moss-Morris, R. Booth, R., Kaptein, A. and Kolbe, K. (2003). The use of reliever medication in asthma: The role of negative mood and asthma symptoms. *Journal of Asthma* 40(4), 357–65.

Marks, R. (2001). Efficacy theory and its utility in arthritis rehabilitation: review and recommendations. *Disability & Rehabilitation* 23, 271–80.

Meyer, D., Leventhal, H. and Gutmann, M. (1985). Common-sense models of illness: the example of hypertension. *Health Psychology* 4, 115–35.

Michela, J. L. and Wood, J. V. (1986). Causal attribution in health and illness. In P. C. Kendall, ed., *Advances in Cognitive-behavioral Research and Therapy.* New York: Academic Press, 179–235.

Moss-Morris, R. and Petrie, K. J. (2001). Discriminating between chronic fatigue syndrome and depression: a cognitive analysis. *Psychological Medicine* 31, 469–79.

Moss-Morris, R., Petrie, K. J. and Weinman, J. (1996). Functioning in chronic fatigue syndrome: do illness perceptions play a regulatory role? *British Journal of Health Psychology* 1, 15–25.

Moss-Morris, R., Weinman, J., Petrie, K. J., Horne, R., Cameron, L. D. and Buick, D. (2002). The Revised Illness Perception Questionnaire (IPQ-R). *Psychology & Health* 17, 1–16.

Moyers, B. (1993). *Healing and the Mind.* New York: Doubleday.

Murdock, G. P. (1980). *Theories of Illness: A World Survey.* Pittsburgh, PA: University of Pittsburgh Press.

Nerenz, D. R., Leventhal, H. and Love, R. (1982). Factors contributing to emotional distress during cancer chemotherapy. *Cancer* 50, 1020–7.

Newby, L. K., Rutsch, W. R., Califf, R. M., Simoons, M. L., Aylward, P. E., Armstrong, P. W., Woodlief, L. H., Lee, K. L., Topol, E. J., Van de Werf, F., for the Gusto-I Investigators (1996). Time from symptom onset to treatment and outcomes after thrombolytic therapy. *Journal of the American College of Cardiology* 27, 1646–55.

Orbell, S., Johnston, M., Rowley, D., Espley, A. and Davey, P. (1998). Cognitive representations of illness and functional and affective adjustment following surgery for osteoarthritis. *Social Science & Medicine* 47, 93–102.

O'Rourke, A. and Hampson, S. (1999). Psychosocial outcomes after an MI: an evaluation of two approaches to rehabilitation. *Psychology, Health & Medicine* 4, 393–402.

Pennebaker, J. W. (1982). *The Psychology of Physical Symptoms.* New York: Springer.

Perry, K., Petrie, K. J., Ellis, C. J., Horne, R. and Moss-Morris, R. (2001). Symptom expectations and delay in acute myocardial infarction patients. *Heart* 86, 91–3.

Petrie, K. J., Cameron, L. D., Ellis, C., Buick, D. and Weinman, J. (2002). Changing illness perceptions following myocardial infarction: an early intervention randomized controlled trial. *Psychosomatic Medicine* 64, 580–6.

Petrie, K. J., Weinman, J., Sharpe, N. and Buckley, J. (1996). Role of patients' view of their illness in predicting return to work and functioning after myocardial infarction: longitudinal study. *British Medical Journal* 312, 1191–4.

Robbins, J. M. and Kirmayer, L. J. (1990). Illness worry and disability in fibromyalgia syndrome. *International Journal of Psychiatry in Medicine* 20(1), 49–63.

Roesch, S. C. and Weiner, B. (2001). A meta-analytic review of coping with illness: do causal attributions matter? *Journal of Psychosomatic Research* 50, 205–19.

Salovey, P. (1992). Mood induced self-focused attention. *Journal of Personality & Social Psychology* 62, 699–707.

Salovey, P. and Birnbaum, D. (1989). Influence of mood on health-relevant cognitions. *Journal of Personality & Social Psychology* 57, 539–51.

Scharloo, M. and Kaptein, A. A. (1997). Measurement of illness perceptions in patients with chronic somatic illness: a review. In K. J. Petrie and J. A. Weinman, eds., *Perceptions of Health and Illness*. Reading, UK: Harwood Academic, 103–54.

Scharloo, M., Kaptein, A. A., Weinman, J., Bergman, W., Vermeer, B. J. and Rooijmans, H. G. M. (2000). Patients' illness perceptions and coping as predictors of functional status in psoriasis: a 1-year follow up. *British Journal of Dermatology* 142, 899–907.

Scharloo, M., Kaptein, A. A., Weinman, J., Hazes, J. M., Breedveld, F. C. and Rooijmans, H. G. M. (1999). Predicting functional status in patients with rheumatoid arthritis. *Journal of Rheumatology* 26, 1686–93.

Scharloo, M., Kaptein, A. A., Weinman, J., Hazes, J. M., Willems, L. N. A., Bergman, W. and Rooijmans, H. G. M. (1998). Illness perceptions, coping and functioning in patients with rheumatoid arthritis, chronic obstructive pulmonary disease and psoriasis. *Journal of Psychosomatic Research* 44, 573–85.

Sissons Joshi, M. (1995). Lay explanations of the causes of diabetes in India and the UK. In I. Markova and R. M. Farr, eds., *Representations of Health, Illness, and Handicap*. Reading, UK: Harwood Academic, 163–88.

Spector, R. E. (1996). *Cultural Diversity in Health and Illness*, 2nd edn. New York: Appleton Century Crofts.

Taylor, S. E. and Brown, J. D. (1988). Illusion and well-being: a social psychological perspective on mental health. *Psychological Bulletin* 103, 193–210.

Taylor, S. E., Lichtman, R. R. and Wood, J. V. (1984). Attributions, beliefs about control, and adjustment to breast cancer. *Journal of Personality & Social Psychology* 46, 489–502.

Tennen, H., Affleck, G. and Gershman, K. (1986). Self-blame among parents of infants with perinatal complications: the role of self-protective motives. *Journal of Personality & Social Psychology* 50, 690–6.

Tennen, H., Affleck, G., Urrows, S., Higgins, P. and Mendola, R. (1992). Perceiving control, construing benefits, and daily processes in rheumatoid arthritis. *Canadian Journal of Behavioural Science* 24, 186–203.

Turnquist, D. C., Harvey, J. H. and Anderson, B. L. (1988). Attributions and adjustment to life-threatening illness. *British Journal of Clinical Psychology* 27, 55–65.

Watson, D. and Pennebaker, J. W. (1989). Health complaints, stress, and distress: exploring the central role of negative affectivity. *Psychological Review* 96, 234–64.

Weiner, B. (1986). *An Attributional Theory of Motivation and Emotion*. New York: Springer.

Weinman, J., Petrie, K. J., Moss-Morris, R. and Horne, R. (1996). The Illness Perception Questionnaire: a new method for assessing the cognitive representation of illness. *Psychology & Health* 11, 431–45.

Weinstein, N. D. (1998). Accuracy of smokers' risk perceptions. *Annals of Behavioral Medicine* 20, 135–40.

Weinstein, N. D. and Klein, W. M. (1995). Resistance of personal risk perceptions to debiasing interventions. *Health Psychology* 14, 132–40.

White, N., Mavoa, H. and Bassett, S. F. (1999). Perceptions of health, illness and physiotherapy of Maori identifying with Ngati Tama iwi. *New Zealand Journal of Physiotherapy* 27, 5–15.

Wilcox, S. and Stefanick, M. L. (1999). Knowledge and perceived risk of major diseases in middle-aged and older women. *Health Psychology* 18, 346–53.

Wober, M. (1987). Perceived risk of disease from alcohol, asbestos and AIDS: links with television viewing? *Health Education Research* 2, 175–84.

Chapter Five

STRESS

Ad Vingerhoets

Chapter Outline

In this chapter, we focus on the issue of stress. We make clear that the term stress is currently used to refer to a process, in which stressors, appraisal, coping and stress reactions are the main components. Each of these concepts is discussed extensively with special attention being given to stressors in the medical context. It is emphasized that stress is an important concept for health psychologists, because there is strong evidence that it may stimulate the seeking of medical help, facilitate the development of several physical disorders, negatively influence recovery processes, and interfere with medical treatment. We review research illustrating these effects and we show how the nature of the relationships between these stress concepts and health status may vary, depending on one's perspective. In addition, we pay attention to the concepts of stress resistance, assessment issues and stress management.

Key Concepts

coping
strain
stress
stressor
strain

social support
stress–disease relationship
stress and health care
stress management

On Defining Stress

Although lay people and professionals generally feel that they know what the concept 'stress' refers to, a more critical evaluation of the use of this term both in the lay and the professional literature reveals that there is a serious lack of agreement with respect to the terminology. A journalist once pithily summarized this disagreement and confusion by stating that stress 'in addition to being itself, and the result of itself, is also the cause of itself.' Indeed, sometimes the term stress is used to refer to situations, stimuli and conditions that may trigger emotional reactions and distress. For example, an exam, the loss of a close friend, marital problems, or a severe illness may all be considered examples of stress.

However, in other texts, the term stress may be used to indicate the reactions or responses of a person to situations such as those just described. Historically, this is the oldest meaning of the term stress, which was introduced by the endocrinologist Hans Selye (1956/1976). This author introduced the term to refer to 'the non-specific (biologic) reaction of the body to any demand made upon it' and labelled it as the General Adaptation Syndrome (GAS). The GAS evolves through three stages: (1) the Alarm reaction, (2) the phase of Resistance, and (3) Exhaustion, all accompanied by specific biological and behavioural characteristics (see figure 5.1).

Finally, there is a third type of definition which emphasizes that stress refers to a process, in which different components should be distinguished, including the antecedents and the consequences of stress. In this view stress refers to a state of an individual that occurs when an individual perceives the environmental demands as exceeding her/his appraised capabilities. In other words, stress is a condition that ensues when a person is aware that (s)he cannot deal adequately with the situation in which (s)he is involved. This state typically occurs when a person is exposed to taxing situations, and it manifests itself in stress reactions.

In this chapter, we will take this psychological process stress model as a starting point. Below, we will discuss each of the [different] crucial components of this stress model. These include the following concepts: stressors, appraisal, (short-term) stress reactions or strains, and long-term health outcomes. In addition, factors moderating the short- and long-term effects of stressor exposure will be discussed briefly.

The psychological stress model

For the stress model presented in this chapter, the following three aspects can be discerned: (1) antecedents, (2) moderators, and (3) consequences (see figure 5.2).

Antecedents of stress are indicated as stressors. A stressor can best be defined as any stimulus, situation or circumstance with the potential to induce stress reactions. Whether such a situation indeed evokes a stress response, however, not only depends on the characteristics of the stressor, but in particular on the individual's appraisal of the situation and on several moderators including his or her coping capabilities

---

Stage 1: Alarm reaction
Physiological response
- Enlargement of the adrenal cortex
- Enlargement of the lymphatic system
- Increase in hormone levels, including adrenalin

Behavioural response
- Increased sensitivity to changes in the environment

If stage 1 is prolonged, the organism moves into stage 2

Stage 2: Resistance
Physiological response
- Shrinkage of adrenal cortex
- Lymph nodes return to normal size
- High hormone levels are maintained
- Increased activity of the parasympathetic nervous system in an attempt to counteract the high arousal

Behavioural response
- Increased sensitivity to stressors
- Individual attempts to resist the stressor

If the organism continues to be exposed to the intense stressor, stage 3 may be reached

Stage 3: Exhaustion
Physiological response
- Lymphatic structures become enlarged and/or dysfunctional
- Levels of some hormones are further increased or high levels are maintained
- Adaptive hormones are depleted

Behavioural response
- Resistance is reduced – giving up
- Increased risk of depression
- Increased risk of physical disease

Figure 5.1 Schematic representation of a psychological stress model
Source: Selye, 1956/1976.

and social support. Appraisal, coping and social support are assumed to be related to personality, psychological and physical state and previous life experiences. Stress reactions may occur at four levels: the physiological level; the subjective, emotional level; the cognitive level; and the behavioural level. In case of chronic exposure to stressful conditions, the enduring physiological stress responses may exhaust the body, decrease its resistance, and make it more vulnerable to all kinds of disease. These effects are also dependent on lifestyle (e.g. smoking, diet, exercising, etc.), physical shape and genetic predispositions.

Each of these stress components will be discussed in more detail below.

Ad Vingerhoets

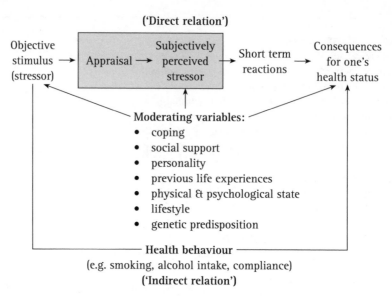

Figure 5.2 The stress model presented in this chapter

STRESSORS AND APPRAISAL

As already indicated, stressors are situations or stimuli that have the potential to evoke stress reactions. Most important, however, is how the stressor is appraised. *Appraisal* is a core concept in psychological stress theory. Lazarus and Folkman (1984) distinguish primary and secondary appraisal, which refer to the questions 'What is at stake?' and 'What can I do about it?', respectively.

The former question may lead to the conclusion that the situation is not relevant for the individual or that it is relevant, but positive. Only if the situation is appraised as negative and harmful or a potential threat, rather than a challenge, may a state of stress be induced. However, also the secondary appraisal is relevant, because this process yields an answer to the question whether or not the individual expects that (s)he can cope with the stressor. For example, previous experience with a similar situation, or reliance on a good social network that will provide support, or a high self-esteem may contribute to the conviction that one is capable to deal adequately with that kind of challenging situation. In this way, any objective situation is converted into a 'subjective' situation, which may or may not have a special meaning for the individual.

In the literature, there are several ways to categorize stressors. Some investigators emphasize the importance of the duration or time dimension of the stressor and make a distinction between *acute* and *chronic* and, sometimes, *chronic intermittent* stressors (e.g. Burchfield, 1979; O'Keefe & Baum, 1990). This distinction is important because, as we will see later, it appears that biological stress responses show a development over time, indicating that responses to acute and to chronic stressful conditions may vary considerably and in important ways.

Examples of acute stressors are exams, arguments, job loss (but not unemployment), painful medical procedures, or being involved in an accident. Marital problems, having a handicap or suffering from a chronic disease, and having a demanding job may be considered chronic stressors. Finally, situations and challenges that return with a certain regularity, such as demanding or emotional events in the work of servicemen, police officers, nurses, etc., are referred to as chronic intermittent stressors.

Other authors classify stressors according to life areas and make a distinction between family stressors, job stressors, disease-related stressors, natural disasters, etc. (e.g. Noshpitz & Coddington, 1990). In addition, there is a categorization which has its roots mainly in the history of stress measurement, where a distinction has been made between life changes or life events, daily hassles, chronic stressors and role stressors (e.g. Hahn & Smith, 1999; Wethington et al., 2001).

The life-events approach is the oldest approach, and has its origin in the work of Holmes and Rahe (1967). These researchers identified events and conditions that frequently precede the seeking of medical help. This yielded a list of events, with fixed, predetermined weights, such as the loss of a spouse, marriage and a change in residence, but also Christmas and minor violations of the law were included.

Not surprisingly, several theorists have criticized this approach, because it obviously conflicts with the relevance of the appraisal process, described above. In addition, it has been noted that these questionnaires cover only a limited subset of all important life changes and stressful conditions, and fail to include several other kinds of stressors. Examples of stressors not included are daily stressors, chronic stressors, traumatic experiences, disasters, and 'non-events', i.e. when certain anticipated and hoped for events do not happen (e.g. women who do not become pregnant, an expected job promotion which is cancelled, etc.). This approach also failed to take into account physical and psychological stressors associated with specific jobs or living and working environments (e.g. shift work, high temperatures, noise, air pollution, other ergonomically less than optimal conditions) (see e.g. European Commission, 2000). Finally, important stressors for specific groups of people (such as foot and mouth disease or a failed crop for farmers) are not included in any of these questionnaires.

Kanner et al. (1981) have emphasized the importance of daily hassles as an important category of stressors. Daily hassles are experiences and conditions of daily living that have been appraised as salient and harmful or threatening to the endorser's well-being. According to them, these kinds of stressors were more influential than life changes in predicting the health status of people. However, the proponents of this approach have apparently overlooked the rather strong interrelations between daily hassles and life events. Daily hassles may precede life events or may be the consequence of a major life event. In addition, daily stressors may exacerbate the effects of life events or vice versa. For example, a serious disease, divorce, or the death of a partner (life events) may cause many other life events (e.g. move, decrease in income) and/or chronic or role stressors or daily hassles (e.g. problems with children, combining work and parenting, etc.) (Wethington et al., 2001).

Another problematic aspect of daily hassles is that – more than is the case with life events – they may be the consequence, rather than the cause of, disease or mental distress. The finding that patients report more daily hassles than do healthy individuals does not necessarily imply that these stressors have contributed to the development of the disease. Both researchers and clinicians should be aware of the fact that stressors are not by definition situations that one is exposed to by chance or fate. Rather, people are active in creating, to a great extent, their own preferred environment with a greater or lesser risk of being confronted with stressful conditions. Research has shown that certain personality factors are associated with a decreased or increased risk of exposure to stressors. For example, extraverts, and especially sensation seekers, are more likely to be involved in risky situations than introverts who prefer to refrain from exciting and adventurous undertakings (see Rice, 1999). Also drug addicts and hostile individuals are examples of people who are more likely to be exposed to stressors than the average person. In the same vein, suffering from a disease may also increase the likelihood of being exposed to taxing circumstances.

Classic examples of role stressors are found in the work of Pearlin and Schooler (1978), who make a distinction between stressors related to one's role as worker, partner, parent, student or supervisor. Each role that we play in life is inherently associated with exposure to specific kinds of stressors. Students have to take exams, deadlines in our work may put pressure on us, we may have serious disagreements with our partner concerning money or how to raise the children, etc.

In sum, although stressors may differ considerably in nature and can be encountered in very different settings, in the research literature, measurement is often limited to just one or two categories. That means that assessment is often confined to only life events, or daily hassles, or a certain type of role stressors. However, neither for theoretical nor for clinical reasons does it make sense to limit the assessment of stressors to just one category. For an extensive discussion of the assessment of stressors, the reader is referred to Wethington et al., 2001.

Stressors, be they acute, chronic or chronic intermittent, may occur in all life areas. As shown in figure 5.3, stressors can be identified as associated with the person him- or herself (disease, handicap, etc.; cf. Patrick et al., 1992; Prugh & Thompson, 1990; Schechter & Leigh, 1990), the family (conflicts, severely ill family members, financial problems; cf. Cohen, 1999; Dyck, Short & Vitaliano, 1999; Kiecolt-Glaser et al., 1995; Rice, 1999), the social environment (disagreements with friends or problems with social relationships; cf. Rice, 1999), the work setting (problems with colleagues or superiors, too-demanding tasks, feeling unjustly treated; cf. European Commission, 2000; Rice, 1999), society at large including the health-care system (living in an unsafe or crowded environment, hospitalization, being involved in an accident; Rice, 1999), and nature (a wide variety of disasters like floods, hurricanes, bush fires; Rice, 1999). Figure 5.3 schematically shows that stressors can be identified in all aspects of life. It further wants to make clear that disease may also be a stressor of itself and that, in addition, disease increases the risk of being exposed to stressors in different life areas.

Of special interest to (clinical) health psychologists are stressors associated with disease and health care. First, one should realize that a serious disease or an otherwise not properly functioning body, such as in the case of infertility, may be

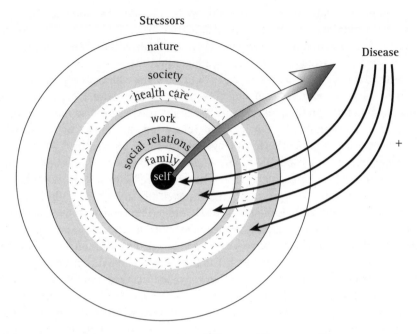

Figure 5.3 Stressors occur in many different life areas. Disease can be conceived of as a stressor associated to the self. Disease also increases the likelihood of being exposed to stressors in other life areas

a serious stressor for a patient. Any condition that limits the individual's autonomy and freedom, interferes with his or her life goals, negatively influences his or her self-esteem, causes pain and discomfort, or implies a life threat can be considered as stressor. Second, as already indicated, illness may increase the risk of exposure to other stressors, including a disturbed relationship with one's partner, a necessary change in life goals, job loss, financial problems, or stigmatization and isolation. In addition, a sick person faces confrontation with the health-care system and maybe even hospitalization and painful medical procedures. Research has demonstrated that introduction into the health-care system may be accompanied by many minor and major stressors (Koenig et al., 1995; Van der Ploeg, 1988; Van Servellen, Lewis & Leake, 1990; White & Ritchie, 1984). Patients are often uncertain about their illnesses because physicians are not very clear in their communication or provide information at inappropriate times. In addition, they may fear medical procedures and examinations.

A few studies have focused on which specific aspects of hospitalization and the confrontation with health care are considered to be most stressful. The study by Koenig et al. (1995) yielded the following list: (1) problems with health-care professionals (in particular lack of information; not responding to questions); (2) diagnostic and therapeutic procedures; (3) the hospital environment (noise, rigid routines, lack of facilities, etc); (4) worries about the home situation and the separation from home; (5) insufficient information about diagnosis and prognosis; and (6) fear of dependency, loss of autonomy, and lack of controllability. In addition, for some specific groups such as AIDS patients, evidence of discriminative behaviour by nurses and fellow patients has been reported (Van Servellen, Lewis & Leake, 1990). An interesting study by Russek and Schwartz (1998) further demonstrated that a stay in an intensive care unit with its alarm signals was perceived as extremely stressful not only by the patients, but also by visiting relatives and nurses working at the ward. This study revealed that people generally prefer silent alarms to the distressing loud sounds that are currently used in most hospitals. For a recent review on the impact of medical illness and treatment on the patient's well-being, see Tedstone and Tarrier (2003).

Of further relevance as sources of stress are the illnesses or handicaps of children or other relatives. There are several examples of studies showing the decreased well-being of parents coping with a seriously ill or physically and/or mentally handicapped child (Dyson, 1993; Floyd & Gallagher, 1997). The psychological state of parents with a newborn in an intensive care unit has been described as an 'emotional roller-coaster' (Schum, 1989). Recent studies have also revealed the negative effects of caring for Alzheimer and schizophrenic patients. It has been demonstrated that the physical condition of these carers is affected, as is shown by the delayed healing of wounds and increased vulnerability to infectious disease (Dyck, Short & Vitaliano, 1999; Kiecolt-Glaser et al., 1995). In addition, members of families which have one hospitalized member have over the years significantly increased costs of using health services (Patrick et al., 1992). Recent research has also suggested an increase in the death rates of older people having to take care of ill family members (Schulz & Beach, 1999).

MODERATORS

The nature and intensity of stress reactions is not only determined by the type and intensity of the stressor; other psycho-social factors having to do with the individual involved and his/her social environment play a role as well. We will briefly mention them here, since this volume contains chapters that are specifically devoted to these concepts. Very important and best known are coping and social support, but certain personality factors, one's physical and psychological state, and previous life experiences are also relevant. In addition, genetic predispositions and lifestyle may interact with the short-term physiological stress responses and co-determine the health effects of stressor exposure.

Coping has been defined as 'the constantly changing cognitive and behavioral efforts to manage specific external and/or internal demands that are appraised as taxing or exceeding the resources of the person' (Lazarus & Folkman, 1984: 141). There is a general consensus that at least two broad classes of coping behaviours can be distinguished: problem-focused coping and emotion-focused coping. The former kind of coping refers to efforts to remove or eliminate stressors or to reduce their intensity. This can be attempted by behavioural or cognitive efforts. For example, a problem can be solved with the assistance of others, a solution can be found for a high workload, or the individual can learn to appraise the situation differently and as less threatening. The goal of emotion-focused coping is to diminish the emotional impact of a stressor, again either by cognitive or behavioural approaches. For instance, one can start drinking alcohol or smoking, go jogging, or follow a course of yoga, or go to an entertaining movie to seek diversion. These examples illustrate that emotional focused coping can be done in a healthy or unhealthy way, thereby possibly decreasing the resistance against disease.

Some theorists feel that this dichotomy does not do justice to the complexity of coping with stress and suggest one or more additional categories, such as avoidance coping, or appraisal coping (e.g. Endler & Johnson, 2001). Other authors make a distinction between combative and preventive coping, referring to efforts aimed at solving a problem or reducing its impact, and actions with the goal of preventing exposure to stressful conditions, respectively (Matheny et al., 1986). There is general agreement that, within each broad category, several specific coping strategies can be distinguished, explaining why several coping assessment devices generally contain several subscales (see Chapter 6, this volume).

It has been suggested that problem-focused coping is superior to emotion-focused coping and more effective in preventing the development of health problems. However, the nature of the stressor is often not taken into account (Penley, Tomaka & Wiebe, 2002). For example, uncontrollable stressors, such as the death of an intimate, may exclude the application of problem-focused coping strategies. As a consequence, such stressors are often appraised as much more stressful than controllable ones. In research, such differences in the perceived intensity of the stressors need to be taken into account. Another important factor is that the effects of coping may also be dependent on the time elapsed since the occurrence of the stressor. For example, denial may be very helpful in the short term, because it prevents the interference of strong emotional reactions with proper functioning. However, in the long run, this coping mechanism may prevent proper adjustment to the new situation.

For health psychologists, it is important to consider that health complaints and illness behaviour may function as coping strategies. Such behaviours may result in secondary gains and may be reinforced according to the principles of operant conditioning. For example, health complaints are generally considered a valid reason not to work or not to engage in several kinds of activities. Health complaints may thus serve the purpose of removing or reducing the impact of stressors. Examples can be given from the work context, but also in the context of marital or family problems. This concept has been elaborated successfully for chronic pain. Interventions have been developed to stop the rewarding of pain behaviours (e.g. Morley, Eccleston & Williams, 1999).

Crying and coping

In order to illustrate the complexity of the coping concept, it is interesting to discuss the relationship between coping and crying. Crying can be considered in at least three ways. It can be seen as an expression of distress. As such, it can be conceptualized as an outcome measure and one could examine which coping style predicts crying in a specific situation (e.g. after having lost a good friend or when failing an exam). On the other hand, crying may also itself be regarded as a coping style. Although there is lack of empirical evidence, it is often proposed that crying brings relief and reduces tension. If this can be demonstrated in future research, crying should be considered as an *emotion-focused* coping strategy, because it facilitates the resolution of distress. In addition, psychologists have put forth evidence that crying has a major impact on the behaviour of others; the mere sight of tears may stop aggression, and induce comforting behaviour and the provision of emotional and other support. Also, there is some evidence that crying may be used to manipulate others. From that perspective, crying could be considered as a *problem-focused* coping strategy.

This example demonstrates that the theoretical distinctions made in models between predictors and outcomes are in practice not always easy to make. The same line of reasoning can be made with respect to depressive symptoms, pain behaviour, or any other illness behaviour. (See Vingerhoets et al., 2000.)

Social support is another important moderator of stress reactions (see Chapter 7, this volume). The availability of an adequate social network that offers informational, instrumental and emotional support is considered an important buffer against the possible negative health consequences of stressor exposure. However, many studies have failed to find these positive effects of social support. Several factors may be responsible for these contradictory findings. Owing to space limitations, we will only briefly mention some of the problems with the different operationalizations of both stress and social support, which can partly explain the seemingly discrepant findings, as was shown by Barrera (1986). For example, the expression of distress may facilitate the provision of social support, thus resulting in a positive association between these two factors, whereas a negative association might be expected.

As can be understood from the stress model, depending on personality, individuals may vary considerably in the extent to which exposure to stressors actually leads to short-term reactions and long-term health consequences. The concepts of *resilience*, *stress resistance* and *stress vulnerability* refer to these individual differences. These terms are commonly used in the popular media and organizations are eager to recruit 'stress-resistant' employees. Although at first glance these concepts seem to be clear and to make sense, a critical analysis reveals several major problems. We have already shown that stress reactions can manifest themselves at four levels: the physiological, emotional, cognitive and behavioural levels, with no clear association between them. In order to qualify a person as stress resistant, all four levels should be assessed. In addition, as was already mentioned, a distinction should be made between short-term reactions and long-term consequences, which are also not always closely related. When a person shows no apparent short-term stress reactions, this does not rule out the possibility that (s)he will develop health complaints in the long run. Finally, there is a wide variety in the nature of stressors, ranging from a high workload to divorce, and from failing an important examination to the death of a loved one. However, we cannot be certain that a person's reactions to one kind of stressor have any predictive power with respect to the question how one will react when exposed to a different kind of stressor. In conclusion, in the strictest sense of the term, it is not possible to determine that someone is stress resistant. When exposed to stressful conditions, we can be certain that every healthy living organism will show a stress reaction at one time or another, and at one level or another. Obviously, the term stress resistant is used in popular texts to indicate that the person functions properly when under much pressure at work, which, however, does not necessarily imply (1) that there is no bodily arousal or a negative mood; (2) that it has no consequences for his health in the long term; and (3) that this person also will function adequately when confronted with a totally different stressor (e.g. the death of his partner).

Nevertheless, in the research literature, a number of *personality characteristics* have been proposed as making people more or less stress resistant (Rice, 1999). The best known of these are hardiness, sense of coherence, optimism, internal locus of control, and self-esteem. In addition, there is increasing evidence that, when confronted with stressful situations, people should not keep it secret, but should share it with others or write about it. There are strong indications that concealment and emotional inhibition may increase health risks (Nyklicek, Vingerhoets & Denollet, 2002). Finally, there is some evidence supporting the relevance and validity of the stress diathesis model (Gatchel, 1993). Each of these concepts will be discussed briefly below.

Hardiness is a concept introduced by Kobasa (1979). It contains three elements: (1) commitment, (2) control, and (3) challenge. Commitment may be defined as a sense of self and purpose. Control refers to the concept of locus of control. An internal locus of control is associated with resilience. Individuals with an internal locus of control believe that they themselves determine to a great extent what happens in their lives and they do not believe that positive and negative events in their lives are all beyond their control. Challenge reflects the degree to which safety, stability and predictability are important. Some studies have shown that managers with these characteristics reported fewer symptoms after being exposed to stressful conditions than managers who did not have these personality features (see Funk, 1992, for an overview). However, there is some serious criticism relating to the construct of hardiness. For example, it has been suggested that hardiness simply implies the absence of neuroticism. Others claim that the most important factor is the concept of control, whereas commitment and challenge do not make much sense. In addition, there is much disagreement about the best way of assessing this concept (Mowinski-Jennings & Staggers, 1994; Sinclair & Tetrick, 2000).

Sense of coherence stems from the work of Antonovsky (1987), who examined Jewish people who had been in concentration camps during the Second World War, but who have remained both mentally and physically healthy. This concept also includes three dimensions: (1) meaningfulness, (2) commitment, and (3) control. Crucial here is that people had the feeling that what happened to them was meaningful, and that they were able to place their experiences in a positive perspective.

Optimism is also a personality characteristic associated with good health (e.g. Aspinwall & Brunhart, 2000; Scheier, Carver & Bridges, 2001). However, until now, there have been a limited number of studies which have shown that optimism may buffer the negative health effects of stressor exposure. The same holds for *self-esteem*.

This may be explained in terms of differences in appraisal and coping styles. Optimistic people and individuals with a high self-esteem have been shown to cope more efficiently (Chang, 2000). On the other hand, some investigators also suggest that unrealistic optimism may make people more likely to engage in high-risk behaviours, such as not wearing a safety belt, practising unsafe sex, etc. (Davidson & Prkachin, 1997).

The basis for stress resistance is believed to be formed in childhood (Haggerty et al., 1996). There is evidence that resilient people were confronted with adverse situations as children. However, during these stressful situations, they received the necessary emotional support and guidance from their parents or carers/guardians. As a result, the stressor exposure was an important learning experience, which stimulated their personal growth and self-esteem. A more or less similar concept is stress inoculation, which is also applied as a stress management technique (Meichenbaum & Deffenbacher, 1988). The basic idea of stress inoculation is that, analogous to the way in which vaccination with an innocuous germ triggers the body to develop immunity against it, exposure to low doses of psycho-social threat combined with skills to deal with that threat results in stress resistance. Having experienced challenging situations that were dealt with adequately may also have positive effects for an adult's self-esteem.

People who talk about their problems or express their emotions in other ways have been found to suffer less from negative health problems. There is a whole body of literature providing support for this thesis (Nyklicek et al., 2002; Smyth, 1998). Not only retrospective studies, but also a number of prospective and experimental studies have yielded converging evidence. Well known in this respect is the work of Pennebaker, who introduced the writing paradigm, requesting participants to write about stressful experiences, three to four times for about 20 minutes. This simple intervention has yielded impressive results, in particular in relation to physical health and psycho-biological processes (Pennebaker, 1997; Smyth, 1998). Compared to a control group who had to write about their daily activities, the experimental group showed a decrease in the number of physician visits, increased immune activity, changes in autonomic muscle activity, behavioural markers (e.g. grade-point average for students, absenteeism from work, re-employment following job loss), and self-reported well-being. In addition, more recent studies also suggest that this intervention may have a positive effect on the course of disease in asthma and rheumatoid arthritis patients (Kelley, Lumley & Leisen, 1997; Smyth et al., 1999).

A final relevant concept is *stress diathesis*, which refers to a predisposition – be it inherited or acquired – to react (physiologically) abnormally to stressors, resulting in increased vulnerability to stress-related disorders (Gatchel, 1993; Weisberg & Clavel, 1999). In other words, a parallel may be drawn with allergies, which are also characterized by abnormal reactions to specific essentially innocuous antigens. According to the diathesis stress model, in order for stressor exposure to produce illness, two conditions must be met. First, the individual must have a predisposition to develop a certain kind of disease. Second, the person must be exposed to a stressful condition of a minimal intensity. Most research with respect to the stress diathesis model has been concerned with depression, but the results have not been consistent; in some cases, the findings provide support for the stress diathesis model, but other research findings seem to contradict it. Monroe and Simons (1991) present some alternative models showing how the diathesis and exposure to stressors may link and interact in their contribution to the development of disease. Weisberg and Clavel (1999) convincingly demonstrate how chronic pain may result from a complex process with *predisposing factors, initiating factors, perpetuating factors* and *factors that are barriers to treatment* as the main players. As might be clear from this chapter, both chronic and acute stressors may play all these roles.

Finally, lifestyle and health behaviours as well as genetic predispositions are supposed to co-determine the effects of the biological stress reactions for one's physical health status. Stressor exposure may have limited effect on someone who is in a physical good shape and who is free from any specific genetically determined or via bad health risk acquired vulnerabilities. In other words, someone whose body is compromised by heavy smoking and bad eating habits is more likely to experience negative health effects of stressor exposure.

STRESS REACTIONS

If an individual appraises a situation as a potential threat, stress reactions may occur. These can occur at each of the following four different levels, which is why we speak of a multi-dimensional stress response:

The physiological level. Exposure to a threatening situation may induce the so-called fight-or-flight reaction, which is characterized by increased activation of the sympathetic system which results in increased heart rate, elevated blood pressure, redistribution of the blood from internal organs to muscles, and release of catecholamines (adrenaline and noradrenaline), which prepare the body for action. Less known is the so-called conservation-withdrawal reaction, although it may include Selye's GAS, which in many respects is a counterpart of the fight-or-flight reaction. In a conservation-withdrawal reaction, the individual feels helpless and hopeless and there is no tendency to act, but rather passivity and giving-up prevail. The heart rate slows down and there is no increased activation of the sympathetic nervous system but rather of the parasympathetic system and the pituitary-adrenal system (cf. Vingerhoets & Perski, 2000). The immune system also displays differential responses in these two reactions, activation versus depression (Bosch et al., 2001). Recently, Taylor et al. (2000) described what they consider to be an additional specific female stress response, the tend-and-befriend reaction. Tending refers to nurturing activities aimed at protecting the self and the offspring, while the term befriending describes establishing and maintaining social networks that may facilitate the former activities. It has been hypothesized that oxytocin, a hormone that also plays a major role in the onset of the delivery, is involved as the main specific psycho-biologic substrate. In conclusion, a specific hormone or autonomic nervous system indicator may behave very differently, depending on the kind of stress reaction which occurs. Note that this indicates that it is not possible to denote one specific physiological parameter as the objective standard for the determination of stress.

The emotional level. Stressful conditions may evoke feelings of helplessness, depression, frustration, anger or anxiety. A wide variety of negative emotions and moods may be activated by stressor exposure. In case of more severe stressors, such as rape, sexual or physical abuse, disasters or accidents, the victims are often additionally afflicted with feelings of intense guilt and/or shame. Remarkably, there is also the possibility that these individuals become emotionally numb and lose their ability to experience and express emotions (Litz, 1992).

The cognitive level. During stressful episodes, people may worry and not be able to concentrate. They may become obsessively focused on certain thoughts and their memories may show problems with storage. Obtrusive thoughts, flashbacks, re-experiences of the events, and worrying are the most characteristic consequences of exposure to traumatic events. Thayer and Lane (2000) consider worry as the most important aspect of the stress response and speculate that it actually intensifies and prolongs the effects of stressors. Stress may also affect memory processes and other cognitive processes (Reason, 1988).

The behavioural level. At this level, there is a wide variety of reactions, including crying, smoking, social withdrawal, use of alcohol or drugs, absenteeism, aggression, etc. It is important to be aware of these kinds of stress reactions, because many of these behaviours may have damaging effects on a person's physical well-being. Occasionally, stress may also have seemingly positive effects on work performance, for example, a man who fully concentrates on his work during his divorce proceedings in an attempt to find distraction.

The major problem in determining whether or not a person is 'under stress' is that the links between these four different levels of reactions are weak at best. An important and serious limitation in stress research is the lack of an objective standard to establish whether or not a person is in a state of stress. The heart rate may show either of two reactions – increase or slow down – and the same holds for all other physiological systems, including the catecholamines and cortisol, which may show enhanced release, but also decreased levels. In addition, immune parameters may demonstrate divergent reaction patterns. Whereas one person may feel well but have difficulties with concentrating on work, another person may stay away from work and have elevated cortisol levels, while a third person may start smoking, feel bad and withdraw socially, but at the physiological level hardly any changes or differences may be detected.

Note that, thus far, we have only discussed the short-term effects of stressor exposure. In many cases, the stressor is acute and its effects dissipate in due course. However, when the stressor is intense and becomes chronic, the person's well-being and health may be in jeopardy. In particular, chronic stressors are accompanied by psycho-biological changes that increase the individual's susceptibility to disease. This happens when the bodily activation, yielding energy for overt behaviour, exceeds the actual demands of the body, or when the body becomes exhausted and no longer adequately supports the physiological need to adapt successfully to environmental challenges (see below).

The consequences for well-being and health

Exposure to stressors may result in a number of effects on health-related outcomes, including the following:

A   People exposed to a high level of stressors may notice and report more symptoms and may be more likely present themselves to the health-care system and seek help from health professionals, although they are often not ill in a biomedical sense.
B   Stressor exposure may facilitate the development of mental and somatic disease.
C   Taxing events may influence the course of disease and may delay recovery.
D   The effects of medical interventions may be nullified or diminished as a consequence of stressor exposure.
E   The information-processing capacity of patients under stress may be affected, preventing a clear understanding of medical information and resulting, among other things, in a lack of compliance.

Below we will discuss each of these consequences briefly.

Ad A. One of the possible explanations as to why stressor exposure makes people *feel* ill is clarified by Pennebaker's symptom perception model (Pennebaker, 1982; 1994). Central to this model is the proposal that bodily processes caused by the emotions that accompany the confrontation with stressful experiences may be incorrectly interpreted as signs of a disease. Pennebaker assumes that there is competition between the perception of external stimuli and of internal, proprioceptive information. The implication is that bodily signals are more likely to be perceived when they are intense, when the external environment is not stimulating, or when the person has a preoccupation with his/her body and focuses his/her attention on the body. This model may be helpful in explaining phenomena such as 'medical student's disease', and the high number of symptoms reported by people who have been exposed to stressful experiences. If, in addition, there is uncertainty about whether or not a person has also been exposed to toxic substances or radiation, more attention will be focused on bodily symptoms, resulting in an increased risk of the perception of bodily signals that may be interpreted incorrectly as signs of diseases (Pennebaker, 1994).

Ad B. The mechanisms involved in the patho-physiology of stress-related disorders have already been discussed: the autonomic nervous system (with the sympathetic and para-sympathetic nervous branches), the neuro-endocrine system and the immune system all play a significant role in rendering the individual more susceptible to disease (cf. Lovallo, 1997; Marsland et al., 2002; Vingerhoets & Perski, 2000). It is interesting to note that, while the lay person is generally convinced of the import- ant role of stress in the development of such disorders as hypertension, headache, coronary heart disease and stomach ulcers, seen from the scientific point of view, the most convincing evidence for a role of stress in the development of disease in humans has been demonstrated for infectious diseases including the common cold, influenza and dental infections (Marsland et al., 2002).

Since there is increasing evidence (e.g. Muhlestein, 2000; Wierzbicki & Hagmeyer, 2000) that pathogens are involved in the development of diseases until recently not known to be associated with infection and inflammatory processes, including stomach ulcer (helicobacter pylori) and myocardial infarction (e.g. cytomegalus virus, chlamydia pneumoniae, herpes viruses, and, again, helicobacter pylori), the potential role of psycho-neuro-immunological processes has gained additional clinical relevance. This is important because it provides us with insight into the mechanisms through which psycho-social factors exert their influence on bodily processes relevant for the devel- opment of disease. In addition, there is impressive evidence from animal work that stress has a significant influence not only on the development of these diseases, but also on tumour growth (McCabe et al., 2000; Strange et al., 2000).

For a proper understanding of the long-term physiological consequences of stress, it is of utmost importance to be aware of the differential, even opposite, effects of acute stress and chronic stress. For example, with respect to immune function, there is suggestive evidence showing that acute stress actually enhances immune functions, rather than suppressing them, which is what typically happens in a state of chronic stress (cf. McEwen & Stellar, 1993; Vingerhoets & Perski, 2000).

Whereas research into the effects of stressor exposure generally focuses on the consequences for the health status of the exposed individual, there is also evidence that stressor exposure in pregnant women may have consequences for the develop- ing foetuses. Recent studies have demonstrated that maternal stressor exposure not only increases the risk of premature birth but may also interfere with the proper development of the foetus, resulting in low birth weight. In addition, some studies demonstrate an increased risk of hypertension and pre-eclampsia in the mother (see Paarlberg et al., 1995; Wadhwa, Sanman & Garite, 2001). Moreover, follow-up studies on the children suggest an association with a wide variety of mental and physical health problems in the first years of their development (Huizink, Mulder & Buitelaar, 2004).

Whereas we have emphasized the importance of psycho-biological stress reactions as mediators of health consequences, as already indicated, another way in which con- frontation with emotional and taxing situations may have a major impact on health concerns changes in health habits, including relapse into the habit of smoking, lack of compliance with medical regimens, and sleep deprivation.

Ad C and D. The same psycho-biological mechanisms and behaviours that may be important for the development of disease are also hypothesized to play a major role in the course of disease and the patients' subjective well-being or quality of life.

There are a wide variety of diseases, including myocardial infarction, breast cancer, HIV infection, rheumatoid arthritis, multiple sclerosis, systemic lupus erythematosus and herpes infections, for which there is some evidence of a role of psycho-social factors on disease outcome (e.g. Chrousos & Gold, 1992; Lovallo, 1997; McEwen, 1998; McEwen & Stellar, 1993; Rice, 1999). However, the results are not always consistent and much more research is needed to settle this question definitively and to clarify the precise conditions which render a negative (or a positive, in the case of inter-ventions) effect of psycho-social factors more likely.

In addition to its influence on the course of disease, there is now evidence of the effects of stress exposure on wound healing. Research has shown that the wounds of carers of patients with dementia and of students during exams take more time to heal than those of a control group not exposed to stressful conditions. Extrapolating these findings to a clinical setting, one may wonder whether psycho-social factors also can affect recovery from surgery (Kiecolt-Glaser et al., 1998).

There are indications that recovery after a surgical operation can be delayed when the patient feels anxious pre-operatively. However, since recovery should be con-sidered as a multi-dimensional concept, with physical state (including pain, fatigue and behaviour), emotional, psychological state, and psycho-biological stress responses as distinct components, the results of different studies do not always show a clear and uniform pattern. Nevertheless, there is sufficient reason to help the patient to reduce his/her level of stress before undergoing a major medical procedure (see Devine, 1992; Johnston & Vögele, 1993; Salmon, 1992 for reviews).

Among the medical interventions which may be less effective when the patient is under stress are vaccinations and *in vitro* fertilization (IVF). For example, it has been shown that individuals under stress when receiving anti-hepatitis, anti-influenza, or pneumococcal vaccines may develop fewer antibodies, implying less protection against these diseases, than low-stress control subjects (Cohen, Miller & Rabin, 2001; Glaser et al., 2000). In a gynaecological setting, there is some evidence suggesting that high-stress IVF candidates are less likely to conceive than their low-stress counterparts (Boivin & Takefman, 1995).

Ad E. In the medical setting, stress may also have a negative effect on health out-comes, because stress impacts on the patient's understanding of the information pro-vided by the physician (Smith, 1990). For example, lack of compliance can be the result of stress-related disruptions in information processing. Physicians should, there-fore, carefully structure the information they provide to meet the needs of patients and to prevent the negative effects of stress on patient understanding and recall (see also Chapter 11, this volume).

Stress research: some methodological issues

How can we be certain that stress affects our health status? The only way to get a reliable answer is to do research. But stress research is often flawed by serious methodological weaknesses. Without pretending to be exhaustive, here we will discuss some of these problems (see Kasl & Jones, 2001 for a review).

First, for a proper understanding of the possible influence of stress on health, it should be realized that there are strong links between stress and other psycho-social and behavioural factors. For example, as indicated before, stressors are not always events or conditions that occur independently of the personality or psychological functioning of the individual. Sensation seekers and extroverts are more likely to be exposed to stressful conditions than introverts, who prefer to live a quiet life. In the same vein, there is reason to assume that smokers and drinkers may have a higher risk of being exposed to stressors. As we have already discussed, being ill or handicapped may also increase the likelihood of being confronted with stressful conditions. In addition, coping, personality, social support and lifestyle are not completely independent factors. For example, shy people are less likely to have an adequate social network (Jackson et al., 2002) and individuals with high internal control beliefs may be more likely to apply a problem-focused coping strategy than those with more external control beliefs (Beasley, Thompson & Davidson, 2003). Stressor exposure may stimulate people to engage in bad health habits, such as (relapse in) smoking or overeating (Fukuda et al., 1999; Hudd et al., 2000; Weidner et al., 1996). These possible interconnections make it difficult to draw valid conclusions about the precise nature of the relationship between stressor exposure and disease.

Moreover, there are many other problems inherent in the study of stress and disease. For instance, for many disorders (cancer, hypertension, diabetes, etc.) it is not possible to date exactly the onset of the disease. That implies that one can never be sure that a certain factor has been involved it its development. In addition, many diseases, including cancer, hypertension, depression, diabetes and rheumatoid arthritis, develop slowly and show a rather capricious course. In practice, often only the moment of the definitive medical diagnosis made by a physician is known – which may differ considerably from the moment of the real onset of the disease. Another pitfall may be the confounding of the onset of disease and the seeking of medical help – which might be under the influence of certain psycho-social factors, different from those that are related to the development of disease. One should also consider the possibility of a reverse relationship (i.e. that the stressor exposure is the result rather than the cause of the disease) or the involvement of a third variable, such as personality, which is connected to both stressor exposure and health status, resulting in a spurious relationship between the latter two variables. Therefore, in psycho-social epidemiology, guidelines have been drawn which help to determine whether or not there is a causal relationship between the confrontation with stressful conditions and the onset of disease (cf. Kasl & Jones, 2001).

The assessment of stress

The logical implications of the conceptualization of stress as a process, as discussed above, are that the assessment of stress must include the measurement of stressors, appraisal, and stress reactions. Wethington et al. 2001 provide an excellent overview of the measurement of stressors, in which they make a distinction between (1) life events; (2) chronic stressors; (3) daily hassles; and (4) stressor appraisals. These authors conclude that, in future research, more sophisticated interview methods should be applied, since most of the currently applied methods suffer from serious drawbacks.

Stress research has a long tradition of measuring stressors. As mentioned before, in the mid-1960s, Holmes and Rahe (1967) developed their Social Readjustment Rating Scale, which contained a list of 43 events, each with a predetermined weight according to the extent to which the event requires adjustment. For example, the death of a spouse received a weighting of 100, marriage had a weighting of 50, and trouble with the boss was given a rating of 23. This questionnaire included both positive and negative situations, based on the assumption that any time an organism has to make a substantial adjustment to a new environment, this may have physiological costs. The situations were derived from pilot studies among people visiting their general practitioners who were asked about certain life events in the period before their visit. This questionnaire and its many copies are widely used, but they have also met with much criticism, which has led to several adaptations. In some cases, the positive events were removed. In addition, questions were added focusing on the extent to which the event was anticipated, to what extent the respondent had control over the situation, and how long the impact of the event lasted (e.g. Antoni & Goodkin, 1989). Although the numbers of items differ considerably among the different stressor lists, ranging from 40 to 150, these checklists or inventories, by definition, are never complete or exhaustive, which may mean that, for specific populations, important stressors are not included. For example, when investigating stressors among farmers, it would be important to apply stressor inventories containing items relating to problems with the harvest or cattle.

More recently, the focus has shifted to daily hassles (cf. Eckenrode & Bolger, 1995; Wethington et al., 2001). It was found that these measures generally demonstrated more substantial associations with health status. However, as some critics have pointed out, compared to life events, it is more likely that hassles may be the consequences rather than the cause of disease, which may explain the generally stronger associations between such stressors and, in particular, subjective health complaints.

Finally, tailor-made measures may focus on specific categories of stressors such as role stressors, job stressors or stressors in the hospital.

In addition to questionnaires, interview methods have been developed to assess stressors (see also Wethington et al., 2001). The best known of these is the Life Events and Difficulties Schedule (LEDS), developed by Harris and Brown (cf. Brown, 1989). The results obtained using this method are impressive in that they often reveal rather strong associations with diseases. However, applying this method not only requires intensive training, but it is also a time-consuming procedure and not appropriate for application with large numbers of participants. On the other hand, the method is reliable and valid and has many strengths, including taking into account the context and timing of the event, which renders it superior to the commonly used life change self-report inventories.

A wide variety of questionnaires is available to assess stress symptoms, well-being and specific mood states like anxiety or depression (cf. Furer, König-Zahn & Tax, 2001; Stone, 1995). In research, there are also examples of performance tests such as proofreading or reaction time tests being applied to measure the effects of stress (e.g. Fleming & Baum, 1986). Of course, many other factors may influence performance, once more emphasizing the need to measure stress at different levels, including self-reported mood and physiological variables. For a detailed discussion of the methodology of measuring stress hormones or immune measures that may be relevant for stress research, the reader is referred to Hawk and Baum, 2001, or Baum and Grunberg, 1995; and Vedhara et al., 2001, or Kiecolt-Glaser & Glaser, 1995, respectively.

Stress management

Stress management programmes have been employed extensively and successfully with people who suffer from a wide variety of stress-related symptoms and illnesses. In the lay literature, stress management is mainly associated with techniques to reduce symptoms or to facilitate relaxation. Although this is a major aim in stress management, the stress model presented above indicates that there are additional possibilities for intervention goals. Focusing on the most important elements of the stress model, stressors–appraisal–coping–social support–strain, there is potential for intervention at all of these levels, as is discussed below.

1) *Stressors*: is it possible to reduce the number and/or intensity of the stressors? This step requires a careful assessment of the stressors the patient is exposed to. In some cases, this may be easy; in other cases this may be a difficult task. And the same holds for the possibilities to manipulate stressors. To eliminate the stressors, a social worker may be needed, but in some cases, the stressors may be relatively easily reduced by the patient him/herself. For example, as a result of training or habituation procedures, the patient may be better prepared for new conditions; or in other cases, assertiveness training may be effective in helping individuals to protect themselves from overload.

2) *Appraisal*: people are not always realistic in their perception of events. People may exaggerate, and see events from the wrong perspective, for example, because they are too perfectionist, not tolerating the slightest inadequacies, or because they take much responsibility. As a consequence, basically neutral stimuli may be appraised as stressful because they may be considered a threat for the ego.

3) *Coping*: although it is impossible to state beforehand which coping strategy will be most effective, because that depends on the characteristics of the stressor and in which phase of stressor exposure the individual is, it may nevertheless be useful to assess aspects of the individual's coping repertoire. In addition, there is some evidence

that people with a rigid coping style, who lack the flexibility to try different ways of dealing with stressors, run a higher risk of developing stress symptoms (Lester, Smart & Baum, 1994). Flexibility may, therefore, also be an important focus of assessment. Currently there is an increasing range of interventions which focus on coping with specific health problems or medical procedures (see also Chapters 6, 9, 12, 13, 14, this volume).

4) *Social support*: social support can be conceived in different ways. It has been made clear that a distinction should be made between the structure of a person's network, perceived social support, and enacted support (Barrera, 1986). On the basis of the proper assessment of social support (see also Van Sonderen & Sanderman, 2001), it is possible to determine whether or not it is necessary and how to intervene in order to facilitate the receipt of social support, be it formal (e.g. visits by a nurse) or informal (e.g. stimulating the person to engage in social activities). Learning social skills may be very helpful for some individuals lacking social support.

5) *Combating stress symptoms*: There is a wide variety of techniques aimed at facilitating relaxation, including systematic desensitization, autogenic training, meditation, yoga, self-hypnosis, etc. In serious cases, the temporary prescription of psychopharmacological agents may be recommended in order to quieten the body (see Lehrer & Woolfolk, 1993; Rice, 1999).

Whereas all of the above suggestions for interventions mainly focus on the individual, interventions may also be applied to groups, organizations (in particular the work setting), or society at large (see also Chapter 15, this volume).

CONCLUSION

Stress is an important concept in health psychology. According to modern stress theories, stress should be considered a process. The key elements in that process are stressors, appraisal, multi-dimensional short-term stress reactions, and long-term outcomes. In addition, the role of moderating factors, such as coping, social support and personality, which either facilitate or reduce the stress reactions, is important. For the link with disease, the role of the autonomic nervous system, the endocrine system and the immune system need to be considered. Moreover, the effects of stress-related changes in health behaviours for a person's physical well-being should not be neglected. In the context of health care, the relevance of stress factors is not limited to their influence on objective health status: it is also important to consider symptoms resulting from incorrectly interpreted bodily arousal.

Further, stress may affect the outcome of medical treatment and interfere with effective doctor–patient communication. For the health psychologist, it is also important to take notice of the fact that disease and health problems can be considered as both stressors as well as (problem-focused) coping. All these perspectives should be taken into account in integral assessment procedures at all levels of the stress process in order to obtain a complete insight into the dynamics of stress.

DISCUSSION POINTS

1. Discuss how the concepts stressor, stress, and strain relate to each other.
2. What is the main cause of the confusion resulting from the use of the term 'stress'?
3. Outline how stressor exposure and disease may be interconnected.
4. List the short-term effects of stressor exposure.
5. Which effects of stressor exposure are particularly relevant for the medical setting?
6. What kinds of stressors are distinguished in the literature?
7. Give examples of stressors that one is more likely to be exposed to when being ill.
8. Discuss how coping and health problems can be related in at least two different ways.
9. Why is it important to make a distinction between acute and chronic stressors?
10. Explain why it is important to have a stress model when developing stress management interventions.

FURTHER READING

Cohen, M. S. (1999). Families coping with childhood chronic illness: A research review. *Families, Systems and Health* 17, 149–64.

Cohen, S., Kessler, R. C. and Underwood-Gordon, L., eds. (1995). *Measuring Stress: A Guide for Health and Social Scientists*. New York: Oxford University Press.

Glaser, R. and Kiecolt-Glaser, J. K., eds. (1994). *Handbook of Human Stress and Immunity*. San Diego, CA: Academic Press.

Johnston, M. and Wallace, L., eds. (1990). *Stress and Medical Procedures*. Oxford: Oxford University Press.

Lazarus, R. S. and Folkman, S. (1984). *Stress, Appraisal, and Coping*. New York: Springer.

Lehrer, P. M. and Woolfolk, R. L., eds. (1993). *Principles and Practice of Stress Management*, 2nd edn. New York: Guilford.

Lovallo, W. R. (1997). *Stress and Health: Biological and Psychological Interactions*. Thousand Oaks, CA: Sage.

McEwen, B. S. (1998). Protective and damaging effects of stress mediators. *New England Journal of Medicine* 338, 171–9.

Rice, P. L. (1999). *Stress and Health*. Pacific Grove, CA: Brooks/Cole.

Sapolsky, R. M. (1994). *Why Zebras Do Not Get Ulcers: A Guide to Stress, Stress Related Disease, and Coping*. New York: W. H. Freeman.

Selye, H. (1956/1976). *The Stress of Life*. New York: McGraw-Hill.

Tsigos, C. and Chrousos, G. P. (1996). Stress, endocrine manifestations, and diseases. In C. L. Cooper, ed., *Handbook of Stress, Medicine, and Health*. Boca Raton, FL: CRC Press, 61–85.

Vingerhoets, A. J. J. M., ed. (2001). *Assessment in Behavioural Medicine*. Hove, UK: Brunner-Routledge.

KEY STUDIES

Cohen, S., Tyrrel, D. A. J. and Smith, A. P. (1991). Psychological stress and susceptibility to the common cold. *New England Journal of Medicine* 325, 306–12.

Kiecolt-Glaser, J. K., Marucha, P. T., Malarkey, W. B., Mercado, A. M. and Glaser, R. (1995). Slowing of wound healing by psychological stress. *The Lancet* 346, 1194–6.

REFERENCES

Antoni, M. H. and Goodkin, K. (1989). Life stress and moderator variables in the promotion of cervical neoplasia, II: life event dimensions. *Journal of Psychosomatic Research* 33, 457–67.

Antonovsky, A. (1987). *Unraveling the Mystery of Health: How People Manage Stress and Stay Well.* San Francisco: Jossey-Bass.

Aspinwall, L. G. and Brunhart, S. M. (2000). What I do know won't hurt me: optimism, attention to negative information, coping, and health. In J. E. Gilham, ed., *The Science of Optimism and Hope: Research Essays in Honor of Mark E. P. Seligman.* Philadelphia PA: Templeton Foundation Press, 163–200.

Barrera, M., Jr. (1986). Distinctions between social support concepts, measures, and models. *American Journal of Community Psychology* 14, 413–45.

Baum, A. and Grunberg, N. (1995). Measurement of stress hormones. In S. Cohen, R. C. Kessler and L. Underwood Gordon, eds., *Measuring Stress: A Guide for Health and Social Scientists.* New York: Oxford University Press, 175–92.

Beasley, M., Thompson, T. and Davidson, J. (2003). Resilience in response to life stress: the effects of coping style and cognitive hardiness. *Personality and Individual Differences* 34, 77–95.

Boivin, J. and Takefman, J. E. (1995). Stress level across stages of in vitro fertilization in subsequently pregnant and nonpregnant women. *Fertility & Sterility* 64, 802–10.

Bosch, J. A., De Geus, E. J. C., Kelder, A., Veerman, E. C. I., Hoogstraten, J. and Van Nieuw Amerongen, A. (2001). Differential effects of active versus passive coping on secretory immunity. *Psychophysiology* 38, 836–46.

Brown, G. W. (1989). Life events and measurement. In G. W. Brown and T. O. Harris, eds., *Life Events and Illness.* New York: Guilford, 3–45.

Burchfield, S. R. (1979). The stress response: a new perspective. *Psychosomatic Medicine* 41, 661–72.

Chang, E. C., ed. (2000). *Optimism and Pessimism: Implication for Theory, Research, and Practice.* Washington, DC: American Psychological Association.

Chrousos, G. P. and Gold, P. W. (1992). The concept of stress and stress system disorders. *JAMA* 267, 1244–52.

Cohen, M. S. (1999). Families coping with childhood chronic illness: a research review. *Families, Systems and Health* 17, 149–64.

Cohen, S., Miller, G. E. and Rabin, B. S. (2001). Psychological stress and antibody response to immunization: a critical review of the human literature. *Psychosomatic Medicine* 63, 7–18.

Davidson, K. and Prkachin, K. (1997). Optimism and unrealistic optimism have an interacting impact on health-promoting behavior and knowledge changes. *Personality and Social Psychology Bulletin* 23, 617–25.

Devine, E. C. (1992). Effects of psycho-educational care for adult surgical patients: a meta-analysis of 191 studies. *Patient Education & Counseling* 19, 39–51.

Dyck, D. G., Short, R. and Vitaliano, P. P. (1999). Predictors of burden and infectious illness in schizophrenia caregivers. *Psychosomatic Medicine* 61, 411–19.

Dyson, L. L. (1993). Response to the presence of a child with disabilities: parental stress and family functioning over time. *American Journal of Mental Retardation* 98, 207–18.

Eckenrode, J. and Bolger, N. (1995). Daily and within-day event measurement. In S. Cohen, R. C. Kessler and L. Underwood Gordon, eds., *Measuring Stress: A Guide for Health and Social Scientists*. New York: Oxford University Press, 80–101.

Endler, N. S. and Johnson, J. M. (2001). Assessment of coping with health problems. In A. J. J. M. Vingerhoets, ed., *Assessment in Behavioral Medicine*. Hove, UK: Brunner-Routledge, 135–60.

European Commission (2000). *Guidance on Work-related Stress: Spice of Life or Kiss of Death?* Luxembourg: Office for Official Publications of the European Communities.

Fleming, I. and Baum, A. (1986). Stress: psychobiological assessment. *Journal of Organizational Behaviour Management* 8, 117–40.

Floyd, F. J. and Gallagher, E. M. (1997). Parental stress, care demands, and use of support services for school-age children with disabilities and behavior problems. *Family Relations: Interdisciplinary Journal of the Applied Family Studies* 46, 359–71.

Fukuda, S., Morimoto, K., Mure, K. and Maruyama, S. (1999). Post-traumatic stress and change in lifestyle among the Hanshin-Awaji earthquake victims. *Preventive Medicine – An International Journal Devoted to Practice and Theory* 29, 147–51.

Funk, S. C. (1992). Hardiness: a review of theory and research. *Health Psychology* 11, 335–45.

Furer, J., König-Zahn, C. and Tax, B. (2001). Health status measurement. In A. J. J. M. Vingerhoets, ed., *Assessment in Behavioural Medicine*. Hove, UK: Brunner-Routledge, 330–52.

Gatchel, R. J. (1993). Psychophysiological disorders: past and present perspectives. In R. J. Gatchel and E. B. Blanchard, eds., *Psychophysiological Disorders: Research and Clinical Applications*. Washington, DC: American Psychological Association, 1–21.

Glaser, R., Sheridan, J., Malarkey, W. B., MacCallum, R. C. and Kiecolt-Glaser, J. K. (2000). Chronic stress modulates the immune response to a pneumococcal vaccine. *Psychosomatic Medicine* 62, 804–7.

Haggerty, R. J., Sherrod, L., Garmezy, N. and Rutter, M., eds. (1996). *Stress, Risk, and Resilience in Children and Adolescents: Processes, Mechanisms, and Interventions*. New York: Cambridge University Press.

Hahn, S. E. and Smith, C. S. (1999). Daily hassles and chronic stressors: conceptual and measurement issues. *Stress Medicine* 15, 89–101.

Hawk, L. W., Jr. and Baum, A. (2001). Endocrine assessment in behavioural medicine. In A. J. J. M. Vingerhoets, ed., *Assessment in Behavioural Medicine*. Hove UK: Brunner-Routledge, 413–40.

Holmes, T. H. and Rahe, R. H. (1967). The Social Readjustment Rating Scale. *Journal of Psychosomatic Research* 11, 213–18.

Hudd, S., Dumlao, J., Erdmann-Sager, D., Murray, D., Phan, E., Soukas, N. and Yokozuka, N. (2000). Stress at college: effects on health habits, health status and self-esteem. *College Student Journal* 34, 217–27.

Huizink, A. C., Mulder, E. J. H. and Buitelaar, J. K. (2004). Prenatal stress and risk for psychopathology: specific effects or induction of general susceptibility? *Psychological Bulletin* 130(1), 115–42.

Jackson, T., Fritch, A., Nagasaka, T. and Gunderson, J. (2002). Towards explaining the association between shyness and loneliness: a path analysis with American college students. *Social Behavior and Personality* 30, 263–70.

Johnston, M. and Vögele, C. (1993). Benefits of psychological preparation for surgery: a meta-analysis. *Annals of Behavioral Medicine* 15, 245–56.

Kanner, A. D., Coyne, J. C., Schaefer, C. and Lazarus, R. S. (1981). Comparison of two modes of stress measurement: daily hassles and uplifts versus major life events. *Journal of Behavioral Medicine* 4, 1–39.

Kasl, S. V. and Jones, B. A. (2001). Some methodological considerations in the study of psychosocial influences on health. In A. J. J. M. Vingerhoets, ed., *Assessment in Behavioural Medicine*. Hove, UK: Brunner-Routledge, 25–48.

Kelley, J. E., Lumley, M. A. and Leisen, J. C. (1997). Health effects of emotional disclosure in rheumatoid arthritis patients. *Health Psychology* 16, 331–40.

Kiecolt-Glaser, J. K. and Glaser, R. (1995). Measurement of immune response. In S. Cohen, R. C. Kessler and L. Underwood Gordon, eds., *Measuring Stress: A Guide for Health and Social Scientists*. New York: Oxford University Press, 213–30.

Kiecolt-Glaser, J. K., Marucha, P. T., Malarkey, W. B., Mercado, A. M. and Glaser, R. (1995). Slowing of wound healing by psychological stress. *The Lancet* 346, 1194–6.

Kiecolt-Glaser, J. K., Page, G. G., Marucha, P. T., MacCallum, R. C. and Glaser, R. (1998). Psychological influences on surgical recovery: Perspectives from psychoneuroimmunology. *American Psychologist* 53, 1209–18.

Kobasa, S. C. (1979). Stressful life events and health: an inquiry into hardiness. *Journal of Personality and Social Psychology* 37, 1–11.

Koenig, H. G., George, L. K., Stangl, D. and Tweed, D. L. (1995). Hospital stressors experienced by elderly medical inpatients: developing a hospital stress index. *International Journal of Psychiatry in Medicine* 25, 103–22.

Lazarus, R. S. and Folkman, S. (1984). *Stress, Appraisal, and Coping.* New York: Springer.

Lehrer, P. M. and Woolfolk, R. L., eds. (1993). *Principles and Practice of Stress Management*, 2nd edn. New York: Guilford.

Lester, N., Smart, L. and Baum, A. (1994). Measuring coping flexibility. *Psychology and Health* 9, 409–24.

Litz, B. T. (1992). Emotional numbing in combat related post-traumatic stress disorder: a critical review and reformulation. *Clinical Psychology Review* 12, 417–32.

Lovallo, W. R. (1997). *Stress and Health: Biological and Psychological Interactions.* London and Thousand Oaks, CA: Sage.

Marsland, A. L., Bachen, E. A., Cohen, S., Rabin, B. S. and Manuck, S. (2002). Stress, immune reactivity and susceptibility to infectious disease. *Physiology & Behavior* 77, 711–16.

Matheny, K. B., Aycock, D. W., Pugh, J. L., Curlette, W. L. and Canella, K. A. S. (1986). Stress coping: a qualitative and quantitative synthesis with implications with implications for treatment. *Counseling Psychology* 14, 499–549.

McCabe, P. M., Sheridan, J. F., Weiss, J. M., Natelson, B. H. and Pare, W. P. (2000). Animal models of disease. *Physiology and Behavior* 68, 501–7.

McEwen, B. S. (1998). Protective and damaging effects of stress mediators. *New England Journal of Medicine* 338, 171–8.

McEwen, B. S. and Stellar, E. (1993). Stress and the individual: mechanisms leading to disease. *Archives of Internal Medicine* 153, 2093–101.

Meichenbaum, D. and Deffenbacher, J. L. (1988). Stress incoculation training. *Counselling Psychologist* 16, 69–90.

Monroe, S. M. and Simons, A. D. (1991). Diathesis-stress theories in the context of life stress research: implications for the depressive disorders. *Psychological Bulletin* 110, 406–25.

Montgomery, R. L., Haemerlie, F. M. and Edwards, M. (1991). Social, personal, and interpersonal deficits in socially anxious people. *Journal of Social Behavior and Personality* 6, 859–72.

Morley, S., Eccleston, C. and Williams, A. (1999). Systematic review and meta-analysis of randomized clinical trials of cognitive behavior therapy and behavior therapy for chronic pain in adults, excluding headache. *Pain* 80, 1–13.

Mowinski-Jennings, B. and Staggers, N. (1994). A critical analysis of hardiness. *Nursing Research* 43, 274–81.

Muhlestein, J. B. (2000). Chronic infection and coronary artery disease. *Medical Clinics of North America* 84, 123–48.

Noshpitz, J. D. and Coddington R. D., eds. (1990). *Stressors and the Adjustment Disorders.* New York: Wiley.

Nyklicek, I., Vingerhoets, A. J. J. M. and Denollet, J. (2002). Emotional (non)expression and health: data, questions, and challenges. *Psychology and Health* 17, 517–28.

O' Keefe, M. K. and Baum, A. (1990). Conceptual and methodological issues in the study of chronic stress. *Stress Medicine* 6, 105–15.

Paarlberg, K. M., Vingerhoets, A. J. J. M., Passchier, J., Dekker, G. A. and Van Geijn, H. P. (1995). Psychosocial factors and pregnancy outcome: a review with emphasis on methodological issues. *Journal of Psychosomatic Research* 39, 563–95.

Patrick, C., Padgett, D. K., Schlesinger, H. J., Cohen, J. and Burns, B. J. (1992). Serious physical illness as a stressor: effects on family use of medical services. *General Hospital Psychiatry* 14, 219–27.

Pearlin, L. I. and Schooler, C. (1978). The structure of coping. *Journal of Health and Social Behaviour* 19, 2–21.

Penley, J. A., Tomaka, J. and Wiebe, J. S. (2002). The association of coping to physical and psychological health outcomes: a meta-analytic review. *Journal of Behavioral Medicine* 25, 551–603.

Pennebaker, J. W. (1982). *The Psychology of Physical Symptoms.* New York: Springer.

Pennebaker, J. W. (1994). Psychological symptom reporting: perceptual and emotional aspects of chemical sensitivity: symptom perception. *Toxicology and Industrial Health* 10, 497–511.

Pennebaker, J. W. (1997). Health effects of the expression (and non-expression) of emotions through writing. In A. J. J. M. Vingerhoets, F. J. van Bussel and A. J. W. Boelhouwer, eds., *The (Non)expression of Emotions in Health and Disease.* Tilburg, The Netherlands: Tilburg University Press, 267–78.

Prugh, D. G. and Thompson II, T. L. (1990). Illness as a source of stress: acute illness, chronic illness, and surgical disorders. In J. D. Noshpitz and R. D. Coddington, eds., *Stressors and the Adjustment Disorders.* New York: Wiley, 60–142.

Reason, J. (1988). Stress and cognitive failure. In S. Fisher, ed., *Handbook of Life Stress, Cognition, and Health.* Oxford: Wiley, 405–21.

Rice, P. L. (1999). *Stress and Health.* Pacific Grove, CA: Brooks/Cole.

Russek, L. G. S. and Schwartz, G. E. R. (1998). Reducing stress in the intensive care unit: integrating mind–body values with modern technology. *Advances in Mind–Body Medicine* 14, 71–3.

Salmon, P. (1992). Psychological factors in surgical stress: implications for management. *Clinical Psychology Review* 12, 681–704.

Schechter, J. O. and Leigh, L. (1990). Illness as stress: accidents and toxic ingestions. In J. D. Noshpitz and R. D. Coddington, eds., *Stressors and the Adjustment Disorders.* New York: Wiley, 143–59.

Scheier, M. F., Carver, C. S. and Bridges, M. W. (2001). Optimism, pessimism, and well-being. In E. C. Chang, ed., *Optimism & Pessimism: Implications for Theory, Research, and Practice.* Washington, DC: American Psychological Association, 189–216.

Schulz, R. and Beach, S. R. (1999). Caregiving as a risk factor for mortality: the caregiver health effects study. *JAMA* 282, 2215–19.

Schum, T. R. (1989). Effects of hospitalization derived from a family diary: review of the literature. *Clinical Pediatrics* 28, 366–70.

Selye, H. (1956/1976). *The Stress of Life.* New York: McGraw-Hill.

Sinclair, R. R. and Tetrick, L. E. (2000). Implications of item wording for hardiness structure, relation with neuroticism, and stress buffering. *Journal of Research in Personality* 34, 1–25.

Smith, A. (1990). Stress and information processing. In M. Johnston and L. Wallace, eds., *Stress and Medical Procedures.* Oxford: Oxford University Press, 58–79.

Smyth, J. M. (1998). Written emotional expression: effect sizes, outcome types, and moderating variables. *Journal of Consulting and Clinical Psychology* 66, 174–84.

Smyth, J. M., Stone, A. A., Hurewitz, A. and Kaell, A. (1999). Effects of writing about stressful experiences on symptom reduction in patients with asthma or rheumatoid arthritis. *JAMA* 281, 1304–9.

Stone, A. (1995). Measurement of affective response. In S. Cohen, R. C. Kessler and L. Underwood Gordon, eds., *Measuring Stress: A Guide for Health and Social Scientists.* New York: Oxford University Press, 122–47.

Strange, K. S., Kerr, L. R., Andrews, H. N., Emerman, J. T. and Weinberg, J. (2000). Psychosocial stressors and mammary tumor growth: an animal model. *Neurotoxicology and Teratology* 22, 89–102.

Taylor, S. E., Klein, L. C., Lewis, B. P., Gruenewald, T. L., Gurung, R. A. R. and Updegraff, J. A. (2000). Biobehavioural responses to stress in females: tend-and-befriend, not fight-or-flight. *Psychological Review* 107, 411–29.

Tedstone, J. E. and Tarrier, N. (2003). Posttraumatic stress disorder following medical illness and treatment. *Clinical Psychology Review* 23, 409–48.

Thayer, J. F. and Lane, R. D. (2000). A model of neurovisceral integration, emotion regulation, and dysregulation. *Journal of Affective Disorders* 61, 201–16.

Van der Ploeg, H. M. (1988). Stressful medical events: a survey of patients' perceptions. In S. Maes and C. D. Spielberger, eds., *Topics in Health Psychology.* Chichester: Wiley, 193–203.

Van Servellen, G., Lewis, C. E. and Leake, B. (1990). The stresses of hospitalization among AIDS patients on integrated and special care units. *International Journal of Nursing Studies* 27, 235–47.

Van Sonderen, E. and Sanderman, R. (2001). Social support: conceptual issues and assessment strategies. In A. J. J. M. Vingerhoets, ed., *Assessment in Behavioural Medicine.* Hove, UK: Brunner-Routledge, 161–78.

Vedhara, K., Wang, E. C. Y., Fox, J. D. and Irwin, M. (2001). The measurement of stress-related immune dysfunction in humans: an introduction to psychoneuroimmunology. In A. J. J. M. Vingerhoets, ed., *Assessment in Behavioural Medicine.* Hove, UK: Brunner-Routledge, 441–80.

Vingerhoets, A. J. J. M., Cornelius, R. R., Van Heck, G. L. and Becht, M. C. (2000). Adult crying: a model and review of the literature. *Review of General Psychology* 4, 354–77.

Vingerhoets, A. J. J. M. and Perski, A. (2000). The psychobiology of stress. In A. A. Kaptein, A. W. P. M. Appels and K. Orth-Gomér, eds., *Psychology in Medicine.* Houten: Wolters Kluwer International, 34–49.

Wadhwa, P. D., Sandman, C. A. and Farite, T. (2001). The neurobiology of stress in human pregnancy: implications for prematurity and development of the fetal central nervous system. *Progress in Brain Research* 133, 131–42.

Weidner, G., Kohlman, C. W., Dotzauer, E. and Burns, L. R. (1996). The effects of academic stress on health behaviors in young adults. *Anxiety, Stress, and Coping – An International Journal* 9, 123–33.

Weisberg, M. B. and Clavel, A. L. (1999). Why is chronic pain so difficult to treat? *Postgraduate Medicine* 106, 141–64.

Wethington, E., Almeida, D., Brown, G. W., Frank, E. and Kessler, R. C. (2001). The assessment of stressor exposure. In A. J. J. M. Vingerhoets, ed., *Assessment in Behavioural Medicine*. Hove, UK: Brunner-Routledge, 113–34.

White, M. and Ritchie, J. (1984). Psychological stressors in ante-partum hospitalizations: reports from pregnant women. *Maternal-Child Nursing Journal* 13, 47–56.

Wierzbicki, W. B. and Hagmeyer, K. O. (2000). Helicobacter pylori, chlamydia pneumoniae, and cytomegalovirus: chronic infections and coronary heart disease. *Pharmacotherapy* 20, 52–63.

Chapter Six

COPING

Lynn B. Myers, Stanton P. Newman and Kazuyo Enomoto

CHAPTER OUTLINE

This chapter provides a background to the development of coping research. It then describes two different approaches to coping: the dispositional approach, focusing on the repressive coping style and monitoring and blunting; and the situational approach, focusing on Lazarus and Folkman's (1984) model. The measurement of coping is introduced. This is followed by a section on conceptual and methodological issues in coping research. Finally interventions to improve coping are discussed.

KEY CONCEPTS

coping interventions
defence
dispositional approach
dispositional optimism
emotion-focused coping
individual differences
locus of control
measurement of coping

monitoring and blunting
neuroticism
primary appraisal
problem-focused coping
repressive coping style
secondary appraisal
situational approach
social support

INTRODUCTION

In health psychology, coping is used to describe the different ways in which people try to deal with stress. Some of these ways may be more successful than others. Coping is central to stress research, and since the 1970s there has been a vast amount of research on coping with chronic illnesses, life events and hassles. The concept of coping has come to play a central role in health psychologists' attempts to understand a different range of responses to illness and procedural stress as well as outcomes in the health and disease process.

EARLY RESEARCH

The study of an individual's response to stressful situations, and hence what can be seen as the origins of coping, came about in the nineteenth century with the Freudian notion of the defences, mainly repression (Freud, 1957). There were some attempts to demonstrate defence mechanisms such as repression experimentally (e.g. Wilkinson & Cargill, 1955; McCullough, Smith & Walker, 1976). However, these studies were not very successful, and consequently their study had declined by the 1970s.

The study of coping *per se* entered the psychological literature in the 1960s with the use of the word coping and related terminology such as coping styles and coping resources (see Parker & Endler, 1996). This work initially came directly from research on defence, but, whereas research on defence mechanisms tended to refer to rather rigid ways of dealing with stress, coping behaviour came to be seen to be much more flexible (Haan, 1965). What distinguishes later work on coping from the earlier work on defence mechanisms is that researchers in the 1960s and 1970s studied what they believed to be much more adaptive defences and ended up studying conscious strategies that people used when encountering stressful situations. However, even today there is still is confusion as to exactly what is defence and what is coping (Singer, 1990).

Early research on coping tended to focus on coping in response to acute events such as life-threatening or traumatic life events, whereas later this focus was broadened to include such events as chronic illness and daily hassles. By focusing on these highly stressful events, early coping researchers found that dispositional factors were poor predictors of specific coping responses, because, although individuals may have preferred coping responses, their choices are limited in extreme situations. Hence the study of situational variables became the prominent theme in coping research, and this legacy can be seen today (see Parker & Endler, 1996).

COPING MODELS AND THEORIES

There are predominantly two main approaches to coping. In both, the fundamental question is whether certain forms of coping are more adaptive, in the sense that they lead to better outcomes such as psychological well-being. The *dispositional approach* looks at whether specific coping styles or dispositions enable people to cope better across situations. The *situational approach* looks at the process of coping and whether there are specific strategies that are useful in different situations.

THE DISPOSITIONAL APPROACH

The dispositional view of coping focuses on relatively stable individual differences in coping, often referred to as coping styles. This section focuses on two of these styles: repressive coping and monitoring and blunting.

Repressive Coping Style

As discussed in the introduction, early attempts to demonstrate repression experimentally were problematic partly due to difficulty in identifying repression for empirical research purposes. One solution has been to treat repression as an individual difference variable rather than a state, and to measure it using questionnaires. Most laboratory studies in the 1960s and early 1970s used the Byrne Repression Sensitization Scale (Byrne, 1964) to measure repression. However, the problem with this scale is that it correlates very highly with measures of trait anxiety, and consequently does not discriminate between low-trait anxious individuals and repressors, since scoring as a 'repressor' on the Byrne scale can either mean that you are a repressor or you are truly low anxious. In response, Weinberger, Schwartz & Davidson (1979) redefined repression based on the pattern of scores obtained from self-report measures of trait anxiety and defensiveness. Individuals with a repressive coping style (repressors) were defined by their low scores on a measure of trait anxiety (or the Byrne Repression Sensitization Scale), and high scores on a measure of defensiveness such as the Marlowe–Crowne Social Desirability Scale (Marlowe–Crowne; Crowne & Marlowe, 1964). The Marlowe–Crowne was used as it assesses repressive defensiveness independently of trait anxiety scales. Weinberger et al. (1979) proposed a four-fold classification of individuals differentiated in terms of their coping styles: *low anxious* (low anxiety–low defensiveness), *repressor* (low anxiety–high defensiveness), [non-defensive] *high anxious* (high anxiety–low defensiveness), and *defensive high anxious* (high anxiety–high defensiveness) (see figure 6.1).

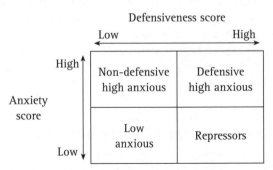

Figure 6.1 The four-fold classification of coping styles (from Weinberger et al., 1979)

One of the defining characteristics of individuals who have a repressive coping style is that when they are put in potentially stressful situations they report low levels of distress but are physiologically very reactive (e.g. increased heart rate, raised blood pressure). This repressive style was noted in the original Weinberger et al. study and is a widely replicated finding in both male and female participants, in students samples, the general population and patients, and using different measures of anxiety and defensiveness (see Myers, 2000 for a review). None of the non-repressor groups exhibit this repressive style.

How do repressors manage to experience such low levels of negative emotion? There is considerable evidence from various studies that repressors use an avoidant style of processing negative information and have a capacity to avoid socially threatening information. For example, in one study undergraduate students watched either an unpleasant film about the after-effects of atomic bomb testing on a pacific island, or a neutral film about Yellowstone National Park. Afterwards, participants were asked to recall a happy memory. Repressors were faster at recalling happy memories after watching the unpleasant film than the neutral film. Non-repressors exhibited the opposite effect (Boden & Baumeister, 1997). So it seems as if repressors use happiness effectively as a way of distracting themselves from distressing information. Avoiding processing negative emotional material may result in poor recall of unpleasant memories, and a number of studies have demonstrated links between repressive coping and the accessibility of negative memories (e.g. Davis, 1987). Other memory studies have found that (a) repressors' own memories are emotionally impoverished, with repressors reporting experiencing less unpleasant affect during daily reporting of moods compared with non-repressors (Cutler, Larson & Bunce, 1996), and (b) repressors have a distinctive style of processing negative material that affects more than their own personal histories. Repressors were significantly worse than non-repressors in recalling negative material in both intentional and incidental recall tasks (Myers & Brewin, 1995; Myers, Brewin & Power, 1998). Consequently, repressors are conceptualized as a group who avoid negative affect.

Although repressors appear to be psychologically healthy, this is not the same for physical health. There is considerable evidence which suggests that the repressive coping style may be associated with adverse physical health, and it has been hypothesized that repressors' not attending to somatic information may be linked with poor health. It has been reported that repressors exhibit impaired immune functioning, increased incidence of cancer, high blood cholesterol and cardiovascular disease (see Myers, 2000, for a review). Therefore, repressors are an important group for health psychologists to study.

Measurement of repressive coping

Although the Weinberger et al. (1979) trait anxiety/defensiveness method has become an increasingly popular method of defining repressive coping, different measures of trait anxiety and defensiveness are used as well as varying ways of identifying repressors and control groups; and later, Weinberger (1990) developed the Weinberger

Adjustment Inventory (WAI) to measure repressive coping which has been found to be a comparable method to the trait anxiety/defensiveness method, with the distress sub-scale of the WAI correlating highly with trait anxiety and the repressive defensiveness and the self-restraint subscales of the WAI correlating with the Marlowe–Crowne.

One of the major difficulties with this area of research is the fact that this method depends on categorizing people into groups based on their location along two dimensions, and it is difficult to determine where to allocate individuals who are not at the extremes of the dimensions. For example, various studies identify their participants at the beginning of the study by screening a large number of potential participants and choosing extreme scorers on trait anxiety and defensiveness to define repressors, low-anxious, high-anxious and (possibly) defensive high-anxious groups. Other studies have used the entire available pool of participants and hence do not use such stringent measures in defining different groups, usually using median splits on trait anxiety and defensiveness to identify repressors and control groups, thereby not losing any potential participants. Therefore, although measuring instruments used to identify repressors are comparable, it is important to note how repressors and control groups have been defined in different studies (see Myers, 2000, for a review).

Monitors and blunters

The construct of monitoring and blunting coping styles was developed by Miller (e.g. Miller & Mangan, 1983) to identify different ways people deal with stress, and has been applied mainly in health contexts. These styles refer to the characteristic ways that individuals respond cognitively and emotionally to potentially distressing information. So, for example, if an individual encounters an aversive situation, such as major surgery, their levels of arousal depend on the amount of attention they direct to the stressor. They can lower such arousal by reducing the impact of threat cues by using such strategies as distraction, denial or re-interpretation. These strategies are called blunting and appear to be adaptive if the situation is out of the control of the individual. Monitoring strategies appear to be more adaptive if some degree of control over the situation is available. The strategies in this case include seeking information about the stressor, monitoring the source of stress. Monitoring strategies tend to be more effective because, although they cause initially increased arousal, they allow the individual to gain control over the stressor in the long term and therefore reduce the impact of threat.

Miller (1996) established that in the face of a health threat, those who have been identified as monitors wanted to know more, and those identified as blunters wanted to know less.

Measurement of monitoring and blunting

Monitoring and blunting is measured by the Miller Behavioural Style Scale (MBSS; Miller, 1987). The MBSS consists of 4 scenarios (e.g. 'imagine you are afraid of flying and have to go somewhere by plane'), each of which is followed by 8 coping options, half of them reflecting monitoring (e.g. 'I would carefully read the information provided about safety features in the plane') and half of them reflecting blunting (e.g. 'I would watch an in-flight film even if I had seen it before').

One of the problems with the MBSS is that it contains only *uncontrollable* fictitious situations, where monitoring may be unadaptive and blunting may be seen as more adaptive. Similarly, whereas repressive coping has been applied in a broad range of situations, the concept of monitoring/blunting is widely applied in the health field, so it may be more sensible to have scenarios reflecting these situations, with some controllable and some uncontrollable. In addition, the blunting scale has been shown to have unacceptably low internal consistency, suggesting that it is not a homogenous scale. For example, in a study investigating information-seeking in daughters of women with early breast cancer, internal consistency of the blunting scale was only 0.41 (Rees & Bath, 2000).

COPING AS PROCESS: THE SITUATIONAL APPROACH

One of the main proponents of coping as a process is Lazarus (e.g. Lazarus, 1993; Lazarus & Folkman, 1984). Although Lazarus has claimed that both dispositional and situational perspectives are essential for understanding coping, he defines coping and its functions from a situational viewpoint: 'constantly changing cognitive and behavioral efforts to manage specific external and/or internal demands that are appraised as taxing or exceeding the resources of the person' (Lazarus & Folkman, 1984: 141).

This is a very broad definition and includes the decisions and actions taken by an individual faced with a stressful life event as well as the accompanying negative emotions to constitute coping and the cognitive and behavioural efforts to manage the stressful situation. Lazarus and Folkman see coping as a psychological mechanism for managing external stress, and coping is our attempt to change a stressor or make a response to the stressful situation. They see the response to a potential stressful situation as encompassing an evaluation process which they termed appraisal. They have described two forms of appraisal (see figure 6.2).

Primary appraisal: The individual appraises the situation in terms of their own well-being. If the situation is perceived as either potentially or actually harmful, then it is regarded as potentially stressful. Alternatively, if the situation is perceived as benign positive, then the individual views the situation as either potentially or actually beneficial to them. It may be that the individual sees no relevance to them in terms of threat to their well-being, either actual or potential, or in terms of benefit to their well-being, and in this case the situation is viewed as irrelevant.

Secondary appraisal: Where the situation is evaluated as a threat or a potential threat to their well-being, the individual will then need to decide on a course of action. The coping strategy that the person uses takes account of the level of threat in relation to the resources they have available. According to the theory, the coping response should aim at reducing the demands placed upon the individual, and hence

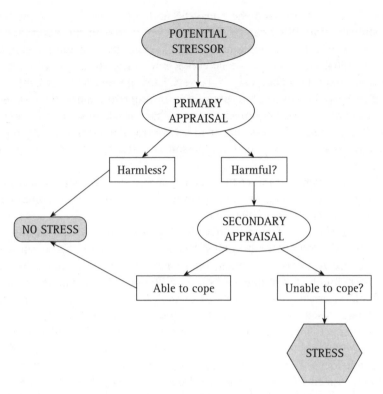

Figure 6.2 Two-stage appraisal of stress (Folkman & Lazarus, 1984)

the level of stress. In any situation stress is related to the relationship between demands and resources available, and this is determined by the relationship between primary and secondary appraisal.

It is rare to find any situation which will remain static, even from a demand or resources point of view, and for this reason situations are continually re-appraised in the light of further information and perceptions. As a result, coping behaviour may change according to the re-appraisal.

Lazarus and Folkman (1984) also identified two general types of coping:

Problem-focused coping: This is directed towards altering the relationship between the demands of the situation and the resources available. Problem-focused coping will only come into existence if the individual perceives that either the problem they are facing or the resources they have available are changeable, and that they can bring about such change. There are many examples of problem-focused coping such as leaving a job which is perceived as stressful or going to college to learn more about a subject in order to feel more comfortable in everyday life.

Emotion-focused coping: When faced with a problem that has no solution and with little or no scope for individual control, the use of problem-focused coping would be much less appropriate. For instance, a relative who is dying in hospital will die regardless of what we do, and there may be nothing which can be done to change the stressful situation. What can be done, however, is to alter the emotional response to such a situation; this can be done either behaviourally or cognitively. Behaviourally the individual may seek out social contacts with friends and loved ones, in order to gain some support, or they may work very hard in order to think of the situation less, or they may turn to alcohol, drugs, etc. in order to change their state of consciousness and awareness. Cognitively, someone may re-appraise the situation in order to reduce the amount of stress that it gives rise to. For instance, with regard to a dying relative one might say that the person is suffering, and dying will stop the suffering.

It is likely, however, that rather than having such clear-cut distinctions as problem-focused coping and an emotion coping strategy, both are used in conjunction with each other for at least part of the time.

There are multitudes of studies investigating the two types of coping in many different illnesses. Research on coping has generally found that problem-focused coping is related to better adjustment than emotion-focused coping (Aldwin, 1994). This has been found in a number of chronic illnesses. For example, in individuals with multiple sclerosis, higher levels of distress have been found to be associated with emotion-focused coping (Beatty et al., 1998; Jean, Paul & Beatty, 1999). Similar findings have been found in breast cancer patients (Ben-Zur, Gilbar & Lev, 2001) and patients with Parkinson's Disease (Sanders-Dewey, Mullins & Chaney, 2001). Moreover, emotion-focused coping and depressive attributional style have been shown to be closely linked (Bruder-Mattson & Hovanitz, 1990). However, sometimes the division between problem-focused and emotion-focused coping is not meaningful, for example, in a study investigating coping strategies and distress in spouses of suspected dementia cases, the distinction between the two types of coping was not important in predicting distress (O'Rourke & Cappeliez, 2002).

Different types of coping may be associated with different treatment options. For example, in a study of over 2,500 obese patients in Sweden, patients either chose conventional treatment or surgery. Surgical patients displayed lower levels of problem-focused coping and higher levels of emotion-focused coping. As in previous studies, emotion-focused coping was positively related to distress (Ryden et al., 2001).

Measurement

Common generic measures include the revised Ways of Coping Questionnaire (WOC; Lazarus & Folkman, 1984), where a particular stressful event is identified and individuals specify how they coped with it on 8 subscales: confrontive coping, distancing, self-controlling, seeking social support, accepting responsibility, escape–avoidance, planful problem solving, and positive reappraisal. These subscales can be combined to reflect either problem-focused or emotion-focused coping.

Another popular generic measure is the COPE (Carver, Scheir & Weintraub, 1989). In this measure the authors further subdivided problem-focused and emotion-focused coping, as they believe that there are a variety of distinct ways to solve problems or to regulate emotions. Problem-focused coping is subdivided into scales measuring active coping, planning, suppression of competing activities, restraint coping and seeking social support for instrumental reasons. Emotion-focused coping is measured by subscales assessing seeking social support for emotional reasons, positive reinterpretation and growth, acceptance, turning to religion, and focus on and venting of emotions. There are two forms of the COPE. One assesses situational or state coping where participants respond on the basis of their most stressful recent experience. The second assesses dispositional or trait coping where participants complete the questionnaire on how they usually respond to a stressful experience. Both the WOC and the COPE are widely used instruments, and an electronic database search using Web of Science indicates that they have both been cited well over 1,000 times.

However, use of checklists to measure coping is not without difficulty, as a study which looked at how students coped with exam-related stress reveals. The researchers devised alternate forms of the revised WOC. One of these took the form of a daily checklist which students had to complete each evening for 7 days prior to an examination. The second form used the traditional retrospective checklist, which students filled in 7 days after the examination. On average only 25 per cent of shared variance was found between daily and retrospective accounts. For students who reported the highest levels of examination stress, less than 10 per cent of the retrospective coping score was predicted by the daily measures. The authors concluded that retrospective coping reports cannot be considered to measure coping obtained in closer proximity to the event (Smith, Leffingwell & Ptacek, 1999). Similarly, in another study of people from the general population, participants were required to give momentary reports of coping via a palm-top computer and short-term retrospective reports of coping. There was relatively poor correspondence between momentary and retrospective coping, with some reports of momentary coping not reported retrospectively and vice versa. Cognitive coping was more likely to be under-reported retrospectively and behavioural coping was over-reported (Stone et al., 1998).

DO PATTERNS OF COPING CHANGE OVER TIME?

Frazier (2002) followed patients with Parkinson's disease (PD) over two years to see whether coping was stable, supporting a dispositional model of coping, or changing, supporting a contextual model of coping. PD can be seen as good example of coping with a chronic illness as it is progressive and creates impairment in physical (e.g. tremor), cognitive (e.g. attentional difficulties) and psychosocial (e.g. loss of control) functioning. It was found that as the disease progressed, distress increased and quality of life decreased. Overall, there was no change in coping strategies used to manage disease-related stress, supporting a dispositional model of coping. However, dispositional coping was correlated with poorer physical and mental outcomes, whereas change in coping strategies (contextual) was correlated with more optimal outcomes. Younger patients who reported their illness was less severe and who experienced less distress were more likely to change their use of coping strategies. So evidence supporting both types of coping was found.

Individual Differences and Situational Coping

A number of individual difference traits have been linked with different types of situational coping. Some of these are briefly discussed below.

Neuroticism: Most research has shown that neuroticism is linked to maladaptive coping. For example, in a sample of adolescents who were rated as exhibiting some degree of maladjustment, neuroticism predicted avoidant coping (Gomez et al., 1999).

Locus of control: This involves individual differences in beliefs about control over reinforcement. Individuals who exhibit an internal locus of control perceive personal mastery over outcomes, whereas those who exhibit an external locus of control perceive that reinforcement is due to external factors. There is an extensive literature indicating that when those with an external locus of control are confronted with stressors they exhibit a wide range of maladaptive coping responses (see Folkman, 1984). For instance, patients who suffer from non-epileptic seizures were found to exhibit a higher external locus of control and more escape–avoidance coping strategies than a non-clinical control group (Goldstein et al., 2000).

Dispositional optimism: Most studies have found that dispositional optimism is associated with adaptive coping in response to physical challenges (Scheier, Weintraub & Carver, 1986). In a study of pregnant women, optimism was associated with less use of avoidance coping and lower emotional distress (Yali & Lobel, 2002).

Social Support and Coping

Social support has been thought only to be beneficial when individuals are coping with stress, with no positive effect at times without stress (Cohen & Wills, 1985). However, social support may lead to not having a life event to deal with. For instance, consider two women each with a young child and a demanding job when the child becomes ill. Friends and relatives of one woman may help look after the child and allow the person to carry on working. Members of the other woman's social network may not help her or be unreliable. Consequently, one woman may be secure in her job whereas the other woman may lose her job. Social support affects how individuals cope with stressful events, and how individuals cope may influence their use of social support in the future. The relationship between social support and coping is complex. (See Pierce, Sarason & Sarason, 1996, for a review.)

Issues in Coping Research

Besides the use of retrospective recall in coping research, there are problems with both its conceptualization and measurement (Coyne & Gottlieb, 1996). Although there have been hundreds of studies using the sorts of measures outlined above, Coyne & Gottlieb (1996) concluded that little progress has been made in understanding the role of coping in adaptation to stress. 'The study of coping has become too narrowly method-bound, defined by uncritical application of standardized checklists to diverse populations and situations. These checklists are used with little regard for their appropriateness and often without a clearly defined specific aim or clearly defined hypothesis' (Coyne & Gottlieb, 1996: 961).

A major conceptual issue in coping research is whether a person is coping with a discrete one-off trauma, or a chronic condition, or illness such as multiple sclerosis or diabetes. In the case of a chronic condition, coping can become automatic and anticipatory. Coyne and Gottlieb take up the issues of coping with chronic illnesses within their paper. They argue that coping checklists do not measure a number of concepts which are central to coping in these situations and that the concept of coping should encompass a wider range of adaptive thought and behaviour. For example, anticipatory coping, which happens before a stressful situation, may avert the stressor, and as a result there will be nothing for a coping inventory to measure, as there will be no stressful situation. So, someone with diabetes, which is controlled with insulin injections, may avoid high or low blood sugars by carefully monitoring blood sugars and balancing the amount of insulin they take with diet and exercise. Thereby there is no stress and nothing to cope with overtly that could be measured by a checklist.

Habitual or automatic behaviour should be included within coping in chronic conditions. For instance, in multiple sclerosis, patients and their families may refine coping strategies that have been effective in the past for dealing with exacerbations of the illness, and these strategies may become a routine. So if the multiple sclerosis patient no longer thinks of a flare up of their illness as a catastrophe, they may not be thinking about it, and dealing effectively with the exacerbation will not be recognized as a coping strategy.

The use of generic scales also has other problems. For example, a scale imposes a specific structure in that it is based on the assumption that people encounter a stressor, make appraisals of what is at stake, select coping strategies, and experience particular emotions as a result. Coyne and co-workers (e.g. Coyne & Calarco 1995; Gottlieb & Gignac, 1996) have found that when comparing checklists to the individual's own narrative, the checklist way of eliciting data only fits some of the people some of the time. There is great variation among respondents and across situations, with some people never making an appraisal of what is at stake, never knowing what their resources are and what they are trying to achieve. Importantly, many people do not make a primary or secondary appraisal until they have to give one in response to the questionnaire.

Another problem is selecting the stressor, as checklists force the individual to choose a stressor. Consequently, different people will complete the same questionnaire for totally different types of stressful events, which may make the comparison between coping profiles quite invalid. It has been suggested that when using standardized questionnaires, the researcher should clearly state the study aims and objectives together with theory-driven hypotheses, and consider whether checklists are suitable and should develop more situation-specific checklists geared to their hypotheses. The use of semi-structured interviews, although labour intensive, should also be considered (Coyne & Gottlieb, 1996).

INTERVENTIONS TO IMPROVE COPING

Despite the difficulties in conceptualizing and assessing coping, there have been an increasing number of studies evaluating interventions aimed at improving adaptation to chronic illness by enhancing coping responses. These interventions usually provide patients with support and specific information and alternative coping skills to improve their adaptation to particular stressors.

Lutgendorf et al. (1998) undertook an intervention study that measured changes in coping skills in a group of HIV-positive gay men. Participants were randomized into a 10-week cognitive behavioural skills management programme which was designed to increase cognitive and behavioural coping skills related to managing the distress of symptomatic HIV, or a waiting-list control condition. Members of the treatment group showed an increase in cognitive coping strategies involving positive reframing (to see their situation in a new light) and acceptance (being HIV positive and having symptoms), whereas controls showed decrements in coping abilities. Increase in acceptance showed the greatest magnitude of post-intervention change, and it mediated the effects of the interventions on distress outcomes.

However, in reviews of the literature both Coyne & Racioppo (2000) and de Ridder & Schreurs (2001) concluded that most intervention studies do not measure coping, and the success of the intervention is usually inferred by improved health outcomes, reduced psychological distress and increased quality of life. Since the publication of these two reviews, a number of intervention studies have measured coping pre and post intervention. Three of these are discussed below with a description of the coping intervention they employed.

Kennedy et al. (2003) undertook a controlled trial comparing spinal cord injury (SCI) patients who received a Coping Effectiveness Training intervention ($n = 45$) with matched controls ($n = 40$). The COPE was used as a measure of coping as well as measures of well-being.

Coping Effectiveness training (CET) is based on Lazurus & Folkman's (1984) theory of stress and coping, but also uses strategies from cognitive behaviour therapy. It was originally developed for use in HIV (Chesney & Folkman, 1994) and was modified for individuals who have recently suffered SCI (King & Kennedy, 1999). The intervention consists of seven, 60- to 75-minute sessions run twice a week for 6 to 9 people. The content of each session is as follows:

Session 1:   The concept of stress is introduced. The need to develop the ability to think critically about appraising and coping with situations are discussed.

Session 2:   In this session the focus is on appraisal skills.

Session 3:   This session introduces problem-solving, including working through several scenarios that are commonly experienced by people with SCI.

Session 4:   Connections and distinctions between thoughts, feelings and behaviour are examined.

Session 5:   How to be aware of and challenge negative assumptions, thoughts and expectations.

Sessions 6 & 7: Description of a 'meta-strategy' is introduced to help patients to chose appropriate ways of coping and to increase social support.

Kennedy et al. (2003) found a decrease in depression and anxiety in the intervention group at post-intervention and 6 weeks follow-up, but not in the control group. There were no differences in coping, although the patients' comments on the most effective part of the intervention involved making more positive appraisals of their situation. It may have been that the COPE was not sensitive enough to detect changes in appraisal and coping over 6 weeks.

Heckman et al. (2001) devised a coping improvement group intervention for HIV-infected older adults. This intervention focuses on teaching patients to accurately appraise sources of stress, develop active coping responses, and access social support resources to facilitate adaptive coping. In a pilot study of this intervention using a small sample ($n = 16$) and no control group, pre-test versus post-test, individuals produced higher perceptions of well-being, engaged in more problem-solving coping, and displayed more optimism about the future.

A coping intervention was devised to teach people with rheumatoid disease to cope actively with their problems (Savelkoul et al., 2001): 168 patients were randomly assigned to a coping intervention group, a mutual support control group, or a wait list control group. The intervention was aimed at improving a form of problem-solving coping and increasing social support. The problem-solving aspect of the intervention involved getting patients to describe the problem, think about all sorts of possible solutions, choose one or more solution, implement the solution or solutions and evaluate the results. Participants were allowed to use the different steps of problem-solving at their own pace, and they had homework assignments to help them to apply the content of the sessions to their own lives. Post-intervention the coping intervention group increased problem-solving coping compared to the mutual support group, but this difference did not last at 6 months follow-up. This suggests that maintenance sessions would be advisable.

SUMMARY AND CONCLUSION

In the last three decades there has been a burgeoning of research on coping since the transactional model of Lazarus in the 1970s. Although the original focus on defence and dispositional measures has been largely superseded by situational approaches, now that coping research also includes chronic stressors, the importance of more stable characteristics should be explored along with situational variables. Coping research is undergoing somewhat of a crisis, with a number of conceptual and methodological problems which have been highlighted in this chapter. However, intervention studies in chronic illness to improve coping with good measures of coping may be the way forward in clarifying the role of coping as well as its measurement. Care needs to be taken in the uncritical use of generic checklists and researchers should look for other measures, possibly specific self-measures, and consider semi-structured interviews, qualitative analyses and daily reports. In addition it remains useful to assess both dispositional and situational determinants of coping, and the incorporation of repressive coping in the wider field of coping may help to illuminate our understanding of coping. The area would also benefit from more theoretical development.

DISCUSSION POINTS

1. Do dispositional and situational approaches to coping complement each other?
2. What are the strengths and weaknesses of the Folkman & Lazarus model of stress and coping?
3. Can coping be effectively measured using self-report? What other methods have been used?
4. How important is the study of individual differences and situational coping?
5. Why is emotion-focused coping considered less effective than problem-focused coping?
6. How would you go about designing an intervention aimed at changing peoples' coping responses?

FURTHER READING

Jones, F. and Bright, J. (2001). *Stress: Myth, Theory and Research*. London: Prentice Hall.
Lazarus, R. and Folkman, S. A. (1984). *Stress, Appraisal and Coping*. New York: Springer.
Singer, J. L., ed. (1990). *Repression and Dissociation*. Chicago: University of Chicago Press.
Myers, L. B. (2000). Identifying repressors: a methodological issue for health psychology. *Psychology and Health* 15, 205–14.
Zeidner, M. and Endler, N. S., eds. (1996). *Handbook of Coping: Theory, Research, Applications*. New York: Wiley & Sons.

KEY STUDIES

Coyne, J. C. and Racioppo, M. W. (2000). Never the twain shall meet? Closing the gap between coping research and clinical intervention research. *American Psychologist* 55, 655–64.

Lutgendorf, S. K., Antoni, M. H., Ironson, G., Starr, K., Costello, N., Zuckerman, M., Klimas, N., Fletcher, A. and Schneiderman, N. (1998). Changes in cognitive coping skills and social support during cognitive behavioral stress management intervention and distress outcomes in symptomatic human immunodeficiency virus (HIV) – seropositive gay men. *Psychosomatic Medicine* 60, 204–14.

REFERENCES

Aldwin, C. (1994). *Stress, Coping and Development: An Integrative Perspective*. New York: Guilford Press.

Beatty, W. W., Hames, K. A., Blanco, C. R., Williamson, S. J., Wilbanks, S. L. and Olsen, A. (1998). Correlates of coping style in patients with multiple sclerosis. *Multiple Sclerosis* 4, 440–3.

Ben-Zur, H., Gilbar, O. and Lev, S. (2001). Coping with breast cancer: patient, spouse and dyad models. *Psychosomatic Medicine* 63, 32–9.

Boden, J. M. and Baumeister, R. M. (1997). Repressive coping: distraction using pleasant thoughts and memories. *Journal of Personality and Social Psychology* 73, 45–62.

Bruder-Mattson, S. F. and Hovanitz, C. A. (1990). Coping and attributional styles as predictors of depression. *Journal of Clinical Psychology* 46, 557–65.

Byrne, D. (1964). Repression-sensitization as a dimension of personality. In B. A. Maher, ed., *Progress in Experimental Personality Research*, volume 1. New York: Academic Press, 169–220.

Carver, C. S., Scheier, M. F. and Weintraub, J. K. (1989). Assessing coping strategies: a theoretically based approach. *Journal of Personality and Social Psychology* 56, 267–83.

Chesney, M. A. and Folkman, S. (1994). Psychological impact of HIV disease and implications for intervention. *Psychiatric Clinics of North America* 17, 163–82.

Cohen, S. and Wills, T. A. (1985). Stress, social support, and the buffering hypothesis. *Psychological Bulletin* 98, 310–57.

Coyne, J. C. and Calarco, V. (1995). Effects of experience of depression: application of focus group and survey methodologies. *Psychiatry* 58, 149–63.

Coyne, J. C. and Gottlieb, B. H. (1996). The mismeasure of coping by checklist. *Journal of Personality* 64, 959–91.

Coyne, J. C. and Racioppo, M. W. (2000). Never the twain shall meet? Closing the gap between coping research and clinical intervention research. *American Psychologist* 55, 655–64.

Crowne, D. P. and Marlowe, D. A. (1964). *The Approval Motive: Studies in Evaluative Dependence*. New York: Wiley.

Cutler, S. E., Larsen, R. J. and Bunce, S. C. (1996). Repressive coping style and the experience and recall of emotion: a naturalistic study of daily affect. *Journal of Personality* 64, 381–405.

Davis, P. J. (1987). Repression and the inaccessibility of affective memories. *Journal of Personality and Social Psychology* 53, 585–93.

de Ridder, D. and Schreurs, K. (2001). Developing interventions for chronically ill patients: is coping a helpful concept? *Clinical Psychology Review* 21, 205–40.

Folkman, S. (1984). Personal control and stress and coping processes: a theoretical analysis. *Journal of Personality and Social Psychology* 46, 839–52.

Frazier, L. (2002). Stability and change in patterns of coping with Parkinson's disease. *International Journal of Aging and Human Development* 55, 207–31.

Freud, S. (1957). Repression. In J. Strachey, ed., *The Standard Edition of the Complete Psychological Works of Sigmund Freud*, vol. 14. London: Hogarth Press, 146–58. (Original work published 1915.)

Goldstein, L. H., Drew, C., Mellers, J., Mithcell-O'Malley, S. and Oakley, D. A. (2000). Dissociation, hypnotizability, coping styles and health locus of control: characteristics of pseudoseizure patients. *Seizure - European Journal of Epilepsy* 9, 314–22.

Gomez, R., Bounds, J., Holmberg, K., Fullarton, C. and Gomez, A. (1999). Effects of neuroticism and avoidant coping style on maladjustment during early adolescence. *Personality and Individual Differences* 26, 305–19.

Gottlieb, B. and Gignac, M. (1996). Content and domain specificity of coping among family caregivers of persons with dementia. *Journal of Aging Studies* 10, 137–55.

Haan, N. (1965). Coping and defense mechanisms related to personal inventories. *Journal of Consulting Psychology* 29, 373–8.

Heckman, T. G., Kochman, A., Sikkema, K. J., Kalichman, S. C., Masters, J., Bergholte, J. and Catz, S. (2001). A pilot coping improvement intervention for late middle-aged and older adults living with HIV/AIDS in the USA. *AIDS Care - Psychological and Socio-medical Aspects of HIV/AIDS* 13, 129–39.

Jean, V. M., Paul, R. H. and Beatty, W. W. (1999). Psychological and neuropsychological predictors of coping patterns by patients with multiple sclerosis. *Journal of Clinical Psychology* 55, 21–6.

Kennedy, P., Duff, J., Evans, M. and Beedie, A. (2003). Coping effectiveness training reduces depression and anxiety following traumatic spinal cord injuries. *British Journal of Clinical Psychology* 42, 41–52.

King, C. and Kennedy, P. (1999). Coping effectiveness training for people with spinal cord injury: Preliminary results of a controlled trial. *British Journal of Clinical Psychology* 38, 5–11.

Lazarus, R. S. (1993). Coping theory and research: past, present and future. *Psychosomatic Medicine* 55, 234–47.

Lazarus, R. and Folkman, S. A. (1984). *Stress, Appraisal and Coping.* New York: Springer.

Lutgendorf, S. K., Antoni, M. H., Ironson, G., Starr, K., Costello, N., Zuckerman, M., Klimas, N., Fletcher, A. and Schneiderman, N. (1998). Changes in cognitive coping skills and social support during cognitive behavioral stress management intervention and distress outcome in symptomatic human immunodeficiency virus (HIV) – seropositive gay men. *Psychosomatic Medicine* 60, 204–14.

McCullough, M. L., Smith, C. D. and Walker, P. (1976). A note on repression. *Bulletin of the British Psychological Society* 29, 235–7.

Miller, S. M. (1987). Monitoring and blunting: validation of a questionnaire to assess styles of information seeking under threat. *Journal of Personality and Social Psychology* 52, 345–53.

Miller, S. M. (1996). Monitoring and blunting of threatening information: cognitive interference and facilitation in the coping process, In I. G. Sarason, G. R. Pierce and B. R. Sarason, eds., *Cognitive Interference: Theories, Methods, and Findings.* Mahwah, NJ: Lawrence Erlbaum, 175–90.

Miller, S. M. and Mangan, C. E. (1983). The interacting effects of information and coping style in adapting to gynecologic stress: should the doctor tell all? *Journal of Personality and Social Psychology* 45, 223–36.

Myers, L. B. (2000). Identifying repressors: a methodological issue for health psychology. *Psychology and Health* 15, 205–14.

Myers, L. B. and Brewin, C. R. (1995). Repressive coping and the recall of emotional material. *Cognition and Emotion* 9, 637–42.

Myers, L. B., Brewin, C. R. and Power, M. J. (1998). Repressive coping and the directed forgetting of emotional material. *Journal of Abnormal Psychology* 107, 141–8.

O'Rourke, N. and Cappeliez, P. (2002). Perceived control, coping and expressed burden among spouses of suspected dementia patients: analysis of the goodness-of-fit hypothesis. *Canadian Journal of Aging* 21, 385–92.

Parker, J. D. A. and Endler, N. S. (1996). Coping and defense: a historical overview. In M. Zeidner and N. S. Endler, eds., *Handbook of Coping: Theory, Research and Applications*. New York: Wiley, 3–20.

Pierce, G. R., Sarason, B. R. and Sarason, I. G., eds. (1996). *The Handbook of Social Support and the Family*. New York: Plenum.

Rees, C. E. and Bath, P. A. (2000). The psychometric properties of the Miller Behavioural Style Scale with adult daughters of women with early breast cancer: a literature review and empirical study. *Journal of Advanced Nursing* 32, 366–74.

Rydén, A., Karlsonn, J., Persson, L., Sjöström, L., Taft, C. and Sulivan, M. (2001). Obesity-related coping and distress and relationship to treatment preference. *British Journal of Clinical Psychology* 40, 177–88.

Sanders-Dewey, N. E. J., Mullins, L. L. and Chaney, J. M. (2001). Coping style, perceived uncertainty in illness, and distress in individuals with Parkinson's disease and their caregivers. *Rehabilitation Psychology* 46, 363–81.

Savelkoul, M., de Witte, L. P., Candel, M. J. J. M., Van der Tempel, H. and Van Den Borne, B. (2001). Effects of a coping intervention on patients with rheumatic diseases: results of a randomized control trial. *Arthritis Care & Research* 45, 69–76.

Scheier, M. F., Weintraub, J. K. and Carver, C. (1986). Coping with stress: divergent strategies of optimists and pessimists. *Journal of Personality and Social Psychology* 51, 1257–64.

Singer, J. L., ed. (1990). *Repression and Dissociation*. Chicago: University of Chicago Press.

Smith, R. E., Lefingwell, T. R. and Ptacek, J. T. (1999). Can people remember how they coped? Factors associated with discordance between same-day and retrospective reports. *Journal of Personality and Social Psychology* 76, 1050–61.

Stone, A. A., Schwartz, J. E., Neale, J. M., Shiffman, S., Marco, C. A., Hickcox, M., Paty, J., Porter, L. S. and Cruise, L. J. (1998). A comparison of coping assessed by ecological momentary assessment and retrospective recall. *Journal of Personality and Social Psychology* 74, 1670–80.

Weinberger, D. A. (1990). The construct validity of the repressive coping style. In J. L. Singer, ed., *Repression and Dissociation*. Chicago: University of Chicago Press, 337–86.

Weinberger, D. A., Schwartz, G. E. and Davidson, R. J. (1979). Low-anxious, high-anxious and repressive coping styles: psychometric patterns and behavioral responses to stress. *Journal of Abnormal Psychology* 88, 369–80.

Wilkinson, F. R. and Cargill, D. W. (1955). Repression elicited by story material based on the Oedipus complex. *Journal of Social Psychology* 42, 209–14.

Yali, A. M. and Lobel, M. (2002). Stress-resistance resources and coping in pregnancy. *Anxiety, Stress & Coping* 15, 289–309.

Chapter Seven

SOCIAL SUPPORT

Ralf Schwarzer, Nina Knoll and Nina Rieckmann

CHAPTER OUTLINE

The chapter deals with social factors and how they might exert an influence on health and longevity. First, a distinction is made between the concepts of social integration and social support. Following this, a more fine-grained differentiation of various social support phenomena is offered, and different approaches to their measurement are described. Moreover, individual differences in support provision and receipt are addressed. In a second section, the importance of social network characteristics along with their possible influence on longevity is discussed. Studies are described that provide evidence for the association of social factors with life expectancy, severe medical conditions, and bereavement. A third section examines the role of social factors in the onset and course of severe health conditions, such as myocardial infarction and cancer. Additionally, evidence is reviewed concerning support mobilization as a form of coping with taxing life events and circumstances.

KEY CONCEPTS

bereavement and loss

gender differences

instrumental, informational, tangible
and emotional support

longevity

measures of social network

measures of social support

onset and course of chronic illness

perceived versus received social support

social integration, social networks and
social ties

social support

stress: daily hassles versus critical life
events

support mobilization

survival

SOCIAL INTEGRATION AND SOCIAL SUPPORT: CONCEPTUAL AND MEASUREMENT ISSUES

More than a century ago, the French sociologist Durkheim (1897/1952) observed that suicide occurred more frequently among individuals who had weak connections to other people. Today, it is common knowledge that poor mental health is more prevalent among people with low social integration. Moreover, physical health and longevity appear to depend in part on social factors. What exactly these social factors are, and how they operate, continue to be difficult questions. Bowlby's (1969) Attachment Theory was a theoretical advancement. According to this theory, emotional attachment in early life promotes a sense of security and self-esteem that ultimately provides the basis on which individuals develop lasting, secure and loving relationships in adult life. Subsequent research has established a pattern of psychosocial variables that are connected to diverse health outcomes in a complicated and seemingly inconsistent manner.

This chapter presents an introduction to the relationship between social support and illness and death. Health is determined not only by biological, but also by social and psychological factors. Epidemiological studies have linked mortality rates to social networks, thus indicating that social factors have a beneficial effect on longevity. Moreover, studies on patients attribute increased survival rates to existing close social bonds. In the case of conjugal loss, for example, widowers are particularly at risk of illness and premature death if they lack a compensating network of support providers. Health psychology is searching for the mechanisms that help explain such associations. Conceptually, it is important to distinguish between social integration and social support. Both constructs, although closely related, will be treated separately in the present chapter.

Besides social support and social integration, further differentiation has to be made in order to understand the quality and function of interaction processes that result in favourable health outcomes. People can be predisposed to illness by long-term social isolation, neglect, loneliness and social stress. Before discussing current issues in the relationship between social factors (as predictors) and illness and death (as outcomes), the conceptual background of the former needs to be clarified.

Social networks, social ties and social integration: structure and quantity of social relationships

The term 'social support' is often used in a broad sense, including social networks and social integration. However, these three notions should be clearly distinguished from one another. *Social networks* represent the objective basis for social integration and social support because social networks are the number of people or possible support providers in an individual's environment. Social integration and social support, however, are theoretical constructs that refer to the degree to which individuals are socially embedded and have a sense of belonging, obligation and intimacy. *Social integration* refers to the structure and quantity of social relationships, such as the size and density of networks and the frequency of interaction, but also sometimes to the subjective perception of embeddedness. *Social support*, in contrast, refers to the function and quality of social relationships, such as perceived availability of help or support actually received. It occurs through an interactive process and can be related to altruism, a sense of obligation, and the perception of reciprocity (Schwarzer & Leppin, 1991; see also the section below).

Social networks and social integration can be assessed in a sophisticated manner, but researchers usually choose a straightforward approach: The most common demographic indicator is considered marital status in order to establish relationships between social integration and health or mortality. It makes a difference whether individuals are single, married, divorced, etc. Based on this information only, one can conclude that, on average, married couples live longer than individuals in the other groups. A more comprehensive way to assess these constructs is a social network index that also includes the number of roles one assumes in the family and in organizations, such as church, as well as the frequency of contact to other members of such groups. Duration of contacts and degree of reciprocity are also important. A social network represents a web of relationships that encircles an individual together with network characteristics, such as range or size (number of members), density (degree of interconnection), boundedness (extent of closeness such as kin, workplace, neighbourhood), and homogeneity (similarity of members). There are various ways to assess these aspects (for an overview, see Cohen, Underwood & Gottlieb, 2000; Laireiter & Baumann, 1992).

Social support: function and quality of social relationships

Social support in the narrow sense has been defined in various ways. For example, it may be regarded as resources provided by others, as coping assistance or as an

exchange of resources. Several types of social support have been inve~~~
as instrumental (e.g. assist with a problem), tangible (e.g. donate goo~~
tional (e.g. give advice), and emotional (e.g. give reassurance), among~~~
(1990) contends that health and well-being are not merely the result ~~
port provision, but are the consequence of participation in a meaningf~~~
text. Receiving support gives meaning to individuals' lives by virtue of motivating
them to give in return, to feel obligated and to be attached to their ties. Rook uses
the term companionship to refer to such a harmonious network of mutual support
and obligation. Being embedded in a positive social world might be more powerful
than receiving help.

The most common distinction made is the one between perceived available support and support actually received. The former may pertain to anticipating help in
time of need, and the latter to help provided within a given time period. The former
is often prospective, the latter always retrospective. This is an essential distinction
because these two constructs need not necessarily have much in common. They can
be closely related in some studies, but in others they may be unrelated, depending on
wording and context (Newcomb, 1990). Expecting support in the future appears to
be a stable personality trait (Sarason et al., 1983) that is intertwined with optimism,
whereas support provided in the past is based on actual circumstances. To which
degree this distinction emerges empirically also depends on the amount of specificity
in the item wordings. The more diffuse and general the questions are, the more the
responses may be influenced by the respondents' personality characteristics.

The assessment of social support

There are a multitude of psychometric tools available to assess support (for an overview,
see Cohen et al., 2000). Items from the Berlin Social Support Scales (BSSS; Schwarzer
& Schulz, 2000) serve to illustrate the multiple dimensions of social support (the complete inventory is available at www.coping.de).

Table 7.1 presents sample items for perceived available emotional support. We have
chosen a wording that refers to the present, not the future, in order to reduce the
confounding of perceived support and optimism. It represents a general subjective
assessment without specifying a particular time period. Examples for perceived available instrumental support are given in table 7.2. Again, there is low specificity, such
as running errands, lending money, taking the dog out for a walk, etc. Depending on
the extent of discriminant validity desired, one can create more specific scales for

Table 7.1 Perceived available support (emotional)

1. There are some people who truly like me.
2. Whenever I am not feeling well, other people show me that they are fond of me.
3. Whenever I am sad, there are people who cheer me up.
4. There is always someone there for me when I need comforting.

Table 7.2 Perceived available support (instrumental)

---

1. I know some people upon whom I can always rely.
2. When I am worried, there is someone who helps me.
3. There are people who offer me help when I need it.
4. When everything becomes too much for me to handle, others are there to help me.

Table 7.3 Support actually received

Think about the person who is closest to you, such as your spouse, partner, child, friend and so on. How did this person react to you **during the last week**?

1. This person showed me that he/she loves and accepts me. (EMO)
2. This person suggested activities that might distract me. (INF)
3. This person comforted me when I was feeling bad. (EMO)
4. This person took care of many things for me. (INST)

Note: EMO = emotional support, INST = instrumental support, INF = informational support.

emotional and instrumental support; however, this prevents the production of a joint sum score of both scales.

The main feature of the scale for support actually received (see table 7.3) lies in the specification of a past time period. In this particular case, the instrument was used with cancer surgery patients, and the time window was defined as one week. Moreover, in this scale emotional, instrumental and informational support are distinguished. Inter-correlations among the three subscales typically range between 0.30 and 0.60, depending on the context. Correlations of these three subscales with the two perceived support scales range between 0.15 and 0.49 in the cancer surgery research project. These relationships attest to the convergent and discriminant validity of the inventories.

Some measures of received support also consider the particular *source* that has provided help in a specific situation, such as spouse, friend or colleague. In a study on the multi-dimensional nature of received social support in gay men (Schwarzer, Dunkel-Schetter & Kemeny, 1994), the UCLA Social Support Inventory was used to examine to what degree partners, friends, family and organizations provided assistance, gave advice, were reassuring or listened empathically. The design of such an instrument is displayed in figure 7.1. The four sources were incorporated within each kind of support. There were 16 items, 4 of which measured giving advice, tangible assistance, reassurance and listening. Thus, each individual statement referred to one source and one kind of support. However, it is not necessary to design instruments in a source-specific manner. One can simply spell out in the instructions preceding a scale which source the respondent should have in mind.

To get the full picture of how an individual's social situation is characterized, it is valuable to know about one's *need for support*. Some people feel better when they can

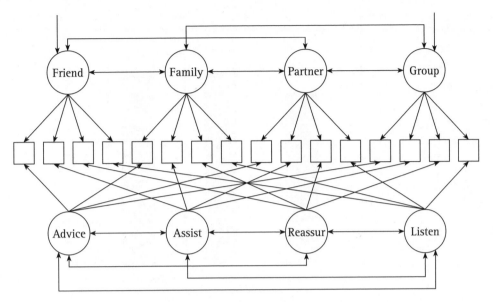

Figure 7.1 Sources and kinds of support (Schwarzer, Dunkel-Schetter & Kemeny, 1994). (Advice = giving advice, Assist = tangible assistance, Reassur = reassurance, Listen = listening.)

Table 7.4 Need for support

1. When I am down, I need someone who boosts my spirits.
2. It is important for me always to have someone who listens to me.
3. Before making any important decisions, I absolutely need a second opinion.

master challenges alone, without help from others, and resort to outside assistance only in the worst case. Others feel more dependent and express a stronger need for support (see table 7.4). Need is positively associated with received support (about 0.30).

Who receives how much social support?

The need for support, its mobilization, perception and receipt, differ systematically between populations. In addition to characteristics of life circumstances and stress situations, there are differences in gender, marital status and age. Gender differences in social networks and social support have been discussed by various authors (e.g. Greenglass, 1982). Throughout the life cycle, women generally have more close friends than men. Commencing in childhood, girls tend to develop more intimate interpersonal relationships than boys, although boys tend to gang together in larger groups. Adult women still have a greater number of close relationships and also seemingly

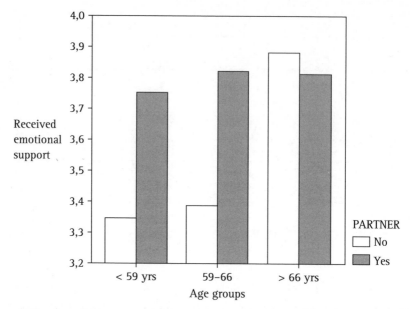

Figure 7.2 Younger cancer patients lack emotional support when they do not have an intimate partner (Schwarzer et al., 2001)

more extensive social networks than men (Laireiter & Baumann, 1992). Additionally, women provide more emotional support to both men and women, and they get more help in return (Klauer & Winkeler, 2002). Explanations for such discrepancies typically focus on gender differences in emotionality and emotional expressiveness. Women emphasize intimacy and self-disclosure in their friendships, and they are generally more empathetic, expressive and disclosing than men. In short, women seem to devote more of themselves to their family and friends than men do.

Individuals who are socially well-integrated receive more support than others. Having an intimate partner is regarded as the best source of support. However, various circumstances can qualify such effects. In our cancer surgery study, living without a partner was associated with receiving less emotional support, but this outcome was observed in 'younger' patients only (below 59 years of age). Figure 7.2 displays emotional support received by 153 patients one month (T3) after surgery. Being single, divorced or widowed is particularly unfortunate for younger patients who, as a consequence, do not receive as much support as the older patients. Younger cancer patients without an intimate partner lack emotional support, whereas older ones seem to be able to compensate for the absence of an intimate partner. If a younger (i.e. middle-aged) patient experiences divorce or widowhood, or was single in the first place, a social deficiency may emerge that is harder to compensate. Older individuals, in contrast, may have developed other social bonds that provide emotional support.

SOCIAL INTEGRATION, SOCIAL SUPPORT AND LONGEVITY: WHO DIES PREMATURELY?

Community-based prospective epidemiological studies have documented a link between lack of social integration on the one hand and morbidity/mortality on the other. Socially isolated people are at the highest risk for a variety of diseases and fatal health outcomes. Social integration, or the lack of it, can influence the onset, progression and recovery from illness. This relationship has been shown for diverse physical health problems, such as the common cold, cancer, HIV infection, cardiovascular diseases and cardiovascular reactivity (Glynn, Christenfeld & Gerin, 1999; Hemingway & Marmot, 1999; Weidner & Messina, 1995). Studies have found a link between social embeddedness and survival rate of patients who had experienced a myocardial infarct (MI). Male survivors of an acute MI who were socially isolated were more than twice as likely to die over a 3-year period than those who were socially integrated. Diagnosis of coronary artery disease and subsequent death was also linked to marital status. Those who were single or without a confidant were more than 3 times as likely to die within 5 years, compared to those who had a close confidant or who were married.

Numerous investigations have documented that social relationships constitute a buffer against premature death. A distinction can be made between large-scale epidemiological studies and life-event studies. *Life-event research* on social support and mortality comes primarily from two sources: after severe medical occurrences or procedures, and after conjugal loss. In *epidemiological studies* in which indicators of social integration (e.g. marital status) were correlated with longevity, it was repeatedly found that the relative risk of dying within a given time period is higher for socially isolated than for socially integrated individuals (Berkman, Leo-Summers & Horwitz, 1992). In the classic Alameda County Study, for example, the mortality risk of people with weak social integration is about twice as high as those who are socially well integrated (Berkman & Syme, 1979). Although the relative risk ratios sometimes appear to be impressive, the effect sizes of these findings are usually very small. In a meta-analysis on this topic, Schwarzer and Leppin (1989) estimated an effect size of $r = -0.07$ between mortality and social integration. This estimate is a weighted average from 18 data sets based on a total of 10,735 individuals. Decomposing this parameter by gender yields $r = -0.06$ for women and $r = -0.08$ for men. Only the latter value is homogeneous enough to be interpreted as a reliable meta-analytic result (Schwarzer & Leppin, 1992).

Hemingway and Marmot (1999) distinguish between two kinds of epidemiological studies: prospective etiological investigations in healthy samples and prognostic studies in patient samples. In a review, they found that 5 out of 8 prospective studies documented an effect of social integration on coronary heart disease. Moreover, they found that 9 out of 10 prognostic studies confirmed evidence for a link between social integration and coronary heart disease.

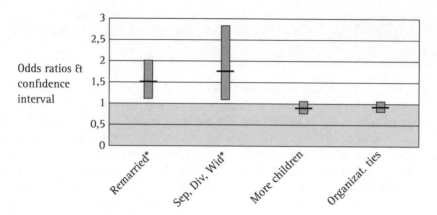

Figure 7.3 Men who were separated or divorced and widowers are at risk of premature death, even after remarriage (Tucker et al., 1999). The horizontal line represents the mortality risk of married men, set to the value of 1. The first bar on the left represents the remarried men with a mortality risk of 1.5, the second bar that of separated, divorced or widowed men (1.75), and the third and fourth bars men with more children or organizational ties that seemingly decrease the mortality risk (but not significantly). All four odds ratios are surrounded by their confidence intervals. (Sep = Separated, Div = Divorced, Wid = Widowed, Organizat. Ties = Organizational ties.) (*Confidence interval excludes 1, i.e. the difference is significant, $p < 0.05$.)

Studies including age differences and cohort differences also account for the fact that the evolution of most diseases involves long-term pathological processes, and that the provision or lack of social support can have both short-term and long-term consequences. Changes in the availability and the subjective importance of presence or absence of different social ties (e.g. partnership, kinship, organizational embeddedness) over the lifespan may go along with changes in their potential protective or detrimental effects. People have a history of social integration and embeddedness and support experience. Loss of intimate partners may be followed by new relationships, social networks may change in size and composition, in meaning and support potential, depending on the specific life context of a person (for example, see Tucker et al., 1999).

In the Terman Life-cycle Study, Tucker et al. (1999) examined the relationship between social ties and mortality in 697 men and 544 women at four assessment points over a period of 51 years (1940–91). They found that men who were married the whole time had a significantly lower mortality risk compared to those who were separated, divorced or widowed, or who had remarried (see figure 7.3). For women, no such effect of marital status emerged. Instead, their mortality risk was lower when they had a greater number of children and belonged to more organizations. However, when conducting separate analyses for two different age groups, namely those younger than

70 years versus those 70 and older, the authors found a protective effect of organizational memberships for the younger group of men, but not for the older group. Also, as they passed the age of 70, remarried men no longer had a higher risk of dying than those who were consistently married. For women, the beneficial effects of having more children were found only for those 70 years and older, but not for the younger ones. With respect to organizational memberships, women showed an opposite age-related change compared to men: For women, these particular social ties exerted their beneficial influence only in the later life period. In sum, these results suggest that lack of social ties other than marriage becomes a stronger predictor of mortality as people age, and that effects are different for men and women. One possible explanation is that age differences and gender differences are due to changing social roles and norms.

In another longitudinal study examining the impact of social integration on mortality in a 15-year follow-up design, Shye et al. (1995) found that among the elderly (aged 70–90), network size was more predictive of mortality than marriage. Interestingly, in this sample, men seemed to gain direct protection through smaller networks than women. Here, also, it remains unclear which internal processes mediate this protective effect. Men might derive a stronger sense of social integration and belonging even from few social ties, whereas, in this age group, women's costs and investments in close ties are higher, thus leading to a greater need for more external support. Whatever the mediating links may be, these results provide strong evidence for the notion that embeddedness in social networks and social participation means something different for older men compared to older women.

Survival rates in sick populations

Having a close confidant has an effect on the life or death of patients. Williams et al. (1992) examined 1,965 patients following an angioplasty. The presence or absence of a confidant or spouse appeared to be the best predictor of time until death, after controlling for other factors, such as family history of heart disease and cigarette smoking. Berkman et al. (1992) found that myocardial infarction (MI) patients with low levels of social support were more likely to die than those with high support, even after accounting for other factors, such as severity of disease. A 10-year follow-up study of MI patients found lower survival rates in unmarried patients. This positive effect of social integration seems to be stronger for men than for women (Chandra et al., 1983). Poor social integration is associated with an increased risk for myocardial infarction. Also, women with few confidants have been found to be at an even greater risk for myocardial infarcts than men (Collijn, Appels & Nijhuis, 1995).

Several major studies have found a link between social integration and survival rate of patients who had experienced MI. Ruberman et al. (1984) studied men who had survived an acute MI and found that cardiac patients who were socially isolated were more than twice as likely to die over a 3-year period than those who were socially integrated. A Swedish study of cardiac patients revealed that those who were socially isolated had a three times higher 10-year mortality rate than those who were socially integrated (Orth-Gomér, Unden & Edwards, 1988). Diagnosis of coronary artery disease and subsequent death was linked to marital status. Patients who were single or without a confidant were more than three times as likely to die within 5 years compared to those who had a close confidant or who were married. Another study of 40,820 patients investigated the effect of marital status on patient outcome (Gordon & Rosenthal, 1995). Here, unmarried surgical patients had a higher risk of dying while in the hospital than those who were married, even after controlling for other factors, such as severity of illness. The risk was even higher for patients who had never been married, compared to patients who were widowed, separated, or divorced.

In another prospective study on MI patients, it was found that mortality rates within a 6-month period were related to the social support these patients reported (Berkman et al., 1992). The authors identified the number of persons providing major sources of emotional support, distinguishing between patients with none, one, two or more such sources. There was a consistent pattern of death rates, the highest of which was associated with social isolation, and the lowest of which pertained to two or more sources of emotional support, independent of age, gender, co-morbidity and severity of MI.

Loss and bereavement

Conjugal loss has also been studied as a source of premature death. In general, marriage is regarded as beneficial for social functioning. Therefore, the loss of a spouse may signal the loss of one's social network, initiating an array of events with severe health consequences. Can the death of a spouse be so detrimental that it results in the premature death of the survivor? For decades, studies have addressed this question and found, on average, that the mortality risk for widows/widowers is increased, compared to those who do not experience this loss (for reviews, see Stroebe, Stroebe & Hansson, 2000). The risk seems to be highest for men during the first 6 months of bereavement. There may be several reasons for this gender difference. Men typically have a smaller social network than women, so their loss has a more profound effect on their social ties (Weidner, 2000). Also, widowhood occurs at an older age for men than for women since men, on average, die earlier than their spouses due to age differences in couples and biological gender differences in longevity. As a result, the death of the spouse leaves a widower who is older and more in need for support than a woman who was just widowed. Moreover, men usually confide in their spouse as their only intimate partner, whereas women cultivate a larger network of family members and friends and find it easier to turn to someone else in time of need. This higher social integration and support may buffer the stressful experience of losing their husbands (Miller & Wortman, 2002).

Traumatic grief has been shown to be a risk factor for mental and physical morbidity (Prigerson et al., 1997). When grieving widowers feel socially isolated, they may develop depression and loneliness, which in turn may lead to more severe consequences. For example, in the weeks and months following conjugal loss, the surviving spouse may be at substantial risk of committing suicide. Suicide following death of a spouse may be five times as likely in widowers compared to widows (Weidner, 2000). In other cases, their immune system or cardiovascular reactivity may be affected in the long run, resulting in illness and eventually in death. The mechanism of pathogenesis needs to be further explored. Not only death from all causes is higher in widowers, but also specific causes of death, such as suicide. Widowed individuals show impaired psychological and social functioning, including depression, and some studies report a significant decline in physical health, mainly for men. Frequency of sick days, use of ambulant physician services, and onset of illness according to medical diagnosis, seem to be about the same for the widowed and for controls (Ferraro, 1989). There is a lack of evidence that the onset of specific diseases such as cancer or coronary heart disease is triggered by conjugal loss or other forms of bereavement, which may be explained by the long time span of pathogenesis. For example, it takes many years to develop chronic degenerative diseases, and numerous additional factors may contribute synergistically to illnesses that emerge during this time period.

SOCIAL SUPPORT AND THE ONSET AND COURSE OF DISEASES

Social support and ill health

Does stress cause illness? Individuals are confronted with a great number of taxing situations, for instance living in a noisy neighbourhood, experiencing difficulties at work, time pressure, problems with their partner, or financial constraints. This list might seem to be an arbitrary array of situations. In fact, probably not everyone would consider these situations as being stressful or of great personal importance. However, the cumulative exposure to a number of aggravating minor daily hassles over a long period of time may have detrimental effects on one's health. In contrast, there is no doubt about the significance of major life events and their potential impact on health. Extreme stressors can create both acute and prolonged psychological distress and ill health or even premature death (Schwarzer & Schulz, 2002).

Most individuals who experience stress, however, do not become ill. Stressful life changes are usually temporary, whereas other risk factors for disease can be longer lasting, for example smoking, alcohol consumption, a high-fat, low-fibre diet, and risky lifestyle in general. When comparing a single life event with those long-term behaviours, the latter seem to be more influential in developing illness. Moreover, experiencing a critical life event is related to coping and social support, whereby these two factors may moderate the stress/illness connection. How can we understand the mechanisms of the stress/illness association? The perception, availability and activation of social support during a life crisis is a major moderator in successfully dealing with stress. A moderator (such as social support) is a variable that statistically interacts with a different factor (such as stress) in producing outcomes (such as illness). Intimate attachment, for example, may buffer the adverse effects of stress.

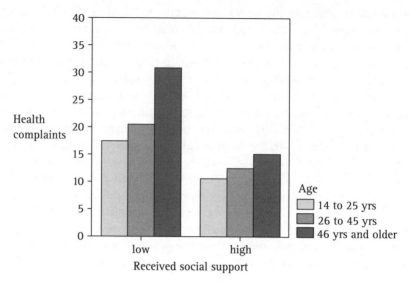

Figure 7.4 Poorly supported middle-aged women feel ill (Knoll & Schwarzer, 2002)

Therefore, this mechanism has been called a 'buffer effect'. In social support research, one always has to be aware of such buffer effects that may emerge instead of or on top of the more frequent main effects. Main effects refer to the generally positive influence of helpful social interactions on health and well-being.

Evidence for the importance of support as a predictor of negative affect and health complaints after a stressful life event comes from a study on East German migrants (Knoll & Schwarzer, 2002). Women who reported the highest social support also reported the fewest health complaints, an effect that could not be replicated for men in this study.

Social support was examined in relation to gender and age among East German migrants in a 2-year follow-up study initiated shortly before the fall of the Berlin Wall. Longitudinal data were collected starting in September 1989. The second and third waves were conducted during the autumn of 1990 and one year later. A total of 126 men and 109 women between the ages of 14 and 66 years participated in all three waves. Young women reported receiving the highest social support, whereas middle-aged and older women indicated relatively low levels of support. Men of all ages reported similar levels of social support. Social support increased for both men and women during the follow-up period.

The experience of migration at a time of macro-social crisis and political ambiguity was clearly stressful for migrants, who needed to draw upon all possible resources, including their social networks (Schwarzer, Jerusalem & Hahn, 1994; Schwarzer & Leppin, 1992). The nature of this experience makes it likely that study participants would manifest physical symptoms and impaired quality of life.

Social support predicted negative affect (depression and anxiety) and health complaints. Figure 7.4 displays levels of ill health for women only. Women receiving a small amount of social support had more health complaints than women receiving more support. Within the group of poorly supported women, those who were the oldest (above 45 years of age) were the worst off.

Women who reported the most social support (younger women) also had the lowest levels of negative affect and health complaints. Interestingly, for men the level of social support did not seem to affect the amount of health complaints. Men reported comparatively low levels of negative affect, and those who were older than 45 years indicated strikingly low levels of health complaints. Analyses predicting health complaints and depression by gender, age and social support showed that women reporting low social support had the highest levels of depression and health complaints, whereas the social support levels of men were unrelated to their depression and health complaints.

According to anecdotal information obtained during the interviews, three typical profiles appear to characterize women in this study. One was the prototype of a healthy young woman who left the East, either bringing along or immediately finding new sources of social support. Another prototypical woman was older and arrived in the West without having any support available. The third was the married, middle-aged woman who involuntarily moved with her husband to the West. The latter two prototypes appeared to be more at risk for anxiety, depression and illness.

Only one pattern of results seems to stand out for the men in this study: regardless of age, they did not seem to be affected by the amount of social support they received, and they appeared to cope fairly well with the situation at hand. Their levels of reported illness, depression and anxiety remained comparatively low.

These results confirm the value of examining the relationships between stress, social support and health in conjunction with demographic factors, such as gender and age. Because morbidity increases as people get older, age and life stage need to be considered closely in studies on social support. (See also Chapters 5 and 6.)

Recovery from myocardial infarction or cardiac surgery

Studies among cardiac patients have found social support to be beneficial for recovery from surgery. Some researchers have focused on the mere existence of social networks, whereas others have examined perceived or actually received social support. Kulik and Mahler (1989), for example, studied men who underwent coronary artery by-pass graft surgery. Those whose spouses visited them often in the hospital were, on average, released earlier than those who received few visits. In a longitudinal study, the same authors also found that emotional support from spouses had positive effects on patients after surgery (Kulik & Mahler, 1993). Other researchers obtained similar results (Fontana et al., 1989). King et al. (1993) found that perceived availability of support was associated with emotional and functional outcomes up to a year following coronary artery surgery. In particular, esteem support (that one is respected and valued by others) appeared to be related to improved health outcomes over the follow-up period. Thus, some types of social support are better than others when

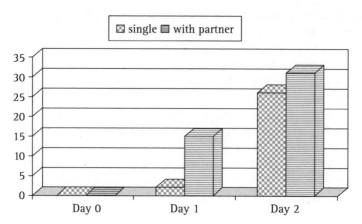

Figure 7.5 Cardiac patients with a partner recover earlier after surgery (Schröder, Schwarzer & Endler, 1997)

matched to the situation at hand. Emotional and esteem support, more so if extended from women to men, may be beneficial because it instils optimistic self-beliefs and equips the patient with more hardiness to cope with barriers and setbacks.

Marital status and recurrent cardiac events were linked in a study by Case et al. (1992), who identified a higher risk of cardiac deaths and nonfatal infarctions among people who lived alone.

Close network members of cardiac patients make a difference in how patients adjust to their disease, depending on their interaction with each other (Bodenmann, 1997; Coyne & Smith, 1991). Marital satisfaction was related to patients' well-being in a study by Waltz (1986). Helgeson (1993) found that patients' perceived availability of information support was a good predictor of recovery. Negative marital interaction predicted poor adjustment, and spousal disclosure predicted patients' life satisfaction.

Within a longitudinal design, 174 patients undergoing coronary artery bypass graft surgery were surveyed before the event (Time 1) and were interviewed one week afterwards (Time 2) (Schröder, Schwarzer & Konertz, 1998). Pre-surgical social resources were examined together with social and ruminative ways of coping in terms of a variety of recovery outcomes. Worry, emotional states, mental activity and physical activity were chosen as indicators of recovery. It was found that social resources predicted recovery.

Having a partner was associated with more reading at Day 1 and Day 2 after surgery (figure 7.5). Patients also wash themselves earlier, ambulate, do fitness exercises, etc., if they are socially integrated. Moreover, coping mediated pre-surgery resources and post-surgery readjustment. Seeking social support emerged as an adaptive way of coping. It was positively associated with recovery indicators, whereas rumination was negatively associated with both resources and outcomes.

In addition, 114 social network members, mostly spouses, reported about their own perceived resources at Time 1 (Schröder, Schwarzer & Endler, 1997). The patient–

spouse dyad was chosen as the unit of analysis. It turned out that characteristics of spouses were related to those of patients. Recovery from surgery at Time 2 and readjustment to normal life after half a year (Time 3) could be partly predicted by spouses' social support as measured at Time 1. Resourceful spouses seemed to transfer their resilient personality to the patients as part of a dyadic coping process.

How does social support influence the onset and progression of illness?

Although much evidence has demonstrated that psychosocial factors play an important role in the aetiology and prognosis of cardiovascular diseases, comparatively little is known about the actual pathways by which these factors influence the onset or progression of specific pathological mechanisms. It is obviously not the mere presence of social network members that results in better physical functioning. Also, the effect of functional support or lack of it is mediated by internal processes (e.g. emotions, affective states, control beliefs) that follow the individual's perception of supportive acts. In general, associations between social support and health can be due to *direct* or *indirect* effects of social support, and these in turn can be beneficial or detrimental. Direct effects refer to social factors being related to health-related outcomes without being further mediated by other variables. Indirect effects, however, involve a third variable that mediates between the predictor and the health outcome. Consider the following example: Elderly patients are supported by their spouses in taking their medication regularly. The medication, in turn, alleviates the illness. Thus, taking medication represents the mediator, and social support improves health indirectly through this mediator. Also, it has been postulated that social support might reveal its beneficial effect on health only in times of distress, in so far as it serves as a buffer to the negative impact of stressful events that people encounter. This moderating impact is known as the so-called *stress buffering effect* (Schwarzer & Leppin, 1991). Moreover, physiological, behavioural and psychological mechanisms have been discussed as potential pathways linking both functional and structural support to illness and subsequent mortality.

Among the multiple *physiological pathways* linking social support to health outcomes and the progression of illness, the focus has been on the cardiovascular, immune and neuro-endocrine systems. Loss and bereavement, for instance, are followed by immune depression, which may compromise natural killer cell activity and cellular immunity (Herbert & Cohen, 1993; Uchino, Cacioppo & Kiecolt-Glaser, 1996). This, in turn, reduces overall host resistance, so that the individual becomes more susceptible to a variety of diseases, including infections and cancer. The quality of social relationships, for example marital quality, has been found to be a predictor of immune functioning. Social stress, in general, tends to suppress immune functioning (Herbert & Cohen, 1993). Acute changes in neuro-endocrine secretion may also be linked to increased cardiovascular reactivity and physiological arousal, which are regarded as antecedents of severe cardiac events. In a study by Seeman et al. (1994), for instance,

emotional support was associated with urinary levels of epinephrine, norepinephrine and cortisol in a sample of elderly people. The link with emotional support was stronger than the link with instrumental support or with mere social integration. In a review of 81 studies relating social support to physiological processes, Uchino et al. (1996) concluded that there is reliable evidence for the beneficial effects of social support on aspects of the cardiovascular as well as the neuro-endocrine and the immune systems.

The *behavioural pathway* has been suggested by studies showing that social networks stimulated health behaviours that prevented the onset of illness, slowed its progression, or influenced the recovery process. For example, abstinence after smoking cessation was facilitated by social support (Murray et al., 1995). Alcohol consumption was lower in socially embedded persons (Berkman & Breslow, 1983), although other studies have found that social reference groups can trigger more risky behaviours, including alcohol consumption (Schwarzer, Jerusalem & Kleine, 1990). Physical exercise is one of those health behaviours that have a close link to social integration and social support. Perceived support by family and friends can help in developing the intention to exercise, as well as initiating the behaviour (Fuchs, 1997). Long-term participation in exercise programmes or the maintenance of self-directed exercise is probably more strongly determined by actual instrumental support than by perceived and informational support. Duncan and McAuley (1993) have found that social support indirectly influences exercise behaviours by improving one's self-efficacy. The latter might be an important mediator in this process. The reason could be that not only a sense of belonging and intimacy is perceived as supportive, but also the verbal persuasion that one is competent or the social modelling of competent behaviours.

There are also *psychological pathways*. It has been shown that social support is closely linked to a variety of other processes, including feelings of distress, depression, loneliness and other emotional states. These can operate as protective or risk factors for patho-physiological processes as well as recovery processes in their own right. Moreover, they might mediate the support/health association. So far, not many studies have directly tested the mediating role of these variables. Some find that the effects of social support are independent from other psychological processes. For example, in three of the studies included in the meta-analytic review by Uchino et al. (1996), depression, anxiety and reported life stress did not mediate the association between social support and immune function.

In sum, our understanding of the processes that mediate the influence of social support on people's physical condition is still limited. There is evidence for direct, indirect, and stress buffering effects with various facets of the social network and functional support operating through a variety of psychological, physiological and behavioural mechanisms that contribute jointly to the long-term evolution of diseases involving the cardiovascular system as well as to the recovery of patients. Preliminary conclusions suggest that for health behaviour changes and their maintenance over time, instrumental support and social embeddedness are crucial, whereas the impact of emotional support on ill health is mostly mediated by neuro-endocrine and immune processes.

Table 7.5 Support-seeking/mobilization

1. In critical situations, I prefer to ask others for their advice.
2. Whenever I am down, I look for someone to cheer me up again.
3. When I am worried, I reach out to someone to talk to.
4. If I do not know how to handle a situation, I ask others what they would do.
5. Whenever I need help, I ask for it.

MOBILIZATION OF SUPPORT AS A WAY OF COPING WITH STRESS

Social support theories are intertwined with the concepts of *stress and coping.* The cognitive appraisal of stress, for example, depends partly on the perceived availability of social resources. Moreover, the mobilization of support can be understood as a coping strategy. Table 7.5 contains sample items from the support-seeking subscale of the BSSS (Schwarzer & Schulz, 2000). It pertains to an individual's preference to request help from others in times of need. Such support mobilization is considered an active and mostly adaptive coping strategy. It is not directly part of the set of social support constructs, but it belongs to the conceptual category of coping. Empirically, it is associated with the amount of support receipt at a subsequent stage of a stress episode.

The study of social relationships requires a conceptual framework that includes activities of the recipient and the provider – although these two common terms are misleading since support is usually not a one-way street. People are embedded in a close network of mutual aid and obligation. These two terms are used for analytic purposes only. Figure 7.6 assumes that recipients enter a stress episode with a habitual level of perceived support, meaning that they anticipate receiving a certain amount

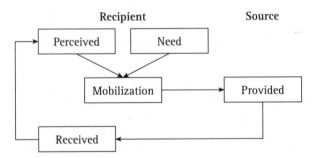

Figure 7.6 The Support Interaction Process: recipients enter a stress episode with a habitual level of perceived support. At the beginning of a stress experience, they may feel a need for support and thus might start mobilizing support. Ideally, a provider will then comfort the person in need, give advice or donate goods. This, in turn, will be considered as received support on the part of the recipient.

of assistance in times of need. At the beginning of the stress experience, they will feel a need for support. As a result, they start coping, which includes active seeking and mobilization of support by implicitly expressing their need or by explicitly calling friends for help. Then, the provider will comfort the person in need, give advice or donate goods. This, in turn, will be considered as received support on the part of the recipient. A fine-grained analysis of such processes requires qualitative research and case studies. Notably, support-seeking is not always associated with better health outcomes.

Aldwin and Yancura (2003) point out that social support conceptualized as social integration (e.g. Berkman & Syme, 1994) or social disclosure (Smythe, 1998) is almost always associated with better mental and physical outcomes. On the other hand, seeking social support – or support utilization, as it is sometimes called – is often associated with poorer outcomes. Monroe and Steiner (1986) maintain that both perception and utilization of support may represent more proximal associations with personality traits than do network size and support quality components. They too mention that measures based on support perception versus support utilization yield discrepant outcomes in relation to psychological symptoms. In that high perceived support is associated with few psychological symptoms, high support utilization predicts greater levels of symptoms. This might be explained by the fact that stress increases both distress and support utilization. Monroe and Steiner (1986) also point to the possibility that support-seeking might bring about a host of consequences, ranging from helpful interactions through disappointment to conflict and rejection. They underscore that at this level personality might determine in part under which circumstances the individual requests support (thus the probability of receiving support) or whom and how the individual asks for support.

CONCLUSION

Engaging in social interaction, be it on the providing or receiving end, emerges as a very complex concept that researchers only recently have started to disentangle. A promising first step seems to be the now often-applied differentiation between social network and social support as well as different subcategories of the latter. The mechanisms by which support concepts seem to act on health and ultimately longevity are also manifold. This chapter reviewed work showing that social relationships may both encourage and disrupt a healthy lifestyle. Support concepts were also shown to influence the human immune system in both positive and negative ways. Social support was furthermore related to lower perceived stress levels and thus to the mastery of taxing situations.

The puzzle on how social interactions may help to improve our health or even prolong our life expectancy is likely to remain complex. Various types of support (e.g. emotional, instrumental) may exert their impact on health and lifetime prolonging factors via a number of behavioural and cognitive mediators that are closely linked to immune functions and cardiovascular reactivity.

A close examination of these mediating mechanisms will advance our understanding of desirable and undesirable aspects of support and help explain individual differences in the ability to benefit from it in terms of physical health. The rapid development of research in this field already promises the unearthing of several crucial pieces of this puzzle in the near future.

DISCUSSION POINTS

1. What is the difference between 'social integration' and 'social support'?
2. Who receives more support, women or men? How is this gender difference in network size, support provision, and receipt usually explained? During which part of the lifespan does this gender gap in support manifest itself?
3. Are there any 'dark sides' to social support and social embeddedness? Which aspect of social embeddedness is associated with (a) surviving a life-threatening illness? (b) longevity following bereavement (especially for men)? How are these associations usually explained?
4. What are the differences between the direct-effect hypothesis and the buffering hypothesis of social support? What might be ideal study designs to test these hypotheses?
5. Is the differentiation between several aspects of social interaction/support useful? Which are the costs and benefits of a differentiated approach to measuring social interaction/support?
6. Is *being single* a health risk? Does this change as people grow older?
7. What are some of the possible health-related consequences of widowhood? Who seems to be more affected by the loss of a partner, women or men? Why?
8. What is the typical range of inter-correlations between emotional, informational and instrumental support?
9. What are some major methodological drawbacks in studies on social support and its correlates?

FURTHER READING

Cohen, S., Underwood, S. and Gottlieb, B. (2000). *Social Support Measures and Intervention*. New York: Oxford University Press.

Kulik, J. A. and Mahler, H. I. M. (1993). Emotional support as a moderator of adjustment and compliance after coronary bypass surgery: a longitudinal study. *Journal of Behavioral Medicine* 16, 45–63.

Miller, E. and Wortman, C. B. (2002). Gender differences in mortality and morbidity following a major stressor: the case of conjugal bereavement. In G. Weidner, M. Kopp and M. Kristenson, eds., *Heart Disease: Environment, Stress, and Gender. NATO Science Series, Series I: Life and Behavioural Sciences, vol. 327.* Amsterdam: IOS Press, 251–66.

Schröder, K., Schwarzer, R. and Endler, N. S. (1997). Predicting cardiac patients' quality of life from the characteristics of their spouses. *Journal of Health Psychology*, 2, 231–44.

Stroebe, M., Stroebe, W. and Hansson, R. O., eds. (2000). *Handbook of Bereavement: Consequences, Coping, and Care.* New York: Cambridge University Press.

Uchino, B. N., Cacioppo, J. T. and Kiecolt-Glaser, J. K. (1996). The relationship between social support and physiological processes: a review with emphasis on underlying mechanisms and implications for health. *Psychological Bulletin* 119, 488–531.

KEY STUDIES

Coyne, J. C. and Smith, D. A. K. (1991). Couples coping with a myocardial infarction: a contextual perspective on wives' distress. *Journal of Personality and Social Psychology* 61, 404–12.

Tucker, J. S., Schwartz, J. E., Clark, K. M. and Friedman, H. S. (1999). Age-related changes in the associations of social network ties with mortality risk. *Psychology and Aging* 14, 564–71.

REFERENCES

Aldwin, C. M. and Yancura, L. A. (2003). Coping and health outcomes: a comparison of the stress and trauma literatures. In P. P. Schnurr and B. L. Green, eds., *Physical Health Consequences of Exposure to Extreme Stress.* Washington, DC: American Psychological Association.

Berkman, L. F. and Breslow, L. (1983). *Health and Ways of Living: The Alameda County Study.* London: Oxford University Press.

Berkman, L. F., Leo-Summers, L. and Horwitz, R. I. (1992). Emotional support and survival following myocardial infarction: a prospective population-based study of the elderly. *Annals of Internal Medicine* 117, 1003–9.

Berkman, L. F. and Syme, S. L. (1979). Social networks, host resistance, and mortality: a nine-year follow-up study of Alameda county residents. *American Journal of Epidemiology* 109, 186–204.

Berkman, L. and Syme, S. L. (1994). Social networks, host resistance, and mortality: a nine-year follow-up study of Alameda County residents. In A. Steptoe and J. Wardle, eds., *Psychosocial Processes and Health: A Reader.* Cambridge: Cambridge University Press, 43–67.

Bodenmann, G. (1997). Dyadic coping – a systemic-transactional view of stress and coping among couples: theory and empirical findings. *European Review of Applied Psychology* 47, 137–40.

Bowlby, J. (1969). *Attachment and Loss.* New York: Basic Books.

Case, R. B., Moss, A. J., Case, N., McDermott, M. and Eberly, S. (1992). Living alone after myocardial infarction. *Journal of the American Medical Association* 267, 515–19.

Chandra, V., Szklo, M., Goldberg, R. and Tonascia, J. (1983). The impact of marital status on survival after an acute myocardial infarction: a population-based study. *American Journal of Epidemiology* 117, 320–5.

Cohen, S., Underwood, S. and Gottlieb, B. (2000). *Social Support Measures and Intervention.* New York: Oxford University Press.

Collijn, D. H., Appels, A. and Nijhuis, F. (1995). Psychosocial risk factors for cardiovascular disease in women: the role of social support. *International Journal of Behavioral Medicine* 2, 219–32.

Coyne, J. C. and Smith, D. A. K. (1991). Couples coping with a myocardial infarction: a contextual perspective on wives' distress. *Journal of Personality and Social Psychology* 61, 404–12.

Duncan, T. E. and McAuley, E. (1993). Social support and efficacy cognitions in exercise adherence: a latent growth curve analysis. *Journal of Behavioral Medicine* 16, 199–218.

Durkheim, E. (1952). *Le suicide: Suicide, a study in sociology.* Glencoe, IL: Free Press. First published 1897 (in French).

Ferraro, K. F. (1989). Widowhood and health. In K. S. Markides and C. L. Cooper, eds., *Aging, Stress and Health.* New York: Wiley, 69–90.

Fontana, A. F., Kerns, R. D., Rosenberg, R. L. and Colonese, K. L. (1989). Support, stress, and recovery from coronary heart disease: a longitudinal model. *Health Psychology* 8, 175–93.

Fuchs, R. (1997). *Psychologie und körperliche Bewegung* [Psychology and physical exercise]. Göttingen, Germany: Hogrefe.

Glynn, L. M., Christenfeld, N. and Gerin, W. (1999). Gender, social support, and cardiovascular responses to stress. *Psychosomatic Medicine* 61, 234–42.

Gordon, H. S. and Rosenthal, G. E. (1995). Impact of marital status on outcomes in hospitalized patients: evidence from an academic medical center. *Archives of Internal Medicine* 155, 2465–71.

Greenglass, E. R. (1982). *A World of Difference: Gender Roles in Perspective.* Toronto: Wiley.

Helgeson, V. S. (1993). The onset of chronic illness: its effect on the patient–spouse relationship. *Journal of Social and Clinical Psychology* 12, 406–28.

Hemingway, H. and Marmot, M. (1999). Psychosocial factors in the aetiology and prognosis of coronary heart disease: systematic review of prospective cohort studies. *British Medical Journal* 318, 1460–7.

Herbert, T. B. and Cohen, S. (1993). Stress and immunity in humans: a meta-analytic review. *Psychosomatic Medicine* 55, 364–79.

King, K. B., Reis, H. T., Porter, L. A. and Norsen, L. H. (1993). Social support and long-term recovery form coronary artery surgery: effects on patients and spouses. *Health Psychology* 12, 56–63.

Klauer, T. and Winkeler, M. (2002). Gender, mental health status, and social support during a stressful event. In G. Weidner, M. Kopp and M. Kristenson, eds., *Heart Disease: Environment, Stress, and Gender. NATO Science Series, Series I: Life and Behavioural Sciences,* vol. *327.* Amsterdam: IOS Press, 223–36.

Knoll, N. and Schwarzer, R. (2002). Gender and age differences in social support: a study on East German refugees. In G. Weidner, M. Kopp and M. Kristenson, eds., *Heart Disease: Environment, Stress, and Gender. NATO Science Series, Series I: Life and Behavioural Sciences,* vol. *327.* Amsterdam: IOS Press, 198–210.

Kulik, J. A. and Mahler, H. I. M. (1989). Social support and recovery from surgery. *Health Psychology* 8, 221–38.

Kulik, J. A. and Mahler, H. I. M. (1993). Emotional support as a moderator of adjustment and compliance after coronary bypass surgery: a longitudinal study. *Journal of Behavioral Medicine* 16, 45–63.

Laireiter, A. and Baumann, U. (1992). Network structures and support functions: theoretical and empirical analyses. In H. O. F. Veiel and U. Baumann, eds., *The Meaning and Measurement of Social Support.* Washington, DC: Hemisphere, 33–55.

Miller, E. and Wortman, C. B. (2002). Gender differences in mortality and morbidity following a major stressor: the case of conjugal bereavement. In G. Weidner, M. Kopp and M. Kristenson, eds., *Heart Disease: Environment, Stress, and Gender. NATO Science Series, Series I: Life and Behavioural Sciences,* vol. *327.* Amsterdam: IOS Press, 251–66.

Monroe, S. M. and Steiner, S. C. (1986). Social support and psychopathology: interrelations with pre-existing disorder, stress, and personality. *Journal of Abnormal Psychology* 95, 29–39.

Murray, R. P., Johnston, J. J., Dolce, J. J., Lee, W. W. and O'Hara, P. (1995). Social support for smoking cessation and abstinence: the Lung Health study. *Addictive Behaviors* 20, 159–70.

Newcomb, M. D. (1990). What structural equation modeling can tell us about social support. In B. R. Sarason, I. G. Sarason and G. R. Pierce, eds., *Social Support: An Interactional View.* New York: Wiley, 26–63.

Orth-Gomér, K., Unden, A. L. and Edwards, M. E. (1988). Social isolation and mortality in ischemic heart disease. *Acta Medica Scandinavica* 224, 205–15.

Prigerson, H. G., Kasl, S. V., Reynolds, C. F., Bierhals, A. J., Frank, E. and Jacobs, S. (1997). Traumatic grief as a risk factor for mental and physical morbidity. *American Journal of Psychiatry* 154, 616–23.

Rook, K. S. (1990). Social relationships as a source of companionship: implications for older adults psychological well being. In B. R. Sarason, I. G. Sarason and G. R. Pierce, eds., *Social Support: An Interactional View.* New York: Wiley, 221–50.

Ruberman, W., Weinblatt, E., Goldberg, J. D. and Chaudhary, B. S. (1984). Psychological influences on mortality after myocardial infarction. *New England Journal of Medicine* 311, 552–9.

Sarason, I. G., Levine, H. M., Basham, R. B. and Sarason, B. R. (1983). Assessing social support: the Social Support Questionnaire. *Journal of Personality and Social Psychology* 44, 127–38.

Schröder, K., Schwarzer, R. and Endler, N. S. (1997). Predicting cardiac patients' quality of life from the characteristics of their spouses. *Journal of Health Psychology* 2, 231–44.

Schröder, K., Schwarzer, R. and Konertz, W. (1998). Coping as a mediator in recovery from cardiac surgery. *Psychology and Health* 13, 83–97.

Schwarzer, R., Dunkel-Schetter, C. and Kemeny, M. (1994). The multidimensional nature of received social support in gay men at risk of HIV infection and AIDS. *American Journal of Community Psychology* 22, 319–39.

Schwarzer, R., Förster, C., Schulz, U. and Taubert, S. (2001). *Coping with Colorectal Cancer Surgery.* Unpublished data.

Schwarzer, R., Jerusalem, M. and Hahn, A. (1994). Unemployment, social support and health complaints: a longitudinal study of stress in East German refugees. *Journal of Community & Applied Social Psychology* 4, 31–45.

Schwarzer, R., Jerusalem, M. and Kleine, D. (1990). Predicting adolescent health complaints by personality and behaviors. *Psychology and Health* 4, 233–44.

Schwarzer, R. and Leppin, A. (1989). Social support and health: a meta-analysis. *Psychology and Health* 3, 1–15.

Schwarzer, R. and Leppin, A. (1991). Social support and health: a theoretical and empirical overview. *Journal of Social and Personal Relationships* 8, 99–127.

Schwarzer, R. and Leppin, A. (1992). Possible impact of social ties and support on morbidity and mortality. In H. O. F. Veiel and U. Baumann, eds., *The Meaning and Measurement of Social Support.* Washington, DC: Hemisphere, 65–83.

Schwarzer, R. and Schulz, U. (2000). *Berlin Social Support Scales (BSSS).* Available from www.coping.de.

Schwarzer, R. and Schulz, U. (2002). The role of stressful life events. In A. M. Nezu, C. M. Nezu and P. A. Geller eds., *Comprehensive Handbook of Psychology,* vol. 9: *Health Psychology.* New York: Wiley, 27–49.

Seeman, T. E., Berkman, L. F., Blazer, D. and Rowe, J. W. (1994). Social ties and support and neuroendocrine function: the MacArthur studies of successful aging. *Annals of Behavioral Medicine* 16, 95–106.

Shye, D., Mullooly, J. P., Freeborn, D. K. and Pope, C. R. (1995). Gender differences in the relationship between social network support and mortality: a longitudinal study of an elderly cohort. *Social Science & Medicine* 41, 935–47.

Smythe, J. M. (1998). Written emotional expression: effect sizes, outcome types, and moderating variables. *Journal of Consulting and Clinical Psychology* 66, 174–84.

Stroebe, M., Stroebe, W. and Hansson, R. O., eds. (2000). *Handbook of Bereavement: Consequences, Coping, and Care.* New York: Cambridge University Press.

Tucker, J. S., Schwartz, J. E., Clark, K. M. and Friedman, H. S. (1999). Age-related changes in the associations of social network ties with mortality risk. *Psychology and Aging* 14, 564–71.

Uchino, B. N., Cacioppo, J. T. and Kiecolt-Glaser, J. K. (1996). The relationship between social support and physiological processes: a review with emphasis on underlying mechanisms and implications for health. *Psychological Bulletin* 119, 488–531.

Waltz, M. (1986). Marital context and postinfarction quality of life: is it social support or something more? *Social Science and Medicine* 22, 791–805.

Weidner, G. (2000). Why do men get more heart disease than women? An international perspective. *Journal of American College Health* 48, 291–4.

Weidner, G. and Messina, C. R. (1995). Effects of gender-typed tasks and gender roles on cardiovascular reactivity. *International Journal of Behavioral Medicine* 2, 66–82.

Williams, R. B., Barefoot, J. C., Califf, R. M., Haney, T. L., Saunders, W. B., Pryor, D. B., Hlatky, M. A., Siegler, I. C. and Mark, D. B. (1992). Prognostic importance of social and economic resources among medically treated patients with angiographically documented coronary artery disease. *Journal of the American Medical Association* 267, 520–4.

Chapter Eight

PAIN AND SYMPTOM PERCEPTION

Suzanne M. Skevington

CHAPTER OUTLINE

Through using pain as an example we have seen how symptom perception goes well beyond the relatively simple process of detecting sensations. The meanings attached to symptoms have profound implications for the action or inaction that follows sensation detection. Many of the influences that affect symptom perception and reporting behaviour are social and cultural as well as psychological and physical. They are to do with the personality of the person concerned. But they are also bound up with this person's history of illness in general, and pain in particular, the beliefs and attitudes they hold about their own health and health care, and these in interaction with the attitudes and beliefs of the health carers with whom they come into contact. In the ambiguity of symptom perception they seek reassurance and information from others about what is the appropriate action to take. These lay informants may be family, friend, colleagues or people in a waiting room, church congregation or train carriage.

Here we see a range of very complex bio-psycho-social processes at work that interact in a multiplicity of ways which make investigations of this area both difficult and complex. Although health psychologists do not have all the answers, one thing is clear, and this is that there is no one-to-one relationship between experiencing a symptom and going to see a doctor. Many influences stop people from going when they need to, and for a small minority predispose them to arrange a visit to seek reassurance for relatively minor complaints. Contrary to popular opinion there is now plentiful evidence to show that many people manage their own symptoms initially at least, and treat themselves using herbal or over-the-counter remedies. They also seek alternative sources of help from non-traditional healers and people outside the formal mental and physical health-care arena, rather than

filling up the waiting rooms of the over-worked primary health-care service. Symptoms that are serious, of sudden onset and disabling, are most
likely to be brought into the consulting room. But because symptoms are
often ambiguous in meaning – especially in the early stages of illness –
and their presentation is influenced by cultural inhibitions like stoicism,
even the most serious and life-threatening symptoms like those announ-
cing an acute myocardial infarction, may not receive the immediate attention they deserve, to save life. So at a practical level the challenge is to
socialize people to know with greater certainty exactly when it is appropriate and even essential to seek care from a professional for a troublesome
symptom, and when to take alternative action such as rest, self-medication,
suitable exercise, booking a holiday or changing their lifestyle in other
ways. In this chapter, one aim is to show how theory and research in health
psychology might provide guidance in this area.

KEY CONCEPTS

attitudes towards pain	pain and gender
decision-making	pain management
fear of pain	pain reports
gate control theory of pain	pain sensations
illness behaviour	reporting behaviour
pain	social comparisons
pain assessment	symptom perception

INTRODUCTION

An ache beneath the sternum, in connoting the possibility of sudden death from heart
failure, can be a wholly unsettling experience, whereas the same intensity and duration
of an ache in a finger is a trivial annoyance, easily disregarded. (Beecher, 1959: 159)

It is Monday morning, and the day of Jane's first exams. She wakes late. Her head
feels fuzzy and feverish and her legs are lethargic and unsteady as she stretches them
to step out of bed. As Jane heads for the bathroom, she tries to swallow and finds
a large lump at the back of her throat. She feels her tender, aching neck and swollen
glands. The thermometer reads 38 degrees Celsius. What does Jane do?

Does she go off to the exam, stopping off at the pharmacy or herbalist en route, to
buy pain relief? Does she stay in bed and keep warm, taking chicken soup and aspirin
periodically? Does she talk to her flatmate to compare symptoms or phone her Mum
and ask her advice? Does she send a message to her tutor in the hope of gaining a

sick note and exemption from taking the exam, or at least a few extra marks, because of illness? Or does Jane join the early morning queue to see her family doctor?

In this chapter we shall discuss the everyday experience of symptom perception and the various bio-psycho-social processes that affect it. In particular the focus is on one of the most common symptoms of all – pain. Before looking at what is known about the psycho-social aspects of pain, we briefly consider a description of the physiology and neuro-anatomy relevant to pain mechanisms, as a biological approach must be an initial departure point for understanding any illness or condition by health psychologists. Later in this chapter, we go on to look at how pain and other symptoms are understood and interpreted, and describe the circumstances that may encourage or deter people from visiting a health-care professional when they perceive pain. Research relating to these decision-making factors will be discussed with primary reference to pain but also with applications to other symptoms. Symptoms are internal and invisible subjective sensations, perceptions and feelings, like nausea, breathlessness and pain. They may be contrasted with signs that are observable, being open to inspection by others, such as spots, lumps, bruises and coughs. Many symptoms such as fatigue, nausea and pain have a significant impact on the quality of life of those with chronic illness (Curt, 2001), and for this reason alone, are worthy of serious consideration by health psychologists.

WHAT IS PAIN?

Pain has been defined as 'an unpleasant sensation and emotional experience that is associated with actual or potential tissue damage, or is described in the terms of such damage' (Merskey et al., 1979). There is a widespread belief that if you are in pain then there must be some physical damage such as injury, disease or malignancy to account for it. However, several conditions that are commonly observed by clinicians provide a challenge to this popular belief. The first situation where this belief demands re-examination is in accident and emergency clinics where extensive damage may be visible, but pain is not experienced at the time of injury or for several hours later (Melzack, Wall & Ty, 1982). This raises the question that if pain is caused by injury then how is it possible to have an amputated limb or deep tissue injury and yet still not feel any pain? The pain is usually experienced within a day of the injury taking place and so it is not permanently absent. From an evolutionary point of view, it is theorized that the onset of pain is delayed to allow the injured person to escape from danger and increase that person's chances of survival.

Secondly, clinicians frequently see patients who have evident pain but no damage (see Melzack & Wall, 1989, for a review). In these cases, there may be have been tissue damage in the past, but complete physical healing has occurred, and the pain still persists in relation to the scar tissue and cannot be accounted for in organic terms. The pain seems to persist in a chronic form, replacing the acute or short-term pain associated with normal healing. Commonly these situations where psychological mechanisms are at work cannot be explained by the presence of psychopathology either, and here the role of the health psychologist is at a premium. Thirdly, some pains appear to the victim to be located in a limb or body part such as the breast, finger or penis that has been removed through surgical amputation or lost through accident. Although having fundamental neurological origins, resulting from severed neurons, this phantom pain is not a psychopathological phenomenon as originally thought, but a very common and normal psychological reaction to losing a part of the body. Together these three scenarios strongly implicate the importance of psychological mechanisms in the generation and maintenance of pain, and for this reason, psychologists have several major roles to play in prevention, assessment, support and treatment.

The physiology of pain is highly complex and detailed, and so only a brief and simplified outline is provided here (see Skevington, 1995, for a more extensive review). Contrary to the assumptions of early pain theorists, neurones carrying impulses that are associated with the painful experience are not entirely or specifically devoted to pain transmission. None are exclusively 'hard-wired' for pain impulses, but some are more specialized in this function than others. Sensory nerves relevant to the understanding of pain are the rapidly transmitting and large, well-insulated myelinated A-beta and A-delta fibres, and the slower, more poorly insulated and smaller C-fibres. A 'gating' mechanism that originates in the substantia gelatinosa of the dorsal horns of the spinal cord responds to the differential inputs from large and small fibres and either permits or prevents information from being transmitted up the spinal cord to the thalamus and cortex of the brain. Feedback from centres in the brain to the dorsal horns completes this communication loop. This mechanism forms the basis of the Gate Control Theory of pain (GCT) (Melzack & Wall, 1965; 1989). Psychological factors like tension and anxiety, for example during childbirth, can 'open' the gate so that pain is perceived and enhanced. Conversely, diverted attention can 'close' the gate; for example, those engaged in sports are sometimes unaware that they have sustained an injury until the game is over. Despite its age, the GCT is still the best theoretical explanation available, guiding research into successful treatments like acupuncture, transcutaneous nerve stimulation and cognitive behaviour therapy. It was the first theory of pain to incorporate psychological factors as an integral part of the mechanism that explains why damage and pain do not necessarily automatically co-occur as often as people suppose. Where earlier theories included psychological factors, they were usually postulated as additional extraneous variables – almost incidental to the central neuro-anatomical and neuro-chemical processes. The GCT has brought the psychological agenda up the priority list in pain research, and more importantly, the GCT has provided excellent guidance to psychologists and other pain researchers about how they should proceed.

Where injury has occurred then immune and vascular changes are associated with tissue damage and the complex bodily changes needed to repair damage (see Wall & Melzack, 1999, for an extensive account). The immediate response to injury is an increase in electrical impulse activity and evidence of cell walls being damaged with the cellular contents seeping into the surrounding tissues. At a second stage, nerve endings emit peptides, and by the tertiary stage, classic inflammation is visible with swelling, redness, heat, tenderness and pain. This is the process associated with the generation of acute pain, but chronic or long-term pain is of greater clinical, personal and economic concern.

So far the explanation has largely concentrated on the sensory components of pain, but the affective components are known to be very important too. Emotional responses to pain are mediated throughout the sympathetic nervous system, so implicating the adrenal glands, the cardiovascular system and so on, in a distinctive spectrum of affective responses. These are associated first with the stress response associated with acute pain, and later in an altered adapted form, if the pain becomes chronic, when depression associated with helplessness is more common than the earlier acute anxiety. Recent research at a molecular level has shown how the RNA cellular component in the neurones of the spinal cord that are involved in the pain mechanism adapt and show 'plastic' changes after about three months of consistent electrical activity. Once beyond this critical level, these molecular changes to the RNA appear to be irreversible and potentially permanent. Cellular RNA activity has for some time known to be associated with learning. This finding starts to explain why chronic pain is so very difficult to treat (Wall & Melzack, 1999). It also provides an important rationale for early intervention to subdue hyper-excitable neurones in the treatment of acute pain generally, and post-surgical pain in particular. This contrasts with the more usual medical practice of 'wait and see' that until very recently has been the main policy adopted by those treating pain in primary care and hospital wards, and which can implicitly allow chronic pain to develop to an intractable state.

It is worth noting, however, that the gate control theory of pain – and the controversial experimental work that has investigated it – provides a much more proficient explanation of acute than chronic pain mechanisms, because it is easier to study acute than chronic pain in laboratory conditions. Consequently the theoretical work that might have been extended and used to underpin new interventions for the treatment of chronic pain has been necessarily hampered by ethical standards relating to the conduct of controlled experiments to induce chronic pain. The new fMRI and PET scanning techniques have instead provided an exciting series of imaging technologies in recent years that can be used initially to map and describe, but have the longer-term potential to enable a better understanding of the processing mechanisms of a brain that is receiving information about pain. These techniques have brought a new frontier to pain research, and new hope to sufferers as well.

PSYCHOLOGY OF PAIN

There are many psychological factors that have been researched to explain the common anomalies listed above, and several models of pain perception that can assist in understanding and interpreting the many psychological factors that have been identified (Melzack & Wall, 1989; Feuerstein & Zastowny, 1996; Gatchel & Turk, 1997; Turk, 1996; Linton, 1994). There appears to be considerable consensus among these model builders that the most important psychological components are cognitions, emotions, motivation and behaviour with physiology (Linton & Skevington, 1999). For example, Linton's (1994) model shows how psychological factors may predispose people to detect and pay attention to pain, while for others, pain is triggered.

Psychological factors such as anxiety are known to maintain pain, and furthermore, can provide a catalyst for the problem. However social support and other psychological components can act as a buffer and provide much-needed resourcefulness to the sufferer (Linton & Skevington, 1999). Skevington's model (1995) adds a range of neglected social and cultural components, and in doing so, takes model building beyond interpretation at a purely individual level.

A psychological perspective is important to the study of pain because it may help to meet the challenge of explaining *why* and not just *who* suffers from a particular pain problem (Turk, 1997). To understand the context of who complains about pain, it is first necessary to briefly revisit early psycho-physiological work on sensory thresholds. Using the usual ascending and descending psycho-physiological methods, it is possible to establish various thresholds associated with painful sensations. The sensation threshold is the lowest level at which any sensation like tickle or warmth is detected (Sternbach & Tursky, 1965). Sternbach and Tursky, together with many other researchers, show that the sensation threshold is a universal characteristic of the human body that appears to be unaffected by learning, and is virtually the same in all social groups, irrespective of culture, gender and experience. The pain perception threshold is the lowest level at which a person reports that a sensation is painful. This was shown for example by Clark and Clark (1980), who tested the pain perception threshold of Nepalese sherpas and European mountaineers under laboratory conditions, and found that the sherpas perceived pain at a significantly higher level of stimulation. The third threshold that can be identified is the pain tolerance level, and this is the point at which pain becomes unbearable. In studies of US minorities, Zborowski (1969) showed how several cultural groups were highly diverse in the level and style of reporting intolerance to pain. In contrast to the sensation threshold, the pain perception and pain tolerance thresholds appear to be dramatically affected by learning, as they vary substantially depending on the cultural background, history, etc. of the person tested. So whether and when people complain of pain, and the style in which they do it, depends to a considerable extent on what they have learned from other people and what they have retained from their own past experience.

Differential learning as a result of being socialized within a particular culture provides insight into individual differences in the response to particular stimuli and their interpretation as painful, as well as explaining why some ethnic groups are less inclined to visit a health professional with painful illness than others (Moore, 1990). Past history with regular painful episodes, such as menstruation and dysmenorrhoea, and positive or negative experiences associated with consulting a health professional about pain, also represent rewards and punishments relating to pain, and shape behaviour accordingly (Turk & Flor, 1987).

The meaning of a symptom is central to the debate about whether or not people are likely to complain of pain, and these meanings will vary considerably depending on the person's experience, background, knowledge, situation and so on, as the quotation at the start of this chapter shows. Many laboratory studies have shown the varied meanings attached to what is ostensibly the same painful experience. However, a basis for the study of the meaning of pain comes from Beecher's classic study of injured soldiers returning from Anzio beach during the Second World War, which provides a naturalistic field study in this area. Beecher observed that soldiers who had been brought to hospital from the battlefield with major injuries, frequently did not require or request pain relief for many hours afterwards, even though they were quite lucid. In contrast, those with minor injuries would often be in agony, requiring large doses of opioids to relieve their pain, so in this situation the pain was not apparently concomitant with the degree of apparent physical damage. The explanation for this ostensibly odd situation was in his records. He found that those with major injuries knew that they would not be returned to the battle field and were intensely relieved when they realized that they had survived and would be sent home. However those with minor injuries knew that they would be returned to the front line once they had recovered, and this was a source of anxiety and anguish (Beecher, 1959).

This study provides powerful evidence to support the view that it is the meaning of pain that is important to that person's pain perception and intensity, and moreover to their response to treatment and eventual recovery. It also demonstrates the case for the GCT. An interpretation based on the psychology of the individual combined with knowledge of the situation taps into a person–environment fit model that is frequently adopted by health psychologists and provides a useful departure point for further psychological understandings of pain. Because of the rich variety of painful interpretations, health professionals need to adopt a patient-centred approach of listening carefully to what a patient says about their pain and its intensity, and to respond to them and their needs without preconceived notions about how much pain this sort of patient 'should' be in. There is evidence that where health professionals develop a framework of pain patient categories, stereotypes and schemata, and cease to respond adaptively to individuals, some patients do not receive adequate pain relief and at the time they need it most (Donovan, Dillon and McGuire, 1987).

PAIN MANAGEMENT

The history of treating chronic pain until relatively recently has been dominated by the use of surgical techniques to cut fibres that carry pain signals or create lesions. However, the results of such neuro-surgery are typically short-lived and often accompanied by substantial supplementary human and economic costs, including the attenuation of pain due to the surgery itself (Melzack & Wall, 1982). Pain returns because the neurons are able to regenerate and because there is a dense, diffuse network of smaller neurons surrounding the major nerves of the spinal cord that continue to function by transmitting signals to the brain. Counter-irritation techniques like acupuncture that stimulate sensory nerves have had only limited, short-term success (Wall & Melzack, 1999). In the light of this history, psychologists have sought less invasive ways to relieve the pain, tension and anxiety cycle that commonly exacerbates pain and maintains it during its transition from the acute to the chronic stage.

Theories of social learning, memory and attention form the historical basis of cognitive behaviour therapy that was developed and tested by psychologists (e.g. Fordyce,

1976; Turner and Clancy, 1988; Turner and Jensen, 1993), and now represents a ~ cessful procedure for the widespread management of chronic pain and disability within pain management programmes. The original social learning theory program designed by Fordyce (1976) and colleagues in Seattle, was based on behaviourist principles and trained a multi-disciplinary team to work together in dedicated hospital wards with inpatients. Reinforcement was used to increase fitness and well behaviours and to discourage pain behaviours like complaining, limping and grimacing; also to reduce harmful levels of multiple medications. The family was engaged and involved so that they could continue using and supporting the program's principles at home. In addition they supplied an impressive structured maintenance schedule to provide supplementary proactive support to patients after the formal course was completed.

Managing disabling chronic pain is more than just its psychological management and the application of the bio-psycho-social model to the area of pain. An international requirement for an accredited course is a multi-disciplinary team, which is typically led by a psychologist and medical director and involves anaesthetists, neurologists, physiotherapists, occupational therapists, nurses, etc., to provide a holistic approach that can address all the salient dimensions of the painful experience and its treatment (Bonica, 1990). This radical breakthrough in psychological therapy for pain was both model based and practically effective, as demonstrated by a series of studies published throughout the 1980s. It was found to be consistently effective in reducing disability in most of the important chronic pain groups, even though it did not claim to reduce pain *per se*. The programme has been modified many times and the original formulation has since been overtaken by the inclusion of a range of cognitive methods.

The components of these programmes vary but have typically included bio-feedback to reduce stress, although with limited success (see Skevington, 1995, for a review). Using visual or auditory information from electrodes, patients are made more aware of muscle tension, for example in neck and forehead muscles for headaches. They may be taught progressive relaxation and deep breathing – with or without bio-feedback – to systematically reduce tension in all or specific muscle groups. Breaking the tension–pain cycle is central to the success of many psychological and pharmacological treatments.

Several cognitive coping techniques have been investigated to ascertain their usefulness in pain management programs. Some people find relief by focusing on or attending to the acute pain of dentistry, for instance; while others seek distraction from the pain by listening to music or inspecting a picture. Attention and distraction may be used spontaneously, but when are these two techniques best applied if taught to those in chronic pain, and how effective are they? A meta-analysis by Suls and Fletcher (1985) showed that avoidance/distraction was a useful short-term strategy for relieving pain for about 3 days, whereas attention strategies like re-interpreting the pain as 'warmth', has a longer-term effect in reducing anxiety, stress and pain (Holmes & Stevenson, 1990). Imagery can also be helpful. Guided by a therapist, pain patients concentrate on a pleasant, unchanging scene like a favourite beach, and are trained to relax. A meta-analysis of 51 studies and over 2,000 patients by Fernandez and Turk (1989) showed that pleasant and emotionally neutral images provided the best pain relief.

More recently, return-to-work rather than improved quality of life has become the valued outcome measure for employers, governments and insurers. Cognitive behaviour therapy harnessed with social and occupational components (Linton, 1986) improves return-to-work rates from CBT courses. An example is the 'work hardening' programme designed by Feuerstein and Zastowny (1996) that extends and applies the cognitive behavioural package to include vocational skills and support, with the aim of facilitating re-entry to work following a pain management programme. Typically this course might include regular appropriate exercise, reduction of medication, training in imagery and relaxation, social skills training, positive and negative reinforcement, vocational guidance with negotiation of suitable work and an appropriate work load. When intensive multi-disciplinary therapy is assessed using data obtained from randomized controlled trials, there is evidence from systematic reviews of definite benefits in restoring functioning when a multi-disciplinary approach is used, compared to inpatient or outpatient treatments from single disciplines (Guzman et al., 2001). However with minor exceptions (e.g. Skevington, Carse & Williams, 2001), few of these trials have properly evaluated the effect of interventions on quality of life. A good quality of life should be a major outcome for almost any patient who is being treated for a chronic painful condition and requires careful measurement. Furthermore this novel but necessary multi-disciplinary initiative in relieving pain and disability is still ignored in relation to the treatment of many other symptoms, such as breathlessness and nausea. It seems plausible that this radical, integrated approach could benefit the understanding and treatment of these other symptoms through similarly applying the bio-psycho-social model in a trans-disciplinary setting.

Recently there has been renewed interest in the fear of pain and the exaggerated pain perceptions that are associated with it. In Fordyce's (1976) original behaviourist model, fear avoidance was instrumentally associated with learning outcomes, but these ideas have resurfaced in a different form through application of the cognitive approach, which is much more appropriate (Philips, 1987). Fear avoidance is important as part of this discussion on symptoms because hyper-vigilance about symptoms or the tendency to give them undue attention can lead to the over-prediction of pain. This is common among anxious chronic pain patients and tends to be associated with poor physical performance (McCraken et al., 1993), disuse, and depression (Vlaeyen & Linton, 2000). Fear avoidance is also one possible result of misinterpreting benign bodily sensations. A fear of taking part in physical exercise has also been identified – especially when it hurts; which is associated with a fear of exacerbating the presumed physical damage (Vlaeyen & Linton, 2000). Indeed Waddell et al. (1993) have suggested that the fear of pain and (re-)injury may be more disabling than the pain itself.

For the many chronic pain patients who participate in pain management programmes – often after a long career of living with chronic pain and having it investigated physically but with no findings – mobilization by taking regular exercise is one of the most important ways in which they can begin to lead a relatively normal life again that is physically, socially, occupationally rewarding. So understanding how to reduce the avoidance associated with a patient's fear of pain is now central to the success of pain management because fear avoidance has the effect of maintaining or even exacerbating fear (Vlaeyen & Linton, 2000). Indeed the fear of pain has been found to be a better predictor of a patient's performance on a pain management programme than the more usual measures of pain intensity (Vlaeyen, personal communication). In public health terms, this finding may also be useful in the prediction of the reporting of painful events in populations who are normally pain free. This work raises interesting evolutionary questions about when it is appropriate to fear pain as an indicator of legitimate physical damage and to decide that the time is right to seek help from a doctor. Conversely, where fear is inappropriate because it predisposes the sufferer towards inactivity and long-term disability, this becomes a potent and urgent problem when mixed with the damaging effects of catastrophization and its potential to generate depression.

PAIN AND SYMPTOM ASSESSMENT

It is very difficult to describe pain, and people in pain are often just simply lost for words. The measurement of pain is important because intensity, quality and duration need to be established. Results of assessments can be a useful aid to diagnosis and contribute to decisions about treatment or a treatment plan; but also because it is essential that changes due to treatment are recorded accurately from a subjective viewpoint. Good pain measures are vital to the establishment of the effectiveness of different types of pain relief (Melzack & Katz, 1999). In trying to better understand and assess the psychological processes that affect the reporting of pain, Melzack (1975) investigated the language of pain and identified 3 classes of pain description; within these dimensions, 102 adjectives are organized in 20 subclasses. Melzack found that sensory adjectives like burning and tearing were most frequently used in the pain vocabulary. Patients were invited to choose one descriptor from every subclass and the weightings used as scores for these descriptions ranged for 1 to 7. For example, they were low for pinching and high for crushing in a subclass that also included pressing, gnawing and cramping as intermediate descriptions. But physical descriptors were often accompanied by affective words relating to the emotions and evaluative descriptors, like gruelling and unbearable. The assessment also includes a scale of Present Pain Intensity and the facility for patients to draw the distribution of their pain on outlines of the body.

The value of the McGill Pain Questionnaire (MPQ) is that it assesses the qualities of pain, in contrast to quantitative pain intensity measures more commonly found in pain research. A short form of 15 items has been designed for rapid assessment (Melzack, 1987) and also shows good psychometric properties. The scale has many uses in understanding pain and the processes of symptom perception. For example, Porzelius (1995) gave the MPQ to 49 patients before, during and after the injection of a local anaesthetic. He found widespread evidence of memory distortions as many patients recalled higher pain levels than were reported at the time of injection, and this may provide some explanation for the avoidance behaviour shown by some patients. The multi-dimensional nature of pain as suggested by the structure of the MPQ has been largely substantiated by subsequent researchers (Melzack & Katz, 1999) and provides an affirmation of construct validity. Despite its age, the development of the MPQ has been commended by Kahneman (1999) as a model, in the careful and rigorous measurement of symptom qualities and intensity.

Commonalities among symptoms are worth noting. Sensory and affective descriptions are often used by people who experience chronic breathlessness (Skevington et al., 1997). Other researchers have recently identified emotion and mood components attached to the symptom of fatigue, in addition to the expected physical or sensory components (Lavidor, Weller & Babkoff, 2002). This confirms its essentially multi-dimensional nature, and raises interesting questions about whether all symptoms other than pain and breathlessness, such as nausea, also have affective components in addition to their sensory content. The existence of a consistent emotional component also has implications for a fuller understanding of the circumstances surrounding people's decisions to report their symptoms to a health professional (addressed below). The findings also have practical and theoretical implications for the potential range of methods that might be used in the psychological management of these symptoms. The affective component of a symptom needs to be addressed in treatment as an integral part of the sensory phenomenon, and not in isolation. In the sections that follow we shall examine some of the explanations that have been documented in explaining the decision-making behaviour that occurs when people detect a symptom such as pain.

WHAT DO PEOPLE DO WHEN THEY HAVE SYMPTOMS?

There is a popular belief that people go to see a doctor when they are ill. However, research has show that the action that people take as a consequence of illness is far less predictable than might be assumed. Egan and Beaton (1987) assessed behaviour resulting from the presence of 13 common complaints, like coughing for 3 days, nausea for 24 hours and so on, and discovered 11 types of response to these symptoms. When ill, people often try to work out a cause. Some just carry on with their lives or even ignore their symptoms; others go to bed early, take more rest, work less or stay at home. Some continue to go to work but may tell their supervisor so that any deficits in performance will be tolerated. They often eat or drink special or different foods, will take non-prescription medication and frequently reduce their social activities. So it is clear that people do not rush to see a doctor but will often make a variety of changes in their lives to accommodate the inconvenience of ill health and take remedial action instead of deciding to go. This diverse range of self-management behaviours shows that people are often pro-active in their self-treatment, especially at this early stage of illness, and hints at the desire to avoid both serious disruption to their lives and the many costs involved in going to see a doctor.

Socialization plays a considerable role in this process – learning to deal with pain starts very early in life. Children learn a great deal from their parents and other children about the social and culturally appropriate ways to respond to symptoms and signs (Craig, 1986). In a survey of more than 7,000 teenagers, Quadrel and Lau (1990) found that when faced with serious conditions like lumps or blood in the urine, influenza or fatigue, adolescents were heavily influenced by the attitudes of their parents about whether to visit a doctor. So what sorts of psycho-social processes might explain these behaviours? Several are addressed below.

ATTENTION TO THE INTERNAL WORKINGS OF THE BODY

Attention has been an important variable in pain research because of its potential uses in pain management. Some approaches have assisted discussion about whether it is productive to focus on sensations such a stabbing pain in a process called monitoring, or whether an inclination to ignore sensations in a process of blunting is more helpful. During monitoring, people are highly attentive to threatening information and very selective about the information that they retain, for example about the discomforts of a surgical procedure. During blunting, they are more inclined to distract themselves from any threatening information, in a strategy that has some similarities with denial. Early research suggested that some people have a consistent tendency to notice symptoms more than others, and hence it was implied that monitoring-blunting could be a stable individual difference or personality trait (Miller, Brody & Summerton, 1988). However, more recently, studies have moved the discussion more towards the view that people have a particular cognitive style which enables them to use both monitoring and blunting in different proportions and at different times, depending on the situation or context. These processes have been applied in trying to understand and explain different responses to pain (Skevington & Mason, 2002). This more flexible cognitive-style approach has provided interesting insights into how people use the health service. Miller et al. (1988) found that those who were high monitors and low blunters were more likely to seek a consultation with a doctor quickly and present less severe problems than high blunters. Although the high monitors also showed less symptom improvement in the week following the consultation, they were equally as distressed, dysfunctional or uncomfortable as the blunters. Such research demonstrates how the psychological orientation of the patient has widespread effects on the interpretation of sensations, the decision-making about whether or not to seek formal help, and the eventual response to treatment.

In recent years this work on attention has been refocused in a number of ways, for example, to look at whether attentional factors are able to explain the sick person's response to illness through the negative affectivity hypothesis. In a study of adolescents with diabetes, Weibe et al. (1994) looked at whether negative emotions were associated with the accuracy of blood glucose symptom perceptions and diabetes control over a two-week period. They found that those who focused on their internal physical sensations were well able to detect blood glucose fluctuations. Those with high anxiety were more likely to make some mistaken attributions about non-blood glucose sensations. However, where high anxiety was combined with attending to internal sensations, metabolic control was the poorest, so the negative affectivity hypothesis alone only seems to supply a partial answer.

A related line of investigation has considered the trade-off between the degree of attention that people pay to the internal workings of their bodies, and the level of stimulation providing distraction from their immediate environment. Applying this person–environment (P–E) fit model, Pennebaker (1982) invited 50 students to view a film lasting 17 minutes and to rate their interest in it every 30 seconds. The mean interest of the group for each segment of time was calculated. They then asked 330 new students to watch the film and simultaneously they audio-taped the number of coughs in each time segment. A correlation of $r = -0.57$ was found between the number of coughs and interest ratings. Drawing from theory it was argued that where there was high interest in the film, people would take in more external information (E) and therefore would pay less attention to their internal bodily sensations (P) and hence cough less than those who were bored, and had more attentional capacity to devote to any discomfort in the throat. This trade-off between internal and external signals and their integration centrally gives us further insights into the experience and reporting of acute pain.

WHO GOES TO SEE THE DOCTOR AND WHY?

Pain is a very common symptom in health care and some estimates suggest that around 80 per cent of people who go to see a doctor are in pain. So the need to seek pain relief is a common motive for booking an appointment. But epidemiological studies also reveal that there are many people in the community who are in pain but who do not go to see their doctor. This feature was first demonstrated in a study of 1,344 primary care patients who were enrolled at a general practice in Glasgow. Hannay (1979) found that three-quarters of these patients had symptoms at any one time, but only one-quarter visited the doctor to consult them about it. This characteristic is referred to as the 'symptom iceberg' by analogy with floating icebergs that only show one-ninth of their total bulk, as eight-ninths are submerged. Hannay also found that many reported symptoms were not considered serious by the patients; they themselves would often describe these symptoms as 'trivia'. Furthermore a significant 10 per cent of consulters had neither pain nor disability. However, the majority of symptoms being presented were mainly characterized either by severe pain and/or disability. This and other studies point to the conclusion that there may be a variety of psycho-social as well as physical factors at work that could explain why those with symptoms decide whether or not to seek formal help from a doctor, so this is a productive area of investigation for health psychology.

There are many reasons why people do not go to see a doctor. Some are too immobilized by pain or disability, or are too highly infectious or seriously ill to leave their home. There are geographical and other structural reasons too. But some illness characteristics are powerful in the way they affect people's response to illness, and one of these is the visibility of illness to the person and to others. These visible features are referred to in a medical context as signs. The more obvious the sign, such as a hacking cough, a wince or grimace, a scar on the face, spots, etc., the more inclined people are to seek a consultation or to be persuaded to do so by others. Then there are invisible symptoms, and it is known that the more severe symptoms tend to predispose individuals to take action, although this has not been altogether borne out by the tenets of the Health Belief Model (see Rutter & Quine, 2002, for a review). The extent to which the symptom interferes with daily life is also known to be an important factor that affects reporting behaviour. Those symptoms that have high levels of interference are more likely to be attended to most rapidly. A fourth factor is the frequency and persistence of symptoms. Frequent symptoms are more problematic for most people than infrequent ones, and intermittent symptoms are less likely to encourage illness behaviour than those that persist unremittingly (Mechanic, 1977). At an individual level, there may be personal reluctance to attend a surgery based on factors such as fears about ill health, painful treatments, previous negative experiences of the consultation and so on. It is also worth noting that most people will advise other people to go to seek help for a symptom but report that they would not themselves go to see the doctor with the same symptom, and so attributional biases as well as other social factors affect the decision-making process. Lastly, there are some inherent methodological problems in the way medical histories have been assessed and recorded. Mechanic (1977) observes that medical histories are much more complex than currently recorded; they are comprised of experiences, referrals from friends, interpretation of sensations and many other factors, but little if any of this is written down or recorded in a systematic way that would help research in unravelling these many factors.

But perhaps one of the more important findings in this area is that there are sources of help other than formal ones. In a Canadian study by Crook, Rideout and Brown (1984) it was found that 75 per cent of health care is undertaken without recourse to professional help. Furthermore, Greenley and Mechanic (1976) carried out a survey of 1,000 US university students seeking mental health consultations over a 2-year period. In addition to medical services, they found that the students sought advice from psychiatric and university counsellors, clergymen, schools, psychologists, social workers, women's groups, training groups, Samaritans, venereal disease clinics, family courts, community law offices, university lecturers and administrators. So it is clear that many and varied sources of help are accessed by those with distressing psychological problems, and these and many other findings show that those providing formal care in the health service do so to only a small proportion of those with ill health at any one time – estimates vary but are around 10 per cent.

AMBIGUOUS SYMPTOMS

Decision-making about whether or not to seek help from a health professional seems to depend in part on the confidence people have in the accuracy with which they can identify their symptoms. As we saw in a previous section, this process begins with an assessment of bodily sensations. If the sensations are recognizable with a high level of confidence, then other parts of the decision-making process come into action. But when they are highly ambiguous, they cannot be properly interpreted. Anderson and Pennebaker (1980) studied this phenomenon by asking students to participate in a laboratory study that involved putting a finger on some vibrating sandpaper for 1 second. One third of the sample signed a consent form to say that they knew they would come into contact with a stimulus that might induce a degree of pain. Another subgroup received a comparable pleasure message, and the control group only a neutrally worded form. Thirteen-point rating scales from pain to pleasure were used to rate the sensation. All those in the pain group said it was painful, while those in the pleasure group reported pleasurable. During debriefing, participants were invited to consider alternative explanations for the labelling of their sensation e.g. pain rather than pleasure or vice versa, but no participant was convinced that the feelings they had experienced could possibly be interpreted in any other way. The results demonstrate how a schema for pain or for pleasure may predispose people to interpret ambiguous information in an unambiguous way. This study provides useful clues to the way in which contextual information can shape the interpretation of ambiguous bodily sensations into ones that are more confident, but possibly misguided. The results also begin to explain the reason for the high levels of resistance that health professionals may encounter in trying to change peoples' views about sensory misinterpretations.

Studying ambiguous symptoms is of more than just academic interest when it comes to the symptoms of a life-threatening event like a heart attack. Theisen et al. (1995) found that acute myocardial infarction (AMI) often goes unrecognized either because the patient does not notice or report their pain or because the physician fails to diagnose it. In an investigation into people who reported chest pain, Hackett and Cassem (1969) found that people frequently misinterpreted the sensations of an acute myocardial infarction (MI) as indigestion (and vice versa), with high physical, financial and psychological costs. Most fatalities from MI occur within an hour of symptom onset and more than 50 per cent of patients in this category die without ever reaching hospital. Since thrombolytic therapy became widely available for treating an acute MI, this has increased the urgency to better understand the delay process because prompt treatment limits heart damage and alters the course of illness (GSSI, 1986). Problems with decision-making about ambiguous symptoms like prolonged chest pain sometimes lead to delays of many hours before calling an ambulance. Furthermore, this lack of certainty also predisposes some sufferers to take up heavy physical exercise, like running up stairs, with the intention of demonstrating to themselves and others that they are not having a heart attack. Such action will increase heart damage if an MI has in fact occurred.

However, it is not clear whether the delay is different for those who have experienced a previous MI compared with those having a first MI – Hackett and Cassem reported that prior experience of symptoms does not shorten the delay when a subsequent attack occurred, suggesting that this prior experience plays only a relatively minor part in the explanation of delay behaviour. But more recently Petrie and Weinman (1997) have said that previous personal experience with heart disease does facilitate a more serious disease model and accelerates attendance following symptom onset. They also found considerable cross-cultural and location variations in getting to hospital. It has been shown that a family history of heart disease is more likely to predispose those with chest pain to consider it as serious more quickly than those without any such history, and therefore gain access to emergency treatment more rapidly (Hedges et al., 1998). Also Kudenchuck et al. (1996) report that older patients, women and those arriving at hospital during daylight hours, had significantly longer delay times. Together these features bolster the case for psycho-social explanations.

In contrast, a review of the literature on non-cardiac chest pain enables us to cast further light on some of the complex factors that may be influential in this context (Thurston et al., 2001). More than 50 per cent of patients referred to a cardiologist with chest pain are diagnosed as having non-cardiac chest pain (NCCP), namely pain that is not due to cardiac ischaemia or other major physical disorders (Bass & Mayou, 1995). Although NCCP patients have a favourable cardiovascular prognosis – 99 per cent are alive after 5 years – their quality of life is substantially impaired due to pain, inability to work and the lack of ability to perform their daily activities.

The bio-psycho-social model can be usefully applied here because treatments that are designed to alter this triad can be used to make improvements in pain and disability. This is because the conventional medical approach of clinical assessment, negative laboratory investigations, reassuring patients and explanation are typically ineffective. Key biological factors that play a role in NCCP are oesophageal motility disorder, especially gastric reflux of acid, and micro-vascular ischaemia where minor occlusions and spasm around the heart occur. A subset of these cases have syndrome X, which is the pain of angina with S-T segment depression in the electrocardiogram during exercise (Thurston et al., 2001). Psychological problems include a low pain threshold that creates an abnormally high sensitivity to stimuli that cause pain. People who develop chronic pain typically show a lowering of the pain threshold as time progresses, for many ostensibly non-painful stimuli such as stroking the skin or tickle, that would not normally be interpreted as painful. There is also evidence of elevated anxiety and depression levels, together with the damaging use of less effective pain coping strategies. Such information may enable physicians to choose a suitable and timely series of interventions. Although cardiac pain has been taken as an example here, the psychological principles associated with perceptual accuracy and health threats associated with delays can be similarly applied to a broad range of other non-painful conditions, such as asthma (Yoos & McMullen, 1999).

SOCIAL FACTORS IN MAKING THE DECISION

Although on the face of it, it might be assumed that the interpretation of symptoms and decisions about symptoms such as pain are an individual process, the business of deciding whether to report them is very much part of an interaction between several salient and complex social processes, as Skevington's model shows (Skevington, 1995, Skevington & Mason 2004). In the following sections we look at some of these socio-cultural processes in more detail and in particular consider how they affect sick-role and illness behaviour.

Through the application of Festinger's (1954) important work on social comparisons, health researchers have been able to better understand that when people are confused about their internal sensations, they turn to others for help in interpreting what they are feeling. Studies utilizing social comparison theory show that in some conditions they make upward comparisons with those who are better off than they are, in this case healthier, while in other situations they will make downward comparisons with those who are in poorer health. These comparisons affect their self-esteem, mental health and other aspects of behaviour connected with health and health care. Furthermore in making direct interpersonal comparisons with others, they not only compare how they are with others who are similar, such as with other patients with arthritis, but also make intergroup comparisons with others from contrasting illness categories or groups. For example, those with chronic disabling arthritis may see other patients with cancer as being worse off than themselves, so using downward comparisons to improve self-esteem in the group (Skevington, 1994). Intrapersonal comparisons are also made with other times or states in life, like when they were younger, healthier, on holiday and how they would ideally like to be. Comparisons can also be made at a global level based on society's expectations about how they should be health-wise (Sartorius, 1987; Skevington, 1994), for instance in view of their age, fitness, working conditions, cultural attitudes, and so on. Health professionals can provide a societal benchmark against which a patient can make comparisons themselves, through statements like whether their health is judged as good or poor 'for a woman of your age'.

Some interesting therapeutic implications have been drawn from applications of research on social comparison processes in health settings. For instance, Kulik and Mahler (1987) studied coronary artery bypass graft surgery patients (CABG), some of whom shared a hospital room with another pre-operative CABG patient while others shared with a similar post-surgical patient. They found that given the choice, more new patients wanted to share with a post-surgical patient than a pre-operative patient. Furthermore, those who shared with post-surgery patients were less anxious and were discharged earlier than those paired with waiting patients, due to the positive comparisons made and reassurance derived from meeting a survivor.

There is other evidence that shows how social comparisons are used within the stages of decision-making. Daily health diaries and interview transcripts were obtained from 50 people in the US by Telles and Pollack (1981) in looking at what people do when they fear that they are becoming ill. The sample for this qualitative study was structured by sex, race and socio-economic status. From the results, they identified 4 stages to the decision-making process. To begin with, people asked others around them to discuss their symptoms and the implications of those symptoms. Feedback on these symptoms helped them to label the sensations as the symptoms of illness or not. They then looked for ways to verify their symptoms, such as obtaining information from other people. If an influenza virus is virulent and at epidemic proportions, then obtaining this knowledge may consolidate the decision-making process about visiting a doctor or going to bed for a few days, for someone with a raised bodily temperature, weakness and loss of appetite. Often making this decision involves drawing comparisons with other people. Lastly they were directed to a legitimator of the sick-role; usually a doctor. Often a concerned family member or friend will urge a visit to the doctor and this may be the encouragement we need to take this step. So we seek assurances from others that our sensations truly represent illness and justify seeking legitimation for our illness from a doctor.

The legitimation of symptoms is the beginning of a much more extended process whereby we come to the point of labelling an illness. Some theoretical models have been elaborated and can be applied to guide thinking about pain. The self-regulatory model of illness developed by Leventhal and colleagues (e.g. Leventhal & Diefenbach, 1991) shows how people construct and represent illness in their lives. They say that people organize their illness schemata along 5 prime dimensions. First, and most relev-ant to the symptom of pain, the problem is identified. This includes the labelling of it together with the labelling of signs ands illness. Illnesses usually consist of several symptoms, and Leventhal & Diefenbach (1991) found that people label their disorder by, first of all, clustering their symptoms to see if they make conceptual sense. Then they link the symptom clusters to illness labels. At the last stage expectations are built up because they subsequently expect to experience other symptoms as a consequence of this labelling process. The other dimensions for pain are the causes of the pain and possible consequences of it, the expected duration of the pain or time-line of it, and beliefs about how far it is controllable or curable. These factors not only provide insight into who goes to see the doctor and why, but they also begin to explain adherence behaviour too.

However, it is clear that various rules are used to modify these judgements. First of all we have a tendency to discount other people's symptoms on days that we know are stressful for them, so consequently this can interfere with the ready, full or smooth legitimation of illness. This predisposition to discount symptoms during stress events is called the stress-illness rule, and can to lead to an increase in self-medication (Leventhal & Crouch, 1997). Common-sense theories about gender and stress produce a gender-biased stress discounting effect, as Martin and Lemos (2002) found when they studied the medical interventions given to women who reported symptoms of chest pain, gallstones and melanoma. These stereotypes linking somatization to gen-der meant that women were less likely to be seen as needing treatment if they were at the same time highly distressed. Such theories, in turn, shape the interpretation of symptoms and the predisposition to self-refer for treatment.

Furthermore, with age, expectations change about the body and its capabilities. For instance, we expect to be less mobile as we get older in accordance with what is known as the age-illness rule. Expectations about athleticism first change when people reach 30 to 40 years of age, and change again for those between 50 and 60. Also, in this age group we have expectations about deteriorating sensory capacities and the increasing likelihood of arthritis (Leventhal & Crouch, 1997). However, this phenomenon is not very easy to investigate. For example, in a study of post-menopausal women, Tradafilopoulos et al. (1998) found that 38 per cent reported bowel dysfunction compared with only 14 per cent of pre-menopausal women studied, even though there were no group differences in pain, diarrhoea and constipation. The irritable bowel syndrome (IBS) complaints peaked at 40 to 49 years, but hormonal status could not account for it. The role of ageing in symptom perception cannot be discounted in this study, despite the more compelling conclusion that IBS is more common and therefore requires careful investigation.

While labelling can be of great assistance in decision-making about whether to seek medical help, in some cases there is also a case for saying that labelling can seriously damage your health! Croyle and Jemmott (1991) conducted an experiment where participants believed there was a chance they had a fictitious enzyme called 'thioamine acetylase' (TAA). One group were told that it was a common enzyme while others believed that it was rare. The results of an enzyme test were perceived to be more serious and emotionally upsetting for the people labelled as having the 'rare' condition (1:5 people) than if they had been reassured by sharing a similar fate with others.

SOCIAL CATEGORIES AND HOW THEY AFFECT THE RESPONSE TO ILLNESS

We have seen that the way we categorize ourselves and are categorized by others can have diverse effects on our health. Some categories like sex and age also have a biological foundation, and here the three parts of the bio-psycho-social model fuse to provide an integrated view of the way these different factors impinge on our health and perceptions of it. In this section, sex is taken as the example of how social categories can affect a person's response to illness and, in interacting with the health-care system, the treatment that they eventually receive.

Many sex differences have been reported in the experience of symptoms and the differential predisposition of men and women to seek health care. Women are consistently reported to show more pain than men; for a detailed review of this field see Berkley and Holdcroft (1999). Experimental psycho-physics shows that although women appear to have lower pain thresholds and a lower tolerance to pain than men, the results vary enormously depending on several important experimental variables. These are the type of stimulus used, whether tolerance or pain thresholds are measured, the bodily location of the stimulus, and physiological features like blood pressure level. Furthermore, environmental factors such as the sex and attractiveness of the experimenter and where the test was carried out also show a significant effect on the results and therefore the conclusions drawn.

Biological sex differences are often associated with diagnosis. Berkley and Holdcroft (1999) conclude that women report many more syndromes than men. These are primarily temporo-mandibular disorder, migraine, fibromyalgia, chest, abdominal and joint pains. Furthermore, the prevalence of some diseases changes as the lifespan progresses, and not always in ways that might be expected. Some painful disorders that are frequently recorded as being more prevalent in women during youth, diminish as they get older. Thirdly, it is now more widely appreciated that symptoms for the same disease may be expressed quite differently by the sexes. Examples include irritable bowel syndrome, acute appendicitis, migraine, coronary heart disease and some rheumatic diseases like ankylosing spondylitis (Calin et al., 1988). An example demonstrates the point: in reviewing the extensive recent literature on acute myocardial infarction, Miller

(2002) found that in addition to chest pain, women commonly reported the less obvious symptoms of breathlessness, back pain, oedema, fatigue and transient non-specific chest pain. The implication for diagnosis here is that these unexpected symptoms require greater attention from health professionals. Berkley and Holdcroft (1999) conclude that the overall burden of pain is greater for women than for men, being more varied and more variable. Although women are more willing to report more pain and seek more consultations in health care as a result, several biological factors found in studies of genetics, physiology, pelvic anatomy and hormones explain a substantial part of the variance in this phenomenon and need to be integrated with cultural and lifestyle factors to provide a much more holistic picture of the patient's condition.

Medical training teaches heuristics to help doctors deal with the vast amount of information they are expected to know and to make decisions under pressure. Clinical wisdom supports the view that gall bladder problems are common in women who are 'fair, fat and forty'. So within this context, it is not surprising to find biases in treatment following labelling. Looking at the general picture, Verbrugge and Steiner (1985) found that women received 5 to 10 per cent more prescriptions for common complaints than men. Women average twice as many visits per year to doctors than men aged 17 to 44 years, and 33 per cent more over 45 years of age. They found that women also have different strategies for dealing with illness; these include greater use of medication and combining several therapies together.

Berkley and Holdcroft (1999) also report that for women, there are more sex-linked biological and gender-related socio-cultural mechanisms for reducing pain, despite the extra burden of pain. So while women are more vulnerable to pain, they do appear to have more ways of dealing with it. One question that has been raised is whether women appear more pleased with the treatment they receive, so giving positive reinforcement to their health-care providers. But even where the incidence of reporting particular illnesses is the same in both sexes, health professionals are inclined to manage these illnesses in different ways. Verbrugge and her colleagues have pursued a series of studies to better understand the train of events that might be at work in this context. Verbrugge and Steiner (1984) found that the consultation frequency for headaches, chest and back pain, fatigue, dizziness and vertigo were similar for both sexes. But when they looked at how doctors responded in terms of providing treatment for these symptoms, they found some interesting differences. A salient finding was that counselling was recommended as a suitable treatment for headaches in women, while men with headaches were more likely to receive injections. Similarly the medical response to chest or back pain in men was a hospital investigation, whereas women with the same conditions were more likely to be sent to a clinic.

This differential interpretation of acute symptoms and their effect on medical management decisions is also demonstrated in a study of painful symptoms. In studying 84 health professionals working in a hospital emergency department with headache, neck and back pain patients, Raftery, Smith-Coggins and Chen (1995) found that in line with previous research findings, health-care providers described women as reporting more pain than men. Although women experienced more pain and received more medication including more potent analgesics than men, they were less likely than men to receive no medication at all. However, in spite of these differences, they found that the severity of pain correlated better with pain practices than did gender. Systematic biases may be perpetuated at different stages in the treatment process. Johnson et al. (1996) studied 1,411 patients attending an emergency department with acute chest pain. The results showed that at the outset women were less likely than men to be admitted to hospital, but they were also less likely to take an exercise stress test within a month of their visit. Of those who were admitted to hospital, the incidence of taking the stress test was equal for the gender groups, but the incidence of cardiac catheterization was lower in women.

So what explanations can be used to explain sex differences? First of all, knowledgeable patients themselves may request more services, and it is very difficult for doctors to refuse these requests if they are relevant to the condition and they want to maintain patient satisfaction and trust and keep lines of communication open. Patients may also refuse services when offered, too. Secondly, for any particular symptom, some patients will be distressed and others will remain calm. Physicians may respond differently to these atmospheres and may well make treatment decisions based in part on this reaction. Thirdly, like other people, physicians may have stereotypic views about ill health in the sexes and how it should be managed, rather than responding to people's problems as individuals, rather than categories. Lastly, and by no means least, a wide and complex range of medical factors determine treatment.

These studies show the insidious effect which social factors like gender may have on access to health care. These processes connected with gender have been carefully unpicked in research, but the findings raise important questions about the effects on health care of other distinctive and visibly different categories of society. They also raise important issues concerning the training of health professionals, which needs to actively incorporate a knowledge base and skills training that will enable practitioners to address the practical problems that confound the fair, equal and socially inclusive distribution of care and treatment at the various points of delivery.

DISCUSSION POINTS

1. What are the main psycho-social factors that influence the decision to seek help from a doctor by those who are experiencing a raised body temperature and painful swollen glands?
2. What psychological theories can be used to better understand this decision-making process?
3. Why are psychological factors central to our understanding of how pain is reported?
4. If a friend broke a toe during a game of tennis in the first set, but did not notice until they were in the changing room an hour later after the game was over, from your knowledge of pain mechanisms, how would you explain this phenomenon?
5. Why do women report more pain than men?

FURTHER READING

1. Melzack, R. and Wall, P. D. (1989). *The Challenge of Pain*. Harmondsworth: Penguin.
2. Taylor, S. E. (2003). *Health Psychology*, 5th edn. New York: McGraw Hill. Especially chapter 8, 'Using Health Services'.
3. Skevington, S. M. (1995). *Psychology of Pain*. Chichester: John Wiley.
4. Petrie, K. and Weinman, J., eds. (1997). *Perceptions of Health and Illness*. Amsterdam: Harwood.
5. Gatchel, R. and Turk, D. C., eds. (1996). *Psychological Approaches to Pain Management: A Practitioner's Handbook*. New York: Guildford.
6. Wall, P. D. and Melzack, R. (1999). *Textbook of Pain*, 4th edn. Edinburgh: Churchill Livingston.

REFERENCES

Anderson, A. D. and Pennebaker, J. W. (1980). Pain and pleasure: an alternative interpretation for identical stimulation. *European Journal of Social Psychology* 10(2), 207–12.

Bass, C. and Mayou, R. A. (1995). Chest pain and palpitations. In R. A. Mayou, C. Bass and M. Sharpe, eds., *Treatment of Functional Symptomatic Symptoms*. Oxford: Oxford University Press.

Beecher, H. K. (1959). *The Measurement of Subjective Responses – Quantitative Measurement of Drugs*. Oxford: Oxford University Press.

Berkley, K. and Holdcroft, A. (1999). Sex and gender differences in pain. In P. D. Wall and R. Melzack, eds., *Textbook of Pain*, vol. IV. Edinburgh: Churchill Livingstone, 951–65.

Bonica, J. J. (1990). Definitions and taxonomy of pain. In J. J. Bonica, *The Management of Pain*, 2nd edn. Philadelphia: Lee and Febinger, 18–27.

Calin, A., Elswood, J., Rigg, S. and Skevington, S. M. (1988). Ankylosing spondylitis – an analytical review of 1,500 patients: the changing pattern of disease. *Journal of Rheumatology* 15(8), 1234–8.

Clark, W. C. and Clark, S. B. (1980). Pain responses in Nepalese porters. *Science* 209, 410–12.

Craig, K. D. (1986). Social modelling influences: pain in context. In R. A. Sternbach, ed., *The Psychology of Pain*, 2nd edn. New York: Raven Press, 67–96.

Crook, J., Rideout, E. and Browne, G. (1984). The prevalence of pain complaints in a general population. *Pain* 18, 299–314.

Croyle, R. T. and Jemmott, J. B. (1991). Psychological reactions to risk factor testing. In J. A. Skelton and R. T. Croyle, eds., *Mental Representation in Health and Illness*. New York: Springer-Verlag, 85–107.

Curt, G. A. (2001). Fatigue in cancer. *British Medical Journal* 322, 1560.

Donovan, M., Dillon, P. and McGuire, L. (1987). Incidence and characteristics of pain in a sample of medical-surgical inpatients. *Pain* 30, 69–78.

Egan, K. J. and Beaton, R. (1987). Response to symptoms in healthy, low utilizers of the health care system. *Journal of Psychosomatic Research* 31(1), 11–21.

Ferguson, R. J. and Ahles, T. A. (1998). Private body consciousness, anxiety and pain symptom reports of chronic pain patients. *Behaviour Research and Therapy* 36(5), 527–35.

Fernandez, E. and Turk, D. C. (1989). The utility of cognitive coping strategies for altering pain perception: a meta-analysis. *Pain* 38(2), 123–36.

Festinger, L. (1954). A theory of social comparison processes. *Human Relations* 7, 117–40.

Feuerstein, M. and Zastowny, T. R. (1996). Occupational rehabilitation: multidisciplinary management of work-related musculo-skeletal pain and disability. In R. Gatchel and D. C. Turk, eds., *Psychological Approaches to Pain Management: A Practitioner's Handbook*. New York, Guildford Publications, 458–85.

Fordyce, W. E. (1976). *Behavioral Methods for Chronic Pain and Illness.* St Louis: Mosby.

Gatchel, R. and Turk, D. C., eds. (1996). *Psychological Approaches to Pain Management: A Practitioner's Handbook.* New York: Guildford Publications.

Greenley, J. R. and Mechanic, D. (1976). Social selection in seeking help for psychological problems. *Journal of Health and Social Behavior* 17, 249–62.

Griffin, K. W., Friend, R., Kaell, A. T., Bennett, R. S. and Wadhwa, N. K. (1999). Negative affect and physical symptom reporting: a test of explanatory models in two chronically ill populations. *Psychology and Health* 14(2), 295–307.

GSSI (1986). Effectiveness of intravenous thrombolytic treatment in acute myocardial infarction. *Lancet* 1, 397–401.

Guzman, J., Esmail, R., Karjalainen, K., Malmivaara, A., Irvin, E. and Bombardier, C. (2001). Multidisciplinary rehabilitation for chronic low back pain: a systematic review. *British Medical Journal* 322, 1511–16.

Hackett, T. P. and Cassem, N. H. (1969). Factors contributing to delay in responding to the signs and symptoms of acute myocardial infarction. *American Journal of Cardiology* 24, 651–8.

Hannay, D. R. (1979). *The Symptom Iceberg: A Study of Community Health.* London: Routledge and Kegan Paul.

Hedges, J. R., Mann, N. C., Meischke, H., Robbins, M., Goldberg, R. and Zapka, J. (1998). Assessment of chest pain onset and out-of-hospital delay using standardised interview questions: the REACT pilot study. *Academic Emergency Medicine* 5(8), 773–80.

Holmes, J. A. and Stevenson, C. A. Z. (1990). Differential effects of avoidant and attentional coping strategies on adaptation to chronic and recent onset pain. *Health Psychology* 9(5), 577–84.

Jemmott, J. B., Ditto, P. H. and Croyle, R. T. (1988). Commonsense epidemiology: self-based judgements from lay-persons and physicians. *Health Psychology* 7, 55–73.

Johnson, P. A., Golma, L., Orav, E. J., et al. (1996). Gender differences in the management of acute chest pain: support for the Yentl syndrome. *Journal of General Internal Medicine* 11, 209–17.

Kahneman, D. (1999). Objective happiness. In D. Kahneman, E. Diener and N. Schwartz, eds., *Well-being: The Foundations of Hedonic Psychology.* New York: Russell Sage, 3–25.

Kudenchuck, P. J., Maynard, C., Martin, J. S., Wirkus, M. and Weaver, W. D. (1996). Comparison of presentation, treatment and outcome of acute myocardial infarction in men versus women – the myocardial infarction triage and intervention registry. *American Journal of Cardiology* 78(1), 9–14.

Kulik, J. A. and Mahler, H. I. M. (1987). Health status, perception of risk and prevention interest for health and non-health problems. *Health Psychology* 6(1), 15–27.

Lavidor, M., Weller, A. and Babkoff, H. (2002). Multidimensional fatigue, somatic symptoms and depression. *British Journal of Health Psychology* 7, 67–75.

Leventhal, E. A. and Crouch, M. (1997). Are there differences in perceptions of illness across the lifespan? In K. J. Petrie and J. A. Weinman, eds., *Perceptions of Health and Illness.* Amsterdam: Harwood Academic, 77–102.

Leventhal, H. and Diefenbach, M. (1991). The active side of illness cognition. In J. A. Skelton and R. T. Croyle, eds., *Mental Representation in Health and Illness.* New York: Springer, 247–72.

Linton, S. J. (1994). The role of psychological factors in back pain and its remediation. *Pain Reviews* 1, 231–41.

Linton, S. J. and Skevington, S. M. (1999). Psychological factors. In *Epidemiology of Pain.* Seattle: International Association for the Study of Pain Press, 25–42.

Martin, R. and Lemos, K. (2002). From heart attacks to melanoma: do common sense models of somatization influence symptom interpretation for female victims? *Health Psychology* 21(1), 25–32.

McCracken, L. M., Gross, R. T., Sorg, P. J. and Edmonds, T. A. (1993). Prediction of pain in patients with chronic low back pain: effects of inaccurate prediction and pain-related anxiety. *Behaviour Research and Therapy* 31, 647–52.

Mechanic, D. (1977). Illness behavior, social adaptation and the management of illness. *Journal of Nervous and Mental Diseases* 165(2), 79–87.

Melzack, R. (1975). The McGill Pain Questionnaire: major properties and scoring method. *Pain* 1, 277–99.

Melzack, R. (1987). The short form McGill Pain Questionnaire. *Pain* 36, 191–7.

Melzack, R. and Katz, J. (1999). Pain measurement in persons in pain. In P. D. Wall and R. Melzack, eds., *Textbook of Pain*, vol. IV. Edinburgh: Churchill Livingstone, 409–26.

Melzack, R. and Wall, P. D. (1965). Pain mechanisms – a new theory. *Science* 150, 971–9.

Melzack, R. and Wall, P. D. (1989). *The Challenge of Pain*, 2nd edn. Harmondsworth: Penguin.

Melzack, R., Wall, P. D. and Ty, T. C. (1982). Acute pain in an emergency clinic: latency of onset and descriptor patterns related to different injuries. *Pain* 14, 33–42.

Merskey, H., Albe-Fessard, D. G., Bonica, J. J., Carmen, A., Dubner, R., Kerr, F. W. L., Lindblom, U., Mumford, J. M., Nathan, P. W., Noordenbos, W., Pagni, C. A., Renaer, M. J., Sternbach, R. A., and Sutherland, S. (1979). IASP subcommittee on taxonomy. *Pain* 6(3), 249–52.

Miller, C. L. (2002). A review of symptoms of coronary artery disease in women. *Journal of Advanced Nursing* 39(1), 17–23.

Miller, S. M., Brody, D. S. and Summerton, J. (1988). Styles of coping with threat: implications for health. *Journal of Personality and Social Psychology* 54(10), 142–8.

Moore, R. A. (1990). Ethnographic assessment of pain coping perceptions. *Psychosomatic Medicine* 52, 171–81.

Pennebaker, J. W. (1982). *The Psychology of Physical Symptoms*. New York: Springer-Verlag.

Petrie, K. J. and Weinman, J. A., eds. (1997). Illness representations and recovery from myocardial infarction. In K. J. Petrie and J. Weinman, eds., *Perceptions of Health and Illness*. Amsterdam: Harwood Academic, 441–62.

Philips, H. C. (1987). Avoidance behaviour and its role in sustaining chronic pain. *Behaviour Research and Therapy* 25, 273–9.

Porzelius, J. (1995). Memory for pain after nerve-block injections. *Clinical Journal of Pain* 11(2), 112–20.

Quadrel, M. J. and Lau, R. R. (1990). A multivariate analysis of adolescent's orientations towards physician use. *Health Psychology* 9, 750–73.

Raftery, K. A., Smith-Coggins, R. and Chen, A. H. M. (1995). Gender-associated differences in emergency department pain management. *Annals of Emergency Medicine* 26, 414–21.

Rutter, D. and Quine, L. (2002). Social cognition models and changing health behaviours. In D. Rutter and L. Quine, eds., *Changing Health Behaviours*. Buckingham, UK: Open University Press, 1–27.

Sartorius, N. (1987). Cross-cultural comparisons of data about quality of life: a sample of issues. In N. K. Aaronson and J. Beckmann, eds., *The Quality of Life of Cancer Patients*. New York: Raven Press, 19–24.

Skevington, S. M. (1994). Social comparisons in cross-cultural quality of life assessment. *International Journal of Mental Health* 23(2), 29–47.

Skevington, S. M. (1995). *Psychology of Pain*. Chichester: Wiley.

Skevington, S. M., Carse, M. and Williams, A. C. de C. (2001). Validation of the WHOQOL-100: pain management improves quality of life for chronic pain patients. *Clinical Journal of Pain* 17, 264–75.

Skevington, S. M. and Mason, V. L. (2004). Social influences on individual differences. In

T. Hadjistavropoulos and K. D. Craig, eds., *Pain: psychological perspectives*. Mahwah, NJ: Lawrence Erlbaum, 179–208.

Skevington, S. M., Pilaar, M., Routh, D. A. and McLeod, R. (1997). On the language of breathlessness. *Psychology and Health* 12, 677–89.

Sternbach, R. A. and Tursky, B. (1965). Ethnic differences among housewives in psychophysiological and skin potential responses to electric shock. *Psychophysiology* 1(3), 217–18.

Taylor, S. E. (2003). *Health Psychology*, 5th edn. New York: McGraw Hill.

Telles, J. L. and Pollack, M. H. (1981). Feeling sick – the experience and legitimation of illness. *Social Science and Medicine* 15A, 243–51.

Theisen, M. E., MacNeill, S. E., Lumley, M. A., Ketterer, M. W., Goldberg, A. D. and Borzak, S. (1995). Psychosocial factors related to unrecognised acute myocardial infarction. *American Journal of Cardiology* 75(17), 1211–13 (June 15).

Thurston, R. C., Keefe, F. J., Bradley, L., Krishnan, K. R. R. and Caldwell, D. S. (2001). Chest pain in the absence of coronary heart disease: a biopsychosocial perspective. *Pain* 93, 95–100.

Triadafilopoulous, G., Finlayson, M. and Grellet, C. (1998). Bowel dysfunction in post-menopausal women. *Women and Health* 27(4), 55–66.

Turk, D. C. (1997). The role of demographic and psychosocial factors in transition from acute to chronic pain. In T. S. Jensen, J. A. Turner and Z. Weisenfeld-Hallin, eds., *Proceedings of the 8th World Congress on Pain, Progress in Pain Research and Management*, vol. 8. Seattle, IASP Press, 185–213.

Turk, D. C., and Flor, H. (1987). Pain behaviours: the utility and limitations of the pain behaviour construct. *Pain* 31, 277–95.

Turner, J. A. and Clancy, S. (1988). Comparison of operant behavioural and cognitive-behavioural group treatment for chronic low back pain. *Journal of Consulting and Clinical Psychology* 56(2), 261–6.

Turner, J. A. and Jensen, M. P. (1993). Efficacy of cognitive therapy for chronic low back pain. *Pain* 52, 169–77.

Vassend, O. (1994). Negative affectivity, subjective somatic complaints and objective health indicators: mind and body still separated? *International Review of Health Psychology*. New York: John Wiley and Sons, 97–118.

Verbrugge, L. M. and Steiner, R. P. (1984). Another look at physician's treatment of men and women with common complaints. *Sex Roles* 11, 11–12.

Verbrugge, L. M. and Steiner, R. P. (1985). Prescribing drugs to men and women. *Health Psychology* 4(1), 79–98.

Vlaeyen, J. W. S. and Linton, S. J. (2000). Fear avoidance and its consequences in chronic musculoskeletal pain: a state of the art. *Pain* 85, 317–32.

Waddell, G., Newton, M., Henderson, I., Somerville, D. and Main, C. (1993). Fear Avoidance Beliefs Questionnaire (FABQ) and the role of fear-avoidance beliefs in chronic low back pain and disability. *Pain* 52, 157–68.

Wall, P. D. and Melzack, R., eds. (1999). *Textbook of Pain*, fourth edn. Edinburgh: Churchill Livingston.

Weibe, D. J., Alderfer, M. A., Palmer, S. C. and Lindsay, R. (1994). Behavioural self-regulation in adolescents with type 1 diabetes. *Journal of Consulting and Clinical Psychology* 62(6): 1204–12.

Yoos, H. L. and McMullen, A. (1999). Symptom perception and evaluation in childhood asthma. *Nursing Research* 48(1), 2–8.

Zborowski, M. (1969). *People in Pain*. San Francisco: Jossey-Bass.

Chapter Nine

CHRONIC ILLNESS

Denise de Ridder

CHAPTER OUTLINE

Chronic illnesses are disorders which persist for an extended period of time and are either incurable or result in pathological changes which limit a person's ability to function daily in a normal way. Some chronic diseases, such as arthritis or multiple sclerosis, cannot be cured (yet), but are only treated to relieve symptoms. Other chronic diseases, such as diabetes and asthma, may be medically controlled, but only at the cost of a very strict regime involving adherence to daily performance of disease management behaviours. Chronic illness has the potential to induce profound changes in a person's life with resulting serious negative effects on quality of life and well-being.

This chapter considers a number of psychological issues related to chronic illness. We begin by addressing some figures on types and distribution of chronic illness, and we will consider their categorization according to psychologically relevant characteristics (section 1). Next, we will look at the psychological factors believed to influence the onset and course of chronic illness (section 2). We proceed by discussing psychological processes associated with adjustment to chronic illness (section 3). Several factors may play a role in the adjustment process, such as patient beliefs about illness, personal traits such as optimism and self-efficacy, and illness behaviours such as coping strategies and seeking social support (section 4). In the following section, we will discuss an emerging new perspective on the psychology of chronic illness, highlighting issues related to self-management (section 5). We will close this chapter with a discussion of psychological interventions for the chronically ill (section 6).

Key Concepts

adaptive tasks
adherence
adjustment
coping strategies
disease onset
health behaviour model
illness behaviour model
illness representations
medical demands
optimism

patient education
personal control
personality
progressive course
quality of life
self-efficacy
self-management
social support
stress and emotion
stress moderation model

1 Types and Distribution of Chronic Illness

Although no scientific definition of the concept of chronic illness exists, many researchers agree that chronic illnesses typically involve diseases of a long-lasting nature without a perspective of cure. In addition, most chronic illnesses are characterized by a progressive course, which means that the physical condition of patients gets worse as years go by. Due to improved public health and to better medical control over acute infectious diseases such as influenza, tuberculosis, measles and polio, and to the increased life expectancy of the population associated with it, during the twentieth century chronic diseases have become important health risks in Western societies (e.g. Glasgow et al., 1999; MacKeown, 1979). Reliable epidemiological data from European countries are scarce, but the available figures demonstrate that amongst the most prevalent chronic diseases are various forms of heart disease (coronary heart disease, stroke and heart failure), rheumatoid arthritis, diabetes, asthma, and different types of cancer (WHO, 1994). For example, figures on diabetes prevalence show that about 3 to 10 per cent of the population in European countries are afflicted by this condition (King & Zimmet, 1988). Asthma, on the other hand, is more variable across countries, with a high prevalence in the United Kingdom and a much smaller prevalence in other European countries (ECRHS, 1996). Estimates of European figures on the prevalence of cancer and heart disease can only be derived from mortality statistics (Boyle, 1992). Unfortunately, such figures are difficult to compare across countries as they are related to country-specific differences in screening and registration procedures (Ruwaard et al., 1994). It is expected that in the near future the prevalence of especially diabetes (due to increased unhealthy diet and associated obesity – Seidell, 1995; Zimmet, 2000) and breast cancer and ovarian cancer (due to increased use of hormone suppletion therapy in menopausal women) will rise (Boyle, 1992). In contrast, it is expected that lung cancer will decrease in the future, at least in the north

European countries, because of the decreased smoking behaviour in men; for women, however, the prevalence of lung cancer is rising (Ruwaard et al., 1994).

Taking all chronic conditions together, it is estimated that at any given moment 50 per cent of the population suffers from a chronic illness requiring some form of medical intervention (Taylor & Aspinwall, 1996a). Most chronic illnesses occur in older adults; and as the average age of the population increases, so does the prevalence of chronic illnesses. It is estimated that people aged 60 years and older have, on average, 2.2 chronic conditions (Rothenberg & Koplan, 1990). Most chronic illnesses have a late onset, but some, such as asthma and diabetes, may even manifest themselves in young children (Suris & Blum, 2001). It is estimated that about 35 per cent of young adults aged 18 to 44 years have at least one chronic condition (Taylor & Aspinwall, 1996a). Because chronic diseases are ones with which people often live many years, medical management of these chronic disorders is costly and accounts for 75 per cent of US health spending (Hoffman, Rice & Sung, 1996).

Types of chronic diseases

The term chronic illness refers to a wide variety of diseases which have in common that they are of a long-lasting nature. From a psychological point of view, the extended course without the perspective of cure may be of interest, possibly affecting patients' willingness and ability to perform behaviours related to managing illness and adhering to medical prescriptions (see section 5). It may be important to discriminate between different categories of chronic illness beyond medical diagnostic distinctions. Attempts in this direction are scarce, however. Disease characteristics such as predictability, contagiousness, and life-threateningness have been proposed as factors possibly affecting illness management and support from relatives and friends (Felton & Revenson, 1984). For example, cancer and AIDS, which confront the family of the patient with crisis and possibly even threaten their own health (in case of AIDS), may provoke decreased, sometimes even 'negative', support, resulting in victimizing the patient (Bishop et al., 1991; Manne et al., 1997). Another characteristic of interest relates to controllability of disease, referring to the actual possibilities of influencing the symptoms and course of the illness by performing self-care behaviours, such as maintaining a healthy diet or adjusting medication intake according to activity. Typical diseases which are controllable by the patient (at least to some extent) are diabetes and asthma, requiring the performance of self-care routines (both medication and health habits) on a daily basis. Actual control may increase feelings of *perceived* control, but it may also impose a high burden on self-management routines, confronting the patient with his or her responsibility to take good care of the illness (Eitel et al., 1995). Typical uncontrollable diseases are neurological disorders such as multiple sclerosis, with an unpredictable course and few opportunities for patients to influence symptoms (Felton & Revenson, 1984; Fournier, De Ridder & Bensing, 2002). Uncontrollability of illness may result in feelings of helplessness, although it has been suggested that there may be adaptive benefits to surrendering control in the face of uncontrollable chronic illness (Reid, 1984). Although the issue of actual illness control is important in discriminating between types of chronic diseases, most studies show that there is a remarkably low association between actual control and perceived, subjective control. Moreover, such studies show that perceived control is a stronger predictor of adjustment than actual control (Helgeson, 1992; Taylor et al., 1991; see also section 4).

Adaptive tasks in chronic illness

Other research on features of chronic illness corroborates the importance of subjective evaluations of disease characteristics and proposes the concept of 'adaptive tasks' as a relevant construct for studying psychological aspects of chronic illness (Bensing et al., 2002; De Ridder, Schreurs & Bensing, 1998; Moos & Schaefer, 1984). The concept of adaptive tasks refers to the subjective evaluation of disease-related stressors which challenge adjustment, and comprises such stressors as dealing with pain and incapacity, dealing with hospital environment, developing adequate relationships with health-care staff, preserving emotional balance, preserving a satisfactory self-image, sustaining relationships with family and friends, and preparing for an uncertain future (cf. Dunkel-Schetter et al., 1992; Moos & Schaefer, 1984). The majority of psychological studies on chronic illness have employed a disease-specific framework, elaborating on the typical medical (disease-specific) demands associated with illness as important factors in adaptation. However, there is some evidence that adaptive tasks are similar across a wide range of chronic illnesses, although the relative importance of such tasks may differ due to the variation in medical demands (Heijmans et al., 2001). Some researchers have therefore proposed that a disease-generic framework, highlighting the common psychological demands of chronic illness, may offer a promising perspective for studying the psychological aspects of chronic illness (Glasgow et al., 2000; Heijmans et al., 2001; Stanton, Collins & Sworowski, 2001). Besides similarities in adaptation processes across diseases, another reason for maintaining a generic view on the psychological aspects of chronic illness relates to the fact that many patients suffer from more than one chronic condition at the same time (known as 'comorbidity') (cf. Rothenberg & Koplan, 1990), which inevitably challenges the validity of a disease-specific approach. Taken together, research on a wide variety of chronic illnesses has failed to identify clear categories of chronic illness according to objective disease characteristics. Subjective evaluations of disease are important for understanding the way patients adjust to illness and are similar across a wide range of chronic diseases. In the following sections, we will therefore not discuss diseases separately but focus on psychological issues which are common to a number of chronic diseases.

Psychological models of chronic illness

Psychological studies on chronic illness are generally guided by models of stress and coping which either focus on the role of stress and moderators of stress in the onset and course of illness, or highlight adaptation to stress caused by being chronically ill (Cohen, Kessler & Gordon, 1995; Cohen & Lazarus, 1979; De Ridder & Schreurs, 1996; Stanton et al., 2001; Maes, Leventhal & De Ridder, 1996). These models are derived from more general conceptual frameworks regarding adjustment to stressful experiences, and typically highlight the role of stressors as possibly affecting health outcomes, well-being and adjustment. The impact of stress is believed to be mediated by cognitive appraisals of the stressor and the personal and social resources available to assist coping with stress. Therefore, coping resources, coping strategies, as well as the personal and social context of stress are important areas of psychological research on chronic illness (Lazarus & Folkman, 1984; Moos & Schaefer, 1993; Taylor & Aspinwall, 1996b). In addition, an important area of research is also concerned with clarifying the role of biological pathways between stress on the one hand and health outcomes on the other hand. To date, such models incorporate hormonal, immuno-logical or cardiovascular aspects of adjustment (e.g. Andersen, Kiecolt-Glaser & Glaser, 1994; Baum & Poluszny, 1999). Compared to other social sciences dealing with chronic illness, such as behavioural medicine or medical sociology, psychological models of chronic illness have equally adopted a so-called bio-psycho-social view of chronic illness (Engel, 1977), in which psychological as well as social and biological factors play a role, but with more emphasis on the psychological processes associated with it.

2 PSYCHOLOGICAL FACTORS IN THE ONSET AND COURSE OF CHRONIC ILLNESS

Early research in the 1950s on psychological issues in chronic illness has been char-acterized by a strong desire to identify personality factors which would explain why some individuals run a greater risk of becoming chronically ill than others. In an attempt to link psychological factors to the onset of chronic disease, research was based on the assumption that a particular psychological make-up would increase the risk of becoming chronically ill. It was also assumed that particular psychological char-acteristics would be predictive of specific diseases. Typical examples are the type A personality, with a proneness to coronary artery disease and whose behaviour is char-acterized by competitive drive, impatience, hostility and rapid speech and motor move-ments (Booth-Kewley & Friedman, 1987); the so-called type C cancer personality, whose behaviour is characterized by a passive, acquiescent style (Temoshok, 1987); and the rheumatoid arthritis personality, who is perfectionist, depressed and restricted in the expression of anger (Anderson et al., 1985).

Current psychological research no longer maintains such strong views of the role of psychological factors in the onset of disease because empirical evidence has demon-strated that the behaviours formerly regarded to contribute to disease in fact may represent reactions to being ill. Thus, where prospective designs have been employed to examine these issues, they do not support formerly held assumptions. Although a direct causal role of psychological factors in the aetiology of chronic illness is no longer maintained, related concepts are still being researched, but mostly in the con-text of more complex personality models of illness (Wiebe & Smith, 1997). These

models are derived from the bio-psycho-social framework and suggest complex relationships between psychological, social and physiological aspects of disease which go
beyond a direct impact of psychological factors on disease onset. Three major models
of personality and illness are distinguished, implying three different pathways through
which personality may impact on the development and course of physical illness (Wiebe
& Smith, 1997). These recent models of the role of personality in chronic illness suggest that personality exerts its influence on health and illness through processes, such
as appraisal of stress and subsequent coping responses (the *stress moderation model*);
the tendency to perform particular health behaviours (either health-protective or
health-damaging) believed to influence the onset of illness (the *health behaviour model*);
and the tendency to perform illness-relevant behaviours (e.g. symptom perception,
health-care seeking, self medication) when one is ill (the *illness behaviour model*).
As a result, the conceptual models relating personality to chronic illness have become
more sophisticated in the past decades and examine the role of personality in the
context of stress and adjustment. Recent studies employing these more sophisticated
models of personality and illness have provided considerable evidence that especially
individuals who have a tendency to create more severe, more frequent and enduring stressors through their thoughts and actions run a greater risk of chronic illness
(Smith, 1992). For example, social isolation, low perceived emotional support, hostility (Hemingway & Marmot, 1999; Rozanski, Blumenthal & Kaplan, 1999), and a combination of negative affectivity and social inhibition (also addressed as type D – for
distressed – personality; Denollet, 1998) are characteristic for the behaviour of individuals who run a greater risk of cardiovascular diseases. Reviews on the onset of
rheumatoid arthritis also present evidence on the role of failing strategies to deal with
stress as a relevant predictor of the onset and course of rheumatoid arthritis (Huyser
& Parker, 1998; Zautra et al., 1998). Recent research findings thus have continued
to demonstrate the significant role of personality factors as relevant predictors of
chronic illness, but with more emphasis on the role of personality in dealing with
stress, more attention to the psycho-physiological mechanisms involved, and with
less emphasis on their disease-specific role (Smith, 1992). In addition, in contrast to
the emphasis on the role of personality factors in the onset of chronic illness in earlier studies, recent studies are also concerned with the role of personality factors in
adjustment to chronic illness (see section 4 for the role of optimism in adjustment).

Stress and emotion

Recent research findings regarding the role of personality in dealing with stress fit
into a broader framework highlighting the role of emotions in the onset of chronic
illness. There is accumulating evidence that repression or inhibition of negative emotions may be a risk factor in the onset and course of chronic diseases (Traue &
Pennebaker, 1993), especially in heart disease (DeNollett, 1998). Although the exact
psycho-physiological mechanisms involved are still unclear, it has been suggested
that the more people inhibit their emotions, the more their physiological activity may

increase (Pennebaker, Hughes & O'Heeron, 1987), which in turn may promote disease onset. In contrast, disclosure of emotions by writing or talking to others may have a beneficial impact on disease course (Smyth et al., 1999; see Smyth, 1998, for a meta-analysis of effects). The role of emotional inhibition in the onset of chronic diseases is a promising new approach to study the psychological factors in becoming ill; especially since the concept of emotional inhibition offers the possibility of explaining mediating physiological and immunological pathways between personality factors on the one hand and the biology of disease on the other hand. However, most research on psychological issues in chronic illness has not been concerned with their role in disease onset but with adjustment to illness – a topic which we will discuss in the following sections.

3 Indicators of Adjustment to Chronic Illness

Immediately following the medical diagnosis of chronic illness, patients are often in a state of crisis characterized by emotional distress and finding that their habitual ways of coping do not work (Moos & Schaefer, 1984). As a result, patients may experience feelings of anxiety, fear, depression or even denial (Taylor & Aspinwall, 1996a). Eventually, the crisis phase of chronic illness passes and patients enter a phase in which they make efforts to adapt to the new situation. Depending on the way they handle this phase and depending on the progression of disease, most patients eventually reach a state of adjustment. Attempts to delineate a set of stages of adjustment have proven unsuccessful as disease stage is related inconsistently to adjustment (e.g. Van 't Spijker, Trijsburg & Duivenvoorden, 1997). However, a number of studies suggest that, for most patients, the crisis of illness diminishes within a year following diagnosis (e.g. Cox & Gonder-Frederick, 1992).

Quality of life

Adjustment to disease can be assessed in multiple ways. A typical measure derived from medical practice is health-related quality of life, which is generally assessed by measures of daily functioning (i.e. the ability to conduct daily personal and role-related activities). The widely used Rand 36-item Health Survey (Ware, 1993), for example, assesses physical functioning, social functioning, role limitations due to physical problems, role limitations due to emotional problems, mental health, vitality, pain and general perceptions of health. Such functional measures of adjustment are relevant in the context of medical treatment, but do not capture adequately other indicators of adjustment, such as satisfaction with life or well-being (Taylor & Aspinwall, 1996a).

The basic assumption of psychological theories of well-being is that the successful pursuit of meaningful goals plays an important role in the development and maintenance of psychological well-being (Brunstein, 1993; Ditto et al., 1996; Scheier & Bridges, 1995). As chronic illness may jeopardize the accomplishment of goals, well-being may also be threatened. Therefore, several researchers in the field of quality-of-life research have emphasized the role of personal goals and related constructs in patients' perceptions of their quality of life. According to Calman (1984), for example, quality of life measures the gap between the individual's hopes, dreams and ambitions and his or her present experience of reality. The central element in this definition is that self-reported quality of life is assumed to involve some subjective evaluation of goal attainment. Distinguishing different conceptualizations of quality of life is relevant as patients' reports on good adjustment tend to differ depending on the type of measure of quality of life which has been used. Studies employing a functional measure mostly indicate rather poor quality of life of chronically ill patients, especially in the domains related to physical functioning (e.g. Schlenk et al., 1998). Studies employing a goal-related measure, however, show that quality of life of chronically ill patients is remarkably similar to the quality of life reported by healthy people. Some studies even demonstrate a positive effect of being ill (Folkman, 1997; Petrie et al., 1999; Södergren & Hyland, 2000). For example, Collins and colleagues (Collins, Taylor & Skokan, 1990) reported that 90 per cent of cancer patients in their study named at least some beneficial changes in their lives as a result of the cancer, including an increased ability to appreciate each day and the inspiration to get on with important life tasks, putting more effort in their relationships, and more awareness of other's feelings and more sympathy and compassion for others. Such findings may be dismissed as an artefact demonstrating the existence of defence mechanisms in chronically ill patients, such as denial of their condition (cf. Croyle, Sun & Hart, 1997), but the consistent observation of positive reactions seems to contradict such an interpretation. Recently, the so-called response shift phenomenon (Sprangers & Schwartz, 1999) has been proposed as an explanation for reported positive reactions to chronic illness, implying that, during the course of illness, patients may learn to adopt new standards and values about important things in life in response to their altered life condition. Such reactions may occur because chronically ill people re-order their priorities and find meaning in other activities in response to illness. Another explanation for the apparently positive adjustment to chronic illness is that it only affects specific domains of functioning instead of creating complete maladjustment. For example, Andersen, Woods and Copeland (1997) found that cancer is more likely to produce 'islands' of life disruption in specific realms and at specific points in time than to confer a risk for global dysfunction. Regardless of why they occur, these positive reactions seem to serve a beneficial function in emotional recovery and imply that we should attend to the protective effects of positive biases in adaptation (Taylor & Brown, 1988).

Emotional distress

Other indicators of adjustment involve assessments of negative emotional impact such as anxiety or depression. A number of studies conclude that people with chronic illness in general maintain adequate psychological functioning, although a significant minority of patients may be at risk for anxiety or depression (Cox & Gonder-Frederick, 1992; DeVellis, 1995; Ell & Dunkel-Schetter, 1994). Although anxiety in chronically ill patients may be an expression of a tendency towards anxiety which already existed before illness onset, typical illness-related situations may also increase the experience of anxiety. Examples of such situations are waiting for test results, invasive procedures, side-effects of treatment, dependency on health professionals, and uncertainty about disease course (e.g. Jacobsen, Bovbjerg & Redd, 1993). Depressive reactions are also more common among chronically ill patients. A number of studies on different chronic diseases have reported that about 30 per cent of patients show symptoms of depression (e.g. Clark, Cook & Snow, 1998; Dickens et al., 2002). It has been suggested that depression is a normal reaction related to the first stage of illness confronting patients with crisis and loss, but there is little evidence to support that view (Wells et al., 1993). Unfortunately, not much is known about the course of depression over time to determine whether depression is a normal response to loss. However, some evidence exists that high levels of depression in chronically ill patients are especially found in patients with a family history of affective disorders. Also, disease severity has been linked with increased levels of depression, as well as the absence of coping resources such as adequate social support from family and friends (Manne et al., 1997). Unfortunately, the assessment of depression in chronically ill patients can be problematic, as many physical signs of depression, such as fatigue, sleeplessness or weight loss, may also be an expression of the disease itself (e.g. Clark, Cook & Snow, 1998). At this point, there is no standard to discriminate between 'normal' depressive reactions to illness and reactions which should be treated with psychological interventions.

4 STRATEGIES OF ADJUSTMENT

Despite the raised levels of anxiety and depression in chronically ill patients, studies on quality of life and well-being demonstrate that many patients are eventually able to adjust to disease, but that there is a minority of patients who report consistently negative consequences. In this section, we will focus on the role of self-efficacy and personal control perceptions, optimism, and perceptions of social support as possible psychological factors which can influence adjustment. Such personal factors are believed to promote adjustment as they assist the process of coping with chronic illness. The general framework of studying adjustment in chronically ill patients is provided by the cognitive stress and coping theory which was originally developed by Lazarus and co-workers (Lazarus & Folkman, 1984; see Chapters 5 and 6, this volume), implying that illness creates stress as a result of its threatening nature confronting the patient with adaptive demands or adaptive tasks. In order to manage stress evoked by illness, individuals must cope to alleviate or diminish the negative effects.

Coping can be categorized in a number of ways, but it is often divided into problem-focused efforts aimed at the stressor itself and emotion-focused coping aimed at the emotions resulting from experiencing stress (see Chapter 6, this volume). It is generally assumed that patients who adopt a problem-focused coping style are better able to adjust to chronic disease (Maes et al., 1996). However, as chronic illness raises a variety of uncontrollable stressors (e.g. symptom course), patients are believed to employ fewer problem-focused coping methods (e.g. planned problem solving) and more emotion-focused and avoidance strategies (e.g. wishful thinking), although evidence regarding this assumption is mixed (Maes et al., 1996). Other studies suggest that chronically ill patients do not use a dominant coping style, but employ a wide variety of coping strategies in dealing with their condition (Dunkel-Schetter et al., 1992). From the perspective of the theory of fit between coping and the type of stressor involved, such mixed strategies would prove a good opportunity for effectively dealing with stress (Lazarus & Folkman, 1984). The theory of fit states that, in order to be effective, coping should be attuned to the quality of the stressor. This implies that, when confronted with uncontrollable stressful situations, emotion-focused coping may be superior to fruitless attempts to solve the stressor. In contrast, the challenge of controllable stressors should lead to the employment of problem-focused strategies in order to be most effective (Lazarus & Folkman, 1984). Unfortunately, few studies have explored the assumption of fit in coping with chronic illness. Most empirical studies show weak associations between coping and adjustment regardless of the type of coping involved – which is probably due to poor measurement of coping strategies (De Ridder, 1997). In addition, it has been suggested that the reported low and negative associations between emotion-focused coping and outcomes may be due to confounded measurement including symptoms of emotional distress and venting emotions, and thus neglecting the strategy of confrontation and appreciation of (negative) emotions (Stanton et al., 2000). Identification of an 'unconfounded' emotion-focused strategy may eventually result in stronger associations between emotion-focused coping and well-being of chronically ill patients. Despite the somewhat disappointing findings regarding the role of coping in adjustment to chronic illness, the stress coping framework is considered useful for studying adjustment processes, as it identifies a number of factors which are believed to be important as coping resources helping the patient to cope with illness. In addition, recent approaches to the role of coping in adjustment to chronic illness have examined new research areas, such as the role of social comparison processes in coping (Buunk & Gibbons, 1997; Stanton et al., 1999), the role of positive emotions (Affleck & Tennen, 1996; Folkman et al., 1997) and cognitive appraisals in the coping process (Leventhal, Leventhal & Contrada, 1998), and accounting for the specific problems patients encounter in the adjustment process (Blalock, DeVellis & Giorgino, 1995; Somerfield, 1997).

Self-efficacy and personal control

Self-efficacy perceptions are considered to play an important role in dealing with chronic illness (Holman & Lorig, 1992; LeGanger, Kraft & Røysamb, 2000), because such perceptions determine whether or not individuals will try to initiate certain health-relevant behaviours in the first place. Bandura's (1997) theory regarding the role of self-efficacy states that people tend to avoid situations that they believe will exceed their capabilities. Perceptions of self-efficacy also determine how much effort and persistence people will expend in the face of obstacles. If individuals believe that they will eventually fail, it is unlikely that they will persist in their efforts to accomplish a certain task. Self-efficacy expectations are task-specific, not global judgements of personal ability (Bandura, 1997), and, in the case of chronic illness, pertain to such disease management behaviours as using medication as prescribed, getting adequate exercise, managing stress, following a recommended diet, communicating with health professionals, and maintaining emotional control (Clark & Dodge, 1999).

Studies on the role of self-efficacy in illness adjustment have shown that high perceptions of self-efficacy are indeed associated with higher levels of motivation and with the intention to perform specific behaviours. When it comes to actual behaviour, results vary, however. Some behaviours relevant for illness management, like smoking or diet, are maintained by strong habitual factors which make them difficult to change regardless of initial levels of confidence (Clark & Dodge, 1999). The concept of self-efficacy is related to the concept of personal control, which is a broader conception of the belief that one can determine one's behaviour, influence the environment and bring about desired outcomes. Patients who believe they have personal control over illness are more likely to cope adequately with their illness (Reed, Taylor & Kemeny, 1993; Taylor et al., 1991) and to adhere to their treatment regimen (Helgeson, 1992).

There is some discussion about whether self-efficacy and personal control should be accurate perceptions of reality in order to be effective. Some authors maintain that, even when such perceptions are over-estimations of one's actual ability, they still may produce desired outcomes (Taylor et al., 1991). There is also research, however, indicating that when real control is low, efforts to exert it may be counter-productive. Similar to this line of reasoning are a number of studies that focus on the psychological costs of control. For example, Brownell (1991) has argued that individuals who are focused on controlling illness run the risk of being blamed for their illness, when they do not meet the responsibilities that increased control over treatment places on them. Others believe that the notion of control is less important than the belief that everything will turn out right in the future, regardless one's own role in it (Carver et al., 2000) – referring to the importance of optimistic expectancies about the future.

Optimism

Although several definitions of optimism exist, it is usually considered in terms of generalized positive expectancies about the future (Scheier & Carver, 1985). Beneficial effects of optimism have been reported for a wide variety of chronic illnesses (e.g. Scheier et al., 1989). Positive expectancies are believed to be related to better health outcomes because optimists maintain an active coping style characterized by more use of problem-focused coping, seeking social support, and positive re-interpretation of events, while pessimists engage more frequently in denial, distancing, focusing on negative feelings, and disengagement from valued life goals (Carver et al., 1993). According to Scheier and Carver (1985), the concept of optimism serves as a watershed when individuals are confronted with adversity: optimistic individuals will continue to engage with desired goals, while pessimists are more likely to disengage and give up. Optimism may fluctuate during disease (Shifren, 1996), but is generally quite stable even when patients are confronted with repeated stressors related to disease (Fournier et al., 2002). Inherent in the concept of optimism is a slightly rose-coloured interpretation of reality, over-emphasising the belief that good things will happen in the future. However, it is believed that the positive bias inherent in the concept of optimism is the key factor which makes patients continue coping efforts in the face of adversity (Taylor & Brown, 1988). Interestingly, recent research findings suggest that optimism does not necessarily lead to a biased perception of reality and an underestimation of risks. In fact, just because optimists hold a positive expectancy about the future, they may be better able to process negative self-relevant information (such as information about health threats) and thus be more prepared to confront threats and take appropriate measures to deal with them (Aspinwall, 1998). It has also been suggested that realistic judgements are especially important in the first stage of illness behaviour, when patients intend to perform particular illness behaviours, and that slightly unrealistic perceptions may be useful when these intentions need to be implemented in actual behaviour (Schwarzer, 1999).

Social support

Social relationships are generally regarded as important resources as they help patients to cope with stress caused by chronic illness (Cohen, 1988; Sarason, Sarason & Gurung, 1997). Social support has been defined as information from others that one is loved and cared for, and part of a social network of mutual obligations. It may take different forms, such as tangible assistance (provision of services or goods), informational support (provision of information about what could be done to alleviate the stressful incident), and emotional support (reassurance and acceptance). Studies suggest that social support has beneficial effects on the cardiovascular, endocrine and immune systems (Uchino, Cacioppo & Kiecolt-Glaser, 1996).

The beneficial effects of social support on the course of illness and on dealing with the stresses of illness are partly due to the real benefits friends and family can provide, but there may also be advantages to simply perceiving that social support is available. In fact, perceived social support has been found to be a better predictor of adjustment than the actual support provided by others – partly because not all expressions of support are experienced as beneficial by chronically ill patients (Coyne, Ellard & Smith, 1990; Revenson, 1994). Unfortunately, not all chronically ill patients are able to benefit from social support. Those with lower social competence and poor self-disclosure skills are less effective in mobilizing social support from relatives and friends (Kessler et al., 1992). Such findings indicate that social support is not a unidirectional resource from which patients may benefit, but a relational issue, requiring adequate coping techniques from the patient to seek support (Schreurs & De Ridder, 1997). Sometimes, negative manifestations of support are elicited by the way patients themselves behave, for example by rejecting support or by demonstrating extreme feelings of helplessness. However, patients are not the only ones responsible for the difficulties which may arise in interaction with others, as friends and relatives may have problems in responding to the patient's altered condition. As a result of fear elicited by seeing a loved one being seriously ill, some relatives try to manage their own emotions by responding in an ambiguous way to patients' needs (Holahan et al., 1997; Lepore & Helgeson, 1998; Manne et al., 1997). In many cases, reactions from family and friends are characterized by ambivalence, which results from a confrontation of their own feelings of fear and the simultaneous awareness of the need to provide support (Hatchett et al., 1997). Social support may be especially ineffective when the type of support provided is not the kind that is needed. For example, patients appear to prefer emotional support from family and friends, but they do not appear to appreciate their good advice since they prefer to get this from health professionals.

5 SELF-MANAGEMENT

Due to the incurable nature of chronic illness and due to its extended time course, the daily lives of chronically ill patients are filled with performing all kinds of tasks related to illness management. For example, the typical case of diabetes self-management requires self-monitoring of blood glucose and adjusting insulin treatment, eating regularly and according to a strict diet, controlling body weight, regular exercise, absence of smoking, and moderate consumption of alcohol (Goodall & Halford, 1991). This is quite a list of tasks, and it may not be surprising that many patients fail to perform these self-care routines on a regular basis (e.g. Burke & Dunbar-Jacob, 1995). Traditionally, the role of health professionals in helping patients to perform these tasks has been rather limited, but during the past decades a new perspective has emerged, acknowledging that health professionals have a task in assisting patients to deal with illness and should even share responsibility for illness management with patients (Clark et al., 1991; Clark & Zimmerman, 1990). Such a perspective has been reinforced by scientific and technological developments, making available treatment options which patients can carry out themselves, involving, for example, the adjustment of medication intake according to activity (as is especially the case in asthma and diabetes management). Due to increased emphasis on the role patients themselves may play in illness management, this perspective has been labelled *self-management* of chronic illness (Clark et al., 1991).

Increasing patient involvement in medical treatment has been shown to be an effective means to assist patients in self-management routines. For example, in a study by Greenfield and colleagues (Greenfield et al., 1988), diabetic patients reviewed their medical record assisted by a research assistant to identify issues that were likely to arise during an upcoming doctor's appointment and to rehearse the negotiation skills that they might use in communicating with the doctor. Compared with those in standard patient education, patients in the intervention group had better blood glucose control three months later, lost fewer days from work, and were more successful in obtaining information from their physicians. However, other studies suggest that many patients experience difficulties in carrying out self-management routines, even when encouraged by health professionals, for example because they do not want to be reminded continuously of being a patient or because the performance of self-care tasks interferes with other activities (Glasgow & Eakin, 1998; Goodall & Halford, 1991).

Psychological theories of self-management

Such difficulties in self-management of chronic illness can be explained by psychological theories of self-regulation stating that all behaviour, including behaviour related to managing illness, is goal directed, and that people regulate their behaviour in accordance with these goals (Karoly, 1991). Highlighting the role of goals in behaviour regulation may account for the conditions under which patients are prepared to engage in illness management behaviours. An important prerequisite is that patients evaluate illness-related goals as important and attainable (Brunstein, 1993; cf. Schreurs et al., 2003). For example, chronic illness may threaten a valued goal such as a work career, and thus account for the failure to engage in illness management behaviours since such behaviours would interfere with job performance. In this case, the personal importance of the goal of a work career may explain why a patient fails to adhere to the medical regimen because he or she is not yet prepared to disengage from that goal. Eventually, the performance of illness management may become a goal by itself. Clark and colleagues (Clark & Zimmerman, 1990; Clark & Dodge, 1999) have presented a model of self-management that highlights self-regulation processes giving rise to illness management behaviour. In this model, self-regulation is distinguished from strategies which one would employ to control disease. Whereas control strategies are derived from a medical endpoint (e.g. symptom control), self-regulation strategies are employed to reach a personal goal or endpoint, for instance sleeping through the night or engaging in a desired level of physical activity. The identification of personal goals of illness management may thus be a prerequisite for engaging in self-care behaviours. Once personal goals have been identified, strategies to accomplish those goals are mobilized and patients engage in self-regulation; that is, they observe their behaviour, make judgements about it, and try out new behaviour if considered necessary. In these models, outcome expectancies toward the future (optimism) or regarding one's capability to deal with it (self-efficacy) play an important role as they motivate patients to strive for the desired goal. In addition to these expectancies, personal beliefs regarding chronic illness play an important role in the regulation of illness management behaviours.

The role of illness representations

According to Leventhal's 'common-sense' model of illness representations (e.g. Leventhal, Meyer & Nerenz, 1980), individuals develop implicit cognitive representations of their illness based on stored knowledge about disease, as well as on information they receive from physicians, friends and family. Such 'lay views' are employed to make sense of and manage their condition, and comprise representations of *identity* (e.g. what are typical symptoms of diabetes), *cause* (e.g. smoking is the cause of my heart condition), *consequences* (e.g. due to being ill I am not able to work), *control* (e.g. taking more rest will decrease my symptoms), and *time-line* (e.g. my rheumatoid arthritis is chronic) of illness. It is essential to note that these personal representations of illness may be inaccurate according to medical standards, but it is these representations which drive patients' attempts to manage illness.

A number of studies have demonstrated that personal illness beliefs are important guides of illness management behaviours, including psychological adjustment, symptom recognition, help-seeking behaviour, and adherence to treatment regimens (Leventhal et al., 1998; Schiaffino, Shawaryn & Blum, 1998). A typical example involves the role of illness representations in hypertension management. Although hypertension is an incurable, chronic and asymptomatic condition, many patients hold the belief that hypertension may be cured and is only of short duration, and that absence of symptoms is a signal of improvement of their condition (referring to a belief that hypertension, like most other diseases, is characterized by symptoms). Patients who hold such personal views of hypertension show high levels of non-adherence, as these views make taking medication 'unnecessary' (Meyer, Leventhal & Gutmann, 1985). Compared to other social-cognitive models used to understand and explain illness management behaviours (such as the Theory of Planned Behavior; see Chapter 3, this volume), the common-sense model of illness representations acknowledges the existence of automatic reasoning driven by implicit beliefs about illness which may overrule rational reasoning based on explicit knowledge. This distinction makes the model an interesting heuristic to explain why so many patients fail in adhering to illness management behaviour even though they are aware of its necessity (Leventhal & Cameron, 1987). (See also Chapter 4, this volume.)

The case of adherence

As stated earlier, a particularly important task confronting patients with a chronic condition relates to the daily performance of a number of illness management routines and adherence to medical prescriptions. Adherence to medication prescriptions is known to be low and adherence to lifestyle alterations is reported to be even lower – especially in chronic illness, since such behaviours require lifetime adherence without a prospect of cure (Burke & Dunbar-Jacob, 1995; Dunbar-Jacob, Burke & Puczynski, 1995). Depending on the complexity of the regime, estimates of non-adherence rise as high as 70 to 80 per cent for long-term prescriptions involving lifestyle alterations (Kaplan & Simon, 1990). Traditionally, non-adherence has been regarded as an act of unwillingness to comply with medical regimens or as a failure to understand fully the benefits of such a regimen. However, more recent interpretations of non-adherence, employing a self-management perspective, refute this conceptualization, as many medical prescriptions are not clear in articulating what patients should do and as even full adherence does not guarantee alleviation of symptoms. Also, many patients appear to be 'creative' and intentional in their acts of non-adherence, demonstrating that their behaviour is a result from conviction rather than indifference (Turk & Meichenbaum, 1991). Applying a self-management perspective to adherence acknowledges the role of personal views of adherence and explains why patients may fail to engage in pre-scribed medical regimens (Horne, 1997). For example, Horne and Weinman (2002) demonstrated that specific concerns about side-effects of medication and the person-ally experienced necessity of taking medication are important predictors of adher-ence in asthma patients. A self-management perspective may also help physicians to improve communication about adherence with patients. While non-adherence generally is not an issue of explicit patient–doctor communication, doctors who are aware of the role of difficulties associated with self-management are more inclined to discuss the topic of non-adherence with patients and thus improve patient's ill-ness management strategies (Ockene, 2001). A recent study on this topic demonstrates that general practitioners may be successfully trained to address self-management routines in taking medication and adhering to lifestyle alterations (Theunissen et al., 2002).

6 INTERVENTIONS

The earlier sections have demonstrated that many chronically ill patients are even-tually able to adjust to their altered condition and report levels of well-being com-parable to healthy people. Many chronically ill patients are able to attain rather high levels of adjustment without professional help. In some cases, however, professional help is required to help patients deal with their condition or alleviate symptoms of distress as a result of their condition. Recognizing that the patient's reactions to ill-ness play a role in adjustment processes means that there is potential for influencing these reactions in order to improve outcome. Many types of psychological interven-tion for chronically ill patients exist, varying from brief psychotherapy and cognitive-behavioural interventions to social support groups and minimal interventions to improve patient–doctor communication (De Ridder & Schreurs, 2001; see also Chapter 11, this volume). Two main categories of psychological intervention may be distinguished: (psycho-)therapeutic interventions and patient education interventions. Interventions drawing on psycho-therapeutic knowledge, either in an individual format or a group format, may be required for those patients who experience high levels of anxiety and depression or suffer from serious emotional problems due to their illness. Even if patients are not confronted with overwhelming psychological problems, they may still find it difficult to adjust to new circumstances and may appreciate professional help in addition to medical assistance and support from relatives and friends. In the latter cases, interventions are more of a psycho-educational nature, including the improvement of illness management skills.

THERAPEUTIC APPROACHES

Regardless of their theoretical bases, therapeutic interventions for chronically ill patients typically share a number of common elements, including interpersonal support, validation of feelings, exploration of issues related to threat imposed by the condition, interpretative feedback, and encouragement to maintain hope (Devins & Binik, 1996). Many therapeutic interventions for chronically ill patients are delivered in a group format. Typically, the emphasis in group therapy is on interpersonal exchange and information sharing in the context of an understanding group which provides patients with encouragement and mutual support in contending with illness induced difficulties. Group composition usually comprises individuals sharing a common diagnosis which provides the opportunity to explore issues typical for that condition – although experiences with heterogeneous patient groups are encouraging, as many patients share worries about illness unrelated to the typical medical demands of disease (Lorig et al., 1999). However, group therapy may have disadvantages too (Helgeson et al., 2000; Spira & Spiegel, 1993). Unstructured groups which lack clear and consistent therapist leadership may contribute to the escalation of feelings of distress, while forceful confrontation of avoidant coping styles (e.g. denial or repression) may be destructive if the therapist fails to provide an effective alternative to manage psychosocial threats (Helgeson et al., 2000). Typically, therapeutic interventions do not focus on the acquisition of specific skills. Whereas psycho-dynamically oriented psychotherapy tends to focus on unresolved intra-psychic conflicts and to provide non-specific support, cognitive-behavioural therapies focus specifically on the problematic appraisal (e.g. irrational beliefs about illness or about illness management) that are supposed to account for difficulties in adjusting to life with a chronic illness. Controlled evaluations of psycho-social interventions have been able to demonstrate significant effects on psycho-social and biological risk factors such as cholesterol levels, systolic blood pressure, and weight in cardiovascular disease (Dusseldorp et al., 1999), survival and quality of life in cancer (Classen et al., 1998), and immunological parameters and mood in HIV/AIDS (Lutgendorf et al., 1997). Unfortunately, as many researchers fail to provide a full description of the intervention techniques employed, it has proven difficult to identify core components of effective interventions (De Ridder & Schreurs, 2001).

Patient education approaches

In contrast to therapeutic approaches, patient education interventions typically address issues related to illness management such as recognizing and acting on symptoms, using medication correctly, managing emergencies, maintaining nutrition and diet, maintaining adequate exercise, giving up smoking, using stress reduction techniques, interacting effectively with health-care providers, using community resources, adapting to work, managing relations with significant others, and managing psychological responses to illness (Clark et al., 1991). Traditionally, the focus of patient education approaches has been on providing the patient with information on these topics. Unfortunately, such programmes have minimal benefit if they do not include a component which is explicitly aimed at behaviour change (De Ridder & Schreurs, 2001). Educational interventions aimed at improving illness management have been almost exclusively focused on the so-called motivational stage of behaviour change, particularly on factors influencing patients' intentions to perform self-management behaviours. Evidence shows that patients indeed make intentions to perform such behaviours when the three core components of the Theory of Planned Behaviour (attitudes towards the behaviour in question, beliefs about social norms on the behaviour, and self-efficacy expectancies about the behaviour) are addressed. However, interventions guided by the Theory of Planned Behaviour have been shown to be less effective regarding the so-called volitional or action stage of behaviour change, that is, with regard to implementing behaviours in daily routines (Schwarzer, 1999). In order to address the volitional stage of behaviour change, implementation of intentions should be addressed explicitly by identification of personal goals and rehearsing strategies to attain these goals (Gollwitzer, 1999). More recently, self-management programmes aimed at improving self-efficacy and coping techniques have been shown to be beneficial and may even reduce health-care utilization (Lorig et al., 1999). Effective self-regulation of behaviour is assumed to consist of three components: *self-monitoring* or providing an individual with the information needed to establish realistic goals, *self-evaluation* or comparing one's current behaviour against these goals, and *self-reaction* or providing oneself with either reward or punishment depending on the performance. A meta-analysis of self-management programs shows that effects of these programs are significant, especially when they include all three components which are regarded as essential for self-regulation (Febbraro & Clum, 1998).

Future directions

Chronic illness imposes a wide range of stressors which individuals cope with in a variety of ways. Many factors influence how patients cope with these stressors, including illness characteristics, personality factors and the personal and social resources patients have available. To the extent that psycho-social interventions address such factors in an effective way, they have been able to improve adjustment of chronically ill patients and the psycho-social factors involved in disease progression (Schneiderman et al., 2001). In addition, although psycho-social interventions for the chronically ill have as their primary goal improvement in quality of life and decreased morbidity, they also can provide useful information about the role of psycho-social factors in disease progression, as they provide an opportunity to manipulate psycho-social factors considered to be important (Schneiderman et al., 2001). Future studies on psycho-social interventions should therefore focus on both the causal role of psycho-social factors in chronic illness and ways to change these factors.

Another topic of interest relates to interventions which may improve self-management routines. During the past decade, major improvements have been made in the medical management of chronic illnesses. Whereas these advances have improved quality and duration of life of patients, they also have demonstrated that, in order to be fully effective, patients need to be assisted in adhering to sometimes complex medical regimens requiring medication intake or changes in illness behaviour. More research on the role of adherence of self-management routines is therefore required (Burke, Dunbar-Jacob & Hill, 1997).

DISCUSSION POINTS

1. Why is it important to discriminate between different categories of chronic illness beyond medical distinctions?
2. Why is personal control a more important predictor of adjustment to chronic disease than actual control?
3. Discuss the benefits of a disease-generic approach to chronic disease compared to a disease-specific one.
4. Why are models of stress and coping so important in psychological research on chronic disease?
5. Why are personality factors no longer considered to play a causal role in the onset of chronic disease?
6. Discuss different conceptualizations of quality of life and how they may relate to psychological adjustment to chronic disease.
7. Why do patients find it so difficult to adhere to medical regimens?
8. What kind of intervention would you design if you were asked to improve self-management of chronic illness?

FURTHER READING

Carver, C. S., Pozo, C., Harris, S. D., Noriega, V., Scheier, M. F., Robinson, D. S., Ketcham, A. S., Moffat, F. L., Jr. and Clark, K. C. (1993). How coping mediates the effect of optimism on distress: a study of women with early stage breast cancer. *Journal of Personality and Social Psychology* 65, 375–90.

Dunkel-Schetter, C., Feinstein, L. G., Taylor, S. E. and Falke, R. L. (1992). Patterns of coping with cancer. *Health Psychology* 11, 79–87.

Schiaffino, K. M., Shawaryn, M. A. and Blum, D. (1998). Examining the impact of illness representations on psychological adjustment to chronic illnesses. *Health Psychology* 17, 262–8.

Stanton, A. L., Danoff-Burg, S., Cameron, C. L., Snider, P. and Kirk, S. B. (1999). Social comparison and adjustment to breast cancer: an experimental examination of upward affiliation and downward evaluation. *Health Psychology* 18, 151–8.

REFERENCES

Affleck, G. and Tennen, H. (1996). Construing benefits from adversity: adaptational significance and dispositional underpinnings. *Journal of Personality* 64, 899–922.

Andersen, B. L., Kiecolt-Glaser, J. K. and Glaser, R. (1994). A biobehavioral model of cancer stress and disease course. *American Psychologist* 49, 389–404.

Andersen, B. L., Woods, X. A. and Copeland, L. J. (1997). Sexual self-schema and sexual morbidity among gynaecologic cancer survivors. *Journal of Consulting and Clinical Psychology* 65, 221–9.

Anderson, K. O., Bradley, L. A., Young, L. D., McDaniel, L. K. and Wise, C. M. (1985). Rheumatoid arthritis: review of psychological factors related to aetiology, effects, and treatment. *Psychological Bulletin* 98, 358–87.

Aspinwall, L. G. (1998). Rethinking the role of positive affect in self-regulation. *Motivation and Emotion* 22, 1–32.

Bandura, A. (1997). *Self-efficacy: The Exercise of Control.* New York: Freeman.

Baum, A. and Poluszny, D. M. (1999). Health psychology: mapping biobehavioral contributions to health and illness. *Annual Review of Psychology* 50, 137–63.

Bensing, J. M., Schreurs, K. M. G., De Ridder, D. T. D. and Hulsman, R. (2002). Adaptive tasks in multiple sclerosis: development of an instrument to identify the focus of patients' coping efforts. *Psychology and Health* 17(4), 475–88.

Bishop, G. D., Alva, A. L., Cantu, L. and Rittiman, T. K. (1991). Responses to persons with AIDS: Fear of contagion or stigma? *Journal of Applied Social Psychology* 21, 1877–88.

Blalock, S. J., DeVellis, B. M. and Giorgino, K. B. (1995). The relationship between coping and psychological well-being among people with osteoarthritis: a problem-specific approach. *Annals of Behavioral Medicine* 17, 107–15.

Booth-Kewley, S. and Friedman, H. S. (1987). Psychological predictors of heart disease: a quantitive review. *Psychological Bulletin* 101, 343–62.

Boyle, P. (1992). Trends in cancer mortality in Europe. *European Journal of Cancer* 28, 7–8.

Brownell, K. (1991). Personal responsibility and control over our bodies: when expectation exceeds reality. *Health Psychology* 10, 303–10.

Brunstein, J. C. (1993). Personal goals and subjective well-being: a longitudinal study. *Journal of Personality and Social Psychology* 65, 1061–70.

Burke, L. E. and Dunbar-Jacob, J. M. (1995). Adherence to medication, diet, and activity recommendations: From assessment tot maintenance. *Journal of Cardiovascular Nursing* 9, 62–79.

Burke, L. E., Dunbar-Jacob, J. M. and Hill, M. N. (1997). Compliance with cardiovascular disease prevention strategies: a review of the research. *Annals of Behavioral Medicine* 19, 239–63.

Buunk, B. P. and Gibbons, F. X., eds. (1997). *Health, Coping, and Well-being: Perspectives from Social Comparison Theory.* Mahwah, NJ: Lawrence Erlbaum.

Calman, K. C. (1984). Quality of life in cancer patients – an hypothesis. *Journal of Medical Ethics* 10, 124–7.

Carver, C. S., Pozo, C., Harris, S. D., Noriega, V., Scheier, M. F., Robinson, D. S., Ketcham, A. S., Moffat, F. L., Jr. and Clark, K. C. (1993). How coping mediates the effect of optimism on distress: a study of women with early stage breast cancer. *Journal of Personality and Social Psychology* 65, 375–90.

Carver, C. S., Harris, S. D., Lehman, J. M., Durel, L. A., Antoni, M. H., Spencer, S. M. and Pozo-Kaderman, C. (2000). How important is the perception of personal control? Studies of early stage breast cancer patients. *Personality and Social Psychology Bulletin* 26, 139–49.

Clark, N. M., Becker, M., Janz, N., Lorig, K., Rakowksi, W. and Anderson, L. (1991). Self-management of chronic disease by older adults: a review and questions for research. *Journal of Aging and Health* 3, 3–27.

Clark, D. A., Cook, A. and Snow, D. (1998). Depressive symptom differences in hospitalised, medically ill, depressed psychiatric inpatients, and nonmedical controls. *Journal of Abnormal Psychology* 107, 38–48.

Clark, N. M. and Dodge, J. A. (1999). Exploring self-efficacy as a predictor of disease management. *Health Education and Behavior* 26, 72–89.

Clark, N. M. and Zimmerman, B. J. (1990). A social-cognitive view of self-regulated learning about health. *Health Education Quarterly* 5, 371–9.

Classen, C., Sephton, S. E., Diamond, S. and Spiegel, D. (1998). Studies of life-extending psychosocial interventions. In J. Holland, ed., *Textbook of Psycho-Oncology*. New York: Oxford University Press, 730–42.

Cohen, S. (1988). Psychosocial models of the role of social support in the etiology of physical disease. *Health Psychology* 7, 269–97.

Cohen, S., Kessler, R. C. and Gordon, L. U. (1995). Conceptualizing stress and its relation to disease. In S. Cohen, R. C. Kessler and L. U. Gordon, eds., *Measuring Stress: A Guide for Health and Social Scientists*. New York: Oxford University Press, 3–26.

Cohen, F. and Lazarus, R. S. (1979). Coping with the stresses of illness. In G. C. Stone, F. Cohen and N. E. Adler, eds., *Health Psychology: A Handbook*. San Francisco: Jossey-Bass, 217–54.

Collins, R. L., Taylor, S. E. and Skokan, L. A. (1990). A better world or a shattered vision? Changes in perspectives following vicitimization. *Social Cognition* 8, 263–85.

Cox, D. J. and Gonder-Frederick, L. (1992). Major developments in behavioral diabetes research. *Journal of Consulting and Clinical Psychology* 60, 628–38.

Coyne, J. C., Ellard, J. H. and Smith, D. A. F. (1990). Social support, interdependence, and the dilemmas of helping. In B. R. Sarason, I. G. Sarason and G. R. Pierce, eds., *Social Support: An Interactional View*. New York: Wiley, 129–49.

Croyle, R. T., Sun, Y. and Hart, M. (1997). Processing risk factor information: defensive biases in health-related judgments and memory. In K. J. Petrie and J. A. Weinman, eds., *Perceptions of Health and Illness: Current Research and Applications*. Amsterdam: Harwood, 267–90.

De Ridder, D. T. D. (1997). What is wrong with coping assessment? A review of conceptual and methodological issues. *Psychology and Health* 12, 417–31.

De Ridder, D. T. D. and Schreurs, K. M. G. (1996). Coping, social support, and chronic disease: a research agenda. *Psychology, Health, and Medicine* 1, 71–82.

De Ridder, D. T. D. and Scheurs, K. M. G. (2001). Developing interventions for chronically ill patients: is coping a helpful concept? *Clinical Psychology Review* 21, 205–40.

De Ridder, D. T. D., Schreurs, K. M. G. and Bensing, J. M. (1998). Adaptive tasks, coping, and quality of life: the cases of Parkinson's disease and Chronic Fatigue Syndrome. *Journal of Health Psychology* 3, 87–101.

Denollet, J. (1998). Personality and coronary heart disease: the type-D scale-16. *Annals of Behavioral Medicine* 20, 209–15.

DeVellis, B. M. (1995). Psychological impact of arthritis: prevalence of depression. *Arthritis Care and Research* 8, 284–9.

Devins, G. M. and Binik, Y. M. (1996). Facilitating, coping, and chronic illness. In M. Zeidner and N. S. Endler, eds., *Handbook of Coping: Theory, Research, and Applications*. New York: Wiley, 640–96.

Dickens, C., McGowan, L., Clark-Carter, D. and Creed, F. (2002). Depression in rheumatoid arthritis: a systematic review of the literature with meta-analysis. *Psychosomatic Medicine* 64, 52–60.

Ditto, P. H., Druley, J. A., Moore, K. A., Danks, H. J. and Smucker, W. D. (1996). Fates worse than death: the role of valued life activities in health state evaluations. *Health Psychology* 15, 332–43.

Dunbar-Jacob, J., Burke, L. E. and Puczynski, S. (1995). Clinical assessment and management of adherence to medical regimens. In P. M. Nicassio and T. W. Smith, eds., *Managing Chronic Illness: A Biopsychosocial Perspective*. Washington, DC: American Psychological Association, 313–49.

Dunkel-Schetter, C., Feinstein, L. G., Taylor, S. E. and Falke, R. L. (1992). Patterns of coping with cancer. *Health Psychology* 11, 79–87.

Dusseldorp, E., Van Elderen, T., Maes, S., Meulman, J. and Kraaij, V. (1999). A meta-analysis of psychoeducational programs for coronary heart disease patients. *Health Psychology* 18, 506–19.

ECRHS (1996). Variations in the prevalence of respiratory symptoms, self-reported asthma attacks, and the use of asthma medication in the European Community Respiratory Health Survey (ECRHS). *European Respiratory Journal* 9, 687–95.

Engel, G. L. (1977). The need for a new medical model: a challenge for biomedicine. *Science* 196, 129–36.

Eitel, P., Hatchett, L., Friend, R., Griffin, K. W. and Wadhwa, N. D. (1995). Burden of self-care in seriously ill patients: impact on adjustment. *Health Psychology* 14, 457–63.

Ell, K. and Dunkel-Schetter, C. (1994). Social support and adjustment to myocardial infarction, angioplasty, and coronary artery bypass surgery. In S. A. Shumaker and S. M. Czajkowski, eds., *Social Support and Cardiovascular Disease*. New York: Plenum, 301–32.

Febbraro, G. A. R. and Clum, G. A. (1998). Meta-analytic investigation of the effectiveness of self-regulatory components in the treatment of adult problem behaviors. *Clinical Psychology Review* 18, 143–61.

Felton, B. J. and Revenson, T. A. (1984). Coping with chronic illness: a study of illness controllability and the influence of coping strategies on psychological adjustment. *Journal of Consulting and Clinical Psychology* 52, 343–53.

Folkman, S. (1997). Positive psychological states and coping with severe stress. *Social Science and Medicine* 45, 1207–21.

Folkman, S., Moskowitz, J. T., Ozer, E. M. and Park, C. L. (1997). Positive meaningful events and coping in the context of HIV/AIDS. In B. H. Gottlieb, ed., *Coping with Chronic Stress*. New York: Plenum, 293–314.

Fournier, M., De Ridder, D. T. D. and Bensing, J. M. (2002). Optimism and adaptation to chronic disease: the role of optimism in relation to self-care options of type 1 diabetes mellitus, rheumatoid arthritis, and multiple sclerosis. *British Journal of Health Psychology* 7(4), 409–32.

Glasgow, R. E. and Eakin, E. G. (1998). Issues in diabetes self-management. In S. A. Shumaker et al., eds., *The Handbook of Health Behavior Change*. New York: Springer, 435–61.

Glasgow, R. E., Strycker, L. A., Toobert, D. J. and Eakin, E. (2000). A social-ecologic approach to assessing support for disease self-management: the chronic illness resources survey. *Journal of Behavioral Medicine* 23, 559–83.

Glasgow, R. E., Wagner, E. H., Kaplan, R. M., Vinicor, R., Smith, L. and Norman, J. (1999). If diabetes is a public health problem, why not treat it as one? A population-based approach to chronic illness. *Annals of Behavioral Medicine* 21, 159–70.

Gollwitzer, P. (1999). Implementation intentions: strong effects from simple plans. *American Psychologist* 54, 493–503.

Goodall, T. A. and Halford, W. K. (1991). Self-management of diabetes mellitus: a critical review. *Health Psychology* 10, 1–8.

Greenfield, S., Kaplan, S. H., Ware, J. E., Yano, E. M. and Frank, H. J. L. (1988). Patients' participation in medical care: effects on blood sugar control and quality of life in diabetes. *Journal of General Internal Medicine* 3, 448–57.

Hatchett, L., Friend, R., Symister, P. and Wadhwa, N. D. (1997). Interpersonal expectations, social support, and adjustment to chronic illness. *Journal of Personality and Social Psychology* 73, 560–73.

Heijmans, M., Foets, M., Rijken, M., Schreurs, K., De Ridder, D. and Bensing, J. (2001). Stress in chronic disease: do the perceptions of patients and their general practitioners match? *British Journal of Health Psychology* 6, 229–42.

Helgeson, V. S. (1992). Moderators of the relation between perceived control and adjustment to chronic illness. *Journal of Personality and Social Psychology* 63, 656–66.

Helgeson, V., Cohen, S., Schultz, R. and Yasko, J. (2000). Group support interventions for women with breast cancer: Who benefits from what? *Health Psychology* 19, 107–14.

Hemingway, H. and Marmot, M. (1999). Psychosocial factors in the aetiology and prognosis of coronary heart disease: systematic review of prospective cohort studies. *British Medical Journal* 318, 1460–7.

Hoffman, C., Rice, D. and Sung, H. Y. (1996). Persons with chronic conditions: their prevalence and costs. *Journal of the American Medical Association* 276, 1473–9.

Holahan, C. J., Moos, R. H., Holahan, C. K. and Brennan, L. P. (1997). Social context, coping strategies, and depressive symptoms: an expanded model with cardiac patients. *Journal of Personality and Social Psychology* 72, 918–28.

Holman, H. R. and Lorig, K. (1992). Perceived self-efficacy in self-management of chronic disease. In R. Schwarzer, ed., *Self-efficacy: Thought Control of Action*. Washington, DC: Hemisphere, 305–23.

Horne, R. and Weinman, J. (2002). Self-regulation and self-management in asthma: exploring the role of illness perceptions and treatment beliefs in explaining non-adherence to preventer medication. *Psychology & Health* 17, 17–32.

Huyser, B. and Parker, J. C. (1998). Stress and rheumatoid arthritis: an integrative review. *Arthritis Care and Research* 11, 135–45.

Jacobsen, P. B., Bovbjerg, D. H. and Redd, W. H. (1993). Anticipatory anxiety in patients receiving cancer chemotherapy. *Health Psychology* 12, 469–75.

Kaplan, R. M. and Simon, H. J. (1990). Compliance in medical care: reconsideration of self-predictions. *Annals of Behavioral Medicine* 12, 66–71.

Karoly, P. (1991). Self-management in health-care and illness prevention. In C. R. Snyder and D. R. Forsyth, eds., *Handbook of Social and Clinical Psychology: The Health Perspective*. New York: Pergamon, 579–606.

Kessler, R. C., Kendler, K. S., Heath, A. C., Neale, M. C. and Eaves, L. J. (1992). Social support, depressed mood, and adjustment to stress: a genetic-epidemiological investigation. *Journal of Personality and Social Psychology* 62, 257–72.

King, H. and Zimmet, P. (1988). Trends in the prevalence and incidence of diabetes: non-insulin dependent diabetes mellitus. *World Health Statistics Quarterly* 41, 190–6.

Lazarus, R. S. and Folkman, S. (1984). *Stress, Appraisal, and Coping*. New York: Springer.

Lepore, S. J. and Helgeson, V. S. (1998). Social constraints, intrusive thoughts, and mental health after prostate cancer. *Journal of Behavioral Medicine* 17, 89–106.

LeGanger, A., Kraft, P. and Røysamb, E. (2000). Perceived self-efficacy in health behaviour research: conceptualization, measurement, and correlates. *Psychology and Health* 15, 51–69.

Leventhal, H. and Cameron, L. (1987). Behavioral theories and the problem of compliance. *Patient Education and Counseling* 10, 117–38.

Leventhal, H., Leventhal, E. and Contrada, R. J. (1998). Self-regulation, health, and behavior: a perceptual cognitive approach. *Psychology and Health* 13, 717–34.

Leventhal, H., Meyer, D. and Nerenz, D. (1980). The common sense representation of illness danger. In S. Rachman, ed., *Contributions to Medical Psychology*, vol. 2. New York: Pergamon Press, 7–30.

Lorig, K. R., Sobel, D. S., Stewart, A. L., Brown, B. W., Bandura, A., Ritter, P., Gonzalez, V. M., Laurent, D. D. and Holman, H. R. (1999). Evidence suggesting that a chronic disease self-management program can improve health status while reducing hospitalization. *Medical Care* 37, 5–14.

Lutgendorf, S., Antoni, M., Ironson, G., Klimas, N., Kumar, M. and Starr, K. (1997). Cognitive behavioral stress management decreases dysphoric mood and herpes simplex type-2 antibody titers in symptomatic HIV seropositive gay men. *Journal of Consulting and Clinical Psychology* 65, 31–43.

MacKeown, T. (1979). *The Role of Medicine.* Oxford: Blackwell.

Maes, S., Leventhal, H. and De Ridder, D. T. D. (1996). Coping with chronic diseases. In M. Zeidner and N. S. Endler, eds., *Handbook of Coping: Theory, Research, Applications.* New York: Wiley, 221–51.

Manne, S. L., Taylor, K. L., Dougherty, J. and Kemeny, N. (1997). Supportive and negative responses in the partner relationship: their association with psychological adjustment among individuals with cancer. *Journal of Behavioral Medicine* 20, 101–25.

Meyer, D., Leventhal, H and Gutmann, M. (1985). Common-sense models of illness: the example of hypertension. *Health Psychology* 4, 115–35.

Moos, R. H. and Schaefer, J. A. (1984). The crisis of physical illness: an overview and a conceptual approach. In R. H. Moos, ed., *Coping with Physical Illness: vol. 2: New Perspectives.* New York: Plenum, 3–25.

Moos, R. H. and Schaefer, J. A. (1993). Coping resources and processes: current concepts and measures. In L. Goldberger and S. Breznitz, eds., *Handbook of Stress: Theoretical and Clinical Aspects.* New York: Free Press, 234–57.

Ockene, J. K. (2001). Strategies to increase adherence to treatment. In L. E. Burke and I. S. Ockene, eds., *Compliance in Health Care and Research.* Armonk, NY: Futura Publishing, 43–55.

Pennebaker, J. W., Hughes, C. and O'Heeron, R. C. (1987). The psychophysiology of confession: linking inhibitory and psychosomatic processes. *Journal of Personality and Social Psychology* 52, 781–93.

Petrie, K. J., Buick, D. L., Weinman, J. and Booth, R. J. (1999). Positive effects of illness reported by myocardial infarction and breast cancer patients. *Journal of Psychosomatic Research* 47, 537–43.

Reed, G. M., Taylor, S. E. and Kemeny, M. E. (1993). Perceived control and psychosocial adjustment in gay men with AIDS. *Journal of Applied Social Psychology* 23, 791–824.

Reid, D. (1984). Participatory control and the chronic illness adjustment process. In H. Lefcourt, ed., *Research with the Locus of Control Construct: Extensions and Limitations*, vol. 3. New York: Academic Press, 361–89.

Revenson, T. A. (1994). Social support and marital coping with chronic illness. *Annals of Behavioral Medicine* 16, 122–30.

Rothenberg, R. B. and Koplan, J. P. (1990). Chronic disease in the 1990s. *Annual Review of Public Health* 11, 267–96.

Rozanski, A., Blumenthal, J. A. and Kaplan, J. (1999). Impact of psychological factors on the pathogenesis of cardiovascular disease and implications for therapy. *Circulation* 99, 2192–217.

Ruwaard, D., Kramers, P. G. N., Van den Berg Jeths, A. and Achterberg, P. W., eds. (1994). *Public Health Status and Forecasts: The Health Status of the Dutch Population over the Period 1950–2010.* Den Haag, the Netherlands: Sdu Publishers.

Sarason, B. R., Sarason, I. G. and Gurung, R. A. R. (1997). Close personal relationships and health outcomes: a key to the role of social support. In S. Duck, ed., *Handbook of Personal Relationships.* New York: Wiley, 547–73.

Scheier, M. F. and Bridges, M. W. (1995). Person variables and health: personality predispositions and acute psychological states as shared determinants for disease. *Psychosomatic Medicine* 57, 255–68.

Scheier, M. F. and Carver, C. S. (1985). Optimism, coping, and health: assessment and implications of Generalized Outcome Expectancies. *Health Psychology* 4, 219–47.

Scheier, M. F., Matthews, K. A., Owens, J., Magovern, G. J., Sr, Lefebvre, R. C., Abbott, R. A. and Carver, C. S. (1989). Dispositional optimism and recovery from coronary artery bypass surgery: the beneficial effects on physical and psychological well-being. *Journal of Personality and Social Psychology* 57, 1024–40.

Schiaffino, K. M., Shawaryn, M. A. and Blum, D. (1998). Examining the impact of illness representations on psychological adjustment to chronic illnesses. *Health Psychology* 17, 262–8.

Schlenk, E. A., Erlen, J. A., Dunbar-Jacob, J., et al. (1998). Health-related quality of life in chronic disorders: a comparison across studies using the MOS SF-36. *Quality of Life Research* 7, 57–75.

Schneiderman, N., Antoni, M. H., Saab, P. G. and Ironson, G. (2001). Health psychology: psychosocial and biobehavioral aspects of chronic disease management. *Annual Review of Psychology* 52, 555–80.

Schreurs, K. M. G., Colland, V. T., Kuijer, R. G., De Ridder, D. T. D. and Van Elderen, T. (2003). Development, content, and process evaluation of a short self-management intervention in patients with chronic diseases requiring self-care behavior. *Patient Education and Counseling* 51(2), 133–41.

Schreurs, K. M. G. and De Ridder, D. T. D. (1997). Integration of coping and social support perspectives: implications for the study of adaptation to chronic diseases. *Clinical Psychology Review* 17, 89–112.

Schwarzer, R. (1999). Self-regulatory processes in the adoption and maintenance of health behaviors: the role of optimism, goals, and threats. *Journal of Health Psychology* 4, 115–27.

Seidell, J. C. (1995). Obesity in Europe: scaling an epidemic. *International Journal of Obesity* 19, S3, 1–4.

Shifren, K. (1996). Individual differences in the perception of optimism and disease severity: a study among individuals with Parkinson's disease. *Journal of Behavioral Medicine* 19, 241–72.

Smith, T. W. (1992). Hostility and health: current status of a psychosomatic hypothesis. *Health Psychology* 11, 139–50.

Smyth, J. M., Stone, A. A., Hurewitz, A. and Kaell, A. (1999). Effects of writing about stressful experiences on symptom reduction in patients with asthma or rheumatoid arthritis: a randomized trial. *Journal of the American Medical Association* 281, 1304–9.

Smyth, J. M. (1998). Written emotional expression: effect sizes, outcome types, and moderating variables. *Journal of Consulting and Clinical Psychology* 66, 174–84.

Södergren, S. C. and Hyland, M. E. (2000). What are the positive consequences of illness? *Psychology and Health* 15, 85–97.

Somerfield, M. R. (1997). The utility of systems models of stress and coping for applied research. *Journal of Health Psychology* 2, 133–51.

Spiegel, D. and Diamond, S. (2001). Psychosocial interventions in cancer: group therapy techniques. In A. Baum and B. L. Andersen, eds., *Psychosocial Interventions for Cancer*. Washington, DC: American Psychological Association, 215–33.

Spira, J. L. and Spiegel, D. (1993). Group psychotherapy of the medically ill. In A. Stoudemire and B. S. Fogel, eds., *Psychiatric Care of the Medical Patient*. New York: Oxford University Press, 31–50.

Sprangers, M. A. G. and Schwartz, C. E. (1999). Integrating response shift into health-related quality of life research: a theoretical model. *Social Science and Medicine* 48, 1507–15.

Stanton, A. L., Collins, C. A. and Sworowski, L. A. (2001). Adjustment to chronic illness: theory and research. In A. Baum, T. A. Revenson and J. E. Singer, eds., *Handbook of Health Psychology*. Mahwah, NJ: Lawrence Erlbaum, 387–403.

Stanton, A. L., Danoff-Burg, S., Cameron, C. L., Snider, P. and Kirk, S. B. (1999). Social comparison and adjustment to breast cancer: an experimental examination of upward affiliation and downward evaluation. *Health Psychology* 18, 151–8.

Stanton, A. L., Kirk, S. B., Cameron, C. L. and Danoff-Burg, S. (2000). Coping through emotional approach: scale construction and validation. *Journal of Personality and Social Psychology* 78, 1150–69.

Suris, J. C. and Blum, R. W. (2001). Adolescent health in Europe: an overview. *International Journal of Adolescent Medicine and Health* 13, 91–9.

Taylor, S. E. and Aspinwall, L. G. (1996a). Psychosocial aspects of chronic illness. In P. T. Costa and G. R. VandenBos, eds., *Psychological Aspects of Serious Illness: Chronic Conditions, Fatal Diseases, and Clinical Care*. Washington, DC: American Psychological Association, 7–60.

Taylor, S. E. and Aspinwall, L. G. (1996b). Mediating and moderating processes in psychosocial stress: appraisal, coping, resistance, and vulnerability. In H. B. Kaplan, ed., *Psychosocial Stress: Perspectives on Structure, Theory, Life-course, and Methods*. San Diego, CA: Academic Press, 71–110.

Taylor, S. E. and Brown, J. D. (1988). Illusion and well-being: a social psychological perspective on mental health. *Psychological Bulletin* 103, 193–210.

Taylor, S. E., Helgeson, V. S., Reed, G. M. and Skokan, L. A. (1991). Self-generated feelings of control and adjustment to physical illness. *Journal of Social Issues* 47, 91–109.

Temoshok, L. (1987). Personality, coping style, emotion, and cancer: towards an integrative model. *Cancer Surveys* 6, 545–67.

Theunissen, N. C. M., De Ridder, D. T. D., Bensing, J. M. and Rutten, G. E. H. M. (2002). Manipulation of patient–provider interaction: using the self-regulatory model of illness to discuss adherence. *Patient Education and Counseling* 51(3), 247–58.

Traue, H. C. and Pennebaker, J. W., eds. (1993). *Emotion Inhibition and Health*. Kirkland, WA: Hogrefe & Huber.

Turk, D. C. and Meichenbaum, D. (1991). Adherence to self-care regimens: the patient's perspective. In R. H. Rozensky, J. J. Sweet and S. M. Tovian, eds., *The Handbook of Clinical Psychology in Medical Settings*. New York: Plenum, 249–66.

Uchino, B. N., Cacioppo, J. T. and Kiecolt-Glaser, J. K. (1996). The relationship between social support and physiological processes: a review with emphasis on underlying processes and implications for health. *Psychological Bulletin* 119, 488–531.

Van 't Spijker, A., Trijsburg, R. W. and Duivenvoorden, H. J. (1997). Psychological sequelae of cancer diagnosis: a meta-analytical review of 58 studies after 1980. *Psychosomatic Medicine* 59, 280–93.

Ware, J. E. (1993). *SF-36 Health Survey. Manual and Interpretation Guide*. Boston: The Health Institute, New England Medical Center.

Wells, K. B., Rogers, W. M. P. H., Burnam, M. A. and Camp, P. (1993). Course of depression in patients with hypertension, myocardial infarction or insulin-dependent diabetes. *American Journal of Psychiatry* 150, 632–8.

Wiebe, D. J. and Smith, T. W. (1997). Personality and health: progress and problems in psychosomatics. In R. Hogan, J. Johnson and S. Briggs, eds., *Handbook of Personality Psychology*. San Diego, CA: Academic Press, 891–912.

World Health Organization (1994). *Health in Europe: The 1993/1994 Health for All Monitoring Report*. European Series no. 56. Copenhagen: WHO Regional Publications.

Zautra, A. J., Hoffman, J. M., Matt, K. S., Yocum, D., Potter, P. T., Castro, W. L. and Roth, S. (1998). An examination of individual differences in the relationship between interpersonal stress and disease activity among women with rheumatoid arthritis. *Arthritis Care and Research* 11, 271–9.

Zimmet, P. (2000). Globalization, coca-colanization and the chronic disease epidemic: can the Doomsday scenario be averted? *Journal of Internal Medicine* 247, 301–10.

Chapter Ten

QUALITY OF LIFE

Hannah McGee

CHAPTER OUTLINE

This chapter deals with the concept of quality of life (QoL) in the health context. There has been a virtual explosion of research on the topic of QoL in the past decade, particularly in relation to health and health-care interventions. Much of the impetus of this research has come from applied questions, for instance comparing medical treatment regimes on QoL as well as other outcome parameters. This activity involves instrument development and psychometric evaluation projects crossing continents and languages on an unprecedented scale. This chapter overviews definitions of QoL, the main uses of the concept, the types of measures developed (with examples of the many measurement instruments available), recent developments in QoL research, and the challenges and opportunities of this research area in the future for health psychologists.

KEY CONCEPTS

dimension-specific QoL

disease- (or population-) specific QoL

generic QoL

individualized QoL

proxy (or surrogate) ratings

quality-adjusted life years (QALYs)

response shift

standard gamble techniques

time trade-off techniques

utility-based QoL

INTRODUCTION

How is the concept of quality of life defined?
What are the main uses of quality of life assessment in health settings?
What are the theoretical and practical challenges in quality of life research?

QoL research has been described as a major growth industry. To illustrate the increasing level of activity in this field, a count of Medline keyword citations to 'quality of life' shows an increase of over seven-fold in the past 15 years (from 869 articles in 1987 to 6,147 in 2002). Other indicators of its increasing popularity are specialist websites, professional societies (e.g. the International Society for Quality of Life Research – www.isoqol.org; and the International Society for Quality of Life Studies – http://marketing.cob.vt.edu/isqols/), international conferences, and a journal entitled *Quality of Life Research*. There are many specific texts on, for example, types of illness (childhood asthma: Christie & French, 1994; renal failure: McGee & Bradley, 1994; epilepsy: Baker & Jacoby, 2000); behavioural medicine (Dimsdale & Baum, 1995); clinical trials (Spilker, 1996; Staquet, Hays & Fayers, 1998), and health policy implications (Patrick & Erickson, 1993). The volume of material available is enormous: for instance, one reference text on *Quality of Life and Pharmacoeconomics in Clinical Trials* by Spilker (1996) has 1,259 pages in its second edition. The *British Medical Journal* recently published a series of five articles on various aspects of the issue (series editors: A. J. Carr, I. J. Higginson and P. G. Robinson, 2001). The role of QoL as a concept in health settings and the development of this research field are described here.

DEFINITIONS OF QUALITY OF LIFE

The nature of QoL is little understood. Definitions abound. These range from quite philosophical statements to pragmatic definitions that have been developed to assist operationalization of the concept. Since all agree that the concept is very wide-ranging, many of those who provide more specific and limited definitions typically qualify this by saying that they have addressed an aspect, but not the whole concept, of QoL. The following examples illustrate definitions from the more phenomenological to the more pragmatic approaches. At its most general and phenomenological:

> Quality of life is what the individual says it is. (Joyce, 1988)

Other approaches identify the relative nature of QoL – the fact that QoL requires a comparison between a present and an aspirational state:

> Quality of life measures the difference, or the gap, at a particular period of time, between the hopes and expectations of the individual and the individual's present experiences. (Calman, 1984)

Another approach has been to acknowledge that it is not practical (or perhaps possible) to assess all that is meant by QoL in health settings, and to argue that a more limited and focused form of assessment can be undertaken. This is the approach taken in many health settings where QoL assessment instruments have been specifically devised to be 'health focused'. The argument is that health interventions have been developed to address health-related aspects of an individual's life, and thus should be judged against the yardstick of health-related quality of life (HRQoL) parameters. In this view of QoL, only health-related aspects of life (and not others such as economic status or environment) can be expected to change as a direct consequence of health interventions. Hence it is argued, only these more focused HRQoL assessments should be used to assess the effects of interventions. A widely used definition of HRQoL was proposed by Patrick and Erickson (1993):

> HRQoL is 'the value assigned to the duration of life as modified by the impairments, functional states, perceptions and social opportunities that are influenced by disease, injury, treatment or policy.' (Patrick & Erickson, 1993)

Another similar HRQoL definition, but with a more clearly articulated role for the individual patient as judge of his or her QoL status, was outlined by Schipper et al. (1996):

> 'Quality of life' in clinical medicine represents the functional effect of an illness and its consequent therapy upon a patient as perceived by the patient. (Schipper, Clinch & Olweny, 1996)

The authors go on to specify four main components of the QoL construct: physical and occupational functioning, psychological state, social interaction and somatic sensation (symptoms). This is a typical formulation of QoL from the HRQoL perspective. However, those researchers who advocate both a more generic and individualized approach to QoL assessment challenge the health-related focus by asking how external observers can determine what is health-related and what is not for an individual (Joyce et al., 2003). For instance, income and environment would not typically be assessed by HRQoL instruments as they would be seen to be beyond the domain of influence of health interventions. Yet ability to earn a reasonable income, financial demands of health care itself, and ability to live independently in a safe and healthy environment may all be influenced by illness and health interventions. These factors in turn may not just vary by individual but may vary across cultures and countries. A definition which incorporates many of the features of the previous types of definition and which acknowledges the interplay between health and other factors is that of the World Health Organization QoL Group:

> QoL is 'an individual's perception of their position in life in the context of the culture and value systems in which they live and in relation to their goals and expectations, standards and concerns. It is a broad ranging concept affected in a complex way by a person's physical health, psychological state, level of independence and their relationships to salient features of their environment.' (WHOQoL Group, 1995)

Lively debate exists in the QoL research community concerning the varying perspectives and their resultant definitions. While not a general rule, it is interesting to note that some of the more vocal proponents of a wider and more individualized definition of QoL are those who work in disability and rehabilitation or in oncology and palliative-care settings (e.g. Dijkers, 2003; Faddin & LePlege, 1992). A problem in the general QoL area is that terminology is used inconsistently. Thus some propose using terms such as 'health-related quality of life' or 'health status' when assessing this particular type of QoL. However, in many situations the words HRQoL and QoL are used interchangeably. Bradley (2001) gives a clear outline of the difficulties in interpreting research results when different terms, definitions and types of measures are used interchangeably. While debate continues about definitions, one of the most notable characteristics across QoL-related studies is the relative scarcity of an explicit definition of QoL by authors in their study reports. In parallel, concepts such as life satisfaction, happiness, well-being and QoL are also used interchangeably. Research in this area would be improved considerably if researchers made explicit their definition of QoL and how this related to instrument selection for the study.

THE CONCEPT OF QUALITY OF LIFE

While there is an extensive empirical literature on QoL, conceptual and theoretical development in QoL is more notable by its absence than presence (Joyce et al., 2003). Most writing on QoL in the health setting considers the more pragmatic issue of 'how to measure' than 'what to measure'. Concepts of QoL can be considered from the philosophical perspective. From this perspective, there are two fundamental approaches underlying conceptualization of QoL: the 'needs' and the 'wants' approaches. Hayry (1991) provides a philosophical overview of these perspectives in a historical context. The needs approach views QoL as the extent to which universal human needs are met. From this perspective, if the basic and universal needs are common to all people, then they can be identified objectively and without consulting about the relative value of various aspects of life with the individual to be assessed. Many HRQoL instruments (to be discussed later) conform to the needs approach, i.e. the themes to be discussed, questions to be asked and question weightings used are standardized to deliver the same assessment across individuals. The themes to be assessed are established independent of the person being assessed. The alternative wants approach proposes that it is the individual who determines his or her basic priorities ('wants') in terms of evaluating QoL. Measures reflecting this perspective should thus be developed to allow for a definition of QoL using themes, questions or question weightings determined by the individual being assessed. The methodologies used to achieve the wants approach are individualized (to be discussed below). They typically do not limit the focus of enquiry to health, and they focus more on the individual's perception than on function. A typical 'wants' question would thus ask 'Are you satisfied with your ability to socialize and to meet other people?' whereas a 'needs' question would ask 'How many times per week do you meet family or friends for social activities?'

The wants approach to QoL assessment is more clearly psychological than the needs perspective. An early influential research paper supports the relative nature of sub-jective assessments such as happiness and QoL. Brickman, Coates and Janoff-Bulman (1978) compared major lottery winners with matched community controls and with accident victims who had become paralysed as a consequence of their accident. (From a 'needs' perspective, the paralysed participants would be seen as automatically as having poorer QoL because the ability to walk would be seen as a fundamental 'need'.) The researchers found that participants in all three groups reported quite similar levels of current happiness. When asked to rate how happy they expected to be in the future, those levels became even more similar. This finding is understandable from the 'wants' perspective, since individuals can have differing and changing perspect-ives on what is important in their lives. The authors of this research asked, 'is hap-piness relative?' This is the challenge when considering assessment of QoL in the health setting.

USES OF THE CONCEPT OF QUALITY OF LIFE IN HEALTH SETTINGS

While the primary outcomes of interest in health-care evaluation have traditionally been mortality and morbidity, the past decades have seen a dramatic increase in iden-tifying the impact of interventions on function and QoL. Measurement of aspects of QoL in health settings can be traced to work on performance status by Karnofsky and Burchenal (1947). They were the first to rate aspects other than physical health when evaluating the success of medical interventions. The Karnofsky Performance Index was an observer-rated measure to assess patients on a 0–100 scale (0 for 'dead' and 100 for 'no evidence of disease, able to carry out normal activity and to work'). A number of other performance status measures have been developed since that time, such as the Spitzer, Dobson and Hall (1981) Quality of Life Index, which is a multi-dimensional observer rating scale for cancer patients. These were seen as valuable since they were based on observable, and potentially repeatable and verifiable, informa-tion. Thus QoL-related ratings by professionals continued to be the norm for some decades. Most attention focused on cancer treatment where the question of quality versus 'quantity' or duration of life was particularly evident with the emergence of partially effective treatments with very severe side-effects. There was a gradual shift to asking patients themselves to provide information on aspects of their QoL. This was in part informed by a body of research which showed that physicians were not good at estimating the QoL of their patients. Sprangers and Aaronson (1992) reviewed evid-ence on this point. They found that physician ratings of patient QoL, when compared to ratings of patients themselves, were not just inaccurate but were also typically lower than those of patients. When relative ratings were compared, they fell between ratings of doctors and patients. Thus patients rated their QoL more positively than did their doctors or their relatives. It is now considered standard practice to ask indi-viduals to rate their own QoL.

Proxy or *surrogate ratings*: ratings about an individual's QoL provided by others – usually relatives or professionals.

'Proxy' or surrogate ratings by others are seen as only acceptable where individuals are unable to make judgements for themselves. In these cases, it is now much more acceptable that relatives make such decisions than professionals. This is the case while acknowledging that surrogate decision-makers are likely to use their own assessment, rather than the criteria of their significant other, when making such judgements. Most assessment on this topic concerns decisions about life-sustaining medical treatment preferences (Fagerlin et al., 2001).

While QoL-related research was first developed in the context of cancer research and practice, it has now spread to every area of health care. There are four main uses of QoL assessments in health settings:

- treatment comparisons in clinical trials;
- treatment choices in individual patient care;
- general or patient population studies to evaluate QoL; and
- evaluations to determine the best uses of health-care resources.

Clinical trials set outcome targets against which they will evaluate the success or otherwise of the intervention being tested. The most important outcomes are called primary outcomes. It is acknowledged that other outcomes may be important or informative to assess, but that the success or failure of the trial will not be determined by these (secondary) outcomes. QoL as used in clinical trials is usually considered a secondary outcome where clinical outcomes, such as mortality following cardiac revascularization, are the primary outcome. In such studies, differences in QoL scores only become influential where two or more treatments achieve equivalent benefit on a primary outcome variable. Thus if two medications had equivalent benefits in terms of reducing a primary outcome such as anginal pain, a different QoL impact for the two medications could influence the recommendations about which one to use (other factors such as cost could also influence recommendations). QoL assessment is increasingly incorporated into clinical trials with influential groups such as the National Heart, Lung, and Blood Institute in the US requiring most trials its funds to have a QoL component. In most of these studies, QoL is a secondary outcome. The value of collecting evidence on QoL in such large-scale clinical interventions is to build up a body of research to better understand influences on QoL in the health setting. There are some studies, for instance in oncology (Tannock et al., 1996), where QoL is the primary outcome of the study.

Treatment choices in individual patient care can be influenced by QoL assessment (Higginson & Carr, 2001). Such assessment can be used to screen patients for difficulties with particular aspects of their QoL. This is not widely used as an option at present. However, there is an increasing range of health conditions where more than one feasible treatment option is currently available. The benefits and drawbacks of many treatments mean that there is no clear option which would be best for all individuals. Knowledge of the clinical and QoL effects of different treatment options can help health-care professionals outline the choices available to patients and assist them in selecting the option which is best for them. Prostate cancer is one such problem for men – there are both surgical and hormonal treatment options with a balance of risks, benefits and side-effects for the two options. The treatment choices available depend in part on the patient's age and the status of the cancer, but also, to some extent, on the individual's preferences given the different QoL implications of the two treatments. Thus some men may opt for surgery, preferring to take an early surgical risk and a short period of post-operative discomfort, while others find a monthly hormone injection with mild to moderate side-effects to be a more preferable option for them. Information on QoL in this context can be useful to both professionals and patients when considering what to expect given certain health conditions and treatments. This kind of evidence to inform an individual professional or patient comes from studies of populations of patients who are experiencing the condition or treatment, i.e. a patient population assessment strategy.

At the population level, there has been some research to evaluate the QoL of the general public. The SF-36 has been used at a general population level in countries such as the UK and Australia (see table 10.2). More often, measures have been used to determine the QoL profile of particular groups of patient populations, for example, patients with Parkinson's disease (Peto et al., 1995). These types of study increase our overall understanding of the psycho-social implications of particular health conditions and treatments.

A final common consideration for QoL assessment is resource allocation in health care (Patrick & Erickson, 1993). In the context of scarce resources, every decision to provide a specific type of health intervention is a decision not to provide another. These decisions may be removed in time from the individual location and patient. For instance, a health service may recruit twice as many cardiac surgeons as orthopaedic surgeons. In this way different weightings are applied to the treatment of cardiac and orthopaedic disorders. While some health intervention decisions are about which treatment to provide to an individual patient (e.g. whether to treat anginal pain medically or surgically), many are taken about which treatments to fund across patients. Thus in the example of the recruitment of surgeons above, the decision is to focus more on surgical services for cardiac than for orthopaedic problems. These decisions have often been made in an arbitrary manner or in a manner influenced by the ability of certain individuals or professional groups to argue more successfully for resources. It is in this context that health economists argue that such decisions, and the rationale behind them, should be made explicit. One of the underlying principles of choice of health interventions to fund is value for money, since treatments should provide the greatest benefit to the greatest number of people if they are to be selected for funding in public health systems. Interventions are seen as value for money depending on how they affect QoL and duration of life for a particular cost. A number of methods have been developed to assess QoL in a manner which assists health economic evaluation. These are discussed in the next section.

Table 10.1 Typology of quality of life instruments illustrated with examples which can be used in research with cardiac patients

Type of instrument	Examples of instruments used in cardiac research
Generic: can be used across patient and general population groups	• Short-Form 36 (SF-36) (Ware & Sherbourne, 1992; McHorney et al., 1993, 1994) • Nottingham Health Profile (NHP) (Hunt et al., 1985)
Disease or population specific: focus on aspects of QoL relevant to particular health problems	• Seattle Angina Questionnaire [SAQ] (Spertus et al., 1995) • MacNew Heart Disease HRQL Questionnaire (MacNew) (Oldridge et al., 1991; Valenti et al., 1996) • Minnesota Living with Heart Failure (MLHF) (Rector et al., 1987)
Dimension specific: focus on a particular component of QoL	• Cardiac Depression Scale (Hare & Davis, 1996) • Global Mood Scale (Denollet, 1993; Denollet & Brutsaert, 1995) • Heart Patients' Psychological Questionnaire (Erdman et al., 1986) • Hospital Anxiety and Depression Scale (Zigmond & Snaith, 1983; Herrmann, 1997)
Individualized: focus on aspects of life selected by the individual being assessed	• Schedule for the Evaluation of Individual Quality of Life (SEIQoL) (McGee et al., 1991; O'Boyle et al., 1992; Hickey et al., 1996) • Quality of Life Index (QLI-cardiac) (Ferrans & Powers, 1985)
Utility: focus on hierarchy of preferences assigned by general population or patients for particular health states	• EuroQoL (EQ-5D) (Kind, 1996) • Quality of Well-being Scale (QWB) (Kaplan et al., 1993)

QUALITY OF LIFE MEASUREMENT INSTRUMENTS

QoL instruments can be divided into five main categories: generic, disease or population specific, dimension specific, individualized and utility (Garratt et al., 2002). These types of measures are outlined in table 10.1, with examples focusing on cardiac-related QoL research to illustrate the wide variety of instrument types and instruments that can be used in a specific setting.

The types of measures outlined in table 10.1 will now be discussed in relation to their particular uses and constraints.

Generic measures

Generic measures of QoL can be used in general or disease-focused population studies.

Generic measures: can be used across patient and general population groups.

They are typically profile measures, i.e. they assess a number of dimensions of QoL but do not usually sum them into one single scale. The general assumption is that scores on separate dimensions, such as sleep and social function, cannot readily be added together in a meaningful way. It is noteworthy that while questionnaire designers have started with this principle, there has been a great demand to have a single, interpretable QoL score, and many of the profile measures now provide some form of subscales summary or overall score. Measures differ in the number and focus of the subscales and items included in their instruments. The three most commonly used generic instruments, as found in a recent review (Garratt et al., 2002), are outlined in table 10.2. These are all HRQoL instruments. The Functional Limitations Profile (an English adaptation of an American instrument – the Sickness Impact Profile) is an early and lengthy instrument that, despite its name (SIP), can be completed by any member of the population. Because of its length, selected subscales are sometimes used instead of the whole scale. Another long-established HRQoL measure is the Nottingham Health Profile. More recently the Short-Form 36 scale has been developed from a large American study called the Medical Outcomes Study (MOS). The original aim of the study was to determine which factors influenced health-care use for those who had or did not have financial cover for such services. At present the SF-36 has become the most widely used HRQoL measure internationally and has been translated and validated in many languages. The measures have differing strengths and weaknesses. The FLP is clearly very broad in its coverage but is also very long. It does not have a pain subscale. The NHP focuses on more severe levels of disability and thus is likely to be less sensitive to change in conditions where effects are in the milder range. Conversely, the SF-36 is more sensitive to lower levels of disability.

Not all generic QoL assessment tools are health-related in focus. The World Health Organization has undertaken a major project to quantify QoL cross-culturally. They have sampled almost 5,000 individuals in 15 countries around the world (WHOQOL Group, 1995, 1998). Their aim was to assess if there are universal concepts when describing QoL and then to develop questions to operationalize these concepts in different cultures. Four universal themes were found – physical health, psychological well-being, social relationships and environment. A 100-item questionnaire was developed in different languages to assess QoL (the WHOQOL-100) and more recently a 25-item, briefer measure has become available. Questions differ slightly across languages as the aim of the study was to find conceptual equivalence in the measure rather than exact translations but with different meanings across languages.

Table 10.2 Scale profiles of three commonly used generic health-related quality of life questionnaires

	Functional Limitations Profile (FLP)	Nottingham Health Profile (NHP)	Medical Outcomes Study Short-form 36 (SF-36)
Authors	Charlton et al., 1983	Hunt et al., 1985	Ware & Sherbourne, 1992
Number of items	136	38 (part 1)	36
Number of subscales	12	7 (part 2)	8
Subscale summary scores?	• Physical • Psycho-social	No	• Physical component • Mental health component
Total score?	Yes	No	No
Subscales	Ambulation Body care & movement Mobility Household management Recreation and pastimes Social interaction Emotion Alertness Sleep and rest Eating Communication Work	Energy Pain Emotional reactions Sleep Social isolation Physical mobility	Physical functioning Role limitations due to physical problems Role limitations due to emotional problems Social functioning Mental health Energy/vitality Pain General health perception

Disease-specific or population-specific measures

There now exists a large body of research on instruments developed to measure aspects of QoL for specific diseases or populations.

Disease- or population-specific QoL: focus on aspects of QoL seen as most relevant to particular health problems.

Bowling (1995 and 1997) has produced excellent summaries of many of the available instruments. Examples are given in table 10.3. The impetus behind the development of such a wide variety of disease-specific instruments is to focus on the most salient aspects of QoL for individuals with a particular health condition. These instruments are developed to be sensitive to change in aspects of life believed to be most affected

Table 10.3 Scale profiles of three disease-specific quality of life questionnaires

	Arthritis Impact Measurement Scales (AIMS-2)*	EORTC Quality of Life Scale (30-item version) (EORTC-30)	Parkinson's Disease Questionnaire (PDQ)
Authors	Meenan et al., 1982 & 1992	Aaronson et al., 1993	Peto et al., 1995
Number of items	78	30	39
Number of subscales	12 (+ single items)	5 (+ 3 symptom subscales and single items)	8
Subscale summary score?	No	No	No
Total score?	No	No	Yes
Subscales	Mobility level Walking and bending Hand and finger function Arm function Self-care tasks Household tasks Social activities Social support Pain from arthritis Work Level of tension Mood	Physical functioning Role functioning Cognitive functioning Emotional functioning General QoL Fatigue Nausea and vomiting Pain	Mobility Activities of daily living Emotional well-being Stigma Social support Cognitions

* revised instrument (AIMS-2) described here.

by the condition concerned and its treatments. For instance, mobility and pain are major themes in arthritis-related instruments. Mobility is also an issue in a measure developed from patient interviews for Parkinson's disease, but pain is not; stigma features more prominently for the Parkinson's disease group. The research challenge when using specific instruments is that it is never possible to determine how different a group is in function from the general population. In the arthritis example, it is possible to say if one treatment for arthritis improves an aspect of QoL such as mobility more than another, but it is not possible to determine whether and when the improvement restores function to that of the general level of the population for a particular age group. This makes such assessment problematic from a health economic perspective. Many studies combine specific and generic measures in order to be able to make reference to function in relation to the general population. The challenge when doing this of course is to have questionnaires which do not place excessive burden on participants because of their length. This is one issue to consider when deciding if and how to assess QoL in a given health setting. The caution to have consideration for participants when selecting instruments should be balanced with the need to defend the use of QoL assessments where QoL is an important aspect of the presentation and care of a particular group of patients. It is easy to be dissuaded from using QoL assessment tools because health-care staff unfamiliar with psychological research think that the questionnaires are too long, repetitive or unnecessary. Where QoL is an important variable, it is worth considering that many of the other assessments in clinical settings are complex (e.g. requiring laboratory assessment and specific equipment and training to assess and interpret) and that many of these will be repeated at regular intervals to monitor progress in the patient's condition. QoL may be the only assessment that offers the patient an opportunity to provide his or her perspective on the success or otherwise of the treatment being provided.

Sometimes the distinction of interest does not relate to a health condition but rather to a particular population. The most usual delineations have been by age and gender. For adults, a HRQoL measure called the Women's Health Questionnaire has been developed for women in mid-life (Hunter, Liao & Lih-Mei, 1996). The aim of this instrument is to assess the range of health-related challenges facing women across the time period when they will experience menopause. A HRQoL measure to assess health-related concerns of older men has also been developed – the Ageing Males' Symptoms (AMS) Scale (Heinemann et al., 2001). It assesses three dimensions (psychological symptoms, somato-vegetative symptoms and sexual complaints).

A number of instruments have been developed to assess QoL in children (Drotar, 1998). These face the additional psychometric challenge of needing to be developmentally appropriate for children of different age groups. Such work has been undertaken with asthma-specific instruments where 3 versions are available (Christie & French, 1994). In other situations, adult versions have been tested and adapted, usually for older children and adolescents (e.g. diabetes) (Hoey et al., 2001). Generic, health-related instruments have also been developed. The Child Health Questionnaire is one such measure (Landgraf, Abetz & Ware, 1996). QoL in populations such as those with a learning disability provide an even more complex set of challenges than assessment in children. Discussion of this issue is beyond the scope of the present chapter. The complexities involved are well considered in an edited volume on the issues of QoL and human rights for older people with learning disabilities (Herr & Weber, 1999).

Individualized measures

Some individualized measures are in fact also generic in that they can be completed by either general population or disease-focused populations. They are characterized in this section, however, as their main distinguishing factor is their attempt to provide individualized assessment.

Individualized QoL: focus on aspects of life selected by the individual being assessed.

Acknowledging the relative and variable nature of QoL across individuals and circumstances, a number of research teams have attempted to develop instruments to assess QoL which have a standardized framework but which allow individualization in various aspects of the assessment. Possibly the most individualized QoL assessment system is the Schedule for the Evaluation of Individual Quality of Life (SEIQoL) (McGee et al., 1991; O'Boyle et al., 1992; O'Boyle at al., 1994) and its briefer direct weighting procedure (Hickey et al., 1996; Browne et al., 1997). The SEIQoL philosophy on QoL proposes that the definition of QoL is individual in nature, that the individual assesses his or her QoL on the basis of evaluation of current status on salient aspects of life and compared with his or her own set of standards concerning optimal function, and that these discrete evaluations are combined in a unique formula based on the relative value of each aspect of life by the individual concerned. The SEIQoL attempts to make explicit this process. Individuals are asked to nominate the five aspects of their life which most contribute to their overall QoL at the time of assessment (these do not have to be health-related). They then rate current function on each aspect on visual analogue scales anchored as 'best possible' and 'worst possible'. In order to find out the relative value (or weighting) an individual ascribes to each of the five aspects of life nominated, a decision-making task is introduced. Individuals are asked to provide the QoL rating they would give to 30 hypothetical life situations representing differing profiles of life function on each of the five aspects of life they have nominated as salient. This exercise allows for a multiple regression procedure to calculate the relative weighting of each of the five life domains in determining the QoL judgements. In the direct weighting procedure (SEIQoL-DW), the rating of hypothetical cases is replaced by having individuals explicitly assign weightings to the domains. Current status on each of the five life domains is multiplied by the relative weight of that domain and summed to make a 0 to 10 scale with higher scores indicating better QoL. Studies have shown that SEIQoL is more sensitive to change than generic or illness-related measures (O'Boyle et al., 1992), that health is not always listed as one of the salient aspects of QoL, even for groups with chronic health conditions assessed in medical settings (McGee et al., 1991; Clarke et al., 2001) and that QoL rated in this way can remain high in patients in palliative care settings (Waldron et al., 1999).

A second individualized QoL instrument is the Patient Generated Index (PGI) (Ruta et al., 1994, 1999). Unlike the SEIQoL, the PGI can only be used in the context of a health condition. Patients are asked to name the five most important areas of life that are affected by their health condition. They then rate how badly affected each of these areas is on a rating scale of 0 (worst they can imagine) to 100 (no effect: exactly as they would like it to be). A sixth box is included to cover all other important aspects of life not already mentioned. In order to ascertain their relative weighting or value the individual would ascribe to improvement in each of these listed domains, they are then asked to 'spend' 60 points on these domains in any combination they choose but with the aim being to best improve their overall QoL. Levels are multiplied by the weighting scores to give an overall QoL score. PGI has been shown to be more responsive to health changes than generic instruments in a number of studies, such as back pain and sleep apnoea. SEIQoL and PGI represent ways in which QoL assessment can be individualized in health or other settings.

A number of other instruments include some level of individualization. For instance, the generic Quality of Life Index (QLI) has 32 pre-selected items to rate. The individual rates functioning on each item and then rates the importance of that item. Scoring is a sum of each item function by its weighting or importance. The McMaster–Toronto Arthritis (MACTAR) Patient Function Preference Questionnaire (Tugwell et al., 1987) also identifies activities affected by the patient's disease and ranks them in the order which the individual patient would most like to see improved. Outcomes are then assessed in relation to these rank orders. Another such measure is the disease-specific Audit of Diabetes Dependent Quality of life (ADDQoL) (Bradley et al., 1999).

Utility measures

Utility measures have been developed from a health economics perspective.

> *Utility measures*: focus on hierarchy of preferences assigned by general population or patients for particular health states.

Their aim, as discussed earlier, was to assess the value of health or other interventions in terms of a combination of increased QoL and length of life. The challenge here is how to combine changes in length and quality of life, for instance how to compare a treatment for terminal cancer which extends life by 12 months but with severe nausea as a side-effect with a hip replacement surgery which has no impact on length of life but results in reduced pain and increased mobility for those treated. The main way in which this has been done is to calculate quality-adjusted life years (QALYs).

> *Quality-adjusted life years (QALYs)*: a calculation of the number of life years gained (or lost) because of illness or health intervention multiplied by the change in HRQoL of those treated.

QALYs are calculated from population rather than individual data. HRQoL is rated from 1.0 (best possible life) to 0.0 (dead). Thus a treatment which lengthened life by 5 years and restored or maintained a person in perfect health ($5 \times 1.0 = 5.0$) would provide a health system gain of 5.0 QALYs. The cost per QALY can be calculated from the cost of the treatment and related costings in a traditional health economic calculation. Different treatments can thus be compared for the cost per QALY of the treatment. Comparisons can be done concerning the same patients, e.g. the cost of treating renal failure patients by hospital haemodialysis, home-based continuous ambulatory peritoneal dialysis (CAPD) or renal transplantation. A UK study using 1991 costings showed the costs to be £23,200 per QALY (haemodialysis), £19,700 (CAPD) and £5,000 (transplantation) (Normand, 1994). Hence the treatment of choice from a combined HRQoL and economic perspective was transplantation. However, in a publicly funded health system, QALYs may also be compared across conditions. Thus costs of hospital haemodialysis (at £23,200 per QALY) compare poorly with medication used in the management of cystic fibrosis (£11,500) and coronary artery surgery for left main vessel coronary disease (£1,000). How are health policy-makers to decide which treatments to 'purchase' from their scarce resources?

The challenge in QALY assessment is how to determine the scores for the HRQoL ratings. Three methods have been used to determine the relative value of different health states, i.e. the magnitude estimation. These are time trade-off, standard gamble and rating scale techniques (Bennett & Torrance, 1996; Jenkinson & McGee, 1998).

> *Time trade-off technique*: method of calculating the relative value of different health states for an individual which involves estimating how much time a person would be willing to sacrifice from their duration of life in order to live a completely healthy life.

Time trade-off techniques involve asking participants to ascertain how many years of perfect health they would be willing to sacrifice in order to be free of a chronic health condition. Various options are presented until equilibrium is reached – a point where the person sees the number of years of life lost as equivalent in value to the option of being able to live without the chronic condition. The HRQoL score is calculated as the ratio between the two options.

> *Standard gamble technique*: method of calculating the relative value of different health states for an individual which involves choosing between living with a chronic condition and gambling for either a perfect health or death outcome.

The standard gamble method provides the person with a choice between the certainty of a life with a chronic condition or a gamble. The gamble involves the chance to have perfect health restored or to die. Varying probabilities are presented until the person reaches equilibrium. Rating scales have also been used. Typically a range of gradated health states is rated. One widely used measure, the EuroQol (EQ-5D) (Kind, 1996), uses assessment of 5 QoL-related dimensions (mobility, self-care, usual activity, pain and mood) by 3 levels (none, moderate or severe problem). A level or weighting of difficulty is assigned to each of these parameters. This is usually done by studies in community settings where population weightings for differing health states are derived. A weighting from 0.0 to 1.0 is then calculated for a particular health state based on the population sample providing weightings. For example, a person might be confined to bed (severe problem–mobility dimension), able to wash and dress himself (no problem–self-care), unable to perform some of his other usual daily activities (moderate problems–usual activity), have moderate pain (moderate problem–pain) and be very depressed (severe problem–mood). What differs in these methods from other means of calculating QoL or HRQoL is that the weightings used in many studies are weightings calculated from a validation population rather than the weightings of the individual being assessed. The individual reports his or her health state and the population weighting for that state is then assigned to it. Critics of these methods argue that weights are assigned in an artificial context by general population samples who are not themselves experiencing the levels of ill-health described in the scenarios. Ratings, or relative ratings, might be quite different if the person had some experience of the situation. On the other hand, the view is that the valuations do represent the public's rating of the severity of health conditions and thus their gauge against which to value the impact of interventions to improve health and QoL. A recent comparison of public and patient ratings showed that patients gave higher (i.e. better) QoL ratings than the public to most scenarios that could be generated using the EQ-5D approach (Polsky et al., 2001). Another problem with the health economic perspective on HRQoL is the inherent ageism in its formulation. Any improvement in HRQoL from a treatment, when multiplied by the number of years the individual can expect to benefit, will automatically indicate that the treatment is better value when provided to younger individuals. These issues have resulted in wide-ranging criticism of health economic approaches to HRQoL assessment. Such criticisms notwithstanding, the need is obvious for methods to inform explicit and objective criteria for societal spending on interventions to improve health.

Questionnaire development and coordination

The level and organization of activity in terms of questionnaire development and refinement in QoL is worth noting. In cancer research, the European Organization for Research and Treatment of Cancer (EORTC) researchers have developed a core cancer HRQL instrument (EORTC-30 as outlined above) (Sprangers et al., 1998). It can be supplemented with specific modules (additional sets of questions) for specific cancers. This approach has been highly successful in facilitating cancer clinical trials which include patients across Europe in different centres and with different languages. In rheumatology, a group called OMERACT (Outcome Measures in Rheumatoid Arthritis Clinical Trials) have also been working for some time towards an agreed set of instruments for use across arthritis research. In cardiology, a consortium of the European Society of Cardiology and the European Health Psychology Society has begun the task of developing a core set of QoL instruments for this setting across European languages. More generically, the International Quality of Life Assessment Project (IQOLA) has been working on translations of the SF-36, the WHOQOL Group on cross-cultural use of its questionnaire, and the European Quality of Life Project Group on the use of the EuroQoL Questionnaire across countries and conditions.

CURRENT ISSUES IN QUALITY OF LIFE RESEARCH

The shortage of conceptual development in QoL, and confusion between QoL and related concepts such as health status, means that QoL is in danger of being devalued or becoming redundant as a concept. There is increasing evidence of construct dynamism in QoL: for instance, QoL in populations with chronic disease can be as high or higher than that in healthy populations (e.g. Allison, Locker & Feine, 1997). Similarly, there is evidence that individuals substantially reframe their perceptions in estimating past and present QoL over time (e.g. Bernhard et al., 1999). Such reframing, or response shift (Schwartz & Sprangers, 2000), is probably integral to patient adaptation to disease and treatment.

> *Response shift*: a change in the meaning of one's self-evaluation on a target construct such as QoL.

Response shift can occur as a result of:

- a change in one's internal standards of measurement (i.e. recalibration),
- a change in one's values (i.e. the importance of components constituting QoL), or
- a redefinition of QoL itself (i.e. reconceptualization).

Each of these changes represents both illustrations of the adaptive nature of the human psyche in response to changing conditions and, for the research community, challenges in estimating their influence on QoL assessments. Methods of assessing response shift have been summarized in a recent methods text by Schwartz & Sprangers (2000).

In part because of conceptual confusion, there has been little evidence to date on the relationship of QoL and psychological well-being. It is of theoretical and practical importance to ascertain, for instance, to what extent QoL ratings may be influenced by depression in medical populations.

More practically, user-friendly versions of QoL instruments are needed for health settings if the concept is to be widely used in the clinical as well as research context. User-friendly means ensuring that brief instruments can readily be completed by patients; that the results can be easily scored by health professionals; that results can be clinically interpreted by health professionals (in the way that clinical indices, such as creatinine as a measure of renal function, can be interpreted at present); and, importantly, that the results obtained can guide treatment decisions based on QoL.

CHALLENGES AND OPPORTUNITIES FOR HEALTH PSYCHOLOGISTS

Health psychologists have been actively involved in the QoL research endeavour to date. Many have provided psychometric skills within a largely bio-medical framework to address challenges such as increasing responsiveness to change in evaluative research instruments (Fitzpatrick, 2000). There is, however, a bigger and more psychological task still to be achieved in extending our understanding of QoL. Current concerns within the QoL research community, as outlined in the previous section, are of course ones for which health psychologists can provide a significant contribution to theory and empirical research. Some others as outlined below may provide a much-needed psychological perspective on the overall endeavour.

One problem with current research frameworks is that QoL is almost always seen as a dependent measure – an outcome variable. Some have argued that QoL is in fact better understood as a process (Leventhal & Colman, 1997; Hyland, 1992) and that the focus should be on how QoL is constructed as a judgement by individuals over time and circumstance. Furthermore, some of the concepts used to calculate QoL, such as mood and pain, may in fact be better conceptualized as determinants rather than constituents of QoL.

Where does an individual's construct of QoL come from and how does it change over time? Little is understood about how concepts of QoL are formed and changed for individuals. QoL is assumed to be a judgement of the acceptability of one's present situation *vis-à-vis* expectations and aspirations. These may be set with reference to oneself (past or present) or with reference to others, i.e. social comparisons (Buunk et al., 1990). The role of self or social comparisons in establishing or altering QoL parameters needs to be examined in order to understand more about formulation of the construct of QoL for individuals. The notion of trait or state aspects of QoL is also of interest. Are there some levels or types of assessment of QoL which are very susceptible to environmental changes or changes in mood while other assessments are more trait-like? Concepts of QoL may also be usefully considered in a Developmental Psychology framework: for example, do the salient issues for an individual's QoL change over time across the lifespan? Finally, there is evidence that constructs which parallel QoL, such as well-being and happiness, are very similar across national and international comparisons and over time, and there are proposals for a homeostatic dimension where individuals actively work to maintain a particular pre-set level of function on these dimensions (Diener, 2000). This issue could also be considered in relation to QoL levels and their management by individuals. How do individuals strive to maintain a particular level of QoL in changing circumstances? A widely used model in health psychology, the self-regulatory model of illness behaviour (Leventhal et al., 1997), could usefully be adapted to consider when, if and how individuals change and reconstruct their interpretation, coping and appraisal in order to maintain a previous level of QoL in the face of health or other adversities. The recently developed 'positive psychology' perspective (e.g. Aspinwall & Staudinger, 2003) also has areas of mutual interest with those concerned with QoL research. These briefly listed examples illustrate that existing psychological research and theory can provide useful frameworks to develop a greater understanding of QoL in the future.

CONCLUSIONS

The value of QoL assessment is now widely accepted in health settings. Developing a common language around QoL can facilitate dialogue between physicians and social scientists (including health psychologists) about the experiences, both individually and collectively, of patients. It allows for the development of a greater understanding of the patient's experience of illness using a common language. While physicians may be interested in the overall profile of patients in research models such as randomized clinical trials or in knowledge to inform individual patient care, the same information can facilitate social scientists to develop theoretical models concerning issues such as changing perspectives on illness over time, over intervention and over culture.

The challenge for the coming decades is to find some reconciliation between these two perspectives. In this way QOL assessment can be better used to direct services at individual and societal levels, while expanding our understanding of how QoL is developed, maintained and altered as necessary through the course of illness and health interventions.

DISCUSSION POINTS

1. Can health-related quality of life be distinguished from quality of life *per se*?
2. What factors can influence an individual's rating of quality of life?
3. Can surrogate assessment be called a 'quality of life' assessment of the individual being assessed?
4. Can quality of life and duration of life variables be validly combined as is done for health-economic-type evaluations of QoL?
5. What is the value of QoL assessment if individuals change their definitions of what QoL is to them over time?

FURTHER READING

Albrecht, G. L. and Fitzpatrick, G., eds. (1994). *Advances in Medical Sociology, volume V: Quality of Life in Health Care*. Greenwich, CT: JAI Press. Good, wide-ranging overview of issues in QoL assessment.

Bowling, A. (1995). *Measuring Disease: A Review of Disease-specific Quality of Life Scales*. Birmingham: Open University Press. AND: Bowling, A. (1997). *Measuring Health: A Review of Quality of Life Scales*, 2nd edn. Birmingham: Open University Press. Invaluable companion books including summaries of a large set of QoL-related instruments: descriptions, psychometric properties, key references and typical uses of the instruments.

Bradley, C. (2001). Importance of differentiating health status from quality of life. *Lancet* 357, 7–8. Concise outline of the difficulties posed when using QoL instruments based on very different meanings of the concept. The problems are illustrated by a diabetes research example.

Diener, E. (2000). Subjective well-being: the science of happiness and a proposal for a national index. *American Psychologist* 55, 34–43. Good overview highlighting the similarities in scores of life satisfaction and happiness in studies cross-culturally. He proposes a homeostatic dimension where individuals actively work to keep satisfaction or happiness levels at a particular pre-set level.

Hayry, M. (1991). Measuring the quality of life: why, how and what? *Theoretical Medicine* 12, 97–116. Excellent outline of the basic philosophical challenges underlying efforts to assess QoL.

Joyce, C. R. B., O'Boyle, C. A. and McGee, H. M. (1999). *Individual Quality of Life: Approaches to Conceptualisation and Assessment.* Amsterdam: Harwood. Detailed overview of diverse set of individualized methods of assessing QoL.

Sprangers, M. A. and Aaronson, N. K. (1992). The role of health care providers and significant others in evaluating the quality of life of patients with chronic disease: a review. *Journal of Clinical Epidemiology* 45, 743–60. Demonstrates that physicians and relatives consistently view patient QoL as poorer than do patients themselves.

KEY STUDIES

Allison, P. J., Locker, D. and Feine, J. S. (1997). Quality of life: a dynamic construct. *Social Science and Medicine* 45, 221–30. Good summary of the complexities of QoL assessment.

Stewart, A. L., Greenfield, S., Hays, R. D., Wells, R. D., Rogers, W. H., Berry, S. D., McGlynn, E. A. and Ware, J. E. (1989). Functional status and well-being of patients with chronic conditions: results from the Medical Outcomes Study. *Journal of the American Medical Association* 262, 907–13. Classic study using SF-36 to illustrate the differing HRQoL profile of patients with 1 of 9 chronic health conditions.

REFERENCES

Aaronson, N. K., Ahmedzai, S. and Bergman, B. (1993). The European Organisation for Research and Treatment of Cancer QLQ-30: a quality of life instrument for use in international clinical trials in oncology. *Journal of the National Cancer Institute* 85, 365–76.

Allison, P. J., Locker, D. and Feine, J. S. (1997). Quality of life: a dynamic construct. *Social Science and Medicine* 45, 221–30.

Aspinwall, L. G. and Staudinger, U. M., eds. (2003). *A Psychology of Human Strengths: Fundamental Questions for a Positive Psychology.* Washington, DC: American Psychological Association.

Baker, G. A. and Jacoby, A., eds. (2000). *Quality of Life in Epilepsy.* Amsterdam: Harwood Academic.

Bennett, K. J. and Torrance, G. W. (1996). Measuring health state preferences and utilities: rating scale, time trade-off and standard gamble techniques. In B. Spilker, ed., *Quality of Life and Pharmacoeconomics in Clinical Trials*, 2nd edn. Philadelphia: Lippincott-Raven, 253–66.

Bernhard, J., Huerny, C., Maibach, R., Herrmann, R. and Laffer, U., for the Swiss Group for Clinical Cancer Research (1999). Quality of life as subjective experience: reframing of perception in patients with colon cancer undergoing radical resection with or without chemotherapy. *Annals of Oncology* 10, 775–82.

Bowling, A. (1995). *Measuring Disease: A Review of Disease-specific Quality of Life Scales.* Birmingham: Open University Press.

Bowling, A. (1997). *Measuring Health: A Review of Quality of Life Scales*, 2nd edn. Birmingham: Open University Press.

Bradley, C. (2001). Importance of differentiating health status from quality of life. *Lancet* 357, 7–8.

Bradley, C., Todd, C., Gorton, T., Symonds, E., Martin, A. and Plowright, R. (1999). The development of an individualised questionnaire measure of perceived impact of diabetes on quality of life: the ADDQoL. *Quality of Life Research* 8, 79–91.

Brickman, P., Coates, D. D. and Janoff-Bulman, C. (1978). Lottery winners and accident victims: is happiness relative? *Journal of Personality and Social Psychology* 36, 917–27.

Browne, J. P., O'Boyle, C. A., McGee, H. M., McDonald, N. J. and Joyce, C. R. B. (1997). Development of a direct weighting procedure for quality of life domains. *Quality of Life Research* 6, 301–9.

Buunk, B. P., Collins, R. L., Taylor, S. E., Van Yperen, N. W. and Dakof, G. A. (1990). The affective consequences of social comparison: either direction has its ups and downs. *Journal of Personality and Social Psychology* 59, 1238–49.

Calman, K. C. (1984). The quality of life in cancer patients – an hypothesis. *Journal of Medical Ethics* 10, 124–9.

Charlton, J. R., Patrick, D. L. and Peach, H. (1983). Use of multi-variate measures of disability in health surveys. *Journal of Epidemiology and Community Health* 37, 296–304.

Christie, M. and French, D., eds. (1994). *Assessment of Quality of Life in Childhood Asthma.* Amsterdam: Harwood Academic.

Clarke, S., Hickey, A., O'Boyle, C. and Hardiman, O. (2001). Assessing individual quality of life in amylotrophic lateral sclerosis. *Quality of Life Research* 10, 117–22.

Denollet, J. (1993). Emotional distress and fatigue in coronary heart disease: the Global Mood Scale (GMS). *Psychological Medicine* 23, 111–21.

Denollet, J. and Brutsaert, D. L. (1995). Enhancing emotional well-being by comprehensive rehabilitation in patients with coronary heart disease. *European Heart Journal* 16, 1070–8.

Diener, E. (2000). Subjective well-being: the science of happiness and a proposal for a national index. *American Psychologist* 55, 34–43.

Dijkers, M. P. (2003). Individualization in quality of life measurement: instruments and approaches. *Archives of Physical and Medical Rehabilitation* 84 (suppl. 2), S3–14.

Dimsdale, J. E. and Baum, A., eds. (1995). *Quality of Life in Behavioural Medicine Research.* Mahwah, NJ: Lawrence Erlbaum.

Drotar, D., ed. (1998). *Measuring Health-related Quality of Life in Children and Adolescents.* Mahwah, NJ: Lawrence Erlbaum.

Erdman, R., Duivenvoorden, H., Verhage, F., Krazemier, M. and Hugenholtz, P. (1986). Predictability of beneficial effects in cardiac rehabilitation: a randomised clinical trial of psychosocial variables. *Journal of Cardiopulmonary Rehabilitation* 6, 206–13.

Fadin, R. and Leplege, A. (1992). Assessing quality of life: moral implications for clinical practice. *Medical Care* 30 (suppl. 5), 166–75.

Fagerlin, A., Ditto, P., Danks, J. H. and Houts, R. M. (2001). Projection in surrogate decisions about life-sustaining medical treatments. *Health Psychology* 20, 166–75.

Fayers, P. M. and Machin, D. (2000). *Quality of Life: Assessment, Analysis and Interpretation.* Chichester: Wiley.

Ferrans, C. E. and Powers, M. J. (1985). Quality of life index: development and psychometric properties. *Advances in Nursing Science* 8, 15–24.

Fitzpatrick, R. (2000). Measurement issues in health-related quality of life: challenges for health psychology. *Psychology & Health* 15, 99–108.

Garratt, A., Schmidt, L., Mackintosh, A. and Fitzpatrick, R. (2002). Quality of life measurement: bibliographic study of patient assessed health outcome measures. *British Medical Journal* 324, 1417–21.

Hare, D. and Davis, C. (1996). Cardiac Depression Scale: validation of a new depression scale for cardiac patients. *Journal of Psychosomatic Research* 40, 379–86.

Hayry, M. (1991). Measuring the quality of life: why, how and what? *Theoretical Medicine* 12, 97–116.

Heinemann, L. A. J., Saad, F., Thiele, K. and Wood-Dauphinee, S. (2001). The Ageing Males' Symptoms rating scale: cultural and linguistic validation into English. *Ageing Male* 4, 14–22.

Herr, S. S. and Weber, G., eds. (1999). *Ageing, Rights and Quality of Life: Prospects for Older People with Developmental Difficulties.* Baltimore, MD: Paul H. Brooks.

Herrmann, C. (1997). International experiences with the Hospital Anxiety and Depression Scale – a review of validation data and clinical results. *Journal of Psychosomatic Research* 42, 17–41.

Hickey, A. M., Bury, G., O'Boyle, C. A., Bradley, F., O'Kelly, F. D. and Shannon, W. (1996). A new short-form individual quality of life measure (SEIQoL-DW): application in a cohort of individuals with HIV/AIDS. *British Medical Journal* 313, 29–33.

Higginson, I. J. and Carr, A. J. (2001). Using quality of life measures in the clinical setting. *British Medical Journal* 322, 1297–1300.

Hoey, H., Aanstoot, H. J., Chiarelli, F., Daneman, D., et al., for the Hvidøre Study Group on Childhood Diabetes. (2001). Good metabolic control is associated with better quality of life in 2,101 adolescents with type 1 diabetes. *Diabetes Care* 24, 1923–8.

Hunt, S., McEwan, J. and McKenna, S. (1985). Measuring health status: a new tool for clinicians and epidemiologists. *Journal of the Royal College of General Practitioners* 35, 185–8.

Hunter, M., Liao, S. and Lih-Mei, K. (1996). Evaluation of a four-session cognitive behavioural intervention for menopausal hot flushes. *British Journal of Health Psychology* 1, 113–25.

Hyland, M. (1992). A reformulation of quality of life for medical science. *Quality of Life Research* 1, 267–72.

Jenkinson, C. and McGee, H. M. (1998). *Health Status Measurement: A Brief But Critical Introduction.* Oxford: Radcliffe Medical Press.

Joyce, C. R. B. (1988). Quality of life: the state of the art in clinical assessment. In S. W. Walker and R. M. Rosser, eds., *Quality of Life Assessment and Application.* Lancaster: MTP Press, 169–79.

Joyce, C. R. B., O'Boyle, C. A. and McGee, H. M. (1999). *Individual Quality of Life: Approaches to Conceptualisation and Assessment.* Amsterdam: Harwood Academic.

Joyce, C. R. B., Hickey, A., McGee, H. M. and O'Boyle. C. A. (2003). A theory-based method for the evaluation of individual quality of life: the SEIQoL. *Quality of Life Research* 12, 275–80.

Kaplan, R. M., Anderson, J. P. and Ganiats, T. G. (1993). The Quality of Well-being Scale: rationale for a single quality of life index. In S. R. Walker and R. M. Rosser, eds., *Quality of Life Assessment: Key Issues in the 1990s.* Dordrecht: Kluwer Academic, 65–94.

Karnofsky, D. A. and Burchenal, J. H. (1947). The clinical evaluation of chemotherapeutic agents in cancer. In C. M. MacLeod, ed., *Evaluation of Chemotherapeutic Agents.* New York: Columbia University Press.

Kind, P. (1996). The EuroQol Instrument: an index of health-related quality of life. In B. Spilker, ed., *Quality of Life and Pharmacoeconomics in Clinical Trials*, 2nd edn. Philadelphia: Lippincott-Raven, 191–202.

Landgraf, J. M., Abetz, L. and Ware, J. E., Jr (1996). *The Child Health Questionnaire (CHQ): A User's Manual.* Boston: The Health Institute.

Leventhal, H., Benyamini, Y., Brownlee, S., Diefenbach, M., Leventhal, E. A., Patrick-Miller, L. and Robitaille, C. (1997). Illness representations: theoretical foundations. In K. J. Petrie and J. A. Weinman, eds., *Perceptions of Health and Illness.* Amsterdam: Harwood Academic, 19–45.

Leventhal, H. and Colman, S. (1997). Quality of life: a process view. *Psychology & Health* 12, 753–68.

McGee, H. M. and Bradley, C., eds. (1994). *Quality of Life Following Renal Failure.* Amsterdam: Harwood Academic.

McGee, H. M., O'Boyle, C. A., Hickey, A. M., Joyce, C. R. B. and O'Malley, K. (1991). Assessing the quality of life of the individual: the SEIQoL with a healthy and a gastroenterology unit population. *Psychological Medicine* 21, 749–59.

McHorney, C. A., Ware, J. E., Jr, Lu, J. F. R. and Shelbourne, C. D. (1994). The MOS 36-Item Short-Form Health Survey [SF-36]: III. Tests of data quality, scaling assumptions, and reliability across diverse patient groups. *Medical Care* 32, 40–66.

McHorney, C. A., Ware, J. E., Jr and Raczek, A. (1993). The MOS 36-Item Short-Form Health Survey (SF-36): II. Psychometric and clinical tests of validity in measuring physical and mental health constructs. *Medical Care* 31, 247–63.

Meenan, R. F., Gertman, P. M. and Mason, J. H. (1982). The Arthritis Impact Measurement Scales: further investigations of a health status measure. *Arthritis & Rheumatism* 25, 1048–53.

Meenan, R. F., Mason, J. H. and Anderson, J. J. (1992). AIMS2: the content and properties of a revised and expanded Arthritis Impact Measurement Scales Health Status Questionnaire. *Arthritis & Rheumatism* 35, 1–9.

Normand, C. (1994). Health care resource allocation and the management of renal failure. In H. M. McGee and C. Bradley, eds., *Quality of Life Following Renal Failure.* Amsterdam: Harwood Academic, 145–53.

O'Boyle, C. A., McGee, H. M., Hickey, A. M., O'Malley, K. and Joyce, C. R. B. (1992). Individual quality of life in patients undergoing hip replacement. *Lancet* 339, 1088–91.

O'Boyle, C. A., McGee, H. M. and Joyce, C. R. B. (1994). Quality of life: assessing the individual. *Advances in Medical Sociology* 5, 159–80.

Oldridge, N., Guyatt, G., Jones, N., Crowe, J., et al. (1991). Effects on quality of life with comprehensive rehabilitation after acute myocardial infarction. *American Journal of Cardiology* 67, 1084–9.

Patrick, D. L. and Erickson, P. (1993). *Health Status and Health Policy: Quality of Life in Health Care Evaluation and Resource Allocation.* New York: Oxford University Press.

Peto, V., Jenkinson, C., Fitzpatrick, R. and Greenhall, R. (1995). The development and validation of a short measure of functioning and well-being for individuals with Parkinson's disease. *Quality of Life Research* 4, 241–8.

Polsky, D., Willke, R. J., Scott, K., Schulman, K. A. and Glick, H. A. (2001). A comparison of scoring weights for the EuroQol derived from patients and the general public. *Health Economics* 10(1), 27–37.

Rector, T. S., Kubo, S. H. and Cohn, J. N. (1987). Patients' self-assessment of their congestive heart failure: content, reliability, and validity of a new measure, the Minnesota Living with Heart Failure questionnaire. *Heart Failure* 3, 198–209.

Ruta, D. A., Garratt, A. M. and Russell, I. T. (1999). Patient centred assessment of quality of life for patients with four common conditions. *Quality in Health Care* 8, 22–9.

Ruta, D. A., Garratt, A. M., Rusell, I. T. and MacDonald, L. M. (1994). A new approach to the measurement of quality of life: the Patient-Generated Index. *Medical Care* 32, 1109–26.

Schipper, H., Clinch, J. J., and Olweny, L. M. (1996). Quality of life studies: definitions and conceptual issues. In B. Spilker, ed., *Quality of Life and Pharmacoeconomics in Clinical Trials,* 2nd edn. Philadelphia: Lippincott-Raven, 11–23.

Schwartz, C. E. and Sprangers, M. A. G., eds. (2000). *Adaptation to Changing Health: Response Shift in Quality-of-Life Research.* Washington, DC: American Psychological Association.

Spertus, J. A., Winder, J. A., Dewhurst, T. A., Deyo, R. A., et al. (1995). Development and evaluation of the Seattle Angina Questionnaire: a new functional status measure for coronary artery disease. *Journal of the American College of Cardiology* 25, 333–41.

Spilker, B., ed. (1996). *Quality of Life and Pharmacoeconomics in Clinical Trials*, 2nd edn. Philadelphia: Lippincott-Raven.

Spitzer, W. O., Dobson, A. J. and Hall, J. (1981). Measuring the quality of life of cancer patients: a concise QL index for use by physicians. *Journal of Chronic Diseases* 34, 585–97.

Sprangers, M. A. and Aaronson, N. K. (1992). The role of health care providers and significant others in evaluating the quality of life of patients with chronic disease: a review. *Journal of Clinical Epidemiology* 45, 743–60.

Sprangers, M. A., Cull, A., Groenvold, M., Bjordal, K., Blazeby, J. and Aaronson, N. K. (1998). The European Organization for Research and Treatment of Cancer approach to developing questionnaire modules: an update and overview. EORTC Quality of Life Study Group. *Quality of Life Research* 7, 291–300.

Staquet, M. J., Hays, R. and Fayers, P. M., eds. (1998). *Quality of Life Assessment in Clinical Trials*. Oxford: Oxford University Press.

Tannock, I. F., Osaba, D., Stockler, M. R., et al. (1996). Chemotherapy with mixoxantrone plus prednisone alone for symptomatic hormone-resistant prostate cancer: a Canadian randomized trial with palliative end-points. *Journal of Clinical Oncology* 14, 1756–64.

Tugwell, P., Bombardier, C., Buchanan, W. W., et al. (1987). The MACTAR Patient Preference Disability Questionnaire. *Journal of Rheumatology* 14(3), 446–51.

Valenti, L., Lim, L., Heller, R. F. and Knapp, J. (1996). An improved questionnaire for assessing quality of life after myocardial infarction. *Quality of Life Research* 5, 151–61.

Waldron, D., O'Boyle, C. A., Kearney, M., Moriarty, M. and Carney, D. (1999). Quality of life measurement in advanced cancer: assessing the individual. *Journal of Clinical Oncology* 17, 3603–11.

Ware, J. E., Jr, and Sherbourne, C. D. (1992). The MOS 36-item short-form health survey (SF-36), I: Conceptual framework and item selection. *Medical Care* 30, 473–83.

WHOQOL Group. (1995). The World Health Organization Quality of Life assessment (WHO-QOL): position paper from the World Health Organization. *Social Science & Medicine* 41, 1403–9.

WHOQOL Group. (1998). Development of the World Health Organization WHOQOL-BREF quality of life assessment. *Psychological Medicine* 28, 551–8.

Zigmond, A. S. and Snaith, R. P. (1983). The hospital anxiety and depression scale. *Acta Psychiatrica Scandinavica* 67, 361–70.

Chapter Eleven

COMMUNICATION IN MEDICAL ENCOUNTERS

J. M. Bensing and P. F. M. Verhaak

CHAPTER OUTLINE

The aim of this chapter is to provide a theoretical and empirical basis for the concept of communication as *the* core instrument in the medical encounter. Adequate communication, embedded in a warm and caring relationship, has always been recognized as essential to the concept of good doctoring, but for long periods of time this was considered as 'the *art* of medicine', distinguished and distinguishable from medical *science*. In the last decades empirical research has helped to turn art into science. We will summarize the evidence, focusing on 'the placebo effect'. We will then show that at about the same time that we began to understand the dynamics of the medical encounter, the doctor–patient relationship itself was subject to major changes. Changes in patient morbidity, in the power balance between doctors and patients, and in the amount and availability of medical information for laymen have had profound influences on the doctor-patient relationship. These societal changes have fed and are fed by a paradigm shift in medicine: from supply-induced care to demand-induced care, from doctor-centred medicine to patient-centred medicine, from clinical decisions to shared decision-making. Each of these developments demands a revaluation of communication as a relevant tool in medicine. The doctor–patient relationship is the context within which patients' expectations and beliefs are shaped and management decisions are taken. This relationship is changing over time and between cultures as well. Patient groups and individual patients may have a variety of needs, expectations and preferences, which require tailored communication by physicians. As a consequence, teaching *general* communication skills in medical education is not sufficient anymore. Moreover, the shift from doctor-centred to patient-centred medicine also implies a shift in focus from the physician's to the patient's role in medical encounters, with explicit attention to patients' illness representations and self-regulation in disease management. By applying principles from health psychology, the medical encounter changes from 'powerful placebo' into a place for 'empowering patients'.

KEY CONCEPTS

adherence

affective behaviour

communication

compliance

consumerism

context

demand-induced care

disclosure

doctor-centred medicine

epidemiological transition

expectancies

illness representations

instrumental behaviour

patient-centred medicine

placebo effect

power balance

relationship

satisfaction

self-management

self-regulation

shared decision-making

THE MEDICAL ENCOUNTER AS POWERFUL PLACEBO

Wisdom from history

Since ancient times physicians have been aware of the therapeutic qualities of the doctor–patient relationship. Probably the first and most cited author who mentioned the relevance of the doctor–patient relationship for patients' well-being was Hippocrates, who wrote in 400 BC: 'The patient, though conscious that his condition is perilous, may recover his health simply through his contentment with the goodness of the physician' (DiMatteo & DiNicola, 1982; DeVeugele, 2003). Fifty years ago, the British psychiatrist Michael Balint re-affirmed the importance of doctor–patient interaction, asserting that by far the most frequently used and most effective drug in medical practice is the doctor himself (Balint, 1955). This concept of 'the doctor as the drug' has inspired many graduate and post-graduate medical training programmes ever since. A recent debate in the *British Medical Journal* about 'what is a good doctor' (Coulter, 2002; Hurwitz & Vass, 2002) shows that at the beginning of the twenty-first century, the words of Hippocrates and Balint have lost remarkably little of their former appeal. Many physicians, especially in primary care, internal medicine and psychiatry, still believe in the magic of the medical encounter apart and aside from the highly valued achievements in bio-medical knowledge (Bensing, 2000; Hurwitz & Vass, 2002).

Turning art into science

For long periods of time the therapeutic potential of the doctor–patient relationship was merely based on philosophical literature and described as 'the art of medicine', distinguished and distinguishable from 'the science of medicine': the body of medical knowledge which is based on fundamental research and clinical trials. But this view on the dual identity of good doctoring is now rapidly changing. Recently, many review studies have been published which document empirical evidence of the therapeutic quality of the practitioner's manner (Crow et al., 1999; DiBlasi et al., 2001; van Dulmen & Bensing, 2001; Moerman & Wayne, 2002), showing that the art of medicine *can* be turned into science. A lot of these studies are at least partly inspired by the intriguing fact that the results of clinical trials seldom show a one-to-one relationship between a medical intervention and a therapeutic effect (van Dulmen & Bensing, 2001). This is because, in addition to specific effects of physical or pharmacological interventions, all kind of non-specific therapeutic effects also occur within the healing process (Turner et al., 1994; de Kleijnen et al., 1994). The classic (now considered unethical) example of the power of these non-specific therapeutic effects comes from two studies of ligation of the bilateral internal mammary arteries as a treatment for angina, in which part of the patients only got sham surgery (Cobb et al., 1959; Dimond et al., 1960; Moerman & Wayne, 2002). Patients receiving sham surgery did as well – with 80 per cent of patients substantially improving – as those receiving the active procedure in the trials. The same effect has been shown repeatedly in pharmaceutical trials (White, 1988; Crow et al., 1999; Moerman & Wayne, 2002). This effect, also referred to as the 'placebo effect', appears to be responsible for a considerable therapeutic effect (White, 1988), and therefore to make a positive contribution to the practice of health care. Researchers and research councils in several countries have recognized the importance of this relatively young field of research, resulting in national conferences and programming studies in the United Kingdom (Crow et al., 1999), the USA (National Institute of Health, 2000) and the Netherlands (van Dulmen & Bensing, 2001). The aim of the efforts in all three countries was to gather empirical evidence on the placebo effect and to set a research agenda. As part of this process, the results of empirical research in this field were summarized in several review studies. While most studies focus on physicians' role in the health-care process, there are also a few studies about the role of nurses with – in general – comparable findings (Kwekkeboom, 1997). The results of the empirical studies can be divided into three main groups of factors: patient factors, physician factors and patient–physician/ nurse factors.

Patient factors

If one reviews the literature, there seem to be at least six types of patient factors which might influence the outcome of medical treatment, independently from the characteristics of the treatment itself (van Dulmen & Bensing, 2001): (1) worry and anxiety, (2) confidence and hope, (3) expectations, suggestion and motivation, (4) self-efficacy and control, (5) catastrophizing and pessimism, and (6) attributions. A number of these factors – such as confidence and hope, and the experience of being in control of the situation – have a positive effect on health. Other factors – such as anxiety, helplessness and negative experiences and expectations – have an unfavourable effect (van Dulmen & Bensing, 2001). In a comprehensive systematic review based on 93 empirical studies, a group of British researchers focus on the central role of expectancies in the placebo effect. They conclude that treatment success is often not so much the result of a powerful drug, but much more of patients' expectancies (Crow et al., 1999). Expectancies are defined as treatment-related outcome expectancies (beliefs that treatments will have positive or negative effects on health status) and patient-related self-efficacy expectations (beliefs that one can carry out the actions necessary for successful management of a disease or coping with the treatment). The majority of the studies in their review provided evidence of the power of positive outcome expectancy to enhance the effects of medical treatment. Most of the improvements were patient self-reports of reduced anxiety, pain and distress. There was also some evidence for the effects of negative outcome expectancy ('nocebo effect'), where the frequency of the patient's self-report of symptoms increased. Expectancies were also shown to influence the (self-)management of illness. Benefits included an improvement in the patient's symptoms (mood, anxiety, pain) as well as improvement in disease status (lowered blood pressure, immunological changes and better metabolic control). A few studies also reported a reduction in the use of health services (Crow et al., 1999).

Until now, little has been known about determinants of patients' expectancies. It is supposed that these reflect pre-existing beliefs, which have been formed over time by past health-care experiences of the patient and his/her social network (Crow et al., 1999). There is some evidence that classical conditioning might play a role (van Dulmen & Bensing, 2001). For instance, in cancer research, it has been demonstrated that the association with previous negative experiences (hospital, smell and taste of chemotherapy) is more determinative for the outcome of the encounter (nausea, anxiety) than the expectation that is aroused by suggestion from the practitioner (Bovbjerg et al., 1990; Kvale et al., 1991). This means that practitioners should pay attention to previous experiences to enhance placebo effects and diminish nocebo effects.

Empirical studies which have sought to explain observed placebo effects on the basis of patient characteristics (age, sex, race, socio-economic status, or personality characteristics) have generated disappointing results (Crow et al., 1999, Moerman & Wayne, 2002). Several studies show that even within an individual, the placebo response is not consistent (Crow et al., 1999).

Physician factors

While it is likely that physician/nurse factors may impact on the efficacy of a medical intervention, research into this is remarkably scarce. Two main physician factors have been distinguished: (1) physicians' own expectations and (2) physicians' status (van Dulmen & Bensing, 2001). In the nursing literature on placebo effects, only patient factors and factors in the patient–nurse relationship have been reported (Kwekkeboom, 1997).

A study into the influence of a physician's expectations on the reduction of pain in 46 chronic pain patients showed that the more physicians expect a patient's pain to be relieved, the more this pain does, in fact, diminish (Galer et al., 1997). According to the researchers, these results suggest that physicians in a subtle way transmit their expectations to the patients. Wirth (1995) has even demonstrated that the expectations of the physician are more determinative for health effects in the patient than the expectations of the patient himself.

The influence of physicians' status on health outcomes seems to be ambivalent. There is a well-documented series of studies, in which a negative effect of the physicians' status on patients' blood pressure has been established, widely known as 'the white coat phenomenon': patients consistently have higher blood pressure when measured by a doctor or experimenter in a white coat, as compared to self-measurements or measurements by a nurse. It is important to note that white-coat hypertension is not a harmless phenomenon. Recent evidence showed that white-coat hypertension is frequently associated with increased target-organ damage and often coexists with other cardiovascular risk factors (Tsai, 2002; Mule et al., 2003). In contrast, the above-cited examples of positive health outcomes after sham surgery show that physicians' status can also have a *positive* effect on patient health outcome. Both phenomena (the negative as well as the positive affects) can be understood when we take account of the psychological process of attribution. Moerman and Wayne (2002) introduced the concept of 'the meaning response', which they define as the physiologic or psychological effects of meaning in the origins or treatment of illness. They argue that most so-called placebo effects are in fact meaning responses. In their view, most elements of medicine *are* meaningful, even if practitioners do not intend them to be so. The physician's costume (the white coat with stethoscope hanging out of the pocket), manner (enthusiastic or not), style (therapeutic or experimental) and language are all meaningful and can be shown to affect the outcome. The successes of the sham surgery can be explained by the fact that surgery is particularly meaningful: surgeons are among the elite of medical practitioners; the shedding of blood is inevitably meaningful in and of itself. In addition, surgical procedures usually have compelling rational explanations, which drug treatments often do not. The logic of arthroscopic surgery ('we will clean up a messy joint') is much more sensible and understandable (especially for people in a culture rich in machines and tools), than is the logic of non-steroidal anti-inflammatory drugs (which 'inhibit the production of prostaglandins which are involved in the inflammatory process', something no one would ever tell a patient).

Surgery clearly induces a profound meaning response in modern medical practice (Moerman & Wayne, 2002).

Factors in the patient–physician/nurse relationship

The medical – or, broader the health-care – encounter is the place where patients and physicians or nurses meet. It is also the place where patient factors and physician factors in the placebo effect find expression, get strengthened, or lose their power in the interaction between the two parties. Facts and figures get their meaning in the interaction between physician or nurse and patient. So, many of the documented placebo effects are in one way or another related to the communication between patient and physician or nurse. In several review studies, strong evidence was found linking physician–patient communication to a variety of patient health outcomes, including emotional health, symptom resolution, functional status, physiologic measures (i.e. blood pressure and blood sugar level), and pain control (Ong et al., 1995; Stewart, 1995; Roter, 2000; van Dulmen & Bensing, 2001). The main results can be classified in three categories: (1) social support, (2) affective communication and (3) instrumental communication. Social support has an important function in any relationship. This is all the more applicable in the case of patient–practitioner interaction. It has been shown that the degree of social support has a favourable effect on blood pressure and other cardiovascular parameters (Kamarck et al., 1998). Social support can also have a more indirect effect. Practitioners who adopt a warm, caring, supportive and empathetic attitude may evoke trust in their patients, which might give them confidence and hope (Letvak, 1995). Patients also need to feel that they are in a supportive and trusted environment, because they seldom verbalize their emotions directly and spontaneously, tending to offer clues instead (Suchman et al., 1997). Several empirical studies and review studies have shown that practitioners' affective behaviour (showing concern and empathy) are effective in facilitating patients to disclose their emotions and talk about their real concerns and worries (Bensing, 1991; Roter & Hall, 1992; Roter, 2000; Ong et al., 1995), including the discussion of psycho-social issues (Bensing et al., 1996). In a randomized controlled trial among 509 patients, Bertakis et al. found that attention to emotions had a positive influence on the general state of health (Bertakis et al., 1998). Further supportive evidence for the value of affective communication was found in a review, which showed that empathic interaction – in the form of reassuring words or affective contact – could lead to a reduction in anxiety, pain and blood pressure (van Dulmen & Bensing, 2001).

Instrumental communication such as question asking and the exchange of information is the third category of patient–practitioner interaction which has been shown to contribute to the therapeutic qualities of the medical encounter. Improvements in both self-reported health status and objective measures were obtained in four intervention studies in which patients were stimulated to ask more questions during the consultation (Crow et al., 1999). All four studies concerned patients with chronic diseases (diabetes, hypertension, post-mastectomy breast cancer and peptic ulcer). Questions shape patients' expectations about medical procedures, treatment and prognosis, and have been shown to enhance patients' control and self-efficacy. From the same review study we can learn that agreement between physician and patient about the nature of the patient's complaints and his or her preferred regimen was associated with health benefits. This was attained by giving the patient more opportunity to speak or ask questions (Crow et al., 1999). Another review study, partly based on different empirical studies, also showed that informativeness is a powerful communication function, clearly linked to health outcomes. This study showed that when the physician gives clear information, especially when coupled with emotional support, psychological distress is reduced, symptom resolution enhanced and blood pressure reduced. When physician informativeness was coupled with the provision of informational packages and programmes (particularly for patients undergoing radiation or surgery), pain was reduced, function improved, and mood and anxiety improved (Roter, 2000).

There is limited evidence that placebo effects are not restricted to patient–physician interaction, but also apply to patient–nurse interaction (Kwekkeboom, 1997). Based on a review study, Kwekkeboom states that placebo effects occur in up to 90 per cent of nursing interventions. In the explanation, apart from patient and treatment factors, and nurse demeanour, the patient–provider relationship and the context of the health-care encounter take relevant places. Kwekkeboom advises nurses to take measures to improve the patient's response to treatment, including providing a comfortable environment, using therapeutic communication techniques, helping patients to understand specific mechanisms of their treatment, and encouraging positive expectations and motivation for effectiveness (Kwekkeboom, 1997).

Communication as *the* central tool in the medical encounter

Summarizing the results, it seems that by applying adequate communication techniques, physicians and nurses can help patients to articulate their expectations, reveal the influence of previous experience with health care, disclose emotions such as anxieties and worries, and express their information needs, all of which seems to have important health benefits, directly, and/or indirectly, by enhancing patients' control and self-efficacy. With this central statement we do not want to disregard the enormous value of modern diagnostic and therapeutic medical technology and pharmaceutical products. However, it should be clear that the use of all this technology is possible as well as helpful only by the grace of appropriate communication. Establishing the right diagnosis is dependent on a thorough assessment of patients' symptoms, for which purpose diagnostic technology might be helpful, but it is even more dependent on carefully listening to the patients' story (Cassell, 1991) and on patients' confidence in doctor's capacities (Thomas, 1987). The cited studies show that there is now ample evidence that communication should be considered as perhaps the most powerful tool in medicine, not only in establishing a workable relationship with the patient, but also in both the diagnostic and therapeutic process (White, 1988; Bensing, 1991; Roter

& Hall, 1992; Lipkin et al., 1995; Crow et al., 1999). Moreover, good technical quality care, provided in an unsatisfactory environment and with unsatisfactory interactions, will not produce healthier patients (Koehler et al., 1992), and negative expectancies increase the frequency with which patients report all kinds of symptoms (Crow et al., 1999). Communication plays a crucial role in medicine: in the establishment of the doctor–patient (or nurse–patient) relationship, in the meaning that is given to symptoms, and in the management of disease. Sometimes this process is positive and leads to better understanding and coping, to better treatment decisions and more compliance; sometimes, however, the role of communication is negative and leads to misunderstanding, dissatisfaction, wrong decisions and even malpractice suits (Roter & Hall, 1992). While this area demands a multi-disciplinary research effort, it is clear that theories from health psychology can help to uncover the mechanisms underlying the 'healthy encounter' and make physicians, nurses and other health-care professionals aware of the effects of their communication behaviour and learn to use it as the powerful tool it can be. Before elaborating this in more detail, it is necessary to pay attention to the dynamic nature of the patient–practitioner relationship.

THE PATIENT–PRACTITIONER RELATIONSHIP IN A CHANGING WORLD

Originally, the placebo concept got its significance in the traditional patient–provider relationship, and it is still associated mostly with concepts like confidence and hope, suggestion and persuasion, which fit within a paternalistic doctor–patient relationship. However, there have recently been fundamental changes in the doctor–patient relationship which have introduced relatively new concepts in the literature, such as: consumerism, demand-induced care, shared decision-making. Three silent revolutions are responsible for this paradigmatic shift: (a) changes in patient morbidity, (b) changes in the availability of medical information and (c) changes in the power balance between doctor and patient. Together these changes have altered the roles and responsibilities of both practitioner and patient, which necessitates a redefinition of the patient–practitioner relationship as well as the function of communication as a central instrument in health-care encounters (Bensing et al., 2000).

Changes in morbidity

Medical science was originally developed from the paradigm of the bio-medical model at a time when the prevailing morbidity consisted of acute diseases, from which patients either recovered or died. In this model the medical diagnosis plays a central role: it is the ultimate task of physicians to discover the aetiology of the patient's symptoms in order to decide about the most adequate treatment. Conversely, working from this paradigm means that if the physician cannot name the symptoms, the patient cannot have a disease (White, 1988). The often reported miscommunication between physicians and patients with psychosomatic conditions can be largely contributed to the fact that diseases-without-diagnoses do not fit the bio-medical model. For this reason, physicians who were confronted with many vague complaints and medical unexplained symptoms – such as general practitioners, psychiatrists and specialists in internal medicine – began to challenge the bio-medical model and asked for a bio-psycho-social approach (Engel, 1977; White, 1988; Cassell, 1991). This movement was further strengthened when physicians from a wide variety of disciplines (rheumatologists, oncologists, endocrinologists, neurologists, cardiologists, gastro-enterologists) began to realize that the very foundation of their profession was under pressure, because diagnosis and treatment of acute disease was no longer their core business (McKinlay & Marceau, 2002). In most Western countries mortality and morbidity patterns have altered dramatically during the last century. This phenomenon is described in the medical literature as 'the epidemiological transition', a term coined to describe the transformation of the prevailing health burden in the population, shifting from infectious and communicable pathologies to chronic and degenerative diseases (Paccaud, 2002, Sullivan, 2003). In developed countries, this epidemiological transition has been well documented: mortality rates went spectacularly down, especially in the lower age groups (Mackenbach, 1993). Almost half of the decrease of total mortality was due to infectious diseases, of which respiratory diseases were the most important subgroup. At the same time, in all developed countries the shares of cancer, cardio-vascular diseases and external causes in overall mortality rates increased, while morbidity patterns changed correspondingly (Mackenbach, 1993). In medical practice, patients with chronic and degenerative diseases replaced those who suffered from acute infectious diseases: heart disease, diabetes, cancer, COPD, multiple sclerosis, Parkinson's disease, have become common disorders in medical practice (for a more extensive overview, see De Ridder's Chapter 9, on 'Chronic Illness', in this volume). This epidemiological transition is forcing an epistemological transition on medicine. In other words, because medicine is interested in new types of health, it must also become interested in new types of scientific evidence concerning health (Sullivan, 2003). For patients with chronic diseases – just as for patients with medically un-explained health problems – the traditional diagnosis–therapy model is not an adequate paradigm anymore (Cassell, 1991; McKinlay & Marceau, 2002). In chronic diseases, the diagnosis has another meaning than in acute diseases: the diagnosis is not felt as a relief ('knowing the disease means knowing the therapeutic strategy'), but as a sign that life has changed forever, that nothing will ever be the same again. The diagnosis of a chronic disease means for the patient that a life looms full of suffering, uncertainty, sometimes anxiety, pain, a gradual loss of mobility and perhaps even autonomy, which asks for a continuous process of adaptation (Bensing et al., 2002). As a consequence, the object of medical science is now the patient's *life* rather than the patient's *body* (Sullivan, 2003). Relief of suffering and care have become more important than cure (Cassell, 1991), and burden of disease and quality of life have become increasingly relevant outcome parameters (Sullivan, 2003).

Another important difference from the traditional bio-medical model is that with chronic diseases physicians' role is limited; much has to be done by the chronically ill patients themselves: changes in lifestyle, compliance with therapeutic regimens, adopting new life perspectives and handling the emotions of not being a healthy person anymore, are all very important tasks in coping with chronic disease (Taylor, 1999; Chapter 9, this volume). For most chronically ill patients the consequences of disease are more important than its causes.

This involves a role change for the health-care provider. Physicians are now expected to assume the role of health educator, counsellor, sounding board or motivating agent, which is quite different from what they had been taught in medical education. Activating patients has become another important task for physicians (and nurses). Several studies have shown that active involvement of patients in medical encounters is associated with several desirable outcomes, including less discomfort, greater satisfaction, increased adherence to treatment, greater control of their diseases and positive treatment outcomes (Brody et al., 1989; Crow et al., 1999; Tennstedt, 2000). It is important to note that all these new tasks can only be realized by adequate communication.

Another consequence of this shift in morbidity is that a growing number of patients in the consultation room are becoming an expert on their own disease and know more than the physician – especially the general practitioner, who is not specialized in the particular disease – which leads to a shift in the power balance, as we shall discuss below.

Changes in availability of and access to medical information

Almost all people want as much information as possible about their health problems, probable causes and possible therapeutic solutions; this is especially true for patients with chronic diseases (Ong et al., 1995). Patients used to be dependent on their GP or other health-care professional for the information they wanted, but they are not anymore. The accessibility of health information has substantially improved (Mechanic, 2001). The media routinely cover health news, including the latest information published in leading scientific journals. Major newspapers and television programmes have special health sections, and cable television has channels dedicated to health news (Mechanic, 2001). An increasing number of health and patient education resources are available as stand alone multimedia programs (e.g. CD-ROM). Health-care consumers can learn about a health topic (e.g. options for treating breast cancer) within a sensory-rich environment that presents information in multiple modalities (e.g. narration, animation, text) and that provides users with an interactive interface for self-selecting their path through the information (Street, 2003). One of the most significant developments in health care over the past 25 years has been the widespread deployment of information and communication technologies (Heath et al., 2003). These technologies have had a wide-ranging impact on patients' experience of illness and its management (Heath et al., 2003). Health-care consumers can use the internet to access websites with information and advice on literally thousands of health topics, resources that in turn could facilitate the consumer's involvement in making informed decisions about health (Street, 2003). Even personally identifiable health information about individuals is increasingly available in electronic form in health databases and through online networks (Hodge et al., 2000). Counter-intuitively, some studies show that underserved and disadvantaged populations can have as much benefit as highly educated and privileged people from increased use of information technology in health care. This was convincingly demonstrated in a project in which parents of hospitalized babies from a Medicaid population could monitor their babies from home at any time, and check on the latest available information updates via Daily Reports, Doctor's Notes, Baby Growth Charts (Safran, 2003). Despite the common wisdom that Medicaid families do not have access to the internet, approximately 85 per cent of the (largely Medicaid) parents accessed the database from home, at work, from the library or from some other public access point. The results of a randomized study showed a 75 per cent reduction in reports of quality-of-care problems. Moreover, parents reported better communication and higher levels of satisfaction with care, and tended to take their children home earlier. This study suggests an unmet need with substantial clinical benefits if such collaborative technology could be widely deployed. The results also suggest that families in crisis would embrace internet-based tools and services regardless of their prior use of computers or the net, their socio-economic status, or their educational level, providing they can read English (Safran, 2003).

In several respects, information and telecommunication technologies are transforming the way health-care consumers communicate for health information, advice, services and support. For example, the asynchronous nature of e-mail interactions (i.e. the interaction is not tied to a time or place) provides flexibility for health-care consumers and providers to communicate more frequently and efficiently (Street, 2003). The internet also provides consumers greater access to support groups for contacting other people with similar health problems to learn about their experiences (Street, 2003), which might help them in their preparation for the medical encounter. The physician's role seems to evolve gradually from providing information into giving a second opinion and advice.

It is clear from these examples that proliferation of electronic data within the modern health information infrastructure presents significant benefits for medical providers and patients, including enhanced patient autonomy, improved clinical treatment, advances in health research and public health surveillance, and modern security techniques. However, there are also pitfalls, threats and challenges. The protection of the privacy of identifiable health information is a relevant issue, and so is the reliability and quality of health information (Hodge et al., 2000; Bodenheimer & Grumbach, 2003). Moreover, doctors have to get accustomed to the modern, well-informed patient. Increasingly, knowledgeable patients armed with information from the media, as well as guidelines developed by health plans, government, specialty societies, professional organizations, and advocacy groups, confront physicians with a bewildering array of new expectations and demands (Mechanic, 2001), which is not accepted well by all physicians. Patients have more questions and conceptions about their care than before, requiring doctors to spend more time answering questions, comparing treatments, and dealing with misinformation (Mechanic, 2001). Finally, while many lay people are positive about modern modes of communication, such as email, physicians' reactions seem to be more mixed (Mechanic, 2001), and there is at least one randomized controlled study of a triage-based e-mail system in primary care, which suggests that growth of email communication in primary care settings may not improve the efficiency of clinical care (Katz et al., 2003). While more research is needed to draw conclusions, it is clear that the greater availability of and access to medical information has supported the development of patients into autonomous co-decision-makers. However, differences in information-seeking behaviour between patients (and even within patients) are large and cannot be predicted from demographic and/or socio-economic factors (Roter & Hall, 1992; Crow, 1999).

Changes in the power balance

Since Byrne and Long wrote their classic book, *Doctors Talking to Patients* (Byrne & Long, 1976), many authors have commented on the changing relationship between doctor and patient, which coincides with a general shift from authoritarian towards more egalitarian relationships in modern Western societies. This change is supported by several societal developments (Roter et al., 1992; de Visser et al., 2001; Coulter et al., 2001; McKinlay & Marceau, 2002). Due to the higher average education level, the cultural and educational gap between doctor and patient has been diminished for growing groups of patients, leading to a more egalitarian relationship in the medical consultation. The greater availability of and access to medical information which was described in the last paragraph, has been facilitating this process, but can also be seen as a consequence of this development. In many countries national governments have actively strengthened the patients' position in health care, both financially and legally (de Visser et al., 2001). Patient organizations have become part of the health-care system and consumer organizations often have special departments for health-care issues. Moreover, in many countries attempts are made to change the traditional supply-induced care into a more demand-induced care (McKinlay & Marceau, 2002). Direct marketing by pharmaceutical industries is gaining ground in many Western countries, showing an impressive increase in sales, although there is still a lack of evidence concerning its impact on the health of the public (Lyles, 2002). All these developments might have an influence on the power balance within the patient–physician relationship, thus facilitating more patient autonomy and more active patient participation. At the same time, however, it has been shown in the literature that the shift in power balance is more visible in philosophical literature than in empirical studies, and more in surveys than in video observation research. Survey studies show that patients generally want as much information as possible and (to a lesser degree) to take part in medical decision-making (Robinson, 2001). But, once in the consultation room, patients still ask few questions. In a video observation study which compared GP and patient communication behaviour between six European countries, the average amount of patient questions varied between 3.6 (in the United Kingdom and Spain) and 5.3 (in Belgium) (van Brink-Muinen, et al., 1999). Despite the vast amount of evidence that patients often do not understand exactly what is being said in medical encounters, there seems to be a widespread hesitance on the part of patients to ask doctors for further clarification (Whitcomb, 2000). Some patients do, many do not; resulting in different types of physician–patient relationships. Patients also seldom verbalize their emotions directly and spontaneously, tending to offer clues instead (Suchman et al., 1997, Del Piccolo et al., 2000). In a qualitative study on British General Practice, it was found that only 4 out of 35 patients voiced all their agendas (Barry et al., 2000). The most common unvoiced agenda items were: worries about possible diagnosis and what the future holds; patients' ideas about what is wrong; side-effects; not wanting a prescription; and information relating to social context. Agenda items that were not raised in the consultation often led to specific problem outcomes (for example, major misunderstandings), unwanted prescriptions, non-use of prescriptions, and non-adherence to treatment. In all of the 14 consultations with problem outcomes, at least one of the problems was related to an unvoiced agenda item. There is even some evidence that the situation even gets worse instead of better. In a very recent study based on the analysis of video-taped medical encounters in general practice, which was aimed at uncovering historical shifts in the communication of general practitioners with hypertensive patients between 1986 and 2001, it was shown that – contrary to expectations – patients from the 1986 sample asked fewer questions and talked *less* about worries, concerns and other psycho-social issues as compared to patients in the 2001 sample. Physicians in the 2001 sample gave more medical information, but showed less affective behaviour (empathy, showing concern) and asked their patients less for clarifications or opinions (Bensing et al., under review).

Between the theory and practice of active patient participation is the medical encounter itself, with its two partners, patient and physician, who together shape the consultation. This may result in a wide variety of interaction patterns and types of physician–patient relationship. A theoretical elaboration was given by Roter (2000), who introduced a typology of physician–patient relationships along two axes, depicting the respective influences of physician and patient on the medical encounter (see figure 11.1).

In the upper left sector of figure 11.1, we see the traditional doctor–patient relationship with a paternalistic doctor who takes the lead and a submissive patient who follows. The upper right sector shows an egalitarian relationship between doctor and patient which is characterized by much more information exchange and shared decision-making: this is the ideal consultation for many modern physicians and patients, although for most patients the need for information is higher than the need for shared decision-making, especially in those with life-threatening conditions (Deber et al., 1996). In the lower part of the figure, the doctor exerts little influence in the consultation. In the lower right part, decision-making has been taken over by the patient in a consumerist model: the patient knows what he or she wants and the doctor responds to these demands. The lower left sector shows a consultation in which neither doctor nor patient is very influential; this consultation type reminds us of the former situation in some eastern European countries, where the physician's job had

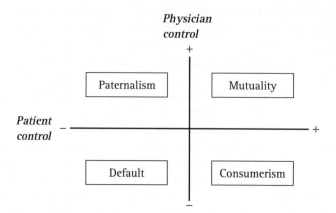

Figure 11.1 A typology of the doctor–patient relationship
Source: Roter, 2000.

a low status and health care was an underprivileged area. In modern Western health care there is a real danger that consultations with patients from minority groups who are not fluent in the country's prevailing language will experience this type of doctor–patient relationship.

The value of typologies like this is that they show the diversity of doctor–patient relationships that emerge in the consultation room, and, as a consequence, the variety in communication strategies that are needed in medical consultations. Talking with young, highly educated, independent persons is different from talking with verbally handicapped or older patients. Moreover, it has been demonstrated that the preferred type of doctor–patient relationship is also dependent on the type and seriousness of the disease. Studies on shared decision-making show that a majority of healthy subjects say that they would want to select their own treatment if they were to have cancer; however, only a minority of patients with cancer shared this view (Degner & Sloan, 1992; Butow et al., 1997). De Haes reflected on the possible reasons that patients could have for *not* wanting control in medical decision-making when confronted with life-threatening diseases (de Haes & Koedoot, 2003). She mentions three reasons. First, while leaving the decision with the clinician, the patient can avoid information. This might be preferable, as information may confront the patient with the probability of negative outcomes. The future may possibly be anxiety provoking and denial may help to cope with such fear. Especially in the most advanced disease stages, patients may thus create a façade of hopefulness to manage fears associated with the potential of negative outcomes. Second, patients may have difficulty understanding or assimilating information and the consequences thereof. Additional information, especially if not well understood, may be confusing and as such provoke uncertainty. Some patients may feel that they lack the intellect or education needed. To be 'a good patient' they would rather have faith in their doctor than ask for information they might not grasp. Third, making a decision makes one responsible for its outcomes. This may result in the mechanism of 'anticipated regret': the mechanism by which people act or refrain from acting to prevent responsibility for outcomes that might occur. Thus, by avoiding information and relying on the physician to make decisions, one would avoid feeling guilty or sorry for the consequences thereof in case these would turn out to be unwanted (de Haes & Koedoot, 2003). Of course, these studies do not imply that the change in power balance is no issue in health care. But they show that it is not easy to tell beforehand which patient will opt for an active role in medical decision-making and which will be more happy with the traditional patient role.

Tailored communication: the new challenge in an ever-changing world

Summarizing, we may conclude that the doctor–patient relationship has changed considerably in the last decades, and is still subject to major changes that can be characterized by the following elements:

*   The overall change in morbidity from acute to chronic diseases has brought a different type of patient into the medical consultation room: patients who *want* to know more, but who also *need* to know more about their disease and the way to cope with its consequences.
*   These patients are supported by the increase in the amount and availability of health information for lay people, especially about chronic diseases. Information technology confronts professionals and patients, researchers and trainers, with challenging prospects.
*   There is a clear tendency towards a more egalitarian relationship between doctor and patient, but at the same time there is more diversity in patient needs and preferences between patients and patient groups, resulting in more variation in types of doctor–patient relationships, the traditional paternalistic model not giving away to another clear model, but diverging into different types that can easily switch, even with the same doctor and the same patient.

In the past, the main concern of most medical educators was to get enough room for the training of communication skills in a primarily bio-medical curriculum, thinking that it was sufficient to teach their medical students one communication model based on general communication skills. Now they have an additional worry, for the empirical studies in this chapter show that they cannot limit their efforts to a one-size-fits-all approach. Apart from the different types of health problems, which call for a variety of communication strategies, it is also the diversity of doctor–patient relationships that demands much more individually tailored communication, based on a sound theoretical framework. It is time for health psychologists to enter the arena.

THE MEDICAL ENCOUNTER REVISITED: TOWARDS A HEALTH PSYCHOLOGY PERSPECTIVE

In the preceding parts of this chapter we have respectively shown that (1) the medical encounter in itself has important therapeutic qualities, with adequate communication being the central instrument, and (2) that a one-size-fits-all approach based on general communication skills is not workable because of the wide variety of patient needs and preferences which need to be addressed by tailored communication strategies. Health care is changing from a strictly bio-medical model to a more comprehensive bio-psycho-social model (Novack, 1995; Graugaard & Finset, 2000; Bensing, 2000; Roter, 2000; de Haes & Koedoot, 2003), from supply-induced to demand-induced care (McKinlay, 2002), from doctor-centred to patient-centred medicine (Stewart, 1995; Bensing, 2000; Mead & Bower, 2002; Sullivan, 2003). Accordingly, the focus in communication research is gradually shifting from physicians (and physician training programmes) towards patients (and patient empowering techniques). Although a multidisciplinary approach is always needed, this is an especially interesting domain for health psychologists, as they focus on health and health behaviour from a patient perspective. In this last part we want to sketch the medical encounter from a health psychology perspective, by incorporating elements from health psychology into existing theoretical notions about the medical encounter – the medical encounter revisited. The term 'sketch' is deliberately chosen: more detailed information about the relevant issues (for instance, illness representations and coping with chronic diseases) can be found in other chapters of the present volume. In order to highlight the paradigm shift from doctor-centred to patient-centred medicine, we will start with discussion of the essentials of patient-centred medicine.

The paradigm of patient-centred medicine

As a result of the changing doctor–patient relationship, there is a growing awareness that health care needs to be individualized. The acknowledgement that patients are not 'objects' of health care, but 'subjects' who want to take an active part and who have their own needs and preferences, has led to the emergence of a new paradigm in medicine: patient-centred medicine. This is a typical example of a fuzzy concept: most people have an inkling of its meaning, but few people can be precise in its definition. The concept is clear in its core, but the boundaries are vague and multi-interpretable. Different authors (summarized by Mead & Bower, 2000, 2002) have tried to define the concept of patient centredness as respectively 'entering the patient's life world', 'seeing the illness through the patient's eyes', or 'understanding the patient as a unique human being'. Moira Stewart was the first to treat the concept of patient centredness as a multidi-mensional concept, distinguishing six relevant elements: (1) exploring the disease and the illness experience; (2) understanding the whole person; (3) finding common ground regarding management; (4) incorporating prevention and health promotion; (5) enhancing the doctor–patient relationship; and (6) 'being realistic' about personal limitations and resources. A slightly different conceptualization has been presented by Nicky Mead, who described five distinct dimensions of 'patient-centred' care (Mead & Bower, 2000): (1)The bio-psycho-social perspective – a perspective on illness that includes consideration of social and psychological (as well as bio-medical) factors. (2) The 'patient-as-person' – understanding the personal meaning of the illness for each individual patient. (3) Sharing power and responsibility – sensitivity to patients' preferences for information and shared decision-making and responding appropriately to these. (4) The therapeutic alliance – developing common therapeutic goals and enhancing the personal bond between doctor and patient. (5) The 'doctor-as-person' – awareness of the influence of the personal qualities and subjectivity of the doctor on the practice of medicine. The results from empirical studies into patient centredness show mixed findings with, overall, Stewart's review being more positive about its effects (Stewart, 1995) than Mead, who concluded in her review that 'the findings of the present review do provide some support for the view that specific evidence of the benefits of patient-centredness is somewhat lacking at present' (Mead, 2002).

Being a fuzzy concept, patient centredness is not easily applicable in empirical research. However, exploring the concept's content can clarify the underlying values that have promoted the paradigm shift, which might be helpful in building a theoretical framework for a better understanding of communication in medical encounters. One way of exploring the concept is by contrasting it with its opposite (Bensing, 2000). With patient-centred medicine this can be done in at least two ways.

The first is to place 'patient-centred' in opposition to 'disease-centred' (Stewart et al., 1995). By making this contrast, it is emphasized that the patient is more than his or her disease, and it is as important to know the patient who has the disease as it is to know the disease which the patient has (McCormick, 1996). Patient-centred medicine in this sense means that health-care providers must be directed to the illness, rather than to the disease, and have to explore patients' needs from a bio-psycho-social model, in which psychological and social factors are as important as the strictly bio-medical elements (Cassell, 1991; Smith & Hoppe, 1991; Bensing, 2000).

Another way to contrast 'patient-centred medicine' is to place the concept opposite 'doctor-centred medicine' (Byrne & Long, 1976; Bensing, 2000). In doing so, this emphasizes that it is not the doctor who can exclusively decide what will happen to the patient, but that it is the patient's right to decide what will be done or not done in terms of diagnostic or therapeutic interventions. This definition of patient-centred medicine demands that health-care providers explore patients' preferences and provide them with information to facilitate decision-making. This belief, originating from the beginning of the patients' rights movement in the sixties, has been articulated in the so-called 'power-shift model' (Byrne & Long, 1976), and since then has been codified in laws in many Western countries (Laine & Davidoff, 1996). In the academic world of health psychology, this movement has been embraced because of the recognition of the health-promoting influence of sense-of-control and self-efficacy (Hyman et al., 1992; Taylor, 1999; Folkman & Greer, 2000).

When 'patient-centred' is contrasted with 'disease-centred', it deals with the content of the consultation, the choice of topics that should or could be addressed, according to patients' needs and expectations. According to this approach, physicians are patient-centred when they don't restrict themselves to 'the disease of the patient', but orient themselves on 'the patient that has the disease'. The physician's ultimate goal is therefore to gain an understanding of the patient's true reasons for encounter, and of the patient's real needs and wishes (McWhinney, 1985). Adequate communication behaviours are derived from psychotherapeutic theories that demonstrate the value of affective behaviour (as opposed to instrumental behaviour) in stimulating patients to talk about everything that is on their mind, including disclosure of emotions (Novack, 1995). In terms of health psychology, the concept of a patient's illness representations refers to the issues that are a consequence of a patient-centred approach, as opposed to a disease-centred one.

When, on the other hand, 'patient-centred' is contrasted with 'doctor-centred', it deals with the issue of control over the consultation, and with whose agenda is dealt with, who is expected and has the power to make decisions, but also with the central question of who takes responsibility for a patient's health. The physician's goals here are to achieve a balance between the doctor's and patient's agendas, and to reach a decision both parties feel comfortable with. The appropriate communication behaviours for reaching this goal can be derived from marketing theories on the elicitation of consumer preferences, as well as from theories on decision-making that demonstrate the value of mutual agreement in reaching a consultation outcome that is satisfying for both parties (Lazare, 1995; Roter et al., 1997). Another important goal in the consultation is the empowerment of patients in order to enable them to take responsibility for their own health and to enhance their self-efficacy. The appropriate communication behaviours for reaching this goal can be derived from health psychology theories, such as stress-coping theory (Lazarus & Folkman, 1984) and self-regulation theory (Leventhal et al., 1997).

The advantage of using a comprehensive theoretical framework is that it allows targeted research questions based on differentiation between patients. In the literature some nice examples can be found. For instance, in an experimental study, Graugaard & Finset (2000) demonstrated that a patient-centred communication style elicited more satisfaction with respondents with low trait anxiety, whereas respondents with high trait anxiety reacted emotionally more positively to a doctor-centred style of communication. Patient-centred communication was defined as aiming at open questions, facilitation of patients' active involvement, exploring both disease and illness experience, taking psycho-social aspects into account and aiming at emotional commitment. Doctor-centred communication was defined as using closed questions, restricting focus to disease experience and somatic aspects, and restricting emotional commitment.

Patients with breast cancer who avoided information about their disease (a 'blunting style') reported fewer communication problems with their doctors. However, in a three-month follow-up, a blunting coping style as well as communication problems added to the prediction of mood disturbances (Lerman et al., 1993). Patients' monitoring coping style is related to certain aspects of their way of communicating: they ask more questions and are more dominant than patients with a low monitoring coping style. A blunting coping style was not related to patients' communication. Physicians' communicative behaviour was not influenced by patients' coping style (Ong et al., 1999).

In summary, we may conclude that the concept of patient-centred medicine refers to two distinct phenomena:

1 to the *content* of the consultation, thereby broadening the bio-medical model to a bio-psycho-social model;
2 to the patient's *influence* in the decision-making process, contrasting the traditional doctor-oriented diagnosis–therapy model with a model of shared decision-making.

Both notions have their impact on the medical consultation, but use different theories in defining adequate communication strategies. Both focus on relevant concepts from health psychology: patients' illness representations and patients' self-management, respectively.

Patients' illness representations

The patient's perspective should be taken into account in several respects. Within the approach of disease-centred medicine, the content and process of the consultation was clearly determined by the doctor's bio-medical disease model, which was silently assumed to be taken for granted by the patient. Over the last 20 years, health psychologists have demonstrated that patients have disease models of their own, and these are referred to as illness representations or illness perceptions. A more detailed overview of illness representations is provided in Chapter 4 in this volume. Here, we will limit ourselves to their consequences for communication in the medical encounter.

Physicians and nurses should be aware of patients' illness representations in order to understand the beliefs and expectations of their patients. Furthermore, as a result of different illness perceptions and attitudes in general, patients cope with their health problems in different ways. Hence, patients have different needs. This again requires an individualized approach from physician or nurse.

There is some evidence that physicians are not always aware of patients' illness perceptions, which results in some topics not being discussed during the medical encounter. Van Dulmen et al. (1994), comparing patients' illness perceptions and doctors' estimations of their patients' perceptions, found large dissimilarities, especial for psycho-social factors. The study group consisted of 120 patients with functional abdominal pain. Doctors over-estimated patients' anxiety, the psycho-social and somatic attributions of their pain, patient catastrophizing, and patient self-efficacy. They under-estimated a number of expectations about doctor's behaviour (to give advice, to discuss emotional problems, to find a somatic explanation). Concerning patients' symptoms, there was considerably higher similarity between patients' and doctors' perceptions (van Dulmen et al., 1994). In another study among patients with hepatitis C, the concordance between patients' values regarding anti-viral therapy and physicians' estimate of patients' values was measured (Cotler et al., 2001). Physicians' estimates were not significantly associated with patients' preference values for hepatitis C health states, treatment side-effects, or with thresholds for accepting treatment. It was found that patients' stated thresholds for taking therapy were related to their ideas about treatment side-effects. Moreover, patients' thresholds for taking treatment were significantly associated with their subsequent treatment choices. It seems that the perspectives that patients held before meeting with the hepatologist played an important role in their decision-making process, and that these views were not well recognized by the physicians (Cotler et al., 2001). Illness perceptions or illness representations are often not voiced during the medical encounter. In a study using the somewhat broader concept of 'patient's agenda', Barry et al. found that only 4 of 35 patients voiced all their agendas in consultation (Barry et al., 2000). The pattern of the main voiced and unvoiced agendas reveals systematic differences between how patients present in consultations with how they present in research interviews. In consultations patients seem only partially present, with only limited autonomy – that is, to make requests but not to suggest solutions. Outside consultations, patients are more fully present: as socially and contextually situated, thinking, feeling people, with their own ideas on their medical condition and opinions and possible criticisms of medical treatments (Barry et al., 2000).

Leventhal et al. (1997), proposing a self-regulation model of health and illness behaviour, distinguished two parallel pathways: cognitive illness representations leading to coping procedures for coping with the problem, and emotional representations leading to coping procedures for coping with fear. Problem-solving coping strategies may be in competition with emotion-focused (often avoidant) coping strategies. Both pathways, the cognitive and emotional one, at last have outcomes of their own, and patients' appraisal of these outcomes will again affect the initial cognitive and emotional representation.

Patients' self-management

The patient's perspective should also be taken into account in disease management. Research interest in this aspect of communication stems originally from the widespread notion that patients tend to be non-compliant with medication and lifestyle recommendations (e.g. exercise) (Sackett & Haynes, 1976; Roter & Hall, 1992; Dimatteo, 1995). Early research was focused upon characteristics of the information provided by the physician, such as its format, understandability, length and content (Ley, 1982). As might be clear from earlier sections in this chapter, the focus of current research is now on the process during the consultation, during which information exchange takes place, as well as on the direct empowering of patients as active participants in the medical encounter. Frederikson (1993) has developed a model in which, as input frames of reference, the motivation, needs and expectations both of doctor and patient are considered important. Outputs of the information exchange process are perceptions, adherence, concern, understanding and relationship, all contributing to patient satisfaction as a final outcome measure. Components of the self-regulation model of Leventhal et al. (1997) can be recognized among the input factors. They suggest that the more explicit and open the talk between doctor and patient, the more effective the process will be. In this respect there is a connection with the patient-centred approach.

There is some evidence regarding the positive effects of a patient-centred approach, which focuses on empowering patients as active participants in health care on the outcomes of the medical consultation. Hall et al. (1988) reviewed a number of studies in which patient satisfaction appeared rather consistently correlated with the amount of information provided, partnership building and socio-emotional behaviour. The associations with compliance were much weaker. Crow et al. (1999) conclude after an extensive literature review: 'although the quality of the research varied, the findings consistently demonstrated beneficial effects on subjective and objective outcomes of interventions that were aimed at enhancing the self-management of chronic illness.'

Some studies show ambiguous results. For instance, in a study among patients who had to undergo urethral surgery it was found that mere information-giving and participation in decision processes did not lead to a decrease in anxiety (Margolith & Shapiro, 1997). On the contrary, those who were not given information nor allowed to choose which treatment they should get showed less anxiety after the initial meeting with the surgeon and comparable anxiety at the time of hospitalization. Regardless of whether they had or had not actually received information or been given choice of treatment, patients with a passive coping strategy who perceived themselves as being informed and involved in decision-making showed a decrease in anxiety after the initial visit. Thus it is the subjective perception of being informed and involved that is the key factor. The results of this study suggest that influencing patient beliefs and behaviours could be more effective than trying to change physician behaviour. Similar results were found in a systematic review of the effects of modification of provider–patient interaction and provider consulting style on patient diabetes self-care and diabetes outcome (van Dam et al., 2003). Eight well-designed studies were identified (all randomized controlled trials). Review of these publications led to the tentative conclusion that focusing on patient behaviour by directly enhancing patient participation is more effective than focusing on provider behaviour, in changing their consultation style into a more patient-centred one. The authors claim that the latter proves hard to sustain, needs intensive support, and is not very effective in improving patient self-care and health outcomes. These results fit nicely within the shift from a doctor-centred towards a more patient-centred approach.

The medical encounter from a patient perspective

In this last section, we want to put the patient perspective in communication research within a comprehensive theoretical framework, combining the bio-psycho-social model in medicine (Engel, 1977) with elements from self-regulation theory (Leventhal et al., 1997) and stress-coping theory (Lazarus & Folkman, 1984). Essential in this framework is that it is not primarily focused on physicians' behaviour and its effect

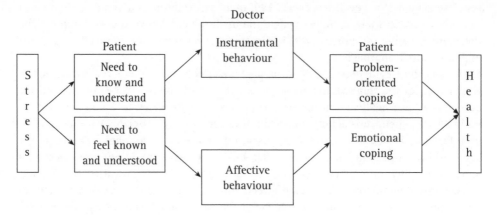

Figure 11.2 Doctor–patient communication from a stress-coping perspective

on patient outcomes, but instead it starts with patients' illness representations, needs and preferences. Physicians' communication is primarily relevant in so far as it helps (or hinders) patients in expressing their concerns and, next, supports (or undermines) patients in coping with illness, including self-management.

Starting from a patient perspective, there appear to be two main questions of concern to patients who enter the consultation room: a cognitive one, 'what is the matter with me?'; and an emotional one, 'is this something to worry about?', and 'will I be taken seriously?' The result is that when patients go to their doctor, they have two sorts of needs (Engel, 1987; Bensing, 1991: Bensing et al., 1996):

a) *the need to know and understand*: the need to know how physical symptoms should be interpreted; the need to know if something is wrong, and – if so – what should be done to cope with it.
b) *the need to feel known and understood*: the need to express concerns, the need to be put at ease, the need for support, acceptance and respect; the need not to be seen as a malingerer.

The first need is a cognitive need and has to be addressed by the physician's instrumental, problem-solving behaviour (clarifying the reason for encounter, structuring the consultation, information exchange). The second need is an emotional need and has to be addressed by the physician's affective, supporting behaviour (listening to patients' worries, showing concern, partnership-building, empathy). In most consultations both types of patient needs are present, although the second need (the need to feel known and understood) is often not articulated by the patient, and therefore remains implicit, unless the physician succeeds in eliciting it by using adequate communication techniques, such as using silence, active listening, reflections and eye-contact (Bensing et al., 1996).

Instrumental behaviour and affective behaviour serve different functions in the medical consultation and have different aims. Viewed from a stress-coping perspective, instrumental behaviour is aimed at problem-solving and strengthening patient's problem-oriented coping, necessary to get control over the experienced health problems and to enable self-management. The aim of affective behaviour is providing emotional support and strengthening patients' emotional coping, necessary to deal with the situation and to give the disease a place in one's life.

It is a challenge for every doctor 'to listen with two ears': that is, symbolically assigning one ear to receive bio-medical and the other ear to receive psycho-social information (Epstein, 1993); or, in our terminology, to listen at two levels: to the instrumental message as well as to the affective message. Another implication of starting from a patient perspective is the need for physicians to be aware that patients often have not one, but a complex, of needs when they enter the consultation room, and that these give rise to multiple goals for the medical consultation, some of which are in the instrumental, task-oriented domain, while others are in the affective, emotional domain. Communication is a powerful tool, but only when it is used as a tool: as a consciously planned and targeted intervention. If doctors are unable to do this, then patients remain to be confronted with doctors who may over-estimate their own communication skills and under-estimate communication's positive and negative impact on the patient. If, on the other hand, they succeed in applying individualized and targeted communication strategies, they can turn the medical encounter from the 'powerful placebo' which is described in the literature into a place for 'empowering the patient'.

REFERENCES

Balint, M. (1955). The doctor, his patient and the illness. *Lancet* 1, 683–8.

Barry, C. A., Bradley, C. P., Britten, N., Stevenson, F. A. and Barber, N. (2000). Patients' unvoiced agendas in general practice consultations: a qualitative study. *British Medical Journal* 320, 1246–50.

Bensing, J. M. (1991). *Doctor–Patient Communication and the Quality of Care: An Observation Study into Affective and Instrumental Behaviour in General Practice.* Utrecht: Nivel/Utrecht University.

Bensing, J. M. (2000). Bridging the gap: the separate worlds of evidence-based medicine and patient-centered medicine. *Patient Education and Counseling* 39, 17–25.

Bensing, J. M., Schreurs, K., de Ridder, D. T. D. and Hulsman, R. L. (2002). Adaptive tasks in multiple sclerosis: development of an instrument to identify the focus of patients' coping efforts. *Psychology & Health* 17(4), 475–88.

Bensing, J. M., Schreurs, K. L. and de Rijk, A. (1996). The role of the general practitioner's affective behaviour in medical encounters. *Psychology and Health* 11, 825–38.

Bensing, J. M., Tromp, F., van Dulmen, A. M. and van den Brink-Muinen, A. (under review). Historical shifts in quality of care and GP communication with hypertension patients.

Bensing, J. M., Verhaak, P. F. M., van Dulmen, A. and Visser, A. P. (2000). Communication: the royal pathway to patient-centered medicine (editorial). *Patient Education and Counseling* 39, 1–3.

Bertakis, K. D., Callahan, E. J., Helms, L. J., Azari, R., Robbins, J. A. and Miller, J. (1998). Physician practice styles and patient outcomes: differences between family practice and general internal medicine. *Medical Care* 36, 879–91.

Bodenheimer, T. and Grumbach, K. (2003). Electronic technology: a spark to revitalize primary care? *Journal of the American Medical Association* 290, 259–64.

Bovbjerg, D. H., Redd, W. H., Maier, L. A., Holland, J. C., Lesko, L. M., Niedzwiecki, D., Rubin, S. C. and Hakes T. B. (1990). Anticipatory immune suppression and nausea in women receiving cyclic chemotherapy for ovarian cancer. *Journal of Consulting and Clinical Psychology* 58, 153–7.

Brody, D. S., Miller, S. M., Lerman, C. E., Smith, D. G. and Caputo, G. C. (1989). Patient perception of involvement in medical care: relationship to illness attitudes and outcomes. *Journal of General Internal Medicine* 4(6), 506–11.

Butow, P. N., Maclean, M., Dunn, S. M., Tattersall, M. H. N. and Boyer, M. J. (1997). The dynamics of change: cancer patient's preferences for information, involvement and support. *Annals of Oncology* 8, 857–63.

Byrne, P. S. and Long, B. E. L. (1976). *Doctors Talking to Patients: A Study of the Verbal Behaviour of General Practitioners Consulting in their Surgeries.* London: HSMO/RCGP.

Cassell, E. (1991). *The Nature of Suffering and the Goals of Medicine.* Oxford: Oxford University Press.

Cobb, L., Thomas, G. I., Dillard, D. H., Merendino, K. A. and Bruce, R. A. (1959). An evaluation of internal-mammary artery ligation by a double blind technique. *New England Journal of Medicine* 260, 1115–18.

Cotler, S. J., Patil, R., McNutt, R. A., Speroff, T., Banaad-Omiotek, G., Ganger, D. R., Rosenblate, H., Kaur, S., Cotler, S. and Jensen, D. M. (2001). Patients' values for health states associated with hepatitis C and physicians' estimates of those values. *The American Journal of Gastroenterology* 96(9), 2730–6.

Coulter, A. (2002). Patients' view of the good doctor. *British Medical Journal* 325, 668–9.

Crow, R., Gage, H., Hampson, S., Hart, J., Kimber, A. and Thomas, H. (1999). The role of expectancies in the placebo effect and their use in the delivery of health care: a systematic review. *Health Technology Assessment* 3(3), 1–96.

De Haes, H. and Koedoot, N. (2003). Patient centered decision-making in palliative cancer treatment: a world of paradoxes. *Patient Education and Counseling* 50(1), 43–9.

De Kleijnen, J., Craen, A. J. M., van Everdingen, J. and Krol, L. (1994). Placebo effect in double blind clinical trials: a review of interactions with medication. *Lancet* 344, 1347–9.

De Visser, A., Deccache, A. and Bensing, J. M. (2001). Patient education in Europe: uniting differences. *Patient Education and Counseling* 44(1), 1–5.

Deber, R. B., Kraetschmer, N. and Irvine, J. (1996). What role do patients wish to play in treatment decision-making? *Archives Internal Medicine* 156(13), 1414–20.

Degner, L. F. and Sloan, J. A. (1992). Decision making during serious illness: what role do patients really want to play? *Journal of Clinical Epidemiology* 45(9), 941–50.

Del Piccolo, L., Saltini, A., Zimmermann, C. and Dunn, G. (2000). Differences in verbal behaviours of patients with an without emotional distress during primary care consultations. *Psychological Medicine* 30, 629–43.

DeVeugele, M. (2003). Doctor–patient communication in general practice. An observational study in six European countries. Thesis, Gent University.

DiBlasi, Z., Harkness, E., Ernst, E., Georgiou, A. and Kleijnen, J. (2001). Influence of context effects on health outcomes: a systematic review. *Lancet* 357, 757–62.

DiMatteo, M. R. (1995). Patient adherence to pharmacotherapy: the importance of effective communication. *Formulary* 30(10), 596–8, 601–2, 605.

Dimatteo, M. R. and DiNicola, D. D. (1982). *Achieving Patient Compliance.* New York: Pergamon Press.

Dimond, E. G., Kittle, C. F. and Crockett, J. E. (1960). Comparison of internal mammary ligation and sham operation for angina pectoris. *American Journal of Cardiology* 5, 483–6.

Engel, G. L. (1977). The need for a new medical model: a challenge for biomedicine. *Science* 196, 129–36.

Epstein, R. M., Campbell, T. L., Cohen-Cole, S. A., McWhinney, I. R. and Smilkstein, G. (1993). Perspectives on patient–doctor communication. *Journal of Family Practice* 37, 377–88.

Folkman, S. and Greer, S. (2000). Promoting psychological well-being in the face of serious illness: when theory, research and practice inform each other. *Psycho-oncology* 9(1), 11–19.

Frederikson, L. G. (1993). Development of an integrative model for medical consultation. *Health Communication* 5, 225–37.

Galer, B. S., Schwartz, L. and Turner, J. A. (1997). Do patients and physician expectations predict response to pain-relieving procedures? *Clinical Journal of Pain* 13, 348–51.

Graugaard, P. K. and Finset, A. (2000). Trait anxiety and reactions to patient-centered and doctor-centered styles of communication: an experimental study. *Psychosomatic Medicine* 62, 33–9.

Hall, J. A., Roter, D. L. and Katz, N. R. (1988). Meta-analysis of correlates of provider behaviour in medical encounters. *Medical Care* 26, 657–75.

Heath, C., Luff, P. and Svensson, M. S. (2003). Technology and medical practice. *Sociology of Health and Illness* 25, 75–96.

Hodge, J. G., Gostin, L. O. and Jacobson P. D. (2000). Legal issues concerning electronic health information: privacy, quality, and liability. *Journal of the American Medical Association* 282(15), 1466–71.

Hurwitz, B. and Vass, A. (2002). What's a good doctor and how can you make one? *British Medical Journal* 325, 667–8.

Hyman, D. J., Maibach, E. W., Flora, J. A. and Fortman, S. P. (1992). Cholesterol treatment practices of primary health care physicians. *Public Health Report* 107, 441–8.

Kamarck, T. W., Peterman, A. H. and Raynor, D. A. (1998). The effects of social environment on stress-related cardiovascular activation: current findings, prospects, and implications. *Annals of Behavioral Medicine* 20, 247–56.

Katz, S. J., Moyer, C. A., Cox, D. T. and Stern D. T. (2003). Effect of a triage-based e-mail system on clinic resource use and patient and physician satisfaction in primary care. *Journal of General Internal Medicine* 18(9), 736–44.

Koehler, W. F., Fottler, M. D. and Swan, J. E. (1992). Physician–patient satisfaction: equity in the health services encounter. *Medical Care Review* 49(4), 455–84.

Kvale, G., Hugdahl, K., Asbjornsen, R. B., Lote, K. and Nordby, H. (1991). Anticipatory nausea and vomiting in cancer patients. *Journal of Consulting and Clinical Psychology* 59, 894–8.

Kwekkeboom, K. L. (1997). The placebo effect in symptom management. *Oncological Nursing Forum* 24(8), 1393–9.

Laine, C. and Davidoff, F. (1996). Patient-centered medicine: a professional evolution. *Journal of the American Medical Association* 275, 152–6.

Lazare, A. (1995). The interview as a clinical negotiation. In M. Lipkin, S. M. Putnam and A. Lazare, *The Medical Interview: Clinical Care, Education and Research*. New York: Springer, 50–62.

Lazare, A., Putnam, S. and Lipkin, M. (1995). Three functions of the medical interview. In M. Lipkin, S. M. Putnam and A. Lazare, *The Medical Interview: Clinical Care, Education and Research*. New York: Springer, 3–19.

Lazarus, R. S. and Folkman, S. (1984). *Stress, Appraisal and Coping*. New York: Springer.

Lerman, C., Daly, M., Walsh, W. P., Resch, N., Seay, J., Barsevick, A., Birenbaum, L., Heggan, T. and Martin, G. (1993). Communication between patients with breast cancer and health care providers. *Cancer* 72, 2612–20.

Letvak, R. (1995). Putting the placebo effect into practice. *Patient Care* 29, 93–102.

Leventhal, H., Benyamini, Y., Brownlee, S., Diefenbach, M., Leventhal, E. A., Patrick-Miller, L. and Robitaille, C. (1997). Illness representations: theoretical foundations. In K. J. Petrie and J. A. Weinman, eds., *Perceptions of Health and Illness*. Amsterdam: Harwood Academic Publishers, 19–45.

Ley, P. (1982). Satisfaction, compliance and communication. *British Journal of Clinical Psychology* 21, 241–54.

Lipkin, M., Putnam, S. M. and Lazare, A. (1995). *The Medical Interview: Clinical Care, Education and Research*. New York: Springer.

Lyles, A. (2002). Direct marketing of pharmaceuticals to consumers. *Annual Review of Public Health* 23, 73–91.

Mackenbach, J. P. (1993). The epidemiological transition in the Netherlands. *Nederlands Tijdschrift voor Geneeskunde* 137(3), 132–8.

Margolith, I. and Shapiro, A. (1997). Anxiety and patient participation in clinical decision-making: the case of patients with urethral calculi. *Social Science & Medicine* 45, 419–27.

McCormick, J. (1996). Death of the personal doctor. *Lancet* 348, 667–8.

McKinlay, J. B. and Marceau, L. D. (2002). The end of the golden age of doctoring. *International Journal of Health Services* 32(2), 379–416.

McWhinney, I. (1985). Patient-centered and doctor-centered models of clinical decision-making. In M. Sheldon, J. Brook and A. Rector, eds., *Decision Making in General Practice*. London: Stockton.

Mead, N. and Bower, P. (2000). Patient-centredness: a conceptual framework and review of the empirical literature. *Social Science and Medicine* 51, 1087–110.

Mead, N. and Bower, P. (2002). Patient-centred consultations and outcomes in primary care: a review of the literature. *Patient Education and Counseling* 48(1), 51–61.

Mechanic, D. (2001). How should hamsters run? Some observations about sufficient patient time in primary care. *British Medical Journal* 323, 266–8.

Moerman, D. E. and Wayne, B. J. (2002). Deconstructing the placebo effect and finding the meaning response. *Annals of Internal Medicine* 136(6), 471–6.

Mule, G., Nardi, E., Cottone, S., Andronico, G., Federico, M. R., Piazza, G., Volpe, V., Ferrara, D. and Cerasola, G. (2003). Relationships between ambulatory white coat effect and left ventricular mass in arterial hypertension. *American Journal of Hypertension* 6(6), 498–501.

National Institute of Health (2000). The science of placebo: towards an interdisciplinary research agenda. www.placebo.nih.gov (accessed Sept. 24, 2003).

Novack, D. H. (1995). Therapeutic aspects of the clinical encounter. In M. Lipkin, S. M. Putnam and A. Lazare, *The Medical Interview: Clinical Care, Education and Research*. New York: Springer.

Ong, L. M. L., de Haes, J. C. J. M., Hoos, A. M. and Lammes, F. B. (1995). Doctor–patient communication: a review of the literature. *Social Science and Medicine* 40(7), 903–18.

Ong, L. M. L., Visser, M. R. M., van Zuuren, F., Rietbroek, R. C., Lammes, F. B. and de Haes, J. C. J. M. (1999). Cancer patients' coping styles and doctor–patient communication. *Psychooncology* 8, 155–66.

Paccaud, F. (2002). Rejuvenating health systems for aging communities. *Aging Clinical Experimental Research* 14(4), 314–18.

Robinson, A. (2001). Variability in patient preferences for participating in medical decision-making: implication for the use of decision support tools. *Quality in Health Care* 10, i34–i38.

Roter, D. L. (2000). The enduring and evolving nature of the patient–physician relationship. *Patient Education and Counseling* 39, 5–15.

Roter, D. L. and Hall, J. A. (1992). *Doctors Talking with Patients/Patients Talking with Doctors: Improving Communication in Medical Visits*. Westport, CT: Auburn House.

Roter, D. L., Stewart, M., Putnam, S. M., Lipkin, M., Stiles, W. and Inui, T. S. (1997). Communication patterns of primary care physicians. *Journal of the American Medical Association* 277(4), 350–6.

Sackett, D. L. and Haynes, R. B. (1976). *Compliance with Therapeutic Regimens*. Baltimore: Johns Hopkins University Press.

Safran, C. (2003). The collaborative edge: patient empowerment for vulnerable populations. *International Journal of Medical Informatics* 69(2–3), 185–90.

Smith, R. C. and Hoppe, R. B. (1991). The patient's story: integrating the patient- and physician-centered approaches to interviewing. *Annals of Internal Medicine* 115, 470–7.

Stewart, M. A. (1995). Effective physician–patient communication and health outcomes: a review. *Canadian Medical Association Journal* 152, 1423–33.

Stewart, M., Brown, J., Weston, W., McWhinney, I., McWilliam, C. and Freeman, T. (1995). *Patient-centred Medicine: Transforming the Clinical Method*. Thousand Oaks, CA: Sage.

Street, R. L. (2003). Mediated consumer–provider communication in cancer care: the empowering potential of new technologies. *Patient Education and Counseling* 50(1), 99–104.

Suchman, A. L., Markakis, K., Beckman, H. B. and Frankel, R. (1997). A model of empathic communication in the medical interview. *Journal of the American Medical Association* 277(8), 678–82.

Sullivan, M. (2003). The new subjective medicine: taking the patient's point of view on health care and health. *Social Science and Medicine* 56(7), 1595–1604.

Taylor, S. (1999). *Health Psychology*. Boston: McGraw-Hill.

Tennstedt, S. L. (2000). Empowering older patients to communicate more effectively in the medical encounter. *Clinical Geriatric Medicine* 16(1), 61–70, ix.

Thomas, K. B. (1987). General practice consultations: is there any point in being positive? *British Medical Journal* 294, 1200–2.

Tsai, P. S. (2002). White coat hypertension: understanding the concept and examining the significance. *Journal of Clinical Nursing* 11(6), 715–22.

Turner, J. A., Deyo, R. A., Loeser, J. D., Von Korff, M. and Fordyce, W. E. (1994). The importance of placebo effects in pain treatment and research. *Journal of the American Medical Academy* 271, 1609–14.

Van Brink-Muinen, A., Verhaak, P. F. M., Bensing, J. M., Bahrs, O., et al. (1999). The Eurocommunication Study: an international comparative study in six European countries on doctor–patient communication in general practice. Utrecht: NIVEL.

Van Dam, H. A., van der Horst, F., van den Borne, B., Ryckman, R. and Crebolder, H. (2003). Provider–patient interaction in diabetes care: effects on patient self-care and outcomes: a systematic review. *Patient Education and Counseling* 41, 17–28.

Van Dulmen, A. M. and Bensing, J. M. (2001). *The Effect of Context in Health Care: A Programming Study*. The Hague: RGO.

Van Dulmen, A. M., Fennis, J. F. M., Mokkink, H. G. A., van der Velden, H. G. M. and Bleijenberg, G. (1994). Doctors' perception of patients' cognitions and complaints in irritable bowel syndrome. *Journal of Psychosomatic Research* 38, 581–90.

Whitcomb, M. E. (2000). Communication and professionalism. *Patient Education and Counseling* 41(2), 137–44.

White, K. L. (1988). *The Task of Medicine: Dialogue at Wickenburg*. Menlo Park, California: The Henri J. Kaiser Family Foundation.

Wirth, D. P. (1995). The significance of belief and expectancy within the spiritual healing encounter. *Social Science and Medicine* 41, 249–60.

Chapter Twelve

HOSPITALIZATION AND STRESSFUL MEDICAL PROCEDURES

Claus Vögele

CHAPTER OUTLINE

Hospitalization can be a stressful experience on its own, but some patients encounter additional stress because they must undergo unpleasant medical procedures. Even some outpatient procedures such as dental treatments or blood donation can be stressful. Normally patients would report increases in anxiety in anticipation of procedures such as surgery, endoscopy, cardiac catheterization or chemotherapy. Among those, surgery is perhaps the most threatening event as it contains many unpredictable and uncontrollable features such as losing consciousness due to the administration of a general anaesthetic, the anticipation of post-operative pain, and the surgical trauma related to the incision. This chapter will concentrate on surgical procedures and describe the stressful characteristics associated with being hospitalized for surgery. Then it will review the literature on psychological and physiological responses to the experience of surgery and summarize findings from studies investigating psychological preparation for surgery. For the purposes of this chapter surgery is identified as that subset of surgical procedures involving general anaesthesia and, therefore, loss of consciousness. Other forms of anaesthesia which do not result in the loss of consciousness include spinal and epidural anaesthesia. They involve the injection of a local anaesthetic into the vertebral canal close to the spinal cord by an anaesthetist. Because patients' experiences of these forms of interventions may differ from having surgery under a general anaesthetic, they are not considered in the current chapter.

KEY CONCEPTS

clinical recovery measures

general anaesthesia

negative affect

post-operative pain

post-operative recovery

pre-operative anxiety

psychological indices

psychological preparation for surgery

recovery process

satisfaction

surgery

surgical outcomes

STRESSFUL CHARACTERISTICS OF THE SURGICAL SITUATION

There are obvious potential threats for the surgical patient: anaesthesia, pain, physical restriction, life-threatening procedures, being away from home. Sleep deprivation may also be a significant stressor, mainly due to early awakening (Murphy et al., 1977). In a study involving 535 medical and surgical patients in a community hospital, Volicer et al. (1977) found surgical patients to be more distressed by the unfamiliarity of their surroundings, loss of independence and the threat of severe illness. Medical patients scored higher on the dimensions of stress due to financial problems and lack of information. These differences remained even after controlling for age and seriousness of illness. More recent evidence suggests that the lack of predictability and control are significant contributors to the stressful experience of surgical patients (Slangen et al., 1993). It is usually the case that we need to be able to predict an event in order to be able to control it. But control does not always imply predictability. Such is the case for elective surgery, which accounts for the vast majority of surgical interventions.

This evidence confirms that there are common characteristics of the surgical situation which are identified by most patients as stressful. However, it seems likely that different types of surgical procedures produce different types of stress. Weinman and Johnston (1988) suggest that a useful way of distinguishing between the various procedures would be by considering the function of the procedure (diagnostic, treatment or both) and the time-line and nature of stress associated with the procedure. Weinman and Johnston (1988) further distinguish between procedural stress (i.e. the stress associated with the negative aspects of the actual procedure itself) and outcome stress (i.e. longer-term fears and concerns related to the results of the treatment or procedure). To illustrate the latter point, some operations, for example, may have more positive characteristics in terms of their expected outcome than others, such as restoration (hip replacement) versus removal of physical function (leg amputation). For a further discussion of stress dimensions of surgery and related methodological issues see Kincey and Saltmore (1990).

RESPONSES OF SURGICAL PATIENTS AT EMOTIONAL, COGNITIVE AND PHYSIOLOGICAL LEVELS

Emotional responses

Most studies investigating emotional responses to surgery have shown elevated levels of anxiety both before and after surgery. In some groups of patients, post-operative anxiety levels may be even higher than those measured pre-operatively and this may reflect different sources of worry (procedural versus outcome). Previous results indicating that anxiety is high before but not after surgery (e.g. Auerbach, 1973; Spielberger et al., 1973) have been dismissed as being methodically flawed, as the post-operative measures were not taken until patients reported they were free from post-operative discomfort (Johnston, 1988).

Vögele and Steptoe (1986) and Vögele (1992) found moderate levels of anxiety on the day before the operation and a significant increase on the days immediately following surgery in patients undergoing total hip replacement. As this particular type of surgery involved the patients getting out of bed on day 2 or 3 after the operation, it seems likely that the observed post-operative increase in anxiety was due to the anticipatory anxiety about the outcome of the operation. Interestingly, a similar pattern of responses could be observed in another patient group undergoing a much more minor orthopaedic surgical procedure (knee arthroscopy, Vögele & Steptoe, 1986).

Although anxiety has been the most frequently assessed emotional response for obvious reasons, it has been shown that surgical patients may also experience high levels of nervousness, depression, anger and boredom (Vögele, 1992).

These results indicate that emotional responses to the surgical situation may vary as a function of the type of operation, and therefore, outcome concerns. They also point to the possibility of effective interventions not only before but also after surgery.

Cognitive responses

Several studies have examined surgical patients' worries (e.g. Johnston, 1987) and it has been suggested that patients' main worries are more related to the outcome of the operation rather than the operation itself (Weinman & Johnston, 1988). Patients also worry significantly about normal everyday matters such as family and home, perhaps exacerbated by hospitalization and the impending surgery. As in the treatment of depression, the cognitive elements of surgical patients' stress response may be critical in indicating the most promising intervention approach to alleviate distress.

Physiological responses

The most thorough research on physiological responses to surgery has been carried out on indices of sympathetic-adrenomedullary activity, both because they are readily measurable in surgical patients and because this highly responsive physiological axis has been widely used in well-controlled laboratory studies of psychological stress. The most consistent finding is that of a reduction in palmar sweat gland activity prior to surgery followed by recovery to normal levels post-operatively (e.g. Vögele & Steptoe, 1986). Due to its ease of application in this setting, palmar sweating has been measured in some studies of surgical patients using the sweat gland count, or palmar sweat index (PSI), assessed using the plastic cast technique. As we have shown (Vögele & Steptoe, 1986), the PSI and the more commonly used skin conductance responses are highly correlated and closely follow the pattern of subjective distress and pain, indicating that sweat gland activity is reduced by the stress of surgery. Some authors, however, have argued that the palmar sweating pattern of surgical patients is related to the effort rather than the distress aspect of stress, i.e. changes in palmar sweating are due to changes in activity levels (Johnston, 1988). Indices of cardio-vascular activity may be even more complicated to interpret. Fleischman et al. (1976) showed reductions in platelet aggregation time and increases in blood pressure between admission and surgery. Goldstein et al. (1982) suggested that the cardiovascular responses to the stress of surgery have multiple determinants and may not be mediated by sympathetic influences. They found pre-operative increases in heart rate, systolic blood pressure and cardiac output, but these persisted when noradrenaline responses were eliminated by diazepam sedation.

The latter two studies investigated patients undergoing relatively minor procedures (dental procedure, e.g. molar extractions) and may therefore not be comparable with the more commonly studied operations such as cholecystectomy or gynaecological operations, neither in severity of the procedure nor in the time-scale investigated. In our own studies (Vögele & Steptoe, 1986; Vögele, 1992), we consistently found elevated heart rates before and after the operation that could not be accounted for by blood loss.

A more recent line of research has investigated neuro-endocrine and immune changes in response to surgery. Post-operative elevations in plasma levels of adrenaline, cortisol and beta-endorphin reflect sympathetic nervous system and hypothalamic–pituitary–adrenal axis activation (Salomaki et al., 1993). Evidence for immune suppression during surgery comes from studies showing suppression of natural killer cell activity (Pollock et al., 1991), lymphocyte proliferative responses to mitogens, and changes in lymphocyte populations (Tonnessen et al., 1987).

In order to interpret these physiological responses to surgery as psycho-physiological phenomena (including the experience of pain), it is necessary to disentangle the effects that are due to the experience of stress from those that are caused by the surgical trauma and other medical interventions (e.g. anaesthesia). Surgery represents in most cases a major trauma with a relatively stereotyped physiological response pattern (Salmon & Hall, 1997). This response pattern involves physiological changes reminiscent of Selye's 'General Adaptation Syndrome' (GAS) (Selye, 1980), and includes the release of catecholamines, glucocorticoids, growth hormone and glucagon, the suppression of insulin secretion, and changes in other endocrine systems. These hormonal responses are assumed to trigger a cascade of metabolic adjustments leading to catabolism (a metabolic state of breakdown of the body's own protein) and substrate mobilization in the post-operative period.

This pattern of responses is sometimes described in the medical literature under the term 'La maladie post-opératoire' or 'Post aggression syndrome' (see Moore, 1976). The implication of a unifying concept of post-operative physiological changes as suggested by this term has, however, been criticized in favour of a more differentiated view (Anand, 1986; Moore, 1976) taking into account site and extent of the surgical trauma. In the simple, uninfected, elective surgical trauma, which usually forms the basis for psychological research reported in this chapter, there is little to note other than the mild tissue injury, with prompt healing, transient starvation, and trivial fluid volume reduction. We would argue, therefore, that any between-patient differences in physiological responses to surgery may be attributable to psychological and behavioural factors, and this – despite all caveats – makes physiological indices of stress an attractive paradigm to study the impact of the surgical situation on post-operative recovery. As we will see in the following section, such differences in physiological responses (including immunological and neuro-endocrine changes) may have an effect on indices of post-operative recovery such as speed of wound healing.

SURGICAL STRESS AND POST-OPERATIVE RECOVERY

There are at least two reasons why psychologists have been interested in the investigation of surgical patients over the last four decades. First, as by far the majority of surgical interventions are planned, or elective, and can therefore be anticipated, surgery provides a useful model for stress in the real world, in that it combines the intense involvement usually found only in field studies with the stringent controls over movement and activity that are normally available only in the laboratory. Secondly, and perhaps more importantly, it is hoped that through a better understanding of the impact of psychological factors on post-operative recovery, high-risk patients may be identified and methods to improve surgical outcome can be developed.

Despite a strong effect of physical factors such as extent of tissue damage caused by the surgical trauma on post-operative recovery, there is variability across patients who have undergone the same procedure. It is unclear what accounts for this variability, and this has led to the suggestion that psychological factors such as anxiety and depression may play some part in determining the duration or quality of post-operative recovery.

There is considerable theoretical and empirical support for the relevance of psychosocial factors to post-operative recovery. These include demographic variables such as age, gender and socio-economic status, and also personality variables such as anxiety, neuroticism, coping style and social support. One of the first studies to investigate the effects of pre-operative anxiety on post-operative recovery was carried out by Janis (1958). He assessed surgical patients' anxiety before the operation and related their degree of anticipatory fear to indices of recovery. On the basis of his findings Janis proposed that moderate levels of pre-operative 'distress' result in optimal post-operative recovery, whereas excessively low or very high levels of distress both are associated with impaired or sub-optimal recovery. The moderate level of distress was coined by Janis as 'the work of worry', which was hypothesized to prepare one-self for the distress and suffering associated with post-operative recovery. This study was very influential as it sparked off a series of studies investigating the effects of psychological factors on post-operative recovery and also on how best to prepare patients in order to optimize recovery. However, the curvilinear relationship between pre-operative anxiety and recovery as proposed by Janis (1958) has never been replic-ated. Instead, most of the available literature today suggests a rather linear associ-ation between pre-operative anxiety and success of recovery, in that the more anxious the patient before the operation the less favourable the post-operative recovery. There is even evidence that pre-operative anxiety is related to intra-operative adjustment (Abbott & Abbott, 1995; de Bruin et al., 2001), though with equivocal results: while in the former study highly anxious patients required more anaesthetic, the latter reports an inverse relationship: the higher pre-operative anxiety levels the less anaesthetic was required during the operation.

In a recent review of studies relating anxiety and post-operative recovery (Munafò & Stevenson, 2001) the authors conclude that there is consistency across studies in finding a linear relationship between pre-operative state anxiety and post-operative mood. A somewhat smaller degree of consistency is reported for the association between pre-operative anxiety and other recovery variables, and the authors use this finding to highlight methodological problems of these studies that prevent any firm conclu-sions to be drawn as yet.

One of these problems concerns the extent to which the potential effect of beha-vioural consistency is not controlled for. The fact, for example, that pre- and post-operative measures of anxiety are frequently reported to be positively correlated may reflect nothing more than behavioural (self-reporting) consistency. The only post-operative recovery measures where an explanation in terms of self-reporting consist-ency would be difficult are physiological correlates of emotional states and other physiological and clinical variables such as wound healing.

Although the number of studies employing such recovery indices is relatively small, there is some compelling evidence for a positive relationship between pre-operative self-report measures and post-operative immune function. Linn et al. (1988) assessed the relevance of differences in pre-operative pain tolerance and stress to post-operative immune function. Physiological responses to a cold pressor test were measured the day before surgery in 24 men undergoing hernia repair. After controlling for pre-operative immunological values (as well as age and social support) lymphocytes from men who reported more recent stressful life events had lower proliferative responses to an antigen (phytohemagglutinin, PHA). In addition, high responders to the cold pressor test (i.e. a lower pain threshold) had significantly lower proliferative responses to a pokeweed mitogen after surgery (i.e. impaired immune function). They also required more pain medication and had more complications.

Across a number of studies, greater self-reported anxiety is typically related to more severe post-operative pain (Johnston, 1988). In addition to direct effects on endocrine and immune function, the greater pain sensitivity of more anxious patients can have further consequences for recovery through altered behaviour. Breathing exercises, for example, can reduce the risk of pneumonia, and ambulation decreases the risk of phlebitis and may improve wound healing (Kehlet, 1997). Highly anxious patients may be more reluctant to follow recommendations for coughing, deep breathing or walking.

Personality variables may moderate post-surgical outcomes via their influence on stress, mood and coping (Mathews & Ridgeway, 1981). For example, neuroticism as assessed by the Eysenck scales has been shown in many studies to be associated with poorer surgical outcomes, such as increased post-operative pain and medical complications. Scheier et al. (1989) assessed the effect of dispositional optimism on recovery from coronary artery bypass surgery. After controlling for a number of confounds (extensiveness of surgery, severity of disease, smoking, hypertension, high cholesterol), the authors found that compared with pessimistic men, optimistic men fared better on peri-operative physiological variables; they also began walking faster after surgery, and rehabilitation staff rated them as showing a more favourable physical recovery.

Some evidence suggests that surgical stress may also interact with both age and psychological stress to increase risk for older adults. In a study by Linn and Jensen (1983) there was no difference immunologically between older and younger adults prior to surgery (hernia repair). However, five days after the operation, immune function was significantly lower in the older sample compared to the younger patients. In a similar study Linn et al. (1983) could show that highly anxious older patients had significantly more complications compared with their low anxious contemporaries and younger patients.

In summary, there is increasing evidence from psycho-neuro-immunological work that stress and pain have a negative effect on endocrine and immune function and may thereby lead to delays in wound healing and other clinical complications. Although wound healing is only one post-operative outcome among a whole range, it is certainly a central parameter for short-term outcome in recovery from surgery. Kiecolt-Glaser et al. (1998) offer a bio-behavioural model suggesting a number of routes through which psychological and behavioural responses can influence surgery and post-operative recovery (figure 12.1).

When investigating the effects of psycho-social variables on post-operative recovery it is important to take into consideration the complexity of post-operative recovery measures. These range from clinical recovery measures, pain medication and length of stay in hospital to physiological indices and subjective ratings of negative affect. It is likely that recovery is not uni-dimensional and that the heterogeneity of recovery variables employed in studies investigating the effects of psychological factors on post-operative recovery has contributed to this rather ambiguous picture. As we shall see, when assessing the impact of psychological preparation for surgery it is just as important to define recovery in terms of outcomes that can be improved.

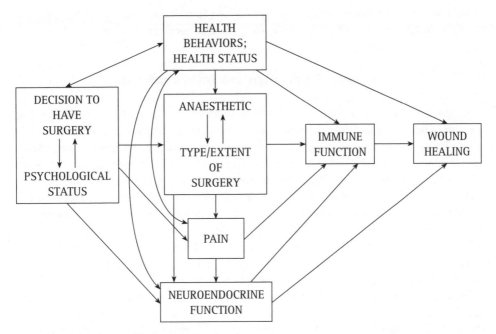

Figure 12.1 A bio-behavioural model of the psychological, behavioural and biological pathways that influence wound healing: the central short-term outcome in recovery from surgery
Source: Kiecolt-Glaser et al., 1998.

Psychological Preparation for Surgery

Most patients cope with preparations for stressful and potentially painful medical procedures as well as they can. However, the evidence reported in the previous sections of this chapter suggests that this coping ability might be compromised by a range of factors such as preceding life events, personality characteristics, demographic variables such as age and gender and previous unfavourable experiences with such procedures.

Efforts to design interventions to help surgical patients with their coping can be traced back to the previously mentioned work by Janis (1958). He found that patients receiving additional information about what would happen before, during and after surgery requested less pain medication, made fewer demands on staff and were discharged earlier than those receiving the usual information. Another early study is reported by Egbert and co-workers (1964). On the night before surgery anaesthetists visited patients to provide information about typical post-surgical physical sensations and also familiarized them with a relaxation technique to reduce pain. The patients receiving this intervention were discharged from hospital on average 2.7 days earlier and required half as much pain medication as patients receiving routine care. This work has prompted numerous studies over the last four decades investigating a diverse range of intervention techniques on equally diverse outcome measures.

Types of pre-surgical interventions

The provision of information of some kind concerning the surgical experience has perhaps been the most frequently employed. There are two types of information provision that can be distinguished: procedural information and sensory information. While the former describes the procedure and sequence of events in more detail, the latter places the emphasis on informing the patient about the sensations they are likely to experience, such as the nature, site and duration of pain after surgery, etc. Another related intervention gives patients instructions on behaviours they should engage in order to promote recovery (e.g. breathing, coughing, walking, eating, etc.). This group of interventions is usually referred to as behavioural instructions. Although both information provision interventions are thought to act through the same mechanism of anxiety reduction, Johnson and Leventhal (1974) and Johnson et al. (1978) present evidence that sensory information may be more effective by creating a 'cognitive map' within which to locate subjective (pain) experiences. It is difficult, however, to prove these claims in the context of preparation for surgery as many researchers in this area have designed interventions that contain mixtures of these three treatments.

That a combination of interventions may be more 'than the sum of its parts' is supported by results from a meta-analysis by Suls and Wan (1989). Results indicated that, in contrast to sensory information, procedural information provided no significant benefits over control group instruction. Combined sensory-procedural preparation, however, yielded the strongest and most consistent benefits in terms of reducing negative affect, pain reports and other-rated distress. The authors conclude that these results are consistent with the dual process preparation hypothesis, which proposes that the information combination is optimal because procedural details provide a map of specific events while sensory information facilitates their interpretation as non-threatening.

Other, less frequently used interventions include cognitive techniques to help the patient re-appraise the surgical situation in a more positive (adaptive) way, relaxation techniques (progressive muscle relaxation, breathing techniques), hypnosis and emotion focused/psychotherapeutic interventions.

There is heterogeneity not only in interventions used, but also in the way they have been delivered. Some studies use a group format, whereas others rely on low-cost alternatives such as booklets, manuals, audio-tapes and video-tapes (e.g. Doering et al., 2000). It may be worth noting, at this point, that most interventions are remarkably brief: the majority of studies employ a single session with an average duration of 30 minutes (Devine, 1992).

Since Janis' (1958) and Egbert et al.'s work (1964), more than 200 studies have investigated the effects of these various forms and formats of psychological preparation for surgery. While being critical of the methodology of some of the studies included, several major literature reviews (e.g. Mathews & Ridgeway, 1984) and meta-analyses (e.g. Mumford et al., 1982; Johnston & Vögele, 1993) are in broad agreement that prepared patients have better post-operative outcomes. In most cases 'better outcome' would relate to statistically significant differences between the group of patients receiving the preparation and an unprepared control group. Contrada et al. (1994), however, argue on the basis of several meta-analyses that these differences are not only statistically but also clinically meaningful. Depending on the meta-analysis, 60 to 75 per cent of prepared patients had better outcomes than untreated controls, and the size of the improvement was in the order of 20 to 28 per cent.

As to the question of how psychological preparation for surgery promotes recovery, two classes of explanation can be distinguished. The first set of assumptions stipulates that the physiological changes accompanying stress reduction resulting from psychological preparation (e.g. reduction in sympathetic arousal) improve patients' immunological responses (Kiecolt-Glaser et al., 1998). There is evidence that interventions that alter appraisal, coping and/or mood may modulate immune and endocrine function (Kiecolt-Glaser & Glaser, 1992; Manyande et al., 1995). An alternative explanation suggests that preparations exert their effects by reducing the frequency and extent of maladaptive behaviours that an unprepared patient might engage in (Mathews & Ridgeway, 1984). These two explanations are not mutually exclusive and can be subsumed under the bio-behavioural model described in above (Kiecolt-Glaser et al., 1998).

Individual differences and psychological preparation for surgery

As discussed in the previous section, personality variables have been shown to moderate post-operative recovery via their influence on stress, mood and coping. Such individual differences may also be important in moderating the effects of psychological preparation for surgery, in particular in the area of preferred styles of coping with threat. For example, patients with a vigilant coping style (monitors) scan for threat-relevant cues, whereas those with a more avoidant coping style (blunters) try to distract themselves from threat cues. The two types of patients appear to show better adjustment in clinical settings when interventions are tailored to their coping style (Miller, 1992). Monitors fare better with voluminous sensory and procedural information, whereas the opposite is true for blunters (Prokop et al., 1991).

Children and psychological preparation for surgery

Hospitalization is a common experience for children as well as for adults. In most cases this involves a number of stressors for children – separation from their parents, an unfamiliar surrounding, diagnostic tests, anaesthesia, surgery and post-operative pain. To help children cope with their fear of treatment presents the health psychologist with a number of problems: limited understanding of the necessity of treatment, the need to prevent the treatment experience from becoming traumatic and thereby providing the basis for later phobias, parental influence (which can be positive or negative), the child's perception and interpretation of the experience as punishment. Melamed and her colleagues have carried out early work to investigate methods to reduce stress in children undergoing elective surgery by using film modelling as preparation for surgery (Melamed, 1974, 1984; Melamed & Siegal, 1975). Modelling is an effective technique for coping with unpleasant medical procedures. Typically, the model appears on film in the same situation that the patient will soon encounter. Melamed's studies provide a range of interesting results. First, the most effective models appear anxious at first, but in the end they successfully cope with the stress of the procedure. Second, viewing the film more than once may be useful. Third, the timing of the viewing seems important: anxiety tends to increase immediately after viewing the film, followed by a decrease. Enough time needs to elapse between the presentation of the model and the procedure in order for the patient to experience the benefit of this intervention.

As is the case for adults (see previous section), however, individual differences in coping styles may also play an important role in children. Field et al. (1988) described children as either using a vigilant or avoidant coping style. Vigilant children tend to be more talkative during hospitalization, seek more information and protest more than avoiders.

As may be apparent from this brief discussion of individual differences and children and psychological preparation for surgery, the focus of research in this area has moved from simple considerations of the best preparation technique to a recognition of the need to provide interventions tailored for different patient populations. Provided we had the appropriate assessment tools to identify these patient groups, it is as yet not clear how such individual treatments could be administered in highly standardized hospital settings.

Outcomes

In view of the heterogeneity of interventions, intervention formats, surgical procedures and the potential of individual differences to interact with treatment outcomes, the results achieved by psychological preparation for surgery are surprising and speak for the robustness of the effect.

The question remains, however: effective in gaining which benefits? It would also seem important to establish if all forms of preparation are equally effective. There are different reasons for an outcome to be valued. Recovery is valued because it indicates the improving health status of the patient and thus, indirectly, the success of the medical procedures. Negative affect is undesirable because it is inherently unpleasant and may be predictive of further poor outcomes. Use of analgesic medication may be used to index health status/recovery or pain/distress or use of resources/

costs of in-patient care. In our own meta-analysis of the literature on preparing adult patients for surgery (Johnston & Vögele, 1993) we examined which benefits were sought, whether they were achieved, and whether all benefits were equally likely to be gained by psychological preparation.

Thirty-eight studies were retrieved which adhered to a number of methodological criteria (e.g. random allocation of patients to treatment or control group), including some unpublished studies which usually go undetected in these kinds of analyses. Based on commonly used variables and classifications in this field, combined with the results of factorially derived outcomes (Johnston, 1984), we grouped outcomes in 8 categories: negative affect, pain, pain medication, length of stay, behavioural and clinical indices of recovery, physiological indices, and satisfaction. The most important conclusion to be drawn from this analysis is that prepared patients show significant improvements in all outcomes analysed. Given the heterogeneity in the data analysed, the consistency of these results seems impressive. They are certainly sufficient to offer useful guidance to the medical or nursing staff or managers of a surgical unit attempting to improve outcomes for patients having routine, elective surgery under general anaesthesia.

In relation to interventions used, we found procedural information and behavioural instructions to show the most ubiquitous effects, both being clearly effective in improving all eight outcomes. Relaxation is also highly effective, showing benefit on all outcomes except behavioural recovery, although sometimes on rather few studies. The results for cognitive interventions suggest that this type of preparation may have a specific effect on negative affect, pain, pain medication and clinical recovery, but not length of stay in hospital, behavioural recovery or physiological indices. It is plausible to assume that these interventions affect a negative affect/symptom complaint dimension, but do not affect physiological or behavioural measures. Finally, we found sensory information, hypnotic and emotion-focused approaches to be rather less effective in improving outcome. However, these interventions have been explored in fewer studies and the procedures may be less well developed. In a more recent study comparing the effects of structured attention, self-hypnotic relaxation and standard care in a group of patients undergoing percutaneous vascular and renal procedures (angiographies), hypnosis had more pronounced effects on pain and anxiety reduction (Lang et al., 2000).

Summarizing these results and those of other reviews and meta-analyses, it can be concluded that psychological preparation for surgery has demonstrable benefits on a range of recovery variables. However, positive effects are not limited to formal interventions. As shown by Ulrich (1984), even small changes such as having a room with a view can result in improved outcome (shorter stay in hospital, less pain medication requested). Another interesting study indicating the potential of informal ways of preparing for surgery comes from a study by Kulik et al. (1993). Patients about to undergo cardiac surgery were assigned a room-mate who was either also awaiting surgery or who already had undergone surgery. Patients with a post-operative room-mate were less anxious before their operation and had a smoother recovery (ambulation, length of stay) than their counterparts. In addition, it made no difference whether the room-mate had a similar surgical procedure. In a follow-up to this study (Kulik et al., 1996), the authors could show that patients without a room-mate had the slowest recovery of all. Kulik and co-workers interpret these effects in terms of affiliation processes in situations involving threat, information provision and modelling.

These processes may be subsumed under the more general construct of interpersonal support. Interpersonal support may be an important element of pre-surgical interventions which is quite independent of the type of intervention. There is ample evidence that social support has a stress buffering effect, and it may be that the benefits associated with psychological preparation for surgery can at least partly be explained by the effects of face-to-face contact provided in studies using a personal approach (as opposed to using a booklet or audio-tape). Whether pre-surgical interventions have any effect over and above the interpersonal support provided by the health-care worker administering the intervention would have to be investigated in studies including an attention-placebo group. Only 5 out of the 38 studies identified in our meta-analysis (Johnston & Vögele, 1993) included such a control group, so that it seems premature to draw any conclusions. What seems more important, however, is the immediate practical applicability of these approaches. The benefits of any such interventions, whether they be formal (e.g. psychological preparation) or informal (e.g. assignment of room-mates) by far outweigh the costs associated with slower recovery.

IMPLICATIONS FOR RESEARCH AND PRACTICE IN THE FUTURE

As a consequence of technical advances in medicine and surgery, many operations are less invasive than in the past. They are, therefore, increasingly performed on an out-patient basis, or with a greatly reduced hospital stay. Kehlet and Wilmore (2002) estimate that in the future most elective surgical procedures will become day surgical procedures or require only one to two days of post-operative hospitalization. In addition to this development, the introduction of managed care in the health care of many countries has led to a further shortening of length of hospitalization. With any extended convalescence at home, family members or carers play a more important role. The additional demands that are placed on carers of surgical patients recovering at home should not be overlooked. Future developments should address these issues in research and in the design of flexible interventions that take into account the psycho-social context in which they take place.

With the advent of health psychology and the establishment of health psychology as a profession, it will become increasingly likely that health psychologists will be asked to provide services in terms of consultancy and interventions in many areas of health care including surgical units. Given the current move towards managed care and the limited resources available in the health-care systems in many countries, it seems probable and desirable that health psychologists will be increasingly involved in the design of interventions (such as booklets, manuals or audio- and video-tapes) rather than the administration of the interventions as such. Only in cases where there is a profound adjustment reaction after surgery, for example in surgery that involves cosmetic consequences, will face-to-face contact be necessary to provide psycho-therapy. It is to be hoped that the development of 'fast track surgery' and 'accelerated care' programmes will result in the use of health psychologists' expertise in this area to further improve multi-modal interventions to achieve a 'pain- and risk-free' peri-operative course.

DISCUSSION POINTS

1. What is stressful about having surgery and how do people cope with it?
2. How does surgical stress affect post-operative recovery?
3. Discuss the different types of psychological preparation for surgery.
4. What is the evidence relating psychological preparation for surgery and better post-operative recovery? Discuss the suggested mechanisms underlying this relationship.
5. Which benefits can be achieved by psychological preparation for surgery, and are all forms of preparation equally effective?
6. How does the psychological preparation of children for invasive medical procedures differ from that used for adults?
7. Discuss the impact of individual differences on post-operative recovery and the effect of psychological preparation for surgery.
8. What is the role of health psychologists in relation to psychological preparation for surgery?

FURTHER READING

Kiecolt-Glaser, J. K., Page, G. G., Marucha, P. T., MacCallum, R. C. and Glaser, R. (1998). Psychological influences on surgical recovery: perspectives from psychoneuroimmunology. *American Psychologist* 53, 1209–18.

Kincey, J. and Saltmore, S. (1990). Surgical treatments. In M. Johnston and L. Wallace, eds., *Stress and Medical Procedures.* Oxford: Oxford University Press, 120–37.

Johnston, M. (1988). Impending surgery. In S. Fisher and J. Reason, eds., *Handbook of Life Stress, Cognition and Health.* Chichester: John Wiley & Sons, 79–100.

Johnston, M. and Wallace, L., eds. (1990). *Stress and Medical Procedures.* Oxford: Oxford University Press.

Johnston, M. and Vögele, C. (1993). Benefits of psychological preparation for surgery: a meta-analysis. *Annals of Behavioral Medicine* 15, 245–56.

KEY STUDIES

Kiecolt-Glaser, J. K., Page, G. G., Marucha, P. T., MacCallum, R. C. and Glaser, R. (1998). Psychological influences on surgical recovery: perspectives from psychoneuroimmunology. *American Psychologist* 53, 1209–18.

Kulik, J. A., Mahler, H. I. and Moore, P. J. (1996). Social comparison and affiliation under threat: effects on recovery from major surgery. *Journal of Personality and Social Psychology* 71, 967–79.

Johnston, M. and Vögele, C. (1993). Benefits of psychological preparation for surgery: a meta-analysis. *Annals of Behavioral Medicine* 15, 245–56.

REFERENCES

Abbott, J. and Abbott, P. (1995). Psychological and cardiovascular predictors of anaesthesia induction, operative and postoperative complications in minor gynecological surgery. *British Journal of Clinical Psychology* 34, 613–25.

Anand, K. J. (1986). The stress-response to surgical trauma: from physiological basis to therapeutic implications. *Progress in Food and Nutritional Science* 10, 67–132.

Auerbach, S. M. (1973). Trait-state anxiety and adjustment to surgery. *Journal of Consulting and Clinical Psychology* 34, 264–71.

Contrada, R. J., Leventhal, E. A. and Anderson, J. R. (1994). Psychological preparation for surgery: marshalling individual and social resources to optimize self-regulation. In S. Maes, H. Leventhal and M. Johnston, eds., *International Review of Health Psychology*, vol. 3. New York: Wiley, 219–66.

De Bruin, J. T., Schaefer, M. K., Krohne, H. W. and Dreyer, A. (2001). Pre-operative anxiety, coping, and intraoperative adjustment: are there mediating effects of stress-induced analgesia? *Psychology & Health* 16, 253–71.

Devine, E. C. (1992). Effects of psychoeducational care for adult surgical patients: a meta-analysis of 191 studies. *Patient Education and Counseling* 19, 129–42.

Doering, S., Katzlberger, F., Rumpold, G., Roessler, S., et al. (2000). Videotape preparation of patients before hip replacement surgery reduces stress. *Psychosomatic Medicine* 62, 365–73.

Egbert, L. D., Battit, G. E., Welch, C. E. and Barlett, M. K. (1964). Reduction of postoperative pain by encouragement and instruction of patients. *New England Journal of Medicine* 270, 825–7.

Field, T., Alpert, B., Vega-Lahr, N., Goldstein, S. and Perry, S. (1988). Hospitalisation stress in children: sensitizer and repressor coping styles. *Health Psychology* 7, 433–45.

Fleischman, A. I., Bierenbaum, M. L. and Stier, A. (1976). Effect of stress due to anticipated minor surgery upon in vivo platelet aggregation in humans. *Journal of Human Stress* 2, 33–7.

Goldstein, D. S., Dionne, R., Sweet, J., Gracely, R., Brewer, H. B. Jr, Gregg, R. and Keiser, H. R. (1982). Circulatory, plasma catecholamine, cortisol, lipid, and psychosocial responses to a real-life stress (third molar extractions): effects of diazepam sedation and of inclusion of epinephrine with the local anaesthetic. *Psychosomatic Medicine* 44, 259–72.

Janis, I. L. (1958). *Psychological Stress: Psychoanalytic and Behavioral Studies of Surgical Patients*. New York: Wiley.

Johnston, M. (1984). Dimensions of recovery from surgery. *International Review of Applied Psychology* 33, 505–20.

Johnston, M. (1987). Emotional and cognitive aspects of anxiety in surgical patients. *Communication & Cognition* 20, 261–76.

Johnston, M. (1988). Impending surgery. In S. Fisher and J. Reason, eds., *Handbook of Life Stress, Cognition and Health*. Chichester: John Wiley & Sons, 79–100.

Johnston, M. and Vögele, C. (1993). Benefits of psychological preparation for surgery: a meta-analysis. *Annals of Behavioral Medicine* 15, 245–56.

Kehlet, H. (1997). Multimodal approach to control postoperative pathophysiology and rehabilitation. *British Journal of Anaesthesia* 78, 606–17.

Kehlet, H. and Wilmore, D. W. (2002). Multimodal strategies to improve surgical outcome. *American Journal of Surgery* 183, 630–41.

Kiecolt-Glaser, J. K. and Glaser, R. (1992). Psychoneuroimmunology: can psychological interventions modulate immunity? *Journal of Consulting and Clinical Psychology* 60, 569–75.

Kiecolt-Glaser, J. K., Page, G. G., Marucha, P. T., MacCallum, R. C. and Glaser, R. (1998). Psychological influences on surgical recovery: perspectives from psychoneuroimmunology. *American Psychologist* 53, 1209–18.

Kincey, J. and Saltmore, S. (1990). Surgical treatments. In M. Johnston and L. Wallace, eds., *Stress and Medical Procedures*. Oxford: Oxford University Press, 120–37.

Kulik, J. A., Moore, P. J. and Mahler, H. I. (1993). Stress and affiliation: hospital room-mate effects on preoperative anxiety and social interaction. *Health Psychology* 12, 118–24.

Kulik, J. A., Mahler, H. I. and Moore, P. J. (1996). Social comparison and affiliation under threat: Effects on recovery from major surgery. *Journal of Personality and Social Psychology* 71, 967–79.

Lang, E. V., Benotsch, E. G., Fick, L. J., Lutgendorf, S., et al. (2000). Adjunctive non-pharmacological analgesia for invasive medical procedures: a randomised trial. *Lancet* 355, 1486–90.

Linn, B. S. and Jensen, J. (1983). Age and immune response to a surgical stress. *Archives of Surgery* 118, 405–9.

Linn, B. S., Linn, M. W. and Jensen, J. (1983). Surgical stress in the healthy elderly. *Journal of the American Geriatric Society* 31, 544–68.

Linn, B. S., Linn, M. W. and Klimas, N. G. (1988). Effects of psycho-physical stress on surgical outcome. *Psychosomatic Medicine* 50, 230–44.

Manyande, A., Simon, B., Gettins, D., Stanford, S. C., et al. (1995). Preoperative rehearsal of active coping imagery influences subjective and hormonal responses to abdominal surgery. *Psychosomatic Medicine* 57, 177–82.

Mathews, A. and Ridgeway, V. (1981). Personality and surgical recovery: a review. *British Journal of Clinical Psychology* 20, 243–60.

Mathews, A. and Ridgeway, V. (1984). Psychological preparation for surgery. In A. Steptoe and A. Mathews, eds., *Health Care and Human Behaviour*. London: Academic Press, 231–59.

Melamed, B. G. (1974). *Ethan has an operation* [Film]. In Cleveland, OH: Western Reserve University, Health Sciences Communication Center.

Melamed, B. G. (1984). Health intervention: collaboration for health and science. In B. L. Hammonds and C. J. Scheier, eds., *Psychology and Health, Master Lecture Series*, vol. 3. Washington, DC: American Psychological Association.

Melamed, B. G. and Siegal, L. J. (1975). Reduction of anxiety in children facing hospitalisation and surgery by use of filmed modelling. *Journal of Consulting and Clinical Psychology* 43, 511–21.

Miller, S. (1992). Monitoring and blunting in the face of threat: implications for adaptation and health. In L. Montada, S. Filipp and M. J. Lerner, eds., *Life Crises and Experiences of Loss in Adulthood*. Hillsdale, NJ: Lawrence Erlbaum, 255–73.

Moore, F. D. (1976). La maladie post-opératoire: is there order in variety? *Surgical Clinics of North America* 56, 803–15.

Mumford, E., Schlesinger, H. J. and Glass, G. V. (1982). The effects of psychological intervention on recovery from surgery and heart attacks: an analysis of the literature. *American Journal of Public Health* 72, 141–51.

Munafò, M. R. and Stevenson, J. (2001). Anxiety and surgical recovery: reinterpreting the literature. *Journal of Psychosomatic Research* 51, 589–96.

Murphy, F., Bentley, S., Ellis, B. W. and Dudley, H. (1977). Sleep deprivation in patients undergoing operation: a factor in the stress of surgery. *British Medical Journal* 2, 1521–2.

Prokop, C. K., Bradley, L. A., Burish, T. G., Anderson, K. O. and Fox, J. E. (1991). Psychological preparation for stressful medical and dental procedures. In C. K. Prokop and L. A. Bradley, eds., *Health Psychology: Clinical Methods and Research*. New York: Macmillan, 159–96.

Pollock, R. E., Lotzova, E. and Stanford, S. D. (1991). Mechanism of surgical stress impairment of human perioperative natural killer cell cytotoxicity. *Archives of Surgery* 126, 338–42.

Salmon, P. and Hall, G. M. (1997). A theory of postoperative fatigue: an interaction of biological, psychological, and social processes. *Pharmacology, Biochemistry and Behavior* 56, 623–8.

Salomaki, T. E., Leppaluoto, J., Laitinen, J. O., Vuolteenaho, O. and Nuutinen, L. S. (1993). Epidural versus intravenous fentanyl for reducing hormonal, metabolic, and physiologic responses after thoracotomy. *Anesthesiology* 79, 672–9.

Scheier, M. F., Matthews, K. A., Owens, J. F., Magovern, G. J., Sr., et al. (1989). Dispositional optimism and recovery from coronary artery bypass surgery: the beneficial effects on physical and psychological well-being. *Journal of Personality and Social Psychology* 57, 1024–40.

Selye, H., ed. (1980). *Guide to Stress Research*. New York: Van Nostrand.

Slangen, K., Krohne, H. W., Stellrecht, S. and Kleemann, P. P. (1993). Dimensionen perioperativer Belastung und ihre Auswirkungen auf intra- und postoperative Anpassung von Chirurgiepatienten. *Zeitschrift für Gesundheitspsychologie* 1, 123–42.

Spielberger, C. D., Auerbach, S. M., Wadsworth, A. P., Dunn, T. M. and Taulbee, E. S. (1973). Emotional reactions to surgery. *Journal of Consulting and Clinical Psychology* 40, 33–8.

Suls, J. and Wan, C. K. (1989). Effects of sensory and procedural information on coping with stressful medical procedures and pain: a meta-analysis. *Journal of Consulting and Clinical Psychology* 57, 372–9.

Tonnessen, E., Brinklov, M. M., Christensen, N. J., Olesen, A. S. and Madsen T. (1987). Natural killer cell activity and lymphocyte function during and after coronary artery bypass grafting in relation to the endocrine stress response. *Anesthesiology* 67, 526–33.

Ulrich, R. S. (1984). View from a window may influence recovery from surgery. *Science* 224, 420–1.

Vögele, C. (1992). Perioperativer Stress. In L. R. Schmidt, ed., *Jahrbuch der Medizinischen Psychologie*, vol. 7. Berlin: Springer, 74–95.

Vögele, C. and Steptoe, A. (1986). Physiological and subjective stress responses in surgical patients. *Journal of Psychosomatic Research* 30, 205–15.

Volicer, B. J., Isenberg, M. and Burns, M. (1977). Medical-surgical differences in hospital stress factors. *Journal of Human Stress* 3, 3–13.

Weinman, J. and Johnston, M. (1988). Stressful medical procedures: an analysis of the effects of psychological interventions and of the stressfulness of the procedures. In S. Maes, P. Defares, I. G. Sarason and C. D. Spielberger, eds., *Topics in Health Psychology*. Chichester: Wiley, 205–17.

Chapter Thirteen

PRIMARY PREVENTION

Brian Oldenburg and Nicola W. Burton

CHAPTER OUTLINE

Primary prevention aims to prevent the occurrence and reduce the incidence of health problems. The science and practice of health psychology has made a significant contribution to primary prevention by generating many of the theories and models that have provided an important link between understanding the modifiable determinants of disease and health, and strategies for promoting health and preventing disease. This chapter discusses the key concepts underlying primary prevention, including the aims, rationale, approaches, targets and settings. A significant proportion of the global burden of morbidity and mortality is preventable, and there is an available evidence base to support such interventions. Primary prevention can target individuals and populations, and can be conducted in a variety of settings such as primary health care, schools, worksites and communities. To address current and future global health challenges, health psychology and primary prevention will need to adopt more socio-ecological ways of thinking about health and human behaviour, and utilize innovative multi-level approaches to target a broader array of social, environmental and economic influences across the human life-course. These approaches can be strengthened and made more sustainable by creating linkage systems and partnerships between traditional health providers and a range of other organizations in the community.

KEY CONCEPTS

community-based interventions/trials	prevention
ecological theory	prevention paradox
health promotion	primary care settings
individual/clinical/high risk approach	programme dose/intensity
inter-sectoral partnerships	programme reach/coverage
life-course factors	public health
lifestyle modification	risk factors
medical model	school-based health promotion
multi-level interventions	tailored interventions
population-based	worksite health promotion
preventable morbidity/mortality	

WHAT IS PRIMARY PREVENTION?

An important distinction is often made between primary, secondary and tertiary levels of prevention and management of poor health and disability. Primary prevention refers to strategies to prevent the occurrence of poor health in individuals, and thereby reduce the incidence of these conditions in the population. Primary prevention targets people who have no signs or symptoms of a condition, with the aim of preventing the condition from developing in as many individuals as possible. Examples of primary prevention strategies include vaccination to limit infectious disease, legislation mandating the wearing of seat-belts to reduce rates of death and injury associated with motor vehicle crashes, and community-wide media campaigns to discourage people from smoking to reduce the incidence of lung cancer and coronary heart disease. Primary prevention is not just relevant to physical disease, as the concepts and methods can apply similarly to a range of social and mental health problems such as depression, domestic violence, child abuse, unplanned pregnancy, suicide, injury and substance abuse.

Primary prevention can be directed at individuals, families, communities and whole populations. At the level of the individual, family or small group, primary prevention typically involves directly or indirectly influencing lifestyle practices or health behaviours. At the level of settings or organizations – such as workplace, schools or health-care organizations – primary prevention may involve the introduction of particular services or policies or programmes aimed at promoting health. At a broader, community-wide and societal level, primary prevention typically involves multiple strategies and the use of media and other communication strategies, as well as changes to environments, government policies, regulations and legislation.

Effective primary prevention at a national level has the potential to improve life expectancy as well as health-related quality of life. Such improvements can significantly reduce the demands placed on the health-care system and associated costs. For example, people who regularly participate in physical activity live significantly longer than those who are sedentary, and have a lower risk of mortality from coronary heart disease, diabetes mellitus and all causes (Vuori, 1998). In addition, active individuals may be better able to perform activities of daily living, and have improved psychological well-being, self-esteem, social skills and self-image (Vuori, 1998). Direct health-care costs attributable to physical inactivity have been estimated as US$24 billion or 2.4 per cent of the US health-care expenditure (Colditz, 1999). Indirect health-care costs, associated with lost productivity, and intangible costs, in terms of reduction of quality of life due to pain, disability, bereavement, anxiety and suffering, are difficult to cost, and perhaps even greater.

At a global level, primary prevention has contributed to marked improvements in life expectancy, from 40 to 63 years during 1950–90 in developing countries (World Bank, 1993). In developed countries, the dramatic reduction in deaths due to cardiovascular disease over the past 40 years has been attributed, at least in part, to primary prevention efforts to influence lifestyle risk behaviours such as tobacco smoking (Winett, King & Altman, 1989). Virtually every major advance in public health has been associated with reducing risk factors to promote health – from prevention targeting sanitation and drinking water through to immunization and environmental legislation.

Primary versus secondary and tertiary prevention

In contrast to primary prevention, secondary and tertiary prevention involve strategies to manage conditions that have already developed in individuals. Secondary prevention (or early detection) aims to identify and intervene with people at the early stage of a condition or disease, so as to slow its progression, lessen its duration, or prevent it from developing into a more serious condition. An example of this type of prevention is screening tests to facilitate the early identification and treatment of cancer. Tertiary prevention (or rehabilitation) involves reducing the complications and minimizing the disability and suffering associated with poor health. For example, physiotherapy rehabilitation programmes for people with injuries aim to improve physical functioning and promote recovery. Medical care typically adopts a tertiary approach to prevention, because of its 'curative' focus. However, medical care is not limited to tertiary prevention, and can include primary and secondary prevention activities, such as immunization and screening.

Kaplan (2000) notes that primary prevention is typically based on a socio-behavioural rather than a disease model – medical diagnosis and treatment play a lesser role, as there is no condition to diagnose and treat. In contrast, secondary and tertiary prevention are typically based on a bio-medical model that involves diagnosis and treatment of an existing condition. This also has implications for the role of individuals in such programmes, because with secondary and tertiary prevention, the participant is often the passive recipient of advice or treatment within the health-care system. However, with primary prevention, the individual is recruited as an active participant in their health (Winett, 1995).

Table 13.1 The relationship between primary, secondary and tertiary levels of prevention

	Primary Prevention	Secondary prevention	Tertiary prevention
Target group:	• Healthy individuals	• Individuals at risk or with early stages of a condition	• Individuals with the condition
Aim:	• Prevent occurrence • Reduce incidence	• Prevent progression • Slow progression • Minimize duration	• Minimize complications • Optimize functioning • Minimize recurrence • Reduce disability
Strategies:	• Promote healthy behaviours, healthy lifestyle, healthy environment, and healthy public policy	• Screening • Early detection • Early intervention • Risk reduction	• Rehabilitation • Reduce psychological, social, physical distress • Enhance support networks • Enhance self-management

While the three levels of prevention are conceptually distinct, in practice the boundaries between them are often unclear, and a coordinated prevention programme can incorporate all three levels. For example, to prevent cardiovascular disease, primary prevention strategies can be used to reduce population rates of risk factors such as physical inactivity, smoking and poor nutrition. Secondary prevention might involve screening for and early detection of hypertension followed by pharmacological treatment. Tertiary prevention would include cardiac rehabilitation programmes to improve physical functioning and minimize the physical, psychological and social sequelae of cardiac events. Programmes can also be used to encourage other family members – for example, the patient's children – to address health behaviours that might place them at increased risk of heart disease when they become adults. The relationship between primary, secondary and tertiary levels of prevention is summarized in table 13.1.

Primary prevention and health psychology

Health psychology . . . the aggregate of the special educational, scientific, and professional contributions of the discipline of psychology to the promotion and maintenance of health, the prevention and treatment of illness, and the identification of the etiologic and diagnostic correlates of health, illness, and related dysfunction. (Matarazzo 1980: 815)

From this definition, it is clear that health psychology can make a valuable contribution to the design, implementation and evaluation of primary prevention. Traditionally, health psychology has focused more on the psychological and social aspects surrounding the treatment and management of poor health, rather than a primary prevention approach. However, the emergence of the fields of behavioural health and behavioural medicine from the late 1970s through to the 1990s facilitated the link between health psychology and primary prevention, with a specific focus on targeting key health behaviours such as smoking, sedentariness and dietary behaviours. This followed the steady increase in evidence emanating from the large prospective epidemiologic studies related to heart disease, cancer and other conditions, following the Second World War. This evidence base began with the landmark study that investigated the relationship between British doctors' smoking habits and disease (Doll & Hill, 1964); the first reports from the Framingham Study that identified a number of 'risk factors' for cardiovascular disease (Kannel & Gordon, 1968); the United States Surgeon General's Report on Smoking and Health (US State Surgeon General's Advisory Committee, 1964), and the Lalonde report (Lalonde, 1974) and the Alameda County study (Belloc & Breslow, 1972) that identified the importance of environmental factors as influences on health. Collectively, these studies enhanced our understanding of the interplay of biological, psychological, behavioural, social and environmental factors associated with the development and pathogenesis of many different diseases and conditions and opportunities for prevention.

Primary prevention almost always involves behaviour change, and therefore incorporates behavioural theories and interventions. The social and behavioural sciences, including health psychology, have generated many of the theories and models that have provided an important link between understanding the modifiable determinants of disease and health, and the development, implementation and evaluation of strategies for disease prevention and health promotion (Oldenburg, 2001). There is an increasingly strong evidence base regarding the association between a range of health and social problems and psycho-social factors, such as a sense of control, social support networks, personal resilience, family environment and chronic stress (Gochman, 1997). Some of the theories that have been used most frequently in the field of primary prevention include Social Cognitive Theory, the Health Belief Model, Health Locus of Control, Protection Motivation Theory and the Theory of Reasoned Action and Planned Behaviour (see Conner & Norman, 1996; Glanz, Lewis & Rimer, 2002). As noted by Winett et al.,

> the health psychology field brings with it a rigorous scientific method for understanding human behaviour, a tradition of delineating the individual contexts of health and disease, and a burgeoning armamentarium of techniques and approaches for modifying behaviour and enhancing motivation and learning. (1989: 27–8)

A number of large primary prevention trials targeting health risk factors for cardiovascular disease have been based on concepts and principles derived from these theories. The Stanford Three Community Study (Farquhar & Maccoby, 1977) demonstrated the feasibility and effectiveness of mass media-based educational campaigns and achieved significant reductions in cholesterol and fat intake. The Minnesota Heart

Health Project (Mittelmark, Luepker & Jacobs, 1986), the Pawtucket Heart Health Programme (Lefebvre et al., 1987) and the Stanford Five-city Project (Farquhar et al., 1990) used interventions aimed at raising public awareness of risk factors for coronary heart disease (cholesterol, obesity, cigarette smoking), and changing risk behaviours through education of health professionals and environmental change programmes such as grocery store and restaurant food labelling.

The North Karelia Project in Finland (Puska et al., 1995) was initiated in response to research demonstrating that Finland had one of the highest rates of heart disease in the world. The prevention strategies were broad, diverse and multi-level, and included tobacco taxation and related restrictions, televised instruction in skills for non-smoking and vegetable growing, and extensive organization and networking to build an education and advocacy organization. Results indicated significant reductions in smoking, systolic blood pressure and cholesterol between 1972 and 1997 (Vartianen et al., 2000), and a decline in cardiovascular disease mortality in Finland by 55 per cent among men and 68 per cent among women between 1972 and 1992, which was primarily attributed to dietary change (Pietinen et al., 1996).

THE CONTEXT FOR PREVENTION: CHANGING PATTERNS OF HEALTH AND ILLNESS

The past 100 years have included significant changes in global patterns of health, disease and death. In the last 40 years, life expectancy has increased more than any other time in human history, with an average 20-year increase in developing countries, and a 50 per cent decline in the number of children dying before 5 years of age (World Health Organization, 1999). Developed countries have seen a decline in the proportion of deaths due to communicable and infectious diseases, such as smallpox and cholera, and a marked increase in non-communicable diseases, particularly chronic diseases such as heart disease and diabetes. These changing patterns of health and illness provide the context for primary prevention, by indicating the major health challenges yet to be addressed, and the proportion of disease burden that is potentially preventable.

Major health challenges for prevention

In developing countries, major health problems continue to include childhood and infectious diseases, under-nutrition and complications of childbirth. Maternal conditions, HIV/AIDS and tuberculosis are three of the major causes of disease burden for adults in developing countries (World Health Organization, 1999). Major contributors to loss of healthy life include childhood and maternal underweight, unsafe sex, unsafe water, sanitation and hygiene, indoor smoke from solid fuels and micronutrient deficiencies (Ezzati et al., 2002). Among children, diarrhoea, acute respiratory infections, malaria, measles and peri-natal conditions account for 21 per cent of all deaths in developing countries, compared to 1 per cent in developed countries (World Health Organization, 1999).

In both developing and developed countries, the incidence and prevalence of non-communicable disease is rapidly increasing. In the early 1990s, ischaemic heart disease and cerebro-vascular disease were identified as the leading causes of mortality, together accounting for 21 per cent of all deaths in the world (World Health Organization, 1999). In high income countries, 81 per cent of the disease burden in 1998 was attributable to non-communicable diseases, in particular, cardiovascular disease, malignant neoplasms and mental health conditions such as depression, with alcohol use being one of the leading identified causes of disability (World Health Organization, 1999). Tobacco, high blood pressure and high cholesterol are also major causes of disease burden (Ezzati et al., 2002).

Injuries are a significant and neglected cause of health problems, accounting for 18 per cent of the global burden of disease (World Health Organization, 1999). In high income countries, road traffic accidents and self-inflicted injuries, such as suicide, are among the 10 leading causes of disease burden (World Health Organization, 1999). In less developed countries, road traffic accidents are the most significant cause of injuries, and war, violence and self-inflicted injuries are among the leading causes of lost years of healthy life (World Health Organization, 1999).

The Global Burden of Disease Study has projected future patterns of mortality and disease burden (Murray & Lopez, 1997). Non-communicable diseases are expected to account for an increasing proportion of disease burden, rising from 43 per cent in 1998 to 73 per cent in 2020. HIV will become one of the 10 leading causes of mortality and disability; in some African countries, it has been the major contributor to life expectancy declining by 10 years and infant death rates doubling in recent years. The leading causes of disease burden will include in descending order: ischaemic heart disease, depression, road traffic accidents, cerebro-vascular disease, chronic obstructive pulmonary disease, lower respiratory infections, tuberculosis, war injuries, diarrhoeal disease and HIV.

Preventable morbidity and mortality

All of these major health challenges are preventable to a large degree. At least 2 million children around the world die each year from diseases for which vaccines are available (World Health Organization, 1999), and in one year, over 3 million children in developing countries will die as a result of being underweight, while half a million people in North America and Europe will die from obesity-related conditions (World Health Organization, 2002). There already exists a body of knowledge and experience regarding the preventability of conditions such as depression, substance abuse, injuries, drowning, HIV/AIDS, diabetes and cardiovascular disease. Furthermore, many conditions share common risk factors (World Health Organization, 2000). Tobacco use is one common and modifiable risk factor, and is predicted to cause more premature death and disability than any single disease, with a projected increase in mortality from 3 million deaths in 1990 to more than 8 million deaths in 2020 (World Health Organization, 1999).

In an attempt to quantify the extent of preventable disease burden, McGinnis and Foege (1993) identified and quantified the major social, behavioural and environmental factors that contribute to premature death. They calculated that approximately half of all deaths that occurred in the United States in 1990 could be attributed to the preventable factors of tobacco (an estimated 400,000 deaths), diet and activity patterns (300,000), alcohol (100,000), microbial agents (90,000), toxic agents (60,000), fire-arms (35,000), sexual behaviour (30,000), motor vehicles (25,000), and illicit use of drugs (20,000). A similar situation exists in Australia, with a significant proportion of total disease burden attributable to tobacco use (12 per cent), physical inactivity (7 per cent), overweight (4 per cent), inadequate fruit and vegetable intake (3 per cent), alcohol consumption (2.2 per cent), illicit drug use (2.2 per cent), occupational exposure to toxins (1.6 per cent) and unsafe sex (1 per cent) (Mathers, Vos & Stevenson, 1999).

The World Health Organization Report (World Health Organization, 2000) identifies the top 10 major preventable risks globally as: childhood and maternal underweight; unsafe sex; high blood pressure; tobacco; alcohol; unsafe water, sanitation and hygiene; high cholesterol; indoor smoke from solid fuels; iron deficiency and overweight/obesity. Together, these factors account for about 40 per cent of the 56 million deaths that occur world-wide annually and one-third of global loss of healthy life years (World Health Organization, 2000). If all of these preventable risks could be addressed as WHO recommends (which is acknowledged as a highly ambitious goal), healthy lifespans could increase an average of 10 years in developing countries and 5 years in developed countries (World Health Organization, 2000).

The current and future global trends in disease and health, the identification of how much of this disease burden may be preventable, and the relatively small number of risks accounting for a large proportion of global death and disability provides a persuasive case for primary prevention. While the clinical management of disease and illness is important, the potential global health gains from primary prevention are clearly substantial.

APPROACHES TO PREVENTION

During the twentieth century, approaches to prevention have evolved through a number of overlapping phases (Labonte, 1992). Traditional prevention focused on individuals' medical factors and behavioural risk factors, while more contemporary prevention focuses on populations and social, ecological and life-course factors.

Medical and healthy lifestyle approaches

The medical approach to prevention was dominant for much of the twentieth century and was very much influenced by the 'disease treatment' model. This approach focused on preventing disease by correcting medically defined or physiological risk factors in individuals. Pharmacological treatment was a common component of such preventive efforts, such as anti-hypertensive medication to reduce incidence of coronary heart disease.

The healthy lifestyle approach was dominant in the 1970s and 1980s, and focused on behavioural risk factors such as smoking, physical inactivity, poor nutrition and diet, and excessive alcohol intake for the prevention of chronic conditions such as heart disease and cancer. This focus on behavioural risk factors became an integral component of many of the landmark community-based prevention programmes conducted in North America, Europe and Australasia, a number of which have already been referred to in this chapter.

Socio-environmental and ecological approaches

The latter years of the twentieth century saw the evolution of socio-environmental and ecological approaches to prevention. These followed on from more complex and sophisticated multi-level social and behavioural epidemiological research demonstrating that individuals' lifestyle and health behaviours were in turn influenced by their family, social and work environments, as well as broader economic and cultural circumstances (Sallis & Owen, 2002). These approaches have led to an increased focus on improving people's environments in which they live, work and play. Examples of such strategies include:

- modifying urban design to enhance street connectivity and include walking paths, to encourage people to walk/bicycle and reduce sedentariness;
- restricting the location of tobacco vending machines and alcohol in areas where young people are likely to be unsupervised so as to reduce illegal use and abuse;
- increasing the amount of natural and structural shade available for sun protection in public recreation areas to reduce the incidence of UV radiation and melanomas;
- ensuring the provision of safe drinking water and appropriate levels of sanitation in remote or developing communities to reduce the incidence of associated disease.

Life-course approaches

As a result of studies on the associations between early life experiences and adult outcomes (e.g. Hertzman et al., 2001; Wadsworth & Kuh, 1997), increasing attention is being given to prevention strategies that incorporate a life-course or lifespan perspective (e.g. Eming Young, 2002; Shonkoff & Meisles, 2000). This approach acknowledges that early life influences have a major impact on health behaviours and health outcomes across the lifespan, and is based on three key conceptual models of human health and development:

- *critical or sensitive periods* during which certain exposures or environmental conditions are necessary for optimal subsequent growth and development (e.g. Nelson, 2000). This model highlights the potential for prevention around key developmental or life transition stages.
- *pathways or cumulative exposures*, which emphasize the accumulation of life circumstances that determine subsequent outcomes. This model highlights that interventions targeting generic risk or protective factors have the potential for widespread positive later life benefits (e.g. Power & Hertzman, 1997).
- *ecological contexts* which emphasize the settings in which individuals develop, such as the family, early childhood settings, schools, communities and the broader socio-economic-political environment (e.g. Bronfenbrenner, 1979; Garbarino & Ganzel, 2000). This model identifies the need to move outside the health sector for delivery of prevention programmes.

Prevention programmes can therefore target influential early life experiences in order to reduce the incidence of poor health outcomes in later life. Examples of these early life influences include:

- childhood overweight and obesity, which is associated with adult obesity, type II diabetes, cardiovascular disease, and some cancers (Deitz, 1998);
- behavioural risk factors including poor eating habits, cigarette smoking, and alcohol and other drug misuse, which have negative health implications in later life (e.g. cancer, cardiovascular disease, liver disease, mental health disorders) (Williams, 1992);
- behavioural and emotional problems, such as conduct disorder, depression and anxiety, which are associated with later life outcomes that include poor educational attainment, relationship difficulties, welfare dependency, delinquency and suicide (Constantino, 1992);
- unfavourable family situations, such as inadequate or abusive care-giving, which have been associated with poor physical health outcomes (Felitti et al., 1998), as well as poor social development, poor mental health, relationship difficulties, and abusive care-giving in the next generation (Osofsky & Thompson, 2000).

Life-course prevention research is increasingly focusing on socio-economic disadvantage and health inequalities (Graham, 2002). This is particularly relevant for indigenous children, children from rural and remote areas, and children disadvantaged by parental unemployment, poor education, low income or single parent status; these children experience a range of poor health and well-being outcomes at higher rates than their more advantaged peers.

Multi-level prevention

Acknowledging the potential gain from each of these different approaches, comprehensive prevention should include strategies aimed directly at individuals, as well as strategies aimed at positively influencing the broad array of social, environmental, economic and life-course factors that in turn influence individuals and their health. This multi-level approach highlights that prevention strategies are not the sole responsibility of the medical or health sector. Table 13.2 provides examples of some of the different foci for primary prevention activities.

Targets for Primary Prevention

Primary prevention programmes can be directed at individuals and/or populations. The following section summarizes a discussion by Rose (1994) on the strengths and limitations of these two approaches. In any population, most people have a mild to moderate level of risk factors, and a minority have a high level. Consequently a comprehensive prevention programme needs to blend synergistically strategies aimed at reducing risk factor levels in the population as a whole, with strategies directed at high risk individuals (World Health Organization, 2000).

Individual or 'high risk' approach

Many primary prevention programmes in health psychology have adopted a clinical or individually focused approach, and targeted individuals at risk of ill health. Typically involving individual or group counselling sessions, programmes have aimed to either reduce the level of risk or provide protection against the effects of the risk, such as psycho-education programmes on safe sex practices for individuals at risk of HIV.

The advantage of this approach is that it is relevant to the individuals involved, and there is limited interference with those who are not specifically at risk. This can facilitate a cost-effective use of resources; programmes reach those who are most likely to benefit, thereby maximizing the cost–benefit ratio. However, prevention often becomes very medical or clinical, and success may be temporary or localized. People are labelled as 'high risk' and may be subsequently stigmatized. The individual can become the focus of blame, and the contributing role of additional factors, such as social and environmental influences, is less likely to be acknowledged. This approach is also limited by our poor ability to predict health outcomes. For example, 'high risk' individuals with multiple cardiac risk factors may not necessarily experience a cardiac event, and 'low risk' individuals with few cardiac risk factors can still develop heart disease. Finally, there are difficulties with feasibility and costs. High risk interventions necessitate identification of high risk individuals or groups, which may be costly and compromise personal privacy, such as identifying individuals with potentially lethal genes or genes associated with socially undesirable conditions.

Population approach

In contrast, population-based prevention targets the whole or large sections of the population. Strategies aim to reduce the average levels of risk in the whole community

Table 13.2 Multi-level foci for prevention

Foci	Concept	Prevention example
Individual development and life-course	Optimizes the early life conditions and developmental settings associated with health and well being in later life	Smoking/substance use cessation programmes for pregnant women to reduce low birth weight and associated developmental delays
Modifying individuals' behavioural risk factors	Assist people to develop the knowledge, attitudes and skills they need to make healthy lifestyle choices	Educational programmes to explain healthy nutrition and demonstrate healthy cooking practices to reduce incidence of obesity
Strengthening individuals and families	Recognizes the inextricable health links between people and their social environment	Child management programmes for parents to reduce the incidence of conduct disorders and child abuse
Improving living and working conditions	Recognizes the inextricable health links between people and their physical environment	Organizational change to improve working conditions and reduce hazardous exposures
Strengthening communities for health	Effective community action in setting priorities, planning strategies and their implementation for health outcomes	Establishment of safe play areas for children to reduce incidence of injury; neighbourhood watch programmes to reduce incidence of crime
Creating macro-level social and economic policies: economic, welfare, health, housing, transport, taxation etc.	Puts health on the agenda of policy-makers in all sectors and at all levels, directing them to be aware of the health consequences of their decisions	Education and training policies to alleviate unemployment, especially for disadvantaged groups; redistribution of wealth through progressive taxation
Improving the health-care system and associated services	Health services to become engaged in providing primary prevention	Providing financial incentives to health-care providers to provide prevention programmes related to smoking, nutrition, physical inactivity and alcohol consumption

by targeting the conditions that contribute to problems at the individual level. Examples of population-level prevention strategies in oral health and nutrition include fluoridation of the water supply to reduce dental caries, and food fortification to improve nutrition. Population-based approaches usually involve multi-level strategies targeting individuals, groups and settings. Tobacco control measures are a common example, incorporating non-smoking policies, regulations controlling relevant advertising, and legislation of various kinds, as well as smoking cessation activities for individuals and groups.

Population prevention strategies have the advantage of being radical and powerful. They move beyond individual blame for ill health and adopt a broader focus on the determinants of health by acknowledging the social, environmental and cultural context in which people live. However, population prevention strategies can be limited by their acceptability, feasibility, costs and safety. Widespread strategies, such as water fluoridation, may compromise individual choice. Large-scale interventions require extensive resources, often for small gains, and these costs are often 'up-front' against a future possibility where the potential benefits are delayed or uncertain. The time taken to implement widespread prevention programmes and see a resultant change in outcomes is typically long and drawn out. Finally, although there is a potential benefit to the population, there may also be risks to individuals. For example, although widespread immunization can contribute to the decline of infectious diseases in the population, there is also the risk of negative reactions, including death, in a small proportion of individuals.

The prevention paradox

An important distinction between these two prevention approaches is the degree of change at the individual versus the population level (Rose, 1994). The high risk approach, while likely to deliver much more clinically significant benefits to the individual, is less significant at a population level because fewer individuals are affected. In contrast, the population approach may bring about a small mean change in individuals, but, if achieved by a large number of people, has the potential to impact much more significantly on disease rates in the whole population. This is the prevention paradox; a preventive measure that brings large benefits to the community offers little to each participating individual.

SETTINGS FOR PRIMARY PREVENTION

Primary prevention can occur in many different settings, including primary health care, worksites, schools and community contexts such as clubs and voluntary organizations. The following section provides an example of and considers the rationale for and limitations of primary prevention within each of these settings.

Primary health care

Primary health care represents a convenient setting for opportunistic prevention, as in most developed countries primary care practitioners represent the first point of contact with the health-care system, and are responsible for on-going care (Oldenburg et al., 1996). In this setting, both the roles and expectations of the practitioners and the patients are conducive to preventing disease and promoting health; practitioners can offer preventive advice and services, and are often identified as credible and preferred sources of such information (Oldenburg et al., 1996).

The Guide to Clinical Preventive Services (US Preventive Services Taskforce, 1996) provides a comprehensive assessment of strategies and interventions for topics that can be appropriately targeted for prevention in the primary health-care setting. Instructional strategies involve the provision of information on the disease process, risk factors and health-enhancing change. Motivational strategies encourage attitudinal change and increase readiness for change. Behavioural approaches aim to modify risk practices, and can be complemented with self-help materials such as books and videos. Appropriate topics for prevention include tobacco use, physical activity, low back pain, gynaecological cancers, dental disease and household and recreational injuries. A meta-analysis of primary prevention trials in clinical settings reported that patient education and counselling for behaviours such as smoking/alcohol use, weight/nutrition, and other behaviours produced quite substantial effects (mean effect sizes 0.5–0.6), with larger effects associated with using behavioural techniques, particularly self-monitoring, and using several communication channels, e.g. media plus personal communication (Mullen et al., 1997).

The Patient-centred Assessment and Counseling on Exercise plus Nutrition (PACE+) Programme is an intervention based in primary care settings to help patients change physical activity and dietary behaviours (Calfas et al., 2002). Patients attending their provider completed computerized screening and assessment and created a tailored action plan to change one behaviour that they then discussed with their provider, who employed brief, behaviourally based counselling. Patients then received follow-up by either mail or telephone. After four months, patients demonstrated improved behaviours in terms of physical activity stage of change, dietary fat, fruit/vegetable intake and over eating behaviours (Calfas et al., 2002).

There are some specific barriers associated with implementing prevention programmes in primary care settings (Oldenburg et al., 1996). Firstly, primary health care tends to be oriented more towards curative care (tertiary prevention) rather than preventive care. As such, primary health-care providers often lack the required behavioural sciences skills and training, and may have mistaken or unrealistic expectations about the efficacy of prevention programmes. Primary health-care providers are often challenged by time constraints, and a lack of incentives to provide preventive services. Depending on the structure of the health-care system, primary health care can also be isolated from other relevant health-care organizations, and be limited by a general lack of resources and referral systems to support preventive services.

Because of these barriers, there is often a gap between evidence-based guidelines for prevention and practice. Learning principles that have been shown to increase effectiveness, such as rewards and feedback, are often not or not adequately applied, and too few interventions focus on possibilities to facilitate desired behaviour, such as reminders, financial stimuli and skills improvement (Kok, van den Borne & Mullen, 1997). A review of interventions to improve the implementation of prevention activities in primary care concluded that there is no evidence to indicate the efficacy of particular strategies to improve prevention implementation such as group education, physician reminders and multi-faceted interventions (Hulscher et al., 2001). While effective interventions to increase prevention in primary care existed, there was considerable variation in the level of change achieved, with only small to moderate effect sizes (Hulscher et al., 2001).

Worksites

The attributes of workplace settings can shape the health and behaviour patterns of individuals. Historically, worksite prevention programmes have tended to focus on safety initiatives, such as reducing injury-related hazards and exposure to harmful substances. More recently, programmes have focused on the characteristics of the workplace that are relevant for promoting health and preventing chronic disease. For example, sedentary occupations may increase physical inactivity; poor implementation of non-smoking policies in work areas can increase passive smoking; and the provision of high calorie and high fat food choices in staff food services may make it difficult to adhere to healthy dietary recommendations. Primary prevention strategies in this setting therefore focus on creating healthy policies and supportive environments, as well as targeting individuals. Because a substantial proportion of the adult population is employed, and because most individuals spend a third of their day at work, workplace programmes have the potential to reach many people, and programme exposure can be substantial (Oldenburg & Harris, 1996).

The Australian National Workplace Health Project aimed to promote health via strategies targeting physical activity, smoking, alcohol consumption, and fruit, vegetable and fat consumption (Simpson et al., 2000). A socio-behavioural intervention involved tailored individual counselling and self-instructional material supplemented by group education sessions aimed at increased awareness of benefits, increased self-efficacy, increased social support and reduced perception of barriers. An environmental intervention aimed to modify key aspects of the physical, information and policy environment. Strategies for the physical environment to encourage healthy eating included the placing of posters at strategic points around the workplace and adding low fat, high fibre food choices to vending machines. Strategies for the information environment included point-of-purchase messages about healthy food choices and take-home messages for healthy lunch tips in employees' pay slips. Strategies for policy level involved consideration of existing policies relating to employee health and the inclusion of specific statements about providing access to healthy food choices.

Outcomes of the programme included an increase and improvement in health-related policies, increased employee perceptions of positive changes to the workplace environment and support from the worksite, but no significant changes in health behaviours.

Most employers can only afford to devote organizational resources to prevention programmes when this provides some benefit to the organization. Three main organizational motives for prevention are to reduce medical costs, enhance productivity and/or enhance the company image (O'Donnell & Harris, 1994). Economic and productivity costs of ill health are common arguments for worksite programmes, however the imprecision in estimating such costs often leads to an overstating of likely economic benefits (Shephard, 2002). Additionally, few worksite studies have provided definitive evidence that primary prevention is a cost-effective means of improving long-term health outcomes and decreasing health-care costs. The dollar value of many indirect benefits of such initiatives, such as social and emotional functioning, is also difficult to cost (Shephard, 2002). Many worksite programmes are adversely influenced by poor employee participation and high rates of attrition, which can be associated with a myriad of employee-related and worksite-related factors (Oldenburg & Harris, 1996). Shephard (2002) reports that in the case of worksite exercise programmes, initial recruitment is likely to be no more than one-third of employees, with as many as half dropping out. Programmes typically enrol individuals who are more committed to a healthy lifestyle (Lerman & Shemer, 1996).

The challenge for worksite-based programmes is to have high reach and sufficient programme exposure, without adversely affecting productivity or profits (Oldenburg & Harris, 1996). Participation of employees, employers and relevant stakeholders, such as union representatives, during the planning, implementation and evaluation process is essential to gain programme support and commitment. However, encouragement by senior personnel can also be interpreted as coercion and compromising individuals' rights to an unhealthy lifestyle (Shephard, 2002). Prevention initiatives and strategies need to be seen as relevant to all participants, and at all levels of management. Prevention programmes need to identify strategies to gain and maintain access to the worksite, build support within the workplace, and develop and win the commitment of employees (e.g. Harris, Oldenburg & Owen, 1999). Finally, any individual changes are unlikely to be sustained without a supportive environment. Structural changes to the wider worksite environment, such as workplace smoking bans, establish cues supportive of change and build social support. However, research evidence on the effectiveness of environmental and structural changes is still only emerging. (See also Chapter 15, this volume.)

Schools

Schools provide an established setting for reaching children, adolescents and their families, to address age-pertinent health issues such as child behaviour problems, smoking, teenage pregnancy and substance use. Schools also have trained staff, policies and environments that can support interventions. The most basic prevention programmes are education based, such as providing instruction in health-related practices as part of the curriculum to target health-related knowledge and attitudes. These programmes have the advantage of seeming highly consistent with the educational focus of schools. Adopting a more comprehensive approach, school-based strategies can also target the physical environment, social reinforcement, peer leaders, social norms, service provision (e.g. food service, medical service) and local ordinances.

The Child and Adolescent Trial for Cardiovascular Health (CATCH) was a multi-site, randomized, controlled field trial to assess the outcomes of health behaviour interventions, focusing on the elementary school environment, classroom curricula, and home programmes for the primary prevention of cardiovascular disease (Luepker et al., 1996). Prevention strategies included food service modifications, enhanced physical education, and classroom health curricula. Results of the trial indicated the CATCH intervention was able to modify the fat content of school lunches, increase moderate-to-vigorous physical activity in physical education, and improve eating and physical activity behaviours in children during third through fifth grades. A follow-up on the three-year maintenance of improved diet and physical activity indicated that the behavioural changes initiated during the elementary school years persisted to early adolescence for self-reported dietary and physical activity behaviours (Nader et al., 1999).

School-based prevention must be consistent with the organizational structure. The Prevention Education Programme (PEP) in Nuremberg Germany was not able to implement strategies to modify school lunches as done by Luepker et al. (1996) in CATCH, as the school system is different from the United States and other European countries and children usually eat lunch at home (Schwandt et al., 1999). Similarly, the school curriculum did not allow for additional health lessons or physical activity programmes. Prevention activities focused instead on dietary modification via a family-oriented home-based intervention programme involving home visits, provision of advice, and a health curriculum for parents outside of the school.

Another challenge for school-based prevention is that unlike primary health care, health is not the 'core business' of schools. Typically, schools have a detailed and mandated curriculum, and prevention activities can be seen as competing with educational and administrative activities, and disrupting a highly regulated system. Therefore the degree to which prevention programmes are viewed as consistent with the service role of the school will influence the receptiveness and commitment to prevention programmes (Linney, 1989). In the context of the complex ecology of the school, collaboration with the school community is essential, but often consuming and complicated. Prevention programmes require the support of the educational system, school principal, teachers, parents and sometimes the wider community. Furthermore, teachers have a high level of professional autonomy in their classrooms, and therefore can offer a wealth of expertise to the design and implementation of prevention programmes with their students, or compromise the fidelity of a programme (Linney, 1989).

One review of school-based drug prevention programmes identified seven evidence-based quality criteria (Cuijpers, 2002). Programmes should have proven effectiveness, and use interactive delivery methods with participant contact and communication opportunities for the exchange of ideas and encouragement of skills learned. Programmes should be based on the social influence model, and focus on norms, commitment and intention towards the targeted behaviour, and use peer leaders. Programme effectiveness can be increased by adding life-skills training and community-based interventions, such as media campaigns. There was no evidence to support the use of booster sessions, resistance skills training or programme intensity.

Communities

Community-based interventions are associated with the concept of population-attributable risk, which reflects the amount of disease in a population that can be attributed to a given level of exposure (Sorensen, Emmons & Hunt, 1998). If a risk factor is distributed widely in the population, then small changes in a large number of people will yield greater improvements in population-attributable risk than large changes in a small number of high risk individuals (Rose, 1994). Community-based prevention typically targets entire populations using media, policy or legislative action, at a national or governmental level. This is an 'upstream' approach to prevention, where activities target the conditions that contribute to and sustain problems appearing at the individual level, and changing social norms. These programmes demonstrate the feasibility of activating entire groups to promote health and reduce disease. They also emphasize the role of collaborative partnerships among the different sectors in society, and that health care is not the sole responsibility of the medical sector.

The Community Intervention Trial for Smoking Cessation (COMMIT) was a community-level, multi-channel, 4-year intervention to increase quit rates among cigarette smokers in the USA and Canada. COMMIT was launched by the National Institute for Cancer and was designed to work through communities, using existing media channels, major organizations and social institutions capable of influencing smoking behaviour in large groups of people. A comprehensive set of activities was organized around four task forces encompassing health-care providers, worksites and organizations, cessation resources and services, and public education. Intervention activities were adapted and implemented in each community through a local community board. Impacting on more than 200,000 adult smokers, a significant intervention effect was observed among light to moderate smokers (COMMIT Research Group, 1995).

Community-based prevention programmes are implemented in the 'real world' and are therefore subject to 'real world' issues and limitations. Compared to laboratory work, there is less control over programme activities, a massive increase in potential participants, and numerous limitations and restrictions to deal with. Widespread programmes are costly, and require extensive planning, coordination, liaison and monitoring. The challenge is to provide sufficient reach and programme exposure to a group that is geographically and socially diverse – participants are not contained in one area, and are very different among themselves. There is also the challenge to coordinate activities to avoid unnecessary duplication and 'health message overload'. Consequently, consultation and collaboration is required with many stakeholders, which is time consuming. In particular, collaboration with stakeholders not directly involved in health promotion as part of their core business can be challenging. One review of prevention for heart disease, substance abuse, violence and HIV infections in US metropolitan areas reported that many programmes did not involve participants in planning, or tailor for targeted sub-population, thereby limiting their effectiveness (Freudenberg et al., 2000).

Often the results of community-based prevention activities are disappointingly small in comparison to the implementation efforts, which is a significant concern for both programme implementers and their financial sponsors. One reason for this is because of the unrealistic change expectations created by clinical or individual approaches to prevention that can yield greater magnitude of change, although in few individuals. The magnitude of the results of community-based prevention must be judged according to population-level effects; using clinical significance alone as the standard for interpretation of results is inappropriate (Sorenson et al., 1998). Small changes at the individual level may result in large benefits at the population level (Rose, 1994). Secondly, the time necessary for desired and sustained health outcomes to appear and therefore validate community-based prevention programmes may be drawn out, often beyond one generation. However, a majority of programmes do not have the resources to conduct long-term follow-up, and can last for less than one year (Freudenberg et al., 2000). Many diseases, such as coronary heart disease and diabetes, have a long-term pathological process that creates a lag time of many years between the initial risk exposure and symptomatic diagnosis. Therefore, successful changes in risk factor modification arising from prevention activities are difficult to evaluate in terms of their impact on incidence at a population level.

There are several difficulties associated with community-based interventions. The characteristics of the evaluation method can account for much of the heterogeneity in the outcomes of community-based heart health programmes, perhaps more so than the characteristics of the interventions (Sellers et al., 1997). Effective evaluation should be cumulative and long term, multi-level (i.e. individual and community level), and include representative samples as well as measures of process as well as outcomes so as to identify the mediators of change. Community prevention trials have been described as the victims of success from other forms of social interventions, as on-going secular changes can nullify the intervention or render intervention effects undetectable (Susser, 1995). That is, specific prevention programmes may be compromised by other influences occurring simultaneously in the wider community, such as changes in legislation, social norms, taxes and current events. This issue highlights the need for on-going population-based monitoring of key health issues, using standardized measures that allow examination of trends over time and across studies.

CURRENT AND FUTURE ISSUES FOR PRIMARY PREVENTION POLICY, RESEARCH AND PRACTICE

The economics of prevention

Rose (1994) states that there are both humanitarian and economic justifications for prevention. From a humanitarian viewpoint, preventable ill health seems unjust, and good health is more desirable than ill health or death. Economically, ill health impairs earning capacity and productivity, and the costs of medical treatment are high and continually escalating. Intuitively, it therefore seems more efficient to prevent ill health before it arises rather than attempt to fix it after it occurs.

However, the economic argument for prevention often fails to meet short-term health-care expectations. Wide-scale community-based prevention programmes can be very expensive while the gains are often negligible in the short term and at the individual level. Rarely does prevention result in the elimination of ill health, and if it does promote a reduction, this may bring with it a different set of problems. For example, as the life expectancy of a population increases due to a decline in preventable mortality, so does the need for social, medical and welfare services for an ageing population.

Most countries spend only a very small proportion of their health-care budgets on prevention compared to medical care. This is despite evidence that improved medical care accounts for a much smaller proportion of preventable mortality (McGinnis, Williams-Russo & Knickman, 2002), and that the cost of primary prevention can be quite low compared to secondary and tertiary prevention efforts. McGinnis et al. (2002) note that 10–15 per cent of preventable mortality could be avoided by better medical care, compared to 40 per cent of deaths that are caused by behaviour patterns that could be modified by prevention interventions. Kaplan (2000) presents a comparison of selective primary and secondary prevention efforts associated with tobacco control, physical activity and safety. Estimates for mammography and cholesterol screening and pharmacological treatment tend to be greater than US$100,000 to produce a quality adjusted life year (QALY: a measure of life expectancy with adjustments for quality of life that can reflect the existence of chronic conditions causing impairment). In contrast, tobacco restrictions and taxations cost less than US$1,000, and regular exercise less than US$12,000 to produce a QALY. Daytime use of lights on automobiles would cost less than US$3 per year from greater fuel consumption, and contribute to a 10 per cent reduction in vehicle crashes.

McGinnis et al. (2002) identify several reasons why less money is devoted to primary prevention compared to medical care. Firstly, while prevention must demonstrate future savings, medical treatment need only demonstrate safety and effectiveness. Secondly, multi-level prevention requires coordination of multiple funding streams. Thirdly, many prevention initiatives depend on policy changes that are outside of traditional health policy. Fourthly, interest group dynamics are such that there are significant commercial forces (such as fast food and tobacco advertising) that can work against prevention efforts. Finally, there is a social preference that while the public expects medical care for when they are ill, there is often resistance to changing health-compromising behaviours when they are still healthy.

Criteria for effective prevention

A review of some of the major prevention 'success stories' in Australia examined a variety of health outcomes including cardiovascular disease, smoking and tobacco control, trauma due to motor vehicle crashes, HIV/AIDS, and cervical cancer. The commonly identified 'critical success' factors for prevention included:

- developing an evidence base about the health issue and what to do about it;
- a quality, focused and sustained research effort over at least 10–20 years;
- the development and implementation of multi-level and cross-sectoral prevention strategies that addressed at least some of the 'causes' and determinants of health behaviours/outcomes, over 20 years or more;
- an active contribution and involvement by the whole of the health-care system;
- collaborative partnerships between health and other sectors, where appropriate,
- political commitment and clear directions beyond a single electoral cycle;
- developing the appropriate workforce development, university education and other training programmes
- a sustained evaluation and monitoring effort so that trends and improvements could be identified and built upon over 10–20 years. (Oldenburg et al., 1997).

Similarly, the World Health Organization (2000) reported that the success of community-based interventions requires community participation, supportive policy decisions, inter-sectoral action, appropriate legislation, health-care reforms, and collaboration with non-governmental organizations, industry and the private sector. It was also noted that decisions made outside the health sector often have a major bearing on influential elements – more health gains in terms of prevention are achieved by influencing public policies in domains such as trade, food and pharmaceutical production, agriculture, urban development and taxation policies, than by changes in health policy (World Health Organization, 2000).

Key future directions

For the developing world, Elder (2001) identifies agro-diversity and sustainable consumption as key targets for future prevention activities. As an advocate for global change and international public health, Elder (2001) describes a need to use the methodologies of the behavioural sciences to advance theory development and broaden the scope of practice and enquiry of primary prevention, as many psycho-social models and theories of behaviour change have limited applicability to prevention in developing worlds where more traditional cultures and subordination of individual to community prevail. To support this, he states that health psychology should consider international opportunities for academic curricula and training, as well as research.

Sorenson et al. (1998) observe that after 15 years of prevention trials conducted in a variety of settings, there is growing concern about the lack of significance in such studies, and if results are significant, about the negligible size of the impact. However these authors state that rather than abandon such trials, we should gather the knowledge necessary to refine them. This could involve developing and utilizing new research designs, methodologies and evaluation methods that are more appropriate to population-based (versus clinical) studies, as well as improving the components and delivery of prevention activities. We also need to better understand the moderators of change; effectiveness and cost effectiveness can vary with individuals' age, gender and other risk factors (Brown & Garber, 1998). Key directions for the next generation of population-level prevention programmes include (a) targeting multiple levels of influence, (b) addressing social inequalities in disease risk, (c) involving communities in programme planning and implementation, (d) incorporating approaches for 'tailoring' interventions, and (e) utilizing rigorous process tracking (Sorenson et al., 1998).

Targeting multiple influences

Although behavioural, social, environmental and socio-economic factors are individually important, it is likely that they are inter-related and will act together, rather than separately, to influence health and disease. As McKinlay and Marceau (2000) note, we need to move from our current obsession with identifying individual risk factors, or 'risk factorology', to much more complex multi-level explanations of human behaviour and health outcomes. Without developing much more sophisticated, multi-level explanations of human behaviour and health outcomes, we shall not be able to develop the evidence base necessary to support prevention activities.

These multi-level approaches need to acknowledge the role of a broad array of influences on health, from the downstream factors such as individual behaviour, through to the more upstream factors such as contextual environments and economic policies. Complex health issues, such as the increasing incidence of obesity and depression, require a multi-faceted response involving action outside of, as well as within, the health system. In the case of obesity, for example, new directions and partnerships could include collaboration with the transport sector, town planners, local government, sport and recreation sector, local communities, and the media to help foster social norms of active living.

Addressing social inequalities in disease risk

Within and among countries, not all sections of the population have benefited equally from the progress attributable to prevention programmes; those in high socio-economic status (SES) groups are more likely to benefit than those in middle and low SES groups (Kawachi & Marmot, 1998). It has long been known that poverty and social and economic disparities are a major cause of poor health (Feinstein, 1993). The disparities in social, mental and physical health between the most advantaged and the most disadvantaged population groups continue, and may be widening (Pappas et al., 1993). Therefore future prevention programmes need to specifically target and evaluate their impact with the more disadvantaged groups in the community as well as target the factors contributing to and maintaining these health inequalities. This is particularly relevant for indigenous populations in many countries.

Research has demonstrated that the role of health professionals as advocates for change in the delivery of health services, public health policy and other community-wide initiatives is extremely important in reducing mortality and improving health outcomes (Oldenburg, McGuffog & Turrell, 2000). Prevention activities to reduce health inequalities include: social and economic policies to reduce poverty and income inequalities; policies that improve economic and geographical access to education and training; improving the living and working conditions of lower occupational groups; improving behavioural risk factors, social support and personal coping skills among people from disadvantaged communities; and improving the equity of the health-care system (Oldenburg et al., 2000). As the major determinants of health inequalities originate outside the health sector (e.g. housing, employment, education, transport, services), prevention needs to target these upstream factors, and involve inter-sectoral collaboration.

Involving communities in prevention planning and implementation

Unfortunately, the availability of relevant and effective prevention does not in itself guarantee sustained implementation. For example, the United States experienced notable success with HIV risk reduction programmes during the first 10 years of the epidemic, however this success has not continued; there have been many documented reports of lapses and relapses in HIV risk behaviours in the gay male population, and limited diffusion to other population groups exhibiting HIV risk behaviours (Kelly et al., 1993).

Therefore, the ultimate value of prevention research may be determined by the extent to which the programmes are widely disseminated, adopted, implemented and maintained within the community, and by the impact on systems and policy at a regional, state and/or national level (i.e. institutionalization). Paradoxically, while considerable effort and resources have been devoted to developing effective primary prevention interventions, relatively little attention has been given to developing and researching effective methods for the diffusion of their use (Oldenburg & Parcel, 2002).

A number of studies have provided consistent evidence to support the importance of collaboration or 'linking agents' to enhance the diffusion process (Steckler, Goodman & Kegler, 2002). There should be a close collaborative partnership between the group promoting the programme ('resource system') and the potential users and beneficiaries of the programme ('user system'). This partnership can involve community representatives in activities such as setting priorities for prevention, identifying opinion leaders and change agents, assessing and building on community resources, planning prevention strategies, problem-solving, and prevention implementation and monitoring strategies. Community participation and input is likely to increase the resources required for programmes, and can create tension with research needs. However, it is also likely to contribute to improved intervention effectiveness, dissemination and durability.

Tailoring interventions

In targeting large groups or whole populations, prevention programmes typically adopt a 'one size fits all' approach. However, it is possible to 'tailor' programmes to enhance their relevance to the daily lives of the target population, thereby increasing the likelihood of effectiveness. Tailoring is consistent with social marketing approaches that recommend the target audience be segmented into subgroups with similar characteristics (Andersen & Armstead, 1995). Groups can be segmented on the basis of geographical, psychological, demographic or problem-relevant characteristics. Interventions may be tailored in terms of literacy level, language and culture. Such programmes may utilize expert systems or theoretical models to personalize and match self-help materials and prevention messages to a limited range of individual contexts, needs, motivation, capacity or readiness to change. In particular, using the internet and other telecommunications technology as part of health service delivery has created exciting options for tailoring and personalizing prevention at a population level (Owen, Fotheringham & Marcus, 2002).

One common approach to tailoring interventions has been associated with individuals' 'readiness to change' or 'motivational readiness'. These approaches are grounded in stage-based models, such as the Trans-theoretical Model (Prochaska, Redding & Evers, 2002), and take into account the current stage an individual has reached in the change process. Despite the widespread use of this approach to tailoring, a systematic review concluded that there is little evidence to suggest stage-based approaches are more effective compared to non-stage based interventions (Riemsma et al., 2002). Practitioners and policy-makers therefore need to acknowledge that this specific approach to tailoring may not be warranted.

Rigorous process tracking

Programme outcomes are the end-points targeted by the intervention, which in the case of primary prevention include risk factors and the incidence of particular conditions. Programme processes are associated with the implementation of component strategies. Tracking these processes provides important information that enhances the interpretation of programme results, costs and overall evaluation. As many community-based trials may show negligible outcomes, process information is particularly important to understand the factors potentially contributing to this lack of success.

Process indicators include measures of dose, fidelity, coverage and degree of participant involvement and satisfaction (Sorensen et al., 1998). Dose refers to the amount or length of the prevention programme. Insufficient dose or programme intensity is a commonly offered interpretation for the modest results obtained in community trials (e.g. Luepker et al., 1996). Fidelity refers to the extent to which implementation occurred as intended and is consistent with the theory and goals underlying the programme conceptualization. Content fidelity refers to the delivery of components specified in the intervention protocol, and process fidelity refers to the manner in which the content is to be delivered. Fidelity is central to the validity of any interventions study, and closely related to the statistical power of outcome analyses (Dumas et al., 2001). The coverage or reach of a programme refers to the proportion and risk characteristics of programme participants (Glasgow, Vogt & Boles, 1999). It is assessed by comparing programme participants to those in the total population targeted for prevention, such as all the employees within a worksite. Typically, individuals with lower levels of education, income and occupational prestige are less likely to participate in health promotion programmes (Glasgow, McCaul & Fisher, 1993), which is of particular concern given their higher rates of risk, morbidity and mortality (Feinstein, 1993). Finally, programme satisfaction refers to the subjective impressions from either participants or other stakeholders. Satisfaction may provide insight into the general acceptability of prevention activities and rates of participation, and need not be associated with programme efficacy. Rogers (1995) notes that many drug abuse prevention programmes diffuse very widely for reasons that are largely unrelated to their proven effectiveness, and often before their effectiveness in reducing drug use has even been determined, because such programmes often provide perceived solutions to a social problem that is identified as a high priority at a local or national level.

CONCLUSIONS

Primary prevention aims to reduce population rates of risk behaviours, morbidity and mortality. Globally, there is an increasing incidence of conditions that have a significant component of preventability, such as ischaemic heart disease, injury, motor vehicle crashes and depression. While traditional prevention has adopted a bio-medical approach, more contemporary prevention targets the social and ecological determinants of health. Comprehensive prevention strategies are multi-level and directed at individuals, the community, media, legislation and policy, across a range of settings such as schools, the workplace, health-care settings and other community contexts. Future challenges for primary prevention include sustaining research and developing a relevant evidence base, economic justification, appropriate resourcing, supportive legislation and policy, and extensive collaborative partnerships. In particular, primary prevention must be differentiated from tertiary health care and be recognized in public health policy (Kaplan, 2000).

The social and behavioural sciences have made, and will continue to make, an important contribution to primary prevention theories and practice. Health psychology provides a rigorous scientific method for understanding health-related behaviour, the social and physical contexts in which behaviour occurs, and approaches for influencing individuals and groups towards positive change. Although health psychology has typically involved an individual and tertiary-level approach to prevention, there are increasing opportunities, and an immediate need for, population-based and primary-level approaches to improve and maintain the health and well-being of our global community.

Acknowledging the significant proportion of preventable disease burden in the world, and the relatively small investment in primary prevention compared to secondary and tertiary prevention efforts in many countries, there is a strong rationale for more resources and research to be dedicated to primary prevention and the related fields of population health, behavioural medicine and health psychology (Oldenburg, 2002). The primary prevention programmes required to deal with the future health challenges confronting the world will need to incorporate an increased understanding of the various issues outlined in this chapter. Current health practice and policy is not oriented towards primary prevention. There will need to be a fundamental paradigm shift to include a focus on the social, economic, environmental and life-course determinants of health. Prevention trials will need to adopt innovative means of multi-level implementation and evaluation, with strong community-based partnerships and multi-sectoral collaborations beyond the health sector. Countries will require health policy and health-care systems that are more population health-oriented, and there will need to be much more exchange of knowledge and resources across traditional boundaries – disciplinary, cultural and national – in order to broaden the scope and practice of heath psychology, and realize the potential of primary prevention.

DISCUSSION POINTS

1. How is primary prevention different from other styles of prevention (i.e. secondary and tertiary)?
2. What is the rationale for primary prevention activities?
3. What are some major health foci for primary prevention activities in developing and developed countries?
4. What are the strengths and limitations of an ecological approach to primary prevention compared to a medical or healthy lifestyle approach?
5. What are life-course factors and how are they relevant to primary prevention?
6. What is a multi-level approach to prevention? Identify a health issue and develop an outline of a multi-level prevention programme.
7. Is an individual or population-based approach to prevention more effective?
8. Identify a health issue (e.g. smoking) and how it could be targeted for primary prevention activities across a range of settings.
9. Why are primary prevention activities less common than secondary or tertiary prevention? What are some of the barriers to primary prevention activities?
10. How could you evaluate a community-based trial aimed at increasing healthy lifestyles? What inter-sectoral partners might be involved in such a programme?

FURTHER READING

Adami, H. O., Day, N. E., Trichopoulos, D. and Willett, W. C. (2001). Primary and secondary prevention in the reduction of cancer morbidity and mortality. *European Journal of Cancer* 37, S118–27.

Conner, M. and Norman, P., eds. (1996). *Predicting Health Behaviour.* Buckingham: Open University Press.

Elder, J. P. (2001). *Behavior Change and Public Health in the Developing World.* Thousand Oaks, CA: Sage.

Glanz, K., Lewis, F. M. and Rimer, B. K., eds. (2002). *Health Behavior and Health Education: Theory, Research and Practice*, 3rd edn. San Francisco: Jossey Bass.

McGinnis, J. M., Williams-Russo, P. and Knickman, J. R. (2002). The case for more active policy attention to health promotion. *Health Affairs* 21, 78–93.

Pearson, T. A., Blair, S. N., Daniels, S. R., Eckel, R. H., et al. (2002). AHA guidelines for primary prevention of cardiovascular disease and stroke: 2002 update: consensus panel guide to risk reduction for adult patients without coronary or other atherosclerotic vascular diseases. *Circulation* 106, 388–91.

Puska, P., Tuomilehto, J., Nissinen, A. and Vartianen, E. (1995). *The North Karelia Project: Twenty-year Results and Experiences.* Helsinki: Helsinki University Printing House.

Rose, G. (1994). *The Strategy of Preventive Medicine.* Oxford: Oxford University Press.

Sallis, J. and Owen, N. (2002). Ecological models. In K. Glanz, F. M. Lewis and B. K. Rimer, eds., *Health Behavior and Health Education: Theory, Research and Practice.* 3rd edn. San Francisco: Jossey Bass, 462–84.

Shonkoff, J. P. and Meisels, S. J., eds. *Handbook of Early Intervention*, 2nd edn. Cambridge: Cambridge University Press.

Susser, M. (1995). The trials and tribulations of trials – interventions in communities. *American Journal of Public Health* 85, 156–8.

Winett, R. A., King, A. C. and Altman, D. G. (1989). *Health Psychology and Public Health, An Integrative Approach.* New York: Pergamon Press.

KEY STUDIES

COMMIT Research Group (1995). Community Intervention Trial for Smoking Cessation (COMMIT): I. Cohort results from a four-year community intervention. *American Journal of Public Health* 85, 183–92.

Farquhar, J. W., Fortmann, S. P., Flora, J. A., Taylor, C. B., et al. (1990). Effects of community-wide education on cardiovascular risk factors: the Stanford Five-City Project. *JAMA* 264, 359–65.

Gomel, M., Oldenburg, B., Simpson, J. and Owen, N. (1993). Worksite cardiovascular risk reduction: randomised trial of health risk assessment, risk factor education, behavioral counselling and incentive strategies. *American Journal of Public Health* 83, 1231–8.

Jousilahti, P., Tuomilehto, J., Korhonen, H. J., Vartiainen, E., Puska, P. and Nissinen, A. (1994). Trends in cardiovascular disease risk factor clustering in eastern Finland: results of 15-year follow-up of the North Karelia project. *Preventive Medicine* 23, 6–14.

Luepker, R. V., Perry, C. L., McKinlay, S. M., Nader, P. R., et al., for the CATCH Collaborative Group (1996). Outcomes of a field trial to improve children's dietary patterns and physical activity: the Child and Adolescent Trial for Cardiovascular Health (CATCH). *JAMA* 275, 768–76.

REFERENCES

Andersen, N. and Armstead, C. (1995). Toward understanding the association of socio-economic status and health: a new challenge for the biopsychosocial approach. *Psychosomatic Medicine* 57, 213–15.

Belloc, N. B. and Breslow, L. (1972). Relationship of physical health status and health practices. *Preventive Medicine* 1, 409–12.

Bronfenbrenner, U. (1979). *The Ecology of Human Development: Experiments by Nature and Design*. Cambridge, MA: Harvard University Press.

Brown, A. D. and Garber, A. M. (1998). Cost effectiveness of coronary heart disease prevention strategies in adults. *PharmacoEconomics* 14, 27–48.

Calfas, K. J., Sallis, J. F., Zabinski, M. F., Wilfley, D. E., et al. (2002). Preliminary evaluation of a multi-component program for nutrition and physical activity change in primary care: PACE+ for adults. *Preventive Medicine* 34, 153–61.

Colditz, G. A. (1999). Economic costs of obesity and inactivity. *Medicine & Science in Sports & Exercise* 31, S663–7.

COMMIT Research Group (1995). Community Intervention Trial for Smoking Cessation (COMMIT): I. Cohort results from a four-year community intervention. *American Journal of Public Health* 85, 183–92.

Conner, M. and Norman, P., eds. (1996). *Predicting Health Behaviour*. Buckingham, UK: Open University Press.

Constantino, J. (1992). On the prevention of conduct disorder: a rationale for initiating preventive efforts. *Infants and Young Children* 5, 29–41.

Cuijpers, P. (2002). Effective ingredients of school-based drug prevention programs: a systematic review. *Addictive Behaviors* 27, 1009–23.

Deitz, W. H. (1998). Childhood weight affects adult morbidity and mortality. *Journal of Nutrition* 128, 411S–14.

Doll, R. and Hill, A. B. (1964). Mortality in relation to smoking: ten years' observations of British doctors. *British Medical Journal* 1, 1399–410.

Dumas, J. E., Lynch, A. M., Laughlin, J. E., Smith, E. P. and Prinz, R. J. (2001). Promoting intervention fidelity: conceptual issues, methods, and preliminary results from the EARLY ALLIANCE prevention trial. *American Journal of Preventive Medicine* 20, 38–47.

Elder, J. P. (2001). *Behavior Change and Public Health in the Developing World*. Thousand Oaks, CA: Sage.

Eming Young, M. (2002). *From Early Child Development to Human Development: Investing in Our Children's Future*. Washington, DC: the World Bank.

Ezzati, M., Lopez, A. D., Rodgers, A., Vander Hoorn, S., Murray, C. J. L. and the Comparative Risk Assessment Collaborating Group (2002). Selected major risk factors and global regional burden of disease. *Lancet* 360, 1347–60.

Farquhar, J. W. and Maccoby, N. (1977). Community education for cardiovascular health. *Lancet* 1, 192–5.

Farquhar, J. W., Fortmann, S. P., Flora, J. A., Taylor, C. B., Haskell, W. L., Williams, P. T., Maccoby, N. and Wood, P. D. (1990). Effects of community-wide education on cardiovascular risk factors: the Stanford Five-city Project. *JAMA* 264, 359–65.

Feinstein, J. S. (1993). The relationship between socio-economic status and health: a review of the literature. *Milbank Q* 71, 279–322.

Felitti, V. J., Anda, R. F., Nordenberg, D., Williamson, D. F., Spitz, A. M., Edwards, V., Koss, M. P. and Marks, J. S. (1998). Relationship of child abuse and household dysfunction to many of the leading causes of death in adults: the Adverse Childhood Experiences (ACE) study. *American Journal of Preventive Medicine* 14, 245–58.

Freudenberg, N., Silver, D., Carmona, J. M., Kass, D., Lancaster, B. and Speers, M. (2000). Health promotion in the city: a structured review of the literature on interventions to prevent heart disease, substance abuse, violence, and HIV infection in US metropolitan areas, 1980–1995. *Journal of Urban Health – Bulletin of the New York Academy of Medicine* 77, 443–57.

Garbarino, J. and Ganzel, B. (2000). The human ecology of early risk. In J. P. Shonkoff and S. J. Meisels, eds., *Handbook of Early Intervention*, 2nd edn. Cambridge: Cambridge University Press, 76–93.

Glanz, K., Lewis, F. M. and Rimer, B. K., eds. (2002). *Health Behavior and Health Education: Theory, Research and Practice*, 3rd edn. San Francisco: Jossey Bass.

Glasgow, R. E., McCaul, K. D. and Fisher, K. J. (1993). Participation in worksite health promotion: a critique of the literature and recommendations for future practice. *Health Education Quarterly* 20, 391–408.

Glasgow, R. E., Vogt, T. M. and Boles, S. M. (1999). Evaluating public health impact of health promotion interventions: the RE-AIM framework. *American Journal of Public Health* 89, 1322–7.

Gochman, D. S., ed. (1997). *Handbook of Health Behaviour Research*. New York: Plenum Press.

Graham, H. (2002). Building an interdisciplinary science of health inequalities: the example of life course research. *Social Science and Medicine* 55, 2005–16.

Graham-Clarke, P. and Oldenburg, B. (1994). The effectiveness of a general-practice-based physical activity intervention on patient physical activity status. *Behaviour Change* 11, 132–44.

Harris, D., Oldenburg, B. and Owen, N. (1999). Australian National Workplace Health Project: strategies for gaining access, support, and commitment. *Health Promotion Journal of Australia* 9, 49–54.

Hertzman, C., Power, C., Matthews, S. and Manor, O. (2001). Using an interactive framework of society and life course to explain self-rated health in early adulthood. *Social Science and Medicine* 53, 1575–85.

Hulscher, M. E., Wensing, M., van Der Weijden, T. and Grol, R. (2001). Interventions to implement prevention in primary care. *Cochrane Database Systematic Review* (1): CD000362.

Kannel, W. B. and Gordon, T. (1968). *An Epidemiological Investigation of Cardiovascular Disease: The Framingham Study*. Washington, DC: US Department of Health Education and Welfare.

Kaplan, R. M. (2000). Two pathways to prevention. *American Psychologist* 55, 382–96.

Kawachi, I. and Marmot, M. G. (1998). Commentary: what can we learn from studies of occupational class and cardiovascular disease? *American Journal of Epidemiology* 148(2), 160–3.

Kelly, J. A., Murphy, D. A., Silkema, K. J. and Kalichman, S. C. (1993). Psychological interventions to prevent HIV infection are urgently needed. *American Psychologist* 48, 1023–34.

Kok, G., van den Borne, B. and Mullen, P. D. (1997). Effectiveness of health education and health promotion: meta-analyses of effect studies and determinants of effectiveness. *Patient Education and Counseling* 30, 19–27.

Labonte, R. (1992). *Community Health and Empowerment: Notes on the New Health Promotion Practice*. Toronto: Health Promotion Centre, University of Toronto.

Lalonde, M. (1974). *A New Perspective on the Health of Canadians: A Working Document*. Ottawa: Government of Canada.

Lefebvre, R. C., Lasater, T. M., Carleton, R. A. and Peterson, G. (1987). Theory and delivery of health programming in the community: the Pawtucket Heart Health Program. *Preventive Medicine* 16, 80–95.

Lerman, Y. and Shemer, J. (1996). Epidemiologic characteristics of participants and non-participants in health promotion programs. *Journal of Occupational and Environmental Medicine* 38, 535–8.

Linney, J. A. (1989). Optimizing research strategies in the schools. In L. A. Bond and B. E. Compas, eds., *Primary Prevention and Promotion in Schools*. Newbury Park, CA: Sage, 50–76.

Luepker, R. V., Perry, C. L., McKinlay, S. M., Nader, P. R., et al., for the CATCH Collaborative Group. (1996). Outcomes of a field trial to improve children's dietary patterns and physical activity: the Child and Adolescent Trial for Cardiovascular Health (CATCH). *Journal of the American Medical Association* 275, 768–76.

Matarazzo, J. D. (1980). Behavioral health and behavioral medicine: frontiers for a new health psychology. *American Psychologist* 35, 807–17.

Mathers, C., Vos, T. and Stevenson, C. (1999). *The Burden of Disease and Injury in Australia*. AIHW cat no. PHE 17. Canberra: AIHW.

McGinnis, J. M. and Foege, W. H. (1993). Actual causes of death in the United States. *Journal of the American Medical Association* 270, 2207–12.

McGinnis, J. M., Williams-Russo, P. and Knickman, J. R. (2002). The case for more active policy attention to health promotion. *Health Affairs* 21, 78–93.

McKinlay, J. B. and Marceau, L. D. (2000). To boldly go . . . *American Journal of Public Health* 90, 25–30.

Mittelmark, M. B., Luepker, R. V. and Jacobs, D. R. (1986). Community-wide prevention: education strategies of the Minnesota Heart Health Program. *Preventive Medicine* 15, 1–17.

Mullen, P. D., Simons-Morton, D. G., Rameriz, G., Frankowski, R. F., Green, L. W. and Mains, D. A. (1997). A meta-analysis of trials evaluating patient education and counselling for three groups of preventive behaviours. *Patient Education and Counseling* 32, 157–73.

Murray, C. J. L. and Lopez, A. D. (1997). Alternative projections of mortality and disability by cause 1990–2020: Global Burden of Disease Study. *The Lancet* 349, 1498–504.

Nader, P. R., Stone, E. J., Lytle, L. A., Perry, C. L., et al. (1999). Three-year maintenance of improved diet and physical activity: the CATCH Cohort. *Archives of Paediatrics and Adolescent Medicine* 153, 695–704.

Nelson, C. (2000). The neurobiological bases of early intervention. In J. P. Shonkoff and S. J. Meisels, eds., *Handbook of Early Intervention*, 2nd edn. Cambridge: Cambridge University Press, 204–27.

O'Donnell, M. P. and Harris, J. S. (1994). *Health Promotion in the Workplace*. New York: Delmar Publishers.

Oldenburg, B. (2001). Public health as a social science. In N. J. Smelser and P. B. Baltes, eds., *The International Encyclopaedia of the Social and Behavioural Sciences*, vol. 18. Oxford: Elsevier, 12450–6.

Oldenburg, B. (2002). Preventing chronic disease and improving health: broadening the scope of behavioral medicine research and practice. *International Journal of Behavioral Medicine* 9, 1–16.

Oldenburg, B., Graham-Clarke, P., Shaw, J. and Walker, S. (1996). Modification of health behaviour and lifestyle mediated by physicians. In K. Orth-Gomer and N. Schneiderman, eds., *Behavioral Medicine Approaches to Cardiovascular Disease Prevention*. Mahwah, NJ: Lawrence Erlbaum.

Oldenburg, B. and Harris, D. (1996). The workplace as a setting for promoting health and preventing disease. *Homeostasis* 37, 226–32.

Oldenburg, B., Hutchins, C., O'Connor, M., Bauman, A., Wise, M. and Sewell, A. (1997). *Case Studies of Achievements in Improving the Health of the Population*. Canberra: National Health and Medical Research Council: Australian Government Publishing Service.

Oldenburg, B., McGuffog, I. and Turrell, G. (2000). Socioeconomic determinants of health in Australia: policy responses and options. *Medical Journal of Australia* 172, 489–92.

Oldenburg, B. and Parcel, G. (2002). Diffusion of innovations. In K. Glanz, F. M. Lewis, and B. K. Rimer, eds., *Health Behavior and Health Education: Theory, Research, and Practice,* 3rd edn. San Francisco: Jossey Bass, 312–34.

Osofsky, J. D. and Thompson, M. D. (2000). Adaptive and maladaptive parenting. In J. P. Shonkoff and S. J. Meisels, eds., *Handbook of Early Intervention,* 2nd edn. Cambridge: Cambridge University Press, 60–75.

Owen, N., Fotheringham, M. and Marcus, B. H. (2002). Communication technology and health behavior change. In K. Glanz, F. M. Lewis, and B. K. Rimer, eds., *Health Behavior and Health Education: Theory, Research, and Practice,* 3rd edn. San Francisco: Jossey Bass, 510–29.

Pappas, G., Queen, S., Hadden, W. and Fisher, G. (1993). The increasing disparity in mortality between socio-economic groups in the United States 1960 and 1986. *New England Journal of Medicine* 329, 103–9.

Pietinen, P., Vartianinen, E., Seppanen, R., Aro, A. and Puska, P. (1996). Changes in diet in Finland from 1972 to 1992: impact on coronary heart disease risk. *Preventive Medicine* 25, 243–50.

Power, C. and Hertzman, C. (1997). Social and biological pathways linking early life and adult disease. *British Medical Bulletin* 53, 210–21.

Prochaska, J. O., Redding, C. A. and Evers, K. (2002). The trans-theoretical model and stages of change. In K. Glanz, F. M. Lewis and B. K. Rimer, eds., *Health Behavior and Health Education: Theory, Research and Practice,* 3rd edn. San Francisco: Jossey Bass, 99–120.

Puska, P., Tuomilehto, J., Nissinen, A. and Vartianen, E. (1995). *The North Karelia Project: Twenty-year Results and Experiences.* Helsinki: Helsinki University Printing House.

Riemsma, R. P., Pattenden, J., Bridle, C., Sowden, A. J., Mather, L., Watt, I. S. and Walker, A. (2002). A systematic review of the effectiveness of interventions based on a stages-of-change approach to promote individual behaviour change. *Health Technology Assessment* 6(24).

Rogers, E. M. (1995). *Diffusion of Innovations,* 4th edn. New York: The Free Press.

Rose, G. (1994). *The Strategy of Preventive Medicine.* Oxford: Oxford University Press.

Sallis, J. and Owen, N. (2002). Ecological models. In K. Glanz, F. M. Lewis and B. K. Rimer, eds., *Health Behavior and Health Education: Theory, Research and Practice,* 3rd edn. San Francisco: Jossey Bass, 462–84.

Schwandt, P., Geib, H. C., Ritter, M. M., Ublacker, C., et al. (1999). The Prevention Education Program (PEP): a prospective study of the efficacy of family oriented lifestyle modification in the reduction of cardiovascular risk and disease: design and baseline data. *Journal of Clinical Epidemiology* 52, 791–800.

Sellers, D. E., Crawford, S. L., Bullock, K. and McKinaly, J. B. (1997). Understanding the variability in the effectiveness of community heart health programs: a meta-analysis. *Social Science and Medicine* 44, 1325–39.

Shephard, R. J. (2002). Issues in worksite health promotion: a personal viewpoint. *Quest* 54, 67–82.

Shonkoff, J. P. and Meisels, S. J., eds. (2000). *Handbook of Early Intervention,* 2nd edn. Cambridge: Cambridge University Press.

Simpson, J., Oldenburg, B., Owen, N., Harris, D., Dobbins, T., Wilson, J., Vita, P., Salmon, A. and Saunders, J. B. (2000). The Australian National Workplace Health Project: design and baseline findings. *Preventive Medicine* 31, 249–60.

Sorensen, G., Emmons, K., Hunt, M. K. and Johnston, D. (1998). Implications of the results of community intervention trials. *Annual Review of Public Health* 19, 379–416.

Steckler, A., Goodman, R. M. and Kegler, M. C. (2002). Mobilizing organizations for health enhancement: theories of organizational change. In K. Glanz, F. M. Lewis and B. K. Rimer, eds., *Health Behavior and Health Education: Theory, Research and Practice*, 3rd edn. San Francisco: Jossey Bass, 335–60.

Susser, M. (1995). The trials and tribulations of trials – interventions in communities. *American Journal of Public Health* 85, 156–8.

US Preventive Services Task Force. (1996). *Guide to Clinical Preventive Services*, 2nd edn. Baltimore: Williams & Wilkins.

US State Surgeon General's Advisory Committee. (1964). *Smoking and Health*. Washington, DC: US Department of Health.

Vartianen, E., Jousilahti, P., Alfthan, G., Sundvall, J., Pietinen, P. and Puska, P. (2000). Cardiovascular risk factor changes in Finland, 1972–1997. *International Journal of Epidemiology* 29, 49–56.

Vuori, I. (1998). Does physical activity enhance health? *Patient Education & Counseling* 33, S95–103.

Wadsworth, M. E. and Kuh, D. J. (1997). Childhood influences on adult health: a review of recent work from the British 1946 national birth cohort study, the MRC National Survey of Health and Development. *Paediatric and Perinatal Epidemiology* 11, 2–20.

Williams, C. L. (1992). Intervention in childhood. In I. S. Ockene and J. K. Ockene, eds., *Prevention of Coronary Heart Disease*. Boston: Little, Brown, 433–68.

Winett, R. A. (1995). A framework for health promotion and disease prevention programs. *American Psychologist* 50, 341–50.

Winett, R. A., King, A. C. and Altman, D. G. (1989). *Health Psychology and Public Health, An Integrative Approach*. New York: Pergamon.

The World Bank. (1993). *World Development Report 1993: Investing in Health*. New York: Oxford University Press.

World Health Organization. (1995). *The World Health Report 1995: Bridging the Gaps*. Geneva: World Health Organization.

World Health Organization. (1999). *The World Health Report 1999: Making a Difference*. Geneva: World Health Organization.

World Health Organization. (2000). *Global Strategy for the Prevention and Control of Non-communicable Diseases*. Geneva: World Health Organization.

World Health Organization. (2002). *The World Health Report 2002: Reducing Risks, Promoting Healthy Life*. Geneva: World Health Organization.

Chapter Fourteen

PSYCHOLOGICAL INTERVENTIONS IN PATIENTS WITH CHRONIC ILLNESS

Paul Bennett

CHAPTER OUTLINE

This chapter focuses on a number of psychological interventions targeted at individuals diagnosed with chronic illnesses. The interventions considered are the provision of information, stress management training, self-management training, the provision of social support, and a relatively new intervention known as written emotional expression. Each section briefly describes the approach before considering its effectiveness in terms of the key goals it is intended to address. The chapter concludes by drawing together some of the issues raised within the various sections and considering future psychological interventions for those with chronic illness. A chapter of this size cannot hope to review all the possible interventions or illness states that have formed their targets. Accordingly, the chapter focuses on some of the most frequently used intervention types and representative illness groups, particularly those with a high prevalence within the general population.

KEY CONCEPTS

changing knowledge	psycho-educational programmes
cognitive behavioural interventions	reducing distress
controlling disease progression	self-management programmes
information provision	social support
managing illness	stress management training
patient education programmes	written emotional expression

INTRODUCTION

Despite, or perhaps because of, significant progress in medical technology, there remains a large group of patients whose illness cannot be cured and who have to cope with a chronic illness for many years. Some conditions may require long-term adherence to medication or routines that minimize the negative impact of the illness. People with insulin-dependent diabetes require careful daily control of insulin levels to prevent acute, possibly fatal, complications; people with arthritis may benefit from engaging in a variety of exercises to maintain joint mobility; and so on. In the case of such disorders, there are clear benefits to managing the illness in a way that maximizes health and minimizes the degree to which it interferes with the individual's quality of life. Other illnesses may progress in the absence of obvious symptoms. Coronary Heart Disease (CHD) may be symptom free until the time of an acute event such as a heart attack (myocardial infarction: MI). However, even in the absence of continuing symptoms, those people who have had an MI may reduce their risk of a further one by making changes to risk behaviours such as cigarette smoking, exercise or diet, in the absence of any day-to-day changes in symptoms. A third area of concern is the often significant emotional distress that may accompany a diagnosis of severe or chronic illness. About one-third of patients with cancer evidence clinical levels of distress (e.g. Zabora et al., 1997), a quarter of patients with CHD develop clinical levels of depression in the year following their MI (Bennett & Connell, 1999), while about 14 per cent of medical and surgical out-patients evidence similar levels of distress (Feldman, Rabinowitz & BenYehuda, 1995). This chapter considers a number of intervention strategies designed to minimize each of the problems faced by chronically ill individuals.

INFORMATION PROVISION

Information can be provided in a number of ways: verbally within a consultation or series of educational meetings, written booklets and handouts, audio- or video-tapes, or via a computer interface. Unfortunately, despite its apparent simplicity, the appropriate provision of information is not a simple process, and there is a wealth of evidence that poorly presented information is of little or no benefit to those receiving it. With this in mind, the findings of Ley (1997) that about a quarter of published medical leaflets would be understood by only 20 to 30 per cent of the adult population, is of particular concern. Verbal information may be usefully augmented by written material. Over three-quarters of patients state they would like some form of permanent information about their condition and its treatment: preferably concise, clear, using appropriate language and syntax, and illustrated with graphics. If provided, about 70 per cent of patients report using such materials (Ley, 1997). Written or other permanent sources of information can have significant benefits over verbal information: the most obvious being that they provide an opportunity to provide carefully prepared information, presented in a way designed to be maximally effective. From the patient's perspective, they provide a record that can be consulted to remind them of salient information. However, permanent information need not necessarily be pre-prepared. Tattersall et al. (1994), for example, compared the impact of an audio-tape of a consultation with that of individualized summary letters sent to patients after their first consultation with a cancer specialist. Patients listened to the tape an average of 2.3 times and read the letter 2.8 times over the following month. Ninety per cent shared the contents of the tape or letter with a friend, relative or doctor. Both methods impacted equally on measures of recall, anxiety or depression. However, the audio-tape proved the more popular method: when asked to rank 6 communication options, 46 per cent of patients gave the highest rank to the tape and 21 per cent to the letter.

Changing knowledge

There is a substantial body of evidence that information provision programmes can enhance knowledge of a condition or its management, at least in the short-term (e.g. Gibson et al., 2000; van den Arend, Stolk & Rutten, 2000). One such study, reported by Marteau et al. (1996), considered the effectiveness of booklets of two levels of complexity providing information to women referred for colposcopy following an abnormal cervical smear. The simple booklet provided brief information about the procedure the women were about to experience, instructions about how they might best cope with the procedure including the use of relaxation and distraction techniques, and information about likely outcomes of the procedure. The complex information provided more detailed information on the nature of cervical abnormalities, as well as details about the procedure and the likely outcomes. It did not suggest any coping strategies that the women might use. The results suggested a specificity of effect. All patients who received the leaflets gained knowledge relative to a group of patients who received no information. However, those that received the complex leaflet, without the coping strategies, did not experience any reduction in anxiety compared to the other groups. By contrast, those patients with the simpler leaflet were least anxious when they attended the hospital for their colposcopy.

The internet is also now increasingly being used as a source of information, both official and unofficial. One official website, developed by the American Heart Association (AHA: Yancy, 2002) called the Heart Profilers (www.americanheart.org/profilers) is a free web-based interactive tool through which patients can obtain a personalized report of 'scientifically accurate' treatment options, a list of questions to ask their doctor on their next visit, and key information they need to participate in their treatment. It is the first of several sites to be provided by the AHA, and addresses problems and treatments of heart failure and CHD, hypertension, high cholesterol and atrial fibrillation. As a tool, it effectiveness is difficult to assess, as access is free and widely based. However, there is increasing evidence that the web is a useful resource for people with a number of medical conditions. Kalichman et al. (2003), for example, reported the results of a survey of 147 HIV-positive people which addressed their use of the internet and its association with their health and well-being. They found that health-related internet use was associated with high levels of HIV illness knowledge, the use of active coping strategies including information seeking, and high levels of social support, suggesting that the internet may prove a useful resource for many people with chronic conditions – particularly those individuals with the skills and resources to utilize its benefits.

Reducing distress

Diagnosis and concerns about prognosis and treatment raise significant anxieties, some of which may be moderated by appropriate information. Rahn et al. (1998), for example, asked women receiving radiotherapy for breast cancer to identify what best helped them cope with their diagnosis and treatment. Ninety-four per cent stated that the most important factor was being kept well informed about the treatment they were receiving. Even simple information about the context of care can prove an extremely valuable means of improving mood. A tour of a clinic, the provision of general information about treatment, and the opportunity to pose questions with an oncology counsellor have been found to be highly effective in reducing stress prior to chemotherapy in patients recently diagnosed as having cancer (Wells et al., 1995). Hospital-based interventions may also contribute to longer-term reductions in anxiety. Tooth, McKenna and Maas (1998) found an educational intervention given prior to cardiac surgery resulted in reduced anxiety levels four months post-surgery and, in comparison to no treatment, improved partner quality of life ratings at one year follow-up. Of interest is that patients may benefit emotionally from an intervention that includes the provision of information via computer. Rawl et al. (2002) evaluated the effect of a computer-based intervention, combined with support from an oncology nurse, which provided users who were newly diagnosed with breast cancer with information on the disease and its treatment as well as symptom management. Following the intervention, participants reported less depression and anxiety than those in a usual care control.

Longer-term educational interventions may also impact on mood. Lewin et al. (1992) compared the effectiveness of a comprehensive, 6-week-long, home-based education programme for cardiac patients known as the 'Heart Manual', with a placebo package of information and informal counselling. The Heart Manual provided a structured rehabilitation package, focusing on the progressive change of risk behaviours and teaching stress reduction techniques. Over the following year, despite its primary focus on disease management, one of the striking results of the Heart Manual intervention was that participants evidenced lower levels of anxiety and depression than those in the control group – a finding echoed in a subsequent trial in the treatment of angina reported below (Lewin et al., 2002). On a more cautionary note, it should be noted that information does not always benefit all patients. McHugh et al. (1995) measured the effect of providing an audio-tape of the consultation in which oncology patients were given their diagnosis and other related information. Although those who received the tape were able to recall more information about their illness than controls at 6-month follow-up, those patients provided with the tape who had a poor prognosis were more likely to be depressed than controls and those with better prognoses.

Managing illness

Educational programmes can impact on how well people manage their illness – sometimes as well as more complex interventions. Nicassio et al. (1997), for example, compared a 10-week education programme that presented information on a range of health-related topics without emphasizing skill acquisition, with a behavioural intervention focused on the practice of a variety of pain coping skills to help participants cope with fibromyalgia (facial nerve pain). Both groups improved following the intervention on measures of depression, self-reported pain behaviours and observed pain behaviours. No differences were found between the behavioural and education conditions.

Despite this success, the majority of studies have shown didactic educational programmes to be less effective than more interactive or skills-based programmes (see Bennett, 2000), even where increases in knowledge are achieved. In a systematic review of 11 educational programmes for people with asthma, for example, Gibson et al. (2000) concluded that while such programmes increased knowledge, there was no evidence that they impacted on measures of medication use, doctor visits, hospitalization and lung function. When didactic information provision programmes have been compared with alternative (and usually more complex) interventions, the alternative programme has generally been found to be superior. In one study in another population, Campbell et al. (1996) compared the effectiveness of educational and behavioural instruction programmes for patients with non-insulin-dependent diabetes, a condition associated with obesity. The goals of the intervention were to improve diet and weight reduction. Both types of intervention proved equally effective in facilitating weight reduction. However, participants in the behavioural programme evidenced greater and more rapid reductions in diastolic blood pressure and cholesterol levels. They also reported the highest treatment satisfaction levels. Similarly, Lewin et al. (2002) compared a standard educational package against a cognitive behavioural approach emphasizing skills acquisition and planning of new activities in the treatment of angina. Their results showed that 6 months after the end of the intervention, patients in the behavioural intervention achieved lower levels of angina, used drugs to control their angina less frequently, and reported less physical restrictions over their activities.

STRESS MANAGEMENT TRAINING

Many illnesses are thought to be either a consequence of stress or to place significant stress on the ill individual (see, for example Chapters 5, 6 and 8 in this volume).

Accordingly, a number of studies have evaluated the impact of interventions designed to moderate the effects of stress on the individual and, on occasion, their illness. Most of these have used stress management techniques, themselves based on more general cognitive behavioural principles.

The theory underlying stress management programmes assumes that the initiator of the stress response is usually an environmental event. This triggers a series of psychological and physiological processes. The first of these involves a cognitive appraisal of the event as 'threatening' in some way (e.g. Lazarus, 1999). Stress management training is most appropriate where these appraisals are unrealistic and distort reality in ways that increase the perception of stress associated with an event. Two levels of cognitions involved in the stress process can be identified (Meichenbaum, 1985). Surface cognitions are the thoughts of which we are aware, and which we can consciously evoke and change. A second order of cognitions, known as cognitive schemata, comprise a set of (usually unconscious) fundamental beliefs about ourselves and the world that guide our interpretation of events and, hence, our surface cognitions. Both sets of cognitions can influence mood, and stress-engendering cognitions may also increase physiological arousal, mediated through the autonomic nervous system. At moderate to high levels of stress, this results in a number of conscious and unconscious physiological changes, including increased physical tension, increased heart rate and output, raised blood pressure and so on. The final outcome of the stress process involves engaging in 'stressed' behaviours, including agitation, loss of temper, use of alcohol or drugs to reduce the experience of stress, and so on.

Each of the components of the stress processes may form the target of stress management procedures. However, two therapeutic strategies may be considered central to stress management: relaxation training and cognitive interventions (Meichenbaum, 1985). Relaxation skills enable the individual to relax as much as is possible and appropriate both throughout the day and at times of particular stress. It reduces levels of physical tension and over-arousal. Two strategies for changing cognitions are frequently employed. The simplest is targeted at surface cognitions. Self-instruction training (Meichenbaum, 1985) involves interrupting the flow of stress-provoking thoughts and replacing them with more realistic or 'coping' ones. A more complex intervention involves identification and challenging the veracity of stress-engendering thoughts. It asks the individual to consider such thoughts as hypotheses, not facts, and to assess their validity without bias. It may involve consideration of both surface cognitions and cognitive schemata. Both skills are practised in the clinic before being used in the 'real world'.

Reducing stress

Stress management procedures have frequently been used with populations considered to be under stress as a consequence of their diagnosis or the illness process. Given that this therapeutic approach has been shown to be highly successful in improving mood in people with mental health problems (Bennett, 2003), it should come as no surprise that the approach has been shown to be effective in improving mood in patients with diagnoses as serious as HIV/AIDS and cancer as well as less life-threatening conditions such as irritable bowel syndrome, psoriasis and arthritis (see Bennett, 2000).

In a relatively early study of the effectiveness of stress management procedures, Fawzy et al. (1993) compared them with usual care in a group of patients with malignant melanoma whose tumour had been surgically excised. The intervention comprised three active components: (i) health education focusing on the nature of melanoma, nutrition, exercise and sun exposure; (ii) stress management techniques – in particular relaxation; and (iii) enhancement of coping skills such as problem-solving and 'general coping alternatives'. Both immediately after the intervention and at 6-month follow-up, only the active intervention group evidenced improvements on mood. This study was particularly important as it also examined the health effects of the intervention – the results of which are reported below. Since then, many studies have shown emotional benefit following this type of intervention. Antoni et al. (2001), for example, found that stress management interventions resulted in a decrease in levels of depression and an increase in what they termed 'benefit finding' (finding positive aspects of their disease) among women in the early stages of breast cancer. These benefits were greatest for women with relatively low levels of optimism at the start of therapy.

A second group for whom stress management programmes have generally proven effective involves individuals with HIV or AIDS. Lutgendorf et al. (1997) explored the effects of a 10-week stress management programme relative to a no-intervention condition in a similar population. Their programme was designed to increase participants' ability to cope with the distress of symptomatic HIV and their use of social support. By the end of the programme, participants reported greater use of cognitive coping strategies and social support than those in the control condition. Both these factors were associated with improvements on measures of anxiety and depression. Showing the specific effects of a stress management programme, Lechner et al. (2003) found that this type of programme improved mental health outcomes in women with AIDS, but did not result in any improvement relative to a psycho-educational intervention on measures including energy/fatigue, pain, role functioning or social functioning.

Managing illness

A second set of interventions have focused on teaching stress management procedures in an effort to control the symptoms of disorders as diverse as chronic obstructive airways disease, arthritis and atopic dermatitis. Some of the relevant literature is reviewed below, focusing on the treatment of the irritable bowel syndrome, angina and diabetes.

One illness process that has captured the interest of many clinical researchers is the irritable bowel syndrome (IBS), the symptoms of which are alternating diarrhoea and constipation and abdominal pain. The interest in IBS stems from an early hypothesis that IBS is a direct consequence of stress. Indeed, the strongest (and subsequently disproved) hypothesis stated that IBS is an alternative presentation of anxiety disorder (Latimer, 1981). This single aetiology model has now been strongly questioned, although there is a strong psychological component in many of the symptoms experienced by patients with IBS. Early studies showed stress management to be as effective as medication or a placebo psychotherapy condition in both the short and long terms (see Bennett, 1997). More recently, Chalder (2003) reported a study in which she examined whether psychological treatment could add to the effectiveness of treatment using a drug which slowed down the gut's activity generally used to treat IBS. All the people in the study were first given the drug treatment. Those that continued to have IBS symptoms 6 weeks later were entered into either a cognitive behavioural programme intended to reduce stress and teach them how best to manage their symptoms, or continued on the drug regime they were already on in the hope that this additional time on the drug would improve their symptoms. Those patients in the combined medical and cognitive behavioural programme faired best and had significant reductions in both negative emotions and a number of measures of IBS activity relative to those on long-term medical treatment.

Angina may be triggered by emotional as well as physical stresses. Accordingly, several studies have explored the potential benefits of stress management procedures in people with angina. One of the first such studies was reported by Bundy et al. (1994), who found that compared to a no-treatment control group, patients who took part in a stress management programme reported reductions in the frequency of angina symptoms, were less reliant on medication, and were able to cope with higher levels of exercise on a treadmill. A much larger study, involving hundreds of participants, was reported by Gallacher et al. (1997). They compared a less intensive intervention, involving a stress management programme delivered in booklet form combined with three group meetings, with a no-treatment control condition. At 6-month follow-up, they found a significant reduction in stress-related, but not exercise-related, angina: a finding consistent with the intervention impacting directly on the stress mechanisms that led to the episodes of angina.

The potential benefits of stress management to the control of diabetes are perhaps less obvious than those related to either IBS or angina. Nevertheless, there are theoretical reasons to presume that they could form an effective element in any programme of diabetes control. Stress often precedes periods of reduced adherence to self-care behaviours and may be associated with inappropriate changes in eating patterns (Viner, McGrath & Trudinger, 1996). In addition, stress hormones reduce insulin sensitivity and may be accompanied by elevations in blood glucose (Surwit & Schneider, 1993). Accordingly, some studies have found relaxation to be an effective intervention in reducing blood glucose levels. Surwit et al. (2002), for example, reported a study comparing the effectiveness of a diabetes education group and a combined education plus stress management group in the long-term control of high blood glucose levels. Their main outcome measure was a substance known as HbA(1c), which indicates levels of blood glucose over the previous 3 months. One year following the intervention, patients in the combined intervention evidenced lower levels of HbA(1c) than those in the education group. Not all people with diabetes may benefit from this type of intervention. Aikens, Kiolbasa and Sobel (1997) found that those people who reported the most stress and who felt that their levels of insulin were most susceptible to changes in stress levels were least likely to use the relaxation methods they were taught. However, those that did practice relaxation did benefit in terms of diabetic control.

Reducing risk of disease progression

Studies of the effect of stress management on disease progression have been of two types. The first have examined the effects of stress management on short-term indicators of disease activity such as immune or cardiovascular function. The second has considered the impact of stress management on the longer-term health outcomes, including survival following diagnoses such as cancer of HIV/AIDS.

There is clear evidence that stress management can impact on short-term immune processes. One innovative way in which the immediate effects of stress management on immune function has been evaluated has been reported by Vedhara et al. (2003). They noted that stress reduces the effectiveness of the immune system to respond to vaccinations, resulting in less than optimal levels of immunity from the illness supposed to be conferred by the vaccination. They argued that stress management should improve immune function, resulting in a greater immune response to vaccination, and therefore afford higher levels of protection from illness. They tested this hypothesis by allocating carers of people with dementia (assumed to be under significant stress) into either a no-treatment condition or a group stress management intervention. In comparison to the group who did not receive the intervention, levels of response to a flu vaccine given after the group were more than double. Indeed, so effective was the intervention in modifying the immune response to the vaccine, that the immune response to the vaccine in the treated group was actually greater than that found in a comparison group of individuals who were under no stress.

In a more acute clinical condition, Antoni et al. (2002) measured the immunological outcomes in 25 HIV-positive men randomly allocated to either a 10-week stress management intervention or a waiting-list control condition. Their measures particularly focused on the impact of the intervention on the level of T-cells (which control the immune response to infection and other physical insults and are depleted in HIV infection) within participants' blood. Immediately following the intervention, those who took part in the intervention had higher T-cell counts than those in the control group, despite there being no pre-treatment differences, suggesting that the stress management influenced levels of a key factor in HIV disease: one which may slow the disease progress and place an individual at less risk of other opportunistic infections.

Follow-up data from the Fawzy et al. (1993) study in melanoma patients described earlier in the chapter suggest these findings may translate into longer survival and increased health. In a series of studies they have reported morbidity and mortality levels among participants in the stress management and no-treatment control group at 6 months, 5–6 years and 10 years after the intervention. By 10-year follow-up

(Fawzy, Canada & Fawzy, 2003), 11 of the 34 people (32 per cent) in the control group had recurrences and had died of cancer: three others had non-fatal recurrences. In the stress management group, 9 of 34 (26 per cent) had died of cancer, and 2 had survived recurrences. After statistically controlling for differences in the severity of the presenting melanoma, these differences were statistically significant. About half the studies that have measured mortality in people with cancer have found similar gains in survival – but half have not, suggesting this effect is inconsistent. However, as Ross et al. (2002) point out, the effects of such interventions may have been stronger if patients had been selected into some studies as a result of their having some distress to ameliorate rather than simply having a diagnosis of cancer.

One of the more controversial risk factors for CHD is known as type-A behaviour. This behaviour complex comprises an excess of time urgency, competitiveness, hostility and easily aroused anger, and has been associated with risk for CHD. Now, it is thought that hostility and easily aroused anger form the 'toxic' element of these behaviours (Smith & Ruiz, 2002). A number of studies have attempted to identify whether changing type-A behaviours may influence risk of disease. The best known of these, the Recurrent Coronary Prevention Program (Friedman et al., 1986), targeted type-A men who had a recent MI. They were randomly allocated into one of three groups: cardiac rehabilitation, cardiac rehabilitation plus type-A management, and a usual care control. Each intervention involved small group meetings at gradually increasing time intervals over a period of four and half years. Evidence of the effectiveness of this process was compelling. Participants in the type-A management programme were at half the risk for further infarction than those in the traditional rehabilitation programme, with total infarction rates over this time of 6 and 12 per cent in each group respectively. A later follow-up study (Friedman et al., 1987) followed participants in the intervention arm of the trial for a further year and reported the outcomes of a group of patients who were previously in the control group who took part in a year-long intervention programme. This latter group also showed a significantly reduced intensity of type-A behaviour and a significant decrease in both the cardiac mortality and morbidity rate over this follow-up period. One other study of this approach was reported by Burell (1996). Project New Life worked with patients who had undergone a coronary artery bypass operation. They were randomly allocated into a type-A management programme involving 17 group meetings over a period of one year and a usual care control. By between 5 and 6 and a half years following surgery, the prognoses of those patients who had taken part in the intervention programme was much better than those in the control group. By this time, a significantly higher proportion of those in the control group than in the intervention group had died from a variety of causes. In addition, the intervention group had suffered significantly fewer cardiac events, including further MI, re-operation or cardiac death, than those in the control group.

A second psychological characteristic which is thought to substantially increase risk for infarction or re-infarction is depression (see Frasure-Smith et al., 2000). Such a relationship suggests that interventions that reduce depression should reduce risk of re-infarction. In the first study to begin to test this hypothesis, Black et al. (1998)

allocated MI patients found to be experiencing significant distress to either usual care or 1 to 7 sessions of behavioural therapy. Thirty-five per cent of participants in the active intervention were hospitalized with cardiac symptoms in the following year, in comparison to 48 per cent of those in the usual care group. However, whether this difference was a consequence of physiological or psychological changes such as less anxiety over cardiac symptoms is not clear.

A much larger study has now examined the impact of treating people for depression on measures of re-infarction and mortality. The ENRICHD study (Berkman et al., 2000) was a large multi-centre study which provided an intervention lasting up to one year for people identified as depressed immediately following their MI. All participants in the active intervention received two treatment components, each aimed at improving their emotional state: (i) group cognitive behaviour therapy, and (ii) social support enhanced by training participants in the social skills necessary to develop their social support network. People who did not evidence any improvement in mood as a result of these interventions were treated using anti-depressants. A comparison group was randomly allocated to the usual care provided by the institutions in which the study took place. At the time of writing, the results of the study have only been reported at conferences, but were commented on by Sheps (2003), who noted that the trial had failed to find any difference between intervention and control conditions. Unfortunately, what these negative findings mean is not clear. The simplest explanation is that the intervention had no effect on mortality. However, there are early indications to suggest that many of the patients who entered the intervention group received a less than optimal intervention, while many of those in the control groups received interventions that did not differ substantially from those provided by the intervention condition (as it was actually implemented). Accordingly, the failure to identify differences in mortality between the two conditions may reflect a failure to achieve clear therapeutic differences between the groups rather than a failure of the intervention to impact on mortality. Nevertheless, the size of this study, and its negative results, suggests that claims that psychological interventions can reduce mortality in cardiac patients should be viewed cautiously.

SELF-MANAGEMENT TRAINING

The goal of self-management programmes is to allow the individual with a chronic illness to gain day-to-day control over their symptoms, in order to increase their quality of life and minimize the degree to which their illness negatively impacts on them. The approach assumes that self-management skills can be learned through practice and watching others, and that success in achieving change will lead to increased confidence and continued application of new skills. Accordingly, the core of self-management training is a structured, progressive, skills training programme that ensures success at each stage before progression to the next. Participants learn to monitor their condition, so they are aware of the impact of these management plans on it. They may be taught a variety of illness-specific management skills as well as generic skills such as relaxation or cognitive restructuring. Practice and integration of these skills into participants' daily life is achieved through the use of rehearsal, problem-solving discussion and role play.

Managing illness

One of the first self-management programmes to be evaluated (Lorig & Holman, 1993) focused on the management of arthritis. The study had no control group. However, there was some evidence of the programme's efficacy, as 20 months after attending the programme participants reported a decreased number of physician visits, as well as reductions in pain and disability – in a condition where one would normally expect a gradual increase in disability. SuperioCabuslay, Ward and Lorig (1996) subsequently reported that, when compared to usual care (usually pharmacological treatments), participants in self-management programmes evidenced gains of 20–30 per cent on measures of pain relief in both osteo-arthritis and rheumatoid arthritis, 40 per cent in functional ability in rheumatoid arthritis, and 60–80 per cent in the reduction in 'tender joint' counts in rheumatoid arthritis.

The intervention model developed by Lorig and colleagues was essentially a 'one size fits all' approach: everyone receives the same intervention. By contrast, tailored programmes provide a series of treatment modules that participants can access according to their differing needs. Evers et al. (2002) reported the effectiveness of one such programme targeted at people with rheumatoid arthritis. Modules included those targeted at helping participants cope with fatigue, negative mood, pain, and maintaining or improving social relationships. The programme resulted in mid- to long-term gains on a number of psychological measures including use of active coping strategies, mood, fatigue and helplessness in comparison to a no-treatment condition. This modular approach may prove a more cost-effective intervention than the generic intervention model.

One of the most complicated conditions to manage is that of being HIV positive. Despite this, there appear to be relatively few evaluations of self-management programmes. Nevertheless, when implemented they do appear to be successful. Gifford et al. (1998), for example, randomly assigned men with symptomatic HIV or AIDS to either a 7-session group self-management programme or usual care. The self-management programme involved the use interactive methods to provide relevant information and a number of illness self-management skills, including symptom assessment and management, medication use, physical exercise, and relaxation skills. Following the intervention, the number of 'significantly troubling symptoms' reported by those in the intervention group fell, while increasing in the control group. Similarly, perceived efficacy in coping with symptoms was maintained in the intervention condition, but fell in the control group.

Teaching self-management techniques can be implemented simply and cheaply using information technology. Glasgow, Toobert and Hampson (1996) combined the use of a touch-screen computer-based programme with phone calls and interactive video or video-tape instruction to teach people with diabetes how to cope with challenges to their dietary control, to problem solve, and to set goals in terms of future dietary targets. People who received this intervention evidenced greater improvements on a number of measures of dietary choice than those in a control condition who did not receive the intervention. Taking this approach one step further, the same research group (Glasgow et al., 2003) have evaluated a self-management programme for diabetes control, called the Diabetes Network (D-Net), provided on the internet. The trial compared the effects of tailored self-management training or peer support components to a basic internet-based, information-focused intervention in a population of 'relatively novice' internet users. The intervention was implemented well and improvements were observed across a variety of patients. There were, however, difficulties in maintaining use of the system over time and the addition of the tailored self-management and peer support components did not significantly improve results. Nevertheless, the programme supports the basic use of easily gained information over the internet as a viable and potentially useful intervention.

SOCIAL SUPPORT

Social support exerts a powerful influence on both mental and physical well-being (see Chapter 7 in this volume). Accordingly, a number of researchers have attempted to determine whether providing social support either through support groups or teaching people the skills to build up there own social support network can improve both well-being and influence health status. Support groups certainly appear to reduce the stress associated with long-term illnesses. Classen et al. (2001), for example, reported on the effectiveness of a year-long weekly support group in which patients with breast cancer were encouraged to explore their emotional reactions to their illness and to gain support from the group. Compared to participants in a control group provided with educational materials, participants in the active intervention reported significantly greater reductions in traumatic stress symptoms and better mood in the long term. This type of intervention may also work in non-Western settings. Montazeri et al. (2001) reported similar benefits following participation in support groups for breast cancer among Iranian women. Group involvement was found to be the most important factor that contributed to improved well-being.

Despite these successes, perhaps the most interest in the benefits of social support has arisen as a consequence of its potential impact on disease status. In the first study to report this outcome, Spiegel, Bloom and Yalom (1989) reported the health outcomes of a group intervention designed initially to influence quality of life in cancer patients. The intervention involved weekly support groups over a period of one year that emphasized building strong supportive bonds, expressing emotions, dealing directly with fears of dying, improving relationships within the family, and active involvement in decisions concerning treatment. To the surprise of the investigators, at 10-year follow-up they found that women in this group lived an average of 18 months longer than those in a no-treatment control, despite being well matched for illness status at the beginning of the trial. These findings generated a great deal of excitement in the research and clinical community when published. Unfortunately, an attempted replication of the study met with only modest success. Gellert, Maxwell and Siegel (1984) compared the effectiveness of the programme developed by Spiegel with a standard treatment condition in a matched sample of breast cancer patients. Although their data showed trends towards a survival gain in the intervention group (by an average of 11 months: 96 versus 85 months), these differences were not statistically significant. Other negative findings have also been reported (e.g. Goodwin et al., 2001). Accordingly, increasing social support has yet to be convincingly shown to impact on illness outcomes in patients with cancer.

By contrast, although not used that frequently, social support has proven a useful adjunct to other interventions targeted at behavioural change. West, Edwards and Hajek (1998), for example, reported on the benefits of a 'buddy system' for individuals attempting to quit smoking. All those involved in the study attended a nurse-led smoker's clinic. Smokers in the buddy condition were paired with another smoker trying to give up at the same time to provide mutual support between clinic sessions. The percentage of smokers still abstinent at the end of treatment was significantly higher in the buddy condition than the solo condition: 27 per cent versus 12 per cent. These findings reflect similar gains in other studies (see May & West, 2000), and similar gains that have been found in programmes as diverse as exercise programmes (Litt, Kleppinger & Judge, 2002) and programmes of diabetic control (Delamater et al., 2001).

WRITTEN EMOTIONAL EXPRESSION

Perhaps one of the most unexpected therapeutic approaches now being developed for people with physical health problems is variously termed narrative or written emotional expression. The work stems from findings of Pennebaker in the 1980s of the psychological benefits of a writing task in which healthy participants, usually students, wrote for about 20 minutes on three consecutive days about an event from the past that had caused them upset or distress in a way that explored their emotional reaction to that event. Following this process, participants typically reported short-term increases in depression or distress, but in the mid- to long-term experienced better mood, and importantly in this context seemed to have better physical health as measured by measures of immune function and the frequency of visiting a doctor (see Esterling et al., 1999).

It took some time for this approach to be tested in patient populations. However, the interventions that have been conducted appear to show significant benefits. Smyth et al. (1999), for example, compared the effects of written expressed emotion and a neutral writing task in patients with rheumatoid arthritis and asthma. Participants in the intervention condition were asked to write about the 'most stressful experience they had ever undergone': those in the control group were asked to write about time management issues as an exercise to reduce stress. Patients with both health problems in the intervention group fared better than their equivalents in the control group at 4-month follow-up on measures of illness status. Those with asthma evidenced improvements in lung function, while those with rheumatoid arthritis showed improvements on a combined index measuring physician-rated factors such as disease activity, joint swelling and tenderness, and the presence and severity of joint deformities, as well as patient reports of any constraints on daily living tasks. Accordingly, the gains reported cannot be attributed to changes in self-report of symptoms as a function of improved mood following the intervention: they appear to be 'objective' gains in disease activity.

A more recent study of the same approach was reported by Stanton et al. (2002). They assigned participants, all of whom were in the early stages of breast cancer, to write about either (i) their deepest thoughts and feelings regarding breast cancer, (ii) positive thoughts and feelings regarding breast cancer, and (iii) facts of their breast cancer experience. Once again, the emotional expression – i.e. condition (i) – seemed to be of benefit. In comparison to the neutral task, participants in the emotional expression condition reported fewer somatic symptoms and fewer visits to the doctor with worries about cancer or related medical conditions. Of interest was that the emotional task appeared to be of most benefit to women who typically did not use avoidant coping strategies – and thus were able to confront the issues raised by their cancer. The positive emotional expression task appeared to benefit those women who were typically avoidant, presumably because it did not force them to confront their fears and other issues raised by their disease.

Summary and Conclusions

The chapter has reviewed the nature and effectiveness of some of the most widely used psychological interventions in a variety of medical conditions and contexts. All of the interventions have proven effective when used in the context to which they are best suited. All have been less effective when used without due consideration to the target population or the goals of that intervention. However, a few general points are suggested by the review. Perhaps the most important one is that where the intervention goal is one of behavioural change, programmes that teach skills and actively consider how they can be applied in the 'real world' of the individual are more likely to be effective than those that provide didactic information only. In addition, the outcomes of interventions are generally specific to the goals or the content of that intervention. Stress management changes levels of stress. Behavioural skills training results in skill changes. Obvious perhaps; but not all interventions have been led by these assumptions: often the hope is for change beyond that specifically provided by the intervention.

Psychological interventions have proven powerful determinants of symptoms, mood, quality of life, use of health service resources, and skills acquisition. These outcomes are worthwhile in themselves. However, for psychologists working in medical settings, there is always the temptation to adopt a bio-medical stance, and to consider whether psychological interventions save lives. Here too there is some evidence of effect. However, the number of studies to address this outcome is limited (the expense of such trials is enormous) and the 'jury must remain out' on the effectiveness of such interventions. Further trials are needed here.

However, perhaps the next real challenge facing clinical health psychology is to move from the scientific study of interventions conducted in centres of research and clinical excellence to the routine use of psychological programmes within the wider health-care system. That goal, unfortunately, remains a long way from being achieved. One way in which this may be achieved is to train other professions in the delivery or routine psychological care, and to supervise that care to ensure quality control. A second approach is to develop brief, cost-effective interventions that require minimal professional input. Here, the work of Lewin et al. (2002) and Gallacher et al. (1997) in developing manualized, structured, written programmes teaching skills required to achieve behavioural change may point to a key intervention strategy for the future. Such interventions need not simply address informational needs or facilitate behavioural change. They may also help people cope with emotional reactions to physical illnesses or the process of care. Written emotional expression provides a further potentially powerful way of influencing well-being as well as basic disease processes.

The key to future interventions may be to identify the minimal intervention that will be of benefit to most patients and to provide this on a large scale, with individual health professionals skilled in psychological therapies only becoming involved in cases where high levels of expertise are required. A further strategy may be to move at least some of the care of people with chronic illness away from hospital and other health-care settings, and to have it more situated in the community. The US Task Force on Community Preventive Services (2001), for example, recommended that public education on self-management of diabetes may be conducted in community gathering places (e.g. community centres or faith institutions) for adults and in the home for children and adolescents with type 1 diabetes. Glasgow (see Glasgow, Wagner & Kaplan, 1999) has adopted a similar public health approach by providing office-based computer programmes on controlling diabetes. Each differing intervention approach may combine to make psychological interventions more accessible to those that would benefit from them.

DISCUSSION POINTS

1. How effective are psychological interventions in the management of disease – which are the most and least effective?
2. Given the financial constraints on the provision of health care, what arguments would you use to justify the use of psychological interventions in patients with chronic disease?
3. Can psychological therapy save lives?
4. Should we be encouraging patients to explore potentially upsetting issues when they are acutely or chronically ill?

FURTHER READING

Berkman, L. F., Carney, R., Blumenthal, J., et al. (2000). Enhancing recovery in coronary heart illness patients (ENRICHD): study design and methods. *American Heart Journal* 139, 1–9. (Likely to be an influential project – although probably not in the way the authors originally intended – impacting on 3,000 patients who had had a myocardial infarction. Look for results papers not available at the time of writing.)

Esterling, B. A., L'Abate, L., Murray, E. J. and Pennebaker, J. (1999). Empirical foundations for writing in prevention and psychotherapy: mental and physical health outcomes. *Clinical Psychology Review* 19, 79–96. (A good review of brief written therapy as a means of improving physical and emotional health status.)

Glasgow, R. E., Wagner E. H., Kaplan R. M., et al. (1999). If diabetes is a public health problem, why not treat it as one? A population-based approach to chronic illness. *Annals of Behavioral Medicine* 21, 159–70. (Suggests a novel public health approach to the treatment of chronic illness.)

Multiple authors. (2002). See a special edition of the *Journal of Consulting and Clinical Psychology* (Volume 70, part 3), which reviews a number of key areas in relation to behavioural medicine and clinical health psychology.

REFERENCES

Aikens, J. E., Kiolbasa, T. A. and Sobel, R. (1997). Psychological predictors of glycemic change with relaxation training in non-insulin-dependent diabetes mellitus. *Psychotherapy and Psychosomatics* 66, 302–6.

Antoni, M. H., Cruess, D. G., Klimas, N., et al. (2002). Stress management and immune system reconstitution in symptomatic HIV-infected gay men over time: effects on transitional naïve T cells (CD4$^+$ CD45RA$^+$ CD29$^+$). *American Journal of Psychiatry* 159, 143–5.

Antoni, M. H., Lehman, J. M., Kilbourn, K. M., et al. (2001). Cognitive-behavioral stress management intervention decreases the prevalence of depression and enhances benefit finding among women under treatment for early-stage breast cancer. *Health Psychology* 20, 20–32.

Appels, A., Bär, F., Lasker, J., et al. (1997). The effect of a psychological intervention program on the risk of a new coronary event after angioplasty: a feasibility study. *Journal of Psychosomatic Research* 43, 209–17.

Bennett, P. (1997). Irritable bowel syndrome. In A. Baum et al., eds., *Cambridge Handbook of Psychology, Health and Medicine.* Cambridge: Cambridge University Press.

Bennett, P. (2000). *Introduction to Clinical Health Psychology.* Buckingham, UK: Open University Press.

Bennett, P. (2003). *Abnormal and Clinical Psychology: An Introductory Textbook.* Buckingham, UK: Open University Press.

Bennett, P. and Connell, H. (1999). Dyadic responses to myocardial infarction. *Psychology, Health and Medicine* 4, 45–55.

Berkman, L. F., Carney, R., Blumenthal, J., et al. (2000). Enhancing recovery in coronary heart illness patients (ENRICHD): study design and methods. *American Heart Journal* 139, 1–9.

Black, J. L., Allison, T. G., Williams, D. E., et al. (1998). Effect of intervention for psychological distress on rehospitalization rates in cardiac rehabilitation patients. *Psychosomatics* 39, 134–43.

Blumenthal, J. A., Jiang, W., Babyak, M. A., et al. (1997). Stress management and exercise training in cardiac patients with myocardial ischemia – effects on prognosis and evaluation of mechanisms. *Archives of Internal Medicine* 157, 2213–23.

Boardway, R. H., Delameter, A. M., Tomakowsky, J. and Gutai, J. P. (1993). Stress management for adolescents with diabetes. *Journal of Pediatric Psychology* 18, 29–45.

Brown, S. J., Lieberman, D. A., Gemeny, B. A., et al. (1997). Educational video game for juvenile diabetes: results of a controlled trial. *Medical Informatics* 22, 77–89.

Bundy, C., Carroll, D., Wallace, L. and Nagle, R. (1994). Psychological treatment of chronic stable angina pectoris. *Psychology and Health* 10, 69–77.

Burell, G. (1996). Group psychotherapy in Project New Life: treatment of coronary-prone behaviors for patients who have had coronary artery bypass graft surgery. In R. Allan and S. Scheidt, eds., *Heart and Mind: The Practice of Cardiac Psychology.* Washington, DC: American Psychological Association.

Campbell, E. M., Redman, S., Moffitt, P. S. and Sanson-Fisher, R. W. (1996). The relative effectiveness of educational and behavioral instruction programs for patients with NIDDM: a randomized trial. *Diabetes Educator* 22, 379–86.

Chalder, T. (2003). Cognitive behavioural therapy and antispasmodic therapy for irritable bowel syndrome in primary care; a randomised controlled trial. Paper presented at 'Psychological Interventions in Physical Health', invited expert conference, Rarotonga.

Classen, C., Butler, L. D., Koopman, C., et al. (2001). Supportive-expressive group therapy and distress in patients with metastatic breast cancer: a randomized clinical intervention trial. *Archives of General Psychiatry* 58, 494–501.

Coates, T. J., McKusick, L., Kuno, R., et al. (1989). Stress reduction training changed number of sexual partners but not immune function in men with HIV. *American Journal of Public Health* 79, 885–7.

Delamater, A. M., Jacobson, A. M., Anderson, B., et al. (2001). Psychosocial therapies in diabetes: report of the Psychosocial Therapies Working Group. *Diabetes Care* 24, 1286–92.

Digiusto, E. and Bird, K. D. (1995). Matching smokers to treatment: self-control versus social support. *Journal of Consulting and Clinical Psychology* 63, 290–5.

Esterling, B. A., L'Abate, L., Murray, E. J., et al. (1999). Empirical foundations for writing in prevention and psychotherapy: mental and physical health outcomes. *Clinical Psychology Review* 19, 79–96.

Evers, A. W., Kraaimaat, F. W., van Riel, P. L., et al. (2002). Tailored cognitive-behavioral therapy in early rheumatoid arthritis for patients at risk: a randomized controlled trial. *Pain* 100, 141–53.

Fawzy, F. I., Canada, A. L. and Fawzy, N. W. (2003). Malignant melanoma: effects of a brief, structured psychiatric intervention on survival and recurrence at 10-year follow-up. *Archives of General Psychiatry* 60, 100–3.

Fawzy, F. I., Fawzy, N. W., Hyun, C. S., et al. (1993). Malignant melanoma: effects of an early structured psychiatric intervention, coping, and affective state on recurrence and survival 6 years later. *Archives of General Psychiatry* 50, 681–9.

Feldman, D., Rabinowitz, J. and BenYehuda, Y. (1995). Detecting psychological distress among patients attending secondary health care clinics – self-report and physician rating. *General Hospital Psychiatry* 17, 425–32.

Frasure-Smith, N., Lesperance, F., Gravel, G., et al. (2000). Social support, depression, and mortality during the first year after myocardial infarction. *Circulation* 101, 1919–24.

Friedman, M., Powell, L. H., Thoresen, C. E., et al. (1987). Effect of discontinuance of type A behavioral counseling on type A behavior and cardiac recurrence rate of post myocardial infarction patients. *American Heart Journal* 114, 483–90.

Friedman, M. Thoresen, C. E., Gill, J. J., et al. (1986). Alteration of type A behavior and its effect on cardiac recurrences in post myocardial infarction patients: summary results of the recurrent coronary prevention project. *American Heart Journal* 112, 653–65.

Gallacher, J., Hopkinson, J., Bennett, P. and Yarnell, J. (1997). Stress management in the treatment of angina. *Psychology and Health* 12, 523–32.

Gellert, G. A., Maxwell, R. M. and Siegel, B. S. (1984). Survival of breast cancer patients receiving adjunctive psychosocial support therapy: a 10-year follow-up study. *Journal of Clinical Oncology* 11, 66–9.

Gibson, P. G., Coughlan, J., Wilson, A. J., et al. (2000). Limited (information only) patient education programs for adults with asthma. *Cochrane Database Systematic Review* 2: CD001005.

Gifford, A. L., Laurent, D. D., Gonzales, V. M., et al. (1998). Pilot randomized trial of education to improve self-management skills of men with symptomatic HIV/AIDS. *Retrovirology* 18, 136–44.

Glasgow, R. E., Boles, S. M., McKay, H. G., et al. (2003). The D-Net diabetes self-management program: long-term implementation, outcomes, and generalization results. *Preventive Medicine* 36, 410–19.

Glasgow, R. E., Toobert, D. J. and Hampson, S. E. (1996). Effects of a brief office-based intervention to facilitate diabetes dietary self-management. *Diabetes Care* 19, 835–42.

Glasgow, R. E., Wagner, E. H., Kaplan, R. M., et al. (1999). If diabetes is a public health problem, why not treat it as one? A population-based approach to chronic illness. *Annals of Behavioral Medicine* 21, 159–70.

Goodwin, P. J., Leszcz, M., Ennis, M., et al. (2001). The effect of group psychosocial support on survival in metastatic breast cancer. *New England Journal of Medicine* 345, 1719–26.

Kalichman, S. C., Benotsch, E. G., Weinhardt, L., et al. (2003). Health-related internet use, coping, social support, and health indicators in people living with HIV/AIDS: preliminary results from a community survey. *Health Psychology* 22, 111–16.

Lazarus, R. S. (1999). *Stress and Emotion: A New Synthesis.* London: Free Association Books.

Lechner, S. C., Antoni, M. H., Lydston, D., et al. (2003). Cognitive-behavioral interventions improve quality of life in women with AIDS. *Journal of Psychosomatic Research* 54, 253–61.

Lewin, B., Robertson, I. H., Irving, J. B. and Campbell, M. (1992). Effects of self-help post-myocardial-infarction rehabilitation on psychological adjustment and use of health services. *Lancet* 339, 1036–40.

Ley, P. (1997). Compliance among patients. In A. Baum et al., eds., *Cambridge Handbook of Psychology, Health and Medicine.* Cambridge: Cambridge University Press, 281–4.

Litt, M. D., Kleppinger, A. and Judge, J. O. (2002). Initiation and maintenance of exercise behavior in older women: predictors from the social learning model. *Journal of Behavioral Medicine* 25, 83–97.

Lorig, K. (1996). *Patient Education: A Practical Approach.* Newbury Park, CA: Sage.

Lorig, K. and Holman, H. (1993). Arthritis self-management studies: a twelve-year review. *Health Education Quarterly* 20, 17–28.

Lorig, K. R., Sobel, D. S., Stewart, A. L., et al. (1999). Evidence suggesting that a chronic illness self-management program can improve health status while reducing hospitalization – a randomized trial. *Medical Care* 37, 5–14.

Lutgendorf, S. K., Antoni, M. H., Ironson, G., et al. (1997). Cognitive-behavioral stress management decreases dysphoric mood and herpes simplex virus-type 2 antibody titers in symptomatic HIV-seropositive gay men. *Journal of Consulting and Clinical Psychology* 65, 31–43.

Marteau, T. M., Kidd, J., Cuddeford, L., et al. (1996). Reducing anxiety in women referred for colposcopy using an information booklet. *British Journal of Health Psychology* 1, 181–9.

May, S. and West, R. (2000) Do social support interventions ('buddy systems') aid smoking cessation? A review. *Tobacco Control* 9, 415–22.

McHugh, P., Lewis, S., Ford, S., et al. (1995). The efficacy of audiotapes in promoting psychological well-being in cancer patients: a randomised, controlled trial. *British Journal of Cancer* 71, 388–92.

Meichenbaum, D. (1985). *Stress Inoculation Training.* New York: Pergamon.

Mendez, F. J. and Belendez, M. (1997). Effects of a behavioral intervention on treatment adherence and stress management in adolescents with IDDM. *Diabetes Care* 20, 1370–5.

Montazeri, A., Jarvandi, S., Haghighat, S., et al. (2001). Anxiety and depression in breast cancer patients before and after participation in a cancer support group. *Patient Education and Counseling* 45, 195–8.

Nicassio, P. M., Radojevic, V., Weisman, M. H., et al. (1997). A comparison of behavioral and educational interventions for fibromyalgia. *Journal of Rheumatology* 24, 2000–7.

Rahn, A. N., Mose, S., ZandeerHeinz, A., et al. (1998). Influence of radiotherapy on psychological health in breast cancer patients after breast conserving surgery. *Anti-cancer Research* 18, 2271–3.

Rawl, S. M., Given, B. A., Given, C. W., et al. (2002). Intervention to improve psychological functioning for newly diagnosed patients with cancer. *Oncology Nursing Forum* 29, 967–75.

Rees, K., Bennett, P., Vedhara, K., et al. (2003). Stress management for coronary heart illness. *The Cochrane Library*, issue 1, 2002. Oxford: Update Software.

Ross, L., Boesen, E. H., Dalton, S. O., et al. (2002). Mind and cancer: does psychological intervention improve survival and psychological well-being? *European Journal of Cancer* 38, 1447–57.

Sheps, D. (2003). ENRICHD and SADHART: implications for future biobehavioral intervention efforts (editorial). *Psychosomatic Medicine* 65, 1–2.

Smith, T. W. and Ruiz, J. M. (2002). Psychosocial influences on the development and course of coronary heart disease: current status and implications for research and practice. *Journal of Consulting and Clinical Psychology* 70, 548–68.

Smyth, J. M., Stone, A. A., Hurewitz, A., et al. (1999). Effects of writing about stressful experiences on symptom reduction in patients with asthma or rheumatoid arthritis: a randomized trial. *Journal of the American Medical Association* 281, 1304–9.

Spiegel, D., Bloom, J. R., Kraemer, H. C., et al. (1989). Effect of psychosocial treatment on survival of patients with metastatic breast cancer. *Lancet* 14(2) (Oct.), 888–91.

Stanton, A. L., Danoff-Burg, S., Sworowski, L. A., et al. (2002). Randomized, controlled trial of written emotional expression and benefit finding in breast cancer patients. *Journal of Clinical Oncology* 15, 4160–8.

SuperioCabuslay, E., Ward, M. M. and Lorig, K. R. (1996). Patient education interventions in osteoarthritis and rheumatoid arthritis: a meta-analytic comparison with nonsteroidal antiinflammatory drug treatment. *Arthritis Care and Research* 9, 292–301.

Surwit, R. S. and Schneider, M. S. (1993). Role of stress in the etiology and treatment of diabetes mellitus. *Psychosomatic Medicine* 55, 380–93.

Tattersall, M. H., Butow, P. N., Griffin, A.-M., et al. (1994). The take-home message: patients prefer consultation audiotapes to summary letters. *Journal of Clinical Oncology* 12, 1305–11.

Tooth, L. R., McKenna, K. T. and Maas, F. (1998). Pre-admission education/counselling for patients undergoing coronary angioplasty: impact on knowledge and risk factors. *Australian and New Zealand Journal of Public Health* 22, 583–8.

US Task Force on Community Preventive Services. (2001). Strategies for reducing morbidity and mortality from diabetes through health-care system interventions and diabetes self-management education in community settings: a report on recommendations of the Task Force on Community Preventive Services. *MMWR Recomm Rep* 28, 1–15.

van den Arend, I. J., Stolk, R. P. and Rutten, G. E. (2000). Education integrated into structured general practice care for type 2 diabetic patients results in sustained improvement of illness knowledge and self-care. *Diabetes Medicine* 17, 190–7.

Vedhara, K., Bennett, P., et al. (2003). Enhancement of antibody responses to influenza vaccination in elderly carers of dementia patients following a cognitive-behavioural stress management intervention. *Psychosomatics and Psychotherapy* 72, 245–52.

Viner, R., McGrath, M. and Trudinger, P. (1996) Family stress and metabolic control in diabetes. *Archives of Diseases in Childhood* 74, 418–42.

Wells, M. E., McQuellon, R. P., Hinkle, J. S., et al. (1995). Reducing anxiety in newly diagnosed cancer patients: a pilot program. *Cancer Practice* 3, 100–4.

West, R., Edwards, M. and Hajek, P. (1998). A randomized controlled trial of a 'buddy' system to improve success at giving up smoking in general practice. *Addiction* 93, 1007–11.

Yancy, C. (2002). Online program aids heart patients and their doctors. *Circulation* 106, 2299.

Zabora, J. R., Blanchard, C. G., Smith, E. D., et al. (1997). Prevalence of psychological distress among cancer patients across the illness continuum. *Journal of Psychosocial Oncology* 15, 73–87.

Chapter Fifteen

WORKSITE HEALTH PROMOTION

Stan Maes and Margot van der Doef

CHAPTER OUTLINE

Worksite Health Promotion (WHP) is concerned with interventions at the worksite which aim to maintain or improve fitness, health and the well-being of employees. After a brief history of WHP this chapter addresses three main issues: (a) reasons why health promotion at the worksite is important, (b) specific examples of WHP programmes, and (c) limitations and opportunities of WHP programmes. Moreover, the chapter will highlight the important differences between American and European WHP programmes and will show that WHP programmes provide unique opportunities to influence a variety of wellness/health outcomes.

KEY CONCEPTS

comprehensive WHP programmes
health education programmes
health risk appraisal
health, wellness and financial outcomes
lifestyles
physical exercise programmes
stress management programmes

programme availability and participation
programme effectiveness and cost
   effectiveness
quality of work life
wellness risk appraisal
work environment and organizational
   interventions

WHY HEALTH PROMOTION AT THE WORKSITE?

As a student you may only be partially aware of the daily pleasures and/or pressures which the majority of the adult population experiences at the workplace. Moreover, you may even be aware that working hard can result in positive outcomes, such as satisfaction, increased morale or self-image (even if you don't get paid). However, stressful events (e.g. exams) may also have less positive consequences for one's individual well-being or lifestyle (even if you would get paid to take exams). Research suggests that during exam periods students feel more stressed, sleep less, are less resistant to colds, smoke more, have less physical exercise and eat more junk food (Weidner et al., 1996). Such adverse health behaviour probably has no long-term health consequences, since exposure to such acute stressful events is usually for brief periods. Yet, one can imagine that a person who is facing comparable or even more demanding stressors on a daily basis at work over a prolonged period may develop wellness/health problems. It is likely that such a stressful environment may also affect one's work performance, presence at work and/or health-care costs. Therefore, it is no surprise that the interest of employers in worksite health promotion has increased over the last decades.

A brief history of WHP

The promotion of well-being, health and safety at the worksite has a long history which can be characterized in a series of stages (Goldbeck, 1984). During the first stage of worksite health promotion (WHP), the worker's health and well-being were not seen as direct goals. Interventions are focused on the quality of the product and physical aspects of safety. For example, a smoking ban was introduced in the food industry in order to prevent contamination of the products and in the petroleum industry in order to prevent fires and explosions. However, there was little if any focus on the harms of smoking on the employees.

During the second stage there was growing attention to the well-being and health of managers. As a consequence, stress management and/or physical fitness programmes were offered to this specific group, which often excluded other employees. Thus, non-managerial staff was unable to reap the benefits of such programmes and were expected to make do with existing safety measures, which were expanded to promote individual safety. During the third stage of WHP, the concept of disease and accident prevention became central: the reduction of recognized health risks (such as smoking, hypertension, high serum cholesterol or unsafe behaviours) was the focus of a range of interventions that consisted primarily of behavioural advice following screening procedures.

In the fourth stage, total 'wellness–health' promotion programmes were introduced. These programmes, which recognized the inter-relation between these two concepts, i.e. wellness and health, were offered to all employees instead of specific subgroups. During this stage of WHP, health promotion, instead of disease prevention, became the ultimate goal.

Two frequently cited examples of these wellness–health programmes are the Johnson & Johnson 'Live for Life' programme and Data Control's 'Stay-well' programme (Cataldo & Coates, 1986). These American programmes were designed to improve well-being and health by promoting individual behaviours (including, for example, smoking cessation, weight control, physical exercise, stress management, improved diet and nutrition, reduced alcohol consumption and blood pressure control) and changes in the working environment to support these behaviours (e.g. smoking bans, provision of space and optimal conditions for physical exercise, changes in food and alcohol supplies) (Cataldo & Coates, 1986). A definition of worksite health promotion reflecting these elements states 'worksite intervention should include (1) periodic or continuing delivery of educational or behaviour change materials, and activities that are designed to maintain or improve employee fitness, health, and well-being, and (2) changes in organisational practices and policies conducive to health promotion' (Terborg, 1998: 204).

To date, a fifth stage can be observed in WHP programmes, especially in Europe, Canada and Australia. Besides interventions focusing on lifestyles and the health risks of employees, the fifth stage WHP programmes intervene on quality of work aspects, which may be the real cause of problems in the area of well-being, health and safety. According to this viewpoint, the workplace is recognized both as an important target (Wilson, Holman & Hammock, 1996) and a determinant of health (Harden et al., 1999). The improvement of working conditions is assumed to enhance wellness and health. In several countries in Europe, legislative guidelines concerning health and wellness at the worksite have stimulated this development. To give an example, in Norway and Sweden the Work Environment Act emphasizes that work conditions must permit the employee to influence his or her own working situation. The work must also be organized to allow the development of competence, social contacts, and the ability to make decisions. In the Netherlands the Dutch Labour Act defines similar healthy work conditions.

Advantages and benefits of WHP

As stated before, work is one of the most central life domains to most people. Over 70 per cent of adults between the ages of 18 and 65 are employees, spending 30 to 50 per cent of their waking hours at work (Terborg, 1988). Taking this into consideration, the worksite is an advantageous setting for health promotion activities, since there is no other single channel through which such a large and concentrated proportion of the adult population can be conveniently and cost-effectively accessed. For many people with low incomes and minimal exposure to traditional forms of health care, the worksite can be the primary channel of health promotion (Terborg, 1988). As such, worksite health promotion interventions have the potential to reach individuals with health risks who might not otherwise be reached (Terborg & Glasgow, 1997). Furthermore, the relative stability of the working population offers possibilities for the implementation of prolonged interventions and for a follow-up of participants over extended periods of time. This is important since it can take several years before the health effects of lifestyle changes occur (Terborg, 1988). In addition, the work setting also has the potential for replication and generalization across worksites and employee populations (Winett, King & Altman, 1989).

The social context of the worksite is one of the most prominent advantages of this setting for health promotion. The unique social environment provides sustained peer support and positive peer pressure, which is a powerful source for enhancing programme participation and for the adoption and maintenance of healthy behaviours (Harden et al., 1999; Terborg, 1988; Wilson et al., 1996; Winett et al., 1989). In addition, an increased awareness of health issues and health behaviour change is not limited to the target population at the worksite, but can be generalized to the family and the social environment of the employees (Craft, 1994; Griffiths, 1995).

Another advantage the worksite offers involves the existence of an organizational structure, including communication and health-care delivery channels, within which a health promotion programme can be embedded (Fielding, 1984; Winett et al., 1989). A final advantage of the worksite is the opportunity to offer health promotion activities at various levels. Besides the possibility of intervening in a systematic way at an individual level, interventions are also focusing at environmental and organizational levels. These environmental and organizational interventions are used to support, encourage and maintain the behavioural changes of the individual employee. Many of the behaviours associated with health risks may be thought of as habitual behaviours that are under stimulus control. Environmental changes that cue and facilitate healthy behaviours produce substantial effects, especially for persons spending a large part of the day at work (Terborg, 1988).

In the US the number of workplace health promotion programmes has grown exponentially since 1980, with 81 per cent of workplaces offering some kind of health promotion programme (Wilson et al., 1996). On the basis of a US Public Health Service national survey of WHP activities, Terborg (1998) indicated that the most notable increases involved programmes on nutrition, weight control, physical fitness, high blood pressure and stress management. Most prevalent activities targeted employee physical fitness and smoking control. Worksite health promotion as such is far more common in the US than in, for instance, the UK. In the UK in 1992 only 40 per cent of the workplaces undertook at least one major health-related activity (Harden et al., 1999). Thus far, in health promotion and stress management programmes, individual behaviour and coping strategies have been the focus rather than the work environment and work organization. Only a few workplaces have implemented health promotion activities to reduce stressors by improving work organization (Harden et al., 1999).

Impressive lists of potential benefits of worksite health promotion programmes for employees and employers have been proposed. Positive effects included increased employee morale; increased employee loyalty; improved work group cohesiveness; improved self-image; improved corporate image; more employee energy and less fatigue; greater employee creativity; increased employee productivity; improved labour–management relations; improved recruiting; improved employee health; reduced absenteeism; reduced tardiness; reduced voluntary turnover; reduced on- and off-the-job accidents; reduced absenteeism due to illness and injury; reduced utilization of medical facilities; reduced company and employee health-care expenditures; and reduced workers' compensation costs (Terborg, 1986, 1998).

However, it should be noted that no single programme has ever produced all these effects. Moreover, presumed benefits for employees are not necessarily equally important to employers and vice versa. Primary reasons for companies to adopt health promotion programmes do not always include the aim to reduce health-care costs and to improve employee productivity. Key reasons include a strong personal commitment to healthy lifestyles by senior management, a response to employee requests, moving to new facilities, the desire to project a favourable corporate image, a belief that health promotion is an important benefit that improves employee recruitment and retention, and a means for improving employee morale and job satisfaction (Fielding, 1990; Terborg, 1998).

EXAMPLES OF US FOURTH GENERATION WHP PROGRAMMES

Two examples of prototypical US WHP programmes of the fourth generation include the 'Live for Life' programme and the 'Working Well Trial'. The 'Live for Life' programme was conducted at the Johnson & Johnson worksites in Pennsylvania and New Jersey in the United States and focused on improving employee health (Wilbur, 1983; Wilbur, Hartwell & Piserchia, 1986). The Working Well Trial is a work-site cancer prevention programme widely implemented in over a hundred worksites in the US (Sorensen et al., 1996).

'Live for Life'

From the beginning, 'Live for Life' has been promoted as a means to improve the health of Johnson & Johnson employees and their families. The short-term objectives of the Live for Life programme included improvements in the quality of life, performance and work attitudes of employees. Some more specific programme objectives included the improvement of physical fitness, nutrition, weight control, blood pressure control, and alcohol use. Furthermore, improved stress management and an increase in smoking cessation and health knowledge were intended. The long-term objective of the Live for Life programme was to reduce health-care costs attributed to unhealthy behaviour and lifestyles that were amenable to modification in the work setting (Wilbur et al., 1986).

It was assumed that employees' daily lifestyles, such as exercise and nutrition intake, would have a direct impact on their present and future health, the quality of their lives and job performance. Furthermore, it was believed that a company-sponsored positive lifestyle change programme, on a voluntary basis and open to all employees, could motivate employees to make positive lifestyle changes sufficient to affect both health and quality of life.

Table 15.1 The Live for Life health screen (based on Wilbur, Hartwell & Piserchia, 1986)

Examples of health and lifestyle variables collected

Biometric measures:	blood lipids
	blood pressure
	body fat
	height and weight
	estimated maximal oxygen uptake
Behavioural measures:	smoking
	alcohol use
	physical activity
	dental hygiene practices
	nutrition practices
	coronary prone behaviour pattern (type-A behaviour)
	stress management skill use
	sleep quality
	human relations
	human potential
Attitudinal measures:	general well-being
	self-reported sick days
	satisfaction with working conditions
	relations with others
	growth opportunities
	ability to handle job strain
	job involvement
	job self-esteem
	organizational commitment

The major components of the programme, which focused on individual employees, included (a) a health screening, followed by (b) a lifestyle seminar, and (c) lifestyle improvement programmes (Wilbur, 1983). In the health screening of each participating employee, a wide range of health and lifestyle measures were taken (see table 15.1). The health screening was followed by a 3-hour lifestyle seminar offered to groups of 50 employees that introduced them to the Live for Life concept. At this point the employees received feedback on their health screening results in the form of a Lifestyle Profile. The Lifestyle Profile is presented as a way to determine 'how healthy you are' and provides a basis for taking action to improve health through participation in lifestyle improvement programmes. Next, employees were offered a variety of programmes, centred on lifestyles such as smoking cessation, physical exercise, stress management, nutrition, weight control and high blood pressure control (see table 15.2). The lifestyle programmes were given in a variety of formats, including group sessions, individual consultation, and self-help kits. To stimulate participation in these

Table 15.2 Description of the core 'Live for Life' interventions (based on Wilbur, Hartwell & Piserchia, 1986)

Lifestyle/risk factor	Lifestyle improvement programmes	Environmental changes to support health behaviour change
Smoking cessation	A 9-session programme that teaches employees how to kick the habit	Smoking policy; Availability of 'thank-you-for-not-smoking' signs
Weight control/nutrition	A 10-session programme that emphasizes eating fewer calories and burning up more through regular exercise; An 8-session programme designed to cover the essential aspects of a prudent eating pattern	Scales in restrooms; Availability of convenient nutrition information where food is sold; Availability of nutritious foods in the company cafeteria and vending machines
Exercise/fitness	A series of 12-week aerobic exercise groups; A 12-session programme that introduces employees to basic yoga exercises and skills	Shower and locker facilities on-site; Exercise facilities either on-site or rented from local organizations
Stress management	An 8-session programme designed to teach basic mental and physical relaxation skills; A 10-session programme to teach employees how to manage stress through improved personal assertiveness	Employee assistance programme to provide professional treatment and referral services to troubled employees; Availability of management training programmes designed to improve boss–subordinate relations; Flextime; carpooling; self-administered blood pressure equipment
High blood pressure	A 4-session educational programme and quarterly follow-up	See 'Stress management'
Alcohol use	A 5-session programme, which allows employees to explore the role alcohol and other substances play in their lives	See 'Stress management'
General		Incentive prizes and awards for participation in activities/ programmes; Newsletter, recruitment brochure, programme bulletin board and information display area, poster displays for upcoming programmes; Health fairs

activities, an incentive system was introduced, and participants received regular feed-back and follow-up results.

The Live for Life programme is based on marketing principles. However, it lacks the systematic use of a conceptual and theoretical framework for the interventions. Mainly, the programme has been determined by more practical considerations and experi-ences from programmes that have worked and those that have not (Fielding, 1984).

In addition to these activities, which focused on the individual employee, changes in the working environment were implemented that supported and encouraged healthy lifestyles. Examples of these changes were the creation of fitness facilities, the avail-ability of healthy food choices in the cafeterias and vending machines, the intro-duction of a clearly stated smoking policy, and the distribution of publicity materials.

In a quasi-experimental design, the results of the intervention programme were evaluated. Four Johnson & Johnson companies introduced the entire Live for Life pro-gramme. Three control companies only offered the annual health screening. However, one must be aware that this screening in combination with the administration of a Health Profile consultation and a group seminar is in itself an important intervention.

One-year findings indicated more favourable changes in the experimental sites with respect to the percentage of employees above ideal weight, physical exercise, blood pressure, cigarette smoking and self-reported sick days (Wilbur et al., 1986). At the two-year follow-up, the interventions had a significant positive impact on exercise, physical fitness and cigarette smoking. A three-year evaluation period was used to assess the effects of the programme on self-reported absenteeism. The results indicated that the impact of the programme on absenteeism was restricted to the lower income class employees. In a comparison to the lower income class employees in control sites, the absenteeism rates in the experimental sites were significantly reduced. No significant differences were found in the absenteeism rates of the higher income classes.

A health-care cost analysis of the programme indicated that in-patient costs for the experimental groups rose at a significantly lower rate than in the control groups; an average of US$42–3 for the programme group compared to $76 for the control group (Bly, Jones & Richardson, 1986). No significant differences in out-patient costs were observed. No true cost–benefit analysis was carried out, as the costs invested in the Life for Live programme were not compared to the financial savings.

The Live for Life programme was followed by the Johnson & Johnson Health & Wellness programme, which concentrated on changing individual behavioural and psycho-social risk factors instead of just focusing on symptom treatment (Ozminkowski et al., 2002). The original Live for Life programme was re-designed into a programme that integrated employee health, occupational medicine, employee assistance pro-grammes, disability management and health promotion. Participation in this programme was approximately 90 per cent, probably the result of the financial incentive of $500 provided for participating employees. An evaluation of the effects of this programme on health-care utilization and expenditures indicated a large reduction in medical care expenditures (approximately $225 per employee per year) over the 4-year pro-gramme period. Conversely, the costs of emergency-department expenditures slightly increased, although there were much larger decreases in expenditures for out-patient and doctor's office visits, mental health visits, and in-patient hospital days. However, as no comparison group was available, one should be careful in attributing these effects (entirely) to the programme.

'The Working Well Trial'

The Working Well Trial is the largest US worksite cancer prevention and control trial to date (Sorensen et al., 1996). This programme differs from the Live for Life programme in many ways. The main focus of this programme is to prevent one single disease outcome, i.e. cancer. The Working Well Trial is widely implemented in 111 worksites, thus including over 28,000 employees. These worksites were randomly assigned to the experimental and control condition. The inclusion of such a large number of worksites in the trial permitted assessment of change at the worksite level.

In line with the objectives of the National Cancer Institute, interventions of the Working Well Trial focused on (a) a reduction of the average consumption of fat, (b) an increase in the average consumption of fibre, (c) an increase in servings of fruit and vegetables, and (d) a reduction in the percentage of adults who smoke. The primary hypothesis of the Working Well Trial was that a sustained 2-year comprehensive cancer control worksite health promotion intervention addressing dietary change and smoking cessation would be more effective than a minimal intervention in achieving both individual behavioural and environmental changes. The WHP intervention was delivered by a participatory strategy and targeted both individuals and the worksite environment. As such, the Working Well Trial can be considered a representative of the fourth generation programme, in that it targeted the individual behaviour of employees and focused on changes in the organizational context, which support individual behaviour change as well.

The study was organized from four research centres that implemented the interventions in the 111 worksites. These four centres used a standard intervention protocol specifying strategies and process objectives. However, they differed to some extent in the interventions they implemented. All centres included the intervention that targeted eating patterns. Only three of the four centres implemented the smoking cessation programme. In one centre all participating worksites had already banned smoking, making this intervention redundant. Instead of smoking, this centre targeted cancer-screening practices in their worksites. Aside from smoking and nutrition, the other three study centres focused on either occupational exposures to carcinogens, exercise, or smokeless tobacco.

The intervention model was based on participatory strategies. In each worksite an employee was appointed as the worksite coordinator for the project. In addition, employee advisory boards were formed as a way to incorporate employee input and concerns. Employees in these advisory boards were trained in the goals and content of the project.

Interventions for individual workers were based on theories of health communication and behaviour change, i.e. Bandura's social cognitive theory and Prochaska and DiClemente's stages of change theory (Sorensen et al., 2002).

In the experimental worksites, core interventions directed at the individual included a kick-off event, interactive activities, posters and brochures, self-assessments, self-help materials, campaigns and contests, and direct education through classes and groups. Besides these interventions aimed primarily at the individual, interventions focusing on environmental changes were also implemented. These interventions included consultation on the formation and implementation of smoking policy, changes in food offerings and/or nutrition education in cafeterias and vending machines, and catering policies.

The control worksites received summary results from the employee survey, which were redistributed to the employees. In the majority of the control worksites a minimal intervention was provided, mainly consisting of the distribution of printed materials such as posters and newsletters. To guard the experimental design, the control worksites were asked to document health promotion activities that were conducted during the two-year trial period.

At base-line and at follow-up three years later, survey data from individual employees was collected. Furthermore, a process evaluation was designed to assess the extent to which the intervention was delivered (based on data from the project staff) and received (based on data from the employees). These measures were assessed to determine whether the independent variable (WHP activity) was in fact differentially manipulated between the intervention and control conditions.

At follow-up, for the trial as whole, small but significant results were observed for two of three individual nutrition outcomes. In comparison to the control sites, the experimental sites exhibited a net reduction in the percentage of energy obtained from fat consumption, and an average increase in fruit and vegetable intake. Although there was no overall significant change found in tobacco use, smoking cessation rates among blue-collar workers more than doubled in the experimental sites, compared with those in the control sites (Sorensen et al., 2002).

Analyses of the data regarding the receipt of the interventions indicated that the level of WHP intervention activity was high in the control worksites, reflecting the overall trend toward increasing health promotion activity in work settings.

Two important things can be learned from these results. The first is, that it becomes increasingly difficult to have real control groups when over 80 per cent of the worksites are offering some form of health promotion activities, as is the case in the US. While this is a positive trend from an employee perspective, it is not facilitating ongoing research. The second point is that evaluation studies should explore effects for subgroups, because it is unlikely that interventions may be equally beneficial for all workers.

'HEALTHIER WORK AT BRABANTIA': AN EXAMPLE OF A EUROPEAN FIFTH GENERATION WHP PROGRAMME

In contrast to American programmes, European programmes tend to focus not only on individual health behaviour, but also on the creation of healthy work conditions.

This latter focus has been stimulated by national legislative guidelines concerning health and wellness at the worksite.

Partly due to their legislative background concerning health and wellness at work, the Scandinavian countries initiated the integration of interventions on quality of work in WHP programmes. Landsbergis and Vivona-Vaughan (1995) developed an occupational stress intervention, in which problem-solving committees were organized to identify stressors and take action to alter them. Likewise, Elo and Leppänen (1999) established health promotion teams that aimed to improve the psycho-social work environment of a metal factory in a 3-year project. The interventions that were implemented concerned the physical activation of personnel, technical improvements in the work process, and social activities. In the same line, Mikkelsen and Saksvik (1999) introduced a participatory organization intervention on job characteristics and job stress in the Postal Service of Norway. The central aim of these intervention studies was to improve employees' physical and mental well-being mainly through improvements in quality of work aspects.

Background and aims of the Brabantia project

The Brabantia project was named after the Dutch manufacturer of household products for which the programme was developed (Maes et al., 1996; Maes et al., 1998). The Brabantia programme can be considered one of the first examples of the fifth stage WHP programmes. Moreover, the programme was unique in that it considered the improvement of working conditions as an important means to enhance employee wellness and health. Interventions were based on principles derived from cognitive behavioural and social learning theory and on Karasek's Demand–Control–Social Support model (Maes et al., 1998).

Description of interventions

During the first year of intervention, activities were mainly targeted at lifestyles. The interventions directed at quality of work were implemented during the second and third year because they required a longer period of preparation (Maes et al., 1998).

At the individual level, all employees were offered the opportunity to participate in 3 half-hour intervention sessions a week. To increase participation, these sessions were held during lunch-time at the worksite and half of the time spent in each session was considered paid work time. During the first intervention year, one 1 of 6 sessions was a health education session, on nutrition (7 sessions), alcohol and drug consumption (2 sessions), working conditions and stress, smoking behaviour, headaches, or back pain (1 session each). In addition to the relevant information, participants in these health education sessions were given the opportunity to join groups that related to themes of smoking cessation, headaches or back pain.

After the first intervention year, these health education sessions were discontinued because of low participation (10 to 20 per cent of the eligible population). In the second intervention year, the initiative for interventions directed at lifestyles was transferred to a special lifestyle committee (a group of workers elected by employees). This resulted in fewer but more comprehensive activities, such as a health fair in the second year and a health exhibition in the third year, with high levels of participation (60 to 70 per cent of the eligible population).

During the whole intervention period, in the remaining half-hour lunch-time sessions, physical exercise training was offered to all employees. The content of the physical exercise sessions was chosen by the participants on the basis of video recordings of various types of physical exercise.

At the organizational and environmental level, an intervention was introduced that gave support to the interventions at the individual level. The measures included, for example, creation of on-site exercise facilities, a smoking policy in the cafeteria, advertising of the programme by means of an information corner in the cafeteria, along with posters, videos, on-site radio messages and newsletter articles, and providing healthy food (and information about nutrition) in the cafeteria. In addition, incentives to promote participation in the programme were used (e.g. T-shirts, sweatshirts, sport bags, and the chance to win a weekend stay at a health and leisure resort).

The second type of intervention at the organizational and environmental level was based on screening for wellness risks at work by means of individual interviews with each employee (see table 15.3). The resulting information was used to construct wellness risk profiles for each function category and each of the 11 production units. A 'wellness committee' consisting of the management team and members of the project team examined these profiles. This committee developed proposals for modifying specific functions and/or aspects of the work organization and environment. After consultation with the employees involved, the wellness committee guided the implementation and evaluation of the proposed changes.

For example, production of the Brabantia potato-chipper had previously been divided into short-cycled tasks. The work was simple, and each worker had always performed the same repetitive task. Decision latitude was almost non-existent. Opportunities for the employees to influence the rate and sequence of work and/or the planning of production were very limited. Employees were well informed about the immediate outcomes of their work; however, they were not informed about the more distant outcomes. In addition, opportunities for social contacts between the workers were limited, partly because of the way in which work areas were designed.

An 'autonomous work group' of workers was established and given authority over the entire production process, from collection of raw materials to delivery of the product to the sales department. This implied additional tasks such as initiating work orders, arranging supply and transport of raw materials and finished products, calculating hours spent on tasks, and performing quality checks. In addition to this greater variety of tasks, rotation of tasks became possible. Workers could take turns in the transport and wrapping of finished products or any other constituent activity. Additional training was necessary for both leaders and the other employees in order to allow these changes in the work process. In addition, a re-organization of the production line was necessary to support these changes and to improve ergonomic conditions.

Table 15.3 Screening of wellness conditions at work by means of the structured interview content and organization of work (Maes et al., 1989)

Wellness condition	Description	Desired wellness condition
Completeness	Percentage of performance, preparational and supportive tasks (e.g. how much time of your total work time is spent on preparational tasks?)	Job includes preparational, performance, and supportive tasks
Complexity	Complexity of the various tasks (e.g. are the supportive tasks you have difficult, partly difficult/partly easy, or easy?)	Job includes a mixture of difficult and easy tasks
Regulation possibilities	Possibility to regulate work procedures, materials, tools (e.g. can you yourself correct a mistake you have made?; do you have the right means (tools, machines, people) to do your work?)	Employee has options to exert control over work procedures (either with or without help or consultation of others)
Organizational tasks	Participation in organization of own work (e.g. are there regular work meetings where topics concerning the organization of work can be discussed seriously?)	Employee has the possibility to solve problems on an organizational level
Autonomy	Decision latitude regarding pace, order and method of work (e.g. can you yourself determine the order in which you perform the given tasks for a day?)	Employee can influence or control work pace, method and order
Contact possibilities	Contact with and support of colleagues and supervisor (e.g. can you ask others for help, when you can not get your job done?)	Job should contain the possibility to have and maintain contact with other people during working hours
Cycle length	Cycle length of the main task (percentage of the day spend on short-cycled tasks (< 90 seconds))	Job should contain tasks that last at least 90 seconds before the same task is repeated
Information	Feedback from own work and communication about general objectives of enterprise (e.g. do you get enough information about the company and the position of your own department in it?)	Employee has to be informed about the aims and results of work on the level of the workplace, department and company

Thus, the entire organizational structure of the experimental site of Brabantia had evolved from a product-oriented structure to a more functional structure. For example, there were 26 foremen and 6 transporters before the intervention, while at the end there were only 13 foremen and no transporters, since the production workers carried out many of the tasks. Another consequence was that the evaluation and gratification system changed from one based on individual performance to a combined individual and group evaluation system.

The evaluation study

The Brabantia project was evaluated in a quasi-experimental pre-test/post-test control group design with repeated measures (Maes et al., 1998). In one experimental site all interventions directed at lifestyle changes and changes in working conditions were implemented. Two other Brabantia sites formed the control group. In these sites no interventions were implemented. The pre-test was administered to both the experimental and control group, followed by a series of post-tests 1, 2 and 3 years after the pre-test. Furthermore, absenteeism data from all employees was gathered during the whole period.

The following outcome variables were incorporated into the study, including a total lifestyle score (based on 6 lifestyles, i.e. smoking, physical exercise, hours of sleep, body mass index, use of alcohol, and fat consumption), a health risk score (representing an employees' risk of developing coronary heart disease during the subsequent 8 years; based on age, serum cholesterol, systolic blood pressure, and smoking status), general stress reactions (a total score covering anxiety, depression, somatic complaints, hostility, and sleep problems), working conditions (four global conditions, i.e. 'psychological demands', 'control', 'social support from colleagues and supervisor', and 'ergonomic conditions'), and absenteeism.

Lifestyle change interventions targeted at the individual level were introduced during the first year, which brought about favourable changes in health risks during the first post-test. This was mainly due to the significant decrease in cholesterol levels in the experimental group. Considering the considerable amount of effort directed at nutrition, the results were not surprising. However, the initial effect on health risk disappeared at post-test 2, which illustrates the need for continuous and more extensive intervention to produce long-lasting effects on health outcomes.

Furthermore, the programme had favourable effects on working conditions, including psychological demands, control and ergonomic conditions. As evidence suggests that higher levels of control and decision latitude are related to increased levels of health and well-being (Karasek & Theorell, 1990), the employees' significant improvement in perceived control in the experimental group was considered an important intervention effect.

Last but not least, the results also show a reduction in absenteeism in the experimental group. This reduction was so substantial that the company had a positive financial return on its investment in the project. The project had no significant effect on the other outcomes included in the evaluation study, i.e. the total lifestyle score, general stress reactions, and social support from colleagues and supervisor.

In conclusion, the Brabantia project emphasized the organization and content of work, in contrast to the American fourth generation WHP programmes that focused primarily on lifestyles. Therefore, it is not surprising that the Brabantia project had the strongest and most enduring effects on perceived working conditions and absenteeism. The American fourth generation programmes focus more exclusively on healthy lifestyles and health risk, and therefore tend to score better on health-related variables. The positive effects these programmes have on outcomes such as absenteeism thus seem to be achieved through a different pathway.

THE STATE OF THE ART AND DIRECTIONS FOR FUTURE RESEARCH

Programme availability and participation

While it is encouraging to observe that over 80 per cent of the worksites in the US (and up to 40 per cent in other Western countries) offer some health promotion programme to their employees, it should be noted that the mean availability of specific health promotion programmes is much lower. According to data from the US National Health Interview Survey, mean availability ranges from 42.5 per cent for smoking cessation programmes, to 31 per cent for health education programmes (focusing on injury prevention, stress management, back care, use of alcohol, nutrition, weight control, sexually transmitted diseases, accident prevention and prenatal information), 30.7 per cent for screening tests (for blood pressure, cholesterol, cancer), 13.9 per cent for the presence of exercise facilities, and 5.9 per cent for exercise programmes (Grosch et al., 1998). Furthermore, participation rates vary greatly. Mean participation rates are as low as 19 per cent for exercise programmes, 32 per cent for health education programmes and 49.3 per cent for screening tests. Surprisingly, the data suggests that participation rates seem to be minimally related to employee characteristics, such as age, gender, ethnicity, occupation and health. This suggests that efforts to increase participation should be focused on programme and workplace factors such as programme implementation strategies, management commitment and incentives for participants (Grosch et al., 1998).

By means of interviews, focus groups and a large employee survey, Crump and colleagues (1996) explored whether the organization context and the implementation process affected participation in WHP activities. Overall, employees participated in fewer than two activities per year. Participation was enhanced when co-workers endorsed the programme. Minority employees and those in lower positions were more likely to participate in fitness activities if the programme was comprehensive, well marketed, provided time off for the participants to participate or had on-site facilities. Management support increased participation among white, male employees, who held upper-level positions. This study shows that employee characteristics apparently interact with programme and workplace characteristics in affecting participation.

Another important issue addressed was the participation of high-risk employees and whether they profited from the instated programmes. Lewis and colleagues (1996) found among employees of a petrochemical research and development company (which offered health risk appraisal and a comprehensive health promotion programme) that, with the exception of programmes for weight control, smoking and blood pressure (which is not surprising), employees at a lower risk had higher participation levels than those at higher risk. This study suggests the importance of evaluating subgroup effects related to risk levels when appraising worksite health promotion programmes.

Programme effectiveness

In terms of interventions, which focus on health outcomes, the strongest support for the effectiveness of WHP seems to exist for effects of stress management and weight control. While the evidence for smoking cessation, physical exercise, safety belt use and reduction of alcohol use is suggestive, the effects of HIV/AIDS prevention and health risk appraisal programmes are weak (Terborg, 1998; Wilson, 1996). It is, however, important to differentiate between health risk appraisal, physical exercise programmes, stress management and health education programmes, which focus on weight control, smoking cessation, safety belt use, nutrition, alcohol use and other health behaviours.

Health risk appraisal (HRA) programmes vary from the other programmes. They consist of bio-medical examinations, interviews or questionnaires to establish bio-medical or behavioural risk factors. They may involve, apart from screening for different types of cancer (breast cancer, colon-rectal cancer and prostate cancer), data collection for fitness risk (frequency, duration and type of exercise), obesity risk (body weight, percentage of body fat and ideal weight), cholesterol risk (high-density lipoprotein levels, low-density lipoprotein levels and cholesterol medication history), blood pressure risk (systolic and diastolic blood pressure and family treatment history), stress risk (clinical stress measures, e.g. for depression), tobacco risk (type, frequency and history of tobacco use) and nutrition risk (body weight, blood pressure, diet, cholesterol and alcohol intake) (Lewis, Huebner & Yarborough, 1996).

In a review of the literature concerning the impact of worksite-based health risk appraisal on health-related outcomes, Anderson and Staufacker (1996) pointed at the fact that there is (weak) evidence for positive changes in seat-belt use, physical activity, systolic blood pressure and body mass index based on solely HRA. Moreover, they state that it is naive to believe that the communication of such risk would motivate large numbers of employees to change their risky health behaviour. However, the authors point out that HRA has evolved over time from a stand-alone procedure to HRA programmes which are fully integrated in a comprehensive health promotion process, including behavioural interventions and follow-up. The review strongly supports that these more comprehensive programmes are effective, and that HRA procedures have the advantage of targeting follow-up behavioural interventions for individuals at risk.

In a review of the methodology and health impact of worksite fitness and exercise programmes, Shephard (1996) points at important methodological shortcomings of effect studies, such as possible Hawthorne effects, substantial sample attrition and a poor definition of the intervention (exercise programme only or part of a compre-hensive program). The author concludes that these programmes show small benefits on a variety of outcomes, including changes in body mass index, skin folds, aero-bic power, muscle strength and flexibility, overall risk-taking behaviour, systolic blood pressure, serum cholesterol and cigarette smoking. However, the present state of research does not allow conclusions regarding (for example) effects on mood state or reduced rates of illness and injury.

Murphy (1996) published a critical review on the health effects of stress manage-ment in work settings. A variety of stress management techniques have been used in worksite studies, such as muscle relaxation, meditation, biofeedback, cognitive-behavioural skills, and combinations of these techniques. In about three-quarters of the studies, stress management was offered to all employees, while for the remain-ing studies high-stress employees were recruited. Only half of the studies included in the review were randomized controlled studies. On the whole, stress management programmes seem to be effective in altering blood pressure, anxiety and somatic com-plaints. The effectiveness varies according to the health outcome measure used. Some techniques, such as cognitive-behavioural skills, were effective for psychological outcomes, whereas muscle relaxation techniques were more effective for physiolo-gical outcomes. Biofeedback was the least used and also the least effective technique. Meditation produced the most consistent effects across outcome measures. In general, studies that used a combination of techniques proved to be the most effective across outcome measures. However, none of the stress interventions produced consistent effects in job/organization relevant outcomes such as absenteeism or job satisfaction. The author suggests that in order to achieve these effects, interventions should alter or modify the sources of stress in the work environment.

The effectiveness of health education programmes varies according to the health behaviours that they target, and methodological shortcomings frequently obscure the validity of conclusions. For example, while some authors state that the strongest sup-port exists for the effectiveness of worksite interventions for weight control as stated above, Hennrikus and Jefferey (1996) seriously question this conclusion in a review paper on this topic. They show that the literature is methodologically weak, consist-ing largely of uncontrolled case studies.

In addition, while worksite interventions for weight control seem to recruit at aver-age as much as about 40 per cent of overweight employees, there is only evidence for short-term weight loss: typically 1 to 2 pounds a week. Long-term weight loss remains to be demonstrated. Likewise, in a review on the health impact of worksite nutrition and cholesterol intervention programmes, Glanz, Sorensen and Farmer (1996) stated that conclusions are limited by the study designs used, which often lacked control groups, used non-randomized designs or suffered from self-selection bias. They further argue that there is evidence that nutrition and cholesterol programmes can have short-term effects, but that there is no conclusive evidence about a causal relationship between these programmes and improved behaviour or health.

However, it can be questioned whether these reviews, which focus on isolated health behaviours, give a fair picture of the state of the art. Many health promotion programmes at the worksite are comprehensive programmes, targeting a variety of health behaviours. It should be noted that the outcome effects of these comprehensive programmes in terms of health behaviours and health risks are probably stronger than in studies, which focus on one single target.

In a review of health-related outcomes of multi-component worksite health promotion programmes, Heaney and Goetzel (1997) recommended cautious optimism about the effectiveness of these programmes. They stated that WHP programmes are preferably multi-component programmes (focusing on different lifestyles or health behaviours), and may enhance productivity or reduce employee health risk if the programmes include (a) individual risk behaviour counselling, and (b) programmatic activities of sufficient intensity and duration to create a supportive environment. In addition, the authors suggested that in order to be effective in reducing preventable morbidity and mortality a programme must attract the participation of high-risk employees. Harden and colleagues (1999) came to the conclusion that most evaluation studies included in their review are not sound enough to allow firm conclusions.

However, it has been suggested that effectiveness of WHP programmes increases if (a) there is support for the interventions from top management, (b) if employees are involved as much as possible in planning, implementation and provision of the interventions, (c) programmes focus on a definable and modifiable risk factor, which is relevant to the workers, and (d) if interventions are tailor-made or otherwise respond to the needs of the workers. Based on a recent review on the effectiveness of comprehensive worksite health promotion and disease management programmes, Pelletier (2001) concluded that providing individualized risk reduction for high-risk employees within the context of comprehensive programming is a critical element of worksite interventions. Moreover, Pelletier suggested that there is now moderate to strong evidence that comprehensive, multi-factorial risk and disease management interventions in worksites are clinical effective and cost-effective.

Cost-effectiveness

Aldana (2001) published a comprehensive review of the literature on the financial impact of health promotion programmes. There is evidence that obesity, high levels of stress, and the presence of multiple risk factors have an important impact on health-care costs and absenteeism. Studies on single risk factors and health behaviours (including hyper-cholesterolaemia, hypertension, diet, alcohol abuse, seat-belt usage, fitness and physical activity) are inconclusive or lacking. However, health promotion programmes designed to ameliorate health risks do seem to reduce absenteeism and health-care costs.

The author attributes these effects to possible non-risk factor related effects such as increased self-responsibility, improved morale or a greater awareness of the use of health-care services. While these suggestions are open to discussion, they certainly raise questions concerning the existing evaluation pathway of most WHP projects, including the over-emphasis on the health behaviour/health risk/health-care cost and productivity relationship. The aforementioned effects of the Brabantia project did not follow this pathway, but rather followed a work content/quality of work life/ productivity channel. This is yet another reason why comprehensive WHP projects should also include interventions to increase quality of work.

Donaldson and colleagues (1999) reported on one of the very few American studies on this alternative pathway. These authors conducted a study with lumber industry employees, which seriously questioned the effects of health behaviour-related WHP activities on increased company profitability. The purpose of the study was to examine whether health behaviour and quality of work life were related to organizational effectiveness outcomes. On the whole, health behaviours (sleep, exercise, having breakfast, eating fatty foods, alcohol consumption, tobacco use) proved to be weakly related or unrelated to outcomes such as organizational commitment, absenteeism, tardiness frequency and well-being. In contrast, quality of work factors (work environment, job stress, co-worker satisfaction, quality of supervision, job security) did significantly predict these outcomes. The authors concluded:

> Given the fact that most employers cannot afford to promote public health at the cost of organizational functioning and profitability, this point [that interventions should enhance quality of work as well as lifestyle] is fundamental for designing comprehensive health promotion systems in the workplace. (Donaldson et al., 1999: 587)

A review by Riedel and colleagues (2001) on the effects of disease prevention and health promotion on workplace productivity may further illustrate the relevance of risk factor screening or health behaviour change programmes for the prevention of performance loss. Early detection or screening programmes provide evidence suggesting that screening for high blood pressure and depression prevents performance loss, whereas the effect of cholesterol or various forms of cancer screening (breast cancer, colon-rectal cancer, prostate cancer) is unknown. For health behaviour change programmes, there is evidence that stress management programmes, vaccination, back-pain-related exercise and smoking cessation programmes have an effect on performance loss, but for general exercise and nutrition programmes the effect is unknown.

The study revealed that there is at least insufficient research on the relationship between several forms of intervention and performance loss. It should also be noted that stress management is the only programme in this review whose impact on performance loss is rated as 'very high'. Again, next to the health risk/health behaviour–productivity, the importance of the quality of work–productivity pathway seems to emerge.

Methodological critique

As already mentioned in some of the previous paragraphs, many evaluations of WHP programmes suffer from methodological shortcomings, even if the methodological rigor of evaluation designs has evolved over the last 10 years. It has been frequently observed that the more rigorous the evaluation design, the smaller and less consistent the results (Pelletier, 1999). As a consequence, many of the aforementioned reviews may over-estimate intervention effects, because many studies included in these reviews were not experimental or quasi-experimental studies.

Another issue regards the sample size. Some studies were conducted with less than 200 employees, whereas others included very large populations of, for instance, ten of thousands of employees. Most reviews were narrative reviews rather than meta-analyses, and as a consequence observed effects may have been over- or under-estimated, depending on the effects of the larger studies.

Many shortcomings appear concerning the existing methodology of the evaluation studies. In many cases, studies relied only on self-report measures rather than on more objective measures of, for example, smoking reduction, alcohol consumption, fat intake or weight reduction, which reduces the reliability of the effects. Even health risk appraisal of important bio-medical risk factors (such as obesity risk, cholesterol risk and blood pressure risk) were frequently assessed by means of self-administered questionnaires, as was the case in a study conducted by Lewis and colleagues (1996), for example. As Anderson and Staufacker (1996) proved, this example is far from being an isolated case.

Moreover, it is not clear which employees are included under the heading of 'participants'. Some studies defined an employee as a participant if the person attended a single session (e.g. one exercise session), while others considered completion of a whole subprogramme as a criterion for participation (Pelletier, 1999). It is clear that the definition of 'participants' (and by default non-participants) was loosely applied within the studies, and can be responsible for variability in the effect size of interventions. The issue of 'participants' brings us to another problematic issue. Many studies suffer from self-selection bias, and programme effects are frequently calculated on the basis of results for voluntary participants, while all other (non-participating) employees are excluded. In several cases effects are even calculated on the basis of differences between participants and non-participants within one worksite over time. Furthermore, drop-out or attrition rates, which (for example) may range for smoking cessation, weight loss or exercise programmes from 0 per cent to 80 per cent, were frequently not taken into account, since effects were mostly calculated on the basis of the remainders (Terborg, 1998).

Finally, very few studies included long-term effect measures. As a consequence, although the present studies inform us about short-term programme effects, they reveal little of maintenance of behaviour change and health or productivity consequences over time. It is quite clear that these shortcomings can seriously threaten the validity of conclusions concerning effectiveness.

The lack of theoretical background

Heaney and Goetzel (1997: 306) have stated in their literature review on multi-component health promotion programmes that, 'With a few notable exceptions, most of the worksite health promotion programmes included in this review were not explicitly and firmly rooted in behavioural science theory.' The two examples described in this chapter are exceptions in this respect, since the Working Well Trial was based on the social cognitive behaviour theory and the Healthier Work at Brabantia project was based on principles derived from cognitive behavioural, social cognitive and behaviour change models and the Job Demand–Control–Support model (JDCS).

One consequence of the lack of theoretical background is that it is difficult to explain successful research findings. Another consequence is that the effectiveness of the interventions can be optimized. For example, the use of behaviour change models such as Prochaska and Di Clemente's (1986) trans-theoretical theory of change implies that behaviour change is not seen as a fact, but as a process, which develops over time. Different phases of behaviour change are identified by this model, including pre-contemplation, contemplation, preparation, action and maintenance. There is a plethora of research which has demonstrated that different interventions are required for individuals at different stages (Herrick, Stone & Mettler, 1997). However, most WHP initiatives offered one standard programme (e.g. for smoking cessation, weight loss, physical exercise, nutrition and other health behaviours) to all employees.

Likewise, the Job Demand–Control–Support model has repeatedly shown that high job demands may have detrimental effects on health and well-being, while higher levels of job control and social support at work can reduce these negative effects (Van der Doef & Maes, 1998, 1999, 2000). In terms of interventions, this model suggests that enhancement of job control (autonomy, skill discretion, task variety) and social support from co-workers and supervisors is beneficial in terms of employees' health and well-being. Apart from the Brabantia project, very few interventions, especially in the United States, have yet addressed these work environment aspects, despite the fact that several authors agree with the importance of such an ecological approach (Murphy, 1996; Donaldson et al., 1999; Stokols, Pelletier & Fielding, 1996).

There is one exception, which will hopefully lead the way for other American projects: a randomized controlled trial of an intervention based on the JDCS model (Pelletier et al., 1998). The intervention was conducted by mail and telephone to manage job strain, which proved to increase employee's knowledge of job strain risk factors and possible solutions, to alter risk behaviour, resulting in self-reported benefits. However, the intervention appeared to be designed to change employee attitude and behaviour rather than the work environment. It has already been pointed out that this difference in approach is typical of American WHP projects.

European and American WHPs seem to rely on a different underlying philosophies. American projects focus more on individual lifestyle changes (supported by environmental measures), while European initiatives focus more on the effects of the work environment on quality of work life (Maes et al., 1996). It is thus no surprise that models which focus more on the work environment, such as the JDCS model, are more popular in Europe than in the US. However, as previously argued, very few authors make these differences explicit at a theory or model level.

Many examples can be given of the relevance of theoretical models for the improvement of programme development and effectiveness. The self-regulation theory is another perspective which could be used as a cornerstone for the improvement of WHP programmes. The core assumption of self-regulation theory is that personal goals guide human behaviour (Maes & Gebhardt, 2000). As a consequence, personal goal facilitation at work may be an important way to improve employee functioning and wellness/health outcomes.

In a study with 1,036 health-care workers, facilitation of personal goals by the workplace proved to contribute directly to the prediction of wellness/health outcomes, explaining additional variance in the outcomes besides the direct effects of demographic variables and job characteristics (JDCS variables). There was also evidence for indirect effects, with goal facilitation mediating the relationships between job characteristics and employee well-being (ter Doest et al., submitted).

In Conclusion

While this section may contain a lot of critical remarks on WHP projects and existing evaluation studies, there is no reason to believe that there isn't a bright future for worksite health promotion projects. Comprehensive projects which (a) are based on sound psychological theory representing a health behaviour change and a quality of work life pathway, (b) are supported by management and employees, (c) which include interventions targeted at individuals at risk based on health risk appraisal and wellness risk appraisal, and (d) are continued over time, will almost certainly improve wellness/health outcomes as well as health-care costs and productivity outcomes in many employees.

As far as effect studies are concerned, we hope that the existing trend, which reflects an increasing rigor of methodological designs, will be continued. However, we should be cautious not to over-sell the benefits of worksite health promotion. Over-commercialization of WHP could easily result in disappointment and drawbacks, while realistic perspectives on possible effects based on empirical evidence are a better guarantee for the continuation, improvement and integration of the many programmes that are initiated. We also recommend that there be an integration of both American and European philosophies with regard to worksite health promotion – that is, health behaviour change and the improvement of quality of work life path – in order to achieve superior effects both on clinical health outcomes and on health-care costs and productivity outcomes.

DISCUSSION POINTS

1. Could you explain how worksite health promotion programmes developed over time?
2. What are the advantages and presumed benefits of WHP?
3. Describe and discuss the 'Live for Life' programme.
4. Describe and discuss the 'Working Well Trial'.
5. Describe and discuss the 'Brabantia' programme.
6. Which important issues relate to programme availability and participation?
7. Is WHP effective? Discuss its strengths and weaknesses.
8. Is WHP cost effective?
9. What are the most important methodological critiques of existing WHP programmes?
10. How, and why, could a sound theoretical background improve WHP?

FURTHER READING

Aldana, S. G. (2001). Financial impact of health promotion programs: a comprehensive review of the literature. *American Journal of Health Promotion* 15, 297–320.

Harden, A., Peersman, G., Oliver, S., Mauthner, M. and Oakley, A. (1999). A systematic review of the effectiveness of health promotion interventions in the workplace. *Occupational Medicine* 49, 540–8.

Maes, S., Verhoeven, C., Kittel, F. and Scholten, H. (1998). Effects of a Dutch work-site wellness–health program: the Brabantia project. *American Journal of Public Health* 88, 1037–41.

Sorensen, G., Stoddard, A. M., LaMontagne, A. D., Emmons, K., et al. (2002). A comprehensive worksite cancer prevention intervention: behavior change results from a randomised controlled trial (United States). *Cancer, Causes and Control* 13, 493–502.

Terborg, J. R. (1998). Health psychology in the United States: a critique and selective review. *Applied Psychology: An International Review* 47, 199–217.

Wilson, M. G. (1996). A comprehensive review of the effects of worksite health promotion on health-related outcomes: an update. *American Journal of Health Promotion* 11, 107–8.

Wilson, M. G., Holman, P. B. and Hammock, A. (1996). A comprehensive review of the effects of worksite health promotion on health-related outcomes. *American Journal of Health Promotion* 10, 429–35.

KEY STUDIES

Maes, S., Verhoeven, C., Kittel, F. and Scholten, H. (1998). Effects of a Dutch work-site wellness–health program: the Brabantia project. *American Journal of Public Health* 88, 1037–41.

Sorensen, G., Stoddard, A. M., LaMontagne, A. D., Emmons, K., et al. (2002). A comprehensive worksite cancer prevention intervention: behavior change results from a randomised controlled trial (United States). *Cancer, Causes and Control* 13, 493–502.

Wilbur, C. S., Hartwell, T. D. and Piserchia, P. V. (1986). The Johnson & Johnson Live for Life program: its organization and evaluation plan. In M. F. Cataldo and T. J. Coates, eds., *Health and Industry: A Behavioral Medicine Perspective.* New York: John Wiley, 338–50.

REFERENCES

Aldana, S. G. (2001). Financial impact of health promotion programs: a comprehensive review of the literature. *American Journal of Health Promotion* 15, 297–320.

Anderson, D. R. and Staufacker, M. J. (1996). The impact of worksite-based health risk appraisal on health-related outcomes: a review of the literature. *American Journal of Health Promotion* 10, 499–508.

Bly, J. L., Jones, R. C. and Richardson, J. E. (1986). Impact of worksite health promotion on health care costs and utilization: evaluation of Johnson & Johnson's Live for Life program. *Journal of the American Medical Association* 256, 3235–40.

Cataldo, M. F. and Coates, T. J., eds. (1986). *Health and Industry: A Behavioral Medicine Perspective.* New York: John Wiley.

Craft, M. (1994). Health at work: a needs assessment in South West Thames Regional Authority. *Promotion & Education* 1, 21–8.

Crump, C. E., Earp, J. A. L., Kozma, C. M. and Hortez-Piciotto, I. (1996). Effect of organization-level variables on differential employee participation in 10 federal worksite health promotion programs. *Health Education Quarterly* 23, 204–33.

Donaldson, S. I., Sussman, S., Dent, C. W., Severson, H. H. and Stoddard, J. L. (1999). Health behavior, quality of work life, and organizational effectiveness in the lumber industry. *Health Education and Behavior* 26, 579–91.

Elo, A.-L. and Leppänen, A. (1999). Efforts of health promotion teams to improve the psychosocial work environment. *Journal of Occupational Health Psychology* 4, 87–94.

Fielding, J. E. (1984). Health promotion and disease prevention at the worksite. *Annual Review of Public Health* 5, 237–65.

Fielding, J. E. (1990). Worksite health promotion programs in the United States: progress, lessons and challenges. *Health Promotion International* 5, 75–81.

Glanz, K., Sorensen, G. and Farmer, A. (1996). The health impact of worksite nutrition and cholesterol intervention programs. *American Journal of Health Promotion* 10, 453–70.

Goldbeck, W. B. (1984). Foreword. In M. P. O'Donnell and T. H. Ainsworth, eds., *Health Promotion in the Workplace.* New York: John Wiley.

Griffiths, J. H. (1995). *A Practical Guide to Health Promotion at the Worksite: Guidelines for Alliance-building and Networking with Companies.* Cardiff, Wales: World Health Organization Europe.

Grosch, J. W., Alterman, T., Petersen, M. R. and Murphy, L. R. (1998). Worksite health promotion programs in the US: factors associated with availability and participation. *American Journal of Health Promotion* 13, 36–45.

Harden, A., Peersman, G., Oliver, S., Mauthner, M. and Oakley, A. (1999). A systematic review of the effectiveness of health promotion interventions in the workplace. *Occupational Medicine* 49, 540–8.

Heaney, C. A. and Goetzel, R. Z. (1997). A review of health-related outcomes of multi-component worksite health promotion programs. *American Journal of Health Promotion* 11, 290–307.

Hennrikus, D. J. and Jeffrey, R. W. (1996). Worksite intervention for weight control: a review of the literature. *American Journal of Health Promotion* 10, 471–98.

Herrick, A. B., Stone, W. J. and Mettler, M. M. (1997). Stages of change, decisional balance, and self-efficacy across four health behaviors in a worksite environment. *American Journal of Health Promotion* 12, 49–56.

Karasek, R. and Theorell, T. (1990). *Healthy Work: Stress, Productivity, and the Reconstruction of Working Life.* New York: Basic Books.

Landsbergis, P. A. and Vivona-Vaughan, E. (1995). Evaluation of an occupational stress intervention in a public agency. *Journal of Organizational Behavior* 16, 29–48.

Lewis, R. J., Huebner, W. W. and Yarborough, C. M. (1996). Characteristics of participants and non-participants in worksite health promotion. *American Journal of Health Promotion* 11, 99–106.

Maes, S. and Gebhardt, W. (2000). Self-regulation and health behavior: the health behavior goal model. In M. Boekaerts, P. Pintrich and M. Zeidner, eds., *Handbook of Self-regulation.* San Diego: Academic Press, 343–68.

Maes, S., Kittel, F., Scholten, H. and Verhoeven, C. (1989). *Gestructureerd interview inhoud en organisatie van de arbeid [Structured interview content and organisation of work, SICOW].* Leiden, the Netherlands: Dept of Health Psychology, Leiden University.

Maes, S., Kittel, F., Scholten, H. and Verhoeven, C. (1996). Health promotion at the worksite, a European perspective. *Japanese Health Psychology* 4, 73–83.

Maes, S., Verhoeven, C., Kittel, F. and Scholten, H. (1998). Effects of a Dutch work-site wellness-health program: the Brabantia project. *American Journal of Public Health* 88, 1037–41.

Mikkelsen, A. and Saksvik, P. O. (1999). Impact of a participatory organizational intervention on job characteristics and job stress. *International Journal of Health Services* 29, 871–93.

Murphy, L. R. (1996). Stress management in work settings: a critical review of the health effects. *American Journal of Health Promotion* 11, 112–35.

Ozminkowski, R. J., Ling, D., Goetzel, R. Z., Bruno, J. A., et al. (2002). Long-term impact of Johnson & Johnson's Health and Wellness program on health care utilization and expenditures. *Journal of Occupational and Environmental Medicine* 44, 21–9.

Pelletier, K. R. (1999). A review and analysis of the clinical and cost-effectiveness studies of comprehensive health promotion and disease management programs at the worksite: 1995–1998 update. *American Journal of Health Promotion* 13, 333–45.

Pelletier, K. R. (2001). A review and analysis of the clinical- and cost-effectiveness studies of comprehensive health promotion and disease management programs at the worksite: 1998–2000 update. *American Journal of Health Promotion* 16, 107–16.

Pelletier, K. R., Rodenburg, A., Chikamoto, Y., Vinther, A., King, A. C. and Farquhar, J. W. (1998). Managing job strain: a randomized controlled trial of an intervention conducted by mail and telephone. *American Journal of Health Promotion* 12, 166–9.

Riedel, J. E., Lynch, W., Baase, C., Hymel, P. and Peterson, K. (2001). The effect of disease prevention and health promotion on workplace productivity: a literature review. *American Journal of Health Promotion* 15, 167–91.

Shephard, R. J. (1996). Worksite fitness and exercise programs: a review of methodology and health impact. *American Journal of Health Promotion* 10, 436–52.

Sorensen, G., Stoddard, A. M., LaMontagne, A. D., Emmons, K., et al. (2002). A comprehensive worksite cancer prevention intervention: behavior change results from a randomised controlled trial (United States). *Cancer, Causes and Control* 13, 493–502.

Sorensen, G., Thompson, B., Glanz, K., Feng, Z., et al. (1996). Work site-based cancer prevention: primary results from the Working Well Trial. *American Journal of Public Health* 86, 939–47.

Stokols, D., Pelletier, K. R. and Fielding, J. E. (1996). The ecology of work and health: research and policy directions for the promotion of employee health. *Health Education Quarterly* 23, 137–58.

Ter Doest, L., Maes, S., Gebhardt, W. and Koelewijn, H. (submitted). Personal goals and employee well-being: goal facilitation at work.

Terborg, J. R. (1986). Health promotion at the worksite: a challenge for personnel and human resources management. *Research in Personnel and Human Resources Management* 4, 225–67.

Terborg, J. R. (1988). The organization as a context for health promotion. In S. Spacapan and S. Oskamp, eds., *The Social Psychology of Health*. Newbury Park, CA: Sage, 129–74.

Terborg, J. R. (1998). Health psychology in the United States: a critique and selective review. *Applied Psychology: An International Review* 47, 199–217.

Terborg, J. R. and Glasgow, R. E. (1997). Worksite interventions. In A. Baum, S. Newman, J. Weinman, R. West and C. McManus, eds., *Cambridge Handbook of Psychology, Health and Medicine*. Cambridge: Cambridge University Press, 264–8.

Van der Doef, M. and Maes, S. (1998). The Job Demand–Control(–Support) model and physical health outcomes: a review of the strain and buffer hypotheses. *Psychology & Health* 13, 909–36.

Van der Doef, M. and Maes, S. (1999). The Job Demand–Control(–Support) model and psychological well-being: a review of 20 years of empirical research. *Work and Stress* 13, 87–114.

Van der Doef, M. and Maes, S. (2000). An examination of the Job Demand–Control–Support model with various occupational strain indicators. *Anxiety, Stress & Coping* 13, 165–85.

Weidner, G., Kohlmann, C.-W., Dotzauer, E. and Burns, L. R. (1996). The effects of academic stress on health behaviors in young adults. *Anxiety, Stress & Coping* 9, 123–33.

Wilbur, C. S. (1983). The Johnson & Johnson program. *Preventive Medicine* 12, 672–81.

Wilbur, C. S., Hartwell, T. D. and Piserchia, P. V. (1986). The Johnson & Johnson Live for Life program: its organization and evaluation plan. In M. F. Cataldo and T. J. Coates, eds., *Health and Industry: A Behavioral Medicine Perspective*. New York: John Wiley, 338–50.

Wilson, M. G. (1996). A comprehensive review of the effects of worksite health promotion on health-related outcomes: an update. *American Journal of Health Promotion* 11, 107–8.

Wilson, M. G., Holman, P. B. and Hammock, A. (1996). A comprehensive review of the effects of worksite health promotion on health-related outcomes. *American Journal of Health Promotion* 10, 429–35.

Winett, R. A., King, A. C. and Altman, D. G. (1989). Health psychology and public health: an integrative approach. In A. P. Goldstein and L. Krasner, eds., *Health in the Workplace*. Elmsford: Pergamon Press, 285–313.

Chapter Sixteen

PROFESSIONAL PRACTICE AND ISSUES IN HEALTH PSYCHOLOGY

Susan Michie

CHAPTER OUTLINE

This chapter deals with the development of health psychology as a profession and some of the issues facing applied psychologists working within health care. It considers the differing roles that health psychologists can play, the competencies necessary to perform these roles and the training required to achieve them. It discusses a range of generic competencies in detail, emphasizes the importance of working with other disciplines within and outside psychology, and highlights the particular contributions that health psychology can make.

KEY CONCEPTS

applied psychology
competence-based qualification
competences
confidentiality
continuing professional development
equal opportunities
ethical approval and practice
evidence-based practice
health promotion

health psychology
informed consent
interventions
multi-disciplinary work
professional practice
public health
supervision
training

ORIGINS AND DEFINITIONS

Health psychology is a rapidly-growing subdiscipline of psychology that emerged some three decades ago from several sources. These included social psychologists' increasing interest in health-related issues, a developing awareness amongst the medical profession that psychological expertise could contribute significantly to understanding and managing disease, and the increasing evidence that lifestyles were major causes of disease, disability and death in the developed world. An international review of the emergence of health psychology (Stone, 1990) also concluded that the development of health psychology was facilitated by two main factors: (i) a strong and independent discipline and profession of psychology within countries, and (ii) relatedly, access to health research and services that are not dominated by medicine or psychiatry. As health psychology developed so behaviour change techniques used in clinical, occupational and educational psychology began to be applied in physical health-care setting such as the treatment of hypertension, obesity, pain and addictions. This in turn created a demand for new professional practice and training.

Health psychology can be succinctly defined as the scientific study of the psychological processes involved in health, illness and health care. Research findings have been applied to:

* promotion and maintenance of health;
* prevention of illness and enhancement of outcomes of those who are ill;
* analysis and improvement of the health-care system and health policy.

Health psychology research has been applied to the development and evaluation of interventions designed to change:

* behaviours influencing health (e.g. smoking, diet and physical activity);
* symptom management and illness behaviour (e.g. self-care in chronic illness and prompt and appropriate seeking of medical help);
* the behaviour of health-care professional and patients (e.g. in relation to doctor–patient communication);
* treatment behaviour (i.e. adherence).

Such interventions may be conducted at individual, group, organizational, community or population levels.

HEALTH PSYCHOLOGY AS A PROFESSION

As the role of health psychology has extended beyond generating knowledge to applying that knowledge, so the professional roles of health psychologists have also developed. While professional skills vary according to type of practice, there are many generic issues and competencies that apply across roles, whether it is conducting laboratory research, teaching undergraduates, acting as an organizational consultant, evaluating and developing services, running smoking cessation clinics or helping individuals to manage pain or stress.

The key role of the professional psychologist has been defined as being able 'to develop and apply psychological principles, knowledge, models and methods in an ethical and scientific way in order to promote the development, well-being and effectiveness of individuals, groups, organizations and society' (European Federation of Professional Psychologists' Associations (EFPPA), 2001).

Professional psychologists apply psychology to everyday problems and questions in order to enhance the well-being of individuals, groups and systems. Health psychologists are informed by many other fields, such as social psychology, clinical psychology, public health, epidemiology, medicine and sociology. This varies in different countries, as does the route developed to achieve professional competence. Becoming a profession ensures minimum standards of competence in relation to academic and research expertise as well as practical skills. Professional bodies also ensure accountability in practice. This benefits not just applied psychologists, but the recipients of psychological services, employers, policy developers, other professions and the public. Health psychologists are represented within national professional associations of psychology world-wide, and the great majority of these represent both the scientific and professional interests.

In the US, health psychology was recognized as a separate professional specialty and proficiency by the American Psychological Association in 1997 (website at www.apa.org). However, this profession is 'clinical health psychology' which focuses on physical health problems and defines its 'client populations' by the physical symptoms or physical illness they experience. This is a narrower conceptualization of health psychology than in other parts of the world, such as Australia and Europe. The Australian College of Health Psychologists, established in 1996 (www.psychsociety.com.au), identifies two areas of practice, health promotion and clinical health. In their definition of health psychology, the first application listed is to 'the promotion and maintenance of health-related behaviour and healthy outcomes'. Professional training involves covering both areas, with the option of specializing in one.

In Europe, countries vary in their emphasis on health promotion activities within health psychology (www.ehps.net). Countries also reflect different stages of professional development, as documented in a report of health psychology in 19 European countries (European Health Psychology Society (EHPS), 2000). This reports that 11 countries had independent post-graduate training in health psychology, 7 had systems of professional regulation and 3 had the profession regulated in law.

In developing countries the picture is even more diverse. Health psychology developed earliest and most rapidly in those countries with strong commitments to community development and centralized planning of health care. A successful example of this is Cuba, where health psychology started in 1969 and enjoys a prominent role within health care and community life (Garcia-Averasturi, 1980, 1985). A preventive and community-based psychology in primary health care is seen as the most effective approach to reduce poverty-related and lifestyle-related ill health and to improve child and family health. Psychologists are central to the multi-disciplinary 'polyclinics' which form the backbone of the Cuban health-care system. Most professional psychologists are generalists, educating other professionals; contributing to health promotion programmes in communities, schools and workplaces; working to improve communication within families, reduce unwanted pregnancies and foster healthy child development (Kristiansen & Søderstrøm, 1990).

THE DEVELOPMENT OF PROFESSIONAL HEALTH PSYCHOLOGY IN EUROPE

In 1981, the European Federation of Professional Psychologists' Associations (EFPPA, www.efppa.org) was founded to organize national professional associations of psychology across Europe (world-wide, the International Association of Applied Psychology serves the same purpose: IAAP, www.iaapsy.org). European, applied psychologists work as independent professionals as part of the health-care services. Health psychologists constitute one of the disciplines of applied psychologists in health and social care: others are clinical psychologists, counselling/psychotherapy psychologists, educational psychologists and occupational psychologists. Overlapping areas between these disciplines have been identified by an EFPPA task force (Marks et al., 1998: 153):

Health, clinical and psychotherapy psychologists work with:
(a)   individuals, couples, families, groups and communities
(b)   people of all ages
(c)   in institutions, organizations and companies
(d)   in the public, private and voluntary sectors.

They undertake:
(a)   assessment and diagnosis
(b)   intervention and treatment
(c)   teaching and training
(d)   supervision, counselling and consultancy
(e)   evaluation, research and development

in various areas of application:
(a)   promotion of well-being
(b)   prevention of deterioration of health
(c)   intervention in psychological aspects of physical health
(d)   intervention in psychological aspects of mental health
(e)   promotion of optimum development and ageing.

They are responsible for:
(a)   the delivery of good services with respect to standards of quality and control
(b)   planning of new services
(c)   informing and influencing the health-care system and policy.

These activities require psychologists to have a good grasp of the evidence that informs these activities and to have the professional skills required to translate this evidence into practice.

PROFESSIONAL ISSUES

Professional health psychologists require an understanding of the place and status of **health psychology in society**, including the health and psychological needs of individuals in their society and their own obligations, rights and restrictions. This involves being well informed of the political, social and legislative context of their work, including national and regional health policies, relevant legislation and the codes of ethics and conduct (especially those of their own professional and/or licensing body). The best way of keeping up to date with changing legislation and government policies and strategies is to regularly consult the key websites (such as those of national government departments of health).

Professional practice also requires a knowledge of the variety of **values and codes of behaviour** held within society, including those held by minority ethnic and disadvantaged groups. This is especially important, since health psychologists rarely represent the socio-economic and ethnic mix of their clients. Health psychologists should aim for equality of opportunity in all their work, such that no colleague, research participant or user of psychological services receives less favourable treatment on the grounds of, for example, gender, colour, ethnic origin, nationality, religion, disability or age. They must not condone values or behaviours which are illegal, immoral or harmful to others and must act to protect those at risk of harm.

Many health psychologists work in multi-disciplinary settings and teams, whether conducting research, providing services or offering consultancy. This requires awareness of other disciplines' theories, practice and ethical principles, and finding ways of respecting others' views while not always agreeing with them.

All professionals have an obligation to the public and to the profession **to continue their professional development** throughout their working lives. Health psychology is evidence-based and theory-based: competence includes updating knowledge of both, and updating skills of their application (Michie & Abraham, 2004). Health psychologists who read current research literature are able to challenge unsubstantiated beliefs about evidence-based practice and keep abreast of the theories for which there is accumulating evidence of their validity. For example, they have pointed out that the popular stages of change, or 'trans-theoretical', model is not supported by evidence (Littrell & Girvin, 2002; Sutton, 2000). This requires time: time to read and attend seminars and conferences. Without this investment professional skills may become outdated and they may not be able to offer the best advice to their clients. For example, in relation to the generation and evaluation of evidence, the ability to perform power calculations to estimate necessary sample sizes in research is fundamental to quality research. Similarly, the competence to plan, conduct and evaluate systematic literature reviews is now expected within health psychology (Petticrew & Gilbody,

2004): 10 years ago, both these skills were regarded as esoteric; now they are part of everyday practice.

There is an expectation that health psychologists will be involved in **training and supervising** psychologists and members of other professions. Psychologists are responsible for monitoring the performance of others in their application of psychological principles and ensuring that they demonstrate competence in their practice. This applies not only to doctoral students and psychology trainees but to nurses, doctors and other professions who psychologists may train. Such training may involve acquisition of the implications of psychological research for practice (e.g. through lectures and seminars in medical and nursing degrees), as well as the development and implementation of skills such as breaking bad news to patients or designing and evaluating behaviour change interventions. The ultimate objective of training should be professional **autonomy and independence**. This requires mutual respect across health-care professions, and may be helped by legislation and regulations, such as the demand for statutory registration.

Quality control mechanisms help to maintain high standards of practice in line with advances in their field, as does supervision of staff at all levels of experience. For senior staff, this may be most appropriately organized outside their professional specialty. Appraisals, whether formal or informal, are most effective when they are regular and linked to goal-setting and continuing professional development. Worthwhile appraisals are geared to future development as well as current practice, addressing the question: 'where does the person want/need to get to, and what is required to make that happen?' Appraisal provides an opportunity for the psychologist to reflect on their recent past achievements, to assess the reasons for strengths and weaknesses, to analyse the potential for progress and to develop strategies to make the most of current opportunities and to create new ones.

Health psychologists cannot always do all the things that others expect of them. Competent practice involves assessing work demands and ensuring that one works **within the limits of one's own competence**. Psychologists must, therefore, be clear about the nature of their qualifications and the limits of their skills techniques and understanding. When they assess demands to be beyond their levels of competence, they have a responsibility to refer the person or issue on to an appropriately qualified professional, either within or across disciplines. For example, psychologists should not provide counselling or implement behaviour change interventions unless they have been specifically trained and qualified in these techniques. One advantage of a competence-based qualification is that it is precise about the competences that an individual has attained in training. Of course individual health psychologists augment their qualifications and competence and so may, or may not, have the ability to advise on policy development. Psychologists have the responsibility to maintain and develop their professional competence, to recognize and work within their limits and to identify and remedy factors which restrict their competence.

Personal conduct is a professional issue. As a professional, whether one is working within a research, teaching, consultancy or behaviour change setting, there are questions of power boundaries and respect for people's rights and dignity. Awareness of differences across culture, ethnic groups, class and gender is key to sensitive communication and challenging prejudice and discrimination. Professional relationships with colleagues, students and clients require awareness of power differentials and monitoring any aspects of these relationships which may involve misuse of that power. They also require clearly established interpersonal boundaries, for example in degree of familiarity and self-disclosure. It is essential that psychologists be familiar with the codes of conduct and ethics of the professional organizations to which they belong. **Conflicts of interest** should always be declared to appropriate managers, colleagues or clients, immediately. Such conflicts may be academic, for example reviewing a journal article reporting work one has been involved with, or professional, for example being asked to provide advice or evaluate a proposal when one has a vested interest in implied resource allocation, or personal, for example when one has a pre-existing relationship with a potential client.

'Psychologists . . . strive to help the public in developing informed judgements and choices regarding human behaviour, and to improve the condition of both the individual and society' (EFPPA, 1995). More specifically, an individual or organization has the right to choose whether to receive psychological assessment or intervention, and to make the choice on the basis of the best information available. Thus psychologists have an obligation to facilitate and ensure **informed consent in health psychology applications**. Consent should be formal, recorded and reviewed, rather than assumed. This is as true for research and teaching as it is for organizational and individual services.

Research is crucial to the advancement of knowledge and its application, and most health psychologists are involved in research. With increasing attention being paid to research governance, there are increasing demands for all research activity to be approved by local or national research ethics committees. A general rule of thumb is that any data collection that may lead to publication or to findings generalizable across settings requires ethical approval. No longer can ethical approval for research be avoided under the guise of audit or service evaluation.

Potential research participants must be informed of all aspects of the research that might influence their willingness to participate, including the aims of the research and any anticipated risks of distress. No pressure for participation should be exerted and patients should be informed that neither consent nor refusal will influence the nature of their care, and that they will be free to withdraw from the research at any time, without giving a reason. This, in turn, has resource implications that need to be taken into account in planning research projects. Informed consent is needed both for research procedures and the publication of results.

The legal duty to ensure **confidentiality** refers to identifiable personal health information. When such information is identifiable, it should be treated with respect and shared only when necessary. The only circumstances in which confidentiality may be broken, without consent, is when the health or safety of others or the public is at risk.

Following informed consent for client material to be published, care needs to be taken to ensure its complete anonymity. This includes clinical audit. When working with other disciplines, psychologists must inform themselves of new confidentiality practices. Psychologists are responsible for ensuring the security of records they keep or contribute to, which includes being aware of the range of access to any such records and knowing when such data should be destroyed. The storage of data on computer is covered by data protection legislation which psychologists must be familiar with.

The ethics of publication also involves appropriate acknowledgement of the contributions that others have made to the work. This implies that authorship rights should be discussed with co-workers at the beginning of the research and as research proceeds towards publication. Different authors may make different contributions, both practical and intellectual (Game & West, 2002), and some journals (e.g. the *British Medical Journal*) now require authors to declare their particular contributions.

Using **the media** to disseminate psychological expertise can be extremely effective. However, psychologists must guard against misrepresentation and sensationalism. Employers may have their own guidelines for dealing with the media and the public, and media training and support from a media officer at work can be invaluable. It is desirable, though not always possible, to see and agree the edited version of what has been said and agreed before transmission. It is also helpful to base one's statements on evidence and clarify their status, for example, whether they are the results of research and how extensive that research was, or personal views or views representing the profession or an employer. Psychologists should not comment on areas beyond their competence, as this may bring the profession into disrepute. It is also wise to be aware of reporters' motivation to heighten the impact of their stories!

Psychologists may want to express concerns publicly about their employers, practices or legislation. In such instances, consulting relevant individuals or organizations (e.g. line manager, trade union, professional body) can ensure that their comments do not breach guidelines and risk disciplinary action.

Psychologists should ensure that they **safeguard their physical and psychological well-being** so that they maintain their **fitness to practise.** In the event that a colleague has become unfit to practise, psychologists have a responsibility to take action on their behalf. Making judgements about one's own and others' fitness to practise involves balancing personal and professional priorities and loyalties with potential costs to clients, colleagues and oneself. Practising while unwell may put others' safety at risk.

PROFESSIONAL COMPETENCES IN HEALTH PSYCHOLOGY

Professional organizations have an absolute responsibility to ensure that training programmes match the demands of psychologists' employment. Professional qualifications (and their assessments) as well as opportunities for continuing professional development must allow psychologists to competently perform their work roles. The emergence of health psychology as a profession has involved identification of:

- required work competencies,
- appropriate methods of teaching and training,

- types of supervised experience necessary to develop skills and confidence, and
- the time needed for people to consolidate their knowledge and skills to the point where they are competent to practise on their own, without supervision. (Michie & Abraham, 2004).

For example, a consultation-based study of professional psychological practice by the British Psychological Society produced a specification of occupational standards in terms of six key roles:

1) Develop, implement and maintain personal and professional standards and ethical practice.
2) Apply psychological and related methods, concepts, models, theories and knowledge derived from reproducible research findings.
3) Research and develop new and existing psychological methods, concepts, models, theories and instruments in psychology.
4) Communicate psychological knowledge, principles, methods, needs and policy requirements.
5) Develop and train the application of psychological skills, knowledge, practices and procedures.
6) Manage the provision of psychological systems, services and resources.

Of these, the first four were considered to apply to all professional psychologists, while the latter two were more specialized roles and more likely to apply once individuals have become independent practitioners rather than being a requirement for practice.

A Competence-based Qualification in Health Psychology

A competence-based qualification in professional development has been developed in the UK, under the auspices of the British Psychological Society (http://www.health-psychology.org.uk). It is the first competence-based psychology qualification in the UK. In specifying the detailed competences required, the qualification achieves two main purposes:

1) It communicates to the public, employers and service users exactly what health psychologists in general (and individual health psychologists with optional competencies) can and cannot do.
2) It allows those who already possess some of the competences to receive accreditation for their prior experience and/or training. One of the advantages of this is to facilitate lateral transfer between different branches of applied psychology.

This qualification requires a first stage of training involving acquisition of a knowledge base (e.g. through an accredited master's programme) and a second stage to acquire and demonstrate a range of 19 core and 8 optional competences. Core competences lie in four areas: generic professional competence, research, consultancy, and teaching and training.

- **Generic professional competence** comprises the competences to implement and maintain systems for legal, ethical and professional standards in applied psychology; contribute to the continuing development of oneself as a professional applied psychologist; provide psychological advice and guidance to others and provide feedback to clients.
- **Research competence** involves skills in a variety of research types, e.g. randomized controlled trials, health service evaluation and clinical audit studies, qualitative studies, analogue or vignette studies as well as systematic reviews of evidence and meta-analyses of quantitative data within. Welcome trends in health psychology research include a shift from understanding causal processes in behavioural regulation to evaluation of interventions to change health behaviours in practice, and the study of observed, rather than self-reported, behaviour.
- **Teaching and training competence** involves the ability to plan, design, deliver and evaluate training programmes to teach psychological knowledge, skills and practices. This may be to individuals, communities or the general population.
- **Consultancy**, the process by which one party (individual or organization) formally seeks and receives the advice of another. The consultee poses the initial questions and the consultant shapes them, proposes a method to address them, implements the process and reports back. The consultant does this on the basis of available relevant evidence and theory and uses research skills to inform and evaluate the consultancy. Communication and negotiation skills are crucial to successful consultancy. Health psychology consultancy is the use of these skills to facilitate, develop or enhance the effectiveness of others in the maintenance and improvement of health. More details of the consultancy role and examples of consultancy work can be found in Michie (1998).

The four main units of generic professional competence outlined above each include three to five components which, in turn, are made up of two to eight specific guidelines on how to acquire and assess the competence described by each component. There are 75 core components of competence and these are used as the unit of assessment. Candidates are also examined on the components of two further optional units. These are outlined in Appendix at the end of this chapter.

A EUROPEAN FRAMEWORK FOR THE TRAINING OF PSYCHOLOGISTS

In 1990, optimal standards for training required for autonomous professional practice in Europe were agreed (EFPPA, 1990). These were of a general nature and have been used by countries to develop their own qualifications. Although the education and training of professional psychologists varies between European countries, particularly in its structure and in the name of the final title, there is considerable overlap in content and required competences.

In order to ensure uniform minimum standards within Europe, to simplify the recognition of qualifications and to facilitate the mobility of psychologists between countries, a 'European Framework for Psychologists' Training' has been developed (see EFPPA website). This project, funded by the EU under its Leonardo da Vinci programme, and involving 12 countries and EFPPA, is developing a 'European Diploma' due to begin in 2003. The project team has considered both 'input' (curriculum) and 'output' (competence) approaches to the development of this framework. There is broad agreement that 6 years' training is required for to prepare for independent professional practice, including 5 years of academic study (providing the basic knowledge base and theoretical foundation and a substantial grounding in research and applications of psychology), and at least one year of supervised practice.

The aim of supervised practice is to enable students to:

- integrate theoretical and practical knowledge,
- apply procedures related to psychological knowledge,
- practise under supervision,
- reflect upon and discuss own and other people's activities,
- work in a setting with professional colleagues.

Supervised practice may be in the following areas: clinical psychology, community psychology, counselling psychology, school and educational psychology, organizational and work psychology, economic psychology, psychological assessment and evaluation, environmental psychology, applied gerontology, forensic psychology, neuropsychology, sport psychology, health psychology, applied cognitive psychology, traffic and transportation psychology, political psychology. In addition, psychologists may be involved in other areas such as disaster, crisis and trauma, consumer behaviour and issues of cultural and ethnic diversity.

PROFESSIONAL HEALTH PSYCHOLOGY IN PRACTICE

Health-care services

Health psychologists have become vital members of multi-disciplinary clinical and research teams in a wide variety of medical fields, including rehabilitation, cardiology, paediatrics, oncology, anaesthesiology, family practice and dentistry. They operate at many levels, assessing and advising on individual behaviour, of both patients and health professionals, and of systems within which they function. Coping with threat, communication and behaviour change are just three issues relevant to both patients and health professionals. Evaluating the effectiveness of services and making recommendations on their development is another area in which health psychologists can make a valuable contribution.

Health promotion and public health

Leading causes of mortality have substantial behavioural components (e.g. drug and alcohol use, unsafe sexual behaviour, smoking and sedentary lifestyle). Thus modifying these behaviours is the main focus of health promotion and disease prevention. While this is most commonly considered in relation to lifestyles and diseases of affluence, it is also true of lifestyles and diseases of poverty, where hygienic behaviours are essential to survival (Aboud, 1998). With increasing appreciation of the economic and social benefits achievable through evidence-based prevention, demand is growing for psychologists to be involved in the design, coordination and evaluation of health promotion programs. For example, health psychologists can identify beliefs, cognitions and regulatory processes that maintain or promote adoption of health risk behaviours and then design health promotion materials that directly target the psychological antecedents of these behaviours (Abraham et al., 2002).

Although it is generally accepted that health education and promotion programmes are more powerful if they are theory-based and evidence-based, they have often been only loosely associated with theory and evidence (Michie & Abraham, 2004). Methods for designing interventions so that they are well grounded in theory and evidence have been developed by health and social psychologists (Kok & Schaalma, 1998). Steps include:

- defining performance objectives,
- selecting theory-based methods on basis of specified criteria for choosing a theory and evaluating evidence,
- translating theoretical methods into practical strategies, for example, by identifying determinants of the component behaviours and tailoring the intervention for sub-populations,
- deciding on scope, sequence, materials, pre-testing and production,
- setting up mechanisms to facilitate awareness, adoption and implementation,
- anticipating evaluation by carefully stating the expected effects and processes in advance.

Health psychologists are also increasingly to be found in Departments of Epidemiology, Public Health or Population Sciences. 'Public health psychology' has been described as the fusion of three elements (Wardle, 2001a):

1) Consideration of the relevance of psychological processes to public health issues. The shift from individual-level to population-level explanations has meant that factors such as ethnicity and socio-economic status are the subjects of interest

rather than potential confounds to be partialled out of statistical analyses. There is a growing interest in understanding how social influences on health get 'under the skin' (Taylor, Repetti & Seeman, 1997).

2) Use of some of the methodological strengths of epidemiology, with its emphasis on rigorous sampling, studies powered to detect small effects and sophisticated statistical multi-level modelling.

3) The extension of psychology's strong empirical tradition to providing convincing evidence for the effectiveness of psychological interventions on a public health scale.

Following initial results of effectiveness, research can refine and improve the interventions to analyse effects on different sectors of the population and to advise on dissemination and implementation. This is the basis from which to persuade social and health policy-makers to use psychological research findings.

Beyond health-care systems

Workplace- and school-based interventions also have the potential to alter health behaviour patterns because people spend a substantial part of their lives in these contexts, and because the earlier that healthy behaviours are established, the more likely they are to persist. Worksite interventions include those aimed at changing individual behaviour and those aimed at organizational change. An example of the former is a trial of a worksite intervention to reduce cardiovascular disease factors, comparing assessment of health risk, education about risk factors and behaviour change counselling (Oldenburg et al., 1995). Behaviour change counselling was both effective at reducing risk after 12 months and cost effective. An example of the latter is the Brabantia project in the Netherlands which intervened to change both lifestyle and working conditions, and found reduced health risks one year later compared to a control group (Maes et al, 1998). (See Chapter 15, this volume.)

School-based interventions focus on establishing health-related behaviours at an early age. This may include promotion of competent problem solving, coping and seeking social support. In such work, educational and health psychologists may benefit from collaboration. Health psychologists have typically been involved in interventions designed to reduce health risk behaviours, such as smoking, drug use or unprotected sex, or to increase health-related behaviours such as exercise and eating fruit and vegetables. An example is the development of theory-driven, research-based school sex education programmes (Kirby et al., 1994; Schaalma et al., 1996). Programmes applying psychological principles to school sex education have also been developed and tested in the UK (e.g. Mellanby et al., 1995; Wight & Abraham, 2000). Wight, Abraham and Scott (1988) describe how psychological and sociological theory were combined to develop a framework for the development of intervention materials used in the SHARE ('Sexual Health and Relationships – Safe, Happy and Responsible') sex education programme, and Wight and Abraham (2000) discuss the practical difficulties of translating theory and research based interventions into sustainable classroom practice.

Working with other professions

Health psychologists work closely with professionals in other fields, such as medicine, nursing, social work, general management. Within multi-disciplinary teams, the psychologist adds a distinct perspective, asks particular types of questions which complement those of other professionals, and uses empirically validated interventions and measures. Psychologists also work with other professionals to help change their behaviour to provide more effective treatment and advice.

While developing multi-disciplinary work, health psychologists will strengthen their contribution by working with other psychology disciplines (e.g. clinical and occupational) and with other applied psychologists internationally. Increasing collaboration across and between disciplines, and across countries will help to gain more resources for research and its application, and to maximize the effective output of those resources.

Disseminating psychological output

Making a difference in practice requires effectively disseminating our findings to those who can make a difference, and helping them find ways of implementing recommendations and maintaining changes (Oldenburg, 2001). While considerable effort and resources have been devoted to developing effective interventions, relatively little attention has been given to developing and researching effective methods for promoting use.

> It's no longer enough to end our papers by saying that our findings have great potential for health gain. We have to prove it. We have to show that our interventions work in the initial test populations, then we have to prove that they work when applied in the real world when administered by individuals not pursuing research, and delivered to individuals who are not subjects in research. We have to assess the potential reach, and therefore the impact of our interventions, and we have to look to developing them into disseminable forms and creating the conditions in which they can readily be adopted. Only by taking this route will we produce evidence that will convince policy makers to take our findings seriously . . . We also need to think how to formulate our work so that we can present it to policy makers. (Wardle, 2001b: 46)

FUTURE DEVELOPMENTS

A central principle of the vision for professional health psychology is the WHO goal that all people have a right to health and health care (WHO, 1995). Despite this, there are glaring inequalities in health throughout the world and within relatively affluent parts of the world, such as Europe. Health inequalities reflect social inequalities, for example, in wealth, educational opportunities, employment security and experience of discrimination and persecution. The content and form of our professional activity should be shaped by awareness of these variations and by a commitment to work to try to reduce them. There are also inequalities in access to health education and services. The principle of equity requires psychologists to provide their services 'to all people regardless of gender, age, religion, ethnic grouping, social class, material circumstances, political affiliation or sexual orientation. When access is low, or when there is evidence of greater needs, special efforts should be made to target service on those with the poorest access or greatest need, for example, refugees, the homeless, lower income groups' (Marks, 1978).

A call has been made for health psychologists to move away from individualistic models of health behaviour to:

- work with more collective and population-based models, interventions and outcomes,
- engage in public policy and debates about resource allocation,
- address causes of ill-health, such as social inequalities and poverty (e.g. Kaplan, 1994; Oldenburg, 2001; Wardle, 2001a).

This will involve a more political role for psychologists:

> For this change to occur, psychologists must assume a more visible profile in lobbying at local, state and national tiers to ensure that behavioral issues are included in policy formation, research agenda, and the allocation of services. This change also dictates an increased involvement of psychologists in public and private efforts and activities that influence health policy. If professional psychology fails to assume this responsibility and meet this challenge, the profession risks being marginalized as a stake holder in the health-care system. (Johnstone et al., 1995: 346–7)

SUMMARY AND CONCLUSIONS

The scientific study of the psychological processes of health, illness and health care has generated potentially useful evidence. Such evidence can be used to promote and maintain health, analyse and improve the health-care system and health policy formation, and prevent illness and disability and enhance outcomes of those who are ill or disabled. To achieve such aims, it is necessary for health psychologists to develop professional skills in research, consultancy and teaching/training. Additional generic professional skills include ensuring legal and ethical standards, continuing professional development and respecting the diversity of colleagues and clients. Knowledge of relevant evidence and the skills to apply it equip health psychologists to work effectively in many settings, ranging from working with individuals to prevent or manage health problems, to intervening in organizational systems such as health service providers to providing advice at a public health policy level.

ACKNOWLEDGEMENTS

This chapter has been informed by the Stage 2 Qualification in Health Psychology developed by the Division of Health Psychology of the British Psychological Society (BPS) and by the Professional Practice Guidelines of the Division of Clinical Psychology, BPS, 1995, and comments on an earlier draft by Professor Suzanne Skevington, University of Bath, and Professor Charles Abraham, University of Sussex.

FURTHER READING

Johnstone, B., Frank, R. G., Belar, C., et al. (1995). Psychology in health care: future directions. *Professional Psychology: Research and Practice* 26, 341–65.

Michie, S. (1998). Consultancy. In D. W. Johnston and M. Johnston, eds., *Comprehensive Clinical Psychology*, vol. 8: *Health Psychology*. Amsterdam: Elsevier, 153–69.

Wardle, J. (2001). Public health psychology: expanding the horizons of health psychology. *British Journal of Health Psychology* 5, 329–36.

REFERENCES

Aboud, F. E. (1998). *Health Psychology in Global Perspective*. London: Sage.

Abraham, C., Krahé, B., Dominic, R. and Fritsche, I. (2002). Does research into the social cognitive antecedents of action contribute to health promotion? A content analysis of safer-sex promotion leaflets. *British Journal of Health Psychology* 7, 227–46.

EFPPA (1990). *Optimal Standards for Training of Professional Psychologists*. Brussels: European Federation of Professional Psychologists' Associations.

EFPPA (1995). *European Federation of Professional Psychologists 'Associations' Metacode of Ethics*. Stockholm: European Federation of Professional Psychologists' Associations.

EFPPA (2001). *A European Framework for Psychologists' Training*. Brussels: European Federation of Professional Psychologists' Associations.

EHPS (2000). *Post-graduate Programs in Health Psychology in Europe: A Reference Guide*. Leiden, the Netherlands: European Health Psychology Society.

Game, A. and West, M. A. (2002). Principles of publishing. *The Psychologist* 15, 126–9.

Garcia-Averasturi, L. (1980). Psychology and health care in Cuba. *American Psychologist* 35, 1090–5.

Garcia-Averasturi, L. (1985). Community health psychology in Cuba. *Journal of Community Psychology* 13, 117–23.

Johnstone, B., Frank, R. G., Belar, C., et al. (1995). Psychology in health care: future directions. *Professional Psychology: Research and Practice* 26, 341–65.

Kaplan, R. M. (1994). The Ziggy theorem: toward an outcomes-focused health psychology. *Health Psychology* 13, 451–60.

Kirby, D., Short, L., Collins, J., Rugg, D., Kolbe, L., et al. (1994). School-based programs to reduce sexual risk behaviours: a review of effectiveness. *Public Health Reports* 10, 339–60.

Kok, G. and Schaalma, H. (1998). Theory-based and evidence-based health education intervention programmes. *Psychology and Health* 13, 747–51.

Kristiansen, S. and Søderstrøm, K. (1990). Cuban health psychology: a priority is the primary health care system. *Psychology and Health* 4, 65–72.

Littrell, J. H. and Girvin, H. (2002). Stages of change: a critique. *Behavior Modification* 26, 223–73.

Maes, S., Verhoeven, C., Kittell, F. and Scholten, H. (1998). Effects of a Dutch work-site wellness-health program: the Brabantia project. *American Journal of Public Health* 88, 1037–41.

Marks, D. (1996). Health psychology in context. *Journal of Health Psychology* 1, 7–21.

Marks, D. F., Brucher-Albers, C., Donker, F. J. S., et al. (1998). Health psychology 2000: the development of professional health psychology. *Journal of Health Psychology* 3, 149–60.

Mellanby, A. R., Phelps, F. A., Crichton, N. J. and Tripp, J. H. (1995). School sex education: an experimental programme with educational and medical benefit. *British Medical Journal* 311, 414–17.

Michie, S. (1998). Consultancy. In D. W. Johnston and M. Johnston, eds., *Comprehensive Clinical Psychology*, vol. 8: *Health Psychology*. Amsterdam: Elsevier, 153–69.

Michie, S. and Abraham, C., eds. (2004). *Health Psychology in Practice*. Oxford: Blackwell.

Michie, S. and Abraham, C. (2004). Interventions to change health behaviours: evidence-based or evidence-inspired? *Psychology and Health* 19, 28–49.

Oldenburg, B., Owen, N., Parle, M. and Gomel, M. (1995). An economic evaluation of four work site based cardiovascular risk factor interventions. *Health Education Quarterly* 22, 9–19.

Oldenburg, B. (2001). Public health as social sciences. In N. J. Smelser and P. B. Baltes, eds., *The International Encyclopaedia of the Social and Behavioral Sciences*. Oxford: Elsevier.

Petticrew, M. and Gilbody, S. (2004). Designing and conducting systematic reviews. In S. Michie and C. Abraham, eds., *Health Psychology in Practice*. Oxford: Blackwell.

Schaalma, H. P., Kok, G., Bosker, R. J., Parcel, G. S., et al. (1996). Planned development and evaluation of AIDS/STD education for secondary-school students in the Netherlands: short-term effects. *Health Education Quarterly* 23, 469–87.

Stone, G. C. (1990). An international review of the emergence and development of health psychology. *Psychology and Health* 4, 3–17.

Sutton, S. (2000). A critical review of the trans-theoretical model applied to smoking cessation. In P. Norman, C. Abraham and M. Conner, eds., *Understanding and Changing Health Behaviour: From Health Beliefs to Self-regulation*. Amsterdam: Harwood Academic, 207–25.

Taylor, S. E., Repetti, R. L. and Seeman, T. E. (1997). Health psychology: what is an unhealthy environment and how does it get under the skin? *Annual Review of Psychology* 48, 411–47.

Wardle, J. (200la). Public health psychology: expanding the horizons of health psychology. *British Journal of Health Psychology* 5, 329–36.

Wardle, J. (2001b). Health psychology in Britain: past, present and future. *Health Psychology Update* 10. Division of Health Psychology, British Psychological Society. Leicester: BPS.

Wight, D. and Abraham C. (2000). From psycho-social theory to sustainable classroom practice: developing a research-based teacher-delivered sex education programme. *Health Education Research* 15, 25–38.

Wight, D., Abraham, C. and Scott, S. (1998). Towards a psycho-social theoretical framework for sexual health promotion. *Health Education Research* 13, 317–30.

World Health Organization (1995). *Renewing the Health-for-all Strategy: Elaboration of a Policy for Equity, Solidarity and Health*. Geneva: Author.

APPENDIX: THE GENERIC PROFESSIONAL COMPETENCES REQUIRED FOR THE UK PROFESSIONAL QUALIFICATION IN HEALTH PSYCHOLOGY

1.1 Implement and maintain systems for legal, ethical and professional standards in applied psychology
1.2 Contribute to the continuing development of self as a professional applied psychologist
1.3 Provide psychological advice and guidance to others
1.4 Provide feedback to clients

1.1 IMPLEMENT AND MAINTAIN SYSTEMS FOR LEGAL, ETHICAL AND PRO-FESSIONAL STANDARDS IN APPLIED PSYCHOLOGY

1.1a Establish, maintain and review systems for the security and control of information
1.1b Ensure compliance with legal, ethical and professional practices for self and others
1.1c Establish, implement and evaluate procedures to ensure competence in psychological practice and research

---

1.1a Establish and maintain systems for the security and control of information

1. Establish and implement:
   - comprehensive systems and security procedures for the collation, storage and retrieval of confidential information
   - comprehensive and differentiated access systems for the retrieval of confidential information

2. Ensure that effective policies regarding the treatment of confidential information are readily accessible for relevant individuals and that these people are clearly informed about their roles and responsibilities to safeguard the confidentiality and security of information

3. Ensure that potentially sensitive information is securely stored to safeguard the confidentiality of its contents

4. Obtain explicit agreements with relevant parties outlining the scope of confidentiality in terms they understand

5. Ensure that:
   - relevant individuals and groups are clearly informed about their roles and responsibilities to prevent unapproved access to sensitive information

- information sources for research and practice remain anonymous unless otherwise agreed

6. Obtain:
    - necessary permissions and written consents prior to the recording, publishing and disclosure of information
    - explicit agreements with relevant parties outlining the scope of confidentiality in terms they understand

7. Obtain and evaluate the advice of experienced and impartial colleagues about the dissemination of information when concerns have been raised about the safety and interests of service recipients and any dangers to third parties

8. Review confidentiality and security policies, systems and procedures regularly

1.1b   To ensure compliance with legal, ethical and professional practices for self and others

1. Establish and implement comprehensive systems for maintaining and monitoring professional practice

2. Inform relevant individuals and groups about their roles and responsibilities in relation to maintaining and reviewing professional practice

3. Identify issues that might affect legal, ethical and professional practice

4. Obtain relevant advice from experienced and disinterested colleagues when concerns have been raised about professional practice and the conduct of self and others

5. Review maintenance and monitoring systems regularly to ensure compliance with acceptable standards and to ensure that the outcomes from the reviews are effectively utilized

1.1c   To establish, implement and evaluate procedures to ensure competence in psychological practice and research

1. Define clearly the boundaries of competence for oneself, and any individuals and groups working with and for health psychologists

2. Identify the strengths and weaknesses of staff carrying out psychological work

3. Allocate work to individuals and groups within the specific boundaries of their competence and identify training needs for competences outside the boundaries specified

4. Ensure that records of personal capabilities, qualifications and competence are accurate and up-to-date

5. Review and compare psychological practice with established competences

6. Identify the strengths and weaknesses of current practice and ensure that appropriate actions are taken to rectify weaknesses

---

1.2 CONTRIBUTE TO THE CONTINUING DEVELOPMENT OF ONESELF AS A PROFESSIONAL APPLIED PSYCHOLOGIST

1.2a   Establish, evaluate and implement processes to develop oneself professionally
1.2b   Elicit, monitor and evaluate knowledge and feedback to inform practice
1.2c   Organize, clarify and utilize access to competent consultation and advice
1.2d   Develop and enhance oneself as a professional applied psychologist
1.2e   Incorporate best practice into one's own work

1.2a: To establish, evaluate and implement processes to develop oneself as a professional health psychologist

1. Use appropriate methods and sources to evaluate personal experiences and knowledge

2. Employ methods of self evaluation to determine needs and consolidate units of competence

3. Identify professional development needs by evaluating strengths and weaknesses of current practice

4. Identify, seek and pursue opportunities to enhance and advance professional performance

5. Review psychological practice and compare it with established competences

6. Identify and assess potential work-related threats to one's physical and emotional well-being

7. Develop strategies to handle threats including seeking and using necessary help and support

8. Identify, acquire and use appropriate resources for own psychological practice

1.2b: To elicit, monitor and evaluate knowledge and feedback to inform practice

1. Actively seek feedback from clients and other relevant individuals and agencies

2. Elicit information about areas of unease, discontent and best practice

3. Monitor and evaluate feedback

4. Use supervision and feedback in one's own practice

5. Monitor and evaluate own knowledge and practice to establish its effectiveness

6. Identify and evaluate sources of new knowledge and practice

1.2c: To organize, clarify and utilize competent consultation and advice

1.   Identify sources of consultation and advice

2.   Identify procedures to access consultation and advice

3.   Actively seek consultation and advice from appropriate sources

4.   Receive consultation and advice in an appropriate manner

5.   Clarify with the appropriate sources areas that are not fully understood

6.   Evaluate consultation and advice for suitability of purpose

7.   Organize, prioritize and integrate relevant consultation material and advice into one's own practice

1.2d: To develop and enhance oneself as a professional health psychologist

1.   Evaluate opportunities to extend and develop professional competence

2.   Take relevant steps to ensure that qualifications, capabilities and views of self as a psychologist are not misrepresented

3.   Accurately and regularly update records of additional capabilities, qualifications and competence

1.2e: To incorporate best practice into one's own

1.   Actively seek and identify:
     - sources of new and emerging knowledge and best practice
     - opportunities to examine new knowledge and experience

2.   Review and evaluate:
     - existing working practices of self and others
     - new working practices

3.   Conduct discussions with colleagues and others to identify best practice

4.   Evaluate and systematically compare best practice models with own practice needs

5.   Incorporate relevant best practice models into own practice

---

1.3   PROVIDE PSYCHOLOGICAL ADVICE AND GUIDANCE TO OTHERS

1.3a   Assess the opportunities, need and context for giving psychological advice
1.3b   Provide psychological advice
1.3c   Evaluate advice given

1.3a   To assess the opportunities, needs and context for giving psychological advice

1.   Recognize and, where appropriate, use opportunities to offer advice on psychological issues

2. Assess the purpose and utility of the advice sought

3. Research literature and other data appropriate to the needs and content of the advice and assess their applicability

4. Identify key people who need to be advised

5. Use relevant criteria to select key people as recipients of advice.

6. Ensure advice is
   - given using media and formats appropriate to the context and the clients
   - supported by relevant, objective, psychological and other evidence and reasoned argument

7. Establish, maintain and agree appropriate levels of confidentiality

1.3b To provide psychological advice

1. Base advice given about psychological knowledge, principles and practices on up to date, relevant and accurate information

2. Formulate advice using appropriate sources of psychological evidence and knowledge

3. Cite sources and give credit to others when appropriate

4. Give advice at appropriate times within an activity cycle when progress for the activity can be maximized

5. Present advice in an intelligible and appropriate manner

6. Assess the context in which the advice is given and its likely impact

7. Establish, maintain and agree levels of confidentiality and security

8. Obtain necessary approval for the use and dissemination of confidential and copyrighted information

1.3c To evaluate the outcome of advice

1. Identify and use strategies for monitoring and adjusting the content of the advice and its communication in response to feedback

2. Evaluate the impact of the psychological advice, using appropriate methods and taking account of the context within which the advice is followed

---

1.4 PROVIDE FEEDBACK TO CLIENTS

1.4a Evaluate feedback needs of clients
1.4b Prepare and structure feedback
1.4c Select methods of communicating feedback
1.4d Present feedback to clients

1.4a: To evaluate feedback needs of client groups

1. Show sensitivity to the feedback situation

2. Identify feedback needs of clients e.g. information and emotional needs, limitations of clients' understanding, the purpose for which feedback will be used

1.4b: To prepare and structure feedback

1. Structure and organize the content to meet clients' needs

2. Prepare materials to facilitate clients' understanding of feedback

3. Support clients to develop methods of recall and identify sources of support and information for follow up of this feedback

4. Select materials to meet needs of clients

5. Structure materials appropriately

6. Pace the presentation of information in response to client needs.

7. Prepare contingency plans

8. Identify the role of others in the client system (e.g. family) in reinforcing feedback and supporting clients

1.4c: To select method of communicating feedback

1. Select communication media and formats of delivery to meet the needs of clients

2. Consider the purposes for which feedback will be used

3. Identify and analyse areas where it is inappropriate to give feedback and select methods for dealing with these

4. Organize appropriate situations and contexts in which to give feedback

5. Offer feedback in an appropriate style and format

1.4d: To present feedback to clients the competent health psychologist will be able to:

1. Present feedback messages in appropriate formats and at appropriate levels

2. Maintain continuous sensitivity to clients' reception and needs in response to the feedback message

3. Give feedback messages within appropriate duration and timings

4. Monitor and evaluate degree of clients' understanding assimilation and acceptance

5. Evaluate feedback processes

Index

Note: page numbers in *italic* refer to tables or figures.

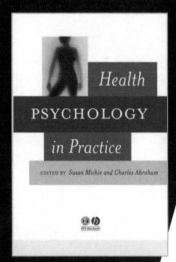

Health
PSYCHOLOGY
in Practice

Edited by Susan Michie
and Charles Abraham

University College London; University of Sussex

"Michie & Abraham have produced a truly comprehensive text based around the competencies required to train as a health psychologist in the UK. It will be required reading for all in such training and, because of the breadth and salience of UK health psychology training, the book will also be of value to a wide range of other applied psychologists and social scientists in the UK and elsewhere."

**Professor Derek Johnston, University of Aberdeen,
Chair Elect Division of Health Psychology**

An essential text for professional training in this field as it provides a comprehensive overview of the UK professional Stage 2 Qualification in Health Psychology. The editors, who helped to establish the British Psychological Society's health psychology professional training programme, have collated insightful material on training models, research, consultancy and interventions, training and teaching, and professional roles and practice.

JUNE 2004 / 1-4051-1089-9 PB / 416 PAGES

BPS Blackwell

www.blackwellpublishing.com